The Anthropology of Globalization

Blackwell Readers in Anthropology

As anthropology moves beyond the limits of so-called area studies, there is an increasing need for texts that do the work of synthesizing the literature while challenging more traditional or subdisciplinary approaches to anthropology. This is the object of this exciting new series, *Blackwell Readers in Anthropology*.

Each volume in the series offers seminal readings on a chosen theme and provides the finest, most thought-provoking recent works in the given thematic area. Many of these volumes bring together for the first time a body of literature on a certain topic. The series thus both presents definitive collections and investigates the very ways in which anthropological inquiry has evolved and is evolving.

1 *The Anthropology of Globalization: A Reader,* Second Edition
 Edited by Jonathan Xavier Inda and Renato Rosaldo

2 *The Anthropology of Media: A Reader*
 Edited by Kelly Askew and Richard R. Wilk

3 *Genocide: An Anthropological Reader*
 Edited by Alexander Laban Hinton

4 *The Anthropology of Space and Place: Locating Culture*
 Edited by Setha Low and Denise Lawrence-Zúñiga

5 *Violence in War and Peace: An Anthology*
 Edited by Nancy Scheper-Hughes and Philippe Bourgois

6 *Same-Sex Cultures and Sexualities: An Anthropological Reader*
 Edited by Jennifer Robertson

7 *Social Movements: An Anthropological Reader*
 Edited by June Nash

8 *The Cultural Politics of Food and Eating: A Reader*
 Edited by James L. Watson and Melissa L. Caldwell

9 *The Anthropology of the State: A Reader*
 Edited by Aradhana Sharma and Akhil Gupta

The Anthropology of Globalization

A Reader

2nd edition

Edited by

Jonathan Xavier Inda and
Renato Rosaldo

Blackwell
Publishing

Editorial material and organization © 2008 by Blackwell Publishing Ltd

BLACKWELL PUBLISHING
350 Main Street, Malden, MA 02148-5020, USA
9600 Garsington Road, Oxford OX4 2DQ, UK
550 Swanston Street, Carlton, Victoria 3053, Australia

First edition published 2002 by Blackwell Publishing Ltd
Second edition published 2008

4   2013

Library of Congress Cataloging-in-Publication Data

The anthropology of globalization : a reader / edited by Jonathan Xavier Inda and Renato Rosaldo.
   p. cm. – (Blackwell readers in anthropology ; 1)
  Includes bibliographical references and index.
  ISBN 978-1-4051-3613-6 (hardback : alk. paper)
  ISBN 978-1-4051-3612-9 (pbk. : alk. paper)
  1. Anthropology. 2. Globalization. I. Inda, Jonathan Xavier. II. Rosaldo, Renato.

GN27.A673 2008
306–dc22

2006037871

A catalogue record for this title is available from the British Library.

Set in 10/12.5pt Sabon
by SPi Publisher Services, Pondicherry, India

For further information on
Blackwell Publishing, visit our website:
www.blackwellpublishing.com

Contents

Contributors

Arjun Appadurai is the John Dewey Professor in the Social Sciences and Senior Advisor for Global Initiatives at The New School, New York.

Tom Boellstorff is Associate Professor of Anthropology at the University of California, Irvine.

Melissa L. Caldwell is Assistant Professor of Anthropology at the University of California, Santa Cruz.

Katherine Pratt Ewing is Associate Professor of Cultural Anthropology at Duke University.

Didier Fassin is Professor of Sociology at the University of Paris North and Director of Studies in Anthropology at the École des Hautes Études en Sciences Sociales in Paris.

Linda Green is Associate Professor of Anthropology at the University of Arizona.

Ariana Hernandez-Reguant is Assistant Professor of Media Studies in the Department of Communication at the University of California, San Diego.

Karen Ho is Assistant Professor of Anthropology at the University of Minnesota, Twin Cities.

Jonathan Xavier Inda is Associate Professor of Chicana/o Studies at the University of California, Santa Barbara.

Jeffrey S. Juris is Assistant Professor of Anthropology and Social and Behavioral Sciences at Arizona State University.

Alan Klima is Associate Professor of Anthropology at the University of California, Davis.

Andrew Lakoff is Assistant Professor of Sociology and Science Studies at the University of California, San Diego.

Brian Larkin is Assistant Professor of Anthropology at Barnard College.

Sally Engle Merry is Professor of Anthropology and Law and Society at New York University.

Kavita Misra is a National Institute of Mental Health Postdoctoral Fellow at Yale University, Center for Interdisciplinary Research on AIDS.

Aihwa Ong is Professor of Anthropology and South and Southeast Asian Studies at the University of California, Berkeley.

Renato Rosaldo is Professor of Anthropology at New York University and Lucie Stern Professor in the Social Sciences Emeritus at Stanford University.

Rachel E. Stern is a graduate student in Political Science at the University of California, Berkeley.

Renée Sylvain is Associate Professor of Anthropology, University of Guelph, Ontario, Canada.

Anna Tsing is Professor of Anthropology at the University of California, Santa Cruz.

Acknowledgments

We owe special thanks to Brian Larkin, Leo Chavez, Susan Bibler Coutin, Aihwa Ong, Matthew Gutmann, and Mayfair Yang for their wonderful suggestions and helpful insights. We are also deeply grateful to our editors at Blackwell, Jane Huber and Emily Martin, for their enthusiastic support of this project. Finally, Jonathan would like to thank Julie Dowling and his colleagues in Chicana/o Studies at the University of California, Santa Barbara for their generosity; and Renato wishes to thank Mary Louise Pratt and his colleagues in the Departments of Anthropology and Social and Cultural Analysis at New York University for their support.

The editors and publisher gratefully acknowledge the following for permission to reproduce copyright material:

Appadurai, Arjun, "Disjuncture and Difference in the Global Cultural Economy," *Modernity at Large: Cultural Dimensions of Globalization.* Minneapolis: University of Minnesota Press, pp. 27–47, 2000.

Tsing, Anna, "The Global Situation," *Cultural Anthropology* 15(3): 327–60, American Anthropological Association, 2000. Reprinted by permission of the American Anthropological Association.

Green, Linda, "Notes on Mayan Youth and Rural Industrialization in Guatemala," *Critique of Anthropology* 23(1): 51–73, London, Thousand Oaks, CA and New Delhi: SAGE Publications, 2003. Reproduced with permission from Linda Green, "Notes on Mayan Youth and Rural Industrialization in Guatemala" Copyright © Sage Publications 2003, by permission of Sage Publications Ltd.

Klima, Alan, "Thai Love Thai: Financing Emotion in Post-crash Thailand," *Ethnos* 69(4): 445–64. Routledge Journals, Taylor and Francis Ltd, on behalf of the Museum of Ethnography, Dec. 2004. Reprinted by permission of the author Alan Klima.

Ho, Karen, "Situating Global Capitalisms: A View from Wall Street Investment Banks," *Cultural Anthropology* 20(1): 68–96, American Anthropological Association, University of California Press, 2005. Reprinted by permission of the American Anthropological Association.

Ong, Aihwa, "Cyberpublics and Diaspora Politics among Transnational Chinese," *Interventions* 5(1): 82–100. Taylor and Francis Ltd, 2003. Also reprinted by permission of the author.

Pratt Ewing, Katherine, "Between Cinema and Social Work: Diasporic Turkish Women and the (Dis)Pleasures of Hybridity," *Cultural Anthropology* 21(2): 265–94. American Anthropological Association: University of California Press, 2006. Reprinted by permission of the American Anthropological Association.

Fassin, Didier, "Compassion and Repression: The Moral Economy of Immigration Policies in France," *Cultural Anthropology* 20(3): 362–87. American Anthropological Association: University of California Press, 2005. Reprinted by permission of the American Anthropological Association.

Caldwell, Melissa L., "Domesticating the French Fry: McDonald's and Consumerism in Moscow," *Journal of Consumer Culture* 4(1): 5–26, 1469–5405, London, Thousand Oaks CA and New Delhi: SAGE Publications, 2004. Reproduced with permission from Melissa L. Caldwell, "Domesticating the French Fry: McDonald's and Consumerism in Moscow," Copyright © SAGE Publications 2004, by permission of SAGE Publications Ltd.

Hernandez-Reguant, Ariana, "Copyrighting Che: Art and Authorship under Cuban Late Socialism," *Public Culture* 16(1): 1–29. Duke University Press, 2004. All rights reserved. Used by permission of the publisher.

Lakoff, Andrew, "Diagnostic Liquidity: Mental Illness and Global Trade in DNA," *Theory and Society* 2005(34): 63–92. Springer, 2005. With kind permission from Springer Science and Business Media.

Boellstorff, Tom, "Dubbing Culture: Indonesian *Gay* and *Lesbi* Subjectivities and Ethnography in an Already Globalized World," *American Ethnologist* 30(2): 225–42. American Anthropological Association, 2003. Reprinted by permission of the American Anthropological Association.

Larkin, Brian, "Itineraries of Indian Cinema: African Videos, Bollywood, and Global Media," in *Multiculturalism, Postcoloniality, and Transnational Media*, eds E. Shohat and R. Stam. New Brunswick, NJ and London: Rutgers University Press, pp. 170–92, 2003.

Shohat, Ella, and Robert Stam, eds. *Multiculturalism, Postcoloniality, and Transnational Media*. Copyright © 2003 by Rutgers, the State University. Reprinted by permission of Rutgers University Press.

Juris, Jeffrey S., "The New Digital Media and Activist Networking within Anti-Corporate Globalization Movements," ANNALS, *AAPSS*, 597, January 2005, pp. 189–208.

Phyllis Kaniss, The ANNALS of the American Academy of Political and Social Science (597/1), pp. 189–208, copyright 2005 by Sage Publications. Reprinted by permission of Sage Publications.

Merry, Sally Engle and Stern, Rachel E., "The Female Inheritance Movement in Hong Kong: Theorizing the Local/Global Interface," *Current Anthropology*

46(3), June 2005: 387–402, 407–9. Reprinted by permission of the publisher The University of Chicago Press and by permission of the authors Sally Engle Merry and Rachel Stern.

Sylvain, Renée, "Disorderly Development: Globalization and the Idea of 'Culture' in the Kalahari," *American Ethnologist* 32(3): 354–70. American Anthropological Association: University of California Press, 2005. Reprinted by permission of the American Anthropological Association.

Misra, Kavita, "Politico-moral Transactions in Indian AIDS Service: Confidentiality, Rights and New Modalities of Governance." *Anthropological Quarterly*, 79(1), 2006: pp. 33–74.

1

Tracking Global Flows

Jonathan Xavier Inda and Renato Rosaldo

Consider the following five snapshots.[1]

Snapshot One: In Guatemala, several thousand Mayan youth – the majority of whom are young unmarried daughters – work as apparel assemblers at the Sam Lucas *maquila* factory. The factory, built from cement blocks with aluminum roofing, is the size of a football field. Inside, long wooden tables divide the workers into production lines of about 30 people. Each person in a line repeats the assigned task over and over, whether it is to sew labels on pants, fasten sleeves to a shirt or cut threads off the almost finished product. Production goals are established for each line. If the production line reaches its goal, then the workers are promised extra pay; if not, money is deducted from their wages, which on average is about US $4 per day for 14 to 16 hours of work.

Snapshot Two: In Germany, there is an increasingly vocal concern about the "refusal" of Turkish Muslims to integrate into German society and the emergence of a self-sufficient "parallel society" that has developed in the heart of German cities. Within this parallel society, it is said, honor killings proliferate and traditionally oriented men prevent their wives and daughters from fully participating in German society. For the most vocal activists and experts, the solution is to "save" these women by offering them shelter when they escape from their families so that they can merge into German society and be "free" of the constraints of the parallel society.

Snapshot Three: In Russia, McDonald's is nowadays a prominent feature in the local landscape. The physical topography of Moscow's streets and pedestrian walkways, for example, is shaped by large red signs with recognizable golden arches and arrows directing pedestrians and motorists to the nearest restaurants. Furthermore, political demonstrators – anti-American or otherwise – often use McDonald's restaurants as landmarks for staging and dispersal areas. And whereas school groups formerly took cultural excursions to sites such as Lenin's tomb, museums and factories, today the same groups take educational tours through McDonald's restaurants and the McComplex production facilities.

Snapshot Four: Meanwhile, in northern Nigeria Indian films have become an integral part of the media scene and form the everyday media environment through which people move. Stickers of Indian stars emblazon trucks, cars, and bikes of the north. Popular stars are given Hausa nicknames, such as *Sarkin Rawa* (King of Dancing) for Govinda, or *Dan daba mai lasin* (licensed hooligan – in the same way that James Bond is licensed to kill). Indian jewelry and clothing have influenced Hausa fashions. Indian film songs and stories have penetrated everyday Hausa popular culture. And Hausa youth draw on the movie world of Indian sexual relations to test the boundaries of their own culture.

Snapshot Five: And in Hong Kong, it is the spring of 1994 and everyone is talking about female inheritance. Women in the New Territories are subject to Chinese customary law and, under British colonialism, still unable to inherit land. A group of rural indigenous women have joined forces with Hong Kong women's groups to demand legal change. In the plaza in front of the Legislative Council building, the indigenous women, dressed in the oversized hats of farm women, sing folk laments with new lyrics about injustice and inequality. Across the plaza, a conservative group representing rural elite interests gathers in large numbers to protest female inheritance on the grounds that it would undermine tradition. One banner carries the plaintive message: "Why are you killing our culture?"

We begin with these snapshots because, at a general level, they illustrate nicely what is now commonly known, not least in anthropological circles, as globalization.[2] This term refers (simply for now) to the intensification of global interconnectedness, suggesting a world full of movement and mixture, contact and linkages, and persistent cultural interaction and exchange. It speaks, in other words, to the complex mobilities and interconnections that characterize the globe today. The general picture these snapshots conjure is thus of an increasingly interconnected world. It is of a world where borders and boundaries have become increasingly porous, allowing more and more peoples and cultures to be cast into intense and immediate contact with each other.

We also commence with these snapshots because, at a more specific level, each highlights a particular mobility or cultural flow – respectively, of capital, people, commodities, images, and ideologies – through which the spaces of the globe are becoming increasingly intertwined.[3] Take, for example, the case of Guatemala. The scene of young women working in an export apparel assembly factory illustrates how, as technologies of communication and transportation have made capital more and more mobile, the search to reduce the costs of production has led corporations farther and farther afield, resulting in a rapid shift of labor-intensive industrial production and service work from the United States, Japan, and western Europe to new and highly dispersed low-wage sites around the globe. Places such as Guatemala have thus become nodes in the rapidly developing and ever-densening network of capital interconnections that epitomize the modern world.

Or take the case of Germany. The presence of Turkish migrants in the heart of German cities represents the extensive post-World War II movement of populations from the less affluent parts of the globe into the major urban centers of the "developed" and "developing" nations; the result being that peoples and cultures formerly located in different parts of the world now find themselves inhabiting the same physical terrains, and the spaces of the "West" find themselves homes to a host of diverse and sometimes incommensurable cultures.[4] This intensification of global mobility and interconnectedness has turned places such as Germany into spaces of juxtaposition and mixture, spaces where disparate cultures converge, collide, and grapple with each other, often in conditions of radical inequality.

Or the case of Russia. The prevalence of McDonald's in this country points to how Russians, and indeed people around the world, increasingly have to wrestle with the global standardization of cultural goods, tastes, and practices. From clothes, food, and music to architecture, film, and television, there is no denying that certain western styles and brands – Coca-Cola, Calvin Klein, Microsoft, Levis, Nike, and, of course, McDonald's – have achieved global prominence, so much prominence, in fact, that they can be found practically anywhere in the world. As this flow of commodities continues apace, as it keeps accelerating across the globe, the cultural lines that connect the world become ever more dense and mass consumption increasingly becomes a primary mediator in the "encounter" between peoples and cultures from around the planet.

Then there is Nigeria. The popularity of Indian film here accentuates the increasing importance of the media in allowing Hausa viewers to partake, as they go about their everyday lives, in the imagined realities of other cultures. More specifically, the snapshot shows the way Indian films participate in the dialogic construction of Hausa popular culture, for they offer Hausa men and women an alternative world, not altogether unlike their own, from which they may envision new forms of fashion, beauty, love, and romance. Indian films thus present Hausa (and other non-western) viewers with a means of creatively engaging with forms of tradition outside their culture but which do not emanate from the West, in effect high-lighting how the circulation of media between non-western countries has become an increasingly important aspect of global cultural flows.

And finally Hong Kong. The fear expressed by rural elites that female inheritance would undermine tradition points to how the question of women's rights excites political and ideological struggles framed in terms of cultural authenticity versus foreign influence. There is thus an important tension in Hong Kong (and elsewhere) about the proper role of women in society. It is a tension between those who seek to place gender equality and human rights at the center of the formation of society and those who would call into question such a project as an alien western imposition. This snapshot can therefore be seen as an instance of the global circulation of western ideologies – most often made up of elements of the Enlightenment worldview such as freedom, welfare, human rights, democracy, and sovereignty – and of the cultural interconnections and tensions that result as these ideologies are localized in various places around the world.

We begin with these pictures, then, because they provide us with a nice panoramic view of the world of globalization. It is a world of motion, of complex interconnections. Here capital traverses frontiers almost effortlessly, drawing more and more places into dense networks of financial interconnections; people readily (although certainly not freely and without difficulty) cut across national boundaries, turning countless territories into spaces where various cultures converge, clash, and struggle with each other; commodities drift briskly from one locality to another, becoming primary mediators in the encounter between culturally distant others; images flicker quickly from screen to screen, providing people with resources with which to fashion new ways of being in the world; and ideologies circulate rapidly through ever-expanding circuits, furnishing fodder for struggles couched in terms of cultural authenticity versus foreign influence. The pictures thus describe a world in which a myriad of processes, operating on a global scale, ceaselessly cut across national boundaries, integrating and connecting cultures and communities in new space-time combinations, and "making the world in reality and in experience more interconnected" (Hall 1996: 619). They speak of an intensely interconnected world – one where the rapid flows of capital, people, goods, images, and ideologies draw more and more of the globe into webs of interconnection, compressing our sense of time and space, and making the world feel smaller and distances shorter. This is the world of globalization.[5]

A few words of caution, however. There is no doubt that the world as a whole is experientially shrinking. Twentieth- and twenty-first-century innovations in technology – particularly in transportation and communication – have made it easier and quicker for people and things to get around. But there are limits to global mobility and connection. It is thus not necessarily the case that the world is shrinking for everyone and in all places (Allen and Hamnett 1995). The experience of globalization is a rather awkward and uneven process. For instance, while some people may possess the political and economic resources to trot across the world, many more have little or no access to transport and means of communication: the price of an airplane ticket or a phone call is just too high for them. And more generally, there are large expanses of the planet only tangentially tied into the webs of interconnection that encompass the globe. According to John Allen and Chris Hamnett, for example, whole areas of Africa "are quite literally off all kinds of maps – maps of telecommunications, maps of world trade and finance, maps of global tourism and the like" (1995: 2).[6] Such places thus have few circuits connecting them to anywhere, only routes of communication and transportation that skip over or bypass them. The point here, then, is that while the world may be full of complex mobilities and interconnections, there are also quite a number of people and places whose experience is marginal to or excluded from these movements and links. Indeed, not everyone and everyplace participates equally in the circuits of interconnection that traverse the globe. For the very processes that produce movement and linkages also promote immobility, exclusion, and disconnection (Coutin et al. 2002; Navaro-Yashin 2003; Ferguson 2006). And this, too, is the world of globalization.

The aim of this reader is to provide an introduction to this world of globalization, to this world of complex mobilities and uneven interconnections. More specifically, it offers an anthropological takes on such a world. The book is an exercise in the anthropology of globalization.[7] Of course, anthropologists are not the only ones interested in this issue. Since the late 1980s or so, globalization has become one of the most important academic topics. It is thus a central concern of quite a number of disciplines, from sociology and economics to media and literary studies. Anthropology, however, brings a unique perspective to bear on the topic. The tendency of much of the literature on globalization is to focus on the macro scope of the phenomenon, thinking of it principally in terms of very large-scale economic, political, or cultural processes. Anthropology, on the other hand, is most concerned with the articulation of the global and the local, that is, with how globalizing processes exist in the context of, and must come to terms with, the realities of particular societies, with their accumulated – that is to say, historical – cultures and ways of life.[8] The anthropology of globalization, in other words, is concerned with the situated and conjunctural nature of globalization. It is preoccupied not just with mapping the shape taken by the particular flows of capital, people, goods, images, and ideologies that crisscross the globe – that is, with tracking global processes as locatable networks of practices and connections – but also with the experiences of people living in specific localities when more and more of their everyday lives are contingent on globally extensive social processes (Foster 1999). What anthropology offers that is often lacking in other disciplines is a concrete attentiveness to human agency, to the practices of everyday life, in short, to how subjects mediate the processes of globalization (Povinelli and Chauncey 1999). Thus, to provide an anthropological introduction to globalization is to focus at once on the large-scale processes (or flows of subjects and objects) through which the world is becoming increasingly, albeit unevenly, interconnected and on how subjects respond to these processes in culturally specific ways.[9] This is precisely what this book does. The articles offered here are concerned with tracking global flows in a way that highlights human agency and imagination. They are a selection of some of the best recent critical anthropological work on globalization.[10] It is material that highlights the great complexity and ingenuity of the anthropology of globalization.

In the rest of this introductory chapter, we present a more comprehensive view of globalization than offered above. First, we provide a more elaborate definition of globalization. We suggest that the term implies something more radical about the world than the mere fact of increasing global interconnectedness: it points to a basic reorganization of time and space. Second, given this more extensive definition, we then consider the cultural dynamics of globalization. This is the realm of global activity that has attracted the most anthropological attention. Third, we focus on the limits of global mobility and connection. The idea is to move beyond the image of unfettered flows and unbound connectivity to conceptualize the manifold practices that both promote and constrain movement and linkage. In the last section, we provide a brief overview of the reader and point to some of its limitations.

The Spaces and Times of Globalization

Earlier we defined "globalization" rather simply as the intensification of global interconnectedness. To be sure, this is in large part what globalization is all about. The world today is witnessing an intensification of circuits of economic, political, cultural, and ecological interdependence. This is a world in which the rapid acceleration in the flows of capital, people, goods, images, and ideologies – subjects and objects, in short – across the face of the globe has brought even the most remote parts of the world in contact with metropolitan centers. However, globalization suggests something much more profound about the modern world than the simple fact of growing global interconnectedness. It implies a fundamental reordering of time and space. We would like to offer, then, a more theoretical take on globalization, one that draws from the work of the two authors who have best captured this profound reorganization of time and space: David Harvey and Anthony Giddens.[11]

Speeding it up

David Harvey (1989) conceptualizes globalization principally as a manifestation of the changing experience of time and space. He captures this change in the notion of "time-space compression," which refers to the manner in which the speeding up of economic and social processes has experientially shrunk the globe, so that distance and time no longer appear to be major constraints on the organization of human activity. In other words, the term points to how the pressures of technological and economic change have continually collapsed time and space: collapsed them in such a way that time has overcome or annihilated the barriers of space. (One brief example of this collapse is the fact that, it is now possible for folks in London to experience the same thing, say, a media event or a business transaction, at the same time as people in Thailand (Waters 1995).) For Harvey, then, globalization involves the "shrinking" of space and the shortening of time. It entails the speeding up of the pace of life, such that the time taken to do things, as well as the experiential distance between different locations in space, becomes progressively shorter. For him, in sum, globalization is intimately linked with the intensification and speeding up of time-space compression in economic and social life.

This process of time-space compression (and hence of globalization), Harvey argues, is not a gradual or continuous occurrence. Rather, it takes place in discrete phases of short and concentrated bursts. The world at any particular moment is not the product of a smooth linear compression of time and space, but the result of a more discontinuous historical unfolding. These eruptions of time-space compression, Harvey notes, can be attributed to the periodic crises of overaccumulation that plague the capitalist system. Today's world, for instance, is in just such a phase, one that started during the early 1970s (Harvey 1989: 141–72). It began with a crisis of overaccumulation in the Fordist system of mass production of western economies. This system, based on Henry Ford's model of centralized mass-assembly production of standardized products, had become so successful and efficient that it began to overproduce, resulting in the massive lay-off of workers, and effectively reducing demand for products. Consumer markets thus became completely saturated. And since there were not enough consumers to buy these goods, corporate profits began to decline, which in turn precipitated a fall in government revenues. This meant the onset of fiscal problems for governments, who consequently found it increasingly difficult to sustain their commitment to their welfare programs. They attempted to solve the problem primarily by printing extra money, but this only set in motion a wave of uncontrollable inflation. This crisis jarred the Fordist system to such a degree that the model of mass production (which entailed rigid arrangements between the state, capitalists, and workers to maintain high levels of employment, investment, and consumption) became unraveled.

In its place, there has emerged a post-Fordist regime of flexible accumulation. This regime, according to Harvey, "rests on flexibility with respect to labor processes, labor markets, products, and patterns of consumption. It is characterized by the emergence of entirely new sectors of production, new ways of providing financial services, new markets, and, above all, greatly intensified rates of commercial, technological, and organizational innovation" (1989: 147). For example, labor markets have become flexible through the introduction of new forms of labor regulation – outsourcing, subcontracting, putting-out and "home work" strategies – and the hiring of large numbers of temporary, part-time, and seasonal workers; production arrangements have become malleable owing to a shift away from rigid centralized firms oriented towards mass production to small, decentralized firms oriented towards niche markets; and capital has become less anchored as a result of the deregulation of the global financial market. This flexibility is aimed at reducing the turnover time of capital: the amount of time necessary for money furnished to fund new production to be recovered with a profit through the sale of services and goods. In other words, the goal is to speed up the process of both production and consumption, for, as the old capitalist adage says, time is money, or rather time costs money. Thus one finds that practices such subcontracting and outsourcing, as well as other organizational shifts, coupled with new technologies of electronic control, have all decreased turnover times in many domains of production (e.g., clothing, electronics, automobiles, machine tools, and construction). Moreover, improved modes of communication and information, together with rationalizations in methods of distribution (e.g., inventory control, packaging, and market feedback), have made it possible for commodities to move around through the market system at a faster pace; 24-hours-a-day financial services and markets have increased the mobility of capital; and the mobilization of fashion in niche markets has facilitated a speed-up in the pace of consumption in clothing, ornaments, and across a wide range of recreational activities and life-styles (e.g., pop music styles, leisure and sporting habits, and video and children's games). In this post-Fordist phase of capitalism, the regime of flexible accumulation reigns – whether in the realm of high finance, production systems, consumption, or labor markets – and the pace of economic and social life has generally accelerated.

The main implication of all this is that, for Harvey, we are currently caught in a particularly intense moment of time-space compression. The general speed-up in the turnover time of capital is rapidly shrinking the world. Time is quickly annihilating space. He puts this in the following terms:

> The satellite communications systems deployed since the early 1970s have rendered the unit cost and time of communication invariant with respect to distance. It costs the same to communicate over 500 miles as it does over 5,000 via satellite. Air freight rates on commodities have likewise come down dramatically, while containerization has reduced the cost of bulk sea and road transport. It is now possible for a large

multinational corporation like Texas Instruments to operate plants with simultaneous decision-making with respect to financial, market, input costs, quality control, and labor process conditions in more than fifty different locations across the globe. Mass television ownership coupled with satellite communication makes it possible to experience a rush of images from different spaces almost simultaneously, collapsing the world's spaces into a series of images on a television screen. The whole world can watch the Olympic Games, the World Cup, the fall of a dictator, a political summit, a deadly tragedy… while mass tourism, films made in spectacular locations, make a wide range of simulated or vicarious experiences of what the world contains available to many people. (Harvey 1989: 293)

The world today, in other words, is subject to the concurrent implosion of space and the speed-up of all facets of economic and social life. Yes, space is shrinking. The pace of life is speeding up. The time taken to do things is becoming progressively shorter. The world, in short, is witnessing the intensification of the compression of time and space. And so, as the world appears to shrink and distances seemingly diminish, as happenings in one place come to impact instantaneously on people and places miles away, "we have to learn how to cope with an overwhelming sense of *compression* of our spatial and temporal worlds" (Harvey 1989: 240).

Stretching it out

Anthony Giddens, like Harvey, considers globalization to involve a profound reorganization of time and space in social and cultural life. However, while Harvey focuses on the general speed-up of economic and social processes, Giddens is more preoccupied with the stretching of social life across time and space. Giddens captures this preoccupation in the notion of "time-space distanciation," which refers to "the conditions under which time and space are organized so as to connect presence and absence" (1990: 14). The basic argument is that social life consists of two fundamental kinds of social interaction. The first entails face-to-face contact. Here people engage directly with each other as they go about their everyday lives in what are often closely bounded local spaces. The second form consists of more remote encounters, those made possible by transport and communications systems, those that people engage in across space and time. The first type of interaction tends to predominate in premodern societies. These are societies in which the "spatial dimensions of social life are, for most of the population, and in most respects, dominated by 'presence' – by localized activities" (1990: 18). With the advent of modernity, however, the second sort of social intercourse becomes increasingly important. Modernity tears the spatial orbit of social life away from the confines of locality, "fostering relations between 'absent' others, locationally distant from any given situation of face-to-face interaction" (1990: 18). In other words, it disembeds or lifts out social relations from local contexts of interaction and rearranges them across extensive spans of time-space. One important effect of this disembedding is to make place, "which refers to the physical settings of social activity as situated geographically," increasingly phantasmagoric (1990: 18). This means that, in conditions of modernity, locales are haunted, so to speak, by that which is absent. They are constituted not just by what is immediately present but also by influences quite removed from them. Modern localities, then, are settings for distanciated relations – for relations at a distance, stretched out across time and space.

It is in terms of space-time distanciation that Giddens understands the process of globalization. For him, globalization broadens the scope of the disembedding process, so that "larger and larger numbers of people live in circumstances in which disembedded institutions, linking local practices with globalized social relations, organize major aspects of day-to-day life" (1990: 79). Said otherwise, it intensifies the level of time-space distanciation and correspondingly stretches out the relations between local and distant social practices and events. Giddens thus defines globalization "as the intensification of worldwide social relations which link distant localities in such a way that local happenings are shaped by events occurring many miles away and vice versa" (1990: 64), emphasizing how the emergence of instantaneous global communication and mass transportation, as well as the expansion of complex global systems of production and exchange, reduce the hold of local environments over people's lives. For example, the jobs of Chinese "Mattel" factory workers may be more dependent on the sale of Barbies in the United States than on the direct actions of local management. This does not mean, however, that place (or locale) has ceased to be significant in the organization of everyday life. It simply means that as social connections extend laterally across time and space, localities around the world become less dependent on circumstances of co-presence (on face-to-face interaction) and more on interactions across distance (on relations with absent others). For Giddens, then, globalization points to the interlocking of the local and the global; that is, it "concerns the intersection of presence and absence, the interlacing of social events and social relations 'at a distance' with local contextualities" (1991: 21). In short, globalization expresses basic aspects of space-time distanciation. It is fundamentally about the transformation of space and time.

The two perspectives sketched out above undoubtedly contain a number of significant differences.[12] For our purposes, however, we want to take them as complementary viewpoints. Together they highlight the basic, present-day spatial-temporal parameters of globalization. Drawing on the work of David Held et al. (1999: 15), we suggest that globalization consists of the following characteristic elements. First of all, given the development of worldwide modes of transport and communication, globalization implies a speeding up of the flows of capital, people, goods, images, and ideas across the world, thus pointing to a general increase in the pace of global interactions and processes. Second, it suggests an intensification of the links, modes of interaction, and flows that interconnect the world, meaning that ties across borders are not sporadic or haphazard but somewhat regularized. Third, globalization entails a stretching of social, cultural, political, and economic practices across frontiers so as to make possible action at a distance – that is, so that happenings, decisions, and practices in one area of the globe can come to have consequences for communities and cultures in other, often quite distant, locales around the world. And finally, as a result of all this speeding up, intensification, and stretching, globalization also implies a heightened entanglement of the global and local such that, while everyone might continue to live local lives, their phenomenal worlds have to some extent become global as distant events come to have an impact on local spaces, and local developments come to have global repercussions.[13] All told, globalization can be seen as referring to those spatial-temporal processes, operating on a global scale, that rapidly cut across national boundaries, drawing more and more of the world into webs of interconnection, integrating and stretching cultures and communities across space and time, and compressing our spatial and temporal horizons. It points to a world in motion, to an interconnected world, to a shrinking world.

The Cultural Dynamics of Globalization

Given this general framework, let us now consider the cultural dynamics of globalization. This is the sphere of global activity that has received the most anthropological attention. This is not to say that anthropologists neglect or fail to consider other aspects of globalization, say, the economic or the political.[14] Indeed, they hardly could. For these are not completely separate realms of activity. What anthropologists tend to do, though, is interpret these other spheres through the prism of the cultural. Indeed, the cultural realm – the realm of meaning, one might say – most often takes conceptual priority. This prioritization is done, however, without necessarily positing the cultural dimension as the master sphere through which everything about globalization must be understood. Anthropologists realize that globalization is a complex, multifaceted process that operates simultaneously in diverse realms – the cultural, the economic, the political, the environmental, and so on – and can thus be embraced from numerous angles (see Nederveen Pieterse 1995). The cultural functions as just one such angle: as one of a number of important ways through which one can grasp the complex creature that is globalization. What does it mean, then, to speak of the cultural dynamics of globalization?

The de/territorialization of culture

Let us begin with the notion of culture itself. The concept has a long and complicated history. Raymond Williams (1976) describes it as one of the two or three most complex words in the English language. "Culture" can thus be a rather slippery idea. We would like to sidestep the problems of definition, however, and propose what might be considered a standard conceptualization of the term. We understand culture, for the purposes of this volume, "as the order of life in which human beings construct meaning through practices of symbolic representation" (Tomlinson 1999: 18). It is the sphere of existence in which people make their lives, individually and collectively, meaningful; and it encompasses both the practices through which meaning is generated and the material forms – popular culture, film, art, literature, and so forth – in which it is embodied.

In anthropology, the historical tendency has been to connect this realm of meaning construction, this realm of culture, very closely to the particularities of place (Clifford 1997; Malkki 1997). The idea of "a culture," for instance, which refers to a group of people – whether a nation, ethnicity, tribe, or so forth – who more or less use a system of shared meanings to interpret and make sense of the world, has traditionally been tied to the idea of a fixed territory. Akhil Gupta and James Ferguson elaborate on this in the following terms:

> The distinctiveness of societies, nations, and cultures is predicated on a seemingly unproblematic division of space, on the fact that they occupy "naturally" discontinuous spaces . . . For example, the representation of the world as a collection of "countries," as on most world maps, sees it as an inherently fragmented space, divided by different colors into diverse national societies, each "rooted" in its proper place . . . It is so taken for granted that each country embodies its own distinctive culture and society that the terms "society" and "culture" are routinely simply appended to the names of nation-states, as when a tourist visits India to understand "Indian culture" and "Indian society" or Thailand to experience "Thai culture" or the United States to get a whiff of "American culture."
>
> Of course, the geographical territories that cultures and societies are believed to map onto do not have to be nations . . . On a smaller scale perhaps are our disciplinary assumptions about the association of culturally unitary groups (tribes or peoples) with "their" territories: thus "the Nuer" live in "Nuerland" and so forth. The clearest illustration of this kind of thinking are the classic "ethnographic maps" that purported to display the spatial distribution of peoples, tribes, and cultures. (2002: 65–6)

The inclination in anthropology, then, has been to assume an isomorphism between place and culture. Culture has been seen as something rooted in "soil." It has been thought of as a bounded entity that occupies a specific physical territory. The idea of culture has thus rested on the assumption of rupture, on the assumption of an intrinsic discontinuity between places as the loci of particular formations of meaning. It has traditionally pointed to a world of human differences conceptualized as a mosaic of cultures – with each culture, as a universe of shared meanings, radically set apart from every other. In short, as James Clifford has noted, "the idea of culture" has historically carried with it an "expectation of roots, of a stable, territorialized existence" (1988: 338).

Nowadays, though, it is impossible, or at least rather unreasonable, to think of culture strictly in such localized terms, to view it as the natural property of spatially circumscribed populations.[15] Globalization has radically pulled culture apart from place. It has visibly dislodged it from particular locales. The signs of this disembedding are everywhere. Just think back to the snapshots we discussed at the beginning of the chapter. These are all essentially about the traffic in meaning. They are about the global mobility of cultural forms and products. Consider the scene of Turkish Muslims in Germany, for example. It illustrates how people, or cultural subjects, nowadays readily traverse national boundaries, a process that brings cultures formerly located in different parts of the world into the same physical terrains, thus turning numerous places into spaces of cultural juxtaposition and mixture. Or take the case of McDonald's in Russia. It shows how cultural objects – clothes, food, music, and so forth – circulate rapidly through ever-expanding networks, networks so extensive that certain styles or brands have achieved an almost ubiquitous presence in the world. Or contemplate the episode of mass media in Nigeria. This, too, is about cultural objects on the move. It highlights how images drift easily across the globe, allowing an increasing number of viewers to participate in the imagined realities of other cultures. This world of the snapshots is thus no "cultural mosaic, of separate pieces with hard, well-defined edges" (Hannerz 1992: 218). Rather, it is a world of culture in motion. It is a world where cultural subjects and objects – that is, meaningful forms such as capital, people, commodities, images, and ideas – have become unhinged from particular localities. The snapshots, in other words, suggest that culture is highly mobile. They point to how cultural interconnections increasingly stretch across the globe, eroding the "natural" connection or isomorphism between culture and place.

On one level, then, anthropologists have come to conceptualize culture as deterritorialized. The term is used to refer to this general weakening of the ties between culture and place, to the dislodging of cultural subjects and objects from particular or fixed locations in space and time. It points to how cultural processes readily transcend specific territorial boundaries. It designates a world of things fundamentally in motion. This should not be taken to mean, though, that anthropologists now think of culture as free-floating, without anchors. Indeed not. For anthropologists realize that the uprooting of culture is only half of the story of globalization. The other half is that the deterritorialization of culture is invariably the occasion for the reinsertion of culture in new time-space contexts. In other words, for anthropologists, cultural flows do not just float ethereally across the globe but are always reinscribed (however partially or fleetingly) in specific cultural environments. The signs of this reinscription, like the marks of deterritorialization, are everywhere evident. We need only turn, again, to our snapshots. Turkish Muslims *in* Germany, for instance, are not aimless wanderers. McDonald's restaurants *in* Russia are not meandering endlessly around the globe. And the Indian films *in* northern Nigeria are not flickering endlessly from screen to screen. They are all, instead, localized in very specific time-space contexts: that of Germany, Russia, and Nigeria respectively. These snapshots are thus not simply of cultural subjects and objects in motion but also of their contingent localizations, of their reinsertion in particular cultural milieus. On another level, then, anthropologists have come to conceptualize culture as reterritorialized. The term refers to this process of reinscribing culture in new time-space contexts, of relocalizing it in specific cultural environments. It suggests that while the connection between culture and specific places may be weakening, it does not mean that culture has altogether lost its place. It just signifies that culture has been placed otherwise, such that it no longer necessarily belongs in or to a particular place. In short, it means that culture continues to have a territorialized existence, albeit a rather unstable one.

The point of all this is that, for anthropologists, globalized culture is never simply deterritorialized. It is also always reterritorialized. We are not dealing, in other words, with two separate processes. Rather, they occur simultaneously. It is a double movement, if you will. We would like to capture this double movement with the neologism de/territorialization. The term captures at once the lifting of cultural subjects and objects from fixed spatial locations and their relocalization in new cultural settings. It refers to processes that simultaneously transcend territorial boundaries and have territorial significance. The key to the meaning of this term is the slash. It allows us to separate "de" from "territorialization," thus calling attention to the fact that deterritorialization always contains territorialization within itself. For us, this means that the root of the word always to some extent undoes the action of the prefix, such that while the "de" may pull culture apart from place, the "territorialization" is always there to pull it back in one way or another. So there is no deterritorialization without some form of reterritorialization. There is no dislodging of everyday meanings from their moorings in particular localities without their simultaneous reinsertion in fresh environments. You can't have one process without the other. It is a matter of both at once. It is a matter of de/territorialization.

Cultural imperialism and the homogenization of the world

One of the important issues that the de/territorialization of culture raises concerns the organization of the flow of meaning in the world, or what might be called the cultural economy of globalization. It may very well be the case that culture is being dislodged from one locality and placed in another, thus generally weakening the ties of culture to particular sites. But this says nothing about the sort of culture that is being disembedded or about its origins and destinations. Does culture, for example, flow equally from and to all locations? Or does its dissemination involve some form of asymmetry? In other words, is there a power geometry to globalization and what might it be (see Massey 1994)?

A powerful answer to this set of questions comes from the discourse of cultural imperialism, a perspective that offers a highly critical stance towards the globalization of culture.[16] One of the central propositions of this discourse is that the de/territorialization of culture is not a benign matter.[17] For there is indeed a power geometry to the processes of globalization. It is one in which the traffic in culture moves primarily in one direction: sometimes it is seen to move from the First World (or West/center) to the Third World (or rest/periphery), other times more specifically from the United States to the rest of the world. In either case, given the asymmetries that putatively structure the flow of meaning, the discourse of cultural imperialism suggests that the processes of globalization involve the domination of certain cultures over others. In other words, this discourse understands the increased global movement of cultural goods primarily as a process of cultural imposition and dominance – of the imposition and dominance of western (predominantly American) culture over the remainder of the globe. The significance of this pattern of domination, from the point of view of this discourse, is that it is leading to the cultural homogenization of the world. The scenario that is often outlined is one in which, as global cultural influences continuously batter the sensibilities of the people of the periphery, "peripheral culture will step by step assimilate more and more of the imported meanings and forms, becoming gradually indistinguishable from the center" (Hannerz 1991: 122). The de/territorialization of culture is thus conceived as promoting a convergence of cultural styles inasmuch as western culture is being embraced in localities around the globe. It is seen, in other words, as leading to the increasing elimination of cultural difference in the world and hence to the crescent production of a world of sameness. The impact of western culture is perceived as rather overwhelming.

This, then, in general terms, is how the discourse of cultural imperialism regards the globalization of culture. The discourse, however, can be broken down and explored a little further. It actually presents us with at least two specific, albeit interrelated, visions of global cultural uniformity (see Tomlinson 1999).[18] The first vision attributes the increasing synchronization of world culture to the ability of transnational capital, most often seen as American-dominated and mass-mediated, to distribute cultural goods around the globe. A dominant version of this vision runs more or less as follows.[19] Since World War II, the global distribution of power points has shifted massively, such that the United States has become increasingly dominant, while European hegemony has diminished. A new empire, that of America, has thus come to replace the western European colonial system that had ensnared much of the world since the nineteenth century. This new imperial regime owes its ascendance to economic might, which germinates principally from the actions of US-based transnational corporations, and communications know-how, which has permitted American business and military interests to largely monopolize the development of electronically based systems of communication. This monopoly has been so strong that the American broadcasting system, which is essentially a commercial system dependent on advertising revenue, has functioned as an archetype for the formation of broadcasting systems around the globe, particularly in the Third World. One problem with the dissemination and adoption of this commercial system of mass media is that it has opened up Third World countries to the large-scale importation of consumer-oriented foreign programs. The outcome has been an electronic invasion that promises to eradicate local traditions everywhere. Local culture, in other words, is meeting with submersion from the mass-produced emissions of commercial broadcasting. It is in danger of being drowned underneath a deluge of commercialized media products and other consumer goods pouring from America and a few other power points in the West. The Third World's adoption of a commercial system of broadcasting has thus been no innocent proposition. These countries have become strapped and buckled to an American-dominated global system of communication and commodity production that threatens to supplant traditional cultural values with the values of consumerism. The scenario often painted, then, is one in which the spread of American/western cultural goods is leading to the absorption of peripheral cultures into a homogenized global monoculture of consumption. It is a vision of a world culturally synchronized to the rhythms of a mass-mediated global marketplace.

The second vision of global uniformity attributes the synchronization of the world to the spread of western culture more generally.[20] This means that globalization entails more than just the simple spread of American/western cultural goods, more than the development of a global taste for McDonald's, Levis, Coca-Cola, and the like. It actually involves, as John Tomlinson points out, "the installation worldwide of western versions of basic social-cultural reality: the West's epistemological and ontological theories, its values, ethical systems, approaches to rationality, technical-scientific worldview, political culture, and so on" (1997: 144). In other words, globalization entails the dissemination of all facets of the West's way of being: from musical forms, architecture, and modes of dress to eating habits, languages (specially English), philosophical ideas, and cultural values and dispositions – those concerning, for example, freedom, democracy, gender and sexuality, human rights, religion, science, and technology. And this is not just a post-World War II development either. Globalization is in fact "the continuation of a long historical process of western 'imperialist' expansion – embracing the colonial expansions of the sixteenth to the nineteenth centuries – and representing an historical pattern of increasing global cultural hegemony" (Tomlinson 1997: 143–4). This vision of cultural uniformity implies that the world is gradually being made over in the image of the West. It indicates that cultural diversity is disappearing as non-western cultures are progressively incorporated into a western-dominated homogenized culture. The ramification here is that western culture has been globalized to such an extent that the West has lost its "natural" connection to a specific geographical territory. The West is no longer an assemblage of cultural practices linked to a particular territorial foundation. It has been deterritorialized, uprooted from its historical birthplace. As such, the West no longer refers simply to Europe. It names instead a worldwide cultural formation.[21] It designates a machine of sorts, one producing planetary unification, one ushering in the worldwide standardization of life-styles. The West describes, in short, the cultural condition of the world. It is simply everywhere, dooming the world to uniformity.

To sum up, then, the discourse of cultural imperialism, taken as a whole, understands the experience of de/territorialization as the global dissemination of certain cultural practices, goods, styles, institutions, and so forth, the result being the increasing cultural homogenization of the world. It suggests that western culture, whether in the form of consumer goods or otherwise, has been lifted from its territorial grounding only to be replicated across the world, leaving a trail of uniformity behind it. Globalization thus becomes coterminous with Americanization or, more generally, with westernization. There is something to be said for this vision of the world. It presents a not entirely implausible scenario. The signs of global uniformity, at least on some level, are there. There is no denying that western cultural forms can be found everywhere (or almost so). Take clothes or food, for example: there are certain styles and brands – we earlier mentioned Coca-Cola, McDonald's, and so forth – that have become household names all over the world (even if not everyone can afford to buy them). Or take film and television: CNN, MTV, the Disney Channel are globally recognized icons; American television shows are broadcast around the world, *Law and Order* and *The Simpsons* being two recent examples; and Hollywood films – *Titanic, Mission Impossible, Pirates of the Caribbean* – and their stars – Leonardo DiCaprio, Tom Cruise, Johnny Depp – have extraordinary worldwide visibility. Or take the realm of ideas: notions of freedom, welfare, rights, democracy, sovereignty seem to be in everyone's vocabulary, indicating that the Enlightenment worldview has much of the world in its thrall. These examples are only the more obvious signs of cultural uniformity. We could point to many others. But we think the point is sufficiently made: there is an abundance of evidence suggesting that western cultural forms have a ubiquitous presence in the world. It would thus appear that there is no denying that the world is becoming to some extent homogenized, that it is becoming to some degree westernized. It is plain as day. All one has to do is look around.

A different picture of the world

From an anthropological perspective, however, the situation is not plain as day. All one has to do is look around – a little harder though. What one finds is that the picture the discourse of cultural imperialism draws of the world fails to adequately capture its complexities. The world, indeed, is a much more complicated place. In what follows, we will explore just how much more complex the world actually is. The tack we will take is to focus on three fundamental problems with the discourse of cultural imperialism, the main goal being to cast doubt on the vision of the world as a homogenized or westernized entity.

The first problem with the discourse of cultural imperialism concerns the fashion in which alien cultural products are said to act upon their consumers in the Third World. An important assumption of the cultural imperialism discourse is

> that TV programs which are made for a commercial television system will unavoidably express consumerist values, both in the programs themselves and in the advertising which constitutes the financial basis of the system; and that these representations will in turn create wants and foster consumerist motivations in their recipients, in such a way that these recipients become harnessed to a western-based system of commodity production and exchange (Thompson 1995: 170–1)

The main problem with this assumption is that it constructs Third World subjects as passive consumers of imported cultural goods. The discourse of cultural imperialism, in other words, relies on what is called the hypodermic model of media effects (Morley and Robins 1995: 126): a model that presupposes that media texts have direct cultural effects on those who view them. This basically means that cultural effects are imputed from an examination of the cultural forms themselves rather than from careful attention to the actual context of viewing. This is too simple a model of cultural reception. The process of reading cultural texts is actually a rather complicated affair, one that entails the active participation of the viewing subject in the construction of meaning (see Morley 1992). Third World consumers faced with an imported text, media or otherwise, will not simply or necessarily absorb its ideologies, values, and life-style positions. Rather, they will bring their own cultural dispositions to bear on such a text, interpreting it according to their own cultural codes (see Ang 1985; Liebes and Katz 1990). What takes place in the viewing encounter is that foreign cultural forms have a tendency to become customized.[22] They are interpreted, translated, and appropriated according to local conditions of reception.[23]

The classic example of this process of customization is Liebes and Katz's (1990) well-known study of the reception of *Dallas* in Israel (focusing on four different ethnic groups: Arabs, Russian Jews, Moroccan Jews, and kibbutz members), the United States, and Japan. The basic finding of the investigation was that viewers from diverse cultural backgrounds attributed very different meanings to the program. The various groups, for example, had different explanations for the motivations of the characters in *Dallas*:

> the Americans and the kibbutz members invoke a sort of Freudian theory, perceiving individuals as governed by irrational drives and connecting these with childhood events.

Thus, JR's personality is thought to derive from his having been second to Bobby in his mother's favor. Interpretations of this kind, of course, relieve individuals of much moral responsibility. In contrast, a large proportion of the Russian statements invoke determinism of another form, as if people behaved in a particular way because their roles impelled them to; as if businessmen, for example, or women, were programmed by society. The Moroccans also blame society, but invoke a Hobbesian model in which individuals must fend for themselves in the jungle of the world. Only the Arabs – who focus not on motivation but on family interrelations and moral dilemmas – find the individual free and responsible enough to struggle against temptation and constraint. (Liebes and Katz 1990: 103)

Given the clear and systematic differences in the ways the various groups interpreted *Dallas*, Liebes and Katz conclude that the process of reception is not a straightforward imposition of meaning but a creative encounter between "the symbolic resources of the viewer and the symbolic offerings of the text" (1990: 6). They suggest, in other words, that the reception of media products is an intricate cultural process that entails the active involvement of individuals in making sense of the images they consume.

Eric Michaels (2002) provides another important example of the customization of alien cultural forms (see also Boellstorff, Chapter 13 in this volume). His work focuses, in part, on the reception of Hollywood videotapes among Warlpiri Aborigines in the western Central Desert of Australia. Michaels's most suggestive finding was that the Aboriginal peoples were not familiar with the genres and conventions of western narrative fiction. They were unable to distinguish, for example, romance from documentary, or to judge the truth value of Hollywood cinema. The reason for this is that in traditional Warlpiri culture all stories are true. Fiction simply does not exist as an epistemological form through which to make sense of the world. This situation produces, according to Michaels, quite extraordinary interpretations of Hollywood programs. He elaborates in the following manner:

> Comparisons between Warlpiri story form and imported video fictions demonstrated that in many instances, content (what is supplied in the narrative) and context (what must be assumed) are so different from one system to the other that they might be said to be reversed. For example, Warlpiri narrative will provide detailed kinship relationships between all characters as well as establishing a kinship domain for each. When Hollywood videos fail to say where Rocky's grandmother is, or who's taking care of his sister-in-law, Warlpiri viewers discuss the matter and need to fill in what for them is missing content. By contrast, personal motivation is unusual in Aboriginal story; characters do things because the class (kin, animal, plant) of which they are members is known to behave this way. This produces interesting indigenous theories, for example, of national character to explain behavior in *Midnight Express* or *The A-Team*. (2002: 319)

The point here is that for Warlpiri viewers Hollywood videos are not necessarily complete, authoritative texts. They are instead partial stories that require "a good deal of interpretive activity on the part of viewers to supply contents as well as context with which to make these stories meaningful" (2002: 321). Michaels's conclusion, then, is that it is not possible to know in advance what the effects of particular television programs might be on traditional Aboriginal audiences. It is only in the actual context of viewing that meaning can be determined.

These two examples should not be taken to imply that foreign texts have no cultural influence at all. It is not our intention to romanticize the process of interpretation. It may be that consuming subjects are active makers of sense. But this does not mean they can therefore do whatever they want with the goods they consume. There are limits to how one can interpret a text.[24] All we mean to suggest is this: that the process of interpretation, and hence the influence that foreign programs have on their audiences, are rather more complicated than the discourse of cultural imperialism, with its hypodermic model, permits. Cultural materials just do not transfer in a unilinear manner (see Tomlinson 1999). They always entail interpretation, translation, and customization on the part of the receiving subject. In short, they can only be understood in the context of their complex reception and appropriation.

The implications of this way of conceptualizing the reception of imported products are rather profound. It gives us cause to rethink the idea that the world is being homogenized. The discourse of cultural imperialism argues that the spread of western cultural goods is leading to the incorporation of peripheral cultures into a synchronized global monoculture. The problem here, though, as Tomlinson points out, is that the cultural imperialism argument makes "unwarranted leaps of inference from the simple presence of cultural goods to the attribution of deeper cultural or ideological effects" (1997: 135). In other words, it simply assumes that the sheer presence of western forms has a self-evident cultural effect on Third World subjects. However, if it is the case (as we are arguing) that consumers do not necessarily absorb the ideologies, values, and life-style positions of the texts they consume, if it is true that subjects always bring their own cultural dispositions to bear on such texts, then the case for the homogenization of the world loses much of its force. The only way to really show that the world is being homogenized is to demonstrate not only the ubiquity of western cultural forms but also that the consumption of these goods is profoundly transforming the way people make sense of their lives. Indeed, the homogenization scenario only makes sense if it can be established that the consumers of foreign cultural products are internalizing the values allegedly contained in them, whatever these values might be. The point, then, is that the ubiquity of western cultural forms around the world cannot in and of itself be taken as evidence that the world is being homogenized. Homogenization entails much more than this: it entails the transformation of the way people fashion their phenomenal worlds (see Tomlinson 1999). This not to say that there has been no cultural convergence at all in the world. It is to suggest, though, that as long as the process of customization is hard at work, the specter of homogenization will be kept somewhat at bay and the world will remain full of difference.

The second problem with the discourse of cultural imperialism's vision of the world has to do with the tendency to analyze globalization simply as a flow from the West to the rest. To be sure, there is substantial asymmetry in the flow of meaning in the world: the center mostly speaks, while the periphery principally listens (Hannerz 1992: 219). But this hardly means that the periphery does not talk back at all. For indeed it does. Culture does move in the opposite direction, that is, from the rest to the West (see, for example, Shannon 2003 and Cook et al. 2004). There is no denying this. The signs of it are everywhere. Take the case of food, for example: there are certain cuisines – such as Indian, Chinese, Korean, Thai, and Mexican – that have become standard eating fare for many in the West. Or take the realm of religion: it is not just Christianity and Judaism that command the attention of the faithful but increasingly also "non-western" religions such as Islam and Buddhism. Or take music: the listening pleasures of those in the West now include not only rock-and-roll and R&B but also samba, salsa, reggae, *rai*, juju, and so forth. Or take, finally, the case of people, which undoubtedly represents the most visible sign of this reverse traffic in culture: since World War II, largely as the result of poverty, economic underdevelopment, civil war, and political unrest, millions of people from the less affluent parts of the world have been driven to seek a future in the major urban centers of the "developed" and "developing" nations.[25] The result is a monumental presence of Third World peoples in the metropolises of the West. One finds, for example, people from the Caribbean basin (Cubans, Dominicans, Haitians, Puerto Ricans, Jamaicans), Asia (Chinese, Cambodian, Indian, Korean, Pakistani, Japanese), and Latin America (Mexicans, Guatemalans, Colombians) in the US; from Algeria, Tunisia, and Morocco in France; from Turkey and North Africa in Germany; from Morocco and the Dominican Republic in Spain; from Indonesia and Suriname in the Netherlands; from Senegal and Albania in Italy; and from the Caribbean, India, Pakistan, and Bangladesh in the United Kingdom (Hall 1996). What has happened, as a result of all this reverse traffic in culture, is that the periphery has set itself up within the very heart of the West. As such, the encounter between the core and the periphery no longer takes place simply "out there." It now also comes to pass "here." The core has been peripheralized, as it were (see Sassen-Koob 1982).

A significant effect of this peripheralization of the core has been that the nation-states of the West have been somewhat unsettled. This unsettling – and we will shortly see what is meant by this – has a lot to do with the nature of contemporary population movements. The interesting thing about migrants nowadays is that, in general, when they move across national boundaries, they do not simply leave their "homelands" behind (see Basch et al. 1994).[26] Rather, they are able to forge and maintain distanciated social relations – relations at a distance, across time and space – that link together their home and host societies. In other words, migrants today often form what might be called diasporic attachments; this refers to this dual affinity or doubled connection that mobile subjects have to localities, to their involvement in webs of cultural, political, and economic ties that encompass multiple national terrains.[27] These are people who have become practiced exponents of cultural bifocality (Rouse 2002). Or, as Stuart Hall has put it:

> They are people who belong to more than one world, speak more than one language (literally and metaphorically), inhabit more than one identity, have more than one home; who have learned to negotiate and translate *between* cultures, and who, because they are irrevocably the product of several interlocking histories and cultures, have learned to live with, and indeed to speak from, *difference*. They speak from the "in-between" of different cultures, always unsettling the assumptions of one culture from the perspective of another, and thus finding ways of being both *the same as* and at the same time *different from* the others amongst whom they live. (1995: 206)

Contemporary migrants (or at least many of them) thus represent different ways of being someone in a shrinking world. They are mobile subjects who draw on diverse assemblages of meanings and locate themselves in different geographies simultaneously.

The classic anthropological example of this diasporic process is Roger Rouse's (1988, 2002) study of the movement of labor migrants from the rural Mexican town of Aguililla, located in the southwest corner of the state of Michoacán, to the North American community of Redwood City, found on the northern edge of California's celebrated Silicon Valley (see also Ong, Chapter 7 in this volume, and Ewing, Chapter 8 in this volume). One of Rouse's basic observations is that the social-spatial image of "community," identified as a "discriminable population with a single, bounded space – a territory or place" (2002: 158), has historically been used to understand the experiences of Mexican migrants to the US as a relatively unproblematic one-way movement from one national space to another, that is, as a movement in which "migrants and their descendants experience a more or less gradual shift from one ordered arrangement to another, either fully converting to the dominant way of life or forging their own form of accommodation in an ordered synthesis of old and new" (2002: 160). Mexican immigrants have thus convention-ally been viewed as persons who uproot themselves, leave behind home, country, and community, and endure the painful process of incorporation into a new society and culture. Rouse argues, however, that since World War II the image of the territorially bounded community "has become increasingly unable to contain the postmodern complexities that it confronts" (2002: 160). For Mexican migrants have developed socio-spatial arrangements that question the received ways of viewing migration and that thus call for alternative cartographies of social space. What has happened, to put it simply, is that the Aguilillan "migrants" who have settled in Redwood City have not severed their ties to "home" but have instead maintained connections so intense that Aguililla and Redwood City can no longer be conceived as separate communities:

> Through the constant migration back and forth and the growing use of telephones, the residents of Aguililla tend to be reproducing their links with people that are two thousand miles away as actively as they maintain their relations with their immediate neighbors. Still more, and more generally, through the continuous circulation of people, money, commodities, and information, the diverse settlements have intermingled with such force that they are probably better understood as forming only one community dispersed in a variety of places. (Rouse 1988: 1–2; quoted in García Canclini 1995: 231–2)

Put otherwise, Aguilillan migrants have not abandoned one national space for another but have formed – through the continuous circulation of people, capital, goods, images, and ideas – a community that stretches across national boundaries. Rouse refers to this territorially unbound community as a transnational migrant circuit, emphasizing that it is here rather than in any particular locale that the lives of Aguilillans take place. Aguilillan migrants thus occupy no singular national space. They live their lives transnationally. They are cultural bifocals who belong simultaneously to more than one home and hence to no one home in particular. They are, in short, the fruit of several interlocking nations and cultures.

What all this indicates is that we are witnessing a world in which significant social relations and the parameters of community are no longer, if they ever were, simply confined within the limits of a single territorial national space. We are witnessing a world, in other words, that has become strewn with migrants who inhabit imagined communities of belonging that cut across and encompass multiple national terrains. The implications of this development for western nation-states, to get back to the question of unsettling, are rather profound. The nation-state, according to Arjun Appadurai, has historically functioned "as a compact and isomorphic organization of territory, ethnos [or people], and governmental apparatus" (1996: 42). This basically means that it has traditionally been constructed as a territorially circum-scribed and culturally homogeneous political space. The main way the nation-state has achieved this cultural homogeneity is through systematically subjecting the individuals living within its spatial frame to a wide array of nationalizing technolo-gies. These technologies of nationhood include the granting of citizenship rights; the development of rules on nationality; the invention of symbols of nationhood such as flags, ceremonials, the celebration of historical figures, and the observance of national holidays; the provision of social welfare policies, conscription, and public bureaucracies; and the building of roads, schools, hospitals and prisons (Axford 1995: 152–3). The nation-state, then, has historically operated with coercive prac-tices designed to forge its subjects into a single homogeneous national community. And it has by and large been very effective at creating this uniform space of nationness, successfully nationalizing not only those folks born on its soil but also the many migrants who settle within its boundaries.[28] Nowadays, however, western nation-states are no longer able to adequately discipline and nationalize all the subjects under their domain. They cannot fully produce proper national subjects – subjects defined by residence in a common territory, a shared cultural heritage, and an undivided loyalty to a common government. A case in point: the many migrants who live their lives across national boundaries. These are people who, because they are intimately linked to more than one place and to no one place in particular, are able to escape, to some degree, the nationalizing apparatuses of the nation-state. These are people, that is, who cannot be fully subjected to the nationalizing or assimilating imperatives of one nation-state since their experience is not limited to that single space. The basic problem here is that these days the nation-state functions less and less as a self-contained, autonomous entity and more and more as a transit depot through which an ever-increasing number of migrants pass, thus making it almost impossible for the technologies of nationhood to do their job and delimit the contours of a singular national order.

The result of this inability to construct a monolithic national community, of the incapacity to turn migrants into proper national subjects, is that the nation-states of the West have become homes to a host of diverse and sometimes incommensurable cultures. They have been turned into meeting places for a broadening array of peoples and cultures. They have developed into sites of extraordinary cultural heterogeneity.[29] Significantly, what this unfolding means is that the isomorphism of territory, ethnos, and legitimate sovereignty has to some extent been undone.

The ethnos and the territory no longer neatly coincide. The nation-state is no longer the place of the ethnos. It has become instead the place of the ethni. Moreover, this unfolding means that the cultural centeredness of the West has been somewhat called into question. For what can it mean to be English or American or French or, simply, western when these countries have become containers of African, Asian, and Latin American cultures? Contemplate, for instance, the following remarks from Jo-Jo, a young white reggae fan in Birmingham's ethnically diverse Balsall Health neighborhood:

> There's no such thing as "England" any more...welcome to India brothers! This is the Caribbean!...Nigeria!...There is no England, man. This is what is coming. Balsall Heath is the center of the melting pot, 'cos all I ever see when I go out is half-Arab, half-Pakistani, half-Jamaican, half-Scottish, half-Irish. I know 'cos I am [half-Scottish/half-Irish]...who am I?...Tell me who I belong to? They criticize me, the good old England. Alright, where do I belong? You know I was brought up with blacks, Pakistanis, Africans, Asians, everything, you name it...who do I belong to?...I'm just a broad person. The earth is mine...you know we was not born in Jamaica...we was not born in "England." We were born here, man. (Hebdige 1987: 158–9, quoted in Gupta and Ferguson 2002: 69)

Jo-Jo no doubt overstates the case a bit. There are many people who continue to define England as a homogenous national space and wish to keep its culture intact, unified within, and with strongly marked borders dividing it from others (Hall 1995). But certainly the idea of a culturally stable and unitary England no longer has the hold it once had. And the same could be said of France, the US, and most other First World nations, whose spaces have similarly become zones of heterogeneity. In a world of motion, the nation-states of the West have indeed been unsettled as antiquated efforts to map the world as an assemblage of homogeneous culture areas or homelands are "bewildered by a dazzling array of postcolonial simulacra, doublings and redoublings, as India and Pakistan seem to reappear in postcolonial simulation in London, prerevolution Teheran rises from the ashes in Los Angeles, and a thousand similar cultural dramas are played out in urban and rural settings all across the globe" (Gupta and Ferguson 2002: 68). In a world of complex mobilities, in short, the normative character of the western nation-state has been called into question and unsettled.[30]

Three general points spring from this discussion of reverse cultural flows. The first is that the process of globalization is much too complex to be thought of merely as a westernizing affair. For it involves not just the circulation of western subjects and objects but also the dissemination of non-western cultural forms. Globalization, in other words, cannot be conceived solely as a matter of one-way, western imperialism. It must be understood instead as a process of mutual, if uneven, infiltration: with the West permeating the rest and vice versa. The second, and related, point is that the process of globalization cannot be thought of merely as a homogenizing affair. For it is also, on some level, about heterogenization. It is about the differentiation of the world. Or, more precisely, it is about the differentiation of the West. The idea here is simply that a primary effect of the peripheralization of the core, or of the reverse traffic in culture, has been to turn the spaces of the West into dense sites of cultural heterogeneity. The final point is that as a result of all this back and forth movement, from the West to the rest and vice versa, the familiar lines between "here" and "there," center and periphery, and West and non-West have to some extent become blurred. That is to say, insofar as the Third World is in the First and the First World is in the Third, it has become difficult to specify with any certitude where one entity begins and the other one ends (see Gupta and Ferguson 2002). Where, for example, does one draw the boundaries of Mexico when so many of "its people" live in the US? Or where does one draw the boundaries of the US when "its capital" has such a strong presence in Mexico? This is not to say that these geopolitical categories have ceased to be useful. Indeed not. But they have become more difficult to map considering that we live in a world of "crisscrossed economies" and "intersecting systems of meaning" (Rouse 2002: 157). In the end, globalization cannot be thought of simply as a westernizing affair, nor can it be viewed solely as a homogenizing one. It must be read instead as a complex process that brings the West to rest and the rest to the West. It must be understood, in short, as a process of mutual imbrication.

The third, and last, problem with the cultural imperialism scenario is that it neglects those circuits of culture that circumvent the West – those which serve primarily to link the countries of the periphery with one another. These circuits can sometimes be more important and influential in shaping local milieus than those that connect the First World to the Third. So it is a major mistake to exclude them from the analysis of globalization. The signs of this peripheral traffic in culture are many. Consider the itineraries of capital: in China, to note just one case, the most important streams of finance come not from the West but from the Chinese communities of Taiwan, Hong Kong, and Southeast Asia (Yang 2002). Or take the flow of commodities: in the northeastern Indian settlement of Rangluwa, for example, the foreign commodities the populace consumes – clothing, cosmetics, and so forth – are more often than not from China rather than from the West (Borooah 2000). Or consider the movement of people: one can find populations from India in South Africa, Fiji, Guyana, and Trinidad and Tobago; from China in Malaysia, Thailand, Indonesia, the Philippines, Mexico, and El Salvador; from Afghanistan in the Islamic Republics of Iran and Pakistan; and from Egypt, Pakistan, Eritrea, India, and the Philippines in Saudi Arabia and other Arab Gulf countries (see Margold 1995; Malkki 1997; Willford 2002; Brodwin 2003; Al-Sharmani 2006). This, of course, is only to cite a few examples. Or take, finally, the case of the mass media, undoubtedly one of the most visible signs of the peripheral flow of culture: the India film industry, for example, serves not only the Indian subcontinent but also Indonesia, Malaysia, and areas of Africa; Mexican and Brazilian soap operas are popular not just in Latin America but in Russia as well; and Hong Kong supplies films not simply for mainland China, Taiwan, and the Chinese diaspora but also for other parts of the Third World. Such are the manifestations of the peripheral flow of culture. What they suggest, above all, is that the global cultural encounter takes place not just between the West and the rest but also within the periphery itself. It also takes place between the countries of the Third World.

There are two significant implications of this peripheral flow of culture. The first is that, for some countries of the periphery, the specter of Americanization or westernization may be less worrisome than, say, the prospects of Indianization, Indonesianization, or Vietnamization (Appadurai, Chapter 2 in this volume). This is the case for Sri Lanka, Irian Jaya, and Cambodia respectively. For some Third World countries, then, the worry is not so much about western domination as it is about the enormous cultural power of other non-western nations. One important analysis of this cultural dynamic is Mayfair Yang's study (2002) of mass media and transnational subjectivity in Shanghai. Yang's central argument is that, for China (or, more specifically, for the Chinese state), the fear of western cultural domination is of minor concern in comparison to the consternation over the subversive influence of overseas Chinese communities. To be sure, she notes, American film and television have made some inroads into China but the far more invasive influence has been Hong Kong and Taiwan popular culture:

> One most vivid indication of this cultural invasion can be found in the pop songs that young people listen to and the popularity of karaoke singing. There is something mesmerizing about the repetition of endless stories of love and disappointment. Hong Kong and Taiwan popular culture has gained a firm foothold in the mainland...with visiting singers giving concerts to packed halls filled with adoring fans paying high prices for tickets. Sixteen- and seventeen-year-old girls want to embrace and kneel in the footsteps of such male idols as Tong Ange and Tang Yongling. The longing to be a star oneself can be temporarily satisfied using the imported karaoke audiovisual systems now found in karaoke bars and in many work units, schools, and restaurants. Music stores have sprung up to sell this music on cassettes. Hong Kong songs are sung in Cantonese by young Shanghainese whose point of comparison these days is not Beijing but Hong Kong. (Yang 2002: 335)

The importance of this Hong Kong and Taiwanese cultural invasion, according to Yang, is that it has exposed Shanghainese subjects to overseas Chinese culture and thus made it possible for them to construct news ways of being Chinese – ways not prescribed by the apparatuses of the centralized state. This cultural invasion, in other words, has enabled Chinese national subjects to fashion identity spaces that "spill out over the constrictive molds of a fixed, state-spatialized Chinese identity and homogeneous national culture" (Yang 2002: 341). One can see, then, how the introduction of Hong Kong and Taiwan popular culture into mainland China might give the Chinese state cause to worry. It is a development that has disrupted the ability of the state to form proper national subjects – subjects whose allegiance and orientation are strictly to the state and the nation it embodies. This is not to suggest, though, that the Chinese state has completely lost its subject-making capacity. This is hardly the case. But it is to suggest that the Chinese state is no longer the sole arbiter of the identity of its subjects: it now has to compete for their minds and allegiances with a host of "foreign" entities. The upshot of all this is that for China, as well as for many other countries of the periphery, the West is not the only, or even the major, cultural power they have to contend with. Just as worrisome are the many cultural forces within the Third World itself. Just as distressing are the cultural powers of the periphery.

The second implication is that, in some cases, the peripheral flow of culture is not perceived as a threat but welcomed as a resource that allows people to participate, on an ongoing basis, in the imagined realities of other cultures. One notable examination of this cultural dynamic is Brian Larkin's study (Chapter 14 in this volume) of Indian films among the Hausa of northern Nigeria. Larkin's basic argument is that Indian films allow Hausa viewers to creatively engage a cultural tradition different from their own and thus to envision new styles of fashion, beauty, love, and romance. The crucial thing about these films, as well as about the styles they inspire, according to Larkin, is that they emanate not from the West but from another Third World country. As such, they are not associated, in the minds of Nigerians, with a cultural imperialist power.[31] This makes their incorporation into Hausa culture much more readily acceptable. Larkin puts this in the following terms:

> In northern Nigeria there is a familiar refrain that Indian culture is "just like" Hausa culture. While indeed, there are many similarities between Hausa and "Indian culture" (at least how it is represented in Indian films) there are many differences, most obviously the fact that Indians are predominantly Hindu and Hausa are Muslim. The popularity of Indian films rests, in part, on this dialectic between difference and sameness – that Indian culture is both like and quite unlike Hausa culture. It is the gap between difference and sameness, the ability to move between the two, that allows Indian films to function as a space for imaginative play in Hausa society. The intra-Third World circulation of Indian film offers Hausa viewers a way of imaginatively engaging with forms of tradition different from their own at the same time as conceiving of a modernity that comes without the political and ideological significance of that of the West. Moreover, when Hausa youth rework Indian films within their own culture by adopting Indian fashions, by copying the music styles for religious purposes, or by using the filmic world of Indian sexual relations to probe the limitations within their own cultural world, they can do this without engaging with the heavy ideological load of "becoming Western."

Larkin's basic argument, in other words, is that Indian films provide Hausa viewers with a meaningful cultural alternative to the aesthetic productions of the West, an alternative that allows them to explore modern forms of existence not linked to the history of western cultural imperialism. Indian films furnish them with a way to fashion new selves without having to take on the West and its ideological baggage. What this example highlights is that peripheral flows of culture figure prominently in generating interconnections between different peoples and cultures – interconnections that allow individuals to construct new ways of being in the world. As such, the traffic in culture within the Third World does not necessarily have to be about cultural domination. It can also be just about allowing people to creatively partake in the imagined realities of different cultures.

The basic point that emerges from all this is that the discourse of cultural imperialism's vision of the West overrunning the Third World, once again, cannot capture what is taking place in the world today. The idea here is that while the circuits that connect the West to the Third World are undoubtedly the prime movers of the global traffic in culture, they are by no means the only important forces around. There are also quite a few circuits that circumvent the West altogether, circuits that serve mainly to interconnect the countries of the periphery with each other. And these can be just as powerful in shaping the local environments of the periphery as any that go through the First World. This means that the West is not necessarily the only or primary foreign influence on many Third World countries. It indicates that the global cultural encounter takes place not just between the core and the periphery but also within the non-western world itself. As such, globalization cannot be thought of simply as a westernizing or homogenizing matter. It must be understood instead as an intricate process that brings not just the West to the rest or the rest to the West but also one part of the periphery to another. It has to be grasped as a much more complex, crisscrossing global affair.[32]

A dislocated world

The argument we have been making is that the discourse of cultural imperialism understands the increased global traffic in culture principally as a process of cultural imposition and dominance: of the imposition and dominance of western culture over the rest of the world. Moreover, we have noted that this pattern of domination is perceived as bringing about the increasing cultural homogenization of the world. The scenario that is often sketched is one in which western cultural practices, institutions, goods, and styles are being lifted from their territorial grounding and replicated across the world; the result being that the cultures of the periphery are being pounded out of existence. The de/territorialization of culture, in other words, is envisioned as leading to the elimination of cultural difference in the world as western culture is increasingly embraced in localities around the globe. It is seen as promoting the production of a world of sameness. We have also suggested, however, that from an anthropological perspective this westernization/homogenization scenario fails to adequately capture what is going on in the world. One basic problem with this take on globalization is that the traffic in culture is conceptualized as simply moving in one direction: from the West to the rest. To be sure, this center to periphery flow is a crucial component of the global cultural economy. But it is not the only thing that globalization is about. Globalization is actually a much more complex process, one that also involves substantial movements of culture from the periphery to the core as well as within the periphery itself. Another basic problem is that western cultural texts are perceived as having a self-evident cultural effect on Third World subjects, the effect being to westernize them. But this is an erroneous perception. The peoples of the periphery do not simply or necessarily absorb the ideologies, values, and life-style positions putatively embedded in the foreign cultural goods they consume. More often than not they actually customize these imported forms, interpreting them according to local conditions of reception. From an anthropological perspective, then, the process of globalization, we have suggested, is much too complex to be thought of merely as a westernizing affair, one that is leading to the obliteration of cultural difference in the world. We have argued that globalization is not in any simple way battering the cultures of the periphery out of existence and bringing forth a world of sameness.

What all of this implies is that the world can no longer be viewed simply as a matter of one-way, western cultural imperialism. It cannot be conceptualized just in terms of core–periphery relations. The world is just too complex a place. What we need, then, is a more nuanced view of the globe than that provided by the discourse of cultural imperialism. We need a different image of the world than the core–periphery model. The image we would like to put forth is that of dislocation. We propose, in other words, to view the world as a dislocated cultural space. The term "dislocation" is borrowed from Ernesto Laclau (1990), who uses it to refer to structures whose center has been displaced – displaced in such a way as to be supplemented not by another center but by a plurality of them. The main structures Laclau has in mind are modern societies or nation-states. But we think that the world as a whole can be conceptualized in similar terms. For the world, like the nation-state, has no single cultural power center from which everything radiates. The West may have historically played this role. But this is no longer the case. The West has been displaced and now has to compete with a plurality of power centers around the world. This is not to suggest, though, that the West has ceased to be the major player in the global cultural economy. It certainly has not. But it does mean that it no longer occupies an unchallenged position of dominance in the world. The world can thus be said to be dislocated to the extent that there is not just one global cultural power center but a plurality of them, even if the West stands out among these. In other words, the world can be thought of as a dislocated cultural space insofar as global cultural power has ceased to be concentrated in the West and become somewhat diffused. It can be considered dislocated, in short, to the degree that the traffic in culture or the flow of meaning does not just originate in the West but also in places all over the globe. To think in terms of dislocation is to view the world not in terms of a monolithic core–periphery model but as a complexly interconnected cultural space, one full of crisscrossing flows and intersecting systems of meaning. It is, in sum, to view the world (and hence globalization) not as a western project but as a global one.

The Limits of Global Mobility and Connection

The world we have described so far is one that is very much in motion. It is a world full of intricate flows and far-flung interconnections. This should not be taken to suggest, though, that the assorted mobilities which traverse the planet are completely foot-loose nor that the links connecting the various parts of the globe to each other are uniform and limitless. Indeed, we do not live in a world of unfettered flows and boundless connectivity. There are definite limits to global mobility and connection (Trouillot 2001; Coutin et al. 2002; Navaro-Yashin 2003; Cunningham and Heyman 2004; Cooper 2005; Tsing 2005; Ferguson 2006). What we would like to do here is explore these limits. First, we will examine what might be called the materiality of the global. This refers to the material practices – infrastructure, institutions, regulatory mechanisms, governmental strategies, and so forth – that both produce and preclude movement. The objective here is to suggest that global flows are patently structured and regulated, such that while certain objects and subjects are permitted to travel, others are not. Immobility and exclusion are thus as much a part of globalization as movement. Second, we will explore what we are calling, inspired by Anna Tsing (2005), awkward connections. This notion captures how the interconnections that typify the globe are highly selective and uneven. The idea here is that while the world might be highly interlinked, it is discriminatingly and unequally so. Indeed, there is a certain patchiness to the global map: while some areas of the world are well networked, others are all but skipped over or bypassed. Disconnection and segregation thus characterize globalization as much as linkage. In this section, then, we aim to round out the picture of globalization, attending to the processes that promote and limit movement and connection.

The materiality of the global

Let us start with the materiality of the global. Too often stories of globalization have imagined the circulation of capital, goods, ideas, images, and people as unrestrained. But the reality is that objects do not generally circulate freely. They require some sort of material infrastructure – encompassing anything from juridical frameworks, governmental strategies, and regulatory mechanisms to highways, airplane routes, and communications technologies – in order to move. By the same token, this very infrastructure (or lack thereof) can serve to limit and constrain mobility. Global flows, then, cannot be adequately apprehended without some attention to the sundry mechanisms that enable or hinder them. Indeed, they very much depend on what Tsing (Chapter 3 in this volume) calls a "material and institutional infrastructure of movement."

A prime example of the how material infrastructures enable movement is Jeffrey Juris's (Chapter 15 in this volume) study of new digital media flows and global activist networking. This work generally focuses on how anti-corporate globalization activists, inspired in large part by the ground-breaking utilization of the Internet by the Zapatistas, have employed new digital technologies – Web pages, open editing software, e-mail lists, and so forth – to create networks, organize mass actions, engage in media activism, and practice an emerging political ideal of open communication and globally networked democracy. Endeavors these activists have spearheaded include global campaigns against the liberalization of trade, drives to abolish the foreign debt of poorer countries, international forums, cross-border information sharing, and global days of action. Through the use of communication networks that span the globe, then, anti-corporate globalization activists have mobilized millions of people around the world in protest against capitalist-driven globalization, as well as brought extensive visibility to issues involving democracy and global economic justice. Significant here is that digital media technologies are a crucial condition of possibility for anti-corporate globalization activism. Juris articulated this as follows:

> By significantly enhancing the speed, flexibility, and global reach of information flows, allowing for communication at a distance in real time, digital networks provide the technological infrastructure for the emergence of contemporary network-based social movement forms...Using the Internet as technological architecture, [anti–corporate globalization] movements operate at local, regional, and global levels, while activists move back and forth between online and offline political activity.

Juris's argument is thus that new digital media provide the technological infrastructure that enables information to traverse the globe and communities to engage in exchanges across vast distances. Without this infrastructure, anti-corporate global-ization activism could hardly thrive.

Also emblematic of how infrastructure makes mobility possible is Kavita Misra's (Chapter 18 in this volume) study of AIDS service organizations in India and the global circulation of ideas. Misra notes that, as her fieldwork developed, she noticed how the transnational idea and practice of "confidentiality" lay behind many key negotiations related to AIDS work. "The uses of this language by AIDS experts," Misra states, "came to signify all that was deemed culturally absent but desirable and ideal for AIDS prevention and management in the Indian context (indeed, in all non-Euro-American contexts), and all that constituted socio-political impediments to health." The notion of "confidentiality" was thus invoked in discussions of AIDS issues ranging from consent, information, and privacy to discrimination, stigma, and institutional neglect. As such, it constituted a key discursive site reflecting changing and contested definitions of health, configurations of citizenship, and arrangements of governance. Importantly, the movement of "confidentially" to India could not have been possible without the expert infrastructure set up to deal with AIDS. As Misra put it:

> The AIDS crisis in India has...produced a community of expertise, a set of transna-tionally mobile individuals and groups, many of whom are situated in the realm of the non-governmental. This space of expert knowledge acts as a self-critical source of cultural commentary as well as transformative trends. It is a conduit for globally established scientific and ideological material to be delivered to local spaces, and the medium through which such material came to be contested, critiqued and reformulated before finding its way back into global sites.

Put otherwise, "confidentiality," as a transnational concept and practice, is very much indebted for its mobility to the assemblage of scientists, biomedical practi-tioners, legal experts, policy-makers, and non-governmental organizations that constitute the Indian AIDS service. This assemblage basically acts as a channel for the circulation of global AIDS ideologies.[33]

Material infrastructures do not only promote mobility, of course. They also hinder and block it. Take, for example, the movement of populations. To be sure, the technological capacity to make people highly mobile generally exists. But the mobility of people is actually rather stratified and subject to often strict state monitoring and control (Coutin et al. 2002; Neumayer 2006). Thus while some people might have the necessary wealth or cultural capital to secure the right to travel, many more do not. Indeed, not everyone has the same capacity for mobility. A particularly significant occurrence is that the immigration policies of First World nations have become progressively stricter, making it more and more difficult for refugees and labor migrants from various parts of the world – Latin America, Eastern Europe, Africa, and Asia – to migrate legally. The case of France is instruct-ive here. Over the last few decades, as Didier Fassin (Chapter 9 in this volume) shows, the attitude of French authorities towards refugees has changed from relative tolerance to almost total mistrust. In 1981, for instance, 80 percent of foreigners who sought asylum in France were granted refugee status. Eighteen years later, in 1999, it was the rejection rate that came to 80 percent. Two developments in the late

1980s were significant in this transformation. One was the end the Cold War, which generated sizable migrations from formerly communist countries toward Western Europe; the other the popular rise of the National Front, an extremely xenophobic political party that loudly decried the "invasion" of France by immigrants. Within this political environment, socialist Prime Minister Michel Rocard famously proclaimed: "France cannot welcome all the misery of the world." What is more, border officials began turning away numerous refugees before they could even apply for asylum and civil servants who assessed claims were instructed to reduce the number of acceptances. Accordingly, the number of foreigners offered political asylum decreased appreciably, gradually settling at approximately 2,000 refugees per year during the 1990s. Today, political asylum has essentially lost much of its legitimacy and asylum seekers are viewed with deep suspicion. As Fassin puts it: "all candidates for refugee status are now considered, until there is evidence to the contrary, to be undocumented immigrants seeking to take advantage of the generosity of the European nations." In other words, asylum seekers are nowadays generally deemed illegitimate and therefore highly unlikely to gain admittance into France, at least not legally.

Just as material infrastructures hamper the movement of people, they can also obstruct the mobility of commodities. In point of fact, goods generally do not move across the globe without friction. Obstacles to the free circulation of commodities include global and regional trade agreements (e.g. North American Free Trade Agreement and the General Agreement on Tariffs and Trade), which specify the rules and protocols of multilateral trade, including the formalities of taxation, export, import, and transit (Chalfin 2006); nation-state customs regimes, which monitor and regulate the movement of goods across state boundaries; and the politics of liquidity, that is, the struggles over the conditions or standards that render objects exchangeable or transferable. A good example of the latter obstacle is Andrew Lakoff's research (Chapter 12 in this volume) on the global trade in DNA. This work tracks the efforts of a French biotechnology company (Genset) to collect and map the DNA of mental patients at a public hospital (Romero) in Argentina, the goal being to uncover the genes or markers associated with susceptibility to bipolar disorder. If found, these genes would be patented and with any luck used to developed new diagnostic and therapeutic tools. The collection of DNA samples turned out to be more difficult than anticipated. It just so happened that bipolar disorder was infrequently diagnosed in Argentina. The Argentine mental health world generally operated according to a psychoanalytic epistemology and not the North American diagnostic system that recognized bipolar disorder. Without appropriate diagnostic standards in place, the mining and exchange of DNA could hardly transpire. Lakoff puts the problem in the following terms:

> Genset's collection process was based on a more general assumption, in cosmopolitan psychiatry, of the existence of an undifferentiated global epidemiological space. The World Health Organization estimated that 2.5% of the world's population between the ages of 15 and 44 suffered from bipolar disorder. If this was the case, where were the Argentine bipolar patients? Why was it so difficult for Romero's doctors to come up with 200 samples? Like the WHO, Genset's research protocol presumed that bipolar disorder was a coherent and stable entity with universal properties. But as a number of analysts of the production of scientific knowledge have argued, the existence of a given

technoscientific object – here, bipolar disorder – is contingent upon its network of production and stabilization. An individual experience of suffering becomes a case of a generalized psychiatric disorder only in an institutional setting in which the disorder can be recognized, through the use of specific concepts and techniques that format the complexities of individual experience into a generalized convention.

In other words, the problem with Genset's gene-hunting effort was that it took for granted the global validity of North American diagnostic standards. Such standards are part of a an infrastructure or epistemic niche that allows technoscientific objects such as bipolar disorder to come into being, take root, and thrive. The difficulty of locating bipolar patients in Argentina signified that a North American diagnostic infrastructure had not quite taken hold there. And in the absence of such an infrastructure, it was difficult to render the illness experience of Argentine mental patients liquid or transferable and thus capable of flowing across administrative boundaries. In the end, Genset did find enough mental patients from whom to collect DNA. But the case shows that the extraction, commodification, and global circulation of genetic material are not a straightforward affair.

Awkward connections

Now let us turn to awkward connections. Not only have stories of globalization tended to imagine global flows as unrestrained; they have also generally envisioned them as ubiquitous, as thoroughly interlinking the globe. The fact is, however, that such flows are not omnipresent and that the world is not uniformly connected. As Frederick Cooper notes: "The world has long been – and still is – a space where economic and political relations are very uneven; it is filled with lumps, places where power coalesces surrounded by those where it does not, places where social relations become dense amid others that are diffuse. Structures and networks penetrate certain places and do certain things with great intensity, but their effects tail off elsewhere" (2005: 91–2). Globalization, then, is at once a matter of selectively dense interconnections and extensive disconnection and abjection (Ferguson 2006).

We can highlight the awkwardness of global connections through examining the circulation of capital. On the issue of dense interconnections, it is clear that most capital movement occurs within or between the poles of what some have called the Triad (Ohmae 1985; Trouillot 2003): an economic zone with major regional centers in North America (the United States and Canada), Western Europe (with Germany at the epicenter), and Asia (with Japan as the focal point). For instance, in the 1980s, the Triad accounted for 88 percent of all capital flows. And of the $317 billion dollars invested across political borders worldwide in 1995, the lion's share, $317 billion, stayed in the United States, Canada, and the European Union (Trouillot 2003: 49). To get a sense of how such an uneven spatial distribution of capital occurs, we can look at the practices of Wall Street global investment banks. As Karen Ho shows (Chapter 6 in this volume), one of the main global strategies of such banks is to concentrate their energies on a few key markets, but simultaneously project the image that they are present (or at least can be) in countless other areas of the world. Being global here is thus not about being everywhere at once but about maintaining lines of access that allows banks to be flexible and move in and out of places as they wish. To achieve this global strategy, Ho observes:

> Wall Street investment banks have empty offices in many places throughout the world, and correspondingly, they focus their material infrastructure, people, and energies on even fewer places such as New York, London, and Tokyo. Such an approach allows investment banks to target their resources and be exclusionary in their sites of capital investment while the empty office secures an entry point, a slight foothold, and a particular global image. This flexible arrangement does not incur the cost of maintaining a fully staffed and operationalized infrastructure, especially if the bank does not have an active business in that location. Given the volatility of financial markets and institutions, the empty office is the kind of unfixed presence that facilitates mobility, even as it diverts from view the particularity and exclusivity of investment banking decisions.

So while Wall Street investment banks might have a presence in numerous places around the world, they actually conduct most of their financial transactions in a limited number of them. They tend to focus their resources on those localities most guaranteed to produce capital returns – on places where, as one of Ho's informants put it, "the markets are big and real, where our clients are big financial institutions, major companies, wealthy individuals." And these places are generally located in the Triad.

Turning to disconnection and abjection, there is no doubt that certain areas of the world are on the whole "excluded" from the global economy. Indeed, it appears that portions of humankind are extraneous to world economic processes and that the global map is increasingly full of "black holes" (Trouillot 2001: 129). Such disconnection is perhaps most visible in relation to Africa (Ferguson 2002, 2006). One of the general tenets of post-World War II development theory was that the impoverished countries of the globe would as a matter of course attract large amounts of capital and that, consequently, they would eventually achieve economic parity with the wealthy industrial nations. These assumptions turned out to be mistaken. Today, the most impoverished countries, including many in Africa, draw hardly any private capital and there is certainly no tendency toward economic convergence with the richer nations. The work of James Ferguson (2002) on Zambia is instructive here. It explores how this African nation has been redlined in global financial markets, as well as generally deprived of governmental aid flows, turning it into an out-and-out ghetto of global capital, a space of economic abandonment. This is not to suggest that Zambia in any way exists outside the world capitalist system. As Ferguson explains,

> "redlined" spaces of decline and disinvestment in the contemporary global economy are as much a part of the geography of capitalism as the booming zones of enterprise and prosperity; they reveal less the outside of the system than its underbelly. Expulsion and abandonment..., disconnection and abjection..., occur within capitalism, not outside of it. They refer to processes through which global capitalism constitutes its categories of social and geographical membership and privilege by constructing and maintaining a category of absolute non-membership: a holding tank for those turned away at the "development" door; a residuum of the economically discarded, disallowed, and disconnected – to put it plainly, a global "Second Class." (2002: 142)

Intrinsic to contemporary global economic processes, then, are practices of exclusion and abjection – the creation of "black holes," of zones of disinvestment and abandonment. Such practices show that capital flows engender not only dense forms of interconnection but forms of disconnection as well. They not only link together the globe but also set it apart. Indeed, connection and disconnection seem go hand in hand.

The perspective sketched out above on the limits of global mobility and connection can undoubtedly be filled out even further. But the fundamental point here is that the various flows which criss-cross the globe are not entirely footloose and the chains linking different parts of the world to each other far from uniform. Thus while capital can certainly traverse frontiers almost effortlessly, there are places where it does not go; while some people may readily cut across national boundaries, many others are stopped at the border's edge; while commodities might be able drift briskly from one locality to another, they are regulated via international trade agreements; while images no doubt can flicker quickly from screen to screen, they are often constrained by national regulatory regimes; and while ideologies may be able to circulate rapidly, they require some sort of material infrastructure in order to move. Indeed, globalization is not about unrestrained mobility and limitless connectivity. The world is not a seamless whole without boundaries. Rather, it is a space of structured circulations, of mobility and immobility. It is a space of dense interconnections and black holes.

The Organization of the Reader

Such is the complex world of globalization. The aim of this reader, as noted earlier, is to provide an anthropological introduction to this world. The articles gathered here are a selection of the most sophisticated recent anthropological work on globalization. We have organized this rich material into an introductory section and five thematic parts (each of which carries a short introduction of its own, along with suggestions for further reading). The introductory section, "Thinking the Global," brings together general theoretical efforts (including this chapter) to map the global condition.[34] The articles suggest that the picture of globalization as a homogenizing, one-way flow of culture from the West to the rest does not adequately capture the complex realities of the contemporary world. Arjun Appadurai's piece, for instance, suggests that the global cultural economy is a complex, overlapping, and disjunctive order – one best understood in terms of the relationship among five dimensions of global cultural flows: ethnoscapes (the moving landscape of people), mediascapes (the distribution of the electronic capabilities to disseminate information), technoscapes (the global configuration of technology), financescapes (the disposition of global capital), and ideoscapes (a chain of ideas composed of elements of the Enlightenment worldview). And Anna Tsing's contribution suggests that anthropologists must investigate global processes "without assuming either their universal extension or their fantastic ability to draw all world-making activities into their grasp." It calls, in other words, for an exploration of the limits of global movement and connectivity. The rest of the book moves away from this broad mapping of globalization to track the trajectories of specific global cultural flows. Part I, "Itinerant Capital," focuses on the mobility of capital, concentrating on its articulations with local cultural formations. Part II, "Mobile Subjects," is concerned with the movement of people, focusing primarily on the extensive post-World War II migrations from the countries of the periphery to the major urban centers of the "developed" and "developing" world.[35] Part III, "Roving Commodities," tracks the global flow of commodities, concentrating on the way the consumption of goods often mediates the "encounter" between peoples and cultures from around the world. Part IV, "Traveling Media," deals with the meanderings of the mass media, highlighting the increasingly important role they play in the quotidian realities of people from all over the globe. And part V, "Nomadic Ideologies," explores the circulation of western ideologies and discourses, focusing on how these narratives both constrict the lives of and create new subject positions for the peoples of the periphery.

The volume as a whole, then, aims to capture the complexities of the globalization process. It is concerned with tracking the paths taken by the numerous cultural flows – of capital, people, goods, images, and ideologies – that traverse the globe, as well as with exploring the local experiences of people as their everyday lives become increasingly contingent on globally stretched out social relations. The volume, in other words, simultaneously focuses on the macro processes through which the globe is becoming increasingly, albeit unevenly, interconnected and on the way subjects mediate these processes in culturally specific ways. It focuses, in short, on the conjunctural and situated character of globalization.

To conclude, we would like to call attention to some of the realities that have shaped the construction of this book. The anthropology of globalization is an exciting and rapidly growing field. We would have liked to capture all of this excitement and growth. Unfortunately, the limitation on space and the realities of budgets necessarily made such a task impossible. The volume therefore contains a number of important gaps. There is no intellectual justification for these exclusions other than the need to erect artificial limits. Let us point to some of the most obvious of these gaps. First, a number of important global phenomena are absent from the volume. They include tourist flows, global religious communities, transnational violence, global cities, and transnational pollution. Second, while the geographical reach of the book is fairly broad, there are a few areas of the world glaringly missing, including the Middle East, Australasia, and Polynesia. Third, we would have liked to pay more attention to issues of gender, race, and sexuality, but the need to broadly map the processes of globalization made this task unfeasible. Nevertheless, a number of the articles do touch on these issues (see Boellstorff; Ewing; Green; Merry and Stern; and Misra). And fourth, we would have liked to include more work dealing with the effects of globalization on the First World. But since most disciplines that deal with globalization tend to focus on the West, we felt this volume should be localized mainly in the Third World. This way the book serves as a corrective to much of the literature on globalization. Such are the omissions of this book, or at least some of them. No doubt there are others. We hope the reader will forgive us for these exclusions and enjoy the material that *is* included here.

NOTES

1 These snapshots are modified quotations taken from various articles included in this volume. See, respectively, Chapter 4, Green; Chapter 8, Ewing; Chapter 10, Caldwell; Chapter 14, Larkin; Chapter 16, Merry and Stern. The quotation marks have been intentionally left off.

2 See Robertson 1992 and Featherstone 2006 for genealogies of the concept of globalization.

3 For a critique of the rhetoric of circulation and flows as the ruling image for global interconnections, see Ferguson 2006 and Tsing Chapter 3 in this volume.

4 In this book, we use the term "western" or "the West" principally as a shorthand for the United States and Western Europe, as well as for the cultural products and practices of these countries.

5 We should note here that globalization is not a wholly new phenomenon. The world has for many centuries been an interconnected space (Wallerstein 1974; Wolf 1982; Abu-Lughod 1989). Arjun Appadurai (Chapter 2 in this volume), for instance, traces this interconnectedness back to the late fifteenth and early sixteenth centuries, when the West's encounter with the rest of the world created an overlapping set of ecumenes in which congeries of conquest, money, migration, and commerce began to form durable cross-cultural bonds. However, the problems of distance and the confines of technology have generally restricted the interactions of the past, so that it has been very difficult (that is, only at great cost and with great effort) to sustain dealings between culturally and spatially separate groups. So it is really only over the course of the past century, with the advent of modern technology – particularly with the innovations in transportation and communication, such as the introduction or improvement of airplanes, telephones, computers and video – that we have entered into a more profound condition of neighborliness, one that encompasses, to varying degrees, even those traditionally most remote from one another. Twentieth-century improvements in technology, then, have made possible interactions of a new magnitude and intensity. Developments in rail and air transport, for example, propel more people faster and longer distances than ever before. High-speed trains dash across the landscape at remarkable speeds, while supersonic jets shrink the extensive landmasses and oceans of the world. And if one prefers not to (or for whatever reason cannot) travel to other regions of the world, people and places reach us in the form of food, clothes, music, television images, and the like; and all kinds of technologies, from the telephone to the internet, enable us to be in touch with people half-way across the world, almost "as if they were present" (Allen and Hamnett 1995: 1). We thus find ourselves in a world that has become smaller over time, one in which borders and boundaries have become more porous than ever, allowing more people and cultures to be cast into "intense and immediate contact with each other," to be brought "closer" together, as it were (Morley and Robins 1995: 115). For the importance of historicizing global connection, see Trouillot 2003 and Cooper 2005.

6 James Ferguson (2002, 2006) thus argues that globalization should not be seen simply as a phenomenon of pure connection. It should also be understood in terms of disconnection.

7 The book is also to some extent concerned with related concepts such as transnationalism. Michael Kearney articulates the difference between transnationalism and globalization as follows: "Transnationalism overlaps globalization but typically has a more limited purview. Whereas global processes are largely decentered from specific national territories and take place in a global space, transnational processes are anchored in and transcend

one or more nation-states. Thus transnationalism is the term of choice when referring, for example, to the migration of nationals across the borders of one or of more nations" (1995: 548). See Hannerz 1996 and Ong 1999 for other articulations of the difference between globalization and transnationalism.

8   To be fair, anthropologists are not the only ones concerned with the articulation of the global and the local. But such discussions in other disciplines tend to stay at a theoretical level. There is hardly ever any concrete engagement with the local. Anthony Giddens, for example, views globalization as concerning "the intersection of presence and absence, the interlacing of social events and social relations 'at a distance' with local contextualities" (1991: 21). However, his analysis doesn't go much beyond this. There is no concrete engagement with these local contextualities.

In reflecting anthropologically on the global/local distinction, we should bear in mind a few things. First of all, the local, as Stacy Leigh Pigg and Vincanne Adams note, "is not a space where indigenous sensibilities reside in any simple sense" (2005: 11). That is to say, the local cannot be seen as a pre-constituted world, a black slate onto which globalizing processes map. Rather, the local is always already the social and historical product of movement, interaction, and exchange. Second, the global, as Pigg and Adams also point out, is not some sort of abstract monolith that hovers "somewhere above localities, imminently transcending the parochial, embodied, particularistic – and by definition limited and small – 'local' worlds" (2005: 30). Rather, it is very much as contingent, rooted, and situated as the local. Indeed, global processes are best thought of as locatable networks of practices and connections. And third, the global and the local should not be thought of as separate processes. Rather they occur simultaneously. At any given time the local is nothing other than the contingent grounding of the global and the global the provisional universalization of the local. The idea here is that what is commonly referred to as the global amounts to the successful circulation of specific localisms. And what we call the local is the "constantly refashioned *product* of forces well beyond itself" (Comaroff and Comaroff 2003: 156). In short, the global is shaped locally while the local is fashioned globally. For recent anthropological takes on the global/local distinction see Comaroff and Comaroff 2003, Mazzarella 2004, Pigg and Adams 2005, and Merry 2006.

9   We should point out that the general tendency in anthropology has been to treat the global as "a taken-for-granted macro context and as an abstract process too big for ethnographic endeavor" (Ho, Chapter 6 in this volume). In other words, the inclination has been to examine "the global simply from the 'rearview' of what it has left in its wake, that is, as a set of received 'effects' or in terms of 'impact'" (Ho, Chapter 6 in this volume). In keeping with such tendency, this volume generally focuses on the local effects of globalization. However, anthropologists have begun to ethnographically engage the global and track it "as cultural action grounded in specific practices and locales that can be thickly described" (Ho, Chapter 6 in this volume; see also Adams and Pigg 2005, Feldman 2005, and Tsing, Chapter 3 in this volume). This means that agency is accorded not just to the local but also to the global. As Gregory Feldman argues, human mediation is not simply at play when "'local' people work over 'global' processes" but also when "specific people *located* in 'macrosystems'... mediate those same processes" (2005: 222). The idea, then, is to treat the global as a project that is humanly mediated.

10 Unlike the first edition of this book, which brought together a blend of new writing and old, of the latest "cutting-edge" material and the best pioneering work, this new version mainly assembles recent anthropological texts on globalization (the one exception being Chapter 2, Arjun Appadurai's contribution. which is an indispensable classic). Over the last half decade, work on the anthropology of globalization has expanded phenomenally.

In order to capture this growth, we felt it best to produce a volume that included as much new work as possible. For earlier work on globalization, readers can turn to the first edition – to its articles and suggestions for further reading.

11 The work of Waters 1995 and McGrew 1996 has been very helpful in conceptualizing this section.

12 One important difference is that while Harvey sees capitalism as the main driving engine of globalization, Giddens views global processes as operating along four dimensions: capitalism; the inter-state system; militarism; and industrialism.

13 We should note here, as Anthony McGrew points out, that these time/space changes

> are not uniformly experienced across the globe. Some regions of the globe are more deeply implicated in global processes than others, and some are more deeply integrated into the global order than others. Within nation-states, some communities (e.g. financial ones) are tightly enmeshed in global networks, while others (e.g. the urban homeless) are totally excluded (although not entirely unaffected) by them. And, even within the same street, some households are more deeply embedded in global processes than others. (1996: 479–80)

We will deal more with the awkwardness and unevenness of global connections later.

14 Globalization as a whole must be understood in terms of simultaneous, complexly related processes in the realms of economy, politics, culture, technology, and so forth. See Held et al. 1999 for one attempt to provide an overall take.

15 To be sure, culture has always been more mobile and less fixed than the classical anthropological approach implies (see Gupta and Ferguson 2002). National, regional, and village boundaries have never enclosed culture in the manner that classical anthropological depictions have often indicated. What the intensification of global interconnectedness means, then, is just that the fiction that such boundaries contain cultures and thoroughly regulate cultural exchange can no longer be maintained.

16 The discourse of cultural imperialism is not as popular in academic circles as it was during the 1970s and 1980s (Tomlinson 1999). Nevertheless, it remains an important critical position for understanding the process of globalization. We find this discourse a useful starting point for discussing the cultural dynamics of globalization because it highlights the global asymmetries in the flow of meaning. Such asymmetries continue to be an important part of the world of globalization.

17 The discourse of cultural imperialism is actually a heterogeneous ensemble of complicated, ambiguous, and contradictory ideas. Here, however, our main concern is to identify some of the central tenets that run through the discourse. We thus necessarily gloss over its tensions and contradictions. See Tomlinson 1991 for a more nuanced view of this discourse.

18 The work of John Tomlinson (1997, 1999) significantly influenced the following discussion of the two visions of global uniformity that follows.

19 This scenario is drawn from one of the most important exponents of this view: the American media critic Herbert Schiller. He articulates this view most powerfully in his 1969 classic *Mass Communications and American Empire*.

20 This second vision of global cultural uniformity is drawn more or less from Latouche 1996.

21 This doesn't mean that the West as a geographical entity has ceased to exist. What has happened, to be more precise, is that "the West" as a cultural formation has been pulled apart from "the West" as a geographic entity. The West, in other words, has been de/territorialized.

22 Other names for this process of interpreting foreign cultural forms according to local conditions of reception are creolization (Hannerz 1992), transculturation (Lull 2000), vernacularization (Merry 2006), and indigenization (Appadurai, Chapter 2 in this volume). We prefer the term "customization" because it is less ideologically loaded than terms such as indigenization, which carry connotations of being rooted in the soil. See Malkki 1997 for a discussion of the problems with metaphors of rootedness.

23 The discussion of customization that follows focuses on the reception of film and television texts. However, this notion is also useful for talking about how people consume commodities (see Caldwell, Chapter 10 in this volume) and for how they interpret foreign ideologies (see Merry and Stern, Chapter 16 in this volume).

24 Morley and Robins, for example, point out that television "programs are usually made in such a way as to 'prefer' one reading over another and to invite the viewer to 'take' the message in some particular way, even if such a 'reading' can never be guaranteed" (1995: 127).

25 It is important to point out that this movement of peoples to the First World has been accompanied by mass-media and commodity flows that cater principally to immigrant populations (see Naficy 1993; Mankekar 2002).

26 The classic literature on immigration has constructed a picture of migrants as beings who leave behind home and country to endure the painful process of incorporation into a new society and culture. Recent scholarship suggests, however, that this picture is not quite accurate, for immigrants have always, to varying degrees and in different ways, maintained networks of interconnection (Glick Schiller et al. 1995). This is not to say that there are no differences between migrants today and those of the past. One main difference is that, given the introduction of modern technologies of transport and communication (telephone, television, airplanes, fax machines, and so forth), it is now a lot easier for immigrants to maintain networks of interconnection. Today's interconnections are thus more dense and intense.

27 The term "diaspora" has a long and complicated history. Unfortunately, we do not have the space to deal with this history here. Suffice it to say that the term has traditionally been used to refer to the Jewish experience of forced exile from Palestine. And nowadays it is commonly employed to designate the experience of forced dispersal more generally (as in the case of Africans) and to speak of those migrant populations that maintain ties with their countries of origin. See Safran 1991 for a discussion of diasporas in modern society.

28 We say "by and large" because nation-states vary (and have historically varied) in their ability to penetrate the nooks and crannies of the everyday lives of the people under their domain. In other words, they are not always (and have not always been) successful in defining and containing the lives of their citizens.

29 This heterogenization of the spaces of the West has not come without its problems, however. There has actually been great resistance in both Europe and the US to this heterogenization. Verena Stolcke (1995), for example, argues that over the past decade or so Europe has witnessed the rise of a political rhetoric of exclusion in which Third World immigrants and their descendants have been constructed as posing a threat to the nation because they are culturally different. Numerous strategies have thus been developed to nationalize, repatriate, and marginalize these populations. See also Ewing Chapter 8 in this volume.

30 This is not to imply that the nation-state has become obsolete. Indeed not. The nation-state continues to operate today with great effectiveness. Aihwa Ong, for example, suggests that "the nation-state – along with its juridical-legislative systems, bureaucratic apparatuses, economic entities, modes of governmentality, and war-making

capacities – continues to define, discipline, control, and regulate all kinds of populations, whether in movement or in residence" (1999: 15). All we mean to suggest, then, is that while the nation-state might continue to exist, its normative character is not going unchallenged.

31 This is not to say that other countries do not view India as a cultural imperialist power. But this is not the case, for the most part, in Nigeria.

32 If we had the space, we would complicate this picture even further by taking into account the numerous flows of culture that take place within the West itself. See Morley and Robins 1995 for a discussion of mass-media flows and Klimt 2000 and Koven 2004 for a discussion of population movements.

33 See Rudnyckyj 2004 for an exploration of the techniques and networks that make possible the movement of migrant laborers, particularly domestics, from Indonesia to wealthy countries in the Pacific and Indian Ocean regions.

34 For other general anthropological takes on globalization see Escobar 2001, Trouillot 2001, Coutin et al. 2002, Moore 2004, Glick Schiller 2005, and Gupta and Sharma 2006.

35 The movement of people is, of course, more complex than this. It involves more than just the flow of populations from the Third World to the First. There are also substantial movements of people from the First World to the Third, most notably tourists (see Ebron 1999), and within both the Third and First Worlds (see Margold 1995; Malkki 1997; Klimt 2000; Willford 2002; Brodwin 2003; Koven 2004; Al-Sharmani 2006). Unfortunately, we do not have room in the reader to cover this complexity.

REFERENCES

Abu-Lughod, Janet L.
  1989 *Before European Hegemony: The World System AD 1250–1350*. New York: Oxford University Press.
Adams, Vincanne and Stacy Leigh Pigg, eds.
  2005 *Sex in Development: Science, Sexuality, and Morality in Global Perspective*. Durham, NC: Duke University Press.
Allen, John and Chris Hamnett
  1995 Introduction. In *A Shrinking World? Global Unevenness and Inequality*. John Allen and Chris Hamnett, eds. Pp. 1–10. New York: Oxford University Press.
Al-Sharmani, Mulki
  2006 Living Transnationally: Somali Diasporic Women in Cairo. *International Migration* 44(1): 55–75.
Ang, Ien
  1985 *Watching Dallas: Soap Opera and the Melodramatic Imagination*. London: Methuen.
Appadurai, Arjun
  1996 Sovereignty without Territoriality: Notes for a Postnational Geography. In *The Geography of Identity*. Patricia Yaeger, ed. Pp. 40–58. Ann Arbor: University of Michigan Press.
Axford, Barrie
  1995 *The Global System: Economics, Politics, and Culture*. New York: St. Martin's Press.
Basch, Linda, Nina Glick Schiller, and Cristina Szanton Blanc
  1994 *Nations Unbound: Transnational Projects, Postcolonial Predicaments, and Deterritorialized Nation-States*. Langhorne, PA: Gordon and Breach.

Borooah, Romy
2000 Transformations in Trade and the Constitution of Gender and Rank in Northeast India. *American Ethnologist* 27(2): 371–99.

Brodwin, Paul
2003 Pentecostalism in Translation: Religion and the Production of Community in the Haitian Diaspora. *American Ethnologist* 30(1): 85–101.

Chalfin, Brenda
2006 Global Customs Regimes and the Traffic in Sovereignty: Enlarging the Anthropology of the State. *Current Anthropology* 47(2): 243–76.

Clifford, James
1988 *The Predicament of Culture*. Cambridge, MA: Harvard University Press.
1997 *Routes: Travel and Translation in the Late Twentieth Century*. Cambridge, MA: Harvard University Press.

Comaroff, Jean and John Comaroff
2003 Ethnography on an Awkward Scale: Postcolonial Anthropology and the Violence of Abstraction. *Ethnography* 4(2): 147–79.

Cook, Ian et al.
2004 Follow the Thing: Papaya. *Antipode* 36(4): 642–64.

Cooper, Frederick
2005 *Colonialism in Question: Theory, Knowledge, History*. Berkeley: University of California Press.

Coutin, Susan Bibler, Bill Maurer, and Barbara Yngvesson
2002 In the Mirror: The Legitimation Work of Globalization. *Law and Social Inquiry* 27(4): 801–43.

Cunningham, Hilary and Josiah McC. Heyman
2004 Introduction: Mobilities and Enclosures at Borders. *Identities: Global Studies in Culture and Power* 11: 289–302.

Ebron, Paulla A.
1999 Tourists as Pilgrims: Commercial Fashioning of Transatlantic Politics. *American Ethnologist* 26(4): 910–32.

Escobar, Arturo
2001 Culture Sits in Place: Reflections on Globalism and Subaltern Strategies of Localization. *Political Geography* 20(2): 139–74.

Featherstone, Mike
2006 Genealogies of the Global. *Theory, Culture & Society* 23(2–3): 387–92.

Feldman, Gregory
2005 Estranged States: Diplomacy and the Containment of National Minorities in Europe. *Anthropological Theory* 5(3): 219–45.

Ferguson, James
2002 Global Disconnect: Abjection and the Aftermath of Modernism. In *The Anthropology of Globalization*. Jonathan Xavier Inda and Renato Rosaldo, eds. Pp. 136–53. Malden, MA: Blackwell Publishing.
2006 *Global Shadows: Africa in the Neoliberal World Order*. Durham, NC: Duke University Press.

Foster, Robert J.
1999 Melanesianist Anthropology in the Era of Globalization. *The Contemporary Pacific* 11(1): 140–58.

García Canclini, Néstor
1995 *Hybrid Cultures: Strategies for Entering and Leaving Modernity*. Minneapolis: University of Minneapolis Press.

Giddens, Anthony
  1990   *The Consequences of Modernity.* Stanford, CA: Stanford University Press.
  1991   *Modernity and Self-Identity.* Cambridge: Polity Press.
Glick Schiller, Nina
  2005   Transnational Social Fields and Imperialism: Bringing a Theory of Power to Transnational Studies. *Anthropological Theory* 5(4): 439–61.
Glick Schiller, Nina, Linda Basch, and Cristina Szanton Blanc
  1995   From Immigrant to Transmigrant: Theorizing Transnational Migration. *Anthropological Quarterly* 68(1): 48–63.
Gupta, Akhil and James Ferguson
  2002   Beyond "Culture": Space, Identity, and the Politics of Difference." In *The Anthropology of Globalization.* Jonathan Xavier Inda and Renato Rosaldo, eds. Pp. 65–80. Malden, MA: Blackwell Publishing.
Gupta, Akhil and Aradhana Sharma
  2006   Globalization and Postcolonial States. *Current Anthropology* 47(2): 277–307.
Hall, Stuart
  1995   New Cultures for Old. In *A Place in the World? Places, Cultures, and Globalization.* Doreen Massey and Pat Jess, eds. Pp. 175–213. New York: Oxford University Press.
  1996   The Question of Cultural Identity. In *Modernity: An Introduction to Modern Societies.* Stuart Hall, David Held, Don Hubert, and Kenneth Thompson, eds. Pp. 595–634. Cambridge, MA: Blackwell Publishers.
Hannerz, Ulf
  1991   Scenarios for Peripheral Cultures. In *Culture, Globalization, and the World-System: Contemporary Conditions for the Representation of Identity.* Anthony D. King, ed. Pp. 107–28. Binghamton: Department of Art and Art History, State University of New York at Binghamton.
  1992   *Cultural Complexity: Studies in the Social Organization of Meaning.* New York: Columbia University Press.
  1996   *Transnational Connections: Culture, People, Places.* London: Routledge.
Harvey, David
  1989   *The Condition of Postmodernity.* Oxford: Blackwell Publishers.
Hebdige, Dick
  1987   *Cut 'n' Mix: Culture, Identity, and Caribbean Music.* London: Methuen.
Held, David, Anthony McGrew, David Goldblatt, and Jonathan Perraton
  1999   *Global Transformations: Politics, Economics, and Culture.* Cambridge: Polity Press.
Kearney, Michael
  1995   The Local and the Global: The Anthropology of Globalization and Transnationalism. *Annual Review of Anthropology* 24: 547–65.
Klimt, Andrea
  2000   Enacting National Selves: Authenticity, Adventure, and Disaffection in the Portuguese Diaspora. *Identities: Global Studies in Culture and Power* 6(4): 513–50.
Koven, Michèle
  2004   Transnational Perspectives on Sociolinguistic Capital among Luso-Descendants in France and Portugal. *American Ethnologist* 31(2): 270–90.
Laclau, Ernesto
  1990   *New Reflections on the Revolution of Our Time.* London: Verso.
Latouche, Serge
  1996   *The Westernization of the World: The Significance, Scope and Limits of the Drive towards Global Uniformity.* Cambridge: Polity Press.

Liebes, Tamar and Elihu Katz
  1990   *The Export of Meaning: Cross-cultural Readings of Dallas.* New York: Oxford
         University Press.
Lull, James
  2000   *Media, Communication, Culture: A Global Approach.* 2nd edn. Cambridge: Polity
         Press.
Malkki, Liisa H.
  1997   National Geographic: The Rooting of Peoples and the Territorialization of National
         Identity among Scholars and Refugees. In *Culture, Power, Place: Explorations in Critical
         Anthropology.* Akhil Gupta and James Ferguson, eds. Pp. 52–74. Durham, NC: Duke
         University Press.
Mankekar, Purnima
  2002   "Indian Shopping:" Indian Grocery Stores and Transnational Configurations of
         Belonging. *Ethnos* 67(1): 75–98.
Margold, Jane A.
  1995   Narratives of Masculinity and Transnational Migration: Filipino Workers in the
         Middle East. In *Bewitching Women, Pious Men: Gender and Body Politics in Southeast
         Asia.* Aihwa Ong and Michael G. Peletz, eds. Pp. 274–98. Berkeley: University of
         California Press.
Massey, Doreen
  1994   *Space, Place, and Gender.* Minneapolis: University of Minnesota Press.
Mazzarella, William
  2004   Culture, Globalization, Mediation. *Annual Review of Anthropology* 33: 345–67.
McGrew, Anthony
  1996   A Global Society? In *Modernity: An Introduction to Modern Societies.* Stuart Hall,
         David Held, Don Hubert, and Kenneth Thompson, eds. Pp. 466–503. Cambridge, MA:
         Blackwell Publishers.
Merry, Sally Engle
  2006   Transnational Human Rights and Local Activism: Mapping the Middle. *American
         Anthropologist* 108(1): 38–51.
Michaels, Eric
  2002   Hollywood Iconography: A Warlpiri Reading. In *The Anthropology of Global-
         ization.* Jonathan Xavier Inda and Renato Rosaldo, eds. Pp. 311–24. Malden, MA:
         Blackwell Publishing.
Moore, Henrietta L.
  2004   Global Anxieties: Concept-metaphors and Pre-theoretical Commitments in Anthro-
         pology. *Anthropological Theory* 4(1): 71–88.
Morley, David
  1992   *Television, Audiences, and Cultural Studies.* London: Routledge.
Morley, David and Kevin Robins
  1995   *Spaces of Identity: Global Media, Electronic Landscapes, and Cultural Boundaries.*
         London: Routledge.
Naficy, Hamid
  1993   *The Making of Exile Cultures: Iranian Television in Los Angeles.* Minneapolis:
         University of Minnesota Press.
Navaro-Yashin, Yael
  2003   "Life is Dead Here:" Sensing the Political in "No Man's Land." *Anthropological
         Theory* 3(1): 107–25.

Nederveen Pieterse, Jan
  1995   Globalization as Hybridization. In *Global Modernities*. Mike Featherstone, Scott Lash, and Roland Robertson, eds. Pp. 45–68. London: Sage Publications.
Neumayer, Eric
  2006   Unequal Access to Foreign Spaces: How States Use Visa Restrictions to Regulate Mobility in a Globalized World. *Transactions of the Institute for British Geographers* 3(1): 72–84.
Ohmae, Kenichi
  1985   *Triad Power: The Coming Shape of Global Competition*. New York: New Press.
Ong, Aihwa
  1999   *Flexible Citizenship: The Cultural Logics of Transnationality*. Durham, NC: Duke University Press.
Pigg, Stacy Leigh and Vincanne Adams
  2005   Introduction: The Moral Object of Sex. In *Sex in Development: Science, Sexuality, and Morality in Global Perspective*. Vincanne Adams and Stacy Leigh Pigg, eds. Pp. 1–38. Durham, NC: Duke University Press.
Povinelli, Elizabeth A. and George Chauncey
  1999   Thinking Sexuality Transnationally: An Introduction. *GLQ: A Journal of Lesbian and Gay Studies* 5(4): 439–50.
Robertson, Roland
  1992   *Globalization: Social Theory and Global Culture*. London: Sage Publications.
Rouse, Roger
  1988   Mexicano, Chicano, Pocho: La Migración Mexicana y el Espacio Social del Posmodernismo. *Página Uno*, supplement to *Unomásuno*, December 31: 1–2.
  2002   Mexican Migration and the Social Space of Postmodernism. In *The Anthropology of Globalization*. Jonathan Xavier Inda and Renato Rosaldo, eds. Pp. 157–71. Malden, MA: Blackwell Publishing.
Rudnyckyj, Daromir
  2004   Technologies of Servitude: Governmentality and Indonesia Transnational Labor Migration. *Anthropological Quarterly* 77(3): 407–34.
Safran, William
  1991   Diasporas in Modern Societies: Myths of Homeland and Return. *Diaspora* 1(1): 83–99.
Sassen-Koob, Saskia
  1982   Recomposition and Peripheralization at the Core. *Contemporary Marxism* 5: 88–100.
Schiller, Herbert I.
  1969   *Mass Communications and American Empire*. New York: Augustus M. Kelly.
Shannon, Jonathan H.
  2003   Sultans of Spin: Syrian Sacred Music on the World Stage. *American Anthropologist* 105(2): 266–77.
Stolcke, Verena
  1995   Talking Culture: New Boundaries, New Rhetorics of Exclusion in Europe. *Current Anthropology* 36(1): 1–24.
Thompson, John B.
  1995   *The Media and Modernity: A Social Theory of the Media*. Stanford, CA: Stanford University Press.
Tomlinson, John
  1991   *Cultural Imperialism*. Baltimore, MD: Johns Hopkins University Press.

1997 Internationalism, Globalization, and Cultural Imperialism. In *Media and Cultural Regulation*. Kenneth Thompson, ed. Pp. 117–62. London: Sage Publications.

1999 *Globalization and Culture*. Chicago: University of Chicago Press.

Trouillot, Michel-Rolph

2001 The Anthropology of the State in the Age of Globalization: Close Encounters of the Deceptive Kind. *Current Anthropology* 42(1): 125–38.

2003 *Global Transformations: Anthropology and the Modern World*. New York: Palgrave Macmillan.

Tsing, Anna Lowenhaupt

2005 *Friction: An Ethnography of Global Connection*. Princeton, NJ: Princeton University Press.

Wallerstein, Immanuel

1974 *The Modern World System*, vol. 1. New York: Academic Press.

Waters, Malcolm

1995 *Globalization*. London: Routledge.

Willford, Andrew

2002 "Weapons of the Meek:" Ecstatic Ritualism and Strategic Ecumenism among Tamil Hindus in Malaysia. *Identities: Global Studies in Culture and Power* 9: 247–80.

Williams, Raymond

1976 *Keywords*. New York: Oxford University Press.

Wolf, Eric R.

1982 *Europe and the People without History*. Berkeley: University of California Press.

Yang, Mayfair

2002 Mass Media and Transnational Subjectivity in Shanghai: Notes on (Re)Cosmopolitanism in a Chinese Metropolis. In *The Anthropology of Globalization*. Jonathan Xavier Inda and Renato Rosaldo, eds. Pp. 325–49. Malden, MA: Blackwell Publishing.

2

Disjuncture and Difference in the Global Cultural Economy

Arjun Appadurai

It takes only the merest acquaintance with the facts of the modern world to note that it is now an interactive system in a sense that is strikingly new. Historians and sociologists, especially those concerned with translocal processes (Hodgson 1974) and the world systems associated with capitalism (Abu-Lughod 1989; Braudel 1981–4; Curtin 1984; Wallerstein 1974; Wolf 1982), have long been aware that the world has been a congeries of large-scale interactions for many centuries. Yet today's world involves interactions of a new order and intensity. Cultural transactions between social groups in the past have generally been restricted, sometimes by the facts of geography and ecology, and at other times by active resistance to interactions with the Other (as in China for much of its history and in Japan before the Meiji Restoration). Where there have been sustained cultural transactions across large parts of the globe, they have usually involved the long-distance journey of commodities (and of the merchants most concerned with them) and of travelers and explorers of every type (Helms 1988; Schafer 1963). The two main forces for sustained cultural interaction before this century have been warfare (and the large-scale political systems sometimes generated by it) and religions of conversion, which have sometimes, as in the case of Islam, taken warfare as one of the legitimate instruments of their expansion. Thus, between travelers and merchants, pilgrims and conquerors, the world has seen much long-distance (and long-term) cultural traffic. This much seems self-evident.

But few will deny that given the problems of time, distance, and limited technologies for the command of resources across vast spaces, cultural dealings between socially and spatially separated groups have, until the past few centuries, been bridged at great cost and sustained over time only with great effort. The forces of

From *Modernity at Large: Cultural Dimensions of Globalization*, pp. 27–47. Minneapolis: University of Minnesota Press, 1996.

cultural gravity seemed always to pull away from the formation of large-scale ecumenes, whether religious, commercial, or political, toward smaller-scale accretions of intimacy and interest.

Sometime in the past few centuries, the nature of this gravitational field seems to have changed. Partly because of the spirit of the expansion of western maritime interests after 1500, and partly because of the relatively autonomous developments of large and aggressive social formations in the America (such as the Aztecs and the Incas), in Eurasia (such as the Mongols and their descendants, the Mughals and Ottomans), in island Southeast Asia (such as the Buginese), and in the kingdoms of precolonial Africa (such as Dahomey), an overlapping set of ecumenes began to emerge, in which congeries of money, commerce, conquest, and migration began to create durable cross-societal bonds. This process was accelerated by the technology transfers and innovations of the late eighteenth and nineteenth centuries (e.g., Bayly 1989), which created complex colonial orders centered on European capitals and spread throughout the non-European world. This intricate and overlapping set of Eurocolonial worlds (first Spanish and Portuguese, later principally English, French, and Dutch) set the basis for a permanent traffic in ideas of people-hood and selfhood, which created the imagined communities (Anderson 1983) of recent nationalisms throughout the world.

With what Benedict Anderson has called "print capitalism," a new power was unleashed in the world, the power of mass literacy and its attendant large-scale production of projects of ethnic affinity that were remarkably free of the need for face-to-face communication or even of indirect communication between persons and groups. The act of reading things together set the stage for movements based on a paradox – the paradox of constructed primordialism. There is, of course, a great deal else that is involved in the story of colonialism and its dialectically generated nationalisms (Chatterjee 1986), but the issue of constructed ethnicities is surely a crucial strand in this tale.

But the revolution of print capitalism and the cultural affinities and dialogues unleashed by it were only modest precursors to the world we live in now. For in the past century, there has been a technological explosion, largely in the domain of transportation and information, that makes the interactions of a print-dominated world seem as hard-won and as easily erased as the print revolution made earlier forms of cultural traffic appear. For with the advent of the steamship, the automobile, the airplane, the camera, the computer, and the telephone, we have entered into an altogether new condition of neighborliness, even with those most distant from ourselves. Marshall McLuhan, among others, sought to theorize about this world as a "global village," but theories such as McLuhan's appear to have overestimated the communitarian implications of the new media order (McLuhan and Powers 1989). We are now aware that with media, each time we are tempted to speak of the global village, we must be reminded that media create communities with "no sense of place" (Meyrowitz 1985). The world we live in now seems rhizomic (Deleuze and Guattari 1987), even schizophrenic, calling for theories of rootlessness, alienation, and psychological distance between individuals and groups on the one hand, and fantasies (or nightmares) of electronic propinquity on the other. Here, we are close to the central problematic of cultural processes in today's world.

Thus, the curiosity that recently drove Pico Iyer to Asia (1988) is in some ways the product of a confusion between some ineffable McDonaldization of the world and the much subtler play of indigenous trajectories of desire and fear with global flows of people and things. Indeed, Iyer's own impressions are testimony to the fact that, if *a* global cultural system is emerging, it is filled with ironies and resistances, sometimes camouflaged as passivity and a bottomless appetite in the Asian world for things western.

Iyer's own account of the uncanny Philippine affinity for American popular music is rich testimony to the global culture of the hyperreal, for somehow Philippine renditions of American popular songs are both more widespread in the Philippines, and more disturbingly faithful to their originals, than they are in the United States today. An entire nation seems to have learned to mimic Kenny Rogers and the Lennon sisters, like a vast Asian Motown chorus. But *Americanization* is certainly a pallid term to apply to such a situation, for not only are there more Filipinos singing perfect renditions of some American songs (often from the American past) than there are Americans doing so, there is also, of course, the fact that the rest of their lives is not in complete synchrony with the referential world that first gave birth to these songs.

In a further globalizing twist on what Fredric Jameson has recently called "nostalgia for the present" (1989), these Filipinos look back to a world they have never lost. This is one of the central ironies of the politics of global cultural flows, especially in the arena of entertainment and leisure. It plays havoc with the hegemony of Eurochronology. American nostalgia feeds on Filipino desire represented as a hypercompetent reproduction. Here, we have nostalgia without memory. The paradox, of course, has its explanations, and they are historical; unpacked, they lay bare the story of the American missionization and political rape of the Philippines, one result of which has been the creation of a nation of make-believe Americans, who tolerated for so long a leading lady who played the piano while the slums of Manila expanded and decayed. Perhaps the most radical postmodernists would argue that this is hardly surprising because in the peculiar chronicities of late capitalism, pastiche and nostalgia are central modes of image production and reception. Americans themselves are hardly in the present anymore as they stumble into the megatechnologies of the twenty-first century garbed in the film-noir scenarios of sixties' chills, fifties' diners, forties' clothing, thirties' houses, twenties' dances, and so on ad infinitum.

As far as the United States is concerned, one might suggest that the issue is no longer one of nostalgia but of a social *imaginaire* built largely around reruns. Jameson was bold to link the politics of nostalgia to the postmodern commodity sensibility, and surely he was right (1983). The drug wars in Colombia recapitulate the tropical sweat of Vietnam, with Ollie North and his succession of masks – Jimmy Stewart concealing John Wayne concealing Spiro Agnew and all of them transmogrifying into Sylvester Stallone, who wins in Afghanistan – thus simultaneously fulfilling the secret American envy of Soviet imperialism and the rerun (this time with a happy ending) of the Vietnam War. The Rolling Stones, in their fifties, gyrate before eighteen-year-olds who do not appear to need the machinery of nostalgia to be sold on their parents' heroes. Paul McCartney is selling the Beatles to a new audience by hitching his oblique nostalgia to their desire for the new that smacks of the old. *Dragnet* is back in nineties drag, and so is *Adam-12*, not to speak of *Batman* and *Mission Impossible*, all dressed up technologically but remarkably faithful to the atmospherics of their originals.

The past is now not a land to return to in a simple politics of memory. It has become a synchronic warehouse of cultural scenarios, a kind of temporal central casting, to which recourse can be taken as appropriate, depending on the movie to be made, the scene to be enacted, the hostages to be rescued. All this is par for the course, if you follow Jean Baudrillard or Jean-François Lyotard into a world of signs wholly unmoored from their social signifiers (all the world's a Disneyland). But I would like to suggest that the apparent increasing substitutability of whole periods and postures for one another, in the cultural styles of advanced capitalism, is tied to larger global forces, which have done much to show Americans that the past is usually another country. If your present is their future (as in much modernization theory and in many self-satisfied tourist fantasies), and their future is your past (as in the case of the Filipino virtuosos of American popular music), then your own past can be made to appear as simply a normalized modality of your present. Thus, although some anthropologists may continue to relegate their Others to temporal spaces that they do not themselves occupy (Fabian 1983), postindustrial cultural productions have entered a postnostalgic phase.

The crucial point, however, is that the United States is no longer the puppeteer of a world system of images but is only one node of a complex transnational construction of imaginary landscapes. The world we live in today is characterized by a new role for the imagination in social life. To grasp this new role, we need to bring together the old idea of images, especially mechanically produced images (in the Frankfurt School sense); the idea of the imagined community (in Anderson's sense); and the French idea of the imaginary (*imaginaire*) as a constructed landscape of collective aspirations, which is no more and no less real than the collective representations of Émile Durkheim, now mediated through the complex prism of modern media.

The image, the imagined, the imaginary – these are all terms that direct us to something critical and new in global cultural processes: *the imagination as a social practice*. No longer mere fantasy (opium for the masses whose real work is elsewhere), no longer simple escape (from a world defined principally by more concrete purposes and structures), no longer elite pastime (thus not relevant to the lives of ordinary people), and no longer mere contemplation (irrelevant for new forms of desire and subjectivity), the imagination has become an organized field of social practices, a form of work (in the sense of both labor and culturally organized practice), and a form of negotiation between sites of agency (individuals) and globally defined fields of possibility. This unleashing of the imagination links the play of pastiche (in some settings) to the terror and coercion of states and their competitors. The imagination is now central to all forms of agency, is itself a social fact, and is the key component of the new global order. But to make this claim meaningful, we must address some other issues.

Homogenization and Heterogenization

The central problem of today's global interactions is the tension between cultural homogenization and cultural heterogenization. A vast array of empirical facts could be brought to bear on the side of the homogenization argument, and much of it has come from the left end of the spectrum of media studies (Hamelink 1983; Mattelart 1983; Schiller 1976), and some from other perspectives (Gans 1985; Iyer 1988). Most often, the homogenization argument subspeciates into either an argument about Americanization or an argument about commoditization, and very often the two arguments are closely linked. What these arguments fail to consider is that at least as rapidly as forces from various metropolises are brought into new societies they tend to become indigenized in one or another way: this is true of music and housing styles as much as it is true of science and terrorism, spectacles and constitutions. The dynamics of such indigenization have just begun to be explored systemically (Barber 1987; Feld 1988; Hannerz 1987, 1989; Ivy 1988; Nicoll 1989; Yoshimoto 1989), and much more needs to be done. But it is worth noticing that for the people of Irian Jaya, Indonesianization may be more worrisome than Americanization, as Japanization may be for Koreans, Indianization for Sri Lankans, Vietnamization for the Cambodians, and Russianization for the people of Soviet Armenia and the Baltic republics. Such a list of alternative fears to Americanization could be greatly expanded, but it is not a shapeless inventory: for polities of smaller scale, there is always a fear of cultural absorption by polities of larger scale, especially those that are nearby. One man's imagined community is another man's political prison.

This scalar dynamic, which has widespread global manifestations, is also tied to the relationship between nations and states, to which I shall return later. For the moment let us note that the simplification of these many forces (and fears) of homogenization can also be exploited by nation-states in relation to their own minorities, by posing global commoditization (or capitalism, or some other such external enemy) as more real than the threat of its own hegemonic strategies.

The new global cultural economy has to be seen as a complex, overlapping, disjunctive order that cannot any longer be understood in terms of existing center-periphery models (even those that might account for multiple centers and peripheries). Nor is it susceptible to simple models of push and pull (in terms of migration theory), or of surpluses and deficits (as in traditional models of balance of trade), or of consumers and producers (as in most neo-Marxist theories of development). Even the most complex and flexible theories of global development that have come out of the Marxist tradition (Amin 1980; Mandel 1978; Wallerstein 1974; Wolf 1982) are inadequately quirky and have failed to come to terms with what Scott Lash and John Urry have called disorganized capitalism (1987). The complexity of the current global economy has to do with certain fundamental disjunctures between economy, culture, and politics that we have only begun to theorize.[1]

I propose that an elementary framework for exploring such disjunctures is to look at the relationship among five dimensions of global cultural flows that can be termed (a) *ethnoscapes*, (b) *mediascapes*, (c) *technoscapes*, (d) *financescapes*, and

(e) *ideoscapes*.[2] The suffix -*scape* allows us to point to the fluid, irregular shapes of these landscapes, shapes that characterize international capital as deeply as they do international clothing styles. These terms with the common suffix -*scape* also indicate that these are not objectively given relations that look the same from every angle of vision but, rather, that they are deeply perspectival constructs, inflected by the historical, linguistic, and political situatedness of different sorts of actors: nation-states, multinationals, diasporic communities, as well as subnational groupings and movements (whether religious, political, or economic), and even intimate face-to-face groups, such as villages, neighborhoods, and families. Indeed, the individual actor is the last locus of this perspectival set of landscapes, for these landscapes are eventually navigated by agents who both experience and constitute larger formations, in part from their own sense of what these landscapes offer.

These landscapes thus are the building blocks of what (extending Benedict Anderson) I would like to call *imagined worlds*, that is, the multiple worlds that are constituted by the historically situated imaginations of persons and groups spread around the globe (see Appadurai 1996: ch. 1). An important fact of the world we live in today is that many persons on the globe live in such imagined worlds (and not just in imagined communities) and thus are able to contest and sometimes even subvert the imagined worlds of the official mind and of the entrepreneurial mentality that surround them.

By *ethnoscape*, I mean the landscape of persons who constitute the shifting world in which we live: tourists, immigrants, refugees, exiles, guest workers, and other moving groups and individuals constitute an essential feature of the world and appear to affect the politics of (and between) nations to a hitherto unprecedented degree. This is not to say that there are no relatively stable communities and networks of kinship, friendship, work, and leisure, as well as of birth, residence, and other filial forms. But it is to say that the warp of these stabilities is everywhere shot through with the woof of human motion, as more persons and groups deal with the realities of having to move or the fantasies of wanting to move. What is more, both these realities and fantasies now function on larger scales, as men and women from villages in India think not just of moving to Poona or Madras but of moving to Dubai and Houston, and refugees from Sri Lanka find themselves in South India as well as in Switzerland, just as the Hmong are driven to London as well as to Philadelphia. And as international capital shifts its needs, as production and technology generate different needs, as nation-states shift their policies on refugee populations, these moving groups can never afford to let their imaginations rest too long, even if they wish to.

By *technoscape*, I mean the global configuration, also ever fluid, of technology and the fact that technology, both high and low, both mechanical and informational, now moves at high speeds across various kinds of previously impervious boundaries. Many countries now are the roots of multinational enterprise: a huge steel complex in Libya may involve interests from India, China, Russia, and Japan, providing different components of new technological configurations. The odd distribution of technologies, and thus the peculiarities of these technoscapes, are increasingly driven not by any obvious economies of scale, of political control, or of market rationality but by increasingly complex relationships among money flows, political possibilities, and the availability of both un- and highly skilled labor. So, while India exports waiters and chauffeurs to Dubai and Sharjah, it also exports software engineers to the United States – indentured briefly to Tata-Burroughs or the World Bank, then laundered through the State Department to become wealthy resident aliens, who are in turn objects of seductive messages to invest their money and know-how in federal and state projects in India.

The global economy can still be described in terms of traditional indicators (as the World Bank continues to do) and studied in terms of traditional comparisons (as in Project Link at the University of Pennsylvania), but the complicated technoscapes (and the shifting ethnoscapes) that underlie these indicators and comparisons are further out of the reach of the queen of social sciences than ever before. How is one to make a meaningful comparison of wages in Japan and the United States or of real-estate costs in New York and Tokyo, without taking sophisticated account of the very complex fiscal and investment flows that link the two economies through a global grid of currency speculation and capital transfer?

Thus it is useful to speak as well of *financescapes*, as the disposition of global capital is now a more mysterious, rapid, and difficult landscape to follow than ever before, as currency markets, national stock exchanges, and commodity speculations move megamonies through national turnstiles at blinding speed, with vast, absolute implications for small differences in percentage points and time units. But the critical point is that the global relationship among ethnoscapes, technoscapes, and financescapes is deeply disjunctive and profoundly unpredictable because each of these landscapes is subject to its own constraints and incentives (some political, some informational, and some technoenvironmental), at the same time as each acts as a constraint and a parameter for movements in the others. Thus, even an elementary model of global political economy must take into account the deeply disjunctive relationships among human movement, technological flow, and financial transfers.

Further refracting these disjunctures (which hardly form a simple, mechanical global infrastructure in any case) are what I call *mediascapes* and *ideoscapes*, which are closely related landscapes of images. *Mediascapes* refer both to the distribution of the electronic capabilities to produce and disseminate information (newspapers, magazines, television stations, and film-production studios), which are now available to a growing number of private and public interests throughout the world, and to the images of the world created by these media. These images involve many complicated inflections, depending on their mode (documentary or entertainment), their hardware (electronic or preelectronic), their audiences (local, national, or transnational), and the interests of those who own and control them. What is most important about these mediascapes is that they provide (especially in their television, film, and cassette forms) large and complex repertoires of images, narratives, and ethnoscapes to viewers throughout the world, in which the world of commodities and the world of news and politics are profoundly mixed. What this means is that many audiences around the world experience the media themselves as a complicated and interconnected repertoire of print, celluloid, electronic screens, and billboards. The lines between the realistic and the fictional landscapes they see are blurred, so that the farther away these audiences are from the direct experiences of metropolitan life, the more likely they are to construct imagined worlds that are chimerical, aesthetic, even fantastic objects, particularly if assessed by the criteria of some other perspective, some other imagined world.

Mediascapes, whether produced by private or state interests, tend to be image-centered, narrative-based accounts of strips of reality, and what they offer to those who experience and transform them is a series of elements (such as characters, plots, and textual forms) out of which scripts can be formed of imagined lives, their own as well as those of others living in other places. These scripts can and do get disaggregated into complex sets of metaphors by which people live (Lakoff and Johnson 1980) as they help to constitute narratives of the Other and protonarratives of possible lives, fantasies that could become prolegomena to the desire for acquisition and movement.

Ideoscapes are also concatenations of images, but they are often directly political and frequently have to do with the ideologies of states and the counterideologies of movements explicitly oriented to capturing state power or a piece of it. These ideoscapes are composed of elements of the Englightenment worldview, which consists of a chain of ideas, terms, and images, including *freedom, welfare, rights, sovereignty, representation*, and the master term *democracy*. The master narrative of the Enlightenment (and its many variants in Britain, France, and the United States) was constructed with a certain internal logic and presupposed a certain relationship between reading, representation, and the public sphere. (For the dynamics of this process in the early history of the United States, see Warner 1990.) But the diaspora of these terms and images across the world, especially since the nineteenth century, has loosened the internal coherence that held them together in a Euro-American master narrative and provided instead a loosely structured synopticon of politics, in which different nation-states, as part of their evolution, have organized their political cultures around different keywords (e.g., Williams 1976).

As a result of the differential diaspora of these keywords, the political narratives that govern communication between elites and followers in different parts of the world involve problems of both a semantic and pragmatic nature: semantic to the extent that words (and their lexical equivalents) require careful translation from context to context in their global movements, and pragmatic to the extent that the use of these words by political actors and their audiences may be subject to very different sets of contextual conventions that mediate their translation into public politics. Such conventions are not only matters of the nature of political rhetoric: for example, what does the aging Chinese leadership mean when it refers to the dangers of hooliganism? What does the South Korean leadership mean when it speaks of discipline as the key to democratic industrial growth?

These conventions also involve the far more subtle question of what sets of communicative genres are valued in what way (newspapers versus cinema, for example) and what sorts of pragmatic genre conventions govern the collective readings of different kinds of text. So, while an Indian audience may be attentive to the resonances of a political speech in terms of some keywords and phrases reminiscent of Hindi cinema, a Korean audience may respond to the subtle codings of Buddhist or neo-Confucian rhetoric encoded in a political document. The very relationship of reading to hearing and seeing may vary in important ways that determine the morphology of these different ideoscapes as they shape themselves in different national and transnational contexts. This globally variable synaesthesia has hardly even been noted, but it demands urgent analysis. Thus *democracy* has clearly become a master term, with powerful echoes from Haiti and Poland to the former Soviet Union and China, but it sits at the center of a variety of ideoscapes, composed of distinctive pragmatic configurations of rough translations of other central terms from the vocabulary of the Enlightenment. This creates ever new terminological kaleidoscopes, as states (and the groups that seek to capture them) seek to pacify populations whose own ethnoscapes are in motion and whose mediascapes may create severe problems for the ideoscapes with which they are presented. The fluidity of ideoscapes is complicated in particular by the growing diasporas (both voluntary and involuntary) of intellectuals who continuously inject new meaning-streams into the discourse of democracy in different parts of the world.

This extended terminological discussion of the five terms I have coined sets the basis for a tentative formulation about the conditions under which current global flows occur: they occur in and through the growing disjunctures among ethnoscapes, technoscapes, financescapes, mediascapes, and ideoscapes. This formulation, the core of my model of global cultural flow, needs some explanation. First, people, machinery, money, images, and ideas now follow increasingly nonisomorphic paths; of course, at all periods in human history, there have been some disjunctures in the flows of these things, but the sheer speed, scale, and volume of each of these flows are now so great that the disjunctures have become central to the politics of global culture. The Japanese are notoriously hospitable to ideas and are stereotyped as inclined to export (all) and import (some) goods, but they are also notoriously closed to immigration, like the Swiss, the Swedes, and the Saudis. Yet the Swiss and the Saudis accept populations of guest workers, thus creating labor diasporas of Turks, Italians, and other circum-Mediterranean groups. Some such guest-worker groups maintain continuous contact with their home nations, like the Turks, but others, like high-level South Asian migrants, tend to desire lives in their new homes, raising anew the problem of reproduction in a deterritorialized context.

Deterritorialization, in general, is one of the central forces of the modern world because it brings laboring populations into the lower-class sectors and spaces of relatively wealthy societies, while sometimes creating exaggerated and intensified senses of criticism or attachment to politics in the home state. Deterritorialization, whether of Hindus, Sikhs, Palestinians, or Ukrainians, is now at the core of a variety of global fundamentalisms, including Islamic and Hindu fundamentalism. In the Hindu case, for example, it is clear that the overseas movement of Indians has been exploited by a variety of interests both within and outside India to create a complicated network of finances and religious identifications, by which the problem of cultural reproduction for Hindus abroad has become tied to the politics of Hindu fundamentalism at home.

At the same time, deterritorialization creates new markets for film companies, art impresarios, and travel agencies, which thrive on the need of the deterritorialized population for contact with its homeland. Naturally, these invented homelands, which constitute the mediascapes of deterritorialized groups, can often become sufficiently fantastic and one-sided that they provide the material for new ideoscapes in which ethnic conflicts can begin to erupt. The creation of Khalistan, an invented homeland of the deterritorialized Sikh population of England, Canada, and the United States, is one example of the bloody potential in such mediascapes as they interact with the internal colonialisms of the nation-state (e.g., Hechter 1975). The West Bank, Namibia, and Eritrea are other theaters for the enactment of the bloody negotiation between existing nation-states and various deterritorialized groupings.

It is in the fertile ground of deterritorialization, in which money, commodities, and persons are involved in ceaselessly chasing each other around the world, that the mediascapes and ideoscapes of the modern world find their fractured and fragmented counterpart. For the ideas and images produced by mass media often are only partial guides to the goods and experiences that deterritorialized populations transfer to one another. In Mira Nair's brilliant film *India Cabaret*, we see the multiple loops of this fractured deterritorialization as young women, barely competent in Bombay's metropolitan glitz, come to seek their fortunes as cabaret dancers and prostitutes in Bombay, entertaining men in clubs with dance formats derived wholly from the prurient dance sequences of Hindi films. These scenes in turn cater to ideas about western and foreign women and their looseness, while they provide tawdry career alibis for these women. Some of these women come from Kerala, where cabaret clubs and the pornographic film industry have blossomed, partly in response to the purses and tastes of Keralites returned from the Middle East, where their diasporic lives away from women distort their very sense of what the relations between men and women might be. These tragedies of displacement could certainly be replayed in a more detailed analysis of the relations between the Japanese and German sex tours to Thailand and the tragedies of the sex trade in Bangkok, and in other similar loops that tie together fantasies about the Other, the conveniences and seductions of travel, the economics of global trade, and the brutal mobility fantasies that dominate gender politics in many parts of Asia and the world at large.

While far more could be said about the cultural politics of deterritorialization and the larger sociology of displacement that it expresses, it is appropriate at this juncture to bring in the role of the nation-state in the disjunctive global economy of culture today. The relationship between states and nations is everywhere an embattled one. It is possible to say that in many societies the nation and the state have become one another's projects. That is, while nations (or more properly groups with ideas about nationhood) seek to capture or co-opt states and state power, states simultaneously seek to capture and monopolize ideas about nationhood (Baruah 1986; Chatterjee 1986; Nandy 1989). In general, separatist transnational movements, including those that have included terror in their methods, exemplify nations in search of states. Sikhs, Tamil Sri Lankans, Basques, Moros, Quebecois – each of these represents imagined communities that seek to create states of their own or carve pieces out of existing states. States, on the other hand, are everywhere seeking to monopolize the moral resources of community, either by flatly claiming perfect coevality between nation and state, or by systematically museumizing and representing all the groups within them in a variety of heritage politics that seems remarkably uniform throughout the world (Handler 1988; Herzfeld 1982; McQueen 1988).

Here, national and international mediascapes are exploited by nation-states to pacify separatists or even the potential fissiparousness of all ideas of difference. Typically, contemporary nation-states do this by exercising taxonomic control over difference, by creating various kinds of international spectacle to domesticate difference, and by seducing small groups with the fantasy of self-display on some sort of global or cosmopolitan stage. One important new feature of global cultural politics, tied to the disjunctive relationships among the various landscapes discussed earlier, is that state and nation are at each other's throats, and the hyphen that links them is now less an icon of conjuncture than an index of disjuncture. This disjunctive relationship between nation and state has two levels: at the level of any given nation-state, it means that there is a battle of the imagination, with state and nation seeking to cannibalize one another. Here is the seedbed of brutal separatisms – majoritarianisms that seem to have appeared from nowhere and microidentities that have become political projects within the nation-state. At another level, this disjunctive relationship is deeply entangled with the global disjunctures discussed throughout this chapter: ideas of nationhood appear to be steadily increasing in scale and regularly crossing existing state boundaries, sometimes, as with the Kurds, because previous identities stretched across vast national spaces or, as with the Tamils in Sri Lanka, the dormant threads of a transnational diaspora have been activated to ignite the micropolitics of a nation-state.

In discussing the cultural politics that have subverted the hyphen that links the nation to the state, it is especially important not to forget the mooring of such politics in the irregularities that now characterize disorganized capital (Kothari 1989; Lash and Urry 1987). Because labor, finance, and technology are now so widely separated, the volatilities that underlie movements for nationhood (as large as transnational Islam on the one hand, or as small as the movement of the Gurkhas for a separate state in Northeast India) grind against the vulnerabilities that characterize the relationships between states. States find themselves pressed to stay open by the forces of media, technology, and travel that have fueled consumerism throughout the world and have increased the craving, even in the non-western world, for new commodities and spectacles. On the other hand, these very cravings can become caught up in new ethnoscapes, mediascapes, and, eventually, ideoscapes, such as democracy in China, that the state cannot tolerate as threats to its own control over ideas of nationhood and peoplehood. States throughout the world are under siege, especially where contests over the ideoscapes of democracy are fierce and fundamental, and where there are radical disjunctures between ideoscapes and technoscapes (as in the case of very small countries that lack contemporary technologies of production and information); or between ideoscapes and finance-scapes (as in countries such as Mexico or Brazil, where international lending influences national politics to a very large degree); or between ideoscapes and ethnoscapes (as in Beirut, where diasporic, local, and translocal filiations are suicidally at battle); or between ideoscapes and mediascapes (as in many countries in the Middle East and Asia) where the lifestyles represented on both national and international TV and cinema completely overwhelm and undermine the rhetoric of national politics. In the Indian case, the myth of the law-breaking hero has emerged to mediate this naked struggle between the pieties and realities of Indian politics, which has grown increasingly brutalized and corrupt (Vachani 1989).

The transnational movement of the martial arts, particularly through Asia, as mediated by the Hollywood and Hong Kong film industries (Zarilli 1995) is a rich illustration of the ways in which long-standing martial arts traditions, reformulated to meet the fantasies of contemporary (sometimes lumpen) youth populations, create new cultures of masculinity and violence, which are in turn the fuel for increased violence in national and international politics. Such violence is in turn the spur to an increasingly rapid and amoral arms trade that penetrates the entire world. The worldwide spread of the AK-47 and the Uzi, in films, in corporate and state security, in terror, and in police and military activity, is a reminder that apparently simple technical uniformities often conceal an increasingly complex set of loops, linking images of violence to aspirations for community in some imagined world.

Returning then to the ethnoscapes with which I began, the central paradox of ethnic politics in today's world is that primordia (whether of language or skin color or neighborhood or kinship) have become globalized. That is, sentiments, whose greatest force is in their ability to ignite intimacy into a political state and turn locality into a staging ground for identity, have become spread over vast and irregular spaces as groups move yet stay linked to one another through sophisticated media capabilities. This is not to deny that such primordia are often the product of invented traditions (Hobsbawm and Ranger 1983) or retrospective affiliations, but to emphasize that because of the disjunctive and unstable interplay of commerce, media, national policies, and consumer fantasies, ethnicity, once a genie contained in the bottle of some sort of locality (however large), has now become a global force, forever slipping in and through the cracks between states and borders.

But the relationship between the cultural and economic levels of this new set of global disjunctures is not a simple one-way street in which the terms of global cultural politics are set wholly by, or confined wholly within, the vicissitudes of international flows of technology, labor, and finance, demanding only a modest modification of existing neo-Marxist models of uneven development and state formation. There is a deeper change, itself driven by the disjunctures among all the landscapes I have discussed and constituted by their continuously fluid and uncertain interplay, that concerns the relationship between production and consumption in today's global economy. Here, I begin with Marx's famous (and often mined) view of the fetishism of the commodity and suggest that this fetishism has been replaced in the world at large (now seeing the world as one large, interactive system, composed of many complex subsystems) by two mutually supportive descendants, the first of which I call production fetishism and the second, the fetishism of the consumer.

By *production fetishism* I mean an illusion created by contemporary transnational production loci that masks translocal capital, transnational earning flows, global management, and often faraway workers (engaged in various kinds of high-tech putting-out operations) in the idiom and spectacle of local (sometimes even worker) control, national productivity, and territorial sovereignty. To the extent that various kinds of free-trade zones have become the models for production at large, especially of high-tech commodities, production has itself become a fetish, obscuring not social relations as such but the relations of production, which are increasingly transnational. The locality (both in the sense of the local factory or site of production and in the extended sense of the nation-state) becomes a fetish that disguises the globally dispersed forces that actually drive the production process. This generates alienation (in Marx's sense) twice intensified, for its social sense is now compounded by a complicated spatial dynamic that is increasingly global.

As for the *fetishism of the consumer*, I mean to indicate here that the consumer has been transformed through commodity flows (and the mediascapes, especially of advertising, that accompany them) into a sign, both in Baudrillard's sense of a simulacrum that only asymptotically approaches the form of a real social agent, and in the sense of a mask for the real seat of agency, which is not the consumer but the producer and the many forces that constitute production. Global advertising is the key technology for the worldwide dissemination of a plethora of creative and culturally well-chosen ideas of consumer agency. These images of agency are increasingly distortions of a world of merchandising so subtle that the consumer is consistently helped to believe that he or she is an actor, where in fact he or she is at best a chooser.

The globalization of culture is not the same as its homogenization, but globalization involves the use of a variety of instruments of homogenization (armaments, advertising techniques, language hegemonies, and clothing styles) that are absorbed into local political and cultural economies, only to be repatriated as heterogeneous dialogues of national sovereignty, free enterprise, and fundamentalism in which the state plays an increasingly delicate role: too much openness to global flows, and the nation-state is threatened by revolt, as in the China syndrome; too little, and the state exits the international stage, as Burma, Albania, and North Korea in various ways have done. In general, the state has become the arbitrageur of this *repatriation of difference* (in the form of goods, signs, slogans, and styles). But this repatriation or export of the designs and commodities of difference continuously exacerbates the internal politics of majoritarianism and homogenization, which is most frequently played out in debates over heritage.

Thus the central feature of global culture today is the politics of the mutual effort of sameness and difference to cannibalize one another and thereby proclaim their successful hijacking of the twin Enlightenment ideas of the triumphantly universal and the resiliently particular. This mutual cannibalization shows its ugly face in riots, refugee flows, state-sponsored torture, and ethnocide (with or without state support). Its brighter side is in the expansion of many individual horizons of hope and fantasy, in the global spread of oral rehydration therapy and other low-tech instruments of well-being, in the susceptibility even of South Africa to the force of global opinion, in the inability of the Polish state to repress its own working classes, and in the growth of a wide range of progressive, transnational alliances. Examples of both sorts could be multiplied. The critical point is that both sides of the coin of global cultural process today are products of the infinitely varied mutual contest of sameness and difference on a stage characterized by radical disjunctures between different sorts of global flows and the uncertain landscapes created in and through these disjunctures.

The Work of Reproduction in an Age of Mechanical Art

I have inverted the key terms of the title of Walter Benjamin's famous essay (1969) to return this rather high-flying discussion to a more manageable level. There is a classic human problem that will not disappear however much global cultural processes might change their dynamics, and this is the problem today typically discussed under the rubric of reproduction (and traditionally referred to in terms of the transmission of culture). In either case, the question is, how do small groups, especially families, the classical loci of socialization, deal with these new global realities as they seek to reproduce themselves and, in so doing, by accident reproduce cultural forms themselves? In traditional anthropological terms, this could be phrased as the problem of enculturation in a period of rapid culture change. So the problem is hardly novel. But it does take on some novel dimensions under the global conditions discussed so far in this chapter.

First, the sort of transgenerational stability of knowledge that was presupposed in most theories of enculturation (or, in slightly broader terms, of socialization) can no longer be assumed. As families move to new locations, or as children move before older generations, or as grown sons and daughters return from time spent in strange parts of the world, family relationships can become volatile; new commodity patterns are negotiated, debts and obligations are recalibrated, and rumors and fantasies about the new setting are maneuvered into existing repertoires of knowledge and practice. Often, global labor diasporas involve immense strains on marriages in general and on women in particular, as marriages become the meeting points of historical patterns of socialization and new ideas of proper behavior. Generations easily divide, as ideas about property, propriety, and collective obligation wither under the siege of distance and time. Most important, the work of cultural reproduction in new settings is profoundly complicated by the politics of representing a family as normal (particularly for the young) to neighbours and peers in the new locale. All this is, of course, not new to the cultural study of immigration.

What is new is that this is a world in which both points of departure and points of arrival are in cultural flux, and thus the search for steady points of reference, as critical life choices are made, can be very difficult. It is in this atmosphere that the invention of tradition (and of ethnicity, kinship, and other identity markers) can become slippery, as the search for certainties is regularly frustrated by the fluidities of transnational communication. As group pasts become increasingly parts of museums, exhibits, and collections, both in national and transnational spectacles, culture becomes less what Pierre Bourdieu would have called a habitus (a tacit realm of reproducible practices and dispositions) and more an arena for conscious choice, justification, and representation, the latter often to multiple and spatially dislocated audiences.

The task of cultural reproduction, even in its most intimate arenas, such as husband–wife and parent–child relations, becomes both politicized and exposed to the traumas of deterritorialization as family members pool and negotiate their mutual understandings and aspirations in sometimes fractured spatial arrangements. At larger levels, such as community, neighborhood, and territory, this politicization is often the emotional fuel for more explicitly violent politics of identity, just as these larger politics sometimes penetrate and ignite domestic politics. When, for example, two offspring in a household split with their father on a key matter of political identification in a transnational setting, preexisting localized norms carry little force. Thus a son who has joined the Hezbollah group in Lebanon may no longer get along with parents or siblings who are affiliated with Amal or some other branch of Shi'i ethnic political identity in Lebanon. Women in particular bear the brunt of this sort of friction, for they become pawns in the heritage politics of the household and are often subject to the abuse and violence of men who are themselves torn about the relation between heritage and opportunity in shifting spatial and political formations.

The pains of cultural reproduction in a disjunctive global world are, of course, not eased by the effects of mechanical art (or mass media), for these media afford powerful resources for counternodes of identity that youth can project against parental wishes or desires. At larger levels of organization, there can be many forms of cultural politics within displaced populations (whether of refugees or of voluntary immigrants), all of which are inflected in important ways by media (and the mediascapes and ideoscapes they offer). A central link between the fragilities of cultural reproduction and the role of the mass media in today's world is the politics of gender and violence. As fantasies of gendered violence dominate the B-grade film industries that blanket the world, they both reflect and refine gendered violence at home and in the streets, as young men (in particular) are swayed by the macho politics of self-assertion in contexts where they are frequently denied real agency, and women are forced to enter the labor force in new ways on the one hand, and continue the maintenance of familial heritage on the other. Thus the honor of women becomes not just an armature of stable (if inhuman) systems of cultural reproduction but a new arena for the formation of sexual identity and family politics, as men and women face new pressures at work and new fantasies of leisure.

Because both work and leisure have lost none of their gendered qualities in this new global order but have acquired ever subtler fetishized representations, the honor of women becomes increasingly a surrogate for the identity of embattled communities of males, while their women in reality have to negotiate increasingly harsh conditions of work at home and in the nondomestic workplace. In short, deterritorialized communities and displaced populations, however much they may enjoy the fruits of new kinds of earning and new dispositions of capital and technology, have to play out the desires and fantasies of these new ethnoscapes, while striving to reproduce the family-as-microcosm of culture. As the shapes of cultures grow less bounded and tacit, more fluid and politicized, the work of cultural reproduction becomes a daily hazard. Far more could, and should, be said about the work of reproduction in an age of mechanical art: the preceding discussion is meant to indicate the contours of the problems that a new, globally informed theory of cultural reproduction will have to face.

Shape and Process in Global Cultural Formations

The deliberations of the arguments that I have made so far constitute the bare bones of an approach to a general theory of global cultural processes. Focusing on disjunctures, I have employed a set of terms (*ethnoscape, financescape, technoscape, mediascape*, and *ideoscape*) to stress different streams or flows along which cultural material may be seen to be moving across national boundaries. I have also sought to exemplify the ways in which these various flows (or landscapes, from the stabilizing perspectives of any given imagined world) are in fundamental disjuncture with respect to one another. What further steps can we take toward a general theory of global cultural processes based on these proposals?

The first is to note that our very models of cultural shape will have to alter, as configurations of people, place, and heritage lose all semblance of isomorphism. Recent work in anthropology has done much to free us of the shackles of highly localized, boundary-oriented, holistic, primordialist images of cultural form and substance (Hannerz 1989; Marcus and Fischer 1986; Thornton 1988). But not very much has been put in their place, except somewhat larger if less mechanical versions of these images, as in Eric Wolf's work on the relationship of Europe to the rest of the world (1982). What I would like to propose is that we begin to think of the configuration of cultural forms in today's world as fundamentally fractal, that is, as possessing no Euclidean boundaries, structures, or regularities. Second, I would suggest that these cultural forms, which we should strive to represent as fully fractal, are also overlapping in ways that have been discussed only in pure mathematics (in set theory, for example) and in biology (in the language of polythetic classifications). Thus we need to combine a fractal metaphor for the shape of cultures (in the plural) with a polythetic account of their overlaps and resemblances. Without this latter step, we shall remain mired in comparative work that relies on the clear separation of the entities to be compared before serious comparison can begin. How are we to compare fractally shaped cultural forms that are also polythetically overlapping in their coverage of terrestrial space?

Finally, in order for the theory of global cultural interactions predicated on disjunctive flows to have any force greater than that of a mechanical metaphor, it will have to move into something like a human version of the theory that some scientists are calling chaos theory. That is, we will need to ask not how these complex, overlapping, fractal shapes constitute a simple, stable (even if large-scale) system, but to ask what its dynamics are: Why do ethnic riots occur when and where they do? Why do states wither at greater rates in some places and times than in others? Why do some countries flout conventions of international debt repayment with so much less apparent worry than others? How are international arms flows driving ethnic battles and genocides? Why are some states exiting the global stage while others are clamoring to get in? Why do key events occur at a certain point in a certain place rather than in others? These are, of course, the great traditional questions of causality, contingency, and prediction in the human sciences, but in a world of disjunctive global flows, it is perhaps important to start asking them in a way that relies on images of flow and uncertainty, hence *chaos*, rather than on older images of order, stability, and systematicness. Otherwise, we will have gone far toward a theory of global cultural systems but thrown out process in the bargain. And that would make these notes part of a journey toward the kind of illusion of order that we can no longer afford to impose on a world that is so transparently volatile.

Whatever the directions in which we can push these macrometaphors (fractals, polythetic classifications, and chaos), we need to ask one other old-fashioned question out of the Marxist paradigm: is there some pre-given order to the relative determining force of these global flows? Because I have postulated the dynamics of global cultural systems as driven by the relationships among flows of persons, technologies, finance, information, and ideology, can we speak of some structural-causal order linking these flows by analogy to the role of the economic order in one version of the Marxist paradigm? Can we speak of some of these flows as being, for a priori structural or historical reasons, always prior to and formative of other flows? My own hypothesis, which can only be tentative at this point, is that the relationship of these various flows to one another as they constellate into particular events and social forms will be radically context-dependent. Thus, while labor flows and their loops with financial flows between Kerala and the Middle East may account for the shape of media flows and ideoscapes in Kerala, the reverse may be true of Silicon Valley in California, where intense specialization in a single techno-logical sector (computers) and particular flows of capital may well profoundly determine the shape that ethnoscapes, ideoscapes, and mediascapes may take.

This does not mean that the causal–historical relationship among these various flows is random or meaninglessly contingent but that our current theories of cultural chaos are insufficiently developed to be even parsimonious models at this point, much less to be predictive theories, the golden fleeces of one kind of social science. What I have sought to provide in this chapter is a reasonably economical technical vocabulary and a rudimentary model of disjunctive flows, from which something like a decent global analysis might emerge. Without some such analysis, it will be difficult to construct what John Hinkson calls a "social theory of postmodernity" that is adequately global (1990:84).

NOTES

1   One major exception is Fredric Jameson, whose work on the relationship between post-modernism and late capitalism has in many ways inspired this essay. The debate between Jameson and Aijaz Ahmad in *Social Text*, however, shows that the creation of a global-izing Marxist narrative in cultural matters is difficult territory indeed (Ahmad 1987; Jameson 1986). My own effort in this context is to begin a restructuring of the Marxist narrative (by stressing lags and disjunctures) that many Marxists might find abhorrent. Such a restructuring has to avoid the dangers of obliterating difference within the Third World, eliding the social referent (as some French postmodernists seem inclined to do), and retaining the narrative authority of the Marxist tradition, in favor of greater attention to global fragmentation, uncertainty, and difference.

2   The idea of *ethnoscape* is more fully engaged in Appadurai 1996, ch. 3.

REFERENCES

Abu-Lughod, J. L. (1989) *Before European Hegemony: The World System AD 1250–1350.* New York: Oxford University Press.

Ahmad, A. (1987) Jameson's Rhetoric of Otherness and the "National Allegory," *Social Text* 17: 3–25.

Amin, S. (1980) *Class and Nation: Historically and in the Current Crisis*. New York and London: Monthly Review Press.

Anderson, B. (1983) *Imagined Communities: Reflections on the Origin and Spread of Nationalism*. London: Verso.

Appadurai, A. (1996) *Modernity at Large: Cultural Dimensions of Globalization*. Minneapolis: University of Minnesota Press.

Barber, K. (1987) Popular Arts in Africa, *African Studies Review* 30(3) (September): 1–78.

Baruah, S. (1986) Immigration, Ethnic Conflict and Political Turmoil, Assam 1979–1985, *Asian Survey* 26(11) (November): 1184–206.

Bayly, C. A. (1989) *Imperial Meridian: The British Empire and the World, 1780–1830*. London and New York: Longman.

Benjamin, W. (1969) The Work of Art in the Age of Mechanical Reproduction [1936]. In H. Arendt (ed.) *Illuminations*. H. Zohn (trans.). New York: Schocken Books.

Braudel, F. (1981–4) *Civilization and Capitalism, 15th–18th Century* (3 vols.) London: Collins.

Chatterjee, P. (1986) *Nationalist Thought and the Colonial World: A Derivative Discourse?* London: Zed Books.

Curtin, P. (1984) *Cross-Cultural Trade in World History*. Cambridge: Cambridge University Press.

Deleuze, G., and F. Guattari (1987) *A Thousand Plateaus: Capitalism and Schizophrenia*. B. Massumi (trans.). Minneapolis: University of Minnesota Press.

Fabian, J. (1983) *Time and the Other: How Anthropology Makes Its Object*. New York: Columbia University Press.

Feld, S. (1988) Notes on World Beat, *Public Culture* 1(1): 31–7.

Gans, E. (1985) *The End of Culture: Toward a Generative Anthropology*. Berkeley: University of California Press.

Hamelink, C. (1983) *Cultural Autonomy in Global Communications*. New York: Longman.

Handler, R. (1988) *Nationalism and the Politics of Culture in Quebec*. Madison: University of Wisconsin Press.

Hannerz, U. (1987) The World in Creolization, *Africa* 57(4): 546–59.

——. (1989) Notes on the Global Ecumene, *Public Culture* 1(2) (Spring): 66–75.

Hechter, M. (1975) *Internal Colonialism: The Celtic Fringe in British National Development, 1536–1966*. Berkeley: University of California Press.

Helms, M. W. (1988) *Ulysses' Sail: An Ethnographic Odyssey of Power, Knowledge, and Geographical Distance*. Princeton, NJ: Princeton University Press.

Herzfeld, M. (1982) *Ours Once More: Folklore, Ideology and the Making of Modern Greece*. Austin: University of Texas Press.

Hinkson, J. (1990) Postmodernism and Structural Change, *Public Culture* 2(2) (Spring): 82–101.

Hobsbawm, E., and T. Ranger (eds.) (1983) *The Invention of Tradition*. New York: Cambridge University Press.

Hodgson, M. (1974) *The Venture of Islam, Conscience and History in a World Civilization* (3 vols). Chicago: University of Chicago Press.

Ivy, M. (1988) Tradition and Difference in the Japanese Mass Media, *Public Culture* 1(1): 21–9.

Iyer, P. (1988) *Video Night in Kathmandu*. New York: Knopf.

Jameson, F. (1983) Postmodernism and Consumer Society. In H. Foster (ed.) *The Anti-Aesthetic: Essays on Postmodern Culture*. Port Townsend, WA: Bay Press.

——. (1986) Third World Literature in the Era of Multi-National Capitalism, *Social Text* 15 (Fall): 65–88.

——. (1989) Nostalgia for the Present, *South Atlantic Quarterly* 88(2) (Spring): 517–37.

Kothari, R. (1989) *State against Democracy: In Search of Humane Governance*. New York: New Horizons.

Lakoff, G., and M. Johnson (1980) *Metaphors We Live By*. Chicago and London: University of Chicago Press.

Lash, S., and J. Urry (1987) *The End of Organized Capitalism*. Madison: University of Wisconsin Press.

Mandel, E. (1978) *Late Capitalism*. London: Verso.

Marcus, G., and M. Fischer (1986) *Anthropology as Cultural Critique: An Experimental Moment in the Human Sciences*. Chicago: University of Chicago Press.

Mattelart, A. (1983) *Transnationals and the Third World: The Struggle for Culture*. South Hadley, MA: Bergin and Garvey.

McLuhan, M., and B. R. Powers (1989) *The Global Village: Transformations in World, Life and Media in the 21st Century*. New York: Oxford University Press.

McQueen, H. (1988) The Australian Stamp: Image, Design and Ideology, *Arena* 84 (Spring): 78–96.

Meyrowitz, J. (1985) *No Sense of Place: The Impact of Electronic Media on Social Behavior*. New York: Oxford University Press.

Nandy, A. (1989) The Political Culture of the Indian State, *Daedalus* 118(4): 1–26.

Nicoll, F. (1989) My Trip to Alice, *Criticism, Heresy and Interpretation* 3: 21–32.

Schafer, E. (1963) *Golden Peaches of Samarkand: A Study of T'ang Exotics*. Berkeley: University of California Press.

Schiller, H. (1976) *Communication and Cultural Domination*. White Plains, NY: International Arts and Sciences.

Thornton, R. (1988) The Rhetoric of Ethnographic Holism, *Cultural Anthropology* 3(3) (August): 285–303.

Vachani, L. (1989) Narrative, Pleasure and Ideology in the Hindi Film: An Analysis of the Outsider Formula. MA thesis, Annenberg School of Communication, University of Pennsylvania.

Wallerstein, I. (1974) *The Modern World System* (2 vols.) New York and London: Academic Press.

Warner, M. (1990) *The Letters of the Republic: Publication and the Public Sphere in Eighteenth-Century America*. Cambridge, MA: Harvard University Press.

Williams, R. (1976) *Keywords*. New York: Oxford University Press.

Wolf, E. (1982) *Europe and the People without History*. Berkeley: University of California Press.

Yoshimoto, M. (1989) The Postmodern and Mass Images in Japan, *Public Culture* 1(2): 8–25.

Zarilli, P. (1995) Repositioning the Body: An Indian Martial Art and its Pan-Asian Publics. In C. A. Breckenridge (ed.) *Consuming Modernity: Public Culture in a South Asian World*. Minneapolis: University of Minnesota Press.

3

The Global Situation

Anna Tsing

Click on worldmaking interconnections. Your screen fills with global flows.

Imagine a creek cutting through a hillside. As the water rushes down, it carves rock and moves gravel; it deposits silt on slow turns; it switches courses and breaks earth dams after a sudden storm. As the creek flows, it makes and remakes its channels.

Imagine an internet system, linking up computer users. Or a rush of immigrants across national borders. Or capital investments shuttled to varied offshore locations. These world-making "flows," too, are not just interconnections but also the recarving of channels and the remapping of the possibilities of geography.

Imagine the landscape nourished by the creek. Yet even beyond the creek's "flows," there are no stable landscape elements: Trees sprout up, transforming meadows into forests; cattle browse on saplings, spreading meadows past forest edges. Nor are forests and meadows the only way to divide up the landscape. Consider the perspective of the earthworm, looking for rich soils, or the weed, able to flourish in both meadow and forest, though only when each meets certain conditions. To tell the story of this landscape requires an appreciation not only of changing landscape elements but also of the partial, tentative, and shifting ability of the storyteller to identify elements at all.

Imagine ethnic groups, corporations, refugees, nongovernmental organizations (NGOs), nation-states, consumers, social movements, media moguls, trade organizations, social scientists, international lawyers, and bankers, all swarming alongside creeks and earthworms to compose the landscape, to define its elements, carve its channels of flow, and establish its units of historical agency. We live in a time of self-consciousness about units and scales: Where shall we draw the boundaries of

From *Cultural Anthropology* 15(3): 327–360. Copyright © 2000, American Anthropological Association.

regions? How are local communities composed? And, most important for this essay, what is this thing we call the globe? If social scientists have had a lot to say about these questions of late, so have other people. Contestants form themselves in shifting alliances, mobilized for reasons of power, passion, discipline, or dis-ease and mounting campaigns for particular configurations of scale. Some of the most excited campaigning in the last 25 years has concerned the globe, that planet-wide space for all humanity and its encompassing habitat. Moreover, in the last ten years, talk about the globe has heated up to the point that many commentators imagine a global *era*, a time in which no units or scales count for much except the globe. "Globalization," the process taking us into that era, has caught up enthusiasts ranging from corporate managers to social activists, from advertisers to cultural theorists.

For many years, the creek makes only gradual changes in the landscape. Then a storm sweeps the flux beyond its accustomed boundaries, shifting every bank and eddy. Trees are uprooted, and what was once on the right side is now on the left. So, too, the social world has shifted around us. Market enthusiasms have replaced communism; national governments prostrate themselves before international finance; social movements market "culture" on a global scale. How should social scientists analyze these changes? This question is muddied by the fact that social science changes too. "Global" practices challenge social scientists to internationalize their venues, as North American and European scholars are brought into discussion with scholars from the South. Social science theories no longer take Western genealogies for granted but, rather, require fluency with a wider range of perspectives, from Latin American dependency theories to South Asian subaltern studies. The excitement of this internationalization of scholarship encourages many of us to throw ourselves into endorsements of globalization as a multilayered evolution, drawing us into the future. Sometimes our critical distance seems less useful than our participation. And yet, can we understand either our own involvement or the changing world without our critical skills? This essay argues that we cannot.

Is Globalization like Modernization?

Consider another moment in which social science was remade together with the world: the period after World War II, when social scientists were called on to participate in the international project of modernization and development. Modernization frameworks brought together scholars, policy makers, politicians, and social activists in a common program for social betterment. It offered the hope of moving beyond the colonial segregation of Europeans and natives to a world in which every nation could aspire to the highest standards of livelihood and culture. Even social scientists who feared its destructiveness or despised its imperiousness thus came to imagine modernization as the world-making process of the times. The charisma of the notion of an era of globalization is comparable in many ways to the charm of modernization in that postwar period. Like modernization theory, the global-future program has swept together scholars and public thinkers to imagine a new world in the making. Do globalization theories contain pitfalls for engaged social scientists similar to those of modernization theory?

Modernization, like globalization, was seductive. It was many years before social scientists moved beyond endorsements, refusals, and reforms of modernization to describe modernization as a set of *projects* with cultural and institutional specificities and limitations. Only when the shine of modernization began to fade did scholars ask how it managed to capture the hopes and dreams of so many experts, how its formulas were communicated to such a variety of social groups and within such a diversity of situations, and how its features were transformed in the process for multiple uses. Recent literature on modernization in its guise as "development" for the Third World is exemplary in this regard. A number of analysts, including Escobar (1995) and Ferguson (1990), have shown the discursive specificities of development, which often thrived more through the coherence of its internal logic than through any insight into the social situations in which it was expected to intervene. The commitment of experts to development drew material and institutional resources to its programs even when they were quite obviously destructive of the human well-being that formed its ostensible goal. Meanwhile, development was also reformulated through its constant negotiation and translation within particular settings, and it assumed multiple forms. Recent studies have shown how development policies diversified as they become entangled in regional political struggles (e.g., Peters 1994) and as they were reinterpreted in varied cultural settings (e.g., Pigg 1992). This rich literature has inspired new attention to the making of modernization. Its example can stimulate attention to the multiple projects of imagining and making globality.

Studies of modernization as a set of projects look in at least three directions. First, analysts attend to the cultural specificity of commitments to modernization. They may make these commitments seem exotic to remove them from the reader's common sense. (How odd, the analyst might say, that sitting in uncomfortable chairs is considered more modern than squatting.) Analysts explore the elements through which modernization projects make assumptions about the world. For example, modernization projects create notions of time through which groups and activities can be situated in relation to stories of progress. Second, analysts attend to the social practices, material infrastructure, cultural negotiations, institutions, and power relations through which modernization projects work – and are opposed, contested, and reformulated. Modernization projects do their work through educational practices, military coercion, administrative policies, resource entitlements, community reorganization, and much more; these arenas and practices both make and are transformed by modernization. To examine the effects of modernization commitments requires attention to the social worlds both of and beyond modernization visions. Third, analysts use the promise of questions and dilemmas brought up in modernization programs without becoming caught in their prescriptions for social change. For example, through its emphasis on critical reflection as a mode of "modern" thought, modernization draws attention to the awkward relationship between representation and its object and to the craft and creativity through which social life must be described. Analysts of modernization projects make use of this insight without assuming the framework of progress that helped generate it.

These directions of analysis seem equally useful to understanding projects of imagining and making globality. Certainly, commitments to globalism are strange enough to warrant cultural analysis. Furthermore, as globalization becomes institutionalized as a program not only in the academy but in corporate policy, politics, and popular culture, it is important to attend to these sites to understand what projects of globalization *do* in the world – and what else goes on with and around them. Finally, I think there is enormous analytic promise in tracing global interconnections without subsuming them to any one program of global-future commitments. A global framework allows one to consider the making and remaking of geographical and historical agents and the forms of their agency in relation to movement, interaction, and shifting, competing claims about community, culture, and scale. Places are made through their connections with each other, not their isolation: This kind of analysis seems too important to relegate only to studying the best-promoted "global" trends; indeed, among other uses, we can employ it to specify the uneven and contested global terrain of global promotion.

In this essay, I use these three directions of analysis to learn something about social science commitments to the newly emerging significance of a global scale. First, I examine the charisma of social science globalisms. By *globalism*, I refer to endorsements of the importance of the global. I want to know how the idea of the global has worked to excite and inspire social scientists. I pick out a number of elements that add to this charisma and argue for their obfuscating as well as enlivening features.

Second, to see how this charisma produces effects in the world, I examine reading and discussion practices in the field of anthropology, as these produce and reproduce commitments to globalization. As an observer, I try to track the excitement of my students and colleagues; yet, as a participant, I want to argue for a *better* use of the charisma of global frameworks.

Thus, third, I show how questions about global interconnections might be detached from the most problematic globalist commitments to offer a more nuanced and critical analysis of culture and history, including recent shifts that have turned attention to the global. I argue that we can investigate globalist projects and dreams without assuming that they remake the world just as they want. The task of understanding planet-wide interconnections requires locating and specifying globalist projects and dreams, with their contradictory as well as charismatic logics and their messy as well as effective encounters and translations.

Globalization draws our enthusiasm because it helps us imagine interconnection, travel, and sudden transformation. Yet it also draws us inside its rhetoric until we take its claims for true descriptions. In the imagery with which I began, flow is valorized but not the carving of the channel; national and regional units are mapped as the baseline of change without attention to their shifting and contested ability to define the landscape. We lose sight of the coalitions of claimants as well as their partial and shifting claims. We lose touch with the material and institutional components through which powerful and central sites are constructed, from which convincing claims about units and scales can be made. We describe the landscape imagined within these claims rather than the culture and politics of scale making. This essay suggests approaches to the study of the global that seem to me to hold onto the excitement of this endorsement of planetary interconnection without trading our critical stance for globalist wishes and fantasies.

Hurtling through Space

To invoke the global at the turn of the second millennium is to call attention to the speed and density of interconnections among people and places. In this imagery, the planet overwhelms us in its rush toward the future; we must either sit on top of it or be swamped and overcome.[1] It seems worth hesitating for a moment to consider the difference between this aggressive globe, hurtling through space, and an only slightly earlier fragile planet, floating gently in its cloud cover. This fertile yet vulnerable green planet was conjured by the global environmentalism that emerged in the United States and Europe at the end of the 1960s and blossomed in the 1970s, 1980s, and early 1990s. As Yaakov Garb (1990) has shown, the global environmentalists' globe gained its power from the visual image of the earth first seen in photographs from space in the 1960s; this awe-inspiring image was repeated in many forms and contexts to mobilize sentiment for the kind of nature that most needed our respect, love, and protection.[2] It became possible to imagine this nature as extending across the planet because global environmentalism brought together the universalist morality of 1960s social justice politics and the transboundary expertise of an emergent ecological science (Haas 1992; Taylor and Buttel 1992). Politics and science, working together, conjured an earth worth studying, managing, and fighting for at multiple but compatibly stratified scales and levels of advocacy and analysis.

Global environmentalism also participated in building another image of the global, in which globality represented the goal of a *process* of building transnational political and cultural ties. Beginning most intensely in the 1980s, social movements – including environmentalism, human rights, indigenous rights, and feminist causes – extended themselves through NGOs; they sought to work around the restrictions of nation-states by forging transnational lines of financial, scientific, and political support (Keck and Sikkink 1998). Activists put pressure on their respective governments with these resources; national policies were also pressed to respond to international agreements. The global here is a never-ending process of "networking" and building lines of support. Annelise Riles (1998b) has shown how the aesthetics of global network formation developed such charisma within NGOs that it became a major objective in itself. Global process here encourages participants to speak up, to learn from each other, and to extend themselves. But it does not yet push us over the edge of an evolutionary abyss.

It was only at the beginning of the 1990s that the process of "globalization," as the definitional characteristic of an *era*, became popular in the media and advertising. The triumph of the capitalist marketplace had been proclaimed with the dismantling of the Soviet Union, and enthusiasm ran high for national economic deregulation and privatization in the North and more thorough forms of structural adjustment in the South. In this atmosphere, *globalization* came to mean an endorsement of international free trade and the outlawing of protected or public domestic economies (Chomsky 1998). Yet the term came to encompass much more. Corporate reorganizations required not just markets but also the ability to transfer operations and finances transnationally to find the most profitable conditions; these kinds of corporate transfers, although reaching several decades back, became caught up in the talk of globalization. Furthermore, social commentators reminded the public that the new mobility of labor was tied to capital mobility and global market guarantees (e.g., Sassen 1998; Schiller et al. 1992). Cosmopolitan connoisseurs have delighted in the new availability of West African music, Brazilian martial arts, and Thai cuisine, as Southern arts blossomed in wealthy Northern cities (e.g., Appiah and Gates 1997). A variety of public debates and discussions came to be seen as "globally" interconnected: not only labor-and-capital-oriented fights about immigration, unionization, downsizing, subcontracting, and impoverishment but also debates about the worldwide spread of U.S. media productions, the role of national governments, the dangers and promises of multiculturalism, and the growing influence and proper management of new computer-based communications technologies. Indeed, the popularity of "global" terms and approaches drew from their evocation of multiple causes, agendas, and historical layers of imagery.[3]

At the turn of the century, then, globalism is multireferential: part corporate hype and capitalist regulatory agenda, part cultural excitement, part social commentary and protest. Within this shifting agenda, several features attract and engage an expanding audience for imagining the globe: first, its futurism, that is, its ability not only to name an era but to predict its progress; second, its conflations of varied projects through which the populist and the corporate, the scientific and the cultural, the excluded margins and the newly thriving centers, all seem wrapped up in the same energetic movement; and, third, its rhetoric of linkage and circulation as the overcoming of boundaries and restrictions, through which all this excitement appears positive for everyone involved. These elements are worth examining separately.

Futurism

Globalization is a crystal ball that promises to tell us of an almost-but-not-quite-there globality. This is powerful stuff for experts, politicians, and policy makers. Social scientists are particularly caught by the force of this charisma. The rush of prescience returns social science to the period after World War II, when the field charted the development of the new nations of the South and, in the North, the welfare state. Since then, social scientists have been better known – like economists and sociologists – as technicians of the present or – like anthropologists and geographers – as collectors of ancient survivals. Now the opportunity has come to look forward with a new expertise. The crystal ball inspires us to rush anxiously into the future, afraid to be left behind.

The future orientation of this discussion of the global requires the assumption of newness. If global interconnections do not define the contemporary era, setting it off from the past, to examine these interconnections shows us complexity rather than direction. Analysts of globalization force attention to the break that differentiates the present from the past because in the context of that break they can see forward.[4] The assumption of newness has other benefits. It can help us see the distinctiveness of a historical moment. It can inspire a "bandwagon" effect whereby unexpected and creative alliances among different kinds of analysts may be forged.[5] In this spirit, it can break up too-comfortably established fields, inspiring new forms of discussion.[6] However, the assumption of newness can also stifle other lines of inquiry and disallow questions about the construction of the field for which it forms the starting line. In history and anthropology, for example, the idea that global interconnections are *old* has only recently been revitalized, muffled as it was for much of the 20th century by the draw of nationally contained legacies, in history, and functionally contained social worlds, in anthropology; it seems unfortunate to lose this insight so quickly.[7]

Perhaps the worst fault of the assumption of global newness is that it erects stereotypes of the past that get in the way of appreciating both the past and the present. This fault has been particularly glaring in the discussion of the nation inspired by talk of globalization.[8] In interpreting the defeat of various national attempts to control financial capital, analysts have imagined an unprecedented world-historical defeat of the nation, as if nations, until now, were unquestioned, consistent, and everywhere hegemonic. Yet national control of finance may itself have been a recent, ephemeral product. After World War II, economic regulations emerging from the Bretton–Woods agreement made it possible for nation-states to control domestic financial capital, providing funding for welfare states. An earlier free-flowing internationalization of finance was cut off, as national capitalisms were set in place (Helleiner 1993).

Similarly, political commitment to national territorial boundaries and the importance of regulating population movements across national borders has a particular history. The new nation-states that emerged after World War II in Africa and Asia, for example, developed special concerns for territorial sovereignty to declare their autonomy from the colonial condition; their national histories and geographies stress self-development, not regional and transregional flow.[9] To turn nationalist visions from this period into a description of a homogeneous past seems likely to lead to distortions.

Given long-term commitments in the humanities to tracing intellectual lineages and civilizational commitments, it is perhaps surprising that literary critics have embraced the assumption of era-making global newness to put together anthologies on "the cultures of globalization" (Jameson and Miyoshi 1998).[10] The anthologies they have created are in many ways extremely exciting: Here are a variety of themes, a breadth of places discussed, and a diversity of scholars that form a striking intervention into the narrowly Western, textual orientation of most humanities. This is not scholarship as usual; it has the political energy and passion of cultural studies. This development is so important that it is awkward to say anything else. But I am suspicious of cultural stage theories, with their determinations of who is at the peak of human evolution and who will be left behind. Without denying their contribution, it may be useful to question how the articles in these anthologies are connected to each other. To discuss globalization, the editors make the a priori assumption of a cultural political era.[11] The era must have a cultural logic, and the descriptions of culture gathered in the book must form part of that logic.[12] I think we can discuss global projects, links, and situations with a better frame: one that recognizes the making and unmaking of claims about the global, even as it examines the consequences of these powerful claims in the world we know, and one that recognizes new and surprising developments without declaring, by fiat, the beginning of an era.[13]

Yet global futurism is seductive. It can be conjured equally by a technical mathematics or by an enthusiastic and suggestive vagueness. Frederic Jameson (1998b: xi) is perhaps the most up-front about all this, claiming that questions about the definition of the global era to which he devotes his book are not only premature but decidedly uncool. Surely, we will find that the disparate cultural and political processes we investigate in these times will turn out to be the trunk, limbs, and tail of that elephant not recognized as a single beast by the blind men. He disarms critics: Anyone who has questions about the elephant must certainly be a curmudgeonly old elephant hater, who believes that there is nothing new under the sun; this exhausts, for him, the options for dissent (1998a: 54). And yet, might it not be a *newly* productive strategy to pay close and critical attention to these different limb-like global projects and agendas, to appreciate their articulations as well as their disengagements and mismatched encounters?

Conflations

Jameson (1998a) argues that globalization is best understood through the Hegelian dialectic: its ideological logic produces both a dark and a light side. This is a useful reminder that the global developments that we, as social commentators, find promising are often deeply connected to those we find dangerous. But why jump quite so quickly into the assumption that the vast array of transcommunal and transnational ideas and activities around us form a single ideological system? There are some important advantages. Overlaps among ideological projects produce an added intensity all around. When the machinery of corporate and state publicity has converged on a single image, it is doubly hard to avoid the sense of complicity, for better or worse. In analyzing recent developments, it would be silly to argue for autonomous institutional, regional, or political-cause domains. It is clear that the appreciation of synergy among varied globalist projects is at the heart of the new enthusiasm about the globe. My point is that this very search for overlaps, alliances, collaborations, and complicities is one of the most important phenomena we could study. We might look at how particular projects become formulated, how they are tied and transformed in the process, and how they sometimes interrupt each other despite themselves. The "globalization" that is formed from these hit-and-miss convergences would be considerably more unstable, and more interesting, than the one posited by any single claimant as a world-making system. One step in looking for this kind of globalization must be to recognize that there are varied agendas, practices, and processes that may or may not be deeply interconnected at a given historical moment.

Two recent studies of the cultural logic of global "network" formation are useful to compare in this regard. Roger Rouse (1997) analyzes a series of advertisements produced for the telephone company MCI that promote the company's ability to build an interactive multimedia communications network. This communication network is advertised as part of a world-changing, future-making revamping of space and time, in which instantaneous communications within a personalized

web of ties will replace geographically grounded routes and central-place hierarchies. The "network" MCI promotes is simultaneously the material technology of
telephones, computers, and the like and the individualized, flexible, transnational
set of contacts and associates that citizens of the future will be able to maintain
through these technologies.

A similar but contrasting global network-in-the-making is analyzed by Annelise
Riles (1998b), who studied women's organizing in Fiji in preparation for the United
Nations–sponsored international conference on women in Beijing in 1995. The
women she studied had formed NGOs addressing gendered concerns; these organizations were connected to sister organizations, funders, and other kinds of political
supporters all over the world. What they learned from this system of ties, Riles
shows, is the importance of "networks," that is, webs of imagined interconnection
through which groups in one area were to exchange information and support with
other groups on what was seen as an egalitarian, voluntary basis. Riles argues that
networks took on a formal aesthetic value and, through this formalism, the Fijian
women organizers saw themselves as part of an emergent global process.[14]

These two globe-making projects have a lot in common. Both have educational
goals to teach people to visualize a future globalism in which "networks" – rather
than nations or bureaucracies – will be the organizing aesthetic. Both value personal
contacts over long distances and individual initiative over the recognition of preset
roles. Yet it is also clear that each project has come into being along a different
historical trajectory, with different material and political resources and objectives,
and their convergence is broken by those differences. As Rouse shows, MCI's
presentation of its product as a "network" separates wealthy professionals
(i.e., those in the network) from the underpaid workers and other poor people to
whom they have some responsibility in the public space of the nation. Only through
this separation can they build a constituency for the global mobility of corporate
resources and the wealthy niche marketing of corporate products. The globalization
this network promotes, then, is one that ties privileged consumers and their corporate sponsors in a self-conscious forgetting about the rest of the world. In contrast,
the NGO networks discussed by Riles are intended to build a transnational women's
solidarity that brings women's rights *into* particular national contexts rather than
excluding network builders from participation in nations. Attention to national and
regional "levels" of network building is supposed to strengthen the call of public
responsibilities within these units rather than eviscerate them. Even as they bypass
state bureaucracies, the women are called on to act as national representatives; in
this capacity, Riles argues (1998a), the Fijian women bring national cultural sensibilities to the imagination of global network activities by focusing on a formal
aesthetics grounded in other Fijian cultural work.

One further striking contrast between these two images of the network is their
differential gender content. MCI's network, as Rouse explains it, rescues vulnerable
young girls through the patriarchal security of a privatized globe. The Fijian
women's NGO network creates new arenas of all-female sociality that draw on
but extend local forms in transnational translations. The contrast provides rich
grounds for thinking about emergent forms of subjectivity and agency in varied
global projects. There is a lot going on, and it does not all match up. Were we to

limit ourselves to one of these visions as a description of the new global landscape, we would miss the pleasures and dangers of this multiplicity. Furthermore, we might overvalorize connection and circulation rather than attending to the shifting, contested making of channels and landscape elements.

Circulation

Interconnection is everything in the new globalisms. And interconnection is created through circulation. Many things are said to circulate, ranging from people to money; cultures to information; and television programs, to international protocols, to the process called globalization itself. "Circulation" is in global rhetoric what the "penetration" of capitalism was in certain kinds of Marxist world-systems theory: the way powerful institutions and ideas spread geographically and come to have an influence in distant places. The difference is significant; where *penetration* always evokes a kind of rape, a forcing of some people's powerful interests onto other people, *circulation* calls forth images of the healthy flow of blood in the body and the stimulating, evenhanded exchange of the marketplace.

Both bodies and markets as models for understanding social process have been much criticized in social theory in the 20th century. Images of society as organically interconnected like a body were important in establishing the social sciences, but they have been largely discredited as disallowing the study of power, meaning, conflict, disjuncture, and historical change. Images of society as a market have had a different kind of lasting power. Caught up in the endorsement of capitalism as an economic system and free trade as its ideal political context, they have been revived and given new authority in celebration of the end of communism and the Cold War. Marxist scholarship, however, continues a substantial record of criticism of these images. Market models assume a "level playing field" of exchange that erases the inequalities of property and the processes of labor exploitation. Market models appear to be inclusive, but they privilege social actors who, because of their economic resources, are able to participate in markets. Most importantly in the context of the post–Cold War enthusiasm for market models, Marxist scholars have shown how bourgeois governments and social institutions have promoted market thinking to naturalize class and other social distinctions. By training the attention of citizens on the equalities and opportunities of circulation and exchange, they justify policies of domination and discrimination. Recent endorsements of "global circulation" as the process for making the future partake in the obfuscations of inequality for which market models are known.

Global circulation is not just a rhetoric of corporate expansion, however. Leftist social commentators often find as much good use for circulation models as capitalist apologists. Circulation is used to discuss the breaking down of oppressive barriers among cultures, races, languages, and nations, including immigration restrictions and segregation policies. Diasporas circulate, bringing the wealth of their cultural heritage to new locations. Authoritarian regimes prevent the circulation of information, inspiring democratic movements to create underground channels of flow. The circulation of film inspires creative viewing practices. Circulation is thus tapped for the endorsement of multicultural enrichment, freedom, mobility, communication, and creative hybridity.

In part, the acceptability of circulation rhetoric among liberal and leftist social scientists derives from a self-conscious rejection of the Marxist emphasis on capitalist production and its consequent deemphasis on market exchange and consumption (e.g., Appadurai 1986; Baudrillari 1975). Leftist critics of corporate globalization point to the importance of marketing and consumption in contemporary corporate strategies for reaching out to new fields of operation (e.g., Jameson 1998a); these are topics that need to be discussed. The growth of managerial and service professions (e.g., Ong 1999; Sassen 1998) also calls out to critics to abandon an exclusive analytic focus on factory production to attend to the variety of economic forms of contemporary capitalism.

The form and variety of capitalist economic activities are not, however, the only issues to raise about the use of the rhetoric of circulation as a ruling image for global interconnections. There are hidden relations of production here that may have nothing to do with labor in factories: the making of the objects and subjects who circulate, the channels of circulation, and the landscape elements that enclose and frame those channels. A focus on circulation shows us the movement of people, things, ideas, or institutions, but it does not show us how this movement depends on defining tracks and grounds or scales and units of agency. This blindness may not be inherent in the idea of circulation itself but, rather, may be caused by the kinds of circulations that have delineated the model. For historically layered political reasons, the model has been closed to attention to struggles over the terrain of circulation and the privileging of certain kinds of people as players. We focus on the money – the *ur* object of flow – instead of the social conditions that allow or encourage that flow. If we imagined creeks, perhaps the model would be different; we might notice the channel as well as the water moving.

In this spirit, Saskia Sassen (1998) has addressed channel making in relation to global circulations of corporate communications as well as labor. She argues that "global cities" have developed as centers for transnational corporate operations because of the density of corporate real estate, professional service workers, and telecommunication connection grids. Corporate rhetoric aspires to an infinite decentralization and deterritorialization of management operations, but this rhetoric ignores the material requirements for dispersed communication, for example, telephone and computer connections, as well as the specialized labor of advertising, finance, and other services, all of which is concentrated in particular cities. The much touted mobility of information, capital, products, and production facilities depends on these coordinating centers. Similarly, Sassen shows that immigration, often discussed as the mass product of individual mobility, requires the creation of institutional ties linking sending and receiving areas. Histories of direct foreign investment or military intervention, for example, have predictably produced flows of immigrants from the targeted regions to the United States. "Flow" is movement stimulated through political and economic channels.

Sassen's work shows that the alternatives to conventional models of circulation are not just to close off our attention to travel and trade. Analysts can also examine the material and institutional infrastructure of movement and pay special attention to the economic coercions and political guarantees that limit or promote circulation. In order to do this, however, we would need to redefine the common distinction between the "local" and the "global." Most commonly, globalist thinkers imagine the local as the stopping point of global circulations. It is the place where global flows are consumed, incorporated, and resisted (Pred and Watts 1992). It is the place where global flows fragment and are transformed into something place bound and particular (Wilson and Dissanayake 1996b). But if flow itself always involves making terrain, there can be no territorial distinctions between the "global" trans-cending of place and the "local" making of places. Instead, there is place making – and travel – all around, from New York to New Guinea.[15]

Place making is always a cultural as well as a political-economic activity. It involves assumptions about the nature of those subjects authorized to participate in the process and the kinds of claims they can reasonably put forth about their position in national, regional, and world classifications and hierarchies of places. The specificities of these subjects and claims contradict and misstate those of other place makers, even as they may form overlaps and links imaged as "flows." The channel-making activity of circulation, then, is always a contested and tentative formation of scales and landscapes. To avoid letting those who imagine themselves as winners call all of the terms, we need to attend to the missed encounters, clashes, misfires, and confusions that are as much part of global linkages as simple "flow."

Culture, specificity, and place making have conventionally been the domain of the discipline of anthropology, particularly as practiced in the United States. Because these kinds of issues are so often missing from discussions of the global, the stakes are particularly high in seeing their incorporation into global questions in anthropology. Yet it is not these issues that first chaperoned globalism into U.S. anthropology. Instead, the charisma of the global was introduced to forward a disciplinary transition away from an overzealous and nonreflective localism. It is from the perspective of this trajectory that it is possible to examine the specific disciplinary practices through which globalist frameworks are being read by U.S. anthropologists.

Readings in Anthropology

Social science globalisms take particular forms in relation to disciplinary reading and discussion practices. They gain their influence not only because they are adopted in the work of articulate practitioners but, equally importantly, because they enter local trajectories of disciplinary momentum. They are rebuilt to speak to disciplinary challenges as these, in turn, are understood in relation to specific social locations of scholarly practice. In the process, social science globalisms pick up regional and disciplinary frameworks and assumptions, even as they throw themselves as objec-tions against others.

Anthropologists do not merely mimic the understandings of globalism of other experts, even as they are influenced by them. No anthropologist I know argues that the global future will be culturally homogeneous; even those anthropologists most wedded to the idea of a new global era imagine this era as characterized by "local" cultural diversity. Disciplinary concern with cultural diversity overrides the rhetoric of global cultural unification pervasive elsewhere, even though, for those in its sway, globalism still rules: Diversity is generally imagined as forming a reaction or a backdrop to the singular and all-powerful "global forces" that create a new world. (Globalisms are not themselves regularly regarded as diverse.) Politically progressive anthropologists sometimes show how this kind of circumscribed, reactive, self-consciously "local" diversity is a form of resistance to the proliferation of globalist capitalism and hypermodernist governmentality; however, the possibility that capitalisms and governmentalities are themselves situated, contradictory, effervescent, or culturally circumscribed is much less explored. Anthropologists who have argued against simplistic models of "global culture" have also, then, naturalized globalist ideologies of the global.

In the United States, the excitement of this globalism for anthropologists draws from a rather "local" disciplinary heritage: a more than 25-year journey away from analyses of "cultures" as autonomous, self-generating, and bounded entities. In the 1960s and 1970s, U.S. anthropologists criticized the discipline's complicity with colonial projects of conquest and administration. Historical, anticolonial, and world-systems frameworks moved to the discipline's center, ousting functionalism, and interpretive accounts of national and nationalist commitments replaced descriptions of isolated cultures. In the 1980s, ethnographic research and description were interrogated for their role in making cultures appear isolated, and U.S. anthropologists recommitted themselves to more open, reflexive, and textually responsive ways of approaching the inequalities and interconnections among people and places. The recent turn to the global takes its alignment within this pathway of disciplinary self-criticism.

Globalism within this trajectory renews stereotypes of the anthropological past in order to confront them. The "old" anthropology imagined here describes cultures so grounded that they could not move out of place. This anthropology imprisons its objects in a cell; interconnection and movement in the form of "global flows" are thus experienced as a form of liberation. Furthermore, these flows fit most neatly inside the discipline when, in deference to past teachers and conventions, the boundedness of past cultures goes unchallenged; global flows can then take the discipline, and the world, into a freer future.

This "freeing up" variety of globalism is both exhilarating and problematic. On the one hand, it shows us new dreams and schemes of world making; on the other, as an aspect of its liberatory project, it also turns attention away from the quirky eccentricities of culture and history that have perhaps been U.S. anthropology's most vital contribution to critical thought. In the process, too, anthropologists tend to endorse the globalist dreams of the people they study, and thus we lose the opportunity to address the located specificity of those globalist dreams.

The three features I have discussed as creating the charisma of social science globalisms are prominent in U.S. anthropology. Each has been endorsed for good "local" reasons. Yet the very enthusiasm that each of these features has provoked has made it easier to erase specificities to create a misleading portrait of a single global future. It is hard not to universalize a globalist framework. But let me see if I can locate these globalisms – and in the process get them to do some very different work.

Futurism

U.S. anthropologists come to an endorsement of a singular global future from their interest in the macroeconomic context of cultural diversity. An important part of the disciplinary trajectory away from the study of isolated cultures has been attention to the capitalist world system. Anthropologists have been able to show how even out-of-the-way and exotic cultures respond to capitalism's challenges. This is crucial work. At the same time, risks and dilemmas remain in this analysis: In turning one's gaze to the systemic features of world capitalism, it is easy to lose track of the specificity of particular capitalist niches. In coming to terms with the transnational scope of contemporary finance, marketing, and production, it is easy to endorse globalism as a predictive frame. Indeed, it is in this context that anthropologists most commonly imagine singular global futures. Even as critics, we are caught in the hyperboles imagined by advocates of neoliberalism, structural adjustment, and transnationalization.

Particularly in its critical versions, this global future forms part of a narrative of the evolution of capitalism. Furthermore, most anthropologists attracted by this narrative take their model from a single source: David Harvey's *The Condition of Postmodernity* (1989). Within much globalist anthropology, Harvey's book establishes the fact of epochal change, laying the ground for global futurism. Yet I find this a particular, peculiar reading of Harvey, and it is worth considering in its own right: For anthropologists, Harvey provides the evidence for a new era. As readers, they pick out "flexible specialization" and "time-space compression" as the characteristics of this new era.[16]

Yet, when I turn to Harvey's book, it seems to me that the central argument is that the "cultural aesthetic" of postmodernism is related to the economic logic of flexible accumulation. The first section of the book reviews modernism and postmodernism as trends in the arts and letters, including architecture and philosophy. This is "capital C" culture: a genealogy of great men and their ideas. The second section of the book turns to the economic "regimes of accumulation" of Fordism and post-Fordist "flexible accumulation." The book's original idea is to juxtapose these two bodies of literature and to argue that post-modernism mirrors post-Fordism. It takes a certain amount of economic determinism to make this argument, in which Culture acts as a mirror of economic realities.[17] But in this gap, space and time come in. For Harvey, the "experience" of space and time mediates between Culture and the (nonculturally organized) economy.

For me the space and time section is the least satisfying section of the book. Harvey describes categories for understanding human encounters with space and time, representations of space and time in the arts and letters (and, in one chapter, in two films), and anecdotes about space and time in the capitalist workplace. No ethnographic sources for understanding spatial and temporal texture or diversity are consulted. The concept of "experience" is never explained. Because the mirror relation between arts and letters and the economy has already been established, their mediation by experience is a formal requirement, needing no substantiation.

In this context, it is strange that anthropologists so often pick only "the acceleration of space-time compression" along with "flexible accumulation" out of this book. In the process of citation, too, the book's tone changes. Harvey's book is polemical. He ranges over a wide variety of scholarship to criticize post-modern aesthetics. This is not a science experiment but, rather, a book-length essay. Yet somehow Harvey's description of economic evolution comes to have the status of a fact when drawn into globalist anthropology. Harvey brings with him the ability to read economics, a skill few anthropologists have developed. It may be that anthropologists ignore the discussion of aesthetics, thinking they know more about culture than he does, and go for the accumulation strategy and associated space-time requirements because they feel like the macroeconomic facts that are outside of their knowledge base.

The result is that a selection of Harvey's terms is used to build a noncultural and nonsituated futurist framework, "beyond culture" (Gupta and Ferguson 1992). One set of problems derives from the attempt to make this future global; as anthropologist Michael Kearney admits, Harvey's thesis is "not dealing with globalization perse" (1995: 551). Indeed, Harvey has a distinct blindness for everything outside dominant Northern Cultures and economies; to make his story applicable to North–South articulations is not impossible, but it is a challenge. Another set of problems seems even more intractable. If we drop Harvey's discussion of aesthetics (as Culture) but still ignore the ethnographic sources through which anthropologists identify culture, just how do we know the shape of space and time? The pared-down Harvey readings preferred by anthropologists have lost even literary and filmic representations of temporal and spatial processes; we are left with economic facts. Without "Culture" or "culture," we must assume rapid circulation, fragmentation, compression, and globality; certainly, we cannot consult either popular or official representations, discourses, or cultural practices. Anthropological analysis, which could look at scale-making claims and representations in conjunction with the social processes that support and result from those claims and representations, becomes reduced to building starships on millennial fantasies.

Another way Harvey's work could be used is to scale back its epochal claims to look at some limited but powerful alliances between aesthetics and economics. Harvey's claim that postmodernism and flexible accumulation have something to do with each other could be pursued by locating patterns and players more specifically. This kind of project, however, diminishes the excitement of another globalist reading practice, which I have called "conflations." Let me examine how this practice both brings to life and impoverishes the anthropology of global interconnection.

Conflations

Not all anthropological globalism is engaged in understanding the systemics of capitalism; another significant sector attempts to hold onto "culture" as an anthropological object while showing its increased contemporary mobility and range. In this genre, anthropologists have done exciting work to specify modes of cultural interconnection that tie people in far-flung locales or travel with them across heterogeneous terrains. This work offers the possibility of attention to regionalisms and histories of place making within an appreciation of interconnection. However, to the extent that this work has been harnessed for the search for a singular anthropological globalism, it has blurred the differences among places and perspectives to emphasize the break from past localisms. This anthropological globalism renaturalizes global dreams instead of examining and locating them ethnographically. Moreover, it leads readers to assume that all globalisms are at base the same; thus, most readers read globalist anthropologists as an undifferentiated crowd.

Might a different kind of reading practice reestablish the potential for appreciating multiple, overlapping, and sometimes contradictory globalisms? Consider, for example, contrasts among the globalisms of Ulf Hannerz (1996), Michael Kearney (1996), and Arjun Appadurai (1996). I choose these authors because each has elaborated his ideas about globalism in a book-length exposition. Each sees his work as advancing the disciplinary trajectory of anthropology beyond the anthropology of separate, segregated cultures and societies. Each is concerned with migrants and travelers and the worlds they make and are made by; each argues that new analytic tools are necessary for new times.

Yet they conjure different global geographies. The globality of Hannerz, the "global ecumene" (1989), is a space of interaction among once-separate cultures now growing in dialogue and mutual acknowledgment. Its creolization is created by cultural flows – particularly flows from powerful centers to less powerful peripheries; it is carried and extended by cosmopolitans who, of necessity, acknowledge and extend European and North American cultural frameworks even as they incorporate and remake non-Western cultures. Center–periphery relations thus organize world culture (Hannerz 1996).

In contrast, Kearney's postmodern globality is a critique of center–periphery frameworks, which Kearney identifies with the classificatory modernist era that has passed away as we have entered transnational hyperspace and non-teleological, postdevelopmental time. The key feature of the global era is the "implosion" of center and periphery, as distinctions between rural and urban as well as South and North disintegrate. Spatial and cultural discriminations become impossible in a world of global flows, as nonunitary migrant subjects are formed in the interstices of past classificatory principles. In the unruly "reticula" Kearney conjures, however, he retains a dialogue with Marxian political economy that gives his multiplicity of identities and geographies its shape. The organization of the transnational economy creates differences of class, power, and value that forge subaltern and dominant social niches of identity and agency.

In contrast again, Appadurai evokes a globality of contested "scapes" in which no single organizing principle rules. "Financescapes," which include capital flows, are only one of several imaginative geographies that compete to make the globe; Appadurai finds that "ethnoscapes" and "mediascapes" – the cultural worlds conjured by migrants and in movies, respectively – are more decisive features in the "rupture" of the global era, with its heightened dependence on the imagination. Like Kearney's, Appadurai's globalism refuses center–periphery frames, but, like Hannerz, he situates it squarely in modernity's worldwide cultural spread rather than postmodernism's epistemological disruptions. Appadurai's globalism refuses Kearney's sociology of migrants to foreground their cultural worlds; indeed, these kinds of cultural terrains, although ungrounded in space, are those criticized by Kearney as modernist classificatory tricks.

Different subjects are at the center of each of these understandings of the global. In the best spirit of anthropology, one might read each account, indeed, in relation to the author's ethnographic experience. Appadurai imagines global scapes from the perspective of his attention to the Indian diaspora and its cultural world. Kearney theorizes from his encounter with Miztec "postpeasants": Mexican Indian farmers who have become migrants selling crafts in San Diego parking lots. Hannerz is concerned about cosmopolitans, world travelers, journalists, and city people everywhere; he returns often to his knowledge about Africa. These varied subjects assist the authors in evoking different globalisms. If, instead of assuming a single global trajectory, we attended to varied globalist claims and perspectives, what might we see?

Diasporas, almost by definition, conjure deterritorialized areas, worlds of meaning and "home" feeling detached from original territorial boundaries – like Appadurai's scapes. This kind of self-consciousness about the making of cultural worlds contrasts sharply with the cultural commitments of cosmopolitans and poor migrants, as these create focal knowledges for Hannerz and Kearney, respectively. Both cosmopolitans and poor migrants erase the specificity of their cultural tracks, although for different reasons: Poor migrants need to fit in the worlds of others; cosmopolitans want more of the world to be theirs. Cosmopolitans, like diasporas, promote projects of world making, but, as Hannerz stresses, the projects they endorse enlarge the hegemonies of Northern centers even as they incorporate peripheries. In contrast, neither the worldmaking projects of Southern diasporas nor those of poor migrants fit into a center–periphery frame. They limit, rather than spread, Northern hegemonies. In this spirit, Appadurai and Kearney implicitly criticize Hannerz's center–periphery approach. Yet it is also the case that Kearney's and Appadurai's actors diverge. Poor migrants, like those at the center of Kearney's globalism, are particularly aware of their need to survive – politically, economically, and culturally – in worlds that others have made; the imagination is never enough for them to create autonomy and self-determination. Thus, Kearney (1995: 553) refuses Appadurai's imagination-ruled scapes, while Appadurai and Hannerz, thinking through diasporas and cosmopolitans, respectively, stress the world-making power of imaginative perspectives.

The regional specificities of these focal knowledges may also be relevant to the globalisms imagined through them: I think of the strength of the culture and media industries of India and its diaspora, the self-consciousness about Northern cultural impositions of cosmopolitan Africans, and the centrality of transnational capitalism in Latin American studies. It also may be suggestive to compare all these knowledges with other angles for thinking about contemporary culture. Consider, for example, U.S. minority groups who have demanded protection from the nation-state against discrimination; thinking through U.S. minority culture provides a less fertile ground than diasporas, poor migrants, and cosmopolitans to imagine an inclusively postnational era.[18] These differences do not make these perspectives wrong; my point is to show that these are differences that matter theoretically. The next step for readers – and future researchers and writers – is to think about that world in which the respective focal knowledges on which they draw could *all* exist, whether in competition or alliance, in mutual acknowledgment or erasure, in misunderstanding or dialogue.

This task requires that we study folk understandings of the global, and the practices with which they are intertwined, rather than representing globalization as a transcultural historical process. With some modifications, each of the perspectives I have been describing can be used for this task. However, we would have to resituate the authors' theories in relation to histories of their respective knowledges of and experiences with specific people and events. We would have to abandon the search for a single global future.

Appadurai's stress on disjunction as well as on the importance of the imagination is well suited for thinking about the interplay of varied globalist perspectives. Yet imaginative landscapes come in many kinds, and this diversity is more useful to understanding disjunction than a division into functional domains of ethnicity, technology, finance, media, and ideology, for these posit a singular formula for "society." If, instead of hegemonic domain divisions, we turned to the social and cultural struggles through which imaginative visions come to count as "scapes" at all, we might be able to incorporate disjunction not only among domains but also among varied and contested kinds of imaginative landscape making in this framework. We might contrast the cultural world of the Indian diaspora with other globalist scapes. For example, Paulla Ebron (1998, 1999) has described the regional and global claims of African American history and memory landscapes; she traces these landscapes through many formats of discussion, which both enter and interrupt Appadurai's "mediascape" domain. Moving beyond a list of globally settled "scapes," we need to study how scales, geographies, eras, and other imaginative terrains are differentially and dialogically negotiated, refused, or erased.

Hannerz's attention to the cultural specificity of cosmopolitanisms is important to assess the power and limitations of claims about scale, era, and geography without subsuming one's own analysis under the truths these claims promote. Hannerz also usefully reminds us of the power of certain imaginative landscapes, especially those that "make people from western Europe and North America feel as much at home as possible" (1996: 107). Yet these powerful perspectives do not necessarily determine the cultural evolution of the whole world; the key is to *situate* them in relation to the political economies that make them possible and the struggles over meaning in which they participate.

In the process of putting global perspectives in situated dialogue, the political economy engaged (if not often endorsed) by Kearney is essential. Imaginative landscapes mobilize an audience through material and institutional resources. Yet, as discussed in the previous section, it is difficult to give full attention to such mobilizations with a theory of the singular evolution of a monolithic capitalism.[19] As J. K. Gibson-Graham (1996) argues, models that predict the stages of capitalism bow to the ideology of a single world-capitalist system rather than investigating its heterogeneous complexities. Instead, Kearney's concern with political economy, like that of Harvey, might point us toward an investigation of shifting cultural developments among surprisingly diverse capitalisms. The innovations of these approaches are not served well, however, by an overreliance on a vocabulary of "flows."

Circulation

Circulation has a deep genealogy in anthropology. I keep waiting to find an author who takes me through this legacy, perhaps tracing his or her thoughts from French structuralist "exchange" through global "flows." But I have not yet found that author. Instead, it has become easy for anthropologists to talk about global circulations as a sign of everything new and of future making.

Circulations are said to be what we are able to study as global. George Marcus is informative and clear about this in the introduction to the series of essays he edited as *Rereading Cultural Anthropology* (1992). Under the heading "Circulations," he says,

> The other major related trend that concerns contemporary global transformations is a move out from local situations to understand how transcultural processes themselves are constituted in the world of the so-called "system" (modern interlocking institutions of media, markets, states, industries, universities – the worlds of elites and middle classes) that has encapsulated, transformed, and sometimes obliterated local cultures. This work examines the circulation of cultural meanings, objects, and identities in diffuse time-space. *It shows how the global arena is itself constituted by such circulations.* [1992:xiii, emphasis added]

Circulations define the newness of the global epoch. Kearney's review "The Local and the Global: The Anthropology of Globalization and Transnationalism" (1995) offers a useful statement of this. His field is the study of movement, both population movement and "the movement of information, symbols, capital, and commodities in global and transnational spaces.... Special attention is given to the significant contemporary increases in the volume and velocity of such flows for the dynamics of communities and for the identities of their members" (1995: 547).

Newness is defined by increased flow. Because authors and readers focus on the excitement of this newness, there has been almost no discussion about the implied dichotomies here: circulation versus stagnation, new versus old. Does the newness and globality of movement mean that once-immobile "local" places have recently been transcended by "global" flow? If analysts must "move out of local situations" to find circulation, there must be some local folks who are still stuck inside them, being stagnant. These imagined stagnant locals are excluded from the new circulating globality, which leaves them outside, just as progress and modernity were imagined as leaving so many behind. Here we must consider which new Orientalisms will define who is in and who is out of circulation, just as frameworks of race, region, and religion defined those excluded from the idea of progress. Furthermore, if circulation is new, does that mean that the old order was static and segregated? Were there really, after all, isolated autonomous cultures out there until the circulations of the last few years? Each of these misleading dichotomies would encourage analysts to resurrect that very anthropology that has been criticized and reworked for the last 25 years: the anthropology that fixed and segregated cultures. But in each case, it would be resurrected only for special cases: the marginal, the past. A globalist anthropology of movement would reign at the center.[20] This will not do. To move beyond the contrast between past and local stability and present/future global flow, we need to examine different modes of regional-to-global interconnection.

The new attention to global circulation responds to real changes in the world – and in anthropology as practiced in the United States. Anthropologists once set out to study "communities"; they thought they could find society and culture within a relatively narrowly defined social sphere. For some years, it has seemed difficult to do anthropology without paying attention to much wider-ranging objects of study: national visions, elite networks, popular culture, social movements, state policies, histories of colonial thinking, and much more. One piece of the excitement of contemporary anthropology involves new ideas about how to do fieldwork on these complex objects. We rush into interdisciplinary social theory to find innovative, project-oriented suggestions. In this process, it is easy to endorse frameworks of globalization that transcend the limitations of site-oriented local research. Instead, I am arguing that we can study the landscape of circulation as well as the flow. How are people, cultures, and things remade as they travel?

Scale as an Object of Analysis

Understanding the institutional proliferation of particular globalization projects requires a sense of their cultural specificities as well as the travels and interactions through which these projects are reproduced and taken on in new places. In thinking about where one would begin a globally informed investigation of local and global processes that avoids the pitfalls I have been discussing, I might begin with two analytic principles. First, I would pay close attention to *ideologies* of scale, that is, cultural claims about locality, regionality, and globality; about stasis and circulation; and about networks and strategies of proliferation. I would track rhetorics of scale as well as contests over what will count as relevant scales. Second, I would break down the units of culture and political economy through which we make sense of events and social processes. Instead of looking for world-wrapping evolutionary stages, logics, and epistemes, I would begin by finding what I call "projects," that is, relatively coherent bundles of ideas and practices as realized in particular times and places. The choice of what counts as a project depends on what one is trying to learn about, but, in each case, to identify projects is to maintain a commitment to localization, even of the biggest world-making dreams and schemes. The various instantiations of capitalism can be regarded as projects; so can progressive social movements, everyday patterns of living, or university-based intellectual programs. Projects are to be traced in relation to particular historical travels from one place to another; they are caught up in local issues of translation and mobilization; although they may be very powerful, we cannot assume their ability to remake nature and society according to their visions. Projects may articulate with each other, creating moments of fabled stability and power (see Tsing 1999c, 2000). They may also rub up against each other awkwardly, creating messiness and new possibilities. Through joint attention to ideologies of scale and projects of scale making, it is possible to move into those cracks most neglected by unself-conscious reliance on global futurism, globalist conflation, and global circulation.

To illustrate such cracks, I turn to scholarship on the making of projects of environmental modernization. Although the rhetoric of globalization has much affected the reconstruction of cities, it is the rhetoric of modernization that continues to make rural hinterlands into the kinds of places that global capital and globalist planning can best use for their projects. Talk of national and international development still dominates the reshaping of the countryside; yet it is the complement of globalization talk. Global dreams require these rural modernization projects, and, thus, globalist strategies can be studied within them. Indeed, there are certain advantages of tracking the importance of globalism in an arena where this rhetoric does not amass a difficult-to-question hegemony.[21] It is easier to see the exotic particularities and the grounded travels of scale-making commitments where these are not the only goal of the scholarship. It is possible to read against the grain of analyses of modernism to make scale an object of analysis. I offer four examples of such starting points.

Scale Making.   Certainly, a key issue in assuming a critical perspective on global claims and processes is the making of scales – not just the global but also local and regional scales of all sorts. Through what social and material processes and cultural commitments do localities or globalities come, tentatively, into being? How are varied regional geographies made real? Globalism's automatic association of particular scales with particular eras makes it very difficult to notice the details and idiosyncrasies of scale making – thus, more the reason to foreground this issue. And, because the globe is a region made large, asking about the making of global scale brings forward questions of the various forms of region making that both facilitate and interrupt global claims.

Critical studies of environmental modernization offer a number of useful examples about how social scientists might approach the investigation of regional and global scale making. "Bioregions" have been a central feature of environmental policy; how are they made? I think of Warwick Anderson's (2003) research on the hygiene-oriented experiments that helped define "the tropics" as a zone of challenge for scientific modernism, or of Peter Haas's (1990) discussion of the transnational strategies of scientists in shaping the cross-border political treaties that made "the Mediterranean" a zone in which issues of water pollution could be addressed. And what of the making of the global superregion? Richard Grove's (1995) research on the construction of global environmental science is particularly exciting in thinking about the makings of globality. Grove shows how the imperial placement of scientists in botanical gardens and research stations across the European colonies inspired continent-crossing correspondence in the late 18th century. Through this correspondence, informed by widespread fears of climate change caused by colonial deforestation, colonial scientists formulated notions of a "global" climate. This commitment to planet-wide environmental process allowed further developments in imagining both science and policy on a global scale. Obviously, this is not the only global scale that matters. But in tracing its specificity, Grove offers a model for thinking about the many kinds of globality that have become important in the contemporary world.

Close Encounters.   Where circulation models have tended to focus only on message transmission, one might instead investigate interactions involving collaboration, misunderstanding, opposition, and dialogue. Attention to these processes provides an alternative to the conflation of varied scale-making claims, projects, and agents. One literature that has become unusually attentive to mixed encounters is the literature on transnational social movements, which require coalitions among extremely various kinds of people, with disparate goals and perceptions of the issues at hand (e.g., Keck and Sikkink 1998). Thus, for example, the coalitions that have been built for rain forest protection have brought together tribal leaders, union organizers, college professors, wildlife lovers, rural workers, cosmetic entrepreneurs, and activists for democratic reform, among others (see Brosius 1999, 2003; Keck 1995; Tsing 1999a; Turner 1999).

To understand even momentary successes of this kind of motley coalition, analysts must attend to the changing definitions of *interests* and *identity* that both allow and result from collaborative activities. They must focus on the historical specificity of the events that resulted in alliance and the open-ended indeterminacy of the regional processes stimulated by that alliance (Tsing 1999b). These are useful reminders in rethinking transnational interactions.

It is not just in transient and defensive social movements, however, that it is important to look for social processes sparked by coalitions, dialogues, missed messages, and oppositional refusals. In considering developments in transnational capitalism this kind of attention can offer an alternative to the blindfolded dedication to a singular unfolding economic logic that has characterized so much globalist analysis. If we investigate the series of historically specific collaborations that create distinctive cultural forms of capitalism, we might better appreciate global heterogeneity.

Peter Dauvergne (1997), for example has shown how Japanese trading companies, requiring a mass scale of transactions, were able to form productive coalitions with national political leaders in Southeast Asia, who were seeking the support of powerful clients; together they created the distinctive features of the Southeast Asian timber industry, which has devastated regional rain forests for cheap plywood. The cultural and economic specificities of both Japanese trading companies and Southeast Asian national political regimes created a particular and peculiar capitalism that cannot be reduced to the playing out of a singular transnational capitalist logic. Instead, Dauvergne argues, it created economic and ecological "shadows" between Japan and Southeast Asia that redefined and reformulated their separate and combined regional agency. This kind of analysis should prove useful in understanding the many forms of capitalism that help to create regional and global scales.

Definitional Struggles.   Circulation imagery can draw attention away from the transformation of actors, objects, goals, perspectives and terrains that characterizes regional-to-global interaction. Instead, we might pay special attention to the roles of both cultural legacies and power inequalities in creating the institutional arenas and assumptions of world-making transitions. Every globalization project is shaped from somewhat unpredictable interactions among specific cultural legacies. Furthermore, the cultural frames and assumptions of globalization projects cannot be understood without attention to multiple levels of political negotiations, with their idiosyncratic and open-ended histories. "Definitional struggles" call attention to how these arenas are designed and the politics of their development. They can remind us that globalization both requires and exceeds the work of particularly positioned and repositioned globalizers.

Critical studies of environmental modernization can also provide illustrative guidance here. Consider, for example, how agribusiness came to power in the western United States. Donald Worster's (1985) study of the building of the great irrigation projects that stimulated the emergence of agribusiness offers a wealth of detail on the interacting cultural legacies that made the scale and design of these massive irrigation projects possible.[22] The wide streets of Mormon aesthetics inspired irrigation design, breaking it away from Hispanic community water control; the legal precedence of California gold rush mineral claims allowed the fluorescence of water law that privileged state–private coalitions; the opportunity for water engineers to tour the irrigation canals of British colonial India created a parallel vision for the western United States in which the landscape should properly be managed by alien experts. Compromises between populists and business advocates congealed center-oriented land allocation policies. These, and more, legacies shaped the design of the great water apparatus that transformed the U.S. economy, bringing profitable farming from east to west and helping to build U.S. imperial strength.

Not just definition but also struggle is at issue in the formation of projects of world transformation. Studies of the formation of the "frontier" in Amazonia, for example, could be told as the classic story of modernization, with its replacement of native traditional living spaces with cosmopolitan modern economies. But critical histories by scholars such as Hecht and Cockburn (1989) and Schmink and Wood (1992) have shown that the cultural assumptions of property and resource management that modernizers might want us to take for granted have been established unevenly, awkwardly, and tentatively, in the midst of passionate and unfinished struggles. Hecht and Cockburn stress the historically shifting wielders of power who have worked so hard, with varied success, for particular programs of frontier making. Schmink and Wood stress the uncanniness of the frontier, in which the best laid plans produce results opposite to their predictions. The works show varied histories at community, regional, and national scales; their components do not fit easily into a single story. Together, they highlight definitional struggles involved in making the frontier.

Concrete Trajectories and Engagements.   In contrast to the abstract globe conjured by social science globalism, the scholarship I am imagining would stress the concreteness of "movements" in both senses of the word: social mobilizations in which new identities and interests are formed and travels from one place to another through which place-transcending interactions occur. These two senses of *movement* work together in remaking geographies and scales. Tracing them concretely offers more insight into planetary complexity than the endorsement of a heterogeneous globalism whose features ricochet helplessly between an imagined spreading global dynamism and its contained local Other.

How might this be done? A number of scholars have followed modern forestry, as developed in Europe, to examine its deployment in colonial regions. Here I am less interested in the metropole-to-colony transfer and more in the movement from one particular place to another, say of British forest science to India. Ramachandra Guha (1989), Ravi Rajan (1994), and K. Sivaramakrishnan (1996) have all done important research on this movement, as it made and transformed forestry experts, forest-dwelling human communities, and forests themselves. Each tells of the effects of this movement: the development of colonial authority relations, involving dissent and opposition as well as compliance, between forest experts and forest peasants; the importance of reaffirming cultural and scientific standards in empire-wide conferences; the incorporation of local knowledges into Indian forestry policy; and the changing practices of foresters as they learned the Indian landscape and its social and political conventions. The concrete sites of encounter and engagement among people as well as trees shape the trajectories of the forestry project. This kind of attention to particular "routes" of travel (Clifford 1997) is equally important in tracing contemporary social and cultural processes around the globe.

In globalization theories, we have confused what should be *questions* about the global ramifications of new technologies and social processes into *answers* about global change. Each of the starting points I have suggested offers an attempt to reverse this globalist thinking to turn concerns about the global back into researchable questions.

Release

Let me return for a moment to the parallels between modernization and globalization. Many anthropologists are able to look at the dreams and schemes of modernization with a critical distance. We need this critical distance, too, in studying globalization. Globalization is a set of projects that require us to imagine space and time in particular ways. These are curious, powerful projects. Anthropologists need not ignore them; we also need not renaturalize them by assuming that the terms they offer us are true.

At this point, some readers may say, "Why not throw out 'the global' completely, since it exists as a fantasy?" My answer is that even fantasies deserve serious engagement. The best legacies of ethnography allow us to take our objects of study seriously even as we examine them critically. To study ghosts ethnographically means to take issues of haunting seriously. If the analyst merely made fun of beliefs in ghosts, the study would be of little use. Several other steps would be needed: a description of ghost beliefs; an examination of the effects of ghost beliefs on social life; and, in the spirit of taking one's informants seriously, a close attention to the questions that ghosts raise, such as the presence of death and its eerie reminders of things gone. In the same spirit, an analyst of globalism cannot merely toss it out as a vacant deception. Instead, an ethnographic study of the global needs careful attention not only to global claims and their effects on social life but also to questions of interconnection, movement, and boundary crossing that globalist spokespeople have brought to the fore. To take globality as an object of study requires both distance and intimate engagement.

Other readers may object that it is important to reify globalization because of the terrible toll it promises to take on cultural diversity and human well-being. Their endorsement of a self-consciously paranoid vision of total transformation involves the choice to glimpse the terrors of the new world order it promises. Yet I would argue that by reproducing this totalizing framework of social change, critics bind themselves within the assumptions and fantasies of those they oppose. If we want to imagine emergent forms of resistance, new possibilities, and the messiness through which the best laid plans may not yet destroy all hope, we need to attune ourselves to the heterogeneity and open-endedness of the world.

This is not, however, an argument for "local" diversity; if anything, it is an argument for "global" diversity and the wrongheadedness of imagining diversity – from an unquestioning globalist perspective – as a territorially circumscribed, "place-based," and antiglobalist phenomenon. (Since when are globalists not place based?) Unlike most anthropologists working on "global" issues, I have tried to examine some basic assumptions of globalism, using them to form a critical perspective rather than a negative or positive endorsement of projects for making a future imagined as global.

Most global anthropologists embrace the idea of diversity. Anthropologists have been critics of theories of global homogenization; at the same time, those who have joined the argument with globalization theorists have been influenced by the terms of debate to accept most of the premises of these theories in order to join the conversation. The debate about global cultural unification has encouraged anthropologists to agree that we are indeed entering an era properly called global, although that era, according to anthropologists, is characterized by local cultural divergences as much as unification. In the embrace of the argument, the cultural divergence we find must be part of the globalist phenomenon.[23]

This is not, I think, a useful place to be stuck. To get out of its grip, analysts need to give up several of the tools and frames we have found most easy to work with, perhaps because they resound so nicely with popular "common sense," at least in the United States. First, we might stop making a distinction between "global" *forces* and "local" *places*. This is a very seductive set of distinctions, promising as it does to give us both focused detail and the big picture, and I find myself slipping into this vocabulary all the time. But it draws us into globalist fantasies by obscuring the ways that the cultural processes of all "place" making and all "force" making are *both* local and global, that is, both socially and culturally particular and productive of widely spreading interactions. Through these terms, global "forces" gain the power to cause a total rupture that takes over the world.

Second, we might learn to investigate new developments without assuming either their universal extension or their fantastic ability to draw all world-making activities into their grasp. International finance, for example, has surely undergone striking and distinctive transformations in the last 30 years. Certainly this has effects everywhere, but what these effects are is unclear. It seems unlikely to me that a single logic of transformation is being produced – or a singular moment of rupture.[24]

Third, globalisms themselves need to be interrogated as an interconnected, but not homogeneous, set of projects – with their distinctive cultural commitments and their powerful but limited presence in the world. Critical studies of modernization projects provide some thought-provoking examples of analytic direction here.

Freed up in these ways, it might be possible to attend to global visions without imagining their world hegemony. Outside the thrall of globalization, a more nuanced and surprising appreciation of the making and remaking of geography might yet be possible.

NOTES

1   The image of sitting on top of the globe, either with one's body or one's technology, has become a mainstay of advertising. As I write this, for example, I have just received two telephone company advertisements: one, from a local telephone company (US West), features a woman sitting in an office chair on top of the globe while talking into the telephone and typing on her personal computer; the other, from a long-distance telephone company (MCI), shows a telephone receiver resting on top of the globe. This globe is a field to be mastered, managed, and controlled.

2   Garb (1990) argues that the image of the globe also brought with it political understandings about white male mastery and control; environmentalists have fought against these understandings in stressing the fragility of the earth but have also been influenced by them.

3   A fuller genealogy of the idea of globalization – whether incorporate policy, social commentary, or academic analysis – is beyond the scope of this essay. New books and articles appear on the subject every week. The inclusively imagined *Globalization Reader* (Lechner and Boli 2000) reprints a number of social science contributions to the conversation, offering a sense of its heterogeneity and breadth. Of the recent anthologies I have seen, I find *Globalisation and the Asia Pacific* (Olds et al. 1999) the most sensible and insightful.

4   Saskia Sassen nicely articulates this analytic choice, necessary to make globalization a significant field-defining process: "My approach entails...constructing 'the difference,' theoretically and empirically, so as to specify the current period" (1998: 85). She adds, frankly, "I do not deny the existence of many continuities, but my effort has been to understand the strategic discontinuities" (1998: 101).

5   I take the notion of the building of a "bandwagon" effect from Joan Fujimura's (1988) work on cancer research.

6   For example, discussion of globalization has stimulated a rethinking of area studies scholarship in the United States; research and teaching programs are being revamped not only at many universities but also at many of the major research institutes and funding foundations. (See, for example, Abraham and Kassimir 1997 on the Social Science Research Council and Volkman 1998 on the Ford Foundation.) This rethinking allows promising new configurations of training and scholarship. At the same time, the national discussion about area studies illustrates the problems I refer to in describing the limitations of the dogma of global newness. Too many participants, asked to rethink areas in the light of globalization, jump to the conclusion that "areas" are archaic forms beset and overcome by newly emergent global forces. Scholarship, many conclude, should either position itself with the winners, studying global forces, or with the losers, attending to regional resistance. In this configuration of choice, no attention is paid to the continually shifting

formation and negotiation of "areas," the consideration of which might have been the most exciting product of the rethinking of area studies.

7   Mintz (1998) argues in this spirit, reminding anthropologists that massive transcontinental migrations have occurred in past centuries. He suggests, provocatively, that scholars find global migration new because large waves of people of color have recently turned up in the "big white societies" of Europe and its diaspora, where, in the 19th century, they were refused (1998: 123).

8   In their first waves of enthusiasm about globalization, many scholars, social commentators, and policy makers argued that it was forcing nations to disappear. This remains perhaps the most popular argument (see, for example, Appadurai 1996; Miyoshi 1996). More recently, a number of scholars have argued that the nation-state takes new forms in the context of rapid international transfers of capital and labor (e.g., Ong 1997; Sassen 1998). Even the most rapidly mobile of corporations depends on the apparatus of the nation-state to guarantee its property and contracts; in this context, national deregulation reregulates the economic domain in the interest of global capital (Cerny 1993). Nation-states have also been instrumental in forging niches of ethnic and national privilege through which the new "global" entrepreneurs secure their advantage. For these kinds of arguments in particular, an appreciation of the shifting histories of the nation and of the hegemonies of particular nation-states – as I advocate here – seems essential.

9   This set of post–World War II nationalist commitments was brought to my attention in the insightful comments of Malaysian economist Jomo K.S. at the conference "Public Intellectuals in Southeast Asia," in Kuala Lumpur, May 1998. As an example, he pointed out that histories in which nationalism in Southeast Asia was stimulated by conversations with overseas Chinese (e.g., Pramoedya 1996) were suppressed by post–World War II Southeast Asian nations.

10 See also Lowe and Lloyd 1997 and Wilson and Dissanayake 1996a.

11 Why is globalization a new era (rather than, say, an object of reflection or an approach to appreciating culture) for these humanists? Some have come to their acceptance of cultural evolutionary stages from a slightly earlier exploration of "postmodernism" as the latest stage of cultural development; for them, globalization is a variation on postmodern culture. For some, too, the appeal of imagining globalization as a stage of cultural politics is drawn from Marxist evolutionary histories of capitalism; the cultural era is generated by the economic era as superstructure to base. For others, the main appeal seems to be the intervention into earlier civilization-bound humanities studies: the opportunity to draw together a diverse group of scholars who can talk to each other across lines of nation, language, and cultural background. Indeed, I see little evidence that most of the contributors to these volumes are themselves particularly invested in positing a singular global era; even the editors, in their separate articles, contribute to a much more nuanced approach. It seems there is something about introductory material that stimulates era making. There is also an admirable political goal in gathering a diverse group under a common banner: Perhaps a politically united front against unregulated corporate expansion can be formed. However, this political cause can only be aided by building an appreciation of the multiple and conflicting agendas of globalization.

12 Jameson and Miyoshi 1998 does not include an editors' introduction. In lieu of an introduction, the preface and the contributions by the two editors, however, offer the reader a sense of the editors' stakes and stand in that regard.

13 A number of the contributors, including the editors themselves, offer insightful descriptions of the coming together and coming apart of varied agendas of "globalization"; they

describe the scope and the exclusions of varied transnational projects; they ask about the legacies and transformational possibilities of various global interconnections. But these kinds of insights are lost in those parts of the editors' introductions that condense this richness into the definitional homogeneity of a new era.

14 Riles's analysis is not a naive celebration of the possibilities of networks for global feminism. In fact, she emphasizes the strangeness of the object the women she studied called a "network." It did not, for example, include their ordinary collegial social relationships; it was a formal design more suited for documents and diagrams than for everyday living. My goal in contrasting Riles's NGO networks and Rouse's corporate ones is not to show what Jameson would call the light and the dark side of globalization. Instead, from my perspective these are both curious ethnographic objects, and I am interested in how they are produced and maintained, separately and together, in the same world.

15 My comments are not meant as a criticism of the kind of analysis that shows how cosmopolitan ideas and institutions are translated and specified as they come to mean something in particular communities. To the contrary, I would like to see the extension of this kind of work to show the cultural specification of the cosmopolitan.

16 George Marcus makes Harvey's argument about accumulation the basis for his call for new research methods in anthropology:

> For those across disciplines interested in placing their specific projects of research in the unfolding of new arrangements for which past historical narratives were not fully adequate, a firm sense of a world system framework was replaced by various accounts of dissolution, fragmentation, as well as new processes – captured in concepts like "post-Fordism" [Harvey], "time-space compression" [Harvey], "flexible specialization" [Harvey], "the end of organized capitalism" [Lash, Urry], and most recently "globalization" [Featherstone, Hannerz, Sklair] – none of which could be fully understood in terms of earlier macro-models of the capitalist world system. [1995: 98; I have substituted the names of authors for the numbered references included in the original]

Michael Kearney brings up time and space:

> The most cogent and comprehensive analysis of changing images of time and space associated with globalization is Harvey's [1989]. Although not dealing with globalization per se, Harvey's thesis is that a marked acceleration in a secular trend of time-space compression in capitalist political economy is central to current cultural change. [1995: 551]

Kearney usefully calls it a thesis; more often Harvey is mentioned to establish a fact.

17 There is also the suggestion that Culture can provide an aesthetic blueprint for the economy (e.g., Harvey 1989:345).

18 Appadurai begins this comparison in his chapter "Patriotism and Its Futures" (1996: 168–172). However, he is interested in convergences between multicultural and postnational commitments. His goal is to mobilize a forward-looking form of postnationalism, not to assess the contrasts among groups with varied histories of dependence on and opposition to nation-states.

19 While Kearney appears to draw on a theory of capitalist stages in his review article (1995), in his book (1996), he refutes the centrality of capitalist accumulation strategies as producing historical stages. Yet his arguments are completely dependent on the eras he posits, which neatly join scholarly theory and world history. Because he rejects forms of

economic, cultural, and historical logic that might generate these all-encompassing eras, I am not sure how they might appear in such a world-hegemonic form.

20   Some globalist anthropologists conflate the excitement of new postlocal approaches in anthropology and that of new developments in the world. But, thus, they weaken the case for each. Global interconnections are not just a new phenomenon, although they certainly have important new features and permutations. If older anthropological frameworks were unable to handle interconnection and mobility, this is a problem with the frameworks and a reason for new ones but not the mirror of an evolutionary change in the world.

21   Environmental studies has generated its own local globalism. Unlike the globalisms I have been describing, it is not focused on the distinctive features of a future-making epoch. Instead, the most commonly promoted environmental globalism endorses a technical and moral "global" unit. The goal of this environmental globalism is to show the compatibility of all scales into the "global" across all time. (There has been some interest in the kinds of globalisms I have been describing here among environmental scholars, especially social scientists. But to trace the encounter between "globalization" and the technical-moral "global environment" is beyond the scope of this essay.) That "global" domain into which all other scales can be collapsed, across all time, is the domain of agency for global environmental science and activism. Social scientists and historians have been rather disruptive of this global domain, although not always self-consciously, when their descriptions establish the incompatibility of various socially defined spatial scales and historical periods, as nature is made and remade in diverse forms that evade simple conflations. The critical literature on environmental modernization, which I tap here, contributes a sense of the historical and spatial rupture of projects of making nature's modernity. Through this distinctive antiglobalism, it can perhaps offer possibilities for nonglobalist global analyses in a different scholarly conversation, in which we might begin to get around blinding endorsements of futurism, conflation, and circulation.

22   Worster's overriding theoretical interest in framing this book is the relationship of irrigation and state power. My discussion here turns instead to his fascinating account of irrigation history.

23   The power and dilemmas of arguing for diversity are illustrated in Albert Paolini's (1995) insightful review of the intersections between postcolonial literary studies and globalization in sociology. Paolini argues provocatively that the overhomogenization of the Third World in postcolonial studies has led to the ease with which globalist sociologists formulate unitary frameworks of modernist progress. But he cannot give up on these frameworks even as he argues against them – despite the fact that they turn Africa into a "nonplace." His alternative involves recognition of agency and ambiguity in African cultural formation. This seems right, but to avoid separate, segregated arguments for every neglected nonplace, we could demand, instead of worldwide modernist globalism, an examination of when, where, and how such frameworks hold sway.

24   In Tsing 2000, I explore one case of the specificity of international finance in relation to other "scale-making" claims.

REFERENCES

Abraham, Itty, and Ronald Kassimir
    1997   Internationalization of the Social Sciences and Humanities. *Items* 51(2–3): 23–30.

Anderson, Warwick
  2003   The Natures of Culture: Environment and Race in the Colonial Tropics. In *Nature in the Global South: Imagination and Distress in Southern Environmental Projects*. Paul Greenough and Anna Tsing, eds. Pp. 29–46. Durham: Duke University Press.
Appadurai, Arjun
  1986   Introduction: Commodities and the Politics of Value. In *The Social Life of Things*. Arjun Appadurai, ed. Pp. 3–63. Cambridge: Cambridge University Press.
  1996   *Modernity at Large: Cultural Dimensions of Globalization*. Minneapolis: University of Minnesota.
Appiah, Kwame Anthony, and Henry Louis Gates, eds.
  1997   *The Dictionary of Global Culture*. New York: Knopf.
Baudrillard, Jean
  1975   *The Mirror of Production*. Mark Poster, trans. St. Louis: Telos Press.
Brosius, Peter
  1999   Green Dots, Pink Hearts: Displacing Politics from the Malaysian Rain Forest. *American Anthropologist* 101(1): 36–57.
  2003   The Forest and the Nation: Negotiating Citizenship in Sarawak, East Malaysia. In *Cultural Citizenship in Southeast Asia: Nation and Belonging in the Hinterlands*. Renato Rosaldo, ed. Pp. 76–133. Berkeley: University of California Press.
Cerny, Philip
  1993   The Deregulation and Re-Regulation of Financial Markets in a More Open World. In *Finance and World Politics*. Philip Cerny, ed. Pp. 51–85. Hants, UK: Edward Elgar.
Chomsky, Noam
  1998   Free Trade and Free Market: Pretense and Practice. In *The Cultures of Globalization*. Frederic Jameson and Misao Miyoshi, eds. Pp. 356–370. Durham: Duke University Press.
Clifford, James
  1997   *Routes: Travel and Translation in the Late Twentieth Century*. Cambridge, MA: Harvard University Press.
Dauvergne, Peter
  1997   *Shadows in the Forest: Japan and the Politics of Timber in Southeast Asia*. Cambridge, MA: MIT Press.
Ebron, Paulla
  1998   Regional Differences in African American Culture. *American Anthropologist* 100(1): 94–106.
  1999   Tourists as Pilgrims. *American Ethnologist* 26(4): 910–932.
Escobar, Arturo
  1995   *Encountering Development: The Making and Unmaking of the Third World*. Princeton: Princeton University Press.
Ferguson, James
  1990   *The Anti-Politics Machine: "Development," Depoliticization, and Bureaucratic Power in Lesotho*. Cambridge: Cambridge University Press.
Fujimura, Joan
  1988   The Molecular Biological Bandwagon in Cancer Research: Where Social Worlds Meet. *Social Problems* 35(3): 261–284.
Garb, Yaakov
  1990   Perspective or Escape? Ecofeminist Musings on Contemporary Earth Imagery. In *Reweaving the World: The Emergence of Ecofeminism*. Irene Diamond and Gloria Orenstein, eds. Pp. 264–308. San Francisco: Sierra Club Books.

Gibson-Graham, J. K.
   1996   *The End of Capitalism (As We Knew It)*. Cambridge, MA: Blackwell.
Grove, Richard
   1995   *Green Imperialism*. Cambridge: Cambridge University Press.
Guha, Ramachandra
   1989   *The Unquiet Woods*. Berkeley: University of California Press.
Gupta, Akhil, and James Ferguson
   1992   Beyond "Culture": Space, Identity, and the Politics of Difference. *Cultural Anthropology* 7(1): 6–23.
Haas, Peter
   1990   *Saving the Mediterranean: The Politics of International Environmental Cooperation*. New York: Columbia University Press.
   1992   Introduction: Epistemic Communities and International Policy Coordination. *International Organization* 46(1): 1–35.
Hannerz, Ulf
   1989   Notes on the Global Ecumene. *Public Culture* 1(2): 66–75.
   1996   *Transnational Connections*. New York: Routledge.
Harvey, David
   1989   *The Condition of Postmodernity*. Cambridge, MA: Blackwell.
Hecht, Suzannah, and Alexander Cockburn
   1989   *The Fate of the Forest: Developers, Destroyers, and Defenders of the Amazon*. New York: Verso.
Helleiner, Eric
   1993   When Finance Was the Servant: International Capital Movements in the Bretton Woods Order. In *Finance and World Politics*. Philip Cerny, ed. Pp. 20–48. Hants, UK: Edward Elgar.
Jameson, Frederic
   1998a   Notes on Globalization as a Philosophical Issue. In *The Cultures of Globalization*. Frederic Jameson and Misao Miyoshi, eds. Pp. 54–77. Durham: Duke University Press.
   1998b   Preface. In *The Cultures of Globalization*. Frederic Jameson and Misao Miyoshi, eds. Pp. xi–xvii. Durham: Duke University Press.
Jameson, Frederic, and Misao Miyoshi, eds.
   1998   *The Cultures of Globalization*. Durham: Duke University Press.
Kearney, Michael
   1995   The Local and the Global: The Anthropology of Globalization and Transnationalism. *Annual Review of Anthropology* 24: 547–565.
   1996   *Reconceptualizing the Peasantry: Anthropology in Global Perspective*. Boulder: Westview Press.
Keck, Margaret
   1995   Social Equity and Environmental Politics in Brazil: Lessons from the Rubber Tappers of Acre. *Comparative Politics* 27(4): 409–425.
Keck, Margaret, and Kathryn Sikkink
   1998   *Activists beyond Borders*. Ithaca, NY: Cornell University Press.
Lechner, Frank, and John Boli, eds.
   2000   *The Globalization Reader*. Oxford: Blackwell.
Lowe, Lisa, and David Lloyd, eds.
   1997   *The Politics of Culture in the Shadow of Capital*. Durham: Duke University Press.
Marcus, George
   1992   Introduction. In *Rereading Cultural Anthropology*. George Marcus, ed. Pp. vii–xiv. Durham: Duke University Press.

1995 Ethnography in/of the World System: The Emergence of Multi-Sited Ethnography. *Annual Review of Anthropology* 24: 95–117.

Mintz, Sidney
1998 The Localization of Anthropological Practice: From Area Studies to Transnationalism. *Critique of Anthropology* 18(2): 117–133.

Miyoshi, Misao
1996 A Borderless World? From Colonialism to Transnationalism and the Decline of the Nation-State. In *Global/Local: Cultural Production and the Transnational Imaginary*. Rob Wilson and Wimal Dissanayake, eds. Pp. 78–106. Durham: Duke University Press.

Olds, Kris, Peter Dicken, Philip Kelly, Lily Kong, and Henry Wai-chung Yeung, eds.
1999 *Globalisation and the Asia Pacific*. London: Routledge.

Ong, Aihwa
1997 Chinese Modernities: Narratives of Nation and of Capitalism. In *The Cultural Politics of Modern Chinese Transnationalism*. Aihwa Ong and Donald Nonini, eds. Pp. 171–202. New York: Routledge.
1999 *Flexible Citizenship: The Cultural Logics of Transnationality*. Durham: Duke University Press.

Paolini, Albert
1995 The Place of Africa in Discourses about the Postcolonial, the Global, and the Modern. *New Formations* 31 (summer): 83–106.

Peters, Pauline
1994 *Dividing the Commons: Politics, Policy, and Culture in Botswana*. Charlottesville: University Press of Virginia.

Pigg, Stacey
1992 Constructing Social Categories through Place: Social Representations and Development in Nepal. *Comparative Studies in Society and History* 34(3): 491–513.

Pramoedya Ananta Toer
1996 *Child of All Nations*. Max Lane, trans. New York: Penguin.

Pred, Allan, and Michael Watts
1992 *Reworking Modernity: Capitalism and Symbolic Discontent*. New Brunswick, NJ: Rutgers University Press.

Rajan, Ravi
1994 Imperial Environmentalism. Ph.D. dissertation, University of Oxford.

Riles, Annelise
1998a Infinity within Brackets. *American Ethnologist* 25(3): 1–21.
1998b The Network Inside Out: Designs for a Global Reality. Paper presented at the Department of Anthropology, University of California at Santa Cruz.

Rouse, Roger
1997 "There Will Be No More There": Globalization, Privatization, and the Family Form in the U.S. Corporate Imaginary. Unpublished MS, Department of Anthropology, University of California at Davis.

Sassen, Saskia
1998 *Globalization and Its Discontents*. New York: The New Press.

Schiller, Nina Glick, Linda Basch, and Cristina Blanc-Szanton, eds.
1992 *Towards a Transnational Perspective on Migration: Race, Class, Ethnicity, and Nationalism Reconsidered*. New York: New York Academy of Sciences.

Schmink, Marianne, and Charles Wood
1992 *Contested Frontiers in Amazonia*. New York: Columbia University Press.

Sivaramakrishnan, K.

   1996   Forest Politics and Governance in Bengal, 1794–1994. Ph.D. dissertation, Yale
      University.

Taylor, Peter, and Frederick Buttel

   1992   How Do We Know We Have Global Environmental Problems? Science and the
      Globalization of Environmental Discourse. *Geoforum* 23(3): 405–416.

Tsing, Anna

   1999a   Becoming a Tribal Elder, and Other Green Development Fantasies. In *Transform-
      ing the Indonesian Uplands*. Tania Li, ed. Pp. 159–202. London: Harwood Academic
      Press.

   1999b   Finding Our Differences Is the Beginning Not the End of Our Work. In *Culturally
      Conflicting Views of Nature*. Working Paper Series, Discussion Paper, 3. Kent Redford,
      ed. Gainesville, FL: Conservation Development Forum.

   1999c   *Notes on Culture and Natural Resource Management*. Berkeley Workshop on
      Environmental Politics, Working Paper WP 99-4, Institute of International Studies,
      University of California at Berkeley.

   2000   Inside the Economy of Appearances. *Public Culture* 12(1): 115–144.

Turner, Terrence

   1999   Indigenous Rights, Indigenous Cultures, and Environmental Conservation: Conver-
      gence or Divergence? The Case of the Brazilian Kayapo. In *Earth, Air, Fire, Water*. Jill
      Conway, Kenneth Kenniston, and Leo Marx, eds. Pp. 145–169. Amherst: University of
      Massachusetts Press.

Volkman, Toby

   1998   *Crossing Borders: The Case for Area Studies*. Ford Foundation Report (winter):
      28–29.

Wilson, Rob, and Wimal Dissanayake, eds.

   1996a   *Global/Local: Cultural Production and the Transnational Imaginary*. Durham:
      Duke University Press.

   1996b   Introduction: Tracking the Global/Local. In *Global/Local: Cultural Production
      and the Transnational Imaginary*. Rob Wilson and Wimal Dissanayake, eds. Pp. 1–18.
      Durham: Duke University Press.

Worster, Donald

   1985   *Rivers of Empire*. New York: Oxford University Press.

Part I

Itinerant Capital

Part I of our reader deals with the mobility of capital, concentrating on its articulations with local cultural formations. Green's essay, for example, illustrates how the search to reduce the costs of production has led corporations to shift labor-intensive industrial production and service work from the United States, Japan, and Western Europe to highly dispersed low-wage sites around the globe. In particular, it focuses on how Mayan youth in Guatemala have negotiated their incorporation into foreign-owned *maquila* factories. Klima's chapter concentrates on the emotional predicaments of financial globalization. Since the crash of the Thai baht in 1997, Thais have dealt with international financial integration and uncertainly through Buddhist donation ceremonies intended to shore up the national currency reserves, as well as through mass rites staged to aid the sprit of the nation's leader. Such rituals of national sentiment and value, Klima argues, embody the power, tensions, and unstable points of opportunity for liberation and domination that are inherent in the phenomena of globalization. And Ho's contribution highlights the uneven spatial distribution of capital – how globalization is a matter of selectively dense interconnections and not the thorough interlinking of the world. More specifically, it shows that while Wall Street investment banks might have a presence in numerous places around the world, they actually focus their material infrastructure, people, and energies in just a few of them: namely, global cities such as New York, London, and Tokyo.

SUGGESTIONS FOR FURTHER READING

Brodkin, Karen
  2000 Global Capitalism: What's Race Got to Do with It? *American Ethnologist* 27(2): 237–56.

Gibson-Graham, J. K.

   1996/97   Querying Globalization. *Rethinking Marxism* 9(1): 1–27.

Harper, Krista

   2005   "Wild Capitalism" and "Ecocolonialism": A Tale of Two Rivers. *American Anthropologist* 107(2): 221–33.

Hernandez, Ester and Susan Bibler Coutin

   2006   Remitting Subjects: Migrants, Money, and States. *Economy and Society* 35(2): 185–208.

Maurer, Bill

   2001   Islands in the Net: Rewiring Technological and Financial Circuits in the "Offshore" Caribbean. *Comparative Studies in Society and History* 43(3): 467–501.

Mills, Mary Beth

   2005   Engendering Discourses of Displacement: Contesting Mobility and Marginality in Rural Thailand. *Ethnography* 6(3): 385–419.

Mirchandani, Kiran

   2004   Practices of Global Capital: Gaps, Cracks, and Ironies in Transnational Call Centers in India. *Global Networks* 4(4): 355–73.

Miyazaki, Hirokazu

   2006   Economy of Dreams: Hope in Global Capitalism and Its Critiques. *Cultural Anthropology* 21(2): 147–72.

Ong, Aihwa

   2004   The Chinese Axis: Zoning Technologies and Variegated Sovereignty. *Journal of East Asian Studies* 4(1): 69–96.

Povinelli, Elizabeth A.

   2000   Consuming *Geist*: Popontology and the Spirit of Capital in Indigenous Australia. *Public Culture* 12(2): 501–28.

Tsing, Anna

   1999   Inside the Economy of Appearances. *Public Culture* 12(1): 115–44.

Yang, Mayfair Mei-hui

   2000   Putting Global Capitalism in Its Place: Economic Hybridity, Bataille, and Ritual Expenditure. *Current Anthropology* 41(4): 477–509.

4

Notes on Mayan Youth and Rural Industrialization in Guatemala

Linda Green

In this article I explore what might be called 'configurations of production, power and culture' (Watts, 1992) through an explication of the experiences of some Mayan youths as they are increasingly drawn into circuits of the world economy as wage workers in rural *maquilas* – the now infamous export apparel assembly factories. I explore how fundamental restructuring of the world economy and the new international division of labor in the last quarter of the 20th century (Harvey, 1989; Sassen, 1982) has directly impacted some households in rural Guatemala. Initially, export processing zones were located within the confines of the capital city, but by the late 1980s rural industrialization began in the mostly agricultural Departments of Sacatepequez and Chimaltenango with the opening of *maquila* factories, dozens of which now line the *zona libre* (free-trade zone) of the Pan-American Highway. These factories, employing thousands of workers, rely mostly on young Mayan women for their labor force (L. Green, 1998; Salazar y Chile, 1997).

Global capitalism has also penetrated rural subsistence activities on *milpas* (small plots of land where Mayas have traditionally grown corn and beans) as the United States Agency for International Development (USAID) has actively promoted contract farming of non-traditional export crops (AVANCSO, 1994a, 1994b; Peterson, 1992; Rosset, 1991). These new global agricultural practices shift the brunt of risk and failure to peasants (Rosset, 1991; Watts, 1992), who have a diminished ability to procure a livelihood with dignity. Moreover, the social dislocations – caused by

From *Critique of Anthropology* 23(1): 51–73. Copyright © 2003, SAGE Publications.

over 25 years of a brutal internal war that, in its final decade, targeted Mayan civilians, and the fact of ongoing militarization – have been aggravated by neo-liberal economic reforms dictated by multinational lending institutions. Impoverished Mayas who make up the majority of Guatemala's population feel most intensely the impact of drastic reductions in social service expenditures and the lifting of price controls on basic foods; they also experience increasing unemployment and scant work opportunities in low-paid jobs.[1]

In what follows I examine in particular how some Mayan youth, as full-time factory wage workers, and their families experience and give meaning to these new work relations. How are these changes in the organization of work and production, what Gavin Smith (1989, 1999) has called 'livelihood', reshaping social relations among family members? Another concern is how changing relations and conditions in the family, the community and the factory may be re-working Mayan youth's relation to culture and identity that can in recent history be tied to subsistence practices and a sense of collective community membership (see Dombrowski, 2001). Moreover, how have economic changes and the dual legacies of political repression and racism affected not only the meanings Mayan adolescents attach to their social world, but their sense of being able to have an impact on the world in which they live (G. Smith, 1999)? As such, I draw on a larger historical framework to shed light on how *maquila* factories in rural Guatemala may operate as new sites of exploitation by reinforcing and intensifying existing inequalities and intergenerational tensions, and manufacturing powerlessness (see C. Green, 2001) among rural Mayan adolescents, while simultaneously seducing them with modernity's desires.

I begin with a story:

> Martina is a 15-year-old Maya-Kaqchikel, who began working in a *maquila* factory in 1999. The factory is located one and a half hours from the municipal town center, which has an overall population of about 25,000 people, including outlying settlements, in the Department of Chimaltenango. Martina lives at home with her parents and younger siblings. She commutes each day on a company-owned bus to her job in the factory. At first, Martina's parents and in particular her father, Pedro, were against her working in the *maquila*. In the end Martina's father, however, acceded to her wishes and gave his permission for her to join her brother, cousins and many other adolescent residents of the town as a wage worker.

> About five months after Martina began her job in the *maquila* she returned home from work one evening around 7 p.m. and, as usual, her mother served her dinner, this time a tamale, a corn-based food wrapped and steamed in corn husks. Martina told her mother that the tamale looked to her like vomit and she refused to eat. Furthermore, she wanted to know why couldn't her mother serve hot dogs at home. When Pedro heard about Martina's remarks to her mother he beat her. Martina's mother worried for days after that Martina would not return home again because of the beating. About a week later Martina did return home to resume her routine as a factory daughter.

At one level this story could be read as simply one more instance of adolescent insolence and not of great import. Yet, this seemingly innocuous incident typifies several related key arenas that I want to explore within this article – that is, how new economic and sociopolitical dislocations – in this case factory labor by Mayan daughters – re-work in complex ways notions of gender, power, labor, modernity and culture/family for Mayan adolescents. Many of these young Mayan women (and men) are caught between two worlds – one, a 'cultural' world, only partially intact, wholly diminished, with scant resources for creating a future – the other, "modern and globalized" from which they are simultaneously excluded, exploited and seduced. Elsewhere, Mary Beth Mills (1999) has demonstrated some of the challenges faced by rural women who migrate to factory work in the metropolis of Bangkok, and in particular how globalized technologies of mass communication have produced enormous contradictions as these young women try to make sense of themselves and their surroundings.

Theoretical Concerns

There is now a substantial literature on globalization and the new international division of labor that provides important critiques on how increasing women's employment outside the domestic unit in many parts of the Third World affects households, families, gender relations, and social relations of production and reproduction (Dwyer and Bruce, 1988; Nash and Fernandez-Kelly, 1983). These studies have addressed the work/family nexus to examine how household-level factors such as fertility demands, gender role socialization and patriarchal controls impact women's relations to the labor market (Sticheter and Parapart, 1988, 1990). Recent works that have focused on export-oriented industrialization where women's labor predominates, demonstrate that, even when women are employed outside the home, their gains have been varied, but limited, in terms of economic, political or gendered power at the workplace and within the family structure (Benería and Roldan, 1987; Fernandez-Kelly, 1983; Safa, 1995; Tiano, 1986). These studies are an important corrective to a discourse offered by mainstream economists who argue that women are the winners in globalization, conflating an increase in women's waged employment with their liberation (Wichterich, 2000).

Poverty not liberation is what has obliged many women to seek employment outside the household. As subsistence production around the globe is increasingly futile for economic livelihood, more 'post-peasants', as Michael Kearney (1996) has called them, are forced to sell their labor within the circuits of global capitalism. Yet, since the 1960s, with decline in number of agricultural workers in many Third World countries, and the growth of industrial and service sectors, there has been a steady decrease in venues for male employment. Relocation of high labor-intensity industries, such as textiles and clothing, to southern countries has increased the demand for women's and not men's labor. In these low-skill factories young daughters and childless women are the preferred workforce, not only because of their 'natural' dexterity in performing the tasks at hand, but because they do not threaten to cost employers more than men (Wichterich, 2000).[2] Although international development discourse has it that women, until recently, have been left out of national and international development strategies (cf. Kabeer, 1994), in fact they have been the indirect recipients of capitalist development all along, as market processes have steadily undermined the value of their domestic production. What is new now are the vast numbers of women, single and married, who are directly subordinated and exploited through their increasing participation in the wage labor force.

This article builds on the insights of research on factory daughters in export production that have explored the relationship between capitalist exploitation, changes in gendered and family relations, and identity (Mills, 1999; Wolf, 1992). In this article I explore how young Mayan women's experiences with factory work affect their notions of identity, culture and agency, simultaneously providing new opportunities for some but within very delimited social spaces.

Understanding power through a notion of hegemony (Gramsci, 1971; Hall, 1994; Williams, 1977), which explores the interplay between the civilizing processes of the state and the discourse and practices of collective membership under specific historical circumstances, gives insights into the not always obvious paradoxes, contradictions and tensions in human affairs (Roseberry, 1994; Sider and Smith, 1997; G. Smith, 1999). And while the violence of racism and exploitation, let alone that of an attempted genocide, do not determine people's behavior, they do condition the range of options open to them.

Recent work on legacies of violence, both structural and political, have taken note of the ways in which violence in both the public and private spheres has re-worked the identities of men, women and children (Das et al., 2000; Kleinman et al., 1997). Fear, silence and impunity are the lived experiences that have circumscribed the lives of many in violent contexts, the social locus in which their gendered subjectivities are produced. Relations between the sexes and intergenerational connections – the glue of everyday life – are fundamentally weakened by structural violence, and profoundly distorted when communities, families and kinship structures are targeted by state violence. Loss of trust in one's known world and unrelenting engagement with violence in everyday life from which one is not able to extricate oneself influence patterns of sociality.

A growing body of literature on the effects of intergenerational trauma has found that roles, values and behavior adopted by subsequent generations, that are sources of vulnerability as well as resilience and strength through the generations, have a lot to do with family communication patterns, the role of silence as well as family structures and community cohesion (see Danielli, 1998). The lingering and expressive effects of trauma can last well into subsequent generations. Work on social problems among Native Americans in the United States has begun to conceptualize a historical legacy of trauma as 'soul wound' that is collective, cumulative and historical, and which encompasses the effects of racism, oppression and genocide (Duran et al., 1998).

Three Waves of Modernization and the Production of Inequalities

Land and labor

Gross inequalities between Mayan Indians and non-Indian elites, and the exploitation of indigenous labor, are facets of a globalization process that could be traced back to the colonial period in Guatemala. Most historians of the modern period in

Guatemala (Cambranes, 1985; Grandin, 2000; McCreery, 1994), however, agree that the end of the 19th century was an epochal turning point in the lives of Mayan indigenous people, the Guatemalan state and *ladino* elite in terms of social, political and economic organization. As such I explore three waves of modernization (cf. Phillips, 1998) over the course of the 20th century, to situate the changing experiences of work and production, cultural practices and gendered relations within a larger historical framework of labor relations, land tenancy and structural and political violence. I do so to explicate what is new and not so new in the Guatemalan case at the beginning of the 21st century in the continuing attempt by the state and global and national elites to create an eternal underclass of subservient people as a docile, cheap labor force.

By the 1890s the Guatemalan economy was increasingly directed toward large-scale coffee production for export, thus ushering in the first wave of modernization, with particular local variants on a modern Liberal nation-state and Western capitalism. Through the use of coercive strategies – debt contracts, labor drafts and vagrancy laws – the Guatemalan elite, with the active support of the Liberal state, transformed Mayan Indians into a part-time migratory workforce. While highland Maya spent most of the year working their small subsistence farms, where, however meagerly, they were able to provide for their own livelihood, at harvest time they were pressed into service on the large plantations.

The backbone of this agro-export economy was the *latifundia/minifundia* land tenancy system based on a logic of private property. Land titling, state-mandated in the late 19th century, over the next quarter century effectively transferred most community-held lands in the Guatemalan highlands to individual property, creating differentiation, rivalries and internal divisions within and between communities. As land became privatized and commodified throughout the 20th century, an asynchronous and erratic process, the slow, steady intensification of market relations critically reshaped community social relations, altering substantively the connective networks among people in communities. For example, the political, economic and cultural logic of social institutions, such as the *cofradia* and traditional marriage practices, sites of social and cultural reproduction, were undermined. Although far from egalitarian in either class or gendered terms, the social relations that formed the bases of these institutions helped mediate between individual and community, cooperation and opportunism Moreover, the social ties created with others helped to mitigate and negotiate the more lethal effects of everyday social antagonisms and conflicts (Green, 1999). While, increasingly, commodification of the rural Mayan economy did lead to new financial opportunities for some, particularly a Mayan elite, it also contributed to an escalation of economic differentiation among individuals in communities. Elite Mayan men in positions of local power often had to choose between their allegiance and responsibility to fellow community members, their own aspirations, and acting as agents of a racist and increasingly repressive state.

The second wave of modernization began roughly in the late 1930s and early 1940s and can be best characterized as one in which indigenous peasants were more fully integrated into a capitalist system. Mayan Indians were freed from the last vestiges of coerced labor and free at last to sell their labor power. Rural households tried to avoid full dependency on cash by clinging tenaciously to their semi-subsistence strategies. Many, however, were compelled by the exigencies of survival to make their way south perennially to the large coffee plantations in order to earn much-needed cash. As a result of population growth during the 20th century, but no appreciable changes in land tenancy among highland peasants, families were having an increasingly difficult time meeting their subsistence needs.

Between 1944 and 1954, however, modernization took a distinct and anomalous turn in the Guatemalan context. Two successive democratically elected governments initiated laws that, for the first time in Guatemalan history, attempted to enfranchise the indigenous majority.[3] Labor codes, peasant leagues, political parties, suffrage and the controversial agrarian reform laws established bases for Mayan male political participation (see Handy, 1994). However, a 1954 CIA-sponsored coup precipitated a return to and intensification of exploitation and repression against, among others, Mayan Indians who supported social change. One of the first steps of the new regime was to return expropriated and redistributed lands to their former owners. Thus, by the early 1970s, Guatemala had one of the most inequitable land distributions in all of Latin America, as rural Mayas survived on 'plots of land the size of graves' (Galeano, 1967: 5). Nor has land distribution been altered at all over the course of the subsequent quarter century.[4] Repression and surveillance in rural communities became (and remain) strategies of state political rule as a succession of military-controlled dictatorships and elected 'democracies' have continued to hold power into the 21st century (cf. Schirmer, 1998).

Another key turning point in this epic was the introduction of low-cost chemical fertilizers into highland *milpa* agriculture in the 1960s as part of the Green Revolution and in lieu of agrarian reform. The chemical fertilizers turned *milpa* lands into increasingly productive units, easing land tenancy pressures. The high yields, too, allowed some peasant farmers to invest their surplus profits into land and in small-scale commerce (C. Smith, 1990), altering their economic positions within their communities. Yet even as Mayan men's positions in local economic structures were enhanced, Mayan *campesinos'* (peasants') relationship to their lands was also fundamentally transformed. For the first time, cash became a necessary component of subsistence production. For decades cash had been necessary in order to sustain consumption levels throughout the year, as significant land concentration compelled most Mayan families in the *altiplano* (highlands) to buy at least some of their year's supply of food with the cash they earned through wage labor. Now, for the first time, cash became a necessity for subsistence production as rural farmers needed money in hand to buy fertilizers for the *milpa*, rather than the customary organic fertilizer that was commonplace until that time. Initially, it mattered little. Over the subsequent decades, as with the failure of the Green Revolution elsewhere, Guatemalan *milpa* farmers became dependent on chemical fertilizers and pesticides that were very expensive and now mostly ineffectual. Thus, by the mid-1970s, over a half-million peasants were making the annual trek from the *altiplano* to the coastal coffee, cotton and sugar plantation, seeking work, and where labor conditions were increasingly deplorable.

With the decline in the world market commodity prices for Guatemala's leading export crops in the early 1980s, coupled with the massive dislocation of the highland population during the political violence of the late 1970s and early 1980s, the need for an extensive migratory workforce fell dramatically. Many highland villagers fled the escalating counter-insurgency war, to the plantation region of the south coast, to Mexico or Guatemala City; or they hid in the mountains near their villages, resulting in the displacement of over 1 million people during the 1980s (cf. Carmack, 1988). In the Department of Chimaltenango, for example, in some communities there were no corn harvests at all between 1981 and 1983 because of population displacements (Krueger and Enge, 1985).

During this same period, USAID was actively promoting non-traditional export production – particularly in the Departments of Sacate-pequez and Chimaltenango – in an attempt to alleviate rural poverty and promote economic development in the midst of growing political unrest and in lieu of substantive land reform. Several years later, USAID was providing the financial infrastructure for rural industrialization (Peterson, 1992). Yet, the inequities of land tenancy as well as demands for addressing the social and economic inequalities that characterize Guatemalan society formed the basis of much of unarmed (and armed) resistance in the highlands in the 1970s.[5] These issues remain unresolved to this day. Thus the third wave of modernization in Guatemala, with its attendant neo-liberal economic policies, needs to be situated within this context of state violence and repression against the Mayan population.

Moreover, the promised rewards of globalization have failed to manifest themselves in the lives of the majority poor; rather, their levels of poverty and immiseration are far worse than they were a quarter of a century ago. Today, an even partial subsistence livelihood on *milpa* lands is no longer a viable option, as imports of basic grains of corn and beans from the United States flood local markets and undercut domestic crops grown on *milpas*. Older men and women are unemployed and unemployable, and they must make do with whatever is left of their fields and local markets. Their children and grandchildren, however, are not semi-proletarians in the classical sense, but rather short-term, temporary proletarians in a globalized economy.[6] For many Mayan families in the Department of Chimaltenango, rural factory work, cultivation of winter vegetables grown on converted *milpa* land, and international migration to the US – that draws almost exclusively on an adolescent workforce – have become some of their principal economic survival strategies.

Racism

In Guatemala, from the colonial period to the present, the state has depended on racial 'Otherness' as the ideological key to domination of Indians by non-Indians. Yet racism has manifested itself in diverse forms and practices in distinct historical epochs and geographical spaces (Cojti, 1999). In the late 19th century, class differentiation between the majority of the rural Mayan population, white elites and rural *ladinos*,[7] was represented as ethnic divisions, which were underwritten by virulent racism. And racism in the guise of ethnicity was re-worked to stress unalterable biological difference rather than previously held notions of cultural and social distinction (Casaus Arzu, 1998). The Guatemalan state constituted the parameters of its citizenship in which the nation-state as 'imagined community' was constructed on a Liberal ideal of *mestizaje*, or indigenous assimilation. Yet, David McCreery in his masterful account, *Rural Guatemala, 1760–1940* (1994) explicates two competing Liberal strategies of Guatemalan development at the advent of coffee capitalism and liberal state power: (1) 'historical' Liberals promoted internal development of production and markets and the concomitant civilizing project of 'uplifting' of the rural masses; (2) 'radical' Liberals, with the support of coffee planters, proposed developing as rapidly and extensively as possible an agro-export economy tied to the expanding world system that necessitated the use of cheap land and labor. The radical approach held sway with its attendant ideological and material *exclusion* of the indigenous majority from the fruits of 'development', rather than *assimilation*, justified in classic social Darwinist terms – the Indian as the modern primitive. Development in this sense was a class project (McCreery, 1994).

As a result, physical features such as skin, hair color and stature were emphasized, alongside cultural differences of clothes, language and religion, and moral characteristics of laziness, submissiveness and conformity provided 'proof' of inherent Indian inferiority (Casaus Arzu, 1998). Although an intellectual elite continued to expound rhetoric about the need to civilize the Indians through education, and law makers intermittently introduced various laws and proposals to aid their assimilation into national life, these gestures made little difference in the daily lives of most indigenous peoples. The experience for rural Mayas was one of profound exploitation through coerced labor for the plantations, and increased repression and surveillance in their communities. New technologies of control, such as the telegraph and bureaucratic reorganization through the expansion of rural militias, served to uphold *ladino* and state authority (McCreery, 1994).

Over the course of the 20th century the rhetoric of assimilation has continued under various regimes, yet the need for cheap Indian labor has also reinscribed a notion of the Maya as backward and lazy. This belief has supported an ideology that the only language that Indians understand is brute force, thus violence is necessary to make Indians work. Jim Handy, in *Revolution in the Countryside* (1994), details some of the same arguments taking place during the 1944 constitutional assembly. Those who opposed the abolition of vagrancy laws[8] and the granting of voting rights to illiterates argued that Indians were unwilling to work voluntarily and that, with suffrage, Indians would easily and unwittingly be manipulated politically. And, in the 1990s, Marta Elena Casaus Arzu (1998), in her profoundly important study with elite Guatemalan families, found that they continued to reassert the same stereotypes and prejudices against Mayan Indians: Mayas were characterized most often in interviews as submissive, conformists, dark-skinned, short, traditional and introverted.

Gender

Transformations were taking place at the household level too. In rural Mayan households, subsistence activities had long been organized around a complementary division of labor between men and women creating a mutual dependency between them. Since the work of both was crucial to survival, the relationship between men and women was characterized by a degree of respect and cooperation, albeit organized along a gendered hierarchy of power relations. As the modern market economy and new technologies increasingly came to dominate the economy locally, the importance of the subsistence sphere was substantially weakened and the economic partnerships between men and women were destabilized (Bossen, 1984). By mid-century new opportunities created by Western development projects were consistently geared toward men, producing what Tracy Ehlers (1996: 5) has described as the 'individualization of income and concentration of other opportunities in men's hands, with the effect of devaluing and marginalizing women's contributions', a redivision of labor that negatively affected rural women's well-being.

As the last vestiges of *cofradia* power and authority waned, the locus of male power and authority was reconcentrated for many solely in the household. There, elder men with a sufficient land base had the ability to procure labor and allegiance from sons and sons-in-law. When that was no longer a viable option, as shrinking family plots were parceled out to subsequent generations, male heads of households were increasingly losing control of their 'traditional' material and symbolic power over the extended family. Men's participation in these programs served to intensify their economic independence from women, thus increasing women's social vulnerability to male violence. These contradictions arose as Mayan men were locked more tightly into subordinate positions within the market economy, as well as having lost power within their own community social structures. They simultaneously gained the upper hand over women in the household economy even as they were unable to fulfill those very responsibilities. In this nexus lies the potential for domestic violence with its double meaning – at the household level and within the confines of the nation-state.

Today, as a result of capitalist restructuring, many Mayan men are increasingly unable to fulfill their role as provider in the household, producing a situation in which the role of men as central to household survival is becoming superfluous (c.f. Gledhill, 2000).

Culture

The material and cultural dimensions of land are integral because, through territoriality, Mayas have laid claim to material resources and the spiritual meanings ascribed to land. Thus land embodied culture in both senses of the term: as a site in the production of subsistence and a site in the production of cultural meaning and gendered identity through association with the *antepasados* (those who came before them) (Dombrowski, 2001; Green, 1999). The increasing loss of ancestral lands – in the context of ancestor-centered religious praxis – is just one of the complex ways in which local meanings fractured and were reshaped. Yet, in spite of the multiple pressures placed on communities in the late 19th and early 20th centuries, many Mayan men were able, in a limited way, to reshape the hierarchical political and religious structures of the *cofradias* so that corporate land usage continued to be respected, although diminished, along with a sense of mutual aid that reinforced social bonds among the living, and between the living and the dead, alongside and in contradiction to increasing micro-economic differentiation.

Corn has been a particularly important site of material practices but also cultural meaning and Mayan agency. Mayan children have received their 'cultural' education in part through growing, preparing and eating corn. Children learn about the importance of corn through their experiences of everyday life. Young girls copy their mothers as they use their hands to shape the corn dough into tortillas or one of the many other corn-based foods. Young boys learn the fundamentals of subsistence agricultural production in the *milpa*. As they work together, grandfathers, fathers, uncles, cousins and older brothers teach young boys the prayers to the ancestors and spirits that are made at the time of planting. Through social relations of domestic production and consumption, corn weaves a thread that connects Mayan people with their past through their ancestors and sacred spirits, and with their future through their children. As material production practices centered around the cultivation of corn are increasingly moribund, many youths no longer care to work the *milpa* lands of their fathers. Young men, like Martina's 20-year-old brother, Tomás, who has worked in *maquila* factories as a supervisor for over four years, prefer modern factory labor to working the corn fields of their ancestors.

Violence

Any understanding of the social space in which Mayan youths, their families and communities are struggling to survive must be situated in the context of the development and the subsequent utter destruction of the collective political engagement of Mayan people in the western highlands that began in the mid-1970s and abruptly halted when the state waged a brutal counter-insurgency war against them. The role of violence and fear are crucial to an explication of the loss of a sense of social collectivity in many highland communities at the end of the 20th and beginning of the 21st centuries.

A number of political currents shaped Mayan activism that challenged local and regional domination in the final decades of the 20th century. The historian Jim Handy (1994) suggests that one of the lasting legacies of the 1944–54 democratic opening was a demand by some rural indigenous peasants for social justice. By the 1970s, a vast array of groups representing the spectrum of community organizing and popular mobilization was flourishing throughout the highland communities. Most of these groups promoted local participation and leadership, presenting new possibilities for a modicum of economic relief and political empowerment to beleaguered Mayas.

By the early 1980s, the highlands of Guatemala had become infamous in international human rights circles as the 'land of eternal tyranny' because of the carnage wrought by the Guatemalan military. By then Guatemala was notorious not only for political murders, kidnappings and disappearances that had become almost daily occurrences since the mid-1970s in both urban and rural areas, but for its 'scorched earth campaign of rural pacification' – in indigenous villages. The counter-insurgency war left in its wake more than 200,000 civilians dead or disappeared,[9] over 600 rural villages totally razed, 150,000 refugees and over 1 million people internally displaced during the 1980s. A report by the Guatemalan Catholic Church's Office of Human Rights, *Guatemala: Nunca Más* (REHMI, 1998), confirmed publicly what had long been known privately, that the targets of the military war were not only guerrilla insurgents but the civilian Mayan population. *Nunca Más* estimated that three out of

four of those killed were Maya civilians, and over half of them belonged to community organizations such as cooperatives or religious affiliated groups, particularly the
Christian-based communities of Liberation Theology.

Yet, one striking feature in the Guatemalan case – and one that differs from recent
analyses of 'ethnic conflicts' and genocide – is that, during the counter-insurgency
war (1976–85), the majority of the foot soldiers, civil militias and military commis-
sioners responsible for the terror waged against the Mayan civilian population were
Mayan men. Thus, while the UN-sponsored Guatemalan Truth Commission called
the war in part a 'genocide against the Mayan people' – violence that was planned
and perpetrated by a *ladino* (non-Indian) minority state against the indigenous
population – many of those directly responsible for carrying out the brutal acts
were Mayas themselves.

'Indians killing Indians' was a central and very successful component of the
Guatemalan military's doctrine of counter-insurgency that not only produced victims but also created and continues to provide the structure at the local level for
what Jennifer Schirmer, in her masterful book *The Guatemalan Military Project:
A Violence Called Democracy* (1998), has called 'permanent counterinsurgency'.[10]
Many Mayan men were forced to commit monstrous acts by the military, under
penalty of their own torture and death or that of their families. Today, despite the
signing of the Peace Accords in 1996, ongoing repression and intimidation against
people working for human rights and justice continues unabated as perpetrators of
past human rights violations are able to continue to commit crimes without fear of
reprisal. The Guatemalan judicial system, largely ineffective, is unable and in some
cases unwilling to assure citizens of their rights and put an end to impunity. Even in
high-profile cases where convictions have taken place, they often are overturned on
appeal or delayed for years without remedy.[11]

Locally, military commissioner posts and the civil patrol system have been theoretically disbanded yet, in some communities in the highlands, the former commis-
sioners and patrols continue to hold de facto power. Some of the groups have been
renamed 'peace and development committees' but maintain close ties with the army's
civilian affairs and intelligence officers (Popkin, 1996; Schirmer, 1998). Impunity is
crucial to the ways in which power works in rural highland communities today.

Many of the survivors of the war are no longer politically active and have become
members of conservative Catholic and Protestant evangelical congregations (Garard-
Burnett and Stoll, 1993; Green, 1999; Stoll, 1990). Their children, who are the
subjects of this article, were born in the mid-1980s, after the worst of the counter-
insurgency war. These youths know well the legacies of repressive violence locally, yet
they know little first-hand of their parents' struggles for social justice and dignity. It is
fear and silence, not justice, that circumscribes their lives.

Rural Industrialization and the Production of Powerlessness

Powerlessness – or the inability of groups to influence those critical political and
economic decisions that shape their lives – is a necessary condition of the globalization
process.... The manufacture of powerlessness is carried out for a single purpose: to

preserve the interests and hegemony of those in power.... Thus the production and reproduction – the manufacturing – of powerlessness among the youth ensures the continued subjugation of an entire group of people, denying them the possibility of becoming fully integrated into the decision-making process. (C. Green, 2000: 1, 4)

Mundane rounds of daily work are where the contradictions of rural industrialization are perhaps most obvious to the observer, and most seductive for many factory daughters. And here too is where many of the subtle changes in attitudes and meanings are taking shape. There is a newness for Mayan adolescents who work the factory lines – wages for consumption of items never imagined or within reach beforehand, leisure time and short-term freedoms with regard to their relations with young men before marriage. Yet, simultaneously, factory work reinforces the status quo in terms of exploitation of them as young women, as workers and as Indians. It reinforces their subordinate gender roles both at work and at home, and it insinuates them into the modern world, but only as the mirror image and inferior 'Other'. While the benefits of factory work expose them to the desires of and limited participation in 'modern' consumption practices, which they cannot afford, they leave their jobs after five years or so with no marketable skills useful elsewhere and no further job training. They return home ill and exhausted, unemployed and disaffected.

Martina works in one of the first and largest of these *maquilas*, the Korean-owned and run Sam Lucas, which employs several thousand workers to assemble apparel for export. All of the assembly line workers are Mayan adolescents – the majority of whom are young unmarried daughters. Although there are some adolescent men employed, like Martina's brother Tomás, they mostly occupy supervisory positions, while the managers are Korean. The factory, built from cement blocks with aluminum roofing, is the size of a football field. Inside, long wooden tables divide the workers into production lines of about 30 people. Each person in a line repeats the assigned task over and over, whether it is to sew labels on pants, fasten sleeves to a shirt or cut threads off the almost finished product. Production goals are established for each line. For example, one line may have to complete 1,500 shirts that day. If the production line reaches its goal, then the workers are promised extra pay; if not, money is deducted from their wages, which on average is US $100–150 per month or about US $4 per day for 14 to 16 hours of work.

Workers I spoke with complained of harsh conditions – poor ventilation, the intense heat generated by the ceiling lamps, leg and back pain from standing for long hours – verbal and physical harassment, and abuse by the supervisors and managers for perceived laxity in work habits, and the multiple inspections of person and belongings that happen on both entering and exiting the factory. Work discipline and control of time, not unexpectedly, are very important managerial techniques in inculcating these adolescents into capitalist labor practices (Thompson, 1967). Managers continually admonish the workers not to waste time, to finish the work on time, to arrive on time. If workers arrive late, half a day's pay is deducted and, in some instances, s/he is not permitted to enter the factory. If a worker does miss a day, US $8 is deducted from her salary, and if she is absent for two days or more she is summarily dismissed. Workers complained that they often do not receive money for overtime that they are promised. Both the workers and their families are well aware of the exploitative conditions – low wages, unhealthy work conditions, lack of legal protections and unfamiliar forms of labor discipline – under which they are laboring. Yet the necessity of procuring cash, however little, coupled with the lack of sufficient land base on which to subsist in an economy marked by high inflation, has left many families with few other options than to allow their adolescent daughters and sons to work in the *maquilas*. As the young workers themselves have noted – $4 a day is better than nothing.

There are no rural *maquila* unions since the workers are afraid to organize. Although several of the *maquilas* in Guatemala City have been successfully organized, union members have repeatedly been the focus of violent intimidation, including death threats, surveillance and dismissals. Although there have been attempts at labor organizing in rural areas as well as in Guatemala City, many of the organizers have met the same fate as the 40 trade union leaders who have been murdered or disappeared in Guatemala since the early 1990s. The Mayan youths I spoke with have participated in half-day work stoppages and slow downs, but they have done so without a structured organization of support, and thus their demands for better pay and working conditions have been ignored. With such widespread unemployment and poverty, on any given day the gates outside the factory are crowded with hundreds of unemployed youths lined up and desperate for work.

Within the wider context, rural factory labor responds not only to the material realities of agricultural underdevelopment, it also engages these influential meanings and cultural practices of Guatemalan modernity (cf. Mills, 1999). Even as these adolescents are 'subjected to intense capitalist discipline' in Aiwah Ong's words (1987: 113) in the *maquila*, these factory daughters and sons have unprecedented freedom from their families economically, socially and culturally compared to any previous generation. Young women, for example, free from the watchful eyes of their families and communities for long periods of time every day, are able to socialize with young men and women from their own community as well as workers from other communities. They have discretionary funds for consumption and they are exposed in the workplace to goods, services and ideas to which they have had little prior access.

Most young women and men I interviewed did not actually invest much of the cash from the *maquila* in the household economy. The wages were more often used for personal consumption items, or they were saving their money for a particular purpose. This is consistent with findings on factory work in other areas by adolescent women (Mills, 1999; Wolf, 1992). Adolescent women used their wages to buy their traditional clothing, the woven blouse (*huipil*) and the wrap skirt (*corte*), an outfit that can cost upwards of US $500, depending on quality. These young women said that, because of the financial constraints within the family and the rising prices of thread and textiles, it was more difficult for their fathers to provide them with their traditional dress. Through factory work, they were able to garner resources to maintain an important symbolic expression of their indigenous identity, even if they were unable to weave for themselves. For these young women it was particularly important to be dressed 'properly' (as an Indian) as they looked for a suitor. Other studies have found that some factory daughters spent money on make-up and other items not usually worn by Mayan women (Salazar and Chile, 1997).

The consumption practices of adolescent men differed in that they used their wages to buy electronic equipment. In some *maquilas* the vendors come right into the factory to sell to the workers. One father complained to me that his son left the factory at the end of the month with his pay check already spent. Popular items for purchase include cassette players, radios, televisions, hairdryers and cell phones.

But it was the ways in which factory work affects time and social relations that was the most distressing to the families and workers I interviewed. Most of the young workers feel that they have abandoned their families for the long hours of factory work. They have very little time to be at home – rising as early as 4 a.m. and often not returning home until after 9 p.m. in the evening; Sundays are the only days that they have to share time with other family members. The factory production schedule is also at odds with a Mayan sense of mutual aid and obligation to family and neighbors. The young daughters and sons are unable to participate in any community events and, in effect, their work severs the daily connections between themselves, their family and their friends. Thus they are put in the difficult situation of choosing between their individual needs and desires, and their commitments to their family and their community.

Modernity's Desires and Intergenerational Tensions

On the one hand, Martina knows full well why the family does not eat hotdogs – they are prohibitively expensive and this family depends on the *milpa* both for sustenance and for the money generated from the surplus. Also, it is likely that Martina was angry with her mother – as most adolescents are at one point or another during those most difficult years. But Martina also repudiated her mother's life – 'I am not like you.' And there are certainly objective reasons why this may be the case. Her mother, Maria Elena, 55 years old, has struggled for 35 years as a wife and mother of 12 children, rising at 4 a.m. most mornings to grind corn by hand for tortillas. Martina and her family live in a modest adobe two-room house with a dirt floor; a fire ring serves as the kitchen stove. To her credit, none of Maria Elena's children have died. Today, Maria Elena, along with her own youngest daughter who is six years old, is raising three grandchildren, as their mother was widowed and her new partner does not want the children. Martina, too, turned her back on the livelihood of her father who has supported his large family, albeit meagerly, through the arduous work of subsistence agriculture of corn and beans. Moreover, for Martina's parents, it seems that she has rejected her very roots, her culture, understood by her mother and father to be expressed through the material and symbolic practices of the production and consumption of corn.

Although Martina earns less than US 50 cents an hour in the factory, and thus remains dependent economically on her family for her own survival, they have come to depend on the cash that Martina earns to supplement their livelihood, often 'borrowing' money from her to make ends meet. This dynamic, however, has done little to shift the actual balance of power in gender relations in families, even though young daughters are able to generate more cash than their fathers and older brothers who supplement their labor in the *milpa* with irregular local wage work.

But it has affected the symbolic balance of power, as it is the wages of the young factory daughters that parents have come to depend on to survive.

Martina has more freedom than her mother and her older sisters in marriage selection. 'Traditional' gender roles and behaviors sought to restrict physical contact between young women and men by constraining the spatial mobility of daughters, keeping them more closely tied to the parental household and village community. This generation of young Mayan daughters not only have access to cash, they also experience an independence and self-sufficiency that no previous generation of rural Mayan women has shared. Today, for example, Martina's cousins, who are expecting to become engaged to marry soon, still meet their boyfriends outside the gate of the family compound as these young men will not be invited into the household until the engagement has been formalized and accepted by the father. Yet one of Martina's cousin's was able to socialize with her then boyfriend and now husband who was initially rejected as an acceptable suitor by her father. They both worked in the *maquila*. While there were certainly surreptitious meetings among Mayan youth before, what is distinctive is the ease with which such meetings can occur outside the purview of family and community, and the vast numbers of young women who are now able to meet with young men in this way.

After their *maquila* employment, however, the factory daughters return to life in their communities as young married women under the undisputed patriarchal authority of their husbands. While in factory work they transferred their patriarchal notions of obedience and authority, once the prerogatives of their fathers, to the factory managers. In this sense the *maquila* serves as a site of hegemonic reproduction where household patriarchal relations are reinscribed to the factory supervisors in the factory – that are subsequently transferred to husbands upon marriage. At the same time their fathers' authority – and that of their new husbands – has been weakened as it was previously tied to the legitimacy of being a provider, which in turn depended on access to land and labor through kin-ties. Moreover, some of these same young men – only temporarily employed, if at all and without a viable future – are participating in Mayan youth gangs before marriage in rural communities. Some of the young men I have spoken with say that they find sociality and bonds of friendship and community within these groups. They also gain access to a modicum of local power and authority – features of earlier 'traditional' *cofraida* – even while brutalizing their neighbors and kin with the same counter-insurgency tactics utilized by the army – violence, kidnapping and extortion. While some of these gangs have ties to military and paramilitary networks of guns and drugs, many do not. What these young men have learned is that the only power available to local men – since all others have been and continue to be repressed – is both the real and symbolic power of the gun.

The *maquila* experience creates a sense of freedom for the youths as it reinforces modernity's desires. Yet in order to do so, it deprecates the traditional as it celebrates the modern, as the cultural authority of the West insinuates itself below the level of conscious awareness. For young Mayan men and women in particular, the plethora of popular cultural representations has had enormous potential to influence identities and social relations. In Guatemala, a country where over half the population is indigenous, billboards, advertising in newspapers, magazines, on the radio and television, in schools and at the clinic have presented the modern world to the Maya as white and wealthy. As the political violence has left their communities in a shambles, divided and militarized, young Mayan adolescents are pulled in two directions between 'being Indian' as defined by their families and 'being modern' as defined by their increasing access to popular culture, the influx of evangelical churches and increased access to 'Western' ideas. A dramatic increase in access to information and technology in the post-war period has given youth unprecedented exposure to Western popular culture through videos, video game centers and television. Moreover, these young people encounter a plethora of images and ideas that valorize Western consumerism and individualism, and reinforce notions of the 'traditional' as backward and inferior. These competing desires further remove youth from their families and communities, even as they are simultaneously and ultimately denied access to the fruits of a wealthy capitalist lifestyle. While the Guatemalan state promotes the Maya – the traditional exotic Other – as the objects of consumption for the burgeoning tourist industry, these young factory daughters, in particular, dressed in their exquisite *traje*, are caught between the traditional and the modern. They are left with contradictory images and feelings, as they are both proud of being indigenous and at the same time longing to be different. Yet, *maquila* work does not offer these young women a secure future, a viable exit out of poverty, nor does it offer legal rights, or a little leverage in overcoming inequalities in the workplace, the household, or the nation-state. As they attempt to re-work what it means to be Indian on their own terms and in their own way, without the political engagements of previous generations, these youth inadvertently reinforce the status quo even as they are unable – with the threat of repression still looming – to effect more profound social transformations.

NOTES

1   Like South Africa and Bolivia, Guatemala has one of the highest rates of inequality in the world. Guatemala's expenditure on public health is at the very bottom of the scale – about 2 percent of GDP – and if both public and private spending are combined, Guatemala ranks only slightly ahead of Haiti. Guatemala has one the highest maternal and infant mortality rates in Latin America (International Development Bank/World Bank, 2001). Of the 9000 medical doctors in Guatemala, 80 percent are concentrated in Guatemala City. Likewise, Guatemala spends very little of its GDP (about 1.8 percent) on public education. It has the second highest rate of illiteracy (31.9 percent) and the greatest disparity between women and men in Latin America (Sieder et al., 2002).

2   See the Human Rights Watch report (2002) that documents how pregnant women are forced to quit their *maquila* jobs and reports allegations that young women factory workers are forced to take birth control pills.

3   The most bitterly contested policy of the Arbenz administration (1950–54) was Decree 154, that redistributed idle lands to rural peasants. This process was halted abruptly by the CIA-sponsored *coup d'état*. Although it is not known how many rural people were killed during and immediately after the coup, there has been some documentation that points towards a repression aimed at those involved in the processes of social change locally (Gleijeses, 1991; Grandin, 2000).

4   The majority of rural Mayas are unable to subsist even partially on the harvests from their *milpas*. With the rising costs of chemical fertilizers and pesticides it is actually cheaper to buy rather than grow one's basic foodstuffs. The problem for many poor families is that they do not have the cash-flow or the credit to buy either the fertilizers or pesticides they need, nor to buy adequate food to meet their nutritional needs. Thus, currently, well over 80 percent of the Mayan people cannot fulfill their basic daily nutritional needs. One of the gross inequities in Guatemala is the maldistribution of land, where approximately 2 percent own 80 percent of the arable lands. Most young men do not head to the coastal plantations (an earlier strategy), nor to the city (a later strategy) but to the North (the US) in hopes of procuring cash for themselves and remittances for family members who remain behind.

5   Cristobal Kay, in a recent article (2001), argues that in South and Central America nations with highly exclusionary agrarian structures reinforced by state policies can be linked to rural conflicts and violence over the past half century. Moreover, current development strategies, including neo-liberalism, continue to exclude the rural poor, mitigating any real chances for democratization.

6   Perhaps it is here that the reality and everyday experiences of a globalized economy, where the celebrated global flows of creativity and imagination (and of human beings) make possible worlds 'unimaginable' to many beforehand, holds its relevance (Appadurai, 1991) as people are increasingly displaced from their homes, families and communities with little hope of creating a future, and where they have to imagine new ways to survive with experiences often more brutal than earlier generations.

7   *Ladino* in Guatemala today refers to non-Indians and can be used generically to include everyone who is not Indian. White elites, however, distinguish themselves from both Indians and *ladinos* as being pure-blooded descendants of the Spanish. During the early colonial period, the distinction between the Spanish and the Mayas rested on consanguinity and the term *ladino* referred simply to Spanish-speaking Mayas or acculturated Mayas (Sherman, 1979). Later, *ladino* came to mean the offspring of miscegenation, usually between a Mayan mother and a Spanish father and, as Martinez Pelaez (1979) has noted, the first *mestizaje* (mixed-blood) unions were based on violence.

8   Vagrancy laws replaced debt peonage and labor drafts as the principal means of supplying part-time cheap indigenous labor to coffee plantations involved in large-scale export production. The change in laws produced a more intensified stratification among Mayas within communities, between those who did not have sufficient land resources to meet the minimum requirement for exemption from obligatory work and those who did. If a *campesino* had 6 acres of corn under cultivation and two harvests per year, he was exempt from labor service. The law required all those who planted 3 or more acres to work at least 100 days per year on *fincas*, while those with less than 3 acres were required to work 150 days per year, setting up problems between *cofradia* leaders and members.

9   Since the war began in the eastern half of Guatemala in the 1960s, over 45,000 people have disappeared, more than any other nation in Latin America.

10   Schirmer (1998: 258) describes in detail *el proyecto politico militar* – outlined in the Thesis of National Stability where the blueprint is articulated for incorporating counter-in surgency structures into the 'very heart of the civilian State'. It also details the criteria defining 'Opponents of the State' who, as a consequence, can be identified and eliminated 'at their infancy'. This project has a timeline well into the 21st century and appears to have been unaffected by the Peace Accords.

11   See Amnesty International (2002) for a discussion of the cases of Myrna Mack and Bishop Gerardi that are instructive in this regard.

REFERENCES

Amnesty International (2002) *Guatemala's Lethal Legacy: Past Impunity and Renewed Human Rights Violations*. London: Amnesty International.

Appadurai, Arjun (1996) *Modernity at Large: Cultural Dimensions of Globalization*. Minneapolis: University of Minnesota Press.

Asociación para el Avance de las Ciencias Sociales (AVANCSO) (1994a) *El significado de la maquila en Guatemala*. Ciudad de Guatemala: AVANCSO, Textos para Debate.

Asociación para el Avance de las Ciencias Sociales (AVANCSO) (1994b) *Impacto ecológico del los cultivos horticolas no-tradicionales en el altiplano de Guatemala*. Ciudad de Guatemala: AVANCSO, Textos para Debate.

Benería, Lourdes and Martha Roldan (1987) *The Crossroads of Class and Gender: Industrial Homework, Subcontracting and Household Dynamics in Mexico City*. Chicago: University of Chicago Press.

Bossen, Laurel (1984) *The Redivision of Labour: Women and Economic Development in Four Guatemalan Communities*. Albany, NY: SUNY Press.

Cambranes, Julio (1985) *Coffee and Peasants in Guatemala*. Guatemala City: University of San Carlos.

Carmack, Robert, ed. (1988) *Harvest of Violence: The Mayan Indians and the Guatemalan Crisis*. Norman: University of Oklahoma Press.

Casaus Arzu, Marta Elena (1998) *La metamorfosis del racismo en Guatemala*. Ciudad de Guatemala: Editorial Cholsamaj.

Cojti, Demetrio (1999) 'Heterofobia y racismo guatemalteco', in Clara Arenas Bianchi, Charles Hale and Gustavo Palma Murga (eds) *Racismo en Guatemala? Abriendo el debate sobre un tema tabu*. Ciudad de Gautemala: AVANCSO.

Danielli, Yael, ed. (1998) *International Handbook of Multigenerational Legacies of Trauma*. New York and London: Plenum Press.

Das, Veena, Arthur Kleinman, Mamphele Ramphele and Pamela Reynolds, eds (2000) *Violence and Subjectivity*. Berkeley: University of California Press.

Dombrowski, Kirk (2001) *Against Culture: Development, Politics and Religion in Indian Alaska*. Lincoln and London: University of Nebraska Press.

Duran, Eduardo, Bonnie Duran, Maria Yellow Horse Brave Heart and Susan Yellow Horse-Davis (1998) 'Healing the American Indian Soul Wound', in Yael Danielli (ed.) *International Handbook of Multigenerational Legacies of Trauma*, pp. 341–54. New York and London: Plenum Press.

Dwyer, Daisy and Judith Bruce, eds (1988) *A House Divided: Women and Income in the Third World*. Palo Alto, CA: Stanford University Press.

Ehlers, Tracy Bachrach (1996) 'Revisiting San Pedro Sacatepequez: W.R. Smith and the Entrepreneurial Woman', paper presented at the annual meeting of the American Anthropological Association, San Francisco, 18–22 November.

Fernandez-Kelly, Maria Patricia (1983) *For We Are Sold, I and My People: Women and Industry in Mexico's Frontier*. Albany: SUNY Press.

Galeano, Eduardo (1967) *País Ocupado*. Mexico City: Nuestro Tiempo.

Garard-Burnett, Virginia and David Stoll (1993) *Rethinking Protestantism in Latin America*. Philadelphia, PA: Temple University Press.

Gledhill, John (2000) *Power and its Disguises: Anthropological Perspectives on Politics*, 2nd edn. London: Pluto Press.

Gleijeses, Pietro (1991) *Shattered Hope*. Princeton, NJ: Princeton University Press.

Gramsci, Antonio (1971) *Selections from Prison Notebooks*, trans. and ed. Quinton Hoare and Geoffrey Nowell. New York: International Publishers.

Grandin, Greg (2000) *The Blood of Guatemala: A History of Race and Nation*. Durham, NC: Duke University Press.

Green, Charles (2001) *Manufacturing Powerlessness in the Black Diaspora*. Walnut Creek, CA: Altamira Press.

Green, Linda (1998) 'The Localization of the Global: Contemporary Production Practices in a Mayan Community', in Lynne Phillips (ed.) *The Third Wave of Modernization in Latin America: Cultural Perspectives on Neoliberalism*, pp. 51–64. Wilmington, DE: Scholarly Resources.

Green, Linda (1999) *Fear as a Way of Life: Mayan Widows in Rural Guatemala*. New York: Columbia University Press.

Hall, Stuart (1994) 'Cultural Identity and Diaspora', in Patrick Williams and Laura Chrisman (eds) *Colonial Discourse and Post-Colonial Theory: A Reader*, pp. 392–403. New York: Columbia University Press.

Handy, Jim (1994) *Revolution in the Countryside: Rural Conflict and Agrarian Reform in Guatemala 1944–1954*. Chapel Hill: University of North Carolina Press.

Harvey, David (1989) *The Conditions of Postmodernity*. Cambridge, MA: Basil Blackwell.

Harvey, David (2000) *Spaces of Hope*. Berkeley: University of California Press.

Human Rights Watch (2002) *From the Household to the Factory: Sex Discrimination in the Guatemalan Labor Force*. New York: Human Rights Watch.

International Development Bank for Reconstruction and Development/World Bank (2001) *World Development Report, 2000–2001: Attacking Poverty*. International Development Bank for Reconstruction and Development/World Bank. New York: Oxford University Press.

Kabeer, Nalia (1994) *Reversed Realities: Gender Hierarchies in Development Thought*. New York: Verso.

Kay, C. (2001) 'Conflictos y violencia en la Latinoamerica rural', *Nueva Sociedad* 174 (July–August): 107–120.

Kearney, Michael (1996) *Reconceptualizing the Peasantry: Anthropology in Global Perspective*. Boulder, CO: Westview Press.

Kleinman, Arther, Veena Das and Margaret Lock (1997) *Social Suffering*. Berkeley: University of California Press.

Krueger, Chris and Kjell Enge (1985) *Security and Development: Conditions in the Guatemalan Highlands*. Washington, DC: Washington Office on Latin America.

Martinez Pelaez, Severo (1979) *La patria de criollo: en sayo de interpretación de la realidad colonial Guatemalteca*. San José, Costa Rica: Editorial Universidad Centroamerica.

McCreery, David (1994) *Rural Guatemala, 1760–1940*. Stanford, CA: Stanford University Press.

Mills, Mary Beth (1999) *Thai Women in the Global Labor Force: Consuming Desires, Contested Selves*. New Brunswick, NJ: Rutgers University Press.

Nash, June and Maria Patricia Fernandez-Kelly, eds (1983) *Women, Men and the International Division of Labor*. Albany, NY: SUNY Press.

Ong, Aiwah (1987) *Spirits of Resistance and Capitalist Discipline: Factory Women in Malaysia*. Albany, NY: SUNY Press.

Peterson, Kurt (1992) *The Maquiladora Revolution in Guatemala*. New Haven, CT: Center for International Human Rights at Yale Law School.

Phillips, Lynne, ed. (1998) *The Third Wave of Modernization in Latin America: Cultural Perspectives on Neoliberalism*. Wilmington, DE: Scholarly Resources.

Popkin, Margaret (1996) *Civil Patrols and their Legacy: Overcoming Militarization and Polarization in the Guatemalan Countryside*. Washington, DC: Robert F. Kennedy Memorial Center for Human Rights.

REHMI (Recuperation of Historical Memory Report) (1998) *Guatemala: Nunca Más*. Guatemala City: Archdiocese of Guatemala Office of Human Rights.

Roseberry, William (1994) 'Hegemony and the Language of Constestation', in Gil Joseph and Daniel Nugent (eds) *Everyday Forms of State Formation*, pp. 355–66. Durham, NC: Duke University Press.

Rosset, Peter (1991) 'Nontraditional Export Agriculture in Central America: Impact on Peasant Farmers', *Working Paper No. 20*. Santa Cruz: University of California.

Safa, Helen (1995) *The Myth of the Male Breadwinner: Women and Industrialization in the Caribbean*. Boulder, CO: Westview Press.

Salazar, Heliodoro Cumes and Teresa Chocoyo Chile (1997) '. . . Nos hacen llorar': *jovenes trabajadoras en las maquilas coreana de San Lucas, Sacatepequez a el Tejar, Chimatenango*. Cuidad de Guatemala: PAMI Investigación No. 9.

Sassen, Saskia (1982) 'Recomposition and Peripheralization at the Core', *Contemporary Marxism* 5: 88–100.

Schirmer, Jennifer (1998) *The Guatemalan Military Project: A Violence Called Democracy*. Philadelphia: University of Pennsylvania Press.

Sherman, William (1979) *Forced Native Labor in Sixteenth-Century Central America*. Lincoln: University of Nebraska Press.

Sider, Gerald and Gavin Smith (1997) 'Introduction', in Gerald Sider and Gavin Smith (eds) *Between History and Histories*, pp. 3–30. Toronto: University of Toronto Press.

Sieder, Rachel, Megan Thomas, George Vickers and Jack Spence (2002) *Who Governs? Guatemala Five Years after the Peace Accords*. Cambridge, MA: Hemispheric Initiatives.

Smith, Carol (1990) 'The Militarization of Civil Society in Guatemala: Economic Reorganization as a Continuation of War', *Latin American Perspectives* 67(4): 8–41.

Smith, Gavin (1989) *Livelihood and Resistance: Peasants and the Politics of Land in Peru*. Berkeley: University of California Press.

Smith, Gavin (1999) *Confronting the Present: Towards a Politically Engaged Anthropology*. Oxford and New York: Berg.

Sticheter, Sharon and Jane Parapart, eds (1988) *Patriarchy and Class: African Women in the Home and Workforce*. Boulder, CO: Westview Press.

Sticheter, Sharon and Jane Parapart, eds (1990) *Women, Employment and the Family in the International Division of Labour*. London: Macmillan.

Stoll, David (1990) *Is Latin America Turning Protestant? The Politics of Evangelical Growth*. Berkeley: University of California Press.

Thompson, Edward P. (1967) 'Time, Work-Discipline and Industrial Capitalism', *Past and Present* 20(38): 56–97.

Tiano, Susan (1986) 'Women and Industrial Development in Latin America', *Latin American Research Review* 21(3): 157–70.

Watts, Michael (1992) 'Living under Contract: Work, Production, Politics and the Manufacture of Discontent in a Peasant Society', in M. Watts and A. Pred, *Reworking Modernity*, pp. 65–105. New Brunswick, NJ: Rutgers University Press.

Wichterich, Christa (2000) *Globalized Women: Reports from a Future of Inequality*. London and New York: Zed Books.

Williams, Raymond (1977) *Marxism and Literature*. Oxford: Oxford University Press.

Wolf, Diane (1992) *Factory Daughters: Gender Household Dynamics and Rural Industrialization in Java*. Berkeley: University of California Press.

5

Thai Love Thai: Financing Emotion in Post-crash Thailand

Alan Klima

Today hundreds of thousands of Thais, in hundreds of mass Buddhist rituals, hold aloft 'trees' made out of US $100 bills and give the US cash, in nationalistic spirit, over to a Buddhist forest saint who, in turn, gives them over to the national treasury. Almost as many have attended rallies, waving Buddhist flags, in moral support of a wildly successful entre-preneur – the richest man among the new rich in Thailand – who has become Prime Minister. As he teetered in 2001 on the verge of impeach-ment for economically related corruption, tens of thousands attended mass Buddhist rituals held to alter his fate.

In postcrash Thailand, passion and finance are intimately bound in rituals of public life, and may be beginning to reconstitute the dominant affective frames through which the nation is articulated under current global conditions. Nowhere is this more apparent than in new mass Buddhist observances that are aimed at the harder edges of globalization. At points where local currency falls to international markets of capital, as happened in the Thai currency crash of 1997, such a defining edge to the conflict between local and global forces exists powerfully in imagination, as well as in practice. This article will address the financing of emotion under globalized conditions in Thailand by assessing the form and possible political effects of rituals of money and passion since the crash.

From *Ethnos* 69(4): 445–64. Copyright © 2004, Routledge Journals, Taylor and Francis Ltd, on behalf of the Museum of Ethnography.

As the dust settles, as debates over contending rational choice models to explain the massive capital flight from Thailand return, for the most part, to the academic circles that train our world's financial governors, the consequences of financial catastrophe settle with those who have little say in such matters. But the emotional dimensions of economic existence in Thailand after the crash of 1997 cannot be appreciated either by attending to the assumed psychological structure of the rational economic actor, nor to that of the 'primitive' in despair and fetishistic confusion. No less inadequate are assumptions about a dynamic global predicament or about its antagonists, essentially lasting hermetic cultural structures. All of which puts the analysis of emotion and money in Thailand after the crash of 1997 in a particularly engaging position in relation to the anthropology of emotion as it has been more typically explored through emphasis on first-person description of experience followed by analysis stressing the construction of emotion within discrete cultural systems. Such approaches have typically explicated emotions through contrast with and translation to a folk psychology and language of 'Western' self and feeling. Such work is best typified, perhaps, by what I would call a 'classic' line of work, a line that might be drawn through major points in its path, such as Clifford Geertz (1973), Michele Rosaldo (1980, 1984), and Catherine Lutz (1988). It might seem that such a path would no longer be navigable under current circumstances, and that the antidote to anthropological theories of emotional construction within discrete cultural units might be to turn anthropology's attention to patterns of globalizing systems that create commonalities and render discrete cultures no longer heuristically relevant. However, such a rationale would play equally into a similar zero-sum game (even if no longer that between the 'West/rest') that proposes a fundamental theoretical opposition between analysis of locality and translocality, where local difference can only appear, where it appears at all, as a figuring contrast that renders the ground of a global order into more clarity by virtue of its fundamental difference from that global order. Instead, one might follow the lead from twenty years ago of Michele Rosaldo (1984) in identifying the analysis of emotion as identical with an analysis of structured social relations, and so include global relations of power as part of the determining context. At the same time, it is necessary to consider the often overlooked fact that the identification of such relations of power can be fundamentally unstable, except when conceived in terms of a 'center' for which there can be no doubt or substitution (Derrida 1978). Without assuming either a center to a hermetic cultural structure, nor a center to 'globalization' that is the key to understanding it in the whole, it may become possible to see in the construction of emotion in certain localities neither the complete assertion nor rejection of translocal orders of control but complex formations that contain both play and order, that contain elements of both domination and liberation, simultaneous potentials for reproducing and extending the power of global capital power processes as well as disrupting and altering them.

Therefore, rather than debunk the classic approach to local construction of emotion, especially as anthropologists such as Rosaldo or Lutz, for instance, have tied it to the practice and consequences of power, I would argue that a shift in emphasis is more like what is in order: rather than translation between cultural 'worlds' a recognition of a shared and mutually constituted world is the first priority

(Wolf 1983). A 'classic' approach is still useful to address an anthropology of emotion and globalization, but the critical energy needs to be focused not so much to understand the contingency of each particular cultural view, nor the general physics of how the *things* 'language,' 'culture,' and 'emotion' interact, so much as it is to understand the workings of a particular historical configuration: an economic, political, and cultural situation of global proportions. The partial knowledge and angle of leverage gained on this situation, through an analysis of particular localities, could create potentially critical understandings not only, or even primarily, of 'Western' theories and folk psychologies, but rather could create critical angles on understanding this shared, global predicament itself. The shift of interest in the importance of cultural difference, a shift in the relevance of analysis from solely local systems to a situation of global dimensions, provides knowledge, then, not simply about the variability possible in the emotional life of the human being, but instead can indicate the developing ways in which a shared situation of global dimensions becomes shared very differently and from multiple positions, and moreover that therefore there can be no unified field theory of globalization itself.

Passion for money is common globally, is attempting to universalize itself, but can never be universal. There is no emotional gold standard to the interest, fascination, glee, despair and desires – noble and less so – that exist through money, nor is there, as yet, even a commonly accepted world currency in such passions. Nevertheless, surely our global situation is being constituted by varying passionate relations that live in and through money that is exchanged in a global arena heavily influenced by certain limited folk psychologies of how money motivates behavior in ways that are said to be natural, and so must be respected and adapted to. And yet, there are in degrees of power and subjugation under global conditions of passion for money innumerable differences in position and understanding between and within various localities, differences that can matter and for which translation and emphasis on local construction can become a key mode of comprehension, a means to critical understanding of globalization, but not an end in itself.

With this in mind, I would turn the attention here toward some ritual contexts for the public definition of emotion in Thailand after the country's devastating defeat in global currency wars in 1997. Forms of political power and influence created through the public redefinition of certain emotions in Thailand can be neither completely understood through local categories and conceptions nor can be accounted for as simply an extension of globalization, nor likewise can they be understood as simply assertions of local resistance nor an enfoldment into the global order of things. Instead, these rituals of national sentiment and value embody the power, tensions, and unstable points of opportunity for liberation and domination that are inherent in the phenomena of globalization.

Saving the Nation with Your Cash

The followers of Luangta Maha Bua, the most famous living 'forest saint' in the northeast Buddhist peripatetic tradition (Kamala 1997; Tambiah 1984), got together with their teacher to establish the Thai-Help-Thai campaign in 1997 shortly after the crash of the Thai baht. The movement's goal was to exchange the tremendous charismatic power of Luangta Maha Bua for US currency, gold, and Thai baht, in the form of Buddhist donations to the famed monk, to be given over to the national reserves.

In the booming 1990s, international sources had flooded Thailand with loans, most of which were denominated in foreign currency and on short-term. The Thai government had, for six decades, stuck to the equivalent of a fixed exchange rate regime where the Bank of Thailand would always buy back baht on the international market with its foreign currency reserves, to keep demand and the price of baht stable. Over the course of the first half of 1997, after declines in export earnings and with debt mounting in the private sector, the Bank of Thailand's ability to defend the currency on the world market was battered when international speculators organized to hit upon the weakness of foreign-denominated debt, a debt compounded by risky domestic financial distribution schemes. The reserves were depleted in a series of attempts to defend the Thai baht against speculators, eventually leading to a broader financial crisis that, in turn, led to an international monetary panic after the defeat of the Thai baht on July 2, 1997, when the government had no choice but to allow the baht to 'float' on its own on the world currency market.

In response, the famed forest *Arahant* (realized Buddhist) Luangta Maha Bua began his campaign to bolster the kingdom's central treasury fund, the *khlang luang*, and so save the nation. Stressing both valued Buddhist sentiments of 'kindness, compassion, and generosity' (*mettā,*) and nationalistic sentiments of 'love for the nation' (*khuam rak chaad*), Luangta and Thai-Help-Thai turned some traditional practices for generating Buddhist-oriented sentiments in merit-making toward new aims, creating a kind of voluntary taxation that was at the same time a religious observance.

The capstone ritual was held on Bangkok's central commons, Sanam Luang, on April 23, 2001. The campaign was in almost its fourth year, and Luangta was to ceremonially give over a ton of gold and over a million dollars that he had collected during the previous year to the government. This event was the culmination of ritual merit-making ceremonies held at hundreds of public venues, mostly temples all over the country, where after considerable advertising Luangta Maha Bua would appear in the flesh to receive alms gifts of US dollars, Thai baht, and gold jewelry, all for the sake of shoring up the national reserves.

In most cases, the ceremonies replaced the traditional *kathin*, or robes-giving ritual, which is held one day a year at each temple. Ordinarily, groups, families, villages, and individuals save up and pool their money for a *kathin* event, often attempting to outdo each other, and then put their money on kathin trees (*ton kathin*): 'trunks' of tightly bound straw on which money tied to sticks is attached to make symbolic 'money trees.' With the high-value cash attached at the top, the money tree is then held aloft, paraded through the streets, shown off in various ways and finally placed in full bloom at the feet of the monks.

At the mass donation ritual in Bangkok, a new version of *kathin* had assembled upwards of a hundred thousand participants in the money rite to save the nation. The crowd waited out a hot afternoon on the central commons of Bangkok's old city, and then finally the announcer proclaimed that Luangta Maha Bua was entering the scene, to give the bars of gold over to the government. He had been on a campaign for almost four years straight, touring the country to collect gold and cash, making stops at temples everywhere to hold merit-making ceremonies to save the nation. With their money trees in hand, thousands of them, the crowd at the great Bangkok donation ritual eagerly awaited the chance to give it all away. As Luangta chanted a first blessing and began a two-hour sermon that moved, alternately, far from and close to the theme of sacrifice, restless donors continually dug cash out of their pockets or solicited from others, finding some way to keep adding, fussing, and primping over their merit making trees, most of which sported the added touches of a Thai national flag and a photo of Luangta with the Thai king on his knees.

As excitement mounted, as darkness fell, as Luangta began to wrap up his two-hour discourse and then finally settled to the end, the 100,000 plus merit makers were finally free to begin pressing anxiously toward the stage. A 30-foot-wide column of bodies and money trees surged the length of the field and hove forward through the convection of others waiting in the wings. Somehow they managed not to turn it into a stampede, with the announcer nervously pleading with the crowd to remain peaceful and orderly, to not 'waste the merit' or 'spoil the merit' and lose it all by getting their hearts into a frenzy at the last-minute and rendering in an instant all their efforts at collecting money over the past months of time useless and futile.

Merit, *puñña*, is in the Thai Buddhist reckoning of the ritual organizers, ultimately an affair of the 'heart' (*cai*). In theory, the tool of money or other gift to the *Sangha* (order of monks) is the initiator or spark of feelings which are to be enhanced and amplified with good intentions and moral behavior, ultimately refining and developing the heart (*cai*) and improving one's spiritual condition. Of course, the particular Buddhist theories that the organizers subscribe to is not necessarily the 'reality of internal feelings,' however one understands access to such a reality (and my concern here will be solely with performative definition of emotions, not the description, nor interpretive deduction, of internal states). But Buddhist theory is of course relevant here since it is one frame through which emotion is understood by participants in Buddhist rites, and especially by the organizers of such rites, who are monastics and dedicated lay practitioners. According, again, to theory, the enhancement of one's spiritual condition is afforded, oftentimes, not only through one's individual concentration and effort, but through the communal presence of others sharing in the power of the rituals themselves as well as the degree to which the recipient of the gift already embodies a refined and meritorious character. Ostensibly, the act of merit-making connects emotion with the spiritual state of the individual donor, links that process together with others in a synergistic fashion, and connects those connections in turn to the state of merit of the recipient. One of the most common ritual symbols and practical tools in performing such connection is the use of actual string, held in the palms of monks, attached to Buddha statues, relics, and anything holy, wound round spaces in need of blessing or protecting, and physically attached to individuals in similar need. With or without the use of string (some rituals outstrip in size the quantity of string at hand), individuals, groups, and those that embody the highest spiritual values simultaneously share and generate *puñña* together.

In lay Thai Buddhism the primary technology for shaping one's character and destiny, the trajectory of lives of individuals and those they share with, has always been merit-making, the arena of Buddhist practice that stresses a language of sentiment more than any other. In this discourse, it is *mettā* – roughly speaking, loving-kindness, compassion, and generosity – that is the central sentimental value appealed to in eliciting participation in merit-making. At the same time, it should be no surprise that in the practice of such public rituals of generosity, of course *mettā* is mixed with the desire to show off to everyone one's own good merit, as well as one's disposable wealth. Merit-making is, then, one of the most performative of all Buddhist activities in Thailand. And *kathin*, its premiere ritual, has historically been extremely effective in varying political and economic contexts over the years, one resonant example being the campaign by Bangkok-based Thai banks to expand their reach in the provinces through sponsoring elaborate *kathin* rituals in the countryside, as studied by Christine Gray (1986).

While merit-making is the primary Buddhist arena that values sentiments of connection to others, in full public and ceremonial view, it is of course far from the only public validation of such sentiments of connection generally. 'Love,' *rak*, is another staple of Thai theories and practices of community, the word 'rak' itself carrying complex and contradictory meanings in Thai. *Rak* is of course a highly valued sentiment in family and romantic relationships (it is never used on favorite foods, etc.). But *rak*, in strict Buddhist theory, is also involved in *tanha* 'clinging/ desire' and *rag* 'lust/passion.' In that sense it can be and often is referred to as a direct antagonist of *mettā*, loving-compassion, since *mettā*, which in its highest form is 'love' for all without discrimination, can be antagonized by love for particular people and especially those for whom one also has lust.

But *rak* certainly gets valued in wider realms of practice in Thai society, which is of course not oriented toward Buddhist enlightenment alone. The premier venues for valuing *rak*, now and in the past, include the exaltation of mother-child bonds, the realm of dramatized romance, and the insistence of nationalist propaganda, which encourages *rak* for the nation. Nationalist love has in the past been largely articulated in relationship to a fear of internal enemies or potential invaders, and such love has often been espoused in tandem with a hatred for others, especially communists. At times, right-wing extremist Buddhists have associated this hate with Buddhist merit, advocating the killing of communists as a Buddhist merit-making act (Keyes 1978). At the same time, and far more often, love for the nation has been more benignly encouraged as supporting the development of the nation as a distinct geo-political territory. Thongchai Winichakul (1994) has called the object of such love, and generator of such hate, the 'geo-body,' an entity which had to be brought into discursive existence for Thais by transforming their technologies of group self-consciousness, particularly through the technology of mapping.

But today, in spite of the fact that Thai citizens are occasionally kidnapped or killed by Burmese security forces in border areas, the border as a military marker of the national body does not command prominence in media attention. And after a dwindling half-life, the US-Thai cooperatively-generated hatred of internal enemies has also passed to a large extent. The geo-spatial consciousness of national and cultural identity no longer looms as the only technology with great potential reality-effects, not in a world in which the movement of finance capital has instantaneous global transport and the entire country can be brought down by the speculative moves of those who bet on international currency exchange rates, or brought down by the ways in which all forms of economic practice within the country contribute to the relative weakness or strength of the position its national money has in that global market. With the sudden crash of the Thai baht, after months of a failed state effort to keep the market price of the national currency up by buying it back from the global market with the nation's foreign currency reserves, and after the lasting, severe, and shared effects of that defeat across society, it is not geographical boundaries that are the first object of nationalistic focus anymore but the currency itself which is the new 'territory' to be developed and defended, and which transmits the feeling of being bound in a common identity and fate. But it is not as though, despite how recent the dominating equation of money and nation is, there are not already in place ample means by which to work with, and rework, these relations of money and love, and so alter the specific trajectory for growth of the new national money-spirit...

One by one, in rapid succession and sprouting out from the bed of money trees, each bristling tree of cash was placed before the feet of Luangta Maha Bua, who sat impassively on the stage as followers bowed down before him. Big and small trees mixed in the gush forward, with the largest ones garnering oohs and ahhs and gasps, particularly those that were bristling with US hundreds, or else the occasional tree of gold: actual large tree branches laced with gold chains, bracelets and jewelry destined to be melted down into gold bars but now flashing in an infinite succession of camera lights and flickering with traces of the persons who had inhabited them, before the gold's future liquidization and reformation into a stack of thick bricks of national security.

Bringing up the rear, and towering over all, was a 50-foot construction, a 'map' of Thailand made out of bright 500-baht purple bills. Giving away this nation made of money, and wedding the 'geo-body,' or the idea of the nation as circulated through mapping technology, to the national currency, perhaps nothing better embodied the exchange of one national imagination into another, borders for monetary integrity, garnering the rare remarkable glance from Luangta who for the most part seemed to take little interest in the amazing spectacle of a sea of money washing up on the shore of his stage.

As the money was whisked behind the stage, so too was behind the stage the next stop for the thousands of pilgrims for the nation. There, hundreds of volunteers proceeded to defoliate a forest of money trees, creating giant piles of cash. Cordoned back with ropes and under the eyes of police, the crowd watched aghast as almost all present had never been in the presence of so much physical cash. Smiling volunteers cheerfully plucked away at the trees, while some would play to the crowd, sinking their elbows deep in a pile of 20 baht notes and coming up with fistfuls, or wistfully holding up a beautifully manicured and densely foliated tree of US hundreds, as though it were a shame to dismantle it.

After over an hour of sustained, climactic giving, Luangta gave the final blessing. The merit having been made, it was time to share and spread it out. Luangta gave the chant for merit and the crowd was as silent and still as it could manage, hands in a position of respect and reception in order to focus on the wish, or *atitaan*, that accompanies giving. A mix of personal and family desires with the wish to save the nation, each *atitaan* is thought to be in connection with the others, all connected in turn to the great merit of Luangta himself. With a blessing string between his palms, then wound past the stage and hooked up to a fleet of eighteen-wheel trucks of water bottles parked behind stage, Luangta made a mass blessing through the string and into the water. In finale, the crowd rushed on the trucks, sometimes violently pushing, to come away with cases of bottled water charged, through connective merit string, with Luangta's blessing.

More Strings Attached

In an astute move, the latest Prime Minister, Thaksin Shinawatra, made sure to be personally in attendance for this mass ritual, to receive the gold bars from Luangta Maha Bua on behalf of the nation. And his attendance at the event was no mere formality: as a media and telecom tycoon, turned politician, he had successfully trumped previous parties' media image fiascoes since the crash, one of the most prominent of which was the previous administration's diversion of Thai-Help-Thai funds from the *khlang luang* toward what seemed a more prudent use of government funds in the budget current at the time: corporate aid. Luangta Maha Bua complained loudly in the media, while the previous government's response, including reasonable economic arguments from certain perspectives, was that at the time there were pressing needs at hand, and once the government had been given the money all strings of possession of the money were detached. Though exonerated of a legal attack launched by Thai-Help-Thai, the government eventually succumbed to this damaging scandal (as well as others), which virtually insured that the government would not gain ground in the critical Northeast voting bloc, the region from which Luangta Maha Bua and the forest monk movement hails. By contrast with the previous government, the new media-wise Prime Minister Thaksin, when given the chance to speak at the mass donation rally, vowed dramatically that not one baht would be diverted from the reserves.

Thaksin Shinawatra's ability to play to a crowd had already been amply demonstrated. He had already achieved the first legitimate landslide in political history, using his image as a wildly successful entrepreneur to promise he could turn the Thai economy around. Of course he would certainly be there at the Thai-Help-Thai ritual, to personally associate himself with the revered monk, and augment his own image as savior to the nation, an image which he had so carefully cultivated in his campaign and which, it turned out, he needed then more than ever. This was not Thaksin's first time in political office. In 1994, before forming his own party in 1998, he had joined the anti-corruption party 'Moral Force' (Palang Dhamma) of Chamlong Sri-Muang, the former Maj. Gen. turned celibate Buddhist politician who led the pro-democracy protests of 1992 which, while ending in brutality, ousted the last dominant military clique in Thailand (Klima 2002). Given anti-corruption laws demanded by the new constitution ratified in 1997, Thaksin was as a cabinet official required to submit assets reports, which later showed some fuzzy practices, including what appeared to be the hiding of billions of baht in assets by transferring them to maids and chauffeurs. The case was finally brought to the end of deliberations by the nation's top Constitutional Court in 2001, shortly after Thaksin's landslide election in January 2001. With evidence of fraud mounting, the man who was elected as a savior of the nation was on the verge of being cast out of office, pending the vote of the judiciary.

Various popular campaigns were launched to save the Prime Minister, many of which had a Buddhist tone and involved liberal use of Buddhist flag-waving demonstrations, while the lay leaders of Thai-Help-Thai came out actively in support of Thaksin as well. But in fact it was the very severity of the crisis that faced him, the strength of the evidence and clarity of the law, that propelled Thaksin's case even more fervently into realms of Buddhist urgency, and one prominent ritual was particularly stirring in this regard: a high-powered Buddhist blessing and mass ritual to alter what seemed an impending fate, and so save Thaksin days before the court's decision was due . . .

The ritual to 'draw in the spirit-forms' or 'call back one's spirits,' *suu khwan*, is a ritual involving merit and blessing string that is done when embarking on new, important or risky ventures or after a calamity has struck. A disease of the *khwan* involves an instability in one's 'spirit forms,' often coming after a fright or sudden shock. The *khwan* are generally said to be 32 in number (corresponding nominally but not identically with the traditional Buddhist conception of the various parts of a body) and must be assembled back into a coherent, integral composite. The individual's composite of spirited energies can, in states of fright or when subject to powerful spiritual forces, become dispersed and fragmented, rendering one vulnerable to malaise, sickness, misfortune, and death.

Suu khwan, the ritual to re-gather, call back, and draw in the *khwan*, is common across Thailand. Although perceived as a traditional rural practice, in fact it is also widely accessed by urban professionals and students in facing their difficulties and tests. While much of the political protests and Buddhist flag waving for Thaksin were directed at the center of Bangkok, where the support for idealistic democracy and anti-corruption laws runs the highest, the blessing of Thaksin was staged quite deliberately in the provinces, at the great Dhamma Chedi (conical tower erected over relics) that was built recently in the heart of Khon Kaen, arguably something of a capital city of the Northeast region of Thailand, 'Isaan,' where the power of moneyed networks of politicians tied to the largest voting bloc in the country makes for the most important arena at national election time. The Northeast is also, per capita, the poorest region of Thailand and its population are among the hardest hit by the crash. Many of the most senior and influential monks in the North-east were assembled to 'gather,' 'draw in,' and 'call back' the spirit forms (*suu khwan*) of Thaksin and get him through the trouble to come, as the court's decision was due in a matter of days. Or, at least, that was the understanding, as Buddhist monks are not supposed to come out expressly in favor of a single party or candidate. An individual like Thaksin always has a right to a private blessing from monks. But given the amount of media attention focused on the rite, attended by every network and national newspaper, and given the prominent monks who were there to represent the Buddhist establishment, the ritual organizers were careful to point out at every opportunity that this was a ritual to help the nation, not any particular individual.

A day of tens of thousands: this time almost exclusively Northeasterners, over 30,000 lay people, '108' senior monks, and over 1,000 other monks, all filling up the lavishly ornate interior of the Chedi tower and spilling out into the temple yard. Loudspeakers blast the proceedings out to those who assembled for the mass event. As the announcer went to pains to point out that this was a ritual to protect the nation from danger, imminent danger, and not a ritual for the sake of any particular individual, the crowd eagerly awaited Thaksin (who was in imminent danger) to arrive. When he did, the place lit up with excitement. Cameras began flashing and rolling, heads began turning and bodies cramming to get close to him. Thaksin was led to the nine monks who would channel the blessing, all assembled in a small circle, with statues of the Buddha inter-spaced between them. A blessing string of connection was unwound which they would hold between their respective palms, connect to the Buddha statues and to the holy relic said to be housed in the center of the Chedi, and run out to the sofa upon which Thaksin would sit.

Originally, the plan was to follow a more traditional form. Thaksin was to sit not outside the circle on a couch, but in the middle of the circle of monks, with the blessing string wound around his head and held in prayer hands. An individual with dispersed *khwan* who is not gathered is vulnerable to illness, death, and misfortune, and is also particularly susceptible to curses and magic. The ritual seeks to bind, or rebind, the *khwan* together, and ends with a blessing in which a portion of the connective string is cut off and tied around the wrist of the recipient, to lock in the effect. Such a blessing of string wound round the wrist is routinely given by monks, but also by any village ritual specialist, and, equally as often in many regions of the country, by any elderly person to anyone who is their junior. The tying of string locks in the blessing and symbolizes the compaction and discrete integrity of the person's spirit forms. At the same time, the blessing is itself an intersubjective sharing of merit: it is a gift, and especially in explicit Buddhist rites it is tied on the individual with the very string that just previously connected community members each to the other and that instantiates the sharing of merit at these and other important ritual moments.

But the prospect of an image of support for Thaksin by monks, who are supposed to be politically aloof, broadcast across the nation, was considered too problematic, and the normal ritual of *suu khwan* was changed and Thaksin was no longer the explicit focus of the ritual. Instead of getting bound in string in the center of the circle of string, the Prime Minister was relegated to an adjacent seat on a sofa and hooked up from there. On an explicit level this ritual may have been transformed, from one stressing the integrity of the person (in a blessing that is given through the community) to the safety and integrity, and so also unity, of the nation, but of course implicitly the ritual remained focused on one person, Thaksin and his court case. However, changing the explicit reference of the ritual from Thaksin to the nation was anything but unfortunate for him. That his fate and that of the nation are exchangeable, or equivalent, was the foundational argument of the entire campaign to save Thaksin: he was the nation's only hope and could not be impeached. And so the foundational message of his dominant political party, so successful in cornering the market in moral authority since the crash, was repeated here once again.

Before ascending his designated seat for the ritual, Thaksin passed through the crowd, who were adoring him in a way never seen before in Thai politics. With arms open wide he moved through the crowd which surged desperately to touch him, and to tie on his wrist strings of personal blessing. This took almost an hour. He was gently tossed through the crowd as they adoringly tied string after string around his wrist, until it was covered in hundreds of strings, and he, visibly overcome with what seemed a kind of ecstasy, passively smiled back through the showering, pouring rain of love directed to him.

Eventually freed from the crowd, he took to a microphone and began to speak. 'I don't want anything for myself.' Tears were running down his cheeks and eventually his voice cracked, only to further deteriorate into sobs. 'I have everything already. I only want to help our country.'

Cheers, some sobbing, and some country yelps (a self-conscious assertion of *Isaan* identity) ensued as Thaksin characterized the dangers facing him and the nation. With his hand and arm covered in blessing strings, as representing the hope and fate of the nation, with his *khwan* becoming the *khwan* of the nation, the national spirit tied into his, and encircled by string, adoration, and an attentive horde from the entire spectrum of journalism, he became the central router through which this sentimental economy was consummated, broadcast, and received.

The final ceremony of blessing in the circle of monks eventually followed. Though with the climax already over, and while not exactly eclipsed by Thaksin's blessing and bodily sharing in the crowd, the blessings of the monks were as inexorably tied to the spirit of that walk through a shower of hopes, the spirit of a new *khwan* body to the nation, one in which finance and love participate in a new national money-spirit...

Thai Love Thai

When Thaksin first formed the splinter party from Moral Force, the splinter party that went on to become the dominant political mega-party today in Thailand with sweeping powers of Parliamentary majority, he named it Thai-Rak-Thai, 'Thai-Love-Thai.' He then set about his campaign with promises of cash giveaways for small enterprise to every village, promises of affordable health care, and promises to focus on domestic Thai-to-Thai trade (all subsequently delivered on, to some degree), as well as his campaign to heal the wound of the new world order with the salve of communal love and so seem to be able to save the nation from the calamity that had befallen it by what seemed a combination of hostile global forces and corrupt internal elites.

> Cut to commercial: a child watching a nature program, where a pack of hyenas are killing and devouring a wildebeest. As the dirty hyenas viciously tear apart the carcass, the child asks grandma why this is happening and she says 'this is the way of the world today.' The voiceover cuts to an explanation of the virtues of Thai financial institutions and a particular bank. The commercial shows clean, spaceage robots that are meant to represent the bank, robots that are revealed to have, glistening within their cold white metal exteriors, beating human hearts.

With the imagination of, as well as harsh effects dealt by, a technologically global-izing world of novel social commerce, the ascendance of a regime of money/love is becoming ever more compelling. There may be a style akin to this in what Roger Rouse (2002) has called the 'cuddly capitalism' of US political leaders. In the US, cuddly capitalism legitimates merciless neoliberal policies through media fascination with leaders' bodily expressions of affection and sometimes, well . . . desire. Mean-while in Thailand, the dimensions of feeling that are opened up by the simultaneous integration of, and uncertainty in, international finance, the dimensions of feeling afforded by global arenas of money exchange, are engaged by Thai-Love-Thai in its own ways.

For now, Thaksin has passed through his ordeal in court and has won, whether because of the *suu khwan* ritual to save him or because (as has been alleged in the press) it turned out that one of his political allies had stacked the court in a way that is rather traditional in Thai politics. And, for now, the debt since the crash remains as unwieldy as ever, at least until Thaksin's Thai-Love-Thai finalizes his expression of Thais loving Thais by moving the 60 billion dollar debt, mostly corporate and banking debt, to the public sector, where it can be paid off through taxation of the general populace. In exchange for the common person taking on this burden, Thai-Love-Thai has implemented a village entrepreneurship scheme, having pledged at election time one million baht (US $26,000) for every village, to be used as a loan-fund for communal micro-lending to jumpstart local economies. This resembles patronage and dependency politics that were previously constituted between local citizenry and their direct parliament representatives, now cast in a wider, less localized national realm of relationship. In return, the wider national community will take on the debt wracked up by a small coterie of financiers.

Meanwhile, as it turns out, and despite the long, vigorous, and well-supported efforts of Luangta's Thai-Help-Thai, the over two tons of gold and over 200 million baht (US $ five million) generated in this nationally prominent campaign is no match for the sheer scale of the sums of money that move globally through international finance, and does not even come close to figuring 1 percent of the debt. There never was any real chance of this money immediately influencing the nation's financial position globally in the foreseeable future.

And so the question might naturally arise, in the same manner, perhaps, as questions of emotion and money always seem to arise among Western academic elites, of whether these particular demonstrations of the act of love are actually forming new or even progressive social relations under globalization, or are simply a super-structural accouterment – the fetishistic reaction of the globally disenfran-chised to the ethereal and inconceivable realm of international money flows: their desperate, even superstitious, fetishism of money that creates secondary fantasy hopes that grease the wheels for a more primary and structurally real economic transformation that will dominate them. On the one hand, the mass Buddhist donation ceremonies of Luangta Maha Bua might be seen as collective effervescence in which physical cash gets imbued with the bubbling sentiments of the crowd, the money commodity fetish becoming, in turn, an actual so-called 'primitive' fetish, and so representing merely a reactive application of local practice and emotion to a hopeless global situation. Meanwhile, Thaksin's Thai-Love-Thai Party might be more simply the 'Thai-Love-Me' Party, where he is the 'spectral' form that consolidates a new and undesired era of late modernist capitalism through sleights of hand that do not register among an enthralled populace. The structural rationale of global capital plods along according to its unfeeling logic.

But if value cannot be fully apprehended without appreciating how imagination and passion participate in its creation, then the emotional dimensions of economic traumas may lend knowledge and insight into multiple, rather than singular, possibilities for the ways in which the 'logic' of money has potential to play itself out. For instance, the Buddhist merit-making rituals to save the nation are both performing and prescribing certain economic values, and spreading them widely and prominently throughout the country. They are anti-debt rituals. The *khlang luang*, or national treasury reserve, is seen as the productive center of power, the health of which will generate the health of everything to which it is connected. Short-term gain is discredited in relation to long-term and solid position. The ritual, in both its accompanying 'voice-over' on loudspeakers as well as in the bodily performance, says it is time to wake from the dream of the boom, its borrowing and its promises. While in terms of actual monetary value the entire movement cannot even begin to participate on a scale that is statistically significant in terms of global economic processes, culturally it can make statements about economic policy, values, and priorities that can begin to participate in the national consciousness of monetary matters on a scale that can actually rival that of the policy makers, and help bring down a government. Luangta Maha Bua can create a public controversy over a government's disbursing part of the national treasury reserves, claiming it is connected to, and so belongs to, the people rather than the government. Thaksin, in depending on love as well as money, has had to faithfully follow the command that the merit-making money for the nation remain connected to the people who gave it, and has in general become more subject than any other previous leader to the support of the populace, where before leaders were far more dependant on money alone (either that or guns and the US). The ideals that Thai-Love-Thai is pushing may exceed the political moment and its personages. In E.P. Thompson's sense, a moral economy, once established, brings contradictions of its values glaringly into view (1971). What are, for instance, the long-term effects of arguing that the State owes healthcare to everyone, for every disease, at the price of one US dollar? Even if the scheme fails, it will be difficult to erase its memory, as well as the ideals with which it was justified in the first place. Does all this performance of communal love, here and elsewhere, simply serve the hegemon of globalization, or does it instead show us instabilities as well as opportunities to form and reform community? Thaksin will always have the money, but the love may not always be his to control. And if Thai-Help-Thai has a string attached to less than 1 percent of the non-discretionary treasury reserve (*khlang luang*), it has a string attached to all of it, as there is no way to distinguish whether any money withdrawn from the *khlang luang* is the money given by the people, or different money which was there before (as has been explained to me by supporters of Thai-Help-Thai, with rakish smiles). To Thai-Help-Thai, the first baht removed from the *khlang luang* will always be the last baht the people had put in there themselves as collective merit.

The fact that money and nation are bound together is not going to go away. It is not simply an ideology, ritual, etc. that is foisted through propaganda on people. The way in which money, connected to the broader universe of international financial markets, in turn binds most Thais together in a shared social predicament (however differently dispersed) is an effect of identity and economic existence that goes far beyond anything a national propaganda machine can produce. It is not the only effect, but under conditions of currency crisis and depression, it is a most daunting and urgent one. The language of blood and death, sacrifice to the soil and land of the Thai, a conception of love that accompanies the nationalist passion associated with the geo-body under previous global conditions is not up to the task of forming, validating, valuing, propounding, and demanding sentiments that function powerfully under current situations of global financial integration and uncertainty. Recent developments, then, have only heightened the precision of Thongchai's argument about the historical particularity of the geo-body, its arising through certain technologies that are historically contingent and so subject to change (1994). Similarly, the national money-spirit is contingent on changing conditions. The fact that the battles over Thai currency in 1997 took place from abstract positions in a global network of computer trading, that positions were established not along a geo-spatial front-line but from multiple points across the globe, without territorial strategy, the fact that location within the attacked territory does not equal allegiance to it and that transnational elites, whatever their nationality, can always sell their fellows out, is a situation not lost on those who suffer the consequences of such wars, and so why would the language of blood and territory speak to them as powerfully as it once did? Similarly, the language and theory of 'global flows' to capital and finance, the hydraulic theory of global modernity, carries traces of geo-spatial reasoning that may be more adequate for some phenomena (much – but not all – labor and refugee migration, for instance) than for others (much – but not all – international currency trade: the transactions are near instant between any two points on the network and money does not 'flow' or even 'circulate' between those points). If global flow were an adequate metaphor, Thais would certainly have been more than ready to embrace it. Given the long history of Thai irrigated farming, and the dependence on water for rice production, there is of course a highly elaborated language of watered flows, life, power, and production in Thailand but these metaphors of controlling flows are not the ones being currently chosen, are not the primary language used in nationalistic assertions on globalization. The reason for that could be because such water-metaphors are not the best, nor even adequate, ideas for the situation as it stands.

Money may not now resemble a blood that circulates or a water that flows within and without the national body. The geo-body may remain in place, but its spirit, its money-spirit, is dispersed from it, drawn out by international networks, over-extended, vulnerable to the influence of others, and with claims and strings tied upon it from beyond. The more un-gathered and disjointed it becomes the more difficult it is to gain any power over or access to it. Under conditions created in a world that is, in part at least, very much influenced by despatialized and deterritor-ialized forces, there are rites that understand this spiritual value to money, that attempt to call that value back and rebind it, to transmit their energy on another plane than that of the physical body and which link and bind and reclaim this power of money with a spiritual technology that strings new cables of transmission. And in the process, the understanding of what is at stake in passions for money around the world today is re-imagined, re-theorized, and re-instantiated.

In constructing an accounting of emotion that might address situations of globalization, it is necessary to adopt approaches to human community, sentiment, and value that have the flexibility and subtlety to orient the mind toward refined senses of the connections between people when the basis of that connectivity is given its subtle figure in terms of something as elusive as the money form, especially where that form is imbricated in highly abstract and technologically refined means of global exchange. The ritual practices of merit-making and integrating spirit-matter suggest not only how some Thais might influence the significance of money by using particular performative means, but how these 'local' means are in fact some of the *best* means to understand a global situation in which money and identity are more powerfully equated than ever before.

And so, rather counter-intuitively, it is not a need to 'go beyond' local structures of feeling and understanding, beyond local terms and categories that the global situation demands of an anthropologist concerned with the workings of power today, but instead what is called for is to delve even further within these 'local' understandings for insights into new ways to conceive of and address globalization, as this article barely begins. The previous techniques of the anthropology of emotion are anything but outmoded, nor are they in direct, zero-sum tension with the demands of global phenomena. What is called for instead is that the shift in anthropological attention is changed from translation – from one cultural universe to another – toward translations between various positions and understandings of a shared global situation, a situation that is, in turn, shared quite differently. But even more than providing understanding, specific techniques of money and emotion can actually create in practice innovative forms of passionate engagement with community under conditions of global threats. Such definitive performances of acts of love – which are deep plays on globalization – reveal the ways in which emotion is a crucial dimension of the battles under globalization, and so the constructive power of culture must continue to be watched and formed mindfully, as it contains both the play of domination and of freedom, which ultimately may not be under the control of any central power.

REFERENCES

Derrida, Jacques. 1978. Structure, Sign, and Play in the Discourse of the Human Sciences. In *Writing and Difference*, transl. Alan Bass, pp. 278–293. Chicago: University of Chicago Press.

Geertz, Clifford. 1973. Person, Time, and Conduct in Bali. In *The Interpretation of Cultures*. New York: Basic Books.

Gray, Christine E. 1986. Thailand: The Soteriological State in the 1970s. Ph.D. dissertation, University of Chicago.

Kamala Tiyavanich. 1997. *Forest Recollections: Wandering Monks in Twentieth-Century Thailand*. Honolulu: University of Hawai'i Press.

Keyes, Charles F. 1978. Political Crisis and Militant Buddhism in Contemporary Thailand. In *Religion and the Legitimation of Power in Thailand, Laos, and Burma*, edited by Bardwell L. Smith. Chambersburg, PA: Anima Books.

Klima, Alan. 2002. *The Funeral Casino: Meditation, Massacre, and Exchange with the Dead in Thailand*. Princeton: Princeton University Press.

Lutz, Catherine A. 1988. *Unnatural Emotions: Everyday Sentiments on a Micronesian Atoll*. Chicago: University of Chicago Press.

Rosaldo, Michele Z. 1980. *Knowledge and Passion: Ilongot Notions of Self and Social Life*. Cambridge: Cambridge University Press.

———. 1984. Toward an Anthropology of Self and Feeling. In *Culture Theory*, edited by Richard Shweder & Robert Levine. New York: Cambridge University Press.

Rouse, Roger. 2002. Cuddly Capitalism: Neoliberal Legitimation and the Meanings of Bill Clinton's Body. Talk presented to the Graduate Program in Cultural Studies, University of California, Davis, March 7, 2002.

Tambiah, Stanley J. 1984. *Buddhist Saints of the Forest and the Cult of the Amulets*. Cambridge: Cambridge University Press.

Thompson, Edward P. 1971. The Moral Economy of the English Crowd in the Eighteenth Century. *Past and Present*, 50: 76–136.

Thongchai Winichakul. 1994. *Siam Mapped: A History of the Geo-body of a Nation*. Honolulu: University of Hawai'i Press.

Wolf, Eric R. 1983. *Europe and the People without History*. Berkeley: University of California Press.

6

Situating Global Capitalisms: A View from Wall Street Investment Banks

Karen Ho

Many cultural studies theorists and social scientists, by giving emphasis to capitalism's omnipotence, have helped to imagine a world of capitalist totality. In the rush to confront and depict the powerful impact of Western global hegemony, they have often neglected the power-laden political effects of their own representations of this very hegemony. Ironically, these academic representations and critiques sound extremely similar to Wall Street triumphalist discourses of global capitalism, as promulgated in much of the business and financial literature.

In this article, I demonstrate the strategic investment that both social theorists and Wall Street investment bankers have in the analytical frameworks of the global that rely on an overarching construct of global capitalism as well as a seductive rhetoric of the global.[1] Given this often-unacknowledged overlap between my informants and my discipline, as promoters and critics of capitalism, respectively, I explore the politics of academic knowledge production on globalization and capitalism. To what extent do critical theorists, despite their professed awareness of the contingencies, constructed effects, and productive strategies of global capitalism, take capitalist pronouncements at face value, allowing representations of globalization to stand for the world "as it is" instead of querying the multiple internal contradictions, complexities, and implosions in their specific worldviews and practices?

From *Cultural Anthropology* 20(1): 68–96. Copyright © 2005, American Anthropological Association.

It is precisely because of these concerns that I came to study Wall Street investment bankers as primary actors in the globalization of U.S. capitalism.[2] By directly accessing the key agents of change on Wall Street, a site widely deemed to be the epitome of the global, I confront anthropology's conceptual and methodological tendency to approach globalization as a taken-for-granted macro context and as an abstract process too big for ethnographic endeavor. I make the case for an ethnographic engagement that tracks the global as cultural action grounded in specific practices and locales that can be thickly described.[3]

To begin this research, I worked for a year as a management consultant at a Wall Street investment bank to learn the language of finance. After I left my Wall Street job, I began 17 months of fieldwork (February 1998–June 1999) researching a diverse group of Wall Street investment bankers and how they make sense of their worldviews and daily practices.[4] I observed and participated in the lives of these actors both in and out of the workplace, conducted 100 interviews, and traveled from cubicles and trading floors to local bars as well as securities industry conferences. Simultaneously, I researched unemployment and outplacement agencies, workers who had been downsized, alternative investment groups, and economic justice activists. I came across multiple approaches, definitions, and claims of what Wall Street is or should be.

In the argument below, I juxtapose representations of global capitalism by two investment banks headquartered in New York City with academic representations of globalization and late capitalism. In a marketing and recruiting brochure, J. P. Morgan, a prestigious investment bank, declares: "We act as a global problem solver for our clients, moving ideas and insights seamlessly across time and space. Our experience in markets around the world gives clients unparalleled access to insights and opportunities" (J. P. Morgan brochure 1995: centerfold). In its 1995 annual report, Merrill Lynch, one of the largest and most profitable investment banks in the United States, proclaims, "Merrill Lynch is singularly positioned and strategically committed to global leadership as the preeminent financial management and advisory company" (Merrill Lynch 1995: 1).[5] In its 1994 annual report, it unabashedly boasts, "Our global scope and intelligence allow us to respond to opportunities and changes in all markets and in all regions. We serve the needs of our clients across all geographic borders" (Merrill Lynch 1994: centerfold).

Consider now some of the representations of globalization by Marxist cultural theorists and social scientists. Frederic Jameson's writings on late capitalism describe it as a "dimly perceivable," "nonhuman" logic, whose global "network of power and control [is] even more difficult for our minds and imaginations to grasp" (Jameson 1991: 38, 408). Such discourses construct global capitalism as an all-powerful monolith, albeit clothed in a postmodern lingo – the language of flows, decenteredness, and immateriality. In this new metanarrative, capitalism is a "borderless world" whose operational arena is engaged in "the relentless saturation of any remaining voids and empty places" (Jameson 1991: 412). Zygmunt Bauman writes that globalization "refers to... 'anonymous forces,' operating in the vast – foggy and slushy, impassable and untamable – 'no man's land,' stretching beyond the reach of the design-and-action capacity of anybody's in particular" (Bauman 1998: 60).[6]

In addition, many social critics imagine finance capital, in particular, to be the most globalized and abstract form of capitalism. For geographer Ron Martin, the movement toward "global financial integration" exemplifies the most globalized form of capitalism (Martin 1994). In conquering physical space, finance capital allows capitalism to transcend its ties to geography and thereby move into the realm of electronic globalization. Theorists such as Jean Baudrillard (1983, 1989) and Guy Debord (1983) posit a radical disjuncture between the fictitious economy (finance capital) and the "real economy." These theories often assume capitalism's supreme agency – the ability to project itself into immateriality and invisibility, to exist in another plane as "spectacle" in which it acts freely, unbounded by the "real" and cumbersome productive economy.

By comparing the self-representations of financial institutions with academic critiques of global capitalism, I highlight the conspicuous similarity between what investment banks say about themselves (to project images of their global reach) and what much critical scholarship says about capitalism.[7] In their attempts to explain the tumultuous changes in global capitalism since the 1970s, many Marxist cultural theorists and social scientists have privileged the economic flows of capitalism as the main agent in the production of postmodernity. By calling attention to these theorists' representations of capitalism, I point out how decontextualized narratives of capital might detract from their larger political projects. I suggest that the theoretical congruence of such unlikely bedfellows is evidence that the very project of understanding global capitalism by the left relies on the continual upholding of an academic model that is as sure of capitalism's trajectory toward dominance as that promoted by global capitalists working toward the expansion of neoliberal markets (Gibson-Graham 1996: 118).

This congruence is striking even though what differentiates cultural studies and social scientific discourses of capitalism from that of Wall Street investment banks is that Wall Street clearly desires to promote global capitalism through the strategic utilization of its discourses of globalization. As marketing power-houses in their own right, Wall Street banks make no attempt to hide the celebration of their global reach and integration, their technological innovations, and the triumphs of late capitalism. In this context, to what extent do social critics, in their attempts to represent capitalism in all its terrible global glory, support those whose economic imperative is precisely to use proclamations of globalization for their own interests? If the very idea of "the global economy" and "inevitable globalization" is precisely the worldview that capitalist interests desire to construct, then it certainly would not appear to make sense for academics interested in counterhegemonic projects to paint the world using similar colors and tools.

Anthropology has been similarly entranced with the importance of the global. In a panel at the 1999 American Anthropological Association meetings entitled "Unraveling Global Capitalism," a group of anthropologists critiqued the pitfalls of anthropological representations of global capitalism as a deterritorialized, totalizing, homogenizing, economic force in contrast to local groundedness, imagined as "privileged sites of culture" (Rouse 1999: 44).[8] Thinking through the particular limitations and rationales of this social scientific romance with the global, anthropologist Anna Tsing explains that because the trajectory and framework of this global construct is often understood as freedom from traditional notions of cultures as bounded and isolated, anthropologists have "lost touch" with the "located specificity... [of] globalist dreams... [and] with the material and institutional components through which powerful and central sites are constructed, from which convincing claims about units and scales can be made" (2000a: 330). Anthropologists, in their effort to theorize interconnection, blur the "differences among places and perspectives" in search for a singular globalism, which in turn "renaturalizes global dreams instead of examining and locating them ethnographically" (2000a: 342).

Consider the following narrative from one of my informants Andrew Wong, an associate investment banker at Goldman Sachs, one of the most prestigious investment banks on Wall Street.[9] Wong, a mergers and acquisitions (M&A) banker who advises corporate CEOs on domestic and transnational mergers,[10] has a great deal of experience selling Goldman Sachs's "global prowess" to potential clients, usually Fortune 500 corporations.[11] In February 1999, I asked Wong about Wall Street's "global impact" and he painted a picture of the kind (and scope) of globalist dreams that many Wall Street actors engage in:

> **Karen Ho:** In light of the world financial crises occurring from Asia to Russia to Latin America, what is the global impact of U.S. investment banks?
>
> **Andrew Wong:** Oh, hugely. The name of the game is definitely globalization in terms of capital flows [and] competition.... What Wall Street really does is they play an important role in mediating the capital flows between borrowers and lenders, all lenders being people who buy stock and bonds. What Wall Street has been doing over the past 15 years is to make the whole world look like one big pool of capital and the whole world look like one big pool of people who need capital. Wall Street basically brings it all together; they sit in the middle between the pool of global capital and the pool of people who need financing. The other function that Wall Street does – you couldn't possibly have every single person who wants to lend money study every single thing about every single company... so, Wall Street... does all of the work to get people comfortable with the company. They not only intermediate the capital but also act as an information sieve. That is why people get paid so much and why they have to hire such smart people.... Basically, nothing gets done these days on a large-scale basis without Wall Street approving it. You can't build a plant in China. You can't build a highway in China. You can't build a highway in Brazil.... Without Wall Street's stamp of approval, nothing gets done now. Nothing, nothing over any decent size at all.
>
> **KH:** And that is because then they won't get the financing.
>
> **AW:** You can't finance it without Wall Street's blessing. Everything sold on the market is securitized. Like your mortgage, right? It is basically chopped up into little pieces and sold into the Wall Street markets. And [into] the global markets your credit card debt, your student loans. Even banks, when they lend out money to corporations, will sell it into the Wall Street markets, into the global. Everything is basically secured and traded over the markets, and Wall Street presides over all of that. By Wall Street, I mean the whole investment and financial community.... So, even though there is this huge

pool of global capital out there, a lot of it is controlled by a few people on Wall Street because you have given them control because you trust them. This whole Wall Street community basically controls access to capital. There is no government that is above Wall Street now. If the Wall Street community does not like the actions of a particular government, they basically lose their confidence and pull capital away and things cannot get done. Things get much more expensive ... much higher interest rates, which kill your building projects and stuff. The financial critic is very powerful now. And certainly everything that is happening in Asia was basically a complete loss of confidence by the financial community.

In Wong's global speak, he explains how Wall Street has helped to construct a world of buyers and sellers where "everything" – all money and debts – have been packaged and transformed for trading in the global market. In addition to being the creator of this global market of capital, Wall Street is the central arbiter and node through which any sizeable amount of capital must flow to gain approval, and through which all information about securities and companies must pass to be legitimated.

Coming back to anthropology, Wong's narrative contains the very three elements of the global that Tsing describes as seductive to social scientists:

Several features attract and engage an expanding audience for imagining the globe: first, its futurism, that is, its ability not only to name an era but to predict its progress; second, its conflations of varied projects through which the populist and the corporate, the scientific and the cultural, the excluded margins and the newly thriving centers, all seem wrapped up in the same energetic moment; and, third, its rhetoric of linkage and circulation as the overcoming of boundaries and restrictions, through which all this excitement appears positive for everyone involved. [Tsing 2000a: 332]

Wong frames a new future era markedly different from 15 years ago, a world in which globalization and Wall Street sit in the center. He conflates the fortunes of the highway in Brazil, the plant in China, the holders of student loans, and the buyers and sellers of stock. Using the "rhetoric of linkage and circulation," Wong states that disparate geographies and groups are connected through Wall Street, and that for anything of "decent size" to "get done," it must circulate through the global markets. Never before has the world been so "wrapped up in the same energetic moment" or so dependent on Wall Street.

The cultural production of knowledge about processes of globalization is not, of course, restricted to Wall Street financiers. Other discourses of globalization, from environmental movements to advertising agencies, also disseminate their own analytical frameworks of globalization. As such, ethnographic models of late capitalism must be able to identify and locate these intersecting "powerful images ... [that] operate across spatially discontinuous realms" (Martin 1997: 145) because they have critical implications. We need to be vigilant about the unforeseen conflations they may lead to in our ethnographic strategies. Given Wall Street's globalist wishes and given that anthropology is answering Laura Nader's call "to study up,"[12] ethnographies about such actors and developments must take care not to further their power – to conflate, exchange, or impose one decontextualized globalist vision for another. Cultural geographer Nigel Thrift illustrates this tendency in academic accounts of finance:

> There is an account of the modern international financial system which has become dominant, an account which is believed not only by many academic commentators but also by many of its practitioners. Amongst the main elements of this account...the international financial system pushed unimaginable sums of money around the world; the international financial system has become hegemonic over the nation state; the international financial system has achieved a "degree of autonomy from real production unprecedented in capitalism's history"...the international financial system relies on ever more rapid reaction times. [1996: 213–214]

Although Thrift acknowledges that these practices, "though often exaggerated, are founded in the actual situation," his concern is not so much their individual accuracy but, rather, how each of these elements are often represented en masse, "pieced together" and "woven into a story of an abstract and inhuman force, a financial leviathan that is increasingly impossible to withstand" (1996: 214). It is precisely the undifferentiated and conglomerated readings of multiple kinds of globalisms into a singular trajectory that has led to the construction of a dominant academic model of capitalism as overarching as Wall Street's wildest imaginations.

To revamp anthropology's global toolkit, I use in my ethnographic analysis of Wall Street's conception of globalization a narrative strategy that parallels my own ethnographic journey toward making sense of Wall Street's notion of the global. I deploy what anthropologist Dorinne Kondo describes as "the narrative convention of 'the setting'" that "evokes the experience of fieldwork by locating the author and the reader in a world that is initially strange, allowing the author to render that world comprehensible to the reader just as it became familiar to her in the process of doing research" (Kondo 1990: 7). This technique is compelling because it resists the imposition of "order and meaning...when you have left the field, in a sometimes violent attempt to recover meaning in the flux and chaos of everyday life" (Kondo 1990: 7).[13] Paying attention to the global as it was dialogically constructed during fieldwork allows me to reconstruct layers of meaning and contestation as they were grappled with, created, and made familiar. Given my own initial subscription to dominant, normalized accounts of financial capital's role in globalization, tracking my own understanding of the global as it unfolded during my ethnographic journey produced knowledge about the global that was less singular and unidimensional.

Rather than assume that global meanings are identical for all powerful subjects, I detail the specifics of what constitutes the multiple forms of the global for Wall Street together with the conditions of its production, legitimacy, and importance.[14] This article, then, is not only an attempt to portray ethnographically the analytical meaning and purpose of the global from Wall Street's points of view, but in doing so, it also seeks to intervene against powerful social scientific norms of thinking about globalization that presuppose or shape a particular interpretation. Exploring how

Wall Street discourses of the global economy are an important strategy through which capitalist power is expressed, consolidated, and perpetuated is also a political project. In a world in which global claims are integral to the normative process of conducting business in an investment bank, these pronouncements are not simply elaborate ruses or mystifying marketing tools that Wall Street bankers employ to further capitalist expansion; they become beliefs and demands that exert a disciplinary force on bankers themselves as a norm they must live up to.

However, I am also aware of the dangers of challenging how global capitalist discourses are constructed. Anthropologists Akhil Gupta and James Ferguson caution against the "temptation" to celebrate the "inventiveness of those 'consumers' of the culture industry (especially on the periphery)...as a way of dismissing...the 'totalizing' narrative of late capitalism...and thus of evading the powerful political issues associated with Western global hegemony" (Gupta and Ferguson 1992: 19). My strategy, however, is quite different. I do not attempt to dismiss or discursively dismantle capitalist neocolonialism by using scattered exceptions of resistance. Instead, it is precisely because of the very powerful work of global capitalism that I conduct this ethnography in the first place. This article seeks to frame another way of confronting capitalist global hegemony, not evade it.

Recruitment

What better point to begin my discussion of Wall Street investment banks' conceptions of the global than with their method of recruitment, orientation, and training of new employees. This is, after all, how I first entered the cultural world of investment banks as an ethnographer. As important sites of cultural transmission and construction, this process revealed to me how investment banks proclaim and describe themselves as global, thereby delineating their definition of what it means to be a successful subject in this age of global capital.

The recruiting and training of new "officers" to Wall Street investment banks is a continual process that consumes a great deal of time, energy, and resources. Imagine hours spent pouring over thousands of resumes; traveling to elite schools; giving presentations; engaging in multiple rounds of individual and group interviews; inundating potential hires with a barrage of cocktails, socials, presentations, speakers, and dinners. Such practices are repeated throughout the year for four major categories of hires: college internships, college graduates, summer MBA internships, and MBA graduates; each of which has its particular recruitment practices and schedules. Once they are hired, of course, a similar process is repeated during the initiation of new hires through orientation and training.[15]

As a graduate student contemplating research on Wall Street investment banks, I attended some of the recruitment presentations that Wall Street firms were conducting on Princeton University's campus in 1995. In late September or early October, these recruiters arrive with the intention of hiring hundreds of graduating seniors for the position of investment banking analysts.[16] Their presentations and receptions are well advertised, and all interested seniors are invited to attend dressed in casual business attire. On the day of their event, Goldman Sachs, Merrill Lynch, or Morgan Stanley, to name a few of the top companies, would send a group of 30–50 investment bankers to Princeton township's hallowed Nassau Inn.[17]

On one of the days that I attended, I was greeted by a sea of charcoal gray, navy, and black business suits worn by eight white men, five white women, one Latino man, one South Asian woman, and one African American man. Comparing myself with the well-coiffed undergraduates, I felt completely out of place. As the slide and video presentation began, I was told that this business is about "dealing with change." "The world is going to continue to change faster and faster, so we need people like you." When the presentation concluded, an older white man began to speak: "We are a Princeton family. I met my wife here. Princeton students make the best analysts, which is why we recruit heavily here." The other speakers introduced themselves by referring to the schools that they had attended: Harvard, Williams, Harvard, Princeton, Wharton, Princeton, Princeton, Princeton; then the South Asian woman said, "I'm from the University of Chicago; I'm not quite as bright as everyone else." The older man continued, "The two-year program will go by in a flash. Your learning and growth curve will be exponential. You will get actual interaction with clients. You are part of the team at our firm; the last thing you should be doing is photocopying. We hire ten people to do that, and that's all they do. We need your intelligence." Another speaker began, "So why should you work here? Because if you hang out with dumb people, you'll learn dumb things. In investment banking, the people are very smart; that's why they got the job; it's very fast, very challenging, and they'll teach as quickly as you can learn." The next speaker spoke up, "Our analysts can go anywhere in the world. We've got Hong Kong, we've got Sydney, we've got London.... You are all so smart." Such were my first observations of investment banks "in action."

In each of these events, I found consistent patterns in their recruitment strategies.[18] First, investment bankers begin by addressing "the Princeton family" to establish a connection with the audience and to delineate an elite selectivity – just as not everyone can be a student at Princeton, investment banking is not a profession in which all can participate. From there, bankers move on to talk about "smartness" to establish collective meritocracy as the organizational rationale for investment banking elitism. Third, the recruiters emphasize the global opportunities one garners through working at their investment bank. Globalization was invoked to imagine the world as a place where investment bankers could not only travel but also live and work. The global power of their potential employer and the opportunity for world travel were emphasized by the reciting of office branches in "key" cities around the world. This emphasis on proliferation of offices in multiple places as a strategy of spatial expansion not only legitimated investment banking know-how and global market access but also signified home spaces around the world for investment bankers-to-be.[19]

Their presentations were so compelling to me that to understand their global proclamations and promise of global prowess I decided to get a job on Wall Street. By actively participating in this intense recruiting process, I could find out more about how investment banks work as central operators in what seemed like a seamless global network of financial firms, capital, and practices. During my job interview, I was surprised at the active interest my interviewer expressed in anthropological paradigms of "global" circulation and "local" specificity for under-standing the transnational flow of people, capital, and ideas. Such a worldview seemed to mesh perfectly with Wall Street's desire to exploit global interconnections to create local–global economic "partnerships" as well as opportunities for trans-national corporations. I was surprised at the easy translation – not to mention the synergies and similarities – between our discursive strategies.

In June 1996, I was hired by Bankers Trust New York Corporation (also known as BT),[20] a "hybrid" investment and commercial bank,[21] as an "internal management consultant" analyst; who would be part of a group that acted as an "agent and advisor of change" for the different businesses within the bank.[22] Although I learned much from my time at BT, my fieldwork (and much of the ethnography for this article) took place after I left my job with them.[23] Because of the incredibly fast pace of change and volatility in investment banks, the internal management consulting group was eliminated in June 1997, and my entire group (including myself) was downsized. Two years later, the entire corporation was bought by the German monolith Deutsche Bank and was, as the lingo goes, "merged out of existence." As "expert" interpreters and disciplinarians of those corporations who do not follow Wall Street's stock market expectations, investment banks are themselves also sub-jected to these same judgments.

Orientation

In August 1996, after completing a two-month training program at BT where I and my cohort learned the basic tools of financial analysis, we were invited to an off-site gala orientation session. For three days, we stayed at a luxurious corporate park where we ate extravagant meals, participated in team-building exercises, and most importantly, learned about the future prowess of the firm (and our place in it) from senior managers who explicated their worldwide strategy. What a singular ethno-graphic opportunity, I thought. Orientation into an investment bank was quite different from the recruitment process. Recruitment seeks to position the bank in the most favorable light by constructing BT as the place where we all wanted to be; whereas orientation is more revealing of the firm's strategies, worldviews, and even foibles. At this orientation, our speakers included the heads of various divisions, such as BT headquarters in Asia and Latin America, the Private Bank, and M&A.

What struck me was that after two months of training in textbook finance, I barely comprehended anything they were talking about. What I managed to get out of these three days was the extent to which the global was referred to, most likely because it resonated with my anthropological norms and assumptions of what Wall Street would be like. In his opening remarks, the CEO boldly stated that investment banks, especially BT, do not simply operate on a "quasi-global" basis by having a single central location with plenty of satellites. Rather, they have multiple locations that are "really integrated." "It just flows," he stated proudly. Other senior manage-ment speakers spoke generally about the need to combine "global capabilities" with "local relationships," where the global referred to financial techniques, products, and resources from New York; and the local referred to geographic places, people, business customs, cultural misunderstandings, and branch offices in "developing markets." Such a premise that defines the global as mobile technique (eliding where the global is located) and the local as place bound (eliding the reach of the local) not only parallels social scientific conceptual problems but also empowers the global as a world-making force. As such, my experiences during orientation affirmed my beliefs and fears of Wall Street's globalist dreams. I frankly did not understand the nuances of how BT's New York City branch used and understood globalization nor how these differed from those of other branches, not to mention other investment banks. I left the orientation convinced of the seamless global prowess and expertise of investment banks without identifying or contextualizing what was meant by "the global" or how this conception was put into practice.

At every turn during my stay at BT, I came across references to the global, from CEO speeches to discussion panels about emerging market trends. Each time the global was emphasized, I often ignored its context and contingency to accumulate every mention of the global as evidence of investment banking's power. As I heard about the number of offices investment banks had worldwide, the mobility of its employees and monetary flows, and the number of corporate privatizations and merger deals from São Paolo to Shanghai, I worried about Wall Street's increasing power to make the world in its own image. I understood the global to mean the ability to penetrate the national markets of the world and discipline them according to Wall Street standards and make the globe conducive to financial capital and transnational corporations. Most of my coworkers shared my belief in Wall Street's globalness, but whereas I found globalization to be a negative sign of hegemony, my coworkers often took it as a badge of honor, a reason to emphasize their belonging to a particular firm. As employees, we were constantly told how global we were, and we believed it. We didn't just have offices, we had global offices; we did not just understand markets, we had global market access and the capability to exploit all markets.

Given the initial confusion of finding my way in fieldwork, the pressures of employment, and making contacts for future research, I hardly stopped to analyze the particularities of why being global held such an important place in investment banking imagination; why it was a criterion for prestige, for business, and for attracting employees. Instead of trying to figure out why the global so preoccupied BT (not to mention every investment bank I encountered), I took it at face value. My coworkers and I would unselfconsciously use the word global to describe BT in particular and investment banking in general, "The investment banking industry is truly global; Bankers Trust is a global investment bank." We would utter such phrases as a matter of fact.

Global Fissures: What's in a Name?

It was not until the "name-change" event that I first began to notice the fissures of globalization and its importance for contextualization. A few months after I began working at BT, they announced that it was changing all the names and acronyms for the different sectors of the bank. Most of BT's businesses were previously named with the word "global" as the first descriptor; for example, GIM stood for Global Investment Management and GIB stood for Global Investment Banking. But the debate at hand for senior management was that because the global should be an already understood characteristic, why did they have to mention it at every turn? Instead of naming GIM for Global Investment Management, they would simply call it IM because the "global" was (they hoped) implicit. Moreover, some of the more prestigious investment banks on Wall Street did not use the word "global" in their various business names. This change of names soon became the punchline of many jokes among my coworkers and myself. In our PowerPoint presentations, we would often insert footnotes stating "the global, of course, is understood," or we would continually put the word "global" in parentheses.

This name-changing event alerted me to the always incomplete process of global schemes and claims, the politics of global hierarchies, the uniformity of my approach to the global, and the extent to which BT insisted on and attempted to create its own globalness. I began to notice BT's insecurity as a "global investment bank." For example, the financial media annually ranks the top-tier firms (measured by such criteria as the number and size of deals completed in a variety of industries and stocks and bonds issued); those at the top are known on Wall Street as "the bulge bracket." BT, once a bulge-bracket firm in Sales and Trading, had recently plummeted in the ranks.[24] It is only in the context of this insecurity that BT's intense concern for global elitism made sense.

BT's faltering and precarious position among Wall Street investment banks began in 1994, when its name and reputation were derided on the covers of *Business Week*, *The Wall Street Journal*, and much of the financial media. "Who can trust Bankers Trust?" went the refrain (Holland et al. 1995). BT had been one of the most profitable banks in trading derivatives;[25] it was considered entrepreneurial and technically innovative in constructing and distributing these new financial instruments. At the height of its success in 1993, it was caught swindling Proctor and Gamble, one of its corporate clients. BT had sold them expensive financial instruments presumably to "reduce their risk exposure" to interest rate fluctuations, but in practice, these instruments had complex "hidden" caveats that allowed BT, not its clients, to benefit under most monetary conditions; in other words, it had "ripped them off." As a result, these corporations lost millions of dollars.[26]

BT was in the midst of staging a recovery from this major scandal when I arrived. They had just hired a new CEO, along with a slew of change-management consultants, and launched a campaign to reclaim its reputation and stock price. When I began to think about BT's approach to the global within the context of the campaign waged to restore BT to its former glory, I was better able to discern the differing versions and uses of the global. That investment banking globalisms were not everywhere the same was a revelation for me. BT's practice during orientation and its continual gesturing to the global now started to make more complex sense. Revisiting my observations of orientation, I realized that in addition to proclaiming BT as a "truly global" corporation, another main theme was "building relationships." At the time, I did not understand why the latter was so openly emphasized (nor what it had to do with BT's global imaginings) because I had assumed that relationships were interventions and ties that Wall Street depended on but avidly denied, as is typically the case with most representative free-market institutions. For example, BT senior management spoke endlessly about how "the hardest thing to earn is relationships," "money is about reputation and relationships," "money is 'client-driven,'" and "if you are good to your clients, money is never an issue." This relational emphasis on the link between people and money – especially in a context in which most investment banks simultaneously denied the social by assigning agency and responsibility to the market – speaks to the politics of acknowledging the network of relationships that enabled the accumulation of money. Prior to the scandal, BT stood out (even on Wall Street) in its assumption that its financial dealings were so abstract and so transaction-orientated, they could actually remove themselves from the complexities of forming relationships with their clients and other banks. Faced with declining profits and forced to realize that their finances were dependent on an array of institutional connections, they began to speak in terms of clients, rather than abstract market mechanisms. The scandal, then, precipitated BT's admission that social networks exist and, thus, can be understood as their effort to negotiate their fall from power.

Just as the emphasis on relationships signified BT's inability to continually claim that its success rested on abstract global capital flows, the ongoing projection of BT as a truly global company reveals the fragility of its global standing. Although these two practices seem at odds (one being a move away from claiming global, non-located market objectivity, the other a promulgation of globalness), when seen as interventions against a declining and scandal-ridden investment bank, they both turn out to be gasps for legitimacy. Initially, I had inadvertently tuned out BT's emphasis on relationships because of its incongruence with my previous assumptions of Wall Street's global strength and seamlessness. However, BT's very emphasis on global expansion exposed a level of desperation that allowed me to read BT's actions as a set of heterogeneous, even contradictory, strategies within investment banking power relations. Each bank, I realized, has multiple and particular approaches to the global.

In the next section, I explore the complex approaches and uses of the global that Wall Street investment banks share more generally. While I argue for the importance of context and history in ethnographies of the global, I also map out how the systemic collaborations between multiple investment banks create powerful and dominant approaches to globalization. To complicate the global, I combine both scales of analysis.

Global Markets or Marketing?

To explore how the global is achieved and used in everyday investment practice, I asked Edward Randolph, a vice president of Risk Management at Merrill Lynch, to explain why major corporations need "global" investment banks:[27]

> If you're going do a big privatization these days of, say, Australia Telecom, you need a big global investment bank to do that. Take Australia Telecom, which they just privatized, and Deutsche Telecom. I mean, these are five to ten billion dollar deals. There

aren't enough people in individual economies in Australia or Germany to buy all that stock. They're going to issue eight to ten billion dollars worth of shares; there aren't enough people in Australia to buy that. And so you need a global investment bank to kind of distribute [the shares] to different markets around the world, and so as a result, they [the investment banks] will come to the U.S. and say, hey, we've got all this paper, this debt or equity of Australia Telecom. [personal communication, March 1998]

The importance of maintaining and accessing a transnational network of investors to sell corporate stocks and bonds was further explained by Ken Hu, a vice president in Emerging Markets at J. P. Morgan who was involved in "raising" short-term capital by selling bonds for Latin American governments.[28] "Roadshows" are a staple investment banking activity through which banks market and sell their clients' stocks and bonds. As Hu explains, "a roadshow is when an investment bank goes out to all the key cities and sells a company's story so that investors will buy." To execute a deal, an investment bank has to "go on the road," flying from New York, Boston, Chicago, Houston, and Los Angeles to Frankfurt, Buenos Aires, and London to meet in upscale hotel ballrooms with hundreds of potential investors, such as large mutual and pension fund managers, to sell them sizeable pieces of the offering.

Investment banks are under pressure to create hype and gauge "investor appetite."[29] In this context, an investment bank's globalness is measured by its ability to summon the connections and resources necessary to maintain a large transnational network of investors who listen to their advice, believe their stories, and buy the products they sell. To win the deal from a corporate or governmental client or to convince a particular institution that their investment bank should be entrusted with the deal and reap the commissions, the bank needs to evoke a network global enough to successfully distribute the deal. The global, then, not only refers to a broad network of potential investors, but it is part of the "pitch," a strategic way of marketing themselves to win the business in the first place.

For example, what struck me during my March 1998 interview with Anthony Johnson, a college graduate who had only been working at J. P. Morgan for a few months, was how smoothly exaggerated "global talk" slid off his tongue. When I asked Johnson how "global" investment banks are and what impact this might have on the global economy, he replied:

Investment banks, the top investment banks, are in themselves, global. We do the same thing in Hong Kong that we do in the U.S. The hope is that you are able to supply global strategic advice, which means that we can talk to [our clients] about M&A in the U.S. We can talk to them about M&A in Sri Lanka. We can talk to them about M&A in Kuwait. And I think what you are trying to do is if a company feels like there is value in [being global], having a presence around the world, [then] you want to be in a position to advise them how to gain that presence around the world. And so, you essentially want to be able to seek out global opportunities for your client if your think that is the right way to go. [interview, Anthony Johnson, March 1998]

As Johnson explains, one of the goals and uses of the global in investment banks, in general, and in M&A departments, in particular, is to project advising capability in multiple markets around the world.[30] What is so striking about Johnson's explanation is that Sri Lanka and Kuwait are two places in the world where investment banks in the United States have not yet entered despite their global ambitions.[31] In Wall Street's view of the world, they are not "suitable" places for investment activity, and there exists little to no Western investment banking presence there. What was Johnson's purpose in raising Sri Lanka and Kuwait, given that both locations are usually invisible in the investment banking map of the world?

Investment banks must convince the potential corporate client by exaggerating that they are willing to search out the best opportunities for a company, regardless of place, and that they can anticipate what companies around the world their clients might want to acquire. Johnson's intent was to inspire confidence in the bank's capabilities, by speaking about how capable and knowledgeable it must be to keep up with today's mergers. His narrative use of faraway and unlikely places (places that are characterized by the absence of banks) is to emphasize how willing, adept, and mobile J. P. Morgan's M&A business can be. His articulation of the hope of seamless global investment banking is part of Wall Street's strategy for generating deals.

Later, I learned that "the pitch" is also a well-developed practice that is an integral part of the narrative rituals through which investment banks win business. Investment banks compete against each other for a deal by out-pitching and out-boasting one another. For example, weeks before the meeting with the potential client, investment banks have their managing directors and senior vice presidents construct the bank's "pitching strategy;" analysts and associates write "the pitch book" to be used for the dramatic presentation; vice presidents edit the book for carefully worded boastfulness, professional presentation, and dynamic color schemes; and finally print shops pull all-nighters for the finishing touches. Jason Kedd, an investment banking associate from Donaldson, Lufkin, and Jenrette, a small yet respected investment bank, declared, "Yah, we spend so much time on the pitch books, making them look good; they're full of bullshit. After we win the deal, we just toss 'em."

It is, of course, crucial to understand the larger context in which investment banking "pitches" and networks operate – that is, a late-capitalist economy that encourages spectacular financial accumulation as opposed to steady reproduction, rewards the divestment of labor in favor of financial schemes, and is driven by the production, marketing, and circulation of brands and images.[32] This "economy of appearances," primarily focused on attracting or constructing financial capital, depends on simultaneous "economic performance and dramatic performance" and the "self-conscious making of a spectacle [that] is a necessary aid to gathering investment funds" (Tsing 2000b: 118). In such an economy, Wall Street's ability to sell the global is integral to its winning of deals. Wall Street's global marketing skills enable it to execute short-term financial transactions and restructurings and to convince investors to bid up stocks. A bank's capabilities in this regard attract corporate clients who wish to enter into the upper echelons of global competition. However, in an economy so dependent on claims to the global, what constitutes hype and what constitutes actual goals become blurred. Moreover, the global strategies of investment banks – when seen in action – tend to be context specific, prone to change, and continually unstable.

Global Contradictions: Simultaneously
Here and Everywhere?

In investment banking, the meanings of the global would often waver between being spatially exclusive and being everywhere. In May 1999, I attended a recruitment event cosponsored by Goldman Sachs (also known as Goldman) and the SEO Career Program (Sponsors for Educational Opportunity), an organization geared toward placing undergraduates of color attending prestigious universities into investment banking, asset management, and management consulting. During this presentation held at Goldman's main headquarters in New York City, Goldman's CEO Henry Paulson wanted to impart three kernels of wisdom about the financial services industry and why Goldman excels in this milieu. Without much attention to notes or visuals, he spoke with conviction and comfort as if he had made this speech many times before. His first and overall point? Globalness! "It's about global-ness," he states. "Wal-Mart just signed a deal with Woolco, one of the largest department stores in Canada. We live in a global world; it's a fact, and it's getting more global by the second." His second point: "All the global players, all the leading firms [investment banks] are U.S. firms. We think of ourselves as a global firm." And his third point: "The pace of change in business is accelerating; this change is being led by technology and consolidation. Our deals keep on getting bigger and bigger."

He then began to detail why Goldman, because of its focus, its global-ness, its "culture of people," is the leader in this business environment. Most striking was that during the Q&A session afterward, an African American male college student raised his hand and asked, "What is Goldman Sachs planning to do in Africa? Is it investing in the growth of African economies?" Sitting in the back of the auditorium, I thought to myself, what a perfect question for identifying the potential limits of the global. Paulson answered in detail:

> We are not moving or strategizing about moving to other countries in Africa besides South Africa. Similarly, we don't need to be in Russia either. They can wait. We don't need to be in every emerging market. We need to be where the markets are big and real, where our clients are big financial institutions, major companies, wealthy individuals – meaning people with 5 million dollars or more. In South Africa, we were a pioneer, and we pulled out first [because of apartheid]. As soon as Mandela came out from jail, we were there. We worked with the ANC; we trained them. Worldwide, not just Africa, our strategy is paced growth. After the Wall came down, we didn't go to Eastern Europe or Germany. Now, we do more merger deals in Germany than Deutsche Bank [the largest bank in Germany]. We do China. I like India. We can't do it all at once. Once we get better deals, then we'll move on [in]. In Europe and the U.S., people know Goldman Sachs. In the emerging markets, no one knows Goldman Sachs. So, we have to show by performance. We do major things that help to credentialize us. We focus on some of the most important families in Asia. We helped to sell Star [a corporation] to [Rupert] Murdoch. We did the first major privatization in China: China Telecom. We did what the Chinese call "the one beautiful flower in the garden," and now we are credentialized. We want to bring U.S.-style integrity. We want to get a strong group of local nationals. So, we have to focus; we can't be everywhere at once.

The question about Africa forced Paulson to delineate what, in particular, the global meant to Goldman. Instead of reiterating that Goldman was everywhere, that it was an expert in all markets, Paulson was quite clear about not needing or wanting to enter multiple markets around the world. He implied that being global is not simply to penetrate all spaces at once but, rather, to maintain lines of access through which Goldman has the ability to be flexible – to move in and out, to pick and choose as it pleases. Paulson's comment, "We do China; I like India," suggests that if and when he wants to be in India, Goldman could simply "marshal the troops" and move in. The global, here, is not a totalizing strategy; Paulson depicts a situation of choice, flexibility, and focused movement.[33] This notion of globalization as "flexible capability" lies not only at the heart of Goldman's understanding and use of the global but also of many investment banks.

The verbal exchange in this discussion demonstrated that even those who unreservedly proclaim the globalness of their firm also have specific, tentative, and nationally based notions of what this global is. Why would investment banks claim to be everywhere, even in places where they were not, and yet, when pressed, be quite specific about what the global meant for their firm's strategy? Although this discussion helped me to understand the complexities of how the global is understood "on the ground," I was perplexed by how diverging notions of the global were reconciled, if at all. What was the social context that allowed the global to be expressed as both "we are everywhere" and "we focus only on places that produce capital return?"

Constituting Global Presence and Flexibility

In June 1999, I decided to ask Patty Lin, a college friend and one of my main informants, in hopes that she would help me make sense of conflicting global aspirations. "What does the global mean on Wall Street?" "How global is Wall Street, really?" A vice president who works in the Structured Finance Group at J. P. Morgan,[34] Patty began her response with a reply that I had become very accustomed to: many investment banks (especially the ones she respects such as J. P. Morgan) are extremely global in that they have full-scale operations and market access in many countries. She cautioned me, however, to make the distinction between "truly" global investment banks that have trading operations in a particular "foreign" locale, that is, a seat on the local stock exchange, and those banks that do not have fully staffed operations and, thus, can only use the New York Stock Exchange to trade foreign bonds.

Then, to my surprise, she suddenly remarked, "you need an office to call yourself global. I guess many banks can call themselves global even if they only have an empty office in that country." My jaw dropped. She continued to explain that although these empty offices are occasionally staffed, their resources are minimal, and their operations are cyclical, depending on the boom and busts of financial capital. "Some banks just can't get it right; they open, shut down, open, shut down.... They aren't very culturally adept." The more she explained, the more it sounded like all banks – not just "some banks" – were prone to opening and shutting down offices. All banks had the "empty office syndrome." Lin acknowledged that even "truly global" J. P. Morgan had recently laid off most of its Asia operation because of the Asian financial crisis.

Trying to grasp this new revelation – that of global investment banks and empty offices – I asked her, "Wait, so you can have an empty office and still be global? What does being global mean again?" Lin replied emphatically, "Global means as long as you have a presence; it could be an empty office." She reiterated that the crucial factor in being global was "having a presence" and that presence was marked and symbolized by the existence of an office. I revisited the times that I had heard investment banking assertions of "global presence and global capability" and just assumed that they were signs of banking dominance. I had not thought of these assertions as minimalist strategies that enable banks to claim global coverage and generate global confidence.

To further clarify Wall Street's notion of "global presence," I explored this aspect with other informants in a more pointed fashion. Raina Bennet, an analyst in the Emerging Markets Group at Lehman Brothers, explained, "It means having an office in lots of different locations; but at any given time, you might just have a telephone number, fax machine, maybe a receptionist." Sally Han, describing her small investment banking firm, mentioned, "Oh, we always say we're global because we have offices in the U.K. and in Australia, even though it's just two people over there." Although my informants were not advertising to potential recruits or corporate clients that their offices were empty, they were also not embarrassed by the fact.

I then began to reread annual reports to see what investment banks meant by the global in light of these new revelations. Two annual reports are striking in their use of the language of presence and capability:

> One obvious opportunity is in the still nascent markets outside the U.S., where we should be able to leverage the firm's global presence along with our considerable asset management expertise.... We are committed to meeting the global need for asset management services and thereby hope to capture a large share of the growing global market. [Morgan Stanley Dean Witter Discover 1997: 27]

In its 1995 annual report, Merrill Lynch stated that its strategy is one of global presence and local commitment:

> Global leadership requires sophisticated cross-border capabilities and strong presence in select local markets worldwide.... With global markets becoming ever more interdependent, cross-border transactions grow in both volume and importance. Global dominance will require strong cross-border competence and presence in select local markets. [Merrill Lynch 1995: 7–8]

These descriptions of global presence were couched in terms of future requirements or possibility. Instead of proclaiming to be anywhere in particular, they attempted to inspire confidence that they have the necessary potential to capture new business, cross borders, and become global leaders. Perhaps, then, the requirement of being "global" is not simply about how widespread a bank is, but rather, how they "leverage" their presence and capability.

To understand this concept of "leveraging presence," it is important to delineate the multiple meanings of presence, as this notion is central to Wall Street understandings and uses of the global. The word "presence" embodies a tension or separation between presence and absence, between one's physical and spiritual states, that is, one's presence is felt although one is not physically there, or although one is physically present, one is not fully there, in spirit. Presence and absence are simultaneously embodied. In *Webster's Encyclopedic Unabridged Dictionary, Revised*, the first two definitions define *presence* as "the state or fact of being present (being, existing, or occurring at this time or now) as with others or in a place." However, further definitions denote an ambiguity: "The ability to project a sense of ease, poise, or self-assurance, esp. the quality or manner of a person's bearing before an audience; personal appearance or bearing, esp. of a dignified or imposing kind; a divine or supernatural spirit felt to be present (1997: 1138).

Wall Street's approach toward the global can be ascertained in terms of these multiple notions of presence: the tension between presence and absence, between existing at a place, and being able to project such an impression of self-assurance that one is felt to be present at that place. In other words, one of the investment banks' main global strategies is to focus on a few pivotal markets and yet at the same time project the sense that they are and can be present in many other markets with flexibility. As such, they are focused yet capable of expanding, exclusive yet globally concerned.

To achieve this strategy, Wall Street investment banks have empty offices in many places throughout the world, and correspondingly, they focus their material infrastructure, people, and energies on even fewer places such as New York, London, and Tokyo. Such an approach allows investment banks to target their resources and be exclusionary in their sites of capital investment while the empty office secures an entry point, a slight foothold, and a particular global image. This flexible arrangement does not incur the cost of maintaining a fully staffed and operationalized infrastructure, especially if the bank does not have an active business in that location. Given the volatility of financial markets and institutions, the empty office is the kind of unfixed presence that facilitates mobility, even as it diverts from view the particularity and exclusivity of investment banking decisions. It is precisely the global boasting that complements (even masks) the existence of empty offices, for such strategies allow investment banks to create "the impression that something is present."[35] These proclamations of global reach serve as a mask for the spatial practices of Wall Street, as they obscure the partial, incomplete, high-pressured, and ephemeral work of how and what constitutes "global presence." We need to look critically at globalization as not simply a fact, but a hope, a strategy, and a triumphalist ideology. Such a call reminds anthropologists that hegemony is not only hard work but also boastful. It would be too facile, however, to read an empty office as simply a sign of weakness, as a puncture in Wall Street discourses of global seamlessness, as if to state that contrary to what Wall Street discourses say, in practice, they only have empty offices. An analysis that positions proclamations of "we are there" against their "actual" capabilities creates a misplaced antagonism between the two. Wall Street's constant insistence of total market coverage is part of the same project as its discourse and practice of empty offices: they are both strategies to construct flexible global presence. Only by emphasizing how many offices they have, how seamless their ability to respond to clients' needs from New York to Malaysia, can they can afford (literally and figura-tively) not to staff offices in Malaysia.

One of the main reasons why "flexible global presence" is an effective strategy is that it blurs the "presences" that are substantial and those that are superficial or absent. It is precisely by exploiting the elusiveness between the real and the fake that investment banks are able to sustain and attract more business. This ambiguity is a necessary requirement for their often far-fetched performances of globe-reaching capabilities and potentials.[36] As such, these investment banking projections of "the global" are not "neutral frame[s] for viewing the world" but are rather specific ways of constructing and imagining scales and movement to achieve particular goals and positions in a world of demanding financial flexibility (Tsing 2000b: 120). This flexibility comes at a great price even to the investment bankers who celebrate it. The premise that investment banks must immediately respond to the requirements of a new deal puts the burden directly on the shoulders of investment bankers because the very maintenance of "the empty office" attests to the lack of substantive support. To respond quickly and agilely to short-term volatile stock market expectations, investment banks must become "liquid corporations," in the sense that they con-stantly need to open and shut offices peopled by temporary staff, ultimately heeding only financial measures of success. As anthropologist Emily Martin has observed, the new concept of the worker and the corporation, otherwise known as "You, Inc," is one in which the corporation has relinquished responsibility as a long-term social organization (1999: 6). The investment banker, then, with laptop, cell phone, and internet connection, is the flexible, globe-trotting empty office branch, responsible for maintaining the global image of the investment bank and its flexible lines of access.[37]

Global Ambitions and Instabilities

Although the dominant approach to the global is one of asserting flexible presence and lines of access (especially aggressive when recovering their power from times of crisis), there are examples of divergences from this practice. In the late 1990s, during a bull-market period, Merrill Lynch (also known as Merrill) adopted a strategy of widespread global expansion that ultimately failed. By 2002, Merrill had either merged or sold off its global acquisitions and returned to Wall Street's standby strategy of mobile presence to stage a recovery. Adopting the business strategy that Wall Street firms, which historically have only catered to corporate clients, could expand into the "Main Streets" of America to capture the growing market of upper-middle-class individual investors, investment banks such as Merrill opened up, not empty offices, but "brick and mortar" brokerage shops on wealthy main streets across the United States.[38] Merrill, to differentiate itself from its competitors, drew attention to its brokerage services and its widespread global reach.[39] In 1998, Merrill acquired Yamaichi Securities and Midland Walwyn, the largest brokerage firms in Japan and Canada, respectively (Komansky 1998).[40] In Japan, Merrill opened up 33 branch offices "to tap into Japan's fabled $10 trillion-plus in household savings" and convince individual "savers" to become investors by purchasing Merrill's financial products (Bremner 2001; McMillan 2001). Merrill was soon to discover that the practice of investing household savings in stocks did not translate well to Japan.[41] In May 2001, after an initial startup cost of $200 million and "cumulative losses of at least twice that over three years," Merrill began to announce branch closings and job cuts in Japan (Bremner 2001). By the end of the following year, after only two branches out of 33 were left, Merrill announced a complete, "full-scale" retreat from the entire venture and merged its Japan operations with those of Hong Kong (Espig 2003: 9). Merrill's global ambitions had become a widely publicized global scale-back, with a change in CEO, the corresponding "ousting of 19 senior executives" and the "erasing [of] more than 23,000 jobs" – almost a third of all Merrill employees (Landon 2003b). The new CEO, Stan O'Neal, undertook a restructuring plan that reemphasized leverage, not extension, and "disciplined growth," "core strengths," "increasing efficiency," "operating flexibility," and global scale only "where it matters" (O'Neal 2002a, 2002b). This was in sharp contrast to the former CEO, who committed Merrill to a global empire building of "enormous scale and scope" to establish roots in multiple local markets and who soon became "the faded symbol of a global expansion strategy that resulted in the corporate bloat that O'Neal is working so hard to pare" (Landon 2003a; Smith 1998). This event demonstrates the flaws and implosions of Wall Street's seemingly foolproof strategy of global presence. Global proclamations are not simply calculating hegemonic tactics, but they can become actual goals with precarious outcomes.

In this article, I avoid examining the global simply from the "rearview" of what it has left in its wake, that is, as a set of received "effects" or in terms of "impact," in which the causes and motivations are taken for granted. I counter, then, academic tendencies to "believe the global hype" despite their commitment to understanding globalization as a set of constructed events. In this vein, I have demonstrated that Wall Street's global deployments are strategic and based on a variety of proclamations and performances. In the context of a political economy that demands constant change, being global is often more about marketing global capability and potential, not about being fixed in space and time. At the same time, the ideal state that is needed to be successful in conditions of late capitalism is constantly shifting. This was especially apparent at the height of the bull market when a few Wall Street firms were "caught up" in these global dreams. For Merrill Lynch, the global shifted to a vision of realizing itself as "truly" global that foundered on the material limitations of overexpansion and on emergent disruptions of the mythology of globalization as a seamless flow of finance capital. By directly engaging with the global as a specific cultural formation and unpacking the global ethnographically from its black box, particular global meanings and goals become tangible so that its purposes cannot simply be taken as a dominant norm or at face value.

NOTES

1   In my research, although I conceive of "Wall Street" as a cluster of multiply positioned actors who work in the financial services and securities industry, I focus on its central

institutions and actors, namely investment banks such as J. P. Morgan and Merrill Lynch and their bankers. It is important to make a distinction between Wall Street investment banks and corporate America, because although investment banks are corporations in an organizational sense, they also possess a supplementary role as voices of capital markets (i.e., stock and bond markets). Described by many of my informants as the oil that greases the wheels of capitalism, these banks are both financial advisors to most large corporations in the United States and experts on the stock market. Claiming to be the voice for millions of shareholders in the United States, they primarily work with corporations to increase their stock prices. As such, they are financial experts on the operations of both corporate America and the stock market. For example, Wall Street investment banks and institutional investors play a critical role in normalizing how corporations should act based on Wall Street's criteria for increasing shareholder value. By researching every corporation listed on the stock exchanges and developing contacts with key senior executives, they simultaneously evaluate their potency as well as mold their expectations. Wall Street, then, creates a bridge between the stock and bond markets and corporations. In the past two decades, Wall Street has increased its influence and spread the practice of shareholder value to the corporations and markets of many countries around the world. Thus, they occupy multiple roles and sites.

2   Most of my informants took for granted that Wall Street was a central site in the spreading of U.S.-style capitalism and freedom around the globe. Investment banks, they reason, help the world to create mature financial markets, which in turn will raise the quality of life and teach the values of democracy. As I demonstrate later on in this article, many academics also assume that Wall Street "masters of the universe" are making the world into their image.

3   This research is also situated within a burgeoning anthropology of finance; a diverse set of projects that examine the social impacts of global financial markets and institutions, and the internal dynamics and meanings of these markets for financial actors. This literature contributes to cultural critiques and translations of financial and economic theory and practices and serves as an important tool to understand postcolonialism, neoliberalism, and late capitalism. See, for example, Carrier and Miller 1998, Elyachar 2002, Maurer 1999, Miyazaki 2003, Zaloom 2003.

4   I also interviewed Wall Street traders, research analysts, emerging market experts, and management consultants.

5   The audience of corporate annual reports consists mainly of the shareholders; potential clients such as Fortune 500 companies, to whom these banks want to "pitch" their services; consulting and information service firms who use these reports to compile information and generate performance charts; the financial news media; and state regulatory agencies such as the SEC (Securities Exchange Commission).

6   Bauman also states that in this new global modern order, "some of us become fully and truly 'global'; some are fixed in their 'locality' – a predicament neither pleasurable nor endurable in the world in which the 'globals' set the tone and compose the rules of the life-game" (Bauman 1998: 2). This mapping of groups along the hierarchical distinction of local and global, place and space, conflate the global with spatial defiance and the local with place fixity and, in doing so, empower those who are located in the space-defying global. It comes as little surprise that in this schema, investment bankers are equated with "the globals," that is, "masters of the universe," as described by both themselves and academics.

7   It would seem, after reading these two juxtapositions, that Western financial capital has seamlessly penetrated the globe. The excerpts from investment banks, deliberately cursory, are not meant to explicate current Wall Street meanings and trajectories of global

capitalism or to de-emphasize the important contributions of Marxian cultural studies scholarship but, rather, to point out some pitfalls of academic strategies of representing the global.

8   This panel outlined some of the challenges of grappling with global capitalism:

> Capitalist dynamics have long played a major role in shaping ethnographic encounters and the ability to grasp these changing dynamics is crucial.... Yet both the celebratory and the critical emphases on globalization and global capitalism manifest assumptions that, too frequently, are accepted as unquestioned truths.... It is ironic that such totalizing images have rushed in to fill the space left empty by the critique of other totalizing narratives. [Rouse 1999: 44]

It is, however, important to mention that since the late 1990s, many anthropologists have begun to write critically about their own understandings and representations of capitalism and globalization. See, for example, Gregory 1998, Tsing 2000a, and Yanagisako 2002.

9   Throughout my research and this article, I use pseudonyms for all my subjects. I do not, however, disguise the identity of the investment banks, which are all public institutions. In instances in which an informant's identity would be compromised if I did mention the bank, I use the name of another comparable firm.

10 M&A is the combining and breaking up of corporations. This activity burgeoned with the corporate takeover movement of the 1980s. Such practice is evidence of the re-structuring of corporations in the late 20th century as financial assets to be bought and sold, not as long-term social institutions responsible to particular people or localities. Almost all Wall Street investment banks have M&A Departments to help corporations execute such transactions where they charge millions of dollars worth of commission fees.

11 On Wall Street, the clients of investment banks are corporations, Fortune 500 companies, and big institutional investors like Fidelity and Vanguard, rather than individual investors.

12 In a groundbreaking 1972 article, anthropologist Laura Nader, calling for anthropology to confront issues of power in the United States, urged her discipline to "study up," to interrogate "the colonizers rather than the colonized, the culture of power rather than the culture of the powerless, the culture of affluence rather than the culture of poverty" (Nader 1972: 289).

13 Kondo, however, does point out that narratives of setting and of journey are themselves highly constructed strategies that are often "(totalizing) stor[ies] of emerging order," of "epiphanal moments of understanding sparked by particular events" (Kondo 1990: 8). Even so, they allow a compromise between the evocative complexities of fieldwork experience and the assimilation toward the familiar that necessitates the imposition of conventional frameworks to simplify and order such complexities.

14 Nigel Thrift argues that because capitalism is "performative," a "practical order that is constantly in action," its meanings and practices are always context specific (Thrift 1997: 164).

15 Of course, not all potential recruits and new employees are treated with pomp and circumstance. Such fanfare is reserved for "officers" of the bank, the category of privileged employees who are hired from elite universities and business school programs and who work in their "front office." Front office refers to the departments of the bank that "directly" generate revenue such as corporate finance and M&A. Investment bankers, my main informants, are considered front-office workers as they draw in financial

business from corporate America. Correspondingly, employees who work in the "back office" – those sections of the bank that process payments, align ledgers, reconcile trades, field customer service inquiries, and so forth – are considered support staff for those who generate revenue and, thus, are not "officers" of the bank. Moreover, the administrative staff and human resources personnel across the bank, even those who work in front-office locations, are similarly categorized as support staff. These workers are poorly paid and not profiled in brochures, and they are not recruited with extravagant socials or invited to many company functions. Not surprisingly, front- and back-office workers are highly segregated by race, gender, class, and location. The majority of back-office workers are not located in "headquarters" but in less-expensive locations in Manhattan, Brooklyn, or across the river in Jersey City.

16   The analyst program is a two-year program for college graduates recruited from a few elite universities in the United States. Not surprisingly, the vast majority of hires are white, but because analysts are the lowest rung of the elite workers on Wall Street, women, depending on the firm, compose almost half of the entering class. Contrary to the mythologies of the new flat and flexible workplace, power relations in investment banks are still highly hierarchical and concentrated at the top. Many former analysts refer to the program as "two years in boot camp" because they are placed at the lowest rung in the front-office hierarchy. The primary job of the analyst is to gather and process a corporation's financial numbers for the purposes of attracting new corporate clients. As former Morgan Stanley analyst Kate Miller describes, "Analysts think they are going to work on Wall Street and be this hot shot investment banker. They are seduced by thinking they get to live the high life in Manhattan but, come on, they are the lowest on the totem pole, get totally exploited for two years, hate it, go to business school, and then come back in two more years to make a quarter of a million dollars." The next step up the investment banking hierarchy is the associate, usually an MBA graduate from one of the few elite MBA programs. In addition to sharing much of the "number-crunching" work of the analyst, associates are often the liaison between the analyst and the vice president. They supervise the analyst's work and work with the vice president to make the numbers "tell a story." Vice presidents are the links between the corporate client, the managing director, and the rest of the team of associates and analysts. They are in charge of supervising the deals on a regular basis. Finally, the rung above vice president is man-aging director. The managing director is usually the one who generates the deal, has personal contacts with the CEO and CFO of major companies and receives much of the credit (and compensation) for deals done.

17   For the most part, this group of Wall Street workers will include recent hires from Princeton so that current students have a chance to see how their classmates made the transition from undergraduate life to the Wall Street fast-track.

18   Starting around 7 a.m., the investment banks usually begin with a MS PowerPoint presentation typically followed by a panel discussion initiated by an older executive of the firm or a lead recruiter. This is followed by short presentations from recent college graduates about their work at the bank. By 8 p.m., current Princeton students are mingling with investment banking representatives over hors d'oeuvres. Afterward, some investment banks will host students at the Nassau Inn tap room or a local bar and grill.

19   These branch offices are both testing grounds for projects in different markets as well as sites for the introduction of New York banking worldviews and techniques. It is import-ant to underscore that although potential hires were asked during recruitment to imagine where in the world they wanted to be (with the assumption that their wish would be granted), it was also widely understood that only by being trained in "the center"

(in New York City), could one actually work in an overseas office without being dubbed provincial and impairing one's career mobility.

20   Bankers Trust is not a pseudonym, and it is in fact the name of the bank where I worked.

21   Investment banks mainly serve major corporations and "high-net-worth individuals," that is, individuals with 2–5 million dollars in assets. Commercial banks, on the other hand, are the banks with which most Americans are familiar.

22   Business divisions such as The Private Bank, Risk Management, and Investment Management hired us to do a variety of projects for them. We analyzed how much market share a group within the bank had in relation to their competitors, documented how the group could implement better "policies and procedures," and streamlined a group's "workflow" so that they could "run a tighter ship" Projects usually lasted a couple of months.

23   When I do write about my time at BT, I am careful to mainly reflect on my own experience in general, taking care not to describe in detail the thoughts and actions of my coworkers and friends who – although they knew of my research interests – were "on the job" and thought of me as employee first, friend second, and ethnographer third. As such, the experiences that I relate are based on my observations and journal writing and not on any information that was considered private or proprietary.

24   Sales and Trading is a major division of an investment bank that distributes securities and handles transactions for institutional investors for a commission or trades in various stocks and bonds for profit.

25   A derivative is a financial instrument or "security whose value is derived from the value of some other asset, called the underlying asset" (Marshall and Ellis 1995: 261).

26   Of course, scandals on Wall Street and in corporate America are commonplace. However, Bankers Trust's transgressions were particularly egregious in the eyes of both investment banks and Fortune 500 companies for the following reasons. First, as in the case of Enron, Wall Street investment banks and the executives of major corporations often act in concert to take advantage of "market opportunities" at the expense of other constituencies such as its employees, the public, or the state. In this case, Bankers Trust very obviously turned on its own client. Second, the victim was Proctor and Gamble, one of the most powerful corporations in the United States. And third, the transgressions were captured on tape.

27   Risk Management is the part of the investment bank that attempts to assuage the investment bank's technical, strategic, and monetary risk. For example, on the monetary front, they use technical models to measure how much exposure a bank has to an array of scenarios.

28   Financial economists assert that Wall Street investment banks provide a crucial function in capitalist economies in that they help corporations and governments raise much-needed capital via linking these institutions with investors. This claim is highly problematic in that for governments, most of the capital raised is short-term and dependent on austerity programs, and for corporations, much of the capital goes to large shareholders and is not necessarily reinvested into long-term corporate growth. Investment banks often "help" corporations "grow" through short-term financial deals and transactions not through steady, long-term production.

29   As advisors to corporations, Wall Street investment banks have convinced corporations that their primary responsibility is to maximize the returns on their shareholders' investments. By continually encouraging institutional investors to buy shares of corporations, investment banks compel corporations to focus on the demands of their shareholders and listen to the advice of Wall Street. Similarly, when investment banks sell the debt of "developing countries" to institutional investors, repaying that debt becomes the primary responsibility of governments.

30 It is important to point out that Johnson works in the investment bank's M&A division. As I have previously described, M&A groups facilitate the break-ups, takeovers, combinations, spin-offs (and lay-offs) of entire corporations and industry sectors. Because of multiple reasons (including pressure from large institutional shareholders to raise the stock price and investment banks themselves), corporations hire M&A groups to help them acquire other companies or sell themselves. Although most of these combinations occur within the United States, many times, an M&A group will recommend mergers across national boundaries, as happened, for example, in the merger between Daimler Benz (from Germany) and Chrysler (from the United States). In such a case, expertise or familiarity with German corporations and stock and bond markets as well as contacts with investors help a particular investment bank win a deal. In this case, Goldman Sachs, a self-proclaimed "global" investment bank, advised and executed the deal.

31 It is commonsense knowledge on Wall Street that investment banks mainly have offices and "do deals" in places that have "mature" financial markets and a sizeable number of corporations. Investment bankers tell me that in addition to the United States, these places are "Europe, Japan, Hong Kong, and a few other countries." Although a few local investment banks have opened up in Kuwait since 2000, none of the annual reports of the major Wall Street investment banks list any offices or deals done in Kuwait or Sri Lanka.

32 Journalist Naomi Klein writes that corporations today are "competing in a race toward weightlessness," in which "the very process of producing – running one's own factories, being responsible for tens of thousands of full-time, permanent employees" is a "clunky liability" (Klein 2000: 4). Exorbitant profits lie in global marketing via the proliferation of corporate brands, and corporations' expenditures for marketing and "brand management" are growing exponentially (Klein 2000: 483).

33 Dominant academic assumptions of the speed of globalization are put into perspective with Goldman Sachs's emphasis that market building takes time, focus, and local relationships. Paulson speaks about capitalism in national terms, as a reflection of national style and standards: "U.S.-style integrity" must be painstakingly built with "paced" and cautious growth and proven performance, not rapacious global capitalism. This passionate moralism implicit in neoliberal globalization is an important component of Wall Street's beliefs and motivations.

34 The Structured Finance Group of investment banks "engineer" a variety of financial instruments to sell financial solutions to clients or "exploit" financial opportunities.

35 This quotation is another definition of *presence* found on www.dictionary.com, accessed August 20, 2004.

36 Anna Tsing has similarly argued that in contexts and economies (such as the recent dot.com bubble or the Asian miracles) in which "finance capital is the ruling edge of accumulation," accumulation strategies rest on the difficulty of discerning "companies that have long-term production potential from those that are merely good at being on stage" (Tsing 2000b: 127). Those engaged in speculation and financial accumulation rely on the construction of hype to attract capital; the inability to distinguish "between the real and the fake" is a competitive requirement of these speculative practices.

37 There exist enormous human as well as corporate consequences of maintaining this particular kind of potential globalism. As Emily Martin observes,

> As the mechanical regularity avidly sought from the assembly line worker gives way to the ideal of a flexible and constantly changing worker, what will happen to the value previously placed on stability and conformity? . . . The individual [now] consists in *potentials to be realized and capacities to be fulfilled.* Since these *potentials and capacities* take their shape in relation to the requirements of a

continuously changing environment, their content – and even the terms in which they are understood – are also in constant change. The person is made up of a flexible collection of assets; a person is proprietor of his or her self as a portfolio. [1999: 5–6, emphasis added]

Interestingly enough, this notion of the person as potential and capability parallels Wall Street's overall approach to business. Just as the new worker is measured more for his or her potential and capacity to continuously change (rather than the content of the change), Wall Street rewards corporate America (as well as themselves) for its ability to respond to the call of increasing its stock price: to merge, cut, move, upsize, and downsize often regardless of content.

38 Whereas investment banks cater to corporations and large institutional investment funds, "discount brokerages" cater to the "retail market" (i.e., middle- and upper-middle-class individuals). Because discount or retail brokerage businesses are not only less prestigious but also have lower profit margins; the strategy is to amass large client bases, often using the Internet. Because of the incredible success of these brokerages such as E-trade, Ameritrade, and Charles Schwab in the late 1990s, Merrill attempted to enter this market globally.

39 Although Merrill Lynch's strategy of global expansion was the most explicitly articulated in its own representations and in the financial media, I would also argue that Morgan Stanley, to a lesser degree, was entranced by such an approach. For example, in 1997, Morgan Stanley, a "blue-blood" investment bank, merged with Dean Witter, a retail brokerage, in an attempt to broaden the scope of its services (although entering the market of the individual investor was at that time a greater priority than global saturation).

40 During this time, Merrill Lynch also "entered into acquisitions/joint ventures in Canada, the U.K., Spain, Italy, South Africa, Australia, India, Indonesia, Malaysia and Thailand" (Sievwright 1998).

41 Merrill Lynch attempted what its top executives called a "global/local strategy," in which they would not simply impose U.S. business models onto the Japanese and run the business from New York, but attempt to "instill our [global capitalist] value system and meld it with their [Japanese] culture" (Komansky 1998). Of course, the assumption that capitalist values are global and Japanese culture is local is just as problematic as the model that assumes total assimilation to American business models.

REFERENCES

Baudrillard, Jean
    1983   *Simulations*. New York: Semiotexte.
    1989   Panic C. In *Panic Encyclopedia: The Definitive Guide to the Postmodern Scene*. Arthur Kroker, Marilou Kroker, and David Cook, eds. Pp. 64–67. New York: St. Martin's Press.
Bauman, Zygmunt
    1998   *Globalization: The Human Consequences*. New York: Columbia University Press.
Bremner, Brian
    2001   How Merrill Lost Its Way in Japan. Electronic document, http://www. keepmedia.-com/jsp/article_detail_print.jsp, accessed June 30, 2004.

Carrier, James G., and Daniel Miller, eds.
  1998   *Virtualism: A New Political Economy*. Oxford: Berg.
Debord, Guy
  1983   *Society of the Spectacle*. Detroit: Black and Red.
Elyachar, Julia
  2002   Empowerment Money: The World Bank, NGOs, and the Value of Culture in Egypt. *Public Culture* 14(3): 493–513.
Espig, Peter
  2003   The Bull and the Bear Market: Merrill Lynch's Entry into the Japanese Retail Securities Industry. *Chazen Web Journal of International Business*: 1–11.
Gibson-Graham, J. K.
  1996   *The End of Capitalism (as We Knew It): A Feminist Critique of Political Economy*. Cambridge, MA: Blackwell Publishers.
Gregory, Steven
  1998   Globalization and the "Place" of Politics in Contemporary Theory: A Commentary. *City and Society*: 47–64.
Gupta, Akhil, and James Ferguson
  1992   Beyond "Culture": Space, Identity, and the Politics of Difference. *Cultural Anthropology* 7(1): 6–23.
Holland, Kelley, Linda Himelstein, and Zachary Schiller
  1995   The Bankers Trust Tapes. In *Business Week*. October 16: 106–111.
Jameson, Fredric
  1991   *Postmodernism, or, the Cultural Logic of Late Capitalism*. London: Verso.
Klein, Naomi
  2000   *No Logo*. New York: Picador.
Komansky, David
  1998   Interview by Lou Dobbs, Putting Down Global Roots. Electronic document, http://money.cnn.com/1998/07/02/companies/merrill_intv, accessed June 8, 2004.
Kondo, Dorinne
  1990   *Crafting Selves: Power, Gender, and Discourses of Identity in a Japanese Workplace*. Chicago: University or Chicago Press.
Landon, Thomas
  2003a   Merrill Lynch Starts to Look More Like a Bear. Electronic document, http://www.iht.com/articles/82291.html, accessed June 30, 2004.
  2003b   Dismantling a Wall Street Club. Electronic document, http://www.nytimes.com/2003/11/02/business/yourmoney/02stan.html, accessed June 30, 2004.
Marshall, John F., and M. E. Ellis
  1995   *Investment Banking and Brokerage*. Malden, MA: Blackwell Publishers.
Martin, Emily
  1997   Anthropology and the Cultural Study of Science: From Citadels to String Figures. In *Anthropological Locations: Boundaries and Grounds of a Field Science*. Akhil Gupta and James Ferguson, eds. Pp. 131–146. Berkeley: University of California Press.
  1999   Flexible Survivors. *Anthropology News* 40(6): 5–7.
Martin, Ron
  1994   Stateless Monies, Global Financial Integration and National Economic Autonomy: The End of Geography? In *Money, Power, and Space*. Nigel Thrift, Stuart Corbridge, and Ron Martin, eds. Pp. 253–278. London: Blackwell Publishers.
Maurer, Bill
  1999   Forget Locke? From Proprietor to Risk-Bearer in New Logics of Finance. *Public Culture* 11(2): 365–385.

McMillan, Alex Frew
  2001   Merrill Lynch Cuts Offices in Japan. Electronic document, http://www.cnn.com/
    2001/BUSINESS/asia/05/24/japan.merrill/index.html, accessed June 30, 2004.
Merrill Lynch
  1994   *Annual Report.* New York: Merrill Lynch and Company, Inc.
  1995   *Annual Report.* New York: Merrill Lynch and Company, Inc.
Miyazaki, Hirokazu
  2003   The Temporalities of the Market. *American Anthropologist* 105(2): 255–265.
Morgan Stanley Dean Witter Discover
  1997   *Annual Report.* New York: Morgan Stanley Dean Witter Discover and Company,
    Inc.
Nader, Laura
  1972   Up the Anthropologist – Perspectives Gained from Studying Up. In *Reinventing
    Anthropology.* D. Hymes, ed. Pp. 284–311. New York: Pantheon Books.
O'Neal, Stanley
  2002a   Investor Confidence and the Financial Services Industry. Electronic document, http://
    www.ml.com/about/exec_speeches_ml/090320021_investor_confidence_ec.htm, accessed
    June 8, 2004.
  2002b   Merrill Lynch's Platform for Growth. Electronic document, http://www.ml.com/
    about/exec_speeches_ml/01312002–1_stan_oneal_ec.htm, accessed June 8, 2004.
Rouse, Roger
  1999   *Unraveling Global Capitalism. American Anthropological Association Abstracts.*
    Chicago: American Anthropological Association.
Sievwright, John P.
  1998   Merrill Lynch's Strategy in Japan. Electronic document, http://www.ml.com/about/
    exec_speeches_ml/jps111898.htm, accessed June 8, 2004.
Smith, Winthrop
  1998   Expansion of Business into Global Markets. Electronic document, http://www.ml.
    com/about/exec_speeches_ml/ws110498.htm, accessed June 8, 2004.
Thrift, Nigel
  1996   *Spatial Formations.* London: Sage Publications.
  1997   Virtual Capitalism: The Globalisation of Reflexive Business Knowledge. In *Virtual-
    ism: A New Political Economy.* James G. Carrier, and Daniel Miller, eds. Pp. 161–186.
    Oxford: Berg.
Tsing, Anna
  2000a   The Global Situation. *Cultural Anthropology* 15(3): 327–360.
  2000b   Inside the Economy of Appearances. *Public Culture* 12(1): 115–144.
Webster's Encyclopedic Unabridged Dictionary
  1997   *Webster's Encyclopedic Unabridged Dictionary.* New Revised Edition. New York:
    Portland House.
Yanagisako, Sylvia
  2002   *Producing Culture and Capital: Family Firms in Italy.* Princeton: Princeton Univer-
    sity Press.
Zaloom, Caitlin
  2003   Ambiguous Numbers: Trading Technologies and Interpretation in Financial Mar-
    kets. *American Ethnologist* 30(2): 258–272.

Part II

Mobile Subjects

This part of the book is concerned with the movement of people, focusing primarily on the extensive post-World War II migrations from the countries of the periphery to the major urban centers of the "developed" and "developing" world. One of the basic arguments of these essays is that when migrants travel across national boundaries, they do not necessarily leave their homelands behind, but instead often forge cultural, political, and economic relations that link together their home and host societies. Ong, for example, explores how, through cyber-based technologies, oversees Chinese have constructed ethnic coalitions and forms of identification that cut across national spaces. A second argument of the essays is that, as the nation-state has come to operate less as a self-contained unit and more as a way-station through which an increasing number of people shuttle, it has become incredibly difficult for the technologies of nationhood to fashion culturally monolithic national communities; meaning that the nation spaces of the West have been turned into sites of incredible cultural heterogeneity. Ewing's piece, for instance, focuses on the tensions and contradictions arising from the attempt to "integrate" diasporic Turkish women into German society. And a third important argument in this part is that while the technological capacity to make people highly mobile generally exists, such mobility is actually rather stratified and subject to often strict state monitoring and control. Thus, Fassin shows how, over the last few decades, the attitude of French authorities towards refugees has changed from relative tolerance to almost total mistrust. Today, asylum seekers are generally deemed illegitimate and therefore highly unlikely to gain admittance into France, at least not legally.

SUGGESTIONS FOR FURTHER READING

Bernal, Victoria
  2004   Eritrea Goes Global: Reflections on Nationalism in a Transnational Era. *Cultural Anthropology* 19(1): 3–25.
Brodwin, Paul
  2003   Pentecostalism in Translation: Religion and the Production of Community in the Haitian Diaspora. *American Ethnologist* 30(1): 85–101.
Brown, Jacqueline Nassy
  1998   Black Liverpool, Black America, and the Gendering of Diasporic Space. *Cultural Anthropology* 13(3): 291–325.
Chavez, Leo R.
  2004   A Glass Half Empty: Latina Reproduction and Public Discourse. *Human Organization* 63(2): 173–88.
Constable, Nicole
  2003   A Transnational Perspective on Divorce and Marriage: Filipina Wives and Workers. *Identities: Global Studies in Culture and Power* 10(2): 163–80.
Coutin, Susan Bibler
  2005   Being En Route. *American Anthropologist* 107(2): 195–206.
Ebron, Paulla A.
  1999   Tourists as Pilgrims: Commercial Fashioning of Transatlantic Politics. *American Ethnologist* 26(4): 910–32.
Leichtman, Mara A.
  2005   The Legacy of Transnational Lives: Beyond the First Generation of Lebanese in Senegal. *Ethnic and Racial Studies* 28(4): 663–86.
Louie, Andrea
  2000   Re-territorializing Transnationalism: Chinese Americans and the Chinese Motherland. *American Ethnologist* 27(3): 645–69.
Norman, Karin
  2004   Equality and Exclusion: "Racism" in a Swedish Town. *Ethnos* 69(2): 204–28.
Peutz, Nathalie
  2006   Embarking on an Anthropology of Removal. *Current Anthropology* 47(2): 217–41.
Werbner, Pnina
  2004   The Predicament of Diaspora and Millennial Islam: Reflections on September 11, 2001. *Ethnicities* 4(4): 451–76.

7

Cyberpublics and Diaspora Politics among Transnational Chinese

Aihwa Ong

The Triggering Event

In August 1997 a financial firestorm swept through Southeast Asia, bringing chaos and suffering to millions in Suharto's Indonesia. Following the precipitous decline of the rupiah in late 1997, millions of Indonesian workers laid off from their jobs returned to poverty-stricken neighborhoods and villages. A picture of Suharto signing away his power, with the stern IMF chief standing over him, his arms crossed, had been a widely-publicized image of national humiliation.[1] A handful of army generals, indigenous business competitors and Muslim intellectuals deflected anger against the ruling elite by stirring racist nationalist feelings against ethnic Chinese. Indonesian Chinese were called 'new-style colonialists ... who plunder the people's wealth' and traitors who keep their wealth in US dollars and send their money overseas. Rumors flew about Chinese shopkeepers hoarding food, raising food prices, and Chinese 'traitors' fleeing the country with ill-gotten capital. Combined with the invisibility and unpredictability of market forces, such metaphors of evil turned fears into rage.

In May 1998 and the following weeks, ordinary people looted and burned Chinese stores and homes, while soldiers stood by, observing a destruction that mimicked the devastation visited on the lives of the poor. In the chaos of the destruction, soldiers disguised as hooligans were reported to have attacked dozens

From *Interventions* 5(1): 82–100. Copyright © 2003, Taylor & Francis Ltd.

of girls and women, many of whom were ethnic Chinese. Human rights activists claimed that the rapes were organized rampage by military men out of uniform. A related process of witch-hunting was set off by rumors about anonymous men in black called ninjas who killed Muslim leaders and dumped their mutilated bodies in mosques. In some neighborhoods, local vigilante groups hunted for ninjas who were killed on sight, their heads paraded on pikes. Such grisly attacks, and the demands by the masses for some kind of redistribution of 'Chinese' wealth in favor of the *pribumi* (indigenous) population, again made the scapegoat community stand for the ravages of the global markets.

It is important to note that, while ethnic and religious differences have long existed in Indonesia, under Suharto's New Order regime (1969–98) a few Chinese tycoons (*cukong*) enjoyed special political access which enabled them to amass huge fortunes and dominate sectors of the economy. The majority of ethnic Chinese (numbering some four million) are small business operators, professionals and working people who bear the brunt of a historical legacy of anti-Chinese sentiments and suffer from a legal status as racialized citizens.[2] The Suharto government, through inaction, had practically 'legalized' attacks on Chinese property and persons, allowing the army to manipulate events to displace anger against the Suharto regime onto the ethnic Chinese (Coppel 1999). The seeming global indifference sparked an international response among ethnic Chinese communities around the world, linked through the Internet.[3]

The Rise of a Huaren Cyberpublic

On 7 August 1998, and the days following, coordinated rallies protested the anti-Chinese violence in front of Indonesian embassies and consulates in the United States, Canada, Australia, and Asia. These rallies were held mainly in cities in the West – Atlanta, Boston, Calgary, Chicago, Dallas, Houston, Los Angeles, New York, San Francisco, Toronto, Vancouver, and Washington. In Asia, demonstrations took place only in Hong Kong, Manila, and Beijing. China issued a rare warning to Indonesia over redress for the victims of the riots and mass rapes.

The global protests were organized through a new website called Global Huaren ('Global Chinese People'), set up by a Malaysian Chinese emigrant in New Zealand called Joe Tan. Enraged by the seeming indifference of New Zealanders and the world to the anti-Chinese attacks, Tan linked up with ethnic Chinese engineers and professionals in Canada, Australia, and the United States, who saw parallels between the plight of Chinese in Indonesia and European Jews. They established the World Huaren Federation (WHF) in order 'to foster a stronger sense of identity among Chinese people everywhere, not to promote Chinese chauvinism but rather racial harmony' (Arnold 1998). Huaren chapters have been formed mainly in Southeast Asian cities, but they are beginning to appear in all continents, and the federation anticipates a membership of ten million in a few years.

This 'revolution' in Chinese political activism is attributed to the fact that 'at least four million of us around the world are computer users, computer geeks and techies', according to an American Chinese attorney, Edward Liu, who heads the

San Francisco chapter of Huaren. As reported on its website, this construction of a global Chinese public identifies race as the unifying feature. Tan maintains that the WHF is not intended to encourage Chinese chauvinism but 'to eradicate the intimidation which some governments are subjecting Chinese and other ethnic minorities to. We want to ensure that such atrocities will never happen again to anyone of any race and color.' He adds: 'Like any other race, the Chinese are expected to be responsible citizens in their country of birth or adoption.'[4] As a diaspora public set up by overseas Chinese professionals based in New Zealand, Australia, Canada, and the US, many of whom have no prior experience with or links to Indonesia, Global Huaren seeks to act as a kind of disembedded and placeless political watch-dog on behalf of the Chinese race.

Edward Liu, who spoke at a San Francisco rally, criticized President Habibie (President Suharto's successor) for being complicit in a *de facto* 'ethnic cleansing' of Chinese influence in the cultural, economic, and social fabric of Indonesia.[5] He thanked ethnic Indonesians such as Father Sandiawan Sumardi and other pribumi human rights advocates who risked their own safety and lives in support of the victims. He condemned the 'Chinese Indonesians' who were at one time cronies of Suharto but 'now have ingratiated themselves with Habibie in the same rotten system of corruption, cronyism and nepotism'. He went on to lecture the Indonesians:

> Chinese Indonesians have a right to be good Indonesians. They have a right to be Chinese culturally too. They have a right, as I do, as a Chinese American of Filipino background to be proud of my ties. I am proud to be a Chinese. I am also proud to be a Filipino. I am also proud to be a San Franciscan and an American.[6]

This speech demonstrates extreme insensitivity to the situation in Indonesia. Liu makes distinctions in racial terms, and seems to give primacy to Chineseness, when most ethnic Chinese prefer to refer to themselves as Indonesian Chinese, and not the reverse. Liu seems to essentialize the Chinese race and to conflate race with culture. He criticizes Habibie, who though politically weak had worked to improve the citizenship protections of ethnic minorities.

The diaspora politics protesting anti-Chinese activities around the world is cast in the language of moral redemption for the Huaren race, posing the need to balance racial protection against economic advantage. For instance, the World Huaren Federation was lauded by the *Straits Times* in Singapore which claimed:

> Previously, Chinese communities were more concerned with commercial and economic matters. The ethnic Chinese in Indonesia had been pummeled by rioting in the past decades – but they had always absorbed the punishment meekly to preserve their commercial interests. This time around, a landmark shift occurred with modern communications technology becoming the unifying force. (Soh 1998)

In on-line discussions on the Huaren website, the attacks on Indonesian Chinese have become a stimulus for a moral resurgence around the concept of a Chinese race. New American Chinese have logged on to confess their 'shame' for having failed 'to help Huaren refugee[s] in Vietnam and in Cambodia'. A subscriber urges his compatriots: 'Don't sell our pride and value for short-term personal and materialist gain. Wealth without pride and compassion is not success or achievement.' He bemoans the fact that wherever any Chinese was mentally or physically discriminated against, the majority of the 'so-called "successful" business Huaren' were nowhere to be seen.[7] A respondent notes that for the past two decades many Chinese emigrants were ashamed of China and Vietnam for being communist and poor countries, and their lack of sympathy to the Chinese boat people was influenced by the 'Western propaganda machine'. Now his own view has changed:

> How and when I realized that I was not just an internationalist (I was a parasite) but a human first and foremost, I can't pinpoint.... Being racial is not necessarily negative. Racial discrimination and persecution is obnoxious but it is necessary to contribute towards one's race. One is as whole as [what] one's ancestors [have] built in the past, and each man in the present must maintain and build for the descendants.... [The] Chinese must begin to let loose their embrace on self-gain.... the stronger must fend for the weaker, the more able to contribute more. This is something new to [us] Chinese and we must set the example.[8]

The Conflation of Diaspora and Transnationalism

This paper considers differentiations among migrant populations who share an ethnocultural or racial ancestry – a diverse assemblage of co-ethnics who have been conceptually reduced to homogeneous 'diasporic communities'. Popular books such as *Sons of the Yellow Emperor* or the *Encyclopedia of Chinese Overseas* seek to unite diverse flows of people in different parts of the world through their Chinese heritage and ancestral mainland origins (Pan 1990, 1999). In recent decades, as new flows of well-educated, middle-class Chinese from Asia have flocked to North America, there has been an intensification of Asian American interest in a search for cultural roots (see *Daedalus* 1991). The term 'diaspora' has suddenly begun to be invoked by activists and academics in order to claim an overarching framework for heterogeneous peoples who may be able to trace ancestral roots to China.[9] Conceptually speaking, 'diaspora' as widely used today refers not to permanent exile, but rather to the global imaginary invoked by transnational subjects located in metropolitan centers who wish to exercise a new form of power through the use of informational technology.

What is necessary, then, is to differentiate between the political use of the term 'diaspora' and the conceptual meaning of diaspora as exile. Many analytical perspectives however conflate diaspora as permanent exile with contemporary forms of fairly unrestricted mobility. The terms 'transnational migration' and 'diaspora' are often used in the same breath, confusing changes in population flows occasioned by globalizing market forces with earlier forms of permanent exile. While some migrations are involuntary or occasioned by war (hegira in Islamic countries), most cross-border flows today are induced and channeled by the ease of travel and the reorganization of labor markets within the global economy. For instance, the terms 'diasporic communities' and 'global ethnoscapes' have been used to refer to migrant communities that have an unprecedented effect on the politics of the homeland

(Appadurai 1995). But the term 'diasporic communities' seems to suggest that migrant populations who have the potential of belonging to the same ethnic group are internally homogeneous, have similar imaginaries, and seek to affect state politics in the same way. The effect of this is to essentialize migrants as particular kinds of ethnics, when our task is rather to sort out the different categories of people who can be described as, for example, ethnic Chinese traveling abroad, but who are often in different class, gender, and labor circuits, and who form discrepant alliances and pursue divergent politics.

The term 'transnationality' better describes the variety of cultural inter-connections and trans-border movements and networks which have intensified under conditions of late capitalism. Contemporary transnational flows may have overlapped with the paths of earlier migrants from the same country of departure who had left under involuntary conditions. When we think of Southeast Asians refugees in the United States, for instance, we might consider them part of a diaspora created by war and resettlement abroad. But a generation later, many of same refugees and their children are engaged in multiple home visits and cross-border exchanges. They are participating in contemporary movements of people back and forth, propelled by trade, labor markets, and tourism. Indeed, most original diaspora populations – initially occasioned by expulsion with no hope of return – now have the possibility of multiple returns and/or participation in global circuits formed by commerce. The ease of travel today means that few migrants are truly exiles, or experiencing diaspora in its original sense of a lack of hope of return to one's homeland. Diaspora sentiments may linger but it may be more analytically exact to use the term 'transnationalism' to describe the processes of disembedding from a set of localized relations in the homeland nation and re-embedding in new overlapping networks that cut across borders. It seems to me, therefore, that the old meaning of diaspora – of being scattered or in dispersion, with no hope of return – is too limiting an analytical concept to capture the multiplicity of vectors and agendas associated with the majority of contemporary border crossings.

As Zygmunt Bauman reminds us, there is a polarization between those free to move and those forced to move, e.g., between travelers and refugees, businessmen and migrant workers. This 'global hierarchy of mobility' is part of a worldwide and local redistribution of privileges and deprivations; a restratification of humanity (Bauman 1998: 70). The scholarship of overseas Chinese in Southeast Asia has been meticulous in analyzing this internal kind of fragmentation and cultural diversity within seemingly unified diaspora populations, but such works remain largely unfamiliar to contemporary diaspora studies.[10] More recently, *Ungrounded Empires* brought together interdisciplinary analyses of diverse ethnic Chinese flows and transnational subjectivity emerging within situations of 'flexible' capitalism in the Asia Pacific (Ong and Nonini 1997). This volume, among others, has influenced China historians to turn to the study of the Chinese diaspora (heretofore considered a residual phenomenon) and, as mentioned, has opened up Asian American Studies to a whole new field of investigation. One important work documenting unexpected circuits and cultural complexity is Adam McKeown's *Chinese Migrant Networks and Cultural Change: Peru, Chicago, Hawaii 1900–1936* (1999). Nevertheless, despite such studies of multiple trajectories and ambiguity in identity, there is still a dearth of scholarly attention focusing on these tensions between translation networks and local ethnic situations in particular locations. Clearly, one needs to differentiate between diaspora as a set of differentiated phenomena and diaspora as political rhetoric.

Thus, I would consider discourses of diaspora not as descriptions of already formed social entities, but rather as specific political practices projected on a global scale. Ironically, then, diaspora politics describe not an already existing social phenomenon, but rather a social category called into being by newly empowered transnational subjects. The contemporary transnationalization of ethnic groups has engendered a yearning for a new kind of global ethnic identification. The proliferation of discourses of diaspora is part of a political project which aims to weave together diverse populations who can be ethnicized as a single worldwide entity. In other words, diaspora becomes the framing device for contemporary forms of mass customization of global ethnic identities. Aided by electronic technology, the assembly of a variety of co-ethnic groups under an electronic umbrella thus disembeds ethnic formation from particular milieus of social life. Indeed, as the above Indonesian incidents and Global Huaren have shown, information technologies play a big role in engendering and channeling desires for a grand unifying project of global ethnicity that flies in the face of the diversity of peoples and experiences. As we shall see, 'Chinese' peoples from around the world are among the most diverse of the populations that have been lumped into a single category.

Contemporary Flows of Overseas Chinese

There are approximately fifty million people of Chinese ancestry living outside China, and they are dispersed in 135 countries. Analysts and activists have often referred to this linguistically and culturally heterogeneous population as a single diaspora community, even though it has been built up over centuries of countless flows – first of exiles, then of migrants – out of the Chinese mainland. Most of the flows from China stemmed from the late nineteenth century, when British incursions, the disruptions of agriculture and trade, and the resulting famines generated the great south Chinese exodus to Southeast Asia, North and South America. Previously, I have used the phrase 'modern Chinese transnationalism' to describe the re-emigration of overseas Chinese subjects who have settled in postcolonial Southeast Asian countries to North America and other continents.[11] The 1965 family unification law allowed the children of earlier waves of Chinese immigrants to join their parents in the United States. In the early 1980s, new waves of ethnic Chinese flocked into Canada, Australia and the United States. In some cases, these were students seeking higher education; in others, families seeking resettlement abroad before the 1998 return of Hong Kong to China rule. Economic affluence in Southeast Asian countries and in Taiwan also encouraged business migrants and professionals to pursue opportunities in the West. At the same time, events in China opened up opportunities for outmigration. These outflows from the mainland, Hong Kong and Taiwan have been diverse, in some cases more remarkable for their differences than for their similarities.

Since the late 1980s, most ethnic Chinese immigrants to North America have been from China (as opposed to ethnic Chinese from Taiwan and Hong Kong). China's opening to the global economy, the impending return of Hong Kong to China rule, and the Tiananmen Square crackdown were major causes for an outflow of students, business people, professionals and ordinary workers seeking political refuge or economic opportunities in the West. Plunging into the market is referred to as diving into the ocean (*xiahai*), and many ambitious Chinese link expanded business and professional activities with seeking opportunities abroad. Legally, 40,000 leave for the US, Canada, and Australia each year. Currently migrants from China are of a higher professional and economic status than earlier ones in the 1980s, and the perception is that the US embassy is raising the bar for skilled immigrants from China, creating fierce competition among Chinese urban elites to enter the United States by making business investments, using family connections, applying to college or contracting bogus marriages with American citizens. The other major category of mainland Chinese emigrants is that of illegal migrants, mainly from the southern province of Fujian, who seek entry into the United States and Canada. Many end up as exploited restaurant and sweatshop workers (Kwong 1997).

Thus the people with Chinese ancestry in North America include citizens from China and overseas Chinese from a dozen other countries in which their ancestors had settled. Such immigrants do not see themselves as a unity since they have different national origins, cultures, languages, and political and economic agendas. They do not necessarily associate with, or view themselves as having any continuity with, earlier waves of immigrants from the mainland. Indeed, the range of nationality, ethnicity, language, and class origins among Chinese immigrants is vast and unstable, splitting and recombining in new ways. For instance, in Vancouver, affluent Hong Kong emigrants are very insistent in setting themselves apart as 'high-quality people' from poor Chinese illegals smuggled in shipping containers (Ong 2003a). In the United States, even among the recent waves of immigrants from China and Taiwan, great distinctions in terms of class, dialect, and region are brought by the newcomers to the new country. Such divisions are only one example of how one cannot assume a unified diaspora community constituted by people who may be construed as belonging to the same ethnic grouping or hailing from the same homeland. There is great diversity among peoples who may be able to claim Chinese ancestry, and they may or may not use diaspora-like notions in shaping their public interests or political goals. I therefore suggest that, instead of talking about given identities, it may be more fruitful to attend to the variety of publics where specific interests intersect and are given particular formulations.

Translocal Publics among New Chinese Immigrants

Given its currency in the age of transnationalism and multiculturalism, 'diaspora' should not be considered as an objective category, but rather treated as an ethnographic term of self-description by different immigrant groups or publics. More and more, diaspora becomes an emotional and ideologically-loaded term that is invoked by disparate transnational groups as a way to construct broad ethnic coalitions that cut across national spaces. Previously, I have used the term 'translocal publics' to describe the new kinds of borderless ethnic identifications enabled by technologies and forums of opinion-making. These publics play a strategic role in shaping new ethnicizing and cultural discourses for audiences scattered around the world.[12] Here, I identify three kinds of milieus that have different potential in shaping transnational ethnic Chinese fields of political action.

Diaspora as an Extension of the Motherland

One can identify a 'Chinese' public that sees itself as an extension of the homeland and as sharing a continuity with earlier waves of Chinese patriots who possessed the conviction that the experience and status of Chinese abroad was a direct result of the status of China within the international system.

> If Chinese people were bullied locally, that was because China received no respect internationally. To be Chinese, anywhere in the world, was to be a representative of the motherland, to have a stake in the future of China, and to recognize the claims of China and Chinese culture over their loyalty. (Williams 1960: 128)

Today, Chinese who see themselves as an extension of territorial nationalism are primarily new migrants from the Chinese mainland whom the Chinese government calls *haiwai huaren* ('Chinese abroad'). They may be living and working in the United States, but their hearts and politics are tied to the interests of the Chinese nation (Tu 1991; Liu 1999). One can say that there is one transnational public that takes mainland China as its frame of reference, another transnational public which is an extension of Taiwanese nationalism, and also a Hong Kong network. These different publics may overlap at the margins, but their orientations are towards politics and social relations with the home country.

Translational Identities of Southeast Asian Immigrants

Southeast Asian immigrants with some kind of Chinese ancestry do not fall naturally under the category of *haiwai huaren* (or the older term of *huaqiao*), although in their re-migration to North America some conditions exist for re-Sinicization, as I discuss below. Ethnic Chinese whose departures from Southeast Asia have been historically shaped by earlier migrations out of China (since the early sixteenth century), European colonialism, postcolonial nationalist ideologies and globalization tend to stress their nationality rather than their ethnic status. Under colonialism, creolized and mixed-race communities – called Straits Chinese in Malaya, mestizos in the Philippines, and Peranakans in the Dutch East Indies – flourished. But in almost all of postcolonial Southeast Asia, a series of native, colonial and/or postcolonial government actions have integrated different kinds of Chinese immigrant communities as ethnic minorities (Malaysia), as an ethnically marked shop-keeping class (Thailand), or through policies of erasing the stigma of Chinese ethnicity which both encouraged and compelled these immigrants to pass into the dominant native community through intermarriage and the adoption of dominant languages and cultural practices (in degrees of severity: Vietnam, Cambodia, Myanmar, the Philippines, Thailand, and Indonesia). Thus people refer to themselves as Malaysian Chinese, not Chinese Malaysians. Among ethnic Chinese in Indonesia, the Philippines, or Thailand, the Chinese ancestry is often eclipsed or uninscribed by name, language, and cultural practices because of forcible state integration of these minorities. In countries where religion has not played a major role of assimilation, people with Chinese ancestry have become part of the ruling class. In all countries but Singapore, where a majority of the population is of Chinese ancestry, Chinese ethnicity is politically underplayed because of the state emphasis on majority rule. Thus such differences in group identity and relationships to nationalism make for extremely complex assemblages of ethnic, cultural, and national identity among overseas Chinese. After a few centuries of migration and settlement, Southeast Asian peoples who can trace Chinese ancestry think of their identities as produced out of a cultural syncretism which is associated with westernized middle-class attributes and cosmopolitanism, although there has been a revitalization of ethnic Chinese connections to China since the 1980s. But in Southeast Asian countries, any political suggestion of diaspora sentiments is avoided, for it implies disloyalty and lack of patriotism to the country of settlement.

When Southeast Asian Chinese subjects re-migrate to North America (and elsewhere in the West), they tend to identify themselves in terms of their home nationalities, and call themselves Thai, Cambodian, and Filipino American. Ethnic Chinese from these diasporas may be highly conscious of the fluidity of identity formation in the shifting field of modern geopolitics, and are more likely to resist the hegemonic discourses of political nationalism among those immigrant Chinese who closely identify with China and Taiwan. Because they are relatively small in number and have come from different Southeast Asian countries, overseas Chinese from Southeast Asia, and especially Indonesia, have not yet come together in a self-conscious production of an all-inclusive ethnicity.[13] Indeed, many of them would fit Stuart Hall's notion of translated identity, seeing themselves as the product of a rich confluence of traditions, histories, and cultures (Hall 1996). For instance, Southeast Asian immigrants participate simultaneously in various media publics – from homeland print cultures to Chinese kung fu movies – in sharp contrast to people from the Chinese mainland who rarely express interest in other Asian cultural spheres.

Ethnic Absolutism in the Cyber Age

For the disparate groups of immigrants who can claim Chinese ancestry, the whole issue of a broader, collective Chinese ethnicity emerges in multicultural America: should they identify more strongly with their new nationality, their old one, or with a potentially resurgent ethnicity driven by ambitious Asian Americans?

I argue that the translocal publics constituted by professionals on-line are now directly engaged in the production of global ethnicities. Specifically, economic globalization has scattered a new kind of transnational Chinese professional (managers, entrepreneurs, engineers, programmers) throughout the world. Over the past two decades, alongside Chinese business migrants, tens of thousands of ethnic Chinese professionals from Southeast Asia and China have moved abroad to global cities while maintaining family, economic, and professional links with their home countries. These expatriate Chinese professionals have formed middle-class Asian neighborhoods in cities such as Sydney, Vancouver, San Francisco, New York, Washington, London, and Paris, and are beginning to think of their Chinese identity in global terms. In North America, the concentration of ethnic Chinese professionals in particular cities (Sunnyvale), neighborhoods and high-level corporate occupations has produced conditions for a diversity of people who claim ethnic Chinese ancestry to become re-Sinicized through the universalizing forces of cyber-power, and through discourses of human rights and citizenship.

Asian immigrants – professionals, managers, entrepreneurs, and venture capitalists – are powerful members of the American corporate world.[14] In Silicon Valley, a majority of the foreign-born engineers are from Asia, mainly Taiwan and India. Besides their technical skills and wealth, these new immigrants 'have created a rich fabric of professional and associational activities that facilitate immigrant job search, information exchange, access to capital and managerial know-how, and the creation of shared ethnic resources' (Saxenian 1999). They maintain professional and business links with cities in Asia, fostering two-way flows of capital, skills, and information between California and Taipei. The very economic clout of such transnational Asian professional communities is, however, undercut by their invisibility in North American cultural and political life. They do not share the histories of earlier waves of immigration from Asia, but constitute a globalized yet politically amorphous collection of ethnicized professionals, incompletely disembedded from their original homelands but playing a dominant role in international commerce and industry. They exist in a social vacuum, and the imbalance between professional power and political-cultural weakness creates conditions that seem ripe for the emergence of what Stuart Hall calls 'ethnic absolutism'. What can they turn to that will allow a kind of re-territorializing – a way of tracking back to those far-flung and myriad ethnic Chinese communities in Asia – which can help 'restore coherence, "closure", and Tradition' in the face of political displacement, cultural diversity, and existentialist uncertainty (Hall 1996: 630)?

Cyber Huaren: The Vicarious Politics of Electronic Intervention

We can now return to the opening scenes of the paper: why do a group of high-tech ethnic Chinese from disparate places intervene in the 1998 anti-Chinese attacks in Indonesia? How has the Internet allowed for a simplification of identities, such as 'Chinese people in diaspora'? What are the positive and negative effects of rapid Internet interventions on the political sovereignties and the situated realities of peoples in distant lands?

The distinctive practices of international business – space-annihilating technologies, digitalized information, the flexible recombinations of different elements – provide a strategy for producing a unified ethnicity that is seemingly borderless.

The Internet, Saskia Sassen has noted, is a powerful electronic technology that 'is partly embedded in actual societal structures and power dynamics: its topography weaves in and out of non-electronic space' (Sassen 1999: 62). At the same time, the rise of digitalized publics means that people with limited access to the Internet are less powerful in affecting distant events than those connected to websites.[15] Privileged émigrés who control the electronic network to shape diaspora politics seek to subvert and bypass the sovereign power of nation-states, but are they able to control the effects of their rapid-fire interventions? What are the consequences when diaspora is invoked to assert an ethnic solidity and to deploy human rights discourses, thus framing particular conflicts and problems in terms of global racial identity? As we shall see, such rapid and remote electronic responses to localized conflicts can backfire against the very people, situated outside electronic space, that they were intended to help.

Following the international uproar over the anti-Chinese attacks, and appeals by various NGOs in Indonesia, President Habibie quickly tried to reassert state control and to revise legal discriminations against ethnic Chinese minorities. In early October, 1998, he announced a decree that would require all government bodies to provide equal treatment and service to all Indonesians. A new law also seeks to revise all policies and laws that are discriminatory 'in all forms, character and ranks based on ethnicity, religion, race, or family records' (Coppel 1999). The terms 'pribumi' and 'non- pribumi' were to be discontinued in all government offices and activities. This news was greeted by Huaren spokesman Edward Liu with an invective about official 'doublespeak' and an assertion that global Huarens should react with 'a great deal of skepticism and sarcasm'.

> If true, this is indeed a small stride in the right direction ... if this is merely a political placebo – empty rhetoric camouflaging a sinister, bad-faith ... public relations attempt to stem the flight of Chinese Indonesian human and capital ... and sanitize the bad image of Indonesia as a lawless, racist society – then we are afraid the downward spiraling of Indonesia will continue.[16]

Liu goes on to warn that in 'an increasingly globalized and digit[al]ized world, Indonesia can least afford to expunge and erase ten million of its most productive and resourceful citizens of Chinese descent. ... The eyes of the Global Huaren are fixed on Indonesia.' This language of the multinational diaspora subject is shunned by people who consider themselves fundamentally – culturally, socially, legally, and politically – Indonesian. By creating invidious essential difference between races, the diaspora discourse reinforces the alien status of Indonesian Chinese who for long have suffered under the dual citizenship policy of Suharto.

What happens when electronic messages from a cyber community are received in sites of political struggle on the ground? On the one hand, we can applaud the role of Global Huaren for its timely mobilization of protests around the world which has been effective in casting a strong spotlight on the Indonesian atrocities, compelling Habibie to take action protecting minorities. On the other hand, some of the tactics of Global Huaren have misfired and jeopardized efforts to rebuild trust between Indonesian Chinese and the pribumis after the crisis.

The Huaren website has carried repeated stories and pictures, including bogus ones, of ongoing rapes. For instance, in mid-1998 the Huaren website circulated a picture, later found to be false, that depicted an Asian-looking rape victim in a shower-stall. This stirred anger in Indonesia. Another Internet account reported that a woman claimed her rapists invoked the name of Islam. The story went on to note that since the era before the coming of Islam 'the act of raping women has been assumed to be the most effective way to conquer races'. Despite controversy surrounding the truth of this story and these claims, rumors were produced about a Serbian-style masterplan to drive the Chinese out of Indonesia through an ethnic-cleansing operation (Sim 1998).

Indeed, to Indonesian Chinese who fled the country and to many overseas Chinese in Southeast Asia, the attacks might have seemed like the result of a policy of ethnic cleansing.[17] But we have to be wary about making such strong charges, since, after all, a government-sponsored team traced the rapes of minority women to a special branch of the Indonesian army (Kopassus) headed by Suharto's son-in-law, then lieutenant-general Prabowo Subianto. In other words, the attacks on minority women were limited to a renegade faction of Suharto's army, and were not the result of official government policy.[18] There is no evidence that the Indonesian public had been engaged in a campaign to oust Indonesian Chinese. Overseas accusations of ethnic cleansing have been adamantly rejected by Indonesian leaders such as President Habibie and General Wiranto. Furthermore, Abdulrahman Wahid of Indonesia's largest Muslim organization, the 35 million strong Nahdlatul Ulama (NU), and another leader, Amien Rais, went on record to condemn whatever rapes had occurred, and to express their fear that such Internet-fueled rumors could sharpen racial and religious polarizations.[19] Furthermore, disagreements surrounded the reports of the actual number of rape cases.[20] The public, including many pribumi-operated NGOs, seem more likely to believe that the army was directly involved in all kinds of abuses, partly to displace the rage in the streets against the government onto Chinese and other minorities. While these questions will probably never be fully resolved, the Indonesian Chinese who have not fled the country reject the tendency of overseas Chinese to blame *all* of Indonesia for the violence, as well as their talk about ethnic cleansing. Attempts to consider Chinese people in the world as a diaspora race distinct from their citizenship in particular countries may jeopardize the post-crisis efforts of Indonesian Chinese to rebuild their society within the context of a broad-based coalition to fight for human rights within Indonesia.

Embedded Citizenship versus Cyber-based Race

The horrendous events of 1998 have convinced more Indonesian Chinese to participate in human rights activities that serve a variety of marginalized groups. Three national commissions – on human rights, women, and children – are building a coalition around issues of anti-militarism and citizenship based in international law. Feminist NGOs formed a national commission on Violence Against Women (VAW) in the aftermath of the army-instigated rapes of minority women in Java and throughout the archipelago.[21] The Urban Poor Consortium has been fighting for the rights of the unemployed and the homeless. The Commission for Missing Persons and Victims of Violence (Kontras) is urging support for an international tribunal to investigate reports of military collusion in the killing of East Timorese, despite the strong objections of the Indonesian state. Other groups include CARI (Committee Against Racism in Indonesia), which is combating racism and pressuring the Indonesian government to stop the systematic killing in parts of Indonesia (Aceh, Ambon, West Timor, and Irian).

In contrast to Global Huaren, Indonesian Chinese using the Internet to mobilize global support have stressed their sense of embedded citizenship in Indonesia. We can say that such counter- webs seek global support for Indonesians in general, and not exclusively for ethnic Chinese, as is the case with Global Huaren. There are multiple websites set up by Indonesian groups, and their messages focus on the suffering of a range of victims. A website called 'Indo-Chaos' operates in both Bahasa Indonesia and in English, and is directly connected with the United Front for Human Rights in Indonesia.[22] It commemorates the Indonesian Chinese victims of sexual violence, but also deplores the Indonesian army-instigated violence against other ethnic groups in Aceh and East Timor. An NGO called Volunteers for Humanitarian Causes notes that, altogether, 1,190 people were killed in Jakarta alone.[23] Yet another website set up by Indonesians stresses the status of the victims not as Chinese but as Indonesian citizens, and appeals for help in their campaign 'against human rights violations, injustice, and racism'.[24] A leader of CARI, the anti-racism group, noted that humanitarian interventions should be careful to avoid inadvertently inflaming the entire population:

> The responses of the Chinese communities in Australia and the West to the May Tragedy were obviously overwhelming and to large degree welcomed by the Chinese in Indonesia. It is always good to know that the International communities, including governments, defended the Indonesian Chinese rights and condemned Indonesian government for their failure to protect their citizens. The problem with these protests was associated with the way some of the demonstrators expressed their anger. Some of them used anti-Indonesia expressions and burnt Indonesian flags. Some even ridiculed Islam religion. Such attitudes...prompt reactions which further jeopardize the positions of the Indonesian Chinese in Indonesia. We need to urge the International communities to direct their protests to the Indonesian government and military forces, not the people in general. We should avoid actions which induce racial or religious conflicts at all costs.

This statement is not only an expression of the importance of a non-racial approach to humanitarian intervention; it is also a plea for the international community to recognize and respect the embedded citizenship of the majority of Indonesian Chinese who have chosen to remain. Indonesian Chinese have much work to do to re-imagine Indonesian citizenship by repairing their damaged image and reassessing their own relations with the government and with their fellow Indonesians. Besides forming a political party and many associations to fight racism and discrimination, they have lobbied the government to erase all forms of official discrimination. As mentioned above, the government recently banned all forms of discrimination on the basis of distinctions between pribumi and non-pribumi. Indonesian Chinese are now working to induce the government to re-categorize ethnic Chinese from the stigmatizing label 'Indonesian citizens of alien Chinese descent' (*warga negara asing/ keturunan Cina*) into the category of 'ethnic groups' (*suku bangsa*) which they would occupy alongside hundreds of other ethnic groups in the country.[25] Ethnic Chinese groups have reached out to pribumis in a process of 'native' empowerment through the construction of a people's economy (*perekonomian rakyat*). Some have given their support to an affirmative action program to channel economic and social resources towards the uplift of the indigenous majority. Thus what Indonesian Chinese do not need is to allow themselves to become part of an ethnicizing transnational public.

The Promise and the Risk of Cyberpublics

'We live in a world of "overlapping communities of fate"', David Held and others have said,

> where the trajectories of each and every country are more tightly intertwined than ever before.... In a world where [powerful states make decisions not just for their own people but for others as well, and] transnational actors and forces cut across the boundaries of national communities in diverse ways, the questions of who should be accountable to whom, and on what basis, do not easily resolve themselves. (Held *et al.* 1999: 81)

Translocal publics can indeed challenge the sovereignty of nations and can have humanitarian effects, bringing international opinion to bear on the mistreatment of a nation's citizens. International interventions, for instance, have stopped bloodletting in some conflicts (in East Timor, for example). Cyberpublics based on nation or religion, such as the Falun Gong movement that emerged in China, can constitute a community of fate that evades state oppression, exposes injustice, and turns a global gaze on a state's shameful behavior. Cyberpublics thus can put pressure on governments to be accountable to their own citizens, as well as to the global community.

But cyber communities of shared fate may also inspire in their members an unjustified sense that an electronic-based humanitarian intervention will invariably produce positive effects. The actions of Global Huaren have demonstrated both the promise and the risk of romantic appeals to autonomy and citizenship beyond the reach of the state, illustrating the potentially explosive danger of the vicarious politics of diaspora. A resurgent Chinese cyber-identity based on moral high ground may be welcomed in Beijing (though not always), but is not necessarily welcomed by ethnic Chinese minorities elsewhere. The cyber-based articulation of a disembedded global racial citizenship can create invidious essential differences between ethnic others and natives, thus deepening rather than reducing already existing political and social divisions within particular nations. The loyalty of local citizens becomes suspect when they are linked by race to global electronic patrons. Rapid-fire Internet interventions, unaccompanied by a sophisticated understanding of specific situations in different countries, may very well jeopardize localized struggles for national belonging and an embedded concept of citizenship.

As I have argued, transnational populations now have the technological means to express their desire for an inclusive global ethnicity that can claim representation for a multitude of others, both on and off website systems, bringing them under an electronic umbrella of diaspora. By proclaiming itself a cyber watchdog, Global Huaren poses the question of accountability in an even more problematic and elusive fashion. What are the stakes of a cyber-based racial community for diverse social groupings (with and without such global web-postings) around the world? Furthermore, Internet discourses of a racialized diaspora cannot make up for the sheer anonymity of the members, clients, and other participants who can log in randomly from anywhere at any time. Websites allow a 'false' amplification of the power of a few individuals who can proliferate at hurricane-speed, unsubstantiated claims about racial interest and fate. A video-game logic can create instantaneous simplifications of good global activists versus bad governments, racial oppressors versus victims, contributing to rumors that might fuel a chain of violent events. Thus an instantaneous citizenship which can be activated by a keystroke has notoriously uncontrollable effects, putting into play disparate information and actors, thus exponentially confusing and conflating the stakes of particular conflicts and struggles.

NOTES

1 The IMF imposed disciplinary conditions for loans, requiring the Indonesian state to cut subsidies for basic commodities such as flour and cooking oil. Millions of Indonesians driven to the edge of starvation turned their anger against the most visible target, ethnic Chinese shopkeepers.

2 For a brief historical view of anti-Chinese discriminations in Indonesia, see Skinner (1963). For a recent overview of the politics of Chinese economic domination, see Schwarz (1994).

3 At the 1998 Manila meeting of the Association of Southeast Asian Nations (ASEAN), Madeline Albright, the American Secretary of State, condemned the Burmese state for its mistreatment of opposition leader Aung San Suu Kyi, but she made no mention of the ongoing attacks on ethnic Chinese in Indonesia.

4 See <http://www.huaren.org> (downloaded 14 June 1999).

5 The teach-in organized by ICANET (Indonesian Chinese American Network), and sponsored by a San Francisco councilman Leland Yee – one of two American Chinese elected councilmen in America's largest enclave of American Chinese – was dramatized by the personal accounts of the Jakarta riots by three Indonesians of Chinese descent, who spoke anonymously, behind a screen, to protect them from potential retaliation by the dark forces within the Indonesian government. This event was reported on <http://www.huaren.org> (downloaded 14 June 1999).

6 See *San Francisco Chronicle* (1998). Reproduced on <http://www.huaren.org>

7 'JT': 'Our shame for failing to help Huaren refugee[s] in Vietnam and Cambodia in the past' <http://www.huaren.org> (downloaded 14 June 1999).

8 'Dennis': 'Re: Our shame for failing to help Huaren refugee[s] in Vietnam and Cambodia in the past' <http://www.huaren.org> (downloaded 14 June 1999).

9 On American campuses, ethnic studies, which originally framed the study of minorities within the American nation, began to be reoriented towards a study of 'diaspora' and of roots in the homelands of immigrants. This is in part a recognition of the transnational

connections sustained by new immigrant populations, but also a re-articulation of ethnic claims in a global space.

10   The literature is too extensive to be listed here. Skinner (1957) is just one classic study of the stratifications and cultural diversity within emigrant Chinese populations in Southeast Asia.

11   For this historically informed, multi-sited view, see Ong and Nonini (1997).

12   I explore three different kinds of Chinese-identified translocal publics, linked by international Chinese media audiences, networks of ethnic Chinese professionals, and business circles located mainly in Southeast Asia (Ong 1999: 139–84).

13   Policy-makers have stuck the label Southeast Asian American on all immigrants from mainland Southeast Asia. It has come to be an all-inclusive ethnic category for links to major institutions and for gaining access to resources. However, deep cultural, ethnic, and national differences persist among the variety of peoples from the region. See Ong (2003b).

14   For a discussion of various Asian populations in the Silicon Valley economy, see Ong (2004).

15   This observation borrows from the insights of Massey (1993).

16   <http://www.huaren.org> (downloaded 8 October 1998).

17   Tens of thousands of Indonesian Chinese fled to surrounding countries. Some decided to settle in Perth, Australia, but many stayed with relatives or in hotels in Malaysia, Singapore, Hong Kong, and Thailand. The wealthy ones have since settled abroad, while others have returned permanently to Indonesia, their homeland and source of livelihood.

18   Prabowo was also involved in the disappearance of twenty-four activists earlier in the year. See reports in the *Jakarta Post* (14 July 1998) and APS (21 December 1998).

19   In 1999, Wahid succeeded Habibie as President.

20   There is still disagreement as to whether there were eighty-five (verified) cases of rape during the riots, or 168, as many NGOs claim. Twenty of the rape victims subsequently died. See <http://members.xoom.com/>

21   For a UN fact-finding report on the May 1998 rapes of minority ethnic women in Java, Sumatra, and East Timor, see Coomaraswamy (1999).

22   <http://members.xoom.com/Xoom/perkosan/main_menu.html>

23   See <http://members.xoom.com> (downloaded 25 March 1999).

24   See <http://www.geocities.com/Soho/Atrium/5140> (email message from soc@indonesia, 10 August 1998).

25   Coppel (1999). The dual categories of citizenship – which treat ethnic Chinese (citizens of foreign descent) as categorically different from indigenous Indonesians – date from the Dutch colonial era.

REFERENCES

Appadurai, Arjun (1995) *Modernity at Large*, Minneapolis: University of Minnesota Press.

Arnold, Wayne (1998) 'Chinese Diaspora using Internet to aid plight of brethren abroad', *Wall Street Journal*, 23 July.

Bauman, Zygmunt (1998) *Globalization*, Stanford: Stanford University Press.

Coomaraswamy, Radhika (1999) 'The report of UN special rapporteur on violence against women', report presented at the 55th session on the UN High Commission on Human Rights, Geneva, 22 March–30 April.

Coppel, Charles (1999) 'Chinese Indonesians in crisis: 1960s and 1990s', paper presented at the 'Chinese Indonesians: The Way Ahead' workshop, ANU, Canberra, 14–16 February.

Daedalus (1991) Special issue: 'The Living Tree': 120(2).

Hall, Stuart (1996) 'The question of cultural identity', in Stuart Hall, David Held, Don Hubert and Kenneth Thompson (eds) *Modernity: An Introduction to Modern Societies*, Oxford: Blackwell, pp. 596–634.

Held, David, McGrew, Andrew, Goldblatt, David and Perraton, Jonathan (1999) *Global Transformations: Politics, Economics and Culture*, Stanford: Stanford University Press.

Kwong, Peter (1997) *Forbidden Workers: Illegal Chinese Immigrants and American Labor*, New York: The Free Press.

Liu, Lydia (1999) 'Beijing sojourners in New York: postsocialism and the question of ideology in global media culture', *positions* 7(3): 763–97.

Massey, Doreen (1993) 'Power-geometry and progressive sense of place', in Jon Bird, Barry Curtis, Tim Putman, George Robertson and Lisa Tickner (eds) *Mapping the Futures*, London: Routledge.

McKeown, Adam (1999) *Chinese Migrant Networks and Cultural Change: Peru, Chicago, Hawaii, 1900–1936*, Chicago: University of Chicago Press.

Ong, Aihwa (1999) *Flexible Citizenship: The Cultural Logics of Transnationality*, Durham: Duke University Press.

—— (2003a) 'Techno-migrants in the network economy', in Ulrich Beck, Natan Sznader and Rainer Winter (eds) *Global America? The Cultural Consequences of Globalization*, Liverpool: University of Liverpool Press, pp. 153–173.

—— (2003b) *Buddha is Hiding: Refugees, Citizenship, the New America*, Berkeley: University of California Press.

—— (2004) 'Latitudes of citizenship: membership, meaning and multiculturalism', in Alison Brysk and Gershon Shafir (eds) *People out of Place: Globalization, Human Rights, and the Citizenship Gap*, New York: Routledge.

Ong, Aihwa and Nonini, Donald (eds) (1997) *Ungrounded Empires: The Cultural Struggles of Modern Chinese Transnationalism*, New York: Routledge.

Pan, Lynn (1990) *Sons of the Yellow Emperor: A History of the Chinese Diaspora*, Boston: Little, Brown.

—— (ed.) (1999) *The Encyclopedia of the Chinese Overseas*, Harvard: Harvard University Press.

San Francisco Chronicle (1998) 'Large crowd attends teach-in on Indonesia crisis in SF', 1 August.

Sassen, Saskia (1999) 'Digital networks and power', in M. Featherstone and S. Lash (eds) *Spaces of Culture: City, Nation, World*, London: Sage, pp. 49–63.

Saxenian, AnnaLee (1999) *Silicon Valley's New Immigrant Entrepreneurs*, San Francisco: Public Policy Institute of California.

Schwarz, Adam (1994) *A Nation in Waiting: Indonesia in the 1990s*, Sydney: Allen & Unwin.

Sim, Susan (1998) 'What really happened?', *Straits Times*, 8 November.

Skinner, G. William (1957) *Chinese Society in Thailand*, Ithaca: Cornell University Press.

—— (1963) 'The Chinese minority', in Ruth McVey (ed.) *Indonesia*, New Haven: Human Relations Area Files, pp. 97–117.

Soh, Felix (1998) 'Tragedy and technology make overseas Chinese UNITE', *Straits Times*, 20 August.

Tu, Wei-ming (1991) 'Cultural China: the periphery as the center', *Daedalus* 120(2): 1–32.

Williams, Lea (1960) *Overseas Chinese Nationalism: The Genesis of the Pan-Chinese Movement in Indonesia, 1900–1916*, Cambridge: The Center for International Studies, Massachusetts Institute of Technology.

8

Between Cinema and Social Work: Diasporic Turkish Women and the (Dis)Pleasures of Hybridity

Katherine Pratt Ewing

The following story appeared in the German news magazine *Der Spiegel* as part of a cover article on the headscarf controversy in Germany:

> "The purity of the woman is the honor of the man," states a Turkish proverb. The family of the 18-year-old Turkish girl Aylin (pseudonym) was prepared to use all legal means to maintain this purity, although the girl was the third generation living in Germany: Until she was 14, she was only allowed to leave the house in the company of her brother or her mother, with the exception of school.
>
> Then she was raped by her uncle, but out of shame she kept silent about the incident. Her uncle became her tormenter and made her life a living hell. He repeatedly told her mother that he had seen her spending time with boys, and the mother believed him. She threatened her daughter that if she did not stop this disgraceful behavior, the mother would get "five men to rape you, and I will hold your hands myself."
>
> When the girl began an apprenticeship, the net of familial control grew tighter. Her wages went into an account that her mother controlled. The young woman had neither an EC card nor a passport when she turned sixteen. "That is normal – many Turkish girls do not get passports, so that they cannot run away," she said.

From *Cultural Anthropology* 21(2): 265–294. Copyright © American Anthropological Association.

One morning in March of this year, her mother confronted her. The uncle had decided that the girl was no longer allowed to go to work. The girl shouted, "I am cursed because you are my mother," and went to the police. For a month she has lived, disguised, somewhere in Germany. [Cziesche et al. 2003: 86 – 87][1]

Echoing a political discourse about the threat of growing immigrant minorities and failures of integration in Europe and the United States, there is in Germany today an increasingly vocal concern about the refusal of Turkish Muslims to integrate into German society and the emergence of a self-sufficient "parallel society" that has developed in the heart of German cities.[2] Within this parallel society, it is said, honor killings proliferate and traditionally oriented men prevent their wives and daughters from fully participating in German society.[3] Aylin and her uncle are presented in the above passage as a paradigmatic instance of this problem. For the most vocal activists and experts, who have easy and repeated access to the media, the solution is to save these women by offering them shelter when they escape from their families so that they can merge into German society and be free of the constraints of the parallel society.[4] In Aylin's case, the German state stepped in and provided her with a new home, a new identity, and even a new name, absorbing her into German society.

Scholarly, legal, and public debate surrounding cases such as this posits an antinomy between the universal human rights of the individual and the collective rights of a group to maintain distinctive cultural practices that may infringe on an individual's rights. The state is primed to see irreconcilable differences between the freedom of the individual and the customs of the minority community. Aylin's situation was depicted in these terms. The solution of hiding her away, which was carried out by the German police, is quite a drastic one, given the extensive fabric of social services in Germany. The fact that this was seen as the best recourse for a girl whose family had clearly broken the law and all standards of decency, including Islamic ones, indicates how much the force of conceptual polarizations has constrained public imagination to the extent that *Der Spiegel* can plausibly present this case as evidence of the role of the German state in protecting human rights against the evils of Islamic culture – as if it were conceivable that Muslims would defend the right of an uncle to rape his niece.

In this discursive environment, in which cultural difference is dichotomized and social activists have denounced multiculturalism as a policy that encourages the maintenance of a parallel society, a popular solution to the problem of integration has been a celebration of hybridity, an idea originally popularized in the United States and Britain. Although there have been numerous scholarly critiques of the concept of hybridity (e.g., Adelson 2003:131; Werbner and Modood 1997; Young 1995) as a sign and an identity marker, it has nevertheless become a part of popular culture and, along with the principle of multiculturalism, an ideological force in political discourse.[5] The concept of hybridity has been important for valorizing the identities of those who successfully occupy culturally "in-between" spaces, such as the Turkish girl who takes up boxing or the successful German-Turkish entrepreneur. However, the concept of hybridity is not a good model for analyzing how people caught between cultures actually negotiate identity, because it does not explain how individuals manage inconsistency through a variety of cultural and psychological strategies that generate multiple, contextualized identities (Ewing 2003). Nonetheless, it is not simply an analytic tool that can be challenged and discarded. The "hybrid" and the related model of a "hyphenated" identity have become cultural productions projected by the media, to be adopted or rejected by individuals alongside other possible identities.[6]

The paths that youth from immigrant families take are shaped by the political discourses, policies, and everyday practices in which they are positioned. Some life possibilities and identities are blocked while others are promoted. Popular culture, including cinema and the news media, plays a role in constituting the subjectivity of Turkish youth by generating naturalized images that shape identity and by delineating the realm of the possible and even the contours of resistance (Abu-Lughod 1993; Appadurai 1996; Butler 1989; Foucault 1978, 1995; Hall 1990).[7] I argue that cinematic images are particularly powerful when they are consistent with other forms of knowledge that are tied to governmentality: state policies, bureaucratic expertise, and social services, as well as the scholarly apparatus that often guides policy formation. As Aihwa Ong has demonstrated, the everyday techniques of government, including the provision of social services, converge to constitute "particular categories of citizen-subject" (Ong 2003: 6). Given that the German government has been a major source of funding for films in which diasporic Turkish characters and situations are portrayed, many of the concerns of social policy makers have been reflected in guidelines for subsidies to filmmakers (Elsaesser 1989).[8]

When all of these forms of knowledge production are consistent in their articulations of the "problem" of integration or the "plight" of the Turkish or Muslim woman, they draw their legitimacy from the scientist's "objective" view and operate as a discursive regime that actively constitutes and disciplines the subject as a key component of subject formation (Foucault 1978, 1995). Signs become mythic images that recur in a range of discursive contexts and are deployed to articulate, freeze, and naturalize difference, a mythological process (Barthes 1972b) in which the identities and personal attributes of those who are represented in the media are dichotomized and polarized.[9] This process occurs not only in the news media but also in the widely publicized writings of many experts, social activists, and those carrying out social policy such as social workers. Polarized images of the Muslim woman as victim are a product of this process. Within this discourse, the Muslim woman is readily cast as the embodiment of the "other" to the liberated Western woman. She is oppressed by her "culture" and in need of liberation by enlightened Western saviors (Ahmed 1992).

Focusing on representations of the cultural practices of Turks in Germany in social policy literature, the media, and cinema, I argue that an ideology based on the assumption of cultural difference and the celebration of hybridity as a strategy for the mediation of this difference actually makes the process of integration more difficult. Not only does it posit and constitute homogeneous collective identities that hamper recognition of the actual heterogeneity of those who fall within the category of this collective identity; it also exacerbates miscommunications between Germans and Turks and between generations within the immigrant community because of very different perspectives on what constitutes an acceptable mediation or hybrid. Furthermore, such an ideology reinforces the utter misrecognition of practicing Muslims who are involved in Islamic groups or who wear headscarves. I aim to disrupt the common scholarly, political, and media articulation of the need to choose between a policy of multiculturalism that rests on a reified notion of "culture" and a policy of humanistic individualism that universally (and ethnocentrically) claims for itself the values of freedom and equality. When either policy is embraced by a modern state, it usually marginalizes an ethnic and religious other.

To elaborate the effects of the trope of hybridity, I focus here on the play of oppositions and "hybrid" mediators in competing myths of the Turkish woman. From this perspective, political contestation and miscommunication can be understood to center on sharp differences over which figures actually mediate the superficially parallel dichotomies in German, Turkish, and Islamic discourses. German public discourse seeks to mediate or resolve the contradictions of the position of the woman of Turkish background (as these contradictions are understood through this discourse)[10] by generating forms of hybridity that directly challenge and even assault Turkish cultural identity, making the process of coexistence more difficult. What from a German perspective is an effective figure of mediation – often a hybrid – is likely to be perceived quite differently by a Turkish audience. Exacerbating these polarizations is the fact that many in the Turkish diasporic community, especially in the early years, talked about the differences between Germans and Turks in ways that echoed – often in inverted form – many of the dichotomies that are articulated in German discourse. This parallel structure makes it particularly difficult for migrants to resist the negative positions into which they are interpellated. At the risk of reifying this diasporic Turkish perspective, I will call it a "rural Turkish discourse." A third, Islamic discourse deliberately recasts and reorganizes this space of difference, offering quite a different, politically charged solution to the problem of integration. As an alternative to the cultural violence of the dominant German discourse, several Turkish Islamic groups in Germany promote a renewed and purified Islam and at the same time distance themselves from what they see as the corrupt traditional practices of village Muslims. The three competing discourses, by articulating oppositions and offering incompatible mediatory solutions, talk past each other, exacerbating tensions in the relationships among Germans and immigrants from Turkey.

I then turn to articulate the practical effects of a polarized discourse on young Muslim women. Among youth, such images can shape their life trajectories as they move into adulthood. Finally, I suggest an alternative perspective that focuses on the micropolitics of everyday life. Instead of using concepts such as hyphenated identities and hybridity as analytic tools, I suggest that scholars pay close attention to how and when such popular mythologies are actually deployed and by whom. We must consider the effects of such deployments in specific situations by examining how individuals are often classified and misrecognized, contrasting such misrecognitions with an account of how individuals, no matter where they are socially positioned, operate through multiple, contextualized identities in a wide range of social situations and manage an array of contradictions and inconsistencies in their lives.

The Turkish Minority in Germany

Immigrants of Turkish background constitute Germany's largest minority. Turkish guestworkers *(Gastarbeiter)* began to flow into Germany in the 1960s to meet the demand for low-cost labor during Germany's post – World War II economic boom years.[11] Most came directly from rural Anatolia rather than from cosmopolitan urban areas, exacerbating the cultural distance between these immigrants and an urban German population. They were meant to be a rotating work force and were given short-term contracts, housed in hostels apart from established neighborhoods, and given minimal social services. However, these arrangements proved inefficient for employers, who preferred to renew contracts, thereby creating a more long-term labor force (O'Brien 1996). When the economy faltered in the early 1970s, the German government response was a ban on further labor recruitment, but workers already in the country were allowed to remain and to bring their families into Germany. These pragmatic responses to changing conditions led to a gradual modification of policy, without any publicly conscious decision to open the country to immigration.

In the early years, these workers remained on the fringes of German society as temporary residents. At first, both Germans and the migrants themselves imagined that they would one day return home to Turkey, an imaginary that has been called the "myth of return." But by the 1980s it became clear to many of these families and to the German public that most of these Turks were in Germany to stay, and German public discourse began to frame the "problem" of their apparent lack of integration into German society. The adolescent girl who is expected to wear a headscarf, pulled out of school at a young age, kept close to home, and forced to marry a relative from Turkey became a powerful symbol of cultural difference and the failure of Turks to embrace assimilation.

The fall of the Berlin Wall in 1989 and the ensuing reunification of East and West Germany was followed by intense public debate around articulations of national identity and citizenship, including the place of Germany's largest minority in the future of a united Germany. These debates about citizenship were also accompanied by expressions of xenophobia and ethnic violence that targeted the Turkish population. Anti-immigrant sentiment was especially strong in the former eastern states of Germany, which underwent profound social and economic transformations during the reunification process. Turkish communities experienced considerable fear for their safety throughout Germany, but the political rhetoric calling for foreigner-free zones *(ausländerfreie Zonen)* and the rise of neo-Nazi groups sharpened public awareness of integration issues and generated intensified support among liberal Germans for the competing idea of Germany as a "multicultural" society. Citizenship laws that establish eligibility according to place of birth rather than according to descent have been slow in coming and restrictions on dual citizenship are still onerous. Increasing numbers of second-generation Turks have opted for German citizenship and are becoming more involved in the political process. However, many German citizens of Turkish background continue to be troubled by media and political representations of Turks, Muslims, and the problems of integration, a rhetoric that has been exacerbated by the post – September 11, 2001 fear of Muslims and the rising strength of nationalist and socially conservative politicians across Europe.

The Mythologies of German Social Work

In German public culture, the scenario of the adolescent girl who is tightly controlled by her "traditional Turkish" family until she finally rebels is one that has been replayed over and over in media accounts, in cinema and literature, and in social science scholarship. The vignette depicting Aylin's fate appeared in the fall of 2003 as part of a long cover story in *Der Spiegel* in the wake of a Constitutional Court decision in Germany concerning the headscarf. Although the article does not mention whether Aylin wore a headscarf, her story was presented as one piece of evidence among others that Muslim women are oppressed and that the headscarf is a symbol of oppression and Muslim "intolerance." The link made between the headscarf and the oppressiveness of the Turkish family is a powerful rhetorical strategy in the politically charged struggles currently going on in Germany – in many ways parallel to the recent well-publicized struggle in France – as conservatives and liberals alike seek to prevent women who wear headscarves from teaching in public schools.[12] In all of these discussions, which take the struggle for women's rights as one of the hallmarks of a liberal democracy, the "problem" has been cast as one of the oppression of women in a traditional patriarchal order that has spilled over into the Western countries where Muslim guestworkers have migrated.

A study describing the living conditions of Turkish women and girls written by social workers in Berlin (Baumgartner-Karabak and Landesberger 1978) played an important role in shaping this discourse. Regarded at the time as "groundbreaking" (Boos-Nünning 1990: 489), it was viewed as the standard German-language work on the situation of Turkish women and included recommendations on strategies for social work with Turkish women in Germany (Spohn 2002: 53).[13] The authors established their authority as experts on Turkish cultural practices by spending a month in a Turkish village. From their perspective, the father makes decisions concerning the affairs of his children autocratically, with little or no input from his wife. The children, especially daughters, have the status of objects, to be traded off in marriage at the highest price possible (Baumgartner-Karabak and Landesberger 1978: 55). The writers indicate that the position of a woman is unconditional subordination to her father and husband. Male authority is justified in terms of the man's honor and the principles of Islam, which handicap and oppress women.

The book was criticized by German scholars in the 1990s because of its one-sided and exaggerated depictions of Turkish gender relations (e.g., Lutz 1991; Spohn 1993, 2002). Despite the critical attention of scholars, this perspective has continued to pervade the perspective of many social workers and policy-oriented literature through the 1990s. For example, a Turkish scholar based at Bilkent University in Turkey who conducted stints of field research in Germany in the early 1990s wrote: "Girls have a special negative status within the family, as well as in the Islamic environment of Turkey or among relatives and friends in Germany"

(Onder 1996: 20). Moreover, "sons are almost invariably the favorite ones in their families. . . . The Islamic norm-value system determines what is good and what is bad. The new social environment turns all this upside down through another value-norm system. As time elapses, a great conflict grows that can in no way be managed" (Onder 1996: 21 – 22). The rhetorical structure of this statement is transparent: Turkish culture devalues girls and overvalues boys. This is in implicit contrast to the equal treatment of the sexes that is presumed to prevail in German society. Even the inverted relationship assumed to exist between Turkish to German culture is explicit: the Turkish "norm-value system" is, to quote, "upside down."[14]

This example is a particularly unsubtle manifestation of the discourse that pervades the conversation of German social workers, government services personnel, and school teachers whose job is to help Turkish children integrate into German society. Several teachers and social workers I spoke with during my research in Berlin between 1999 and 2004 echoed the stereotypes of this social service literature. Yet most saw themselves as politically liberal, critical of the highly publicized racist attacks on Turks, and concerned for the welfare of the Turkish population. Nonetheless, their perspectives on the situation of Turkish women and the problems of integration can be illustrated by a journal entry I wrote following a conversation in the summer of 2003 with a professional woman who worked in a federal office in Berlin and had considerable contact with people from Turkey: "Her opinions about Turks seemed quite fixed. She felt that a big problem with integration is that the women are uneducated and trapped at home and so can't help their children with their schoolwork. They don't try to learn German. Her depiction of Turks seemed like an image from the early seventies."

Not surprisingly, therefore, young Turkish women who have left their parents' homes are often represented in social work literature as heroic. For example, one study, *The Cost of Freedom: Ten Years in the Life of a Young Woman of Turkish Background*, subtitled *A Long-Term Study of the Difficult Process of Finding One's Way Out of a Turkish Family* (Kultus 1998), articulates the premise that "freedom" must be paid for through pain and struggle. It was written as a tribute to the 743 brave Turkish women who fled their families and sought refuge in PAPATYA (Kriseneinrichtung für Mädchen aus der Türkei [Crisis Center for Girls from Turkey]), a shelter for young women who wish to escape the abuse of their Turkish families. It also affirms the importance of public programs for facilitating the adjustment of Turks to German culture. The book does include a disclaimer that not all Turkish families are like the heroine who is the focus of the book: "Not all young women of Turkish heritage in Germany leave their families under circumstances of conflict. There are also those whose parents are tolerant and who seek to let their daughters grow up in the same manner as German youth. Tolerance generally ends, however, with a girl's friendship with a young man, and with pre-marital sex" (Kultus 1998: 148). Nonetheless, this passage implies a normative goal of the total assimilation of the Turkish young woman into German society, defined in the most liberal terms of total freedom of choice. This is, in effect, a demand for parents of Turkish background to abandon completely any effort to enforce Turkish or Islamic guidelines for the organization of gender relations and sexuality.

However, the provision of social services emphasizes the importance of recognizing cultural difference. Not only has there been government sponsorship of a youth culture that celebrates hybridized art forms (as discussed below), but both state and private welfare organizations have also produced ethnic and cultural differences where they otherwise would not have been salient: "The decisive factor... was the emphasis on religion – a marker migrants themselves would not have used. The combination of language and religion for professional and administrative purposes created 'cultures,' and subsequently 'ethnic groups,' whose special needs the welfare organizations had to meet through particular measures" (Radtke 1997: 252). This process gave rise to a complex administrative apparatus of counseling centers, support systems, and learning courses that reinforced cultural difference along the lines of language and religion. Migrants were no longer dealt with in their social roles as workers or family members or whether they were unemployed, homeless, pregnant, school failures, alcoholics, or drug addicts, but as bearers of a cultural identity and therefore representative of their national culture. Intervention strategies were applied to a generic group rather than to individuals. Until recently, for example, minority children were often segregated by language in school, whether or not they "needed" or wanted to be. This practice could find its justification in the radical cultural differences assumed in social work literature and practice.

Cinematic Interpellations of Turkish Women

Although there is a socially critical genre of film and literature focused on the oppressive working and living conditions of the male guestworker in Germany, especially in the early years of Turkish migration (e.g., Fassbinder 1973; Gförer 1986), the cinematic gaze shifted toward the end of the 1980s to cultural difference and the plight of Turkish wives and daughters who eventually followed these men to Germany.[15] The young woman who is deprived of her freedom and rights by her family was a central figure in the limited repertoire of images of Turkish immigrants constructed by filmmakers in the 1980s. As in the social policy literature, the dominant theme was a clash of cultures. In the Tevfik Başer film *40 Quadratmeter Deutschland* (1986),[16] a Turkish guestworker brings his new bride from his home village in Turkey to his small flat in urban Germany. The film is a relentless depiction of female confinement: the husband works at his job for long hours, while his new bride endures solitary days locked in a claustrophobic apartment and increasingly struggles against her culture and her husband. The film makes it clear that her husband's actions arise from the patriarchalism of rural Turkish culture, magnified by his fear of an alien and threatening German world. When he suddenly dies of a seizure, she cautiously waddles, very pregnant, into the daylight and freedom of the German world outside her door.

In the Hark Bohm film *Yasemin* (1988), a box office hit in Germany, Yasemin becomes the focus of the affections of a German boy Jan. Her father increasingly restricts her activities, pulling her out of school despite her academic promise and keeping her under constant surveillance. When he tries to send her back to Turkey, a place where she has never lived, she flees with Jan. The filmmaker based his depictions of Turkish life and customs on the diaries of two young girls he met while doing research for the film (Pflaum 2002). As one German review described the director of *Yasemin*: "Without taking sides, he deals with the seemingly irreconcilable differences between traditional, patriarchal Muslim values and those of contemporary German society" (Pflaum 2002), an analysis that unquestioningly reproduces the dichotomy. Although there is some acknowledgment of the German prejudices that make integration difficult, the emphasis is on the "freedom" that German culture offers to Turkish youth.[17]

Arguably, these images may depict the reality of a situation faced by many young Turkish women in the early phase of diasporic experience, a reality that some women such as Aylin continue to face a generation later. I have personally met and written about women whose experiences have closely paralleled Yasemin's situation (see Ewing 2002), which would seem to confirm the film's veracity. The genre of social realism encourages such a reading. However, what I find startling in retrospect is how closely the stories and choices of these young woman were, in fact, following the scripted narrative of *Yasemin* and other films of similar structure, for example, Horst and Lottman's (1987) *Aufbrüche* (Departures). This genre of film, its themes echoed by representations in other media and by the power/knowledge constellations of governmentality as manifested in social services, has a certain formative power to script the possibilities and choices of these young women. To use an old phrase of Clifford Geertz, such images operate as a model "for" as well as a model "of" reality in a process that naturalizes the film images (Geertz 1973).

The film emphasizes the gulf dividing the social spaces that Yasemin must cross as she passes back and forth between school and home, transforming her body by hitching up and lowering her skirt, removing and donning her village-style headscarf. Openness and freedom are contrasted with closed spaces and confinement; the value of the self who may freely choose a spouse is contrasted with the value of the group that arranges marriages within the group; education and career ambition contrast with the foreclosing of possibilities for women. One hardly need go on, the contrasts are so obvious and predictable.

The body itself is inscribed in particularly obvious ways in these films, with posture marking identity. In *40 Quadratmeter Deutschland*, the oppressed protagonist walks around with hunched shoulders and eyes cast down. Yasemin, in contrast, carries herself with an assertive, sometimes even defiant, posture and physically resists her male relatives. In *Aufbrüche*, the daughter defies her father's desire to marry her off by running away to live with German friends, but her Turkish identity is marked by the familiar hunched-over posture, even when she is hanging out with her German friends. Only at the very end of the film, when she is alone at work in her photography studio, does she stand up straight.

In German public discourse, the trope of hybridity operates as a mediator between the irreconcilable opposition of Turkish and Islamic traditional values with modern democratic values. A prime figure of mediation is the modern Turkish youth who manages to succeed in German society as a cultural hybrid. In articulating the problem of assimilation and how to accomplish it, a number of German institutions and discursive practices promote and support youth who feel themselves to be a part of German culture. This is evident in the social worker's depiction of Aylin's story

(Kultus 1998). In the opening scene of *Yasemin*, the title character is dressed in a karate outfit and is engaged in hand-to-hand combat with a German boy in an after-school coed karate class while under the watchful eye of her male cousin. For Germans, secular Turkish youth who are participants in cosmopolitan youth culture are the intermediaries between traditional Turks on the one hand and German society on the other hand – some are a sign of the success of integration, whereas those who drop out of school or get caught up in violence and crime are a sign of failure. The latter group reflects the failure of immigrants to appreciate the value of a good education and German efforts to facilitate integration.

Images of hybridity, hyphenation, and multiculturalism are therefore consciously used by "German-Turkish" culture-producers born in Germany. A popular Berlin radio program, for example, is called Multikulti. The Berliner female rapper Azize-A claims an identity in the following terms: "I attempt to erase the question 'are we Turkish or German,' and announce that we are *multi-kulti* and cosmopolitan. I want to show that we are no more sitting between the two chairs, we have got a 'third chair' between those two" (Kaya 2002: 40).[18] But, as Ayse Caglar has argued, although German Turkish rap is celebrated by rappers as the voice of the street against the power of the "center" (1998: 249, 251), German state-sponsored institutions such as youth clubs actively support and popularize such groups. She further points out that "a community worker tone and terminology all find their way into German-Turks' rap" (Caglar 1998: 252), addressing social problems such as racism, drug abuse, and violence and reinscribing existing categories and statuses rather than negotiating new scripts of identity.[19] This "social worker scenario" (Göktürk 2001: 133) also characterizes *Yasemin*, as in a scene in which Yasemin's teacher comes to her father's grocery store to try to persuade him to allow her to return to school.

In recent years, young German directors of Turkish background have produced a number of films, depicting the lives of second- and third-generation youth. Read by critics as resistant to the German discursive positioning of Turks, they have been celebrated as the "neo-neo" German cinema.[20] Deniz Göktürk traces a shift in these films from the social realism of a "cinema of duty" toward the "pleasures of hybridity" (Göktürk 2001: 131). Although voicing the perspectives and the raw choices that face many Turkish youth, many of these images (like those of other genres of popular culture such as hip-hop) also inadvertently reinscribe the dichotomies of the dominant discourse.

Cultural production in this domain has increasingly elaborated a fluid space of integration that is moving away from the dichotomies of earlier films into what Bhabha has called the "third space of enunciation" (Bhabha 1994a: 37). As filmmakers of Turkish background establish themselves in German cinema, cinematic depictions of youth of Turkish background are showing new flexibility, but they continue to be shaped by these founding dichotomies. Bhabha's (1994b) concept of mimicry is apt for characterizing the discursive space of this cultural production: almost German, but with a difference.

Even in the most celebrated of this neo-neo German cinema, the theme of the oppressed young woman remains powerful. Faith Akin's (2004) internationally acclaimed film *Gegen die Wand* (Against the wall), translated as *Head On* in

English, begins with this very theme: To escape from the constraints of her oppressive father, a young woman initiates a marriage of convenience with a culturally hybrid man whose life has descended into alcohol and despair. It is a thoughtful and powerful film that moves between German and Turkish worlds, exploring a hybrid "third space" by disrupting the myth of a woman's escape from family into a German "happily ever after," as well as disturbing the dichotomy between Germany as a cosmopolitan urban space and Turkey as a traditional rural space. Nevertheless, it takes off from the conventional starting point of a young woman's flight from her family, complete with a conventional authoritarian Turkish father.[21]

Even neo-neo films that present the most striking figures of hybridity do not escape a reification of Bhabha's "third space": they create a bounded category that is betwixt and between, in which the hybrid is caught and readily marginalized (Adelson 1990). Consider, for instance, Aysun Bademsoy's (1996) *Ein Mädchen im Ring* (Girl in the ring), a documentary chronicling the training and competition of a teenage German Turkish female boxer – a figure of mediation par excellence. Although this film celebrates the liberation of girls of Turkish background, it nonetheless contains a scene in which the girl's parents, although they support her boxing, indicate that they are planning to send her to Turkey for college and, hopefully, a husband. Their daughter's reaction – to stare silently off into the distance – demonstrates German identity with a difference. The "third space" that this young woman occupies as a boxer does little to resolve the tensions of her position. A Turkish female boxer may indeed be a hybrid figure, but she is a person who is not adequately represented by this figure.

Turkish Rural Discourse

The point of view of the dislocated guestworker who is responsible for the welfare of his family in Germany has had little public representation: this is the subaltern who can rarely speak, whose actions are interpreted through the multiple discursive filters of Orientalism, Turkish and German secularisms, feminism, and Islamic reform.[22] In what I am calling a "rural Turkish discourse," a set of dichotomies about Germany and Turkey can be identified that in many respects parallels the predominant German perspective. The same terms stand as opposites, but there is an inversion of their valence.[23]

The superficial congruence of the perspective of the German public and the first-generation Turkish guestworker community can be seen in the "myth of return," although the significance of this theme of migration and return may be very different in German and Turkish discourse. From the perspective of the Turkish villager, the stay in Germany was experienced as a kind of exile (*gurbet*) (Delaney 1990: 523). In one documentary by a filmmaker of Turkish background, Yüksel Yavuz's (1994) *Mein Vater der Gastarbeiter* (My father the guestworker), the camera cuts back and forth between bucolic farm scenes, nostalgically portrayed, and harsh shots of heavy industrial zones and elevated urban highways, a familiar contrasting trope in diasporic films (see Naficy 2001). The father portrayed in the film had never brought his family to Germany during the many years he had been a guestworker before rejoining his family in their village. When he revisits Germany in the 1990s and tries to gain access to the factory where he had worked in hopes of finding his son a job, he is coldly refused admittance and feels betrayed: "I gave them the best years of my life." In rural Turkish discourse, the safe Turkish village stands as the opposite of the threatening German metropolis. The practicing Muslim confronts a godless and inhumane secularist society.[24]

Although there are clear parallels in the structure of Turkish and German discourses, there are also key differences in what constitutes a satisfactory mediation of the gulf between Turkish village culture and German urban society. For some Turkish parents, the threats of German society are epitomized in the very youth culture that the German media and social work efforts for integrating foreigners promote – with its hybrid figures celebrating sexuality, homosexuality, exotic fashions, alcohol consumption, and the like. First-generation parents and community leaders may not be sensitive to what are key differences for German authorities between violence, drugs, and other illegal activities and the rebellious but safe forms of personal and artistic expression that are promoted by neighborhood associations. When parents in response clamp down on their children's activities for fear of losing them to the corruptions of German society, the result may be conflict and rebellion rather than communication.

For many Turks, the mediations that cushion this harsh, impersonal environment in which they are marginalized are transnational networks of kinship, friendship, and religious institutions. Many parents continue to arrange the marriages of their children with relatives back in Turkey. However, these are precisely the practices that are taken by the media as evidence that Turks are backward, traditional, and do not allow their children free choice in marriage.[25] From a German perspective – as well as a cosmopolitan Turkish perspective – the guestworker seeking to safeguard the honor of his family by protecting his women from corruption in an inhumane metropolis becomes the agent of suffocating oppression who is mired in backward tradition. In situations in which men become violent and abusive – as often happens in situations of intense stress, humiliation, and personal threat – this myth perpetuates the notion that violence is an inevitable manifestation of Turkish Islamic "culture."

An Islamic Solution

The polarization even of mediating spaces and figures, which can be seen in both the negative reactions of immigrant parents to the hybrid figures of pop culture and in the negative reactions of Germans to immigrant efforts at bridging the cultural gap, is one that members of Islamic groups have also recognized. Several moderate Islamic organizations have become established in Germany with the growth of the Turkish population. Most of these promote a discourse that recasts dichotomies of difference in terms allowing for an alternative resolution to conflicts that center on the adolescent German girl of Turkish background. This alternative structure disrupts the Orientalizing dichotomy to create a space for a new and more balanced form of integration. From this perspective, rural Turkish Islamic practices are considered to be a corruption of true Islam by Turkish habits, superstitions, and local culture, a position that most Germans and elite secularist Turks would also agree with. Islamists argue that in the village, people act out of group pressure and conformity and not out of any knowledge about how to form a true relationship with God. At the same time and analogously, these moderate Muslim groups reject many elements of Western consumption and popular culture, with its celebration of sexuality, violence, and the breakdown of morality and the family. This aspect of popular culture is, along with the village, viewed as yet another source of corruption, although of the opposite extreme.

Mediating between these two extremes are the principles of true Islam, which include a freely chosen obedience to God, human rights, gender equality, respect for the body and its health, concern for the environment and the poor, and productive activity in the world. Moderate Muslims assert that the principles of true Islam provide an alternative vision of modernity and are consistent with the principles underlying most of Western law and democracy. These groups, therefore, disrupt the German dichotomy that lines up modernity, secularism, cosmopolitanism, gender equality, and individual rights on one side and, on the other side, tradition, Islam, rural conservatism, patriarchy, and group conformity. Islamic organizations thereby provide a position from which German youth of Turkish background can resist the identity scripts that surround them in German media, schools, and other institutions.

My ethnographic research among Muslims in Germany has focused on the Islamische Gemeinschaft Milli Görüs (IGMG), the largest Turkish Islamic organization in Germany, originally founded in 1976. In practical terms, IGMG claims one of its major goals to be the improvement of relationships between immigrant parents and their children, and it provides social services from which girls can seek help without creating a total rupture with the family. To accomplish this goal, they discourage marriages with relatives still in Turkey, because they feel that this increases the likelihood of problems in the marriage. They educate girls about their rights, including how to interpret the Qur'an as a defense against the father's authority to decide their future. And they also provide a support structure outside the family that helps to avoid positioning these girls as a threatening "modern" or "Western" other to their parents.

A young woman I talked with in Berlin described how she had learned from her teachers at the mosque to resist some of her father's demands:

> My father wants me to marry a boy in Turkey (not a relative), but I don't want him, and my mother doesn't want him. . . . I want someone who practices Islam and prays. Also, my father talked with him and made the decision but didn't ask me beforehand. Then when he asked me, I told him I didn't want him. I want to talk to the boy before making a decision. My father also said that the boy looked very good, but I don't think that this is a good reason. I think this boy wants to marry me because I live in Germany.
>
> My father is a person who makes a decision, and no one can change what he thinks. My father makes problems at home. This thing that my father insisted on made me psychologically ill – I couldn't listen to it anymore. I didn't want to accept my father's wish that I marry that boy. But I heard from the life of the Prophet how someone should marry and who decides. For example, the Prophet talked to his daughter, and the

Prophet was emotional, in tears. He said, "I want you to marry Ali, but you must make the decision; I cannot." This is an example, so you can see that the father cannot make the decision. . . . He didn't change his thinking, but he saw that he couldn't succeed. He cannot do more.

Five young women I met with as participants in a young women's group associated with the Mevlana Mosque in Berlin discussed how their religious education was making them more aware of their rights in Islamic law. One had recently married and said that she had known to sign a contract before marriage giving her the right to divorce and the right to alimony. They discussed how important it is to separate out Turkish custom from Islamic law or principles. One of the women also distinguished between Islamic principles and specific laws meant for particular historical situations and argued that much of German law is consistent with Islamic principles. This is a point that I also heard made by leaders of IGMG. A key example of this is the Qur'anic verse (2: 282), which states that two women must serve in the place of one man as a witness and is interpreted by many to mean that the testimony of a woman is worth only half that of a man. One of the women, echoing a point that I had also heard from an IGMG leader, explained that this particular passage referred to a business situation in which women were not typically expert at the time when the verse was originally written, and they were thus more likely to become uncertain or confused. However, in a context in which women are equally educated and employed, this principle would not apply.

These women characterize themselves as "conscious" Muslims who actively contest the use of the headscarf in political discourse and public media as a sign of the oppression of Muslim women. They cover their heads as an act of personal choice, drawing a contrast with women who wear a headscarf as a "habit" (Turkish: *adet*) learned in childhood and thus wear it "unconsciously." As conscious Muslims, they claim self-awareness in a way that creates a "third" social space: on the one hand, this identity constitutes a Western other (either non-Muslim or non-practicing Muslim) as not-self; on the other hand, it constitutes a "traditional" other as not-self. In this third space, the conscious Muslim woman mediates between the non-Muslim and the traditional villager. These Muslim women stress that the headscarf enhances their freedom in relation to a traditional family. Their parents are not as worried about them when they go out. In many cases, these youth also gain power and authority over their parents. They learn to argue that the practices advocated by Islamists are true Islam and that the "village Islam" of their families has been corrupted by local culture and is practiced out of habit rather than out of a relationship with God. Among the families I have worked with, young women often draw their parents into their practice, giving them books to read and teaching them how to wear a headscarf properly. The young woman who resisted her father's wishes was also able to assert herself without threatening or alienating her mother.

Muslim women associated with IGMG and other Islamic groups stressed that wearing the headscarf properly also entails a specific bodily comportment that requires one to avoid shaking hands with men or making excessive eye contact with them (however, these women do look directly at a man while talking with him) and speaking in a controlled voice in public spaces. Wearing a headscarf does not preclude riding a bicycle or participating in physical activity. This kind of bodily discipline was quite different from the stereotyped submissiveness marked by the hunched shoulders depicted in filmic representations of oppressed women such as *40 Quadratmeter Deutschland* and *Aufbrüche*. On the contrary, these women prided themselves on their assertiveness in social situations.

The IGMG leadership is very concerned with educating both boys and girls for life in German society. One series of textbooks that was used in an IGMG-sponsored course had been prepared for Islamic education in the public schools by the Institut für Internationale Pädagogik und Didaktik. It included a book devoted to recycling, which discussed it in terms of preserving the resources provided by God and cited Qur'anic verses in support of this idea. The IGMG leadership encourages young women to wear headscarves while at the same time urging them to pursue higher education, especially as teachers and doctors.

However, this discourse is one that is adamantly refused by much of the German public, which perceives the Muslim woman with a headscarf as the absolute other and the antithesis of democracy, freedom, and equality. Some German scholars have been actively involved in shaping this attitude of the German public. For example, Wilhelm Heitmeyer, the scholar who invented the term *parallel society*, and his associates accused Turks of resisting integration because of their involvement in Islam (Heitmeyer et al. 1997). Leaders of Islamic organizations I have spoken with have been quite outraged by this assertion.

Aylin's story clearly exhibits this set of contrasts: "The high value of the 'self'-responsible individual, a requirement for each democratic community, cannot be shared by the Islamic Fundamentalist because he thinks best in terms of collectives and groups" (Cziesche et al. 2003: 85). Although her case had nothing to do with headscarves or with Islamists, it is sandwiched between descriptions of two court decisions in which female students were released from required school activities (a field trip and a gym class) because participation in them violated specific religious rulings *(fatawa)*. In the critical words of the *Der Spiegel* author, this decision "shows how lightly German courts deal with the oppression of women by their parents in the name of religious freedom. . . . In the name of religious freedom, orthodox parents may also have the chance to confine and control Muslim girls with the blessing of the German courts – this is what the headscarf symbolizes" (Cziesche et al. 2003: 87). Aylin's story is thus used to illustrate how Muslim parents do not allow their daughters personal autonomy. Although there is no indication of the personal wishes of the girl who was excused from gym classes, it is implied that she, like Aylin, was being forced by her family against her will to dress modestly and be deprived of gym. As presented in *Der Spiegel*, Aylin serves as proof that Islamists do not see their women as having any right to freedom or personal autonomy. German representation of Islamic groups obliterates the extent to which such groups offer a mediating position between Turkish tradition and Western materialism and consumerism for Turkish youth. Young German Turkish women who wear headscarves, succeed in graduating from German universities, and strive for careers in teaching, law, and medicine are presented as symbols for the failure of integration.

Returning to the issue of how popular culture shapes the identity possibilities for German Turkish women, do we see Islamic representations presenting any viable alternatives in popular culture? In the United States, Christian youth have taken up popular music and have even made the music charts. For Islamists, there are a few films, such as Mesut Uçakan's *Yalniz Degilsiniz*! (You are not alone!; 1990). Made in Turkey but well known among young women in Germany who wear headscarves, this film portrays a university student in Turkey who becomes a practicing Muslim and has to struggle against her secularist family, the university, and the mental health system to wear a headscarf. However, most young people of Turkish background who have chosen to go into filmmaking in Germany are not practicing Muslims (although there is at least one exception), and Islam is no more than a background presence in most films. To date, little media representation has been produced from an Islamic perspective.

The Displeasures of Hybridity

Having laid out the relationships among three discourses, each of which posits a dichotomy between urban German cosmopolitanism and rural Turkish traditionalism but with radically different mediatory processes for bridging this divide, I now turn to look at some of the effects of these discursive mythologies on young women who have sought to escape the constraints of their families. In so doing, I argue that the micropolitics of everyday life provides us with an alternative strategy for interpreting and assessing conflicts that are usually understood as a clash of cultures.

Der Spiegel's account of Aylin's plight begins with a Turkish proverb: "The purity of the woman is the honor of the man," to explain her family's treatment. The story moves very quickly from this cultural artifact to Aylin's accusation that her uncle had raped her – clearly a violation of the moral code of the most remote Turkish village and hardly a normal "cultural practice." An analogous use of the concept of culture can be seen at a 1996 Youth Forum in Berlin on "problems facing the migrant youth in Germany" (Soysal 2001: 17). Girls of Turkish background discussed their personal experiences and problems faced at home. Most said that they had few problems with their own parents, because many families over the years have gradually relaxed the restrictions on their daughters. Nevertheless, a recurrent theme was to blame the "culture" – Islamic and Turkish – for the tendency of fathers and brothers to restrict the freedom of girls. In other words, they did not see "culture" operating within their own families but imputed it to the Turkish family in the abstract. However, other participants objected, saying that there was nothing inherent in Turkish culture or Islam that necessitated the repression of women. Instead they put the responsibility on individual persons (Soysal 2001: 18). This distinction points to the micropolitics of the family and allows us to escape or at least evade a seemingly unresolvable conflict between the principles of group rights rooted in a doctrine of multiculturalism and an individualism grounded in universal human rights.

This tension is central to the recent work of Unni Wikan, who has been conducting research on abductions and honor killings in Scandanavia. Wikan used the case of a second-generation Norwegian citizen to argue for the importance of Muslim girls' human rights, understood to be grounded in moral individualism, to take precedence over cultural rights: Nadia was abducted by her Moroccan parents for a forced marriage in Morocco but was able to call the Norwegian Embassy for help. Nadia's parents were prosecuted and sentenced in a Norwegian court. The verdict states: "The case arises from culture conflict.... That they wish to maintain the customs of their country of birth is unobjectionable, so long as these customs do not come into conflict with Norwegian law" (Wikan 2002: 137). Variously positioned spokespersons in the Muslim community were outraged at the verdict against Nadia's parents. Wikan notes that in the November 11, 1998, *Dagbladet*, the chairman of the Islamic Council states, "This is an insult to all Muslims. It implies that we are bushmen who do not follow Norwegian laws and rules! ... The charges and the verdict are an offense against the family and us Muslims. The judge is requiring us to respect Norwegian laws, but does not show us any respect" (2002: 138). Given the alternatives that this verdict sets up, one might be led to ask whether the chairman of the Islamic Council was arguing for the right of Muslim fathers to abduct their daughters?

In her public role as an advocate for the rights and safety of young women in similar situations, Wikan felt this verdict was appropriate because it clearly prioritized the daughter's human rights over the parents' cultural rights. She may well be right in this case, but I cannot help asking whether the outcome of such trials must be so polarized? Is it inevitable that immigrant families be driven to such rifts at all? A journalist whom Wikan cites seems to take a position different from Wikan's: He did not disagree with the sentence but wrote that the premises of the verdict were unacceptable (Wikan 2002: 138). Although Wikan does not indicate what the journalist felt an alternative premise might have been, the young women at the Berlin Youth Forum suggest an alternative: place the responsibility for misconduct on the individual parents and not on the "culture."

To assume that the pathologies exhibited in Aylin's rape or in Nadia's abduction are an inevitable component of the "patriarchal" Muslim family is to impose a distancing stereotype. In many hierarchically organized families, the father maintains his public authority as the head of the extended family and primary decision maker only by privately consulting with other family members and taking into account their attitudes, feelings, and expertise (Ewing 1991). Such families have a complex and fluid political dynamic within the context of an ideal that is based not dominance and submission but on responsibility, love, and care on the part of the elders of the family and deference and respect on the part of the children and other subordinates. Difficulties, abuse, and rebellion arise when the father attempts to maintain exclusive power over his wife and children and are not the inevitable result of the culturally specific structure of the family, even when it is founded on hierarchy.

The case of Seyhan Derin, the daughter of a guestworker who ran away from home at 15, illustrates the classic pattern that is so clearly and stereotypically represented in the German media as a manifestation of Turkish "culture": She and two sisters fled from an authoritarian father who had threatened to send them back to Turkey after their oldest sister eloped with a German boy. Thirteen years later, as a young director, Derin made a documentary film, *Ben Annemin Kiziyim* (I'm my mother's daughter; 1996), which depicts her reconciliation with her parents through the making of the film. The film demonstrates retrospectively the negative effects on Derin's family of the congruent polarizations of German and rural Turkish discourses. As Derin and her family work through their reconciliation, the audience also sees how these polarizations had constrained Derin's possibilities for identity formation as an adolescent and how her parents' relationship had not been a manifestation of Turkish gender inequality but was, rather, an effect of the stresses of migration and discrimination in Germany. From a German perspective, Derin is a prime example of successful integration – a well-educated and successful young filmmaker and the embodiment of a hybrid mediating figure. Yet she had been living a life of total rupture with her past and her parents.

In the film, Derin and her mother visit the family village in Turkey. In this liminal space and time, misunderstandings are overcome through new kinds of interactions. In the village, Derin's aunt tells her that everyone had thought she and her sisters had run off to become prostitutes when they left home. In village discourse, becoming a prostitute is, of course, the most corrupting, dishonoring fate that one can imagine. What from a German perspective would be seen as a case of successful hybridity was, from the perspective of her relatives, an abomination.

Through the process of filmmaking, Derin comes to accept an identity as her mother's daughter, which she had previously disavowed. Near the end of the film, Derin contrasts her new insights into her mother's strengths and independence with the earlier image she had of her mother, which had been based on stereotypes formed in Germany. Derin narrates (in Turkish): "The image of a self-sufficient and independent village woman blatantly contradicts my image formed in Germany of a mother who was withdrawn into herself and had obediently accepted the conditions of life, a picture that gradually becomes blurred before my eye." Before the experience of making the film, she had seen her mother as someone who had been overshadowed by her father and "caught up in traditions that I could not accept as valid for me."

Derin's account provides further evidence for the importance of disentangling explanations based on "culture" from those based on the dynamics of particular families. However, it allows us to also recognize that pathologies of the family are often a consequence of the stresses of migration itself and the circumstances of life in Germany. In her voiceover, Derin describes how her father had worked in a German mine until he was so badly injured that he became completely disabled; he incurred large debts and went off to a gambling hall; he drank too much and was cold to the family. Instead of being gentle, he imposed arbitrary rules. In a difficult situation, he sought to maintain control by becoming authoritarian.[26]

Although this reaction is itself a cultural process, it is not simply a manifestation of "culture." When guestworkers commiserate and strategize, seeking solutions to the difficulties that threaten them, they draw on a range of resources and understandings, many but not all of which they bring with them from Turkey. To identify an active process is quite different from saying that they act in these ways because of their culture, understood as a set of preexisting rules for action that they must give up if they are to assimilate. A German discourse that attributes to Turkish culture all evidence of vice also encourages misrecognition by these men themselves. The "cultural defense" argument in the legal system is often used in precisely this way: a man commits a murder and then claims that his "culture" made him do it.[27]

The complementary polarizations of German and Turkish discourse thus foster miscommunication between children and their immigrant parents and leave few options for the young woman when her family is abusive or overly restrictive. The last resort of turning to the police, courts, or German social services creates a radical rupture, driving the wedge of the German state into the Turkish family. The intrusive authority of the state and the parents' worst fears of losing their daughter to the vices of the West are confirmed.

The potentially powerful role that stereotypes and scripts play stands in tension with the fluidity of actual situations of rupture. These are best analyzed by examining the micropolitics of an evolving situation. Nergis is a young woman of Turkish background whom I met just four days after she had fled her husband. Her husband was a relative from Turkey to whom she had been engaged at age 11 and married at age 17.[28] The husband was uneducated and frustrated by his low economic status as compared to his wife. She had experienced his responses to his humiliation as oppressive, but he had not physically abused her.

Her story as she told it to me was framed in terms of two compartmentalized identities, as a Turkish girl whose life had been tightly circumscribed by her parents and as an educated professional whose career had taken her as far as Curaçao on a business trip. When I met her, she was hiding out with a colleague from work, afraid that her family would find her and commit an "honor killing." Because of her professional connections, she was able to engage a lawyer, who functioned as a mediator between Nergis and her family. They were able to reconcile the conflict in an optimal way: She moved into her own apartment with her son and got a divorce from her husband. Her mother, who had done everything possible to force her into this marriage, resumed caring for her baby during the day and became much more flexible with her younger daughter after her experience with Nergis. A significant role was played by a local religious leader (*molla*) in both creating the initial crisis and in its subsequent resolution. He had initially worked to push Nergis into the marriage but switched his position and later adopted a mediating role, working alongside the lawyer to resolve the conflict.

Although Nergis's family was in many respects typical of immigrants from Turkey, the details of her situation indicate a micropolitics that does not conform to stereotypes. Although she feared the violence of her father, brothers, and husband, it was actually her mother who was the key player at every stage. Nergis herself had considerable power in her family, despite her self-portrayal as the typical Turkish girl who has been victimized by her culture and her family. Even the traditional molla, who had prescribed amulets and other village treatments to force Nergis to accept her husband, demonstrated his flexibility in the end.

Conclusion

Scholarly and political articulations of problems associated with integration have commonly been framed as a choice between a policy of multiculturalism in which rights and requirements are accommodated to the cultural differences of a minority group and a policy of humanistic individualism focused on universal rights and free choice. However, when either policy is embraced by a modern state, it often marginalizes ethnic and religious others. Multiculturalism, on the one hand, assigns individuals to membership in an essentialized cultural category, generating stereotypes such as the Turkish woman as victim. Individualism, on the other hand, often smuggles the cultural particularities of the dominant group into a discourse of universal human rights and justifies forced assimilation to these norms: The woman who wears a headscarf must be liberated so that she is free to expose her body to the male gaze or be free to engage in premarital sex. In difficult cases in which a minority group enforces a cultural practice that, according to the state, may violate the rights of individual group members, state authorities are then put into the quandary of either allowing the practice to go unchecked while "rescuing" those who want out or declaring that the cultural principles of the group are incompatible with a modern democracy and that it must abandon its "culture" and become assimilated. In either case, attention is focused on the difficulties of life "between" cultures, and solutions to individual problems are focused either on strategies for escaping this condition of betweenness through assimilation or on managing this state by "celebrating" it.

The notion of betweenness is itself a product of a mythically structured discourse. One outcome of this discursive structure has been cultural production focused on the mediation of cultural difference and the generation of mediatory figures such as the hybrid. A number of anthropologists, recognizing the limitations of this concept, have challenged its analytic utility. Although I agree that the idea of hybridity, like multiculturalism, is problematic, I have argued here that it cannot be seen as merely an analytic concept that has outlived its usefulness and should be discarded. Rather, it is a powerful category that has been taken up in public discourse and shaped the very process of integration. This figure of betweenness is pervasive and is particularly visible in cinema images produced both by German filmmakers and by filmmakers of Turkish background.

An analysis of the effects of this discourse shows that an ideology based on multiculturalism and celebratory hybridity imagines homogeneous collective identities that hamper recognition of the actual heterogeneity of those who fall within a particular group. In the field of social work, superficial reports on Turkish village life have been used to assess how migrants would fail to adapt to urban life in Germany, often resulting in social policies that increase segregation and make integration more difficult. It also exacerbates miscommunications between Germans and Turks and between generations within the immigrant community as Turkish youth participate in hybrid forms of popular culture that their parents may view as corrupt and dangerous.

Clearly, new solutions to the "problem" of integration must begin by challenging the assumption of a dichotomous cultural difference and reconceptualizing altogether the nature of the obstacles that face immigrants. Islamic solutions disrupt an Orientalism that equates Muslims with those who are backward, traditional, superstitious, patriarchal, and subordinate to a group. Although an Islamic solution may not be appropriate for most immigrants of Turkish background, lessons for social service providers and policy makers could be taken from the specific successes of Islamic organizations. These groups have reduced the disjunction between generations, encouraging education for both boys and girls, while at the same time enhancing the possibilities of young women to resist the sometimes inappropriate demands of their fathers and families.

However, a fear of Islamism has led Western nations to misrecognize the policies and practices of Islamic groups by denying that their activities may be effective integration strategies. A pervasive suspiciousness and condemnation is directed toward explicitly Muslim activities. This is particularly evident in the misrecognition of young women in headscarves, who are viewed as victims of Muslim patriarchal oppression despite their having successfully gone through the German university system. Many of these women who are supported by such organizations are now struggling to gain jobs as public school teachers in the face of hastily passed German laws banning them from teaching if they wear headscarves.

My concern has been to identify the discursive practices that stereotype minorities and the rhetorical maneuvers such as multiculturalism and the celebration of hybridity that justify such practices in the name of a liberal sensitivity to difference. I take my own strategy for evading such polarizations from the perspectives of ordinary individuals who have been misrecognized through minority stereotyping. A spokesman for a U.S. minority church stated this eloquently: "While we, as a church, teach many things different from mainstream Christianity, we are a normal, Christian community with every range of human strength and frailty" (Banerjee 2005: A11). This plea was articulated against the inevitable media stereotyping that follows aberrant behavior within a minority community – in this case a murder rampage by one of its members. Consistent with this plea, I pose the alternative of tracing out the micropolitics of everyday life, foregrounding the multiple position-ings and identities occupied by immigrants and their families and the diverse contradictions and inconsistencies they negotiate, without singling out their situ-ations as uniquely contradictory. They are, like the rest of us, a heterogeneous assortment of people who must live in a heterogeneous, rapidly changing world and who creatively draw on available resources to solve the problems they face.

NOTES

1 All translations from this article are my own.
2 The term *parallel societies* (*Parallelgesellschaften*) was first used in a 1996 newspaper article (see Heitmeyer 1996).
3 The recent murder of Hatun Sürücü by her brothers in what has been labeled an "honor killing" has triggered renewed media focus in Germany on the dangers facing the young Turkish woman who tries to live "like a German." This concern has also been taken up enthusiastically in international media, including PBS, the BBC, and the *New York Times* (Lau 2005; National Public Radio [NPR] 2005; Schneider 2005).
4 The most visible of these activists are Seyran Ateş, Necla Kelek, and Serap Çileli.
5 Working in Trinidad, Aisha Khan has argued analogously that "ideologies about mixing are causal forces in social processes" (Khan 2004: 4) because of the cultural elaboration of the concept of creolization. Jan French has argued that in certain contexts the concept of mestizaje "provides openings for choices about self-identification and political identity-making" (French 2004: 665).

6   For discussion of German-Turkish hyphenated identities, see Caglar 1997, Kaya 2002.

7   Arjun Appadurai in his discussion of "mediascapes" has suggested that the images projected by the media offer "scripts" for imagined lives (Appadurai 1996: 35). Stuart Hall sees cinema as a form of representation that can "constitute us as new kinds of subjects" (Hall 1990: 402). Less optimistically, it is also possible to see media images as being so powerful that they constrain not only their abilities to imagine who they may become but even who they have been, along the lines of the views of scholars of the Frankfurt School such as Theodor Adorno and Herbert Marcuse, who were concerned with the power of mass media to shape consciousness.

8   In the 1970s and 1980s, "many films suggest that state-funded cinema is primarily a force for social work" (Elsaesser 1989: 53). More recently, Germany's federal minister of culture has increasingly tilted subsidy programs to favor filmmakers who have had box office successes.

9   Roland Barthes, in his analysis of diverse modern phenomena such as wrestling, magazine photos, and film, identifies myth as a type of speech in which a sign (signifier plus concept) becomes a signifier in a kind of metalanguage that naturalizes and freezes meaning into stereotypes (Barthes 1972a, 1972b).

10 There are no satisfactory labels for identifying those of Turkish descent, heritage, ethnicity, or citizenship who live in Germany. It is common in scholarly and popular literature to use a hyphenated term such as Turkish-German or German-Turkish, but the hyphenated term foregrounds precisely the element of hybridity that I wish to critique. Recently the phrase "of Turkish descent" has been adopted by some, but this unduly emphasizes biological descent, which is far from a neutral concept in German history. "Ethnically Turkish" foregrounds ethnicity, an import with unnecessary conceptual baggage. I have settled on the phrase "of Turkish background" as a relatively neutral, if awkward, designation that minimizes reification of identity.

11 The need for a large number of foreign laborers developed suddenly with the construction of the Berlin Wall and the sealing of the border between East and West Germany in 1963. These laborers were explicitly called "guests," in contrast to the term used for foreign workers (*Fremdarbeiter*) who were enslaved during the Nazi era (Herbert and Hunn 2001: 191).

12 In France, the controversy has centered on students who wish to wear a headscarf in the secular space of the state school. In Germany, where the state's relationship to secularism is rather different, the debate over a ban on headscarves has focused on teachers as representatives of the neutral state.

13 Similar themes are echoed by Meske (1983).

14 I mentioned in passing that Onder was actually a scholar from Turkey. This is a significant detail, because modernization in Turkey over the course of the 20th century has been shaped by a secularism that closely associated rural traditionalism with Islam as a conservative force in a polarized political environment. Until very recently, virtually all of the Turkish educated elite, from Left to Right, have been unreflexively secularist and supportive of state measures that strictly constrain Muslim practice. If anything, Turkish scholars have contributed to the depiction of Turkish Muslim village culture as the antithesis of modern civilization.

15 Guestworker literature (*Gastarbeiterliteratur*) from the late 1970s was primarily didactic, protesting against inhumane living and working conditions and social discrimination (Horrocks and Kolinsky 1996; Suhr 1989). Similarly, New German Cinema of the 1970s and early 1980s was intensely concerned with social and political questions (Elsaesser 1989: 52). The literature of the late 1980s and early 1990s focused on issues

of deterritorialization and loss of identity, drawing on Turkish traditions to challenge conventions of German literature (Harnisch et al. 1998: 18).

16 Tevfik Başer, born and educated in Turkey as a graphics artist and photographer, studied filmmaking in Hamburg, Germany, in his early thirties (Kuheim 2001).

17 Trumpener has summarized the film's message: "Here it is not the Germans who agitate to send the Turks back to where they came from. . . . Instead it is the Turks themselves who threaten to send back their own Germanicized children, and concerned, caring bureaucrats who must take Turkish children away from their parents, for their own good" (Trumpener 1989: 24).

18 This quotation echoes Bhabha's articulation of a "third space" of creative cultural production.

19 Caglar suggests that Turkish pop from Turkey, in contrast, has become popular among German Turkish youth in the 1990s in ways that open up new spaces that celebrate Turkishness yet disrupt reified identities by referring to "the metropoles and urban spaces, not to Turkey as a cultural system" (1998: 256). Alternatively, Turkish pop could be seen to function as another mediating figure – Turkish yet urban, thereby transcending the dichotomy between the rural, parochial Turkish and the cosmopolitan German.

20 "The German and Turkish language media seem to agree on one point: 'The new German film is Turkish!'" (Deutsch-türkishe Tendenzen im Film? 2000).

21 Akin's (2000) earlier film *Im Juli* (In July) appeared to have avoided this theme, because the primary female character moves freely and independently. However, it, too, does nothing to disrupt stereotypes of the Turkish family because it simply leaves issues of family behind: The film does not show the female protagonist as having any family connections at all – she could be a girl who has fled from her family. Both films, however, do recast gender relationships by recognizing women's power and exploring male anxieties and insecurities.

22 Margret Spohn has attempted to capture the rarely heard voices of first generation male guestworkers in a study that reproduces transcripts of her interviews with several men (2002). One of her goals was to articulate a diversity of orientations among these men who are invisible in public discourse. Although this is a valuable and careful study, the voices of these men are heavily filtered through an interview schedule and theoretical apparatus that categorize them in terms of issues of authority and tradition still shaped by the Orientalizing discourse that Spohn seeks to disrupt. Werner Schiffauer has also interviewed first generation guestworkers, insightfully tracing attitudinal shifts vis-à-vis their own fathers still in Turkey (Schiffauer 1991).

23 Zafer Şenocak, a German writer of Turkish background, recognized the reproduction of the dichotomous terms of German discourse, the "fairy tale Orientalism of the German public" in the work of the well-known Turkish author Emine Sevgi Özdamar, who came to Germany as a guestworker (Jordan 2003: 93; Şenocak 2000).

24 The village, however, is also depicted as a dead end for pragmatic reasons: successful farm life depends on familial continuity from one generation to the next. When this is disrupted by migration and when children and other close relatives leave for the city, it is impossible for parents to grow old and die there with no younger generation to take over the heavy work.

25 Such "arranged marriages" violate the Western model of a marriage based on "love," and the Muslim preference for marriage between cousins is often regarded by Westerners as incest. Ironically, the arranged marriages with Turks back home are encouraged by German immigration policy: the doors to immigration were closed in 1973 to new workers, but from that point, those already in Germany could bring in other members

of their family. Arranged marriage has become an important economic strategy for migrant families, as well as a strategy for preserving their own cultural identity.

26 Conger and Elder (1994) have shown that in rural families under economic pressure in the United States, the husband is likely to become more hostile and aggressive and the wife more depressed; the husband is also more likely to displace his anger experienced at work onto his family. These reactions are consistent with what in Germany is perceived as the Turkish "cultural" pattern of domination of the father and submission of the mother.

27 The notion of "cultural defense" was developed in the United States in the mid-1980s in the wake of a number of cases in which defendants invoked the traditions of their culture to explain or mitigate their actions (Renteln 2004). Feminist literature on multiculturalism has criticized the cultural defense for its reliance on "cultural tradition" to legitimate crimes against women (Okin 1999). Phillips (2003) suggests that, on the whole, the cultural defense has not been successfully employed by male defendants to mitigate crimes against women, although there are troubling exceptions.

28 I have used a pseudonym for this young woman, who lives in the Netherlands, where the conditions facing Turkish immigrants are generally similar to those in Germany (see Ewing 2002).

REFERENCES

Abu-Lughod, Lila
  1993   Finding a Place for Islam: Egyptian Television Serials and the National Interest. *Public Culture* 5(3): 493–514.
Adelson, Leslie
  1990   Migrants' Literature or German Literature? TORKAN's *Tufan*: Brief an einem islamischen Bruder. *German Quarterly* 63 (3–4): 382–389.
  2003   Against Between: A Manifesto. In Zafer Şenocak. Tom Cheesman and Karin Yeilada, eds. Pp. 130–143. Cardiff: University of Wales Press.
Ahmed, Leila
  1992   *Women and Gender in Islam: Historical Roots of a Modern Debate*. New Haven, CT: Yale University Press.
Akin, Fatih, dir.
  2000   *Im Juli*. (In July). 100 min. Wueste Film. Hamburg.
  2004   *Gegen die Wand* (*Against the wall*); *Head-On* (U.S. title). 121 min. Wueste Film. Hamburg.
Appadurai, Arjun
  1996   *Modernity at Large: Cultural Dimensions of Globalization*. Minneapolis: University of Minnesota Press.
Bademsoy, Aysun, dir.
  1996   *Ein Mädchen im Ring* (*Girl in the ring*). 30 min. Berlin.
Banerjee, Neela
  2005   Rampage Puts Spotlight on a Church Community: 7,000 Congregants Struggle with Crises. *New York Times*, March 18: A11.
Barthes, Roland
  1972a   The Lost Continent. In *Mythologies*. Annette Lavers, trans. Pp. 94–96. New York: Hill and Wang.
  1972b   Myth Today. In *Mythologies*. Annette Lavers, trans. Pp. 109–159. New York: Hill and Wang.

Başer, Tevfik, dir.

1986   40 Quadratmeter Deutschland (Forty square meters of Germany). 80 min. Studio Hamburg Film Produktion. Hamburg.

Baumgartner-Karabak, Andrea, and Gisela Landesberger

1978   Die verkauften Bräute. Türkische Frauen zwischen Kreuzberg und Anatolien (Sold brides: Turkish women between Kreuzberg and Anatolia). Hamburg: Rowolt Taschenbuchverlag.

Bhabha, Homi K.

1994a   The Commitment to Theory. In The Location of Culture. Pp. 19–39. London: Routledge.

1994b   Of Mimicry and Man: The Ambivalence of Colonial Discourse. In The Location of Culture. Pp. 85–92. London: Routledge.

Bohm, Hark, dir.

1988   Yasemin. 70 min. Hamburger Kino Kompanie. Hamburg.

Boos-Nünning, Ursula, ed.

1990   Die türkische Migration in deutschsprachigen Büchern 1961–1984. (Turkish migration in German language books 1961–1984). Opladen: Leske and Budrich.

Butler, Judith

1989   Gender Trouble: Feminism and the Subversion of Identity. New York: Routledge.

Caglar, Ayse S.

1997   Hyphenated Identities. In The Politics of Multiculturalism in the New Europe: Racism, Identity and Community (Postcolonial Encounters). Tariq Modood and Pnina Werbner, eds. Pp. 169–185. London: Zed Books.

1998   Popular Culture: Marginality and Institutional Incorporation. Cultural Dynamics 10(3): 243–261.

Conger, Rand D., and Glen H. Elder Jr.

1994   Families in Troubled Times: Adapting to Change in Rural America. New York: Aldine de Gruyter.

Cziesche, Dominik, Dietmar Hipp, Felix Kurz, Barbara Schmid, Matthias Schreiber, Martin Sümening, Silvia Tyburski, and Andreas Ulrich

2003   Das Kreuz mit dem Koran. Der Spiegel, September 29: 82–97.

Delaney, Carol

1990   The hajj: Sacred and Secular. American Ethnologist 17(3): 513–530.

Derin, Seyhan, dir.

1996   Ben Annemin Kiziyim/Ich bin Tochter meiner Mutter (I'm my mother's daughter). 89 min. Derinfilmproduktion. Munich.

Deutsch-türkische Tendenzen im Film?

2000   Das interkulturelle Kino Europas. Electronic document, http://www.interforum.net/2000/200_vorworte_D.htm, accessed October 22.

Elsaesser, Thomas

1989   New German Cinema: A History. New Brunswick, NJ: Rutgers University Press.

Ewing, Katherine Pratt

1991   Can Psychoanalytic Theories Explain the Pakistani Woman? Intrapsychic Autonomy and Interpersonal Engagement in the Extended Family. Ethos 19(2): 131–160.

2002   Images of Order and Authority: Shifting Identities and Legal Consciousness in a Runaway Immigrant Daughter. In Power and the Self. Jeanette Mageo and Bruce Knauft, eds. Pp. 93–113. Cambridge: Cambridge University Press.

2003   Migration, Identity Negotiation and Self Experience. In Worlds on the Move: Globalization, Migration and Cultural Security. Jonathan Friedman and Shalini Randeria, eds. Pp. 117–140. London: I. B. Taurus.

Fassbinder, Rainer Werner, dir.
  1973   *Angst essen Seele auf (Fear eats the soul)*. 93 min. Tango Film. Munich.
Foucault, Michel
  1978   *The History of Sexuality*, vol. 1. New York: Pantheon Books.
  1995   *Discipline and Punish: The Birth of the Prison*. New York: Vintage Books.
French, Jan
  2004   *Mestizaje* and Law Making in Indigenous Identity Formation in Northeast
         Brazil: After the Conflict Came the History. *American Anthropologist* 106(4):
         663–674.
Geertz, Clifford
  1973   Religion as a Cultural System. In *Interpretation of Cultures; Selected Essays*.
         Pp. 87–125. New York: Basic Books.
Gförer, Jörg, dir.
  1986   *Ganz unten (At the bottom of the heap)*. 100 min. KAOS Film. Cologne.
Göktürk, Deniz
  2001   Turkish Delight – German Fright: Migrant Identities in Transnational Cinemas. In
         Mediated Identities. Deniz Derman, Karen Ross, and Nevena Dakovic, eds. Pp. 131–149.
         Istanbul: Bilgi University Press.
Hall, Stuart
  1990   Cultural Identity and Diaspora. In *Identity: Community, Culture, Difference*.
         J. Rutherford, ed. Pp. 222–237. London: Lawrence and Wishart.
Harnisch, Antje, Anne Marie Stokes, and Friedemann Weidauer, eds. and trans.
  1999   *Fringe Voices: An Anthology of Minority Writing in the Federal Republic of
         Germany*. Oxford: Berg.
Heitmeyer, Wilhelm
  1996   Für türkische Jugendliche in Deutschland spielt der Islam eine wichtige Rolle.
         Die Zeit 35. Electronic document, http://www.zeit.de/archiv/1996/35/heitmey.txt.
         19960823.xml, accessed July 22, 2005.
Heitmeyer, Wilhelm, Joachim Müller, and Helmut Schröder
  1997   *Verlockender Fundamentalismus: Türkische jugendliche in Deutschland*. (*Enticing
         fundamentalism: Turkish youth in Germany*). Frankfurt am Main: Suhrkamp.
Herbert, Ulrich, and Karin Hunn
  2001   Guest Workers and Policy on Guest Workers in the Federal Republic: From the
         Beginning of Recruitment in 1955 until Its Halt in 1973. In *The Miracle Years: A Cultural
         History of Germany 1949–1968*. Hanna Schissler, ed. Pp. 187–218. Princeton: Princeton
         University Press.
Horrocks, David, and Eva Kolinsky, eds.
  1996   *Turkish Culture in German Society Today*. Providence: Berghahn.
Horst, Hartmut, and Eckart Lottman, dirs.
  1987   *Aufbrüche (Departures)*. 79 min. Medien Operative. Berlin.
Jordan, James
  2003   Zafer Şenocak's Essays and Early Prose Fiction: From Collective Multiculturalism to
         Fragmented Cultural Identities. In Zafer Şenocak. Tom Cheesman and Karin Yeşilada,
         eds. Pp. 91–105. Cardiff: University of Wales Press.
Kaya, Ayhan
  2002   The Hyphenated Germans: German-Turks. *Private View*. Spring: 36–43.
Khan, Aisha
  2004   *Callalloo Nation: Metaphors of Race and Religious Identity among South Asians in
         Trinidad*. Durham, NC: Duke University Press.

Kuheim, Rosemarie
  2001 Tevfik Baser. Electronic document, http://www.deutsches-filmhaus.de/bio_reg/
     b_bio/regiss/baser_tevfik_bio.htm, accessed July 21, 2004.
Kultus, Eva
  1998 *Der Preis der Freiheit: 10 Jahre im Leben einer jungen Frau türkisher Herkunft (The*
     cost of freedom: 10 years in the life of a young woman of Turkish background).
     Frankfurt: IKO-Verlag für Interkulturelle Kommunikation.
Lau, Jörg
  2005 Wie eine Deutsche. Die Zeit. Electronic document, http://zeus.de/text/2005/09/
     Hatin_S_9fr _9fc_9f_09, accessed September 30.
Lutz, Helma
  1991 *Welten Verbinden. Türkische Sozialarbeiterinnen in den Niederlanden und der*
     Bundesrepublik Deutschland (Connecting Worlds. Turkish Social Work in the Nether-
     lands and the Federal Republic of Germany). Frankfurt am Main: IKO-Verlag für
     Interkulturelle Kommunikation.
Meske, Sigrid
  1983 *Situationsanalyse türkischer Frauen in der BRD. Unter dem Aspekt ihrer kulturellen*
     Neuorientierungen in der Türkei. Berlin: Express Edition.
Naficy, Hamid
  2001 *An Accented Cinema: Exilic and Diasporic Filmmaking*. Princeton: Princeton
     University Press.
National Public Radio (NPR)
  2005 Profile: Turkish Women Murdered in Germany by Their Own families in Honor
     Killings because of Their Lifestyles. Morning Edition, March 29. NPR transcripts.
     Electronic document, http://nl.newsbank.com, accessed March 29.
O'Brien, Peter
  1996 *Beyond the Swastika*. London: Routledge.
Okin, Susan Moller
  1999 Is Multiculturalism Bad For Women? In *Is Multiculturalism Bad for Women?* Susan
     Moller Okin, ed. Pp. 7–24. Princeton: Princeton University Press.
Onder, Zehra
  1996 Muslim-Turkish Children in Germany: Sociocultural Problems. *Migration World*
     Magazine 24(5): 18–24.
Ong, Aihwa
  2003 *Buddha is Hiding: Refugees, Citizenship, the New America*. Berkeley: University of
     California Press.
Pflaum, Hans Günther
  2002 Turkish Cinema Newsletter. Electronic document, http://www.turkfilm.net/arc107.
     html, accessed February 2, 2004.
Phillips, Anne
  2003 When Culture Means Gender: Issues of Cultural Defence in the English Courts.
     Modern Law Review 66(4): 510–531.
Radtke, Frank-Olaf
  1997 Multiculturalism in Welfare States: The Case of Germany. In *The Ethnicity Reader,*
     Nationalism, Multiculturalism and Migration. Montserrat Guibernau and John Rex, eds.
     Pp. 248–256. Cambridge: Polity Press.
Renteln, Alison Dundes
  2004 *The Cultural Defense*. New York: Oxford University Press.

Schiffauer, Werner
  1991   *Die Migranten aus Subay. Türken in Deutschland. Eine Ethnographie.* Stuttgart: Klett-Cotta.
Schneider, Peter
  2005   The New Berlin Wall. *New York Times*, December 4, Section 6: 66.
Şenocak, Zafer
  2000   *Atlas of a Tropical Germany: Essays on Politics and Culture, 1990–1998.* Leslie Adelson, trans. Lincoln: University of Nebraska Press.
Soysal, Levent
  2001   Diversity of Experience, Experience of Diversity: Turkish Migrant Youth Culture in Berlin. *Cultural Dynamics* 13(1): 5–28.
Spohn, Margret
  1993   *Alles getürkt (Everything has become Turkish).* Oldenburg: Bibliotheks-und Informationssystem der Universität Oldenburg.
  2002   *Türkische Männer in Deutschland: Familie und Identität. Migranten der ersten Generation erzählen ihre Geschichte (Turkish men in Germany: Family and Identity. Migrants of the first generation tell their stories).* Bielefeld: Broschiert.
Suhr, Heidrun
  1989   Auslanderliteratur: Minority Literature in the Federal Republic of Germany. *New German Critique* 46: 71–103.
Trumpener, Katie
  1989   On the Road: Labor, Ethnicity and the New "New German Cinema" in the Age of the Multinational. *Public Culture* 2(1): 20–30.
Uçakan, Mesut, dir.
  1990   *Yalniz Degilsiniz! (You are not alone!).* Sur Film. Turkey.
Werbner, Pnina, and Tariq Modood, eds.
  1997   *Debating Cultural Hybridity: Multi-Cultural Identities and the Politics of Anti-Racism.* London: Zed Books.
Wikan, Unni
  2002   Citizenship on Trial: Nadia's Case. In *Engaging Cultural Differences: The Multicultural Challenge in Liberal Democracies.* Richard Shweder, Martha Minow, and Hazel Rose Markus, eds. Pp. 128–143. New York: Russell Sage Foundation.
Yavuz, Yüksel
  1994   *Mein Vater der Gastarbeiter (My father the guestworker).* 52 min. Hamburg.
Young, Robert J. C.
  1995   *Colonial Desire: Hybridity in Theory, Culture and Race.* London: Routledge.

9

Compassion and Repression: The Moral Economy of Immigration Policies in France

Didier Fassin

"Reconcile humanitarian aid to refugees with refusal of clandestine immigration: such is the intention of the *préfet* (chief administrator) – who nevertheless recognizes difficulties in finding the point of equilibrium." So ran the headline of a local newspaper in the north of France (*Nord Littoral* 1999e). A compassionate repression: this could have been the oxymoron used to define the political program of this zealous but sympathetic representative of the left-wing French government. The article referred to the dilemma that national authorities were confronting: Hundreds of immigrants from Kosovo, Kurdistan, and Afghanistan were fleeing oppression to seek asylum in Britain. Invariably costly (with smugglers asking $500–$1,000 to cross the Channel), these trips also proved life threatening, as some asylum seekers fell from the train cars of the Eurostar or died of suffocation in a container. Waiting to make this passage, the "candidates for the British Eldorado" (*Nord Littoral* 1999d) were camped in a park at the heart of Calais, where many inhabitants protested against the transformation of their city into "the funnel of misery" (*Nord Littoral* 1998) of Western Europe. At the same time, others had formed a nongovernmental organization (NGO) to demand "refuge at any price" (*Nord Littoral* 1999b) for these unfortunate foreigners who had been deprived of everything.

From *Cultural Anthropology* 20(3): 362–387. Copyright © American Anthropological Association.

A week later, the state seemed to have made its choice among contradictory alternatives and the paper quoted the *sous-préfet* as saying that he was now going "to switch [his emphasis] from [one of] humanitarianism to security" (*Nord Littoral* 1999a). For an observer of the local scene, this rhetoric both responded to and reversed a shift in policy from three months earlier, asserting that "after announcing securitization, the time had come for humanization" (*Nord Littoral* 1999d). But now times had changed. The police expelled the undocumented immigrants from the park and arrested over 200 of them. Nevertheless, the use of force had to be counterbalanced by more humane measures, and the government decided to open a "refuge" under the patronage of the French Red Cross (*Nord Littoral* 1999c). Ironically, both the media and the local population began to refer to the immigrants as "refugees." However, this term indexed their residential situation and their universal condition rather than a legal status that the state authorities were not eager to grant them. In fact, the asylum seekers would have preferred to seek refugee status in Britain where their networks functioned better and where welfare provision was more favorable.

The Sangatte Center, an unused warehouse of 25,000 square meters (approx. 30,000 square yards) a few kilometers outside of Calais, opened on August 14, 1999. It soon became known as a transit camp because it was supposed to provide accommodation for only a short stay for immigrants on their way to Britain. As it happened, however, during the first two and a half years of its existence, it had accommodated up to 50,000 persons, only 350 of whom asked for asylum in France. The rest managed to cross the Channel, usually after having spent less than a month in the refuge. The French government could thus get off lightly by combining the appearance of "humanitarian aid to the refugees" while refusing "clandestine immigration," to quote the préfet. The situation changed, however, when the British government, under public pressure, decided to restrain access to asylum and block illegal entrance to its territory. In the context of a national debate exacerbated by newspaper headlines such as "Asylum: Yes, Britain Is a Soft Touch!" (*Daily Mail* 2001) and "Kurds on Way: But Will Jack Send Them Back?" (*Sun* 2001), referring to British Minister of Home Affairs Jack Straw and his supposedly weak policy, Tony Blair negotiated with Jacques Chirac during a meeting held in Cahors to gain stricter control of immigration networks in France and a tighter collaboration between the police of the two countries concerning the Eurostar, the high-speed train uniting the two countries under the English Channel. On February 12, 2001, the communist newspaper *L'Humanité*, denouncing the loss of national sovereignty implied by this policy, led with the bellicose headline "The English Recapture Calais." Following this new political turn, getting out of Sangatte became more and more difficult for immigrants, and the Red Cross center increasingly turned into a place of confinement, with as many as 1,500 people in a place initially opened to receive 200–300 persons. "Sangatte emergency center, a small town of 1300 inhabitants who dream of England," was the title of an article in *Le Monde* on 30 May, 2002. However, with its circulation of people among a city of large tents, its huge canteen where long queues waited for meals, its prefab buildings housing administrative and medical services, and its open space for Muslim worship, this "small town" began to acquire distinctively urban features.

During this last period, as the crossing of the Channel became more perilous, the organization of smuggling became more lucrative. Conflicts developed between Kurds and Afghanis for the control of this activity, especially for access to the sites where it was possible to catch the trains or gain access to containers. Violence increased at the center between rival groups, and several immigrants were wounded or murdered (*Le Monde* 2001b, 2002a, 2002e). The Red Cross had to accept the permanent presence of the police in a compromise of humanitarian sentiments with security preoccupations. The state security police parked a bus day and night at the entrance of the center, and policemen making rounds among the tents and the prefabs became a part of everyday life for immigrants. For the French visitor entering Sangatte, the sight of armed men in military uniform on the iron platform looming above the "refugees," however peaceful this appeared, produced a strange feeling of déjà vu. The memory of the concentration camps of World War II gave a polemic tone to most comments on the subject in the public sphere (See Groupe d'Information et de Soutien des Immigrés 2001). For the Red Cross, the situation was extremely uncomfortable as critiques mounted against its collaboration with repressive policies (Red Cross 2002). Sangatte had become a focal point for human rights grievances as well as a potential menace to the public order. For many, the humanitarian center looked more and more like an internment camp.

In May 2002, when the new right-wing government took office following a presidential campaign centered mainly on public security issues, the first act of the French minister of the Interior, Nicolas Sarkozy, was to visit Sangatte and announce that he would close it by the end of the year. Arguments for this decision were twofold: first, such a place was a magnet for illegal immigration, and second, it was shameful for a modern democracy to allow such an institution to persist. The fear of attracting migrants is a classic theme used by a right-wing constituency to justify immigration control. The reference to national shame is more unusual, but quite clever, as it speaks to left-wing critiques that reference the dark memory of German concentration camps. On November 5, 2002, the registration of new inmates for the center was stopped. Under the headline "Farewell to Sangatte," *Libération* told the story of the first three families who had to leave the center on December 3, 2002. Once again asylum seekers invaded the streets of Calais. Some made temporary homes in a blockhouse left by the Germans on the beach at the end of World War II. The police were accused of setting one of the shelters on fire with gasoline (*Le Monde* 2002c). Local and national NGOs called for humanitarian management of the cases. As an increasing number of immigrants gathered in a church hall, the government decided against the use of force, and the new préfet announced that a place would be opened to accommodate them. A year later, the Sangatte warehouse had been destroyed, and the media were no longer interested in Calais; yet immigrants were still trying to get to Britain. While waiting for an opportunity to cross the Channel by boat or by train, they wandered through the streets and slept in the parks of the city.

The drama of Sangatte is paradigmatic of tensions between the discourses and practices of compassion and repression in the policies of immigration and more specifically of asylum in Europe (Bloch and Schuster 2002). In a wider perspective, it offers a basis for understanding the moral economy of contemporary Europe. In his historical study of the British poor, E. P. Thompson (1971: 79) referred to "moral economy" as a "traditional view of social norms and obligations, of the proper economic functions of several parties in the community," which "impinged very generally on eighteenth-century government." In his ethnographic research on Southeast Asian peasants, James Scott (1976: 3) similarly defined "moral economy" as a "notion of economic justice and [a] working definition of exploitation," which permitted us "to move toward a fuller appreciation of the normative roots of peasant politics." Both give a specific economic meaning to the concept, but in their utilization, they obviously open it to a broader sense: the economy of the moral values and norms of a given group in a given moment. I will retain this meaning here in the analysis of the values and norms by which immigration and asylum are thought and acted on and, in a broader sense, which define our moral world (Fassin 2005). This moral economy defines the scope of contemporary biopolitics considered as the politics that deals with the lives of human beings. The study of biopolitics is particularly crucial when it governs the lives of undesired and suffering others (Fassin 2001a), undocumented immigrants in this case, but it would not be so different if we studied the political treatment of the undeserving poor (Geremek 1987), the urban underclass (Wacquant 1999), or delinquent youth (Fassin 2004), oscillating between sentiments of sympathy on the one hand and concern for order on the other hand, between a politics of pity and policies of control.

Reexamining Max Weber's analysis of bureaucracies (1976) and following Mary Douglas's description of institutions (1986), Michael Herzfeld (1992) has proposed a vivid perspective on the culture of European states and more specifically on their "social production of indifference." The question he wants to answer is the following: "How does it come about that in societies justly famed for their hospitality and warmth, we often encounter the pettiest form of bureaucratic indifference to human needs and suffering?" (1992: 1). Exploring a distinct but complementary domain in political anthropology, my purpose here is to unveil the ethic of contemporary states when it comes to the moral evaluation of difference. This evaluation is anything but indifferent: it is full of passion and norms, of feelings and stereotypes. Strong beliefs and deep prejudices are expressed about the legitimacy and utility of certain categories of individuals, about their culture and their future, and about their obligations and their rights. The question I want to address, therefore, is why, in societies hostile to immigrants and lacking in concern for undesirable others, there remains a sense of common humanity collectively expressed through attention paid to human needs and suffering?

In a study of the Swedish welfare state and its responses to a growing presence of refugees, Mark Graham (2003) has shown some of the dilemmas that civil servants face in their everyday contact with immigrants and how a bureaucracy can become "emotional" under such circumstances. Indeed, these emotions may also have their limits, as the repetition of pathetic narratives erodes the affective responses of civil servants and even provokes a general distrust regarding the accumulation of misfortunes told by applicants to welfare personnel (Fassin 2003). However, my intention is somewhat different here in moving beyond the individual difficulties and contradictions of the social agents who have to implement national policies to grasp what Josiah Heyman (1998) calls the "moral heart" of these policies. What values and hierarchies of values are mobilized within states to decide how to manage trans-national human flows and how can we account publicly for these decisions? Such questions cast a light on the contemporary ethos, the "genius" or guiding spirit of an institution or system (following Bateson 1958: 2), in the policies of immigration and asylum.

For Giorgio Agamben, "if refugees represent such a disturbing issue in the organization of the modern nation-state, it is above all because, by breaking the continuity between mankind and citizenship, between birthplace and nationality, they question the original fiction of modern sovereignty" (1997: 142). Confronting Michel Foucault's biopolitics (1978) and Hannah Arendt's vita activa (1958), he develops the distinction between zoë, or bare life, the fact of being alive, and bios, or full life, the social presence in the world. Exploring the genealogy of Western societies, he asserts that "the implication of bare life in the political sphere represents the original but hidden core of the sovereign power" (Agamben 1997: 14). The refugees thus occupy a central place in our moral economy because they reveal the persistence of bare life in contemporary societies: deprived from their human rights by lack of citizenship, they can only claim to stay alive, most of the time confined in camps settled in countries near the one from which they have fled. Our world is thus characterized by "the separation between humanitarianism and politics" (1997: 144), as the former defends human beings reduced to their physical life at the margin or even against the latter. In conclusion, "separated from the political, the humanitarian can only reproduce the isolation of sacred life which founds sovereignty" and "the camp – the pure space of exception – is the biopolitical paradigm with which the humanitarian cannot get through" (1997: 145). Sangatte, with its refugees, would thus be the perfect expression of this paradigm in the new context of the European Community.

However, anthropological anamnesis and ethnographic observation lead to a different diagnosis. If the refugees occupy a crucial space in the biopolitics of Europe today, their collective treatment does not rest on the separation of the "humanitarian" from the "political," but on the increasing confusion between the two, which consequently redefines the contemporary signification of the camp. In this article, I analyze this new configuration within the French context. First, I show how asylum lost much of its legitimacy in the 1990s for victims of political violence, even while a new criterion based on "humanitarianism" was developed for sick immigrants. Second, I suggest that, during the same period, the discrediting of refugees has been accompanied by a "humanitarianization" in the management of asylum seekers. Third, referring to the longer history of camps, I suggest that in the context of the perceived threat to the security of the nation by aliens, compassion has opened new paradigmatic relations between the figures of the camp and polis.

Political Asylum versus Humanitarian Reasons

Marie is a 25-year-old Haitian woman. Her father, a political dissident, was murdered by unknown assailants some years ago. Her mother later disappeared and is thought to have been killed. Marie was raped in the presence of her boyfriend by a group of men who burst into her house. In the following weeks, after having found a temporary refuge with a relative, she decided to leave her country and sought asylum in France. Her request for asylum was rejected by the Office français de protection des réfugiés et des apatrides (the French Office for the Protection of Refugees and Stateless People [OFPRA]). So was her appeal. The absence of corroborating evidence outweighed her testimony, despite confirmations by her boyfriend. After several months of increasing social isolation and feeling more and more depressed, she went to a hospital. The physician she saw was convinced by her symptoms of psychic suffering and sent her to a psychiatrist who immediately started treating her with antidepressants. Both doctors were aware of a legal criterion recently introduced in the 1945 Immigration Act recognizing the possibility that undocumented immigrants who faced severe health problems and who had no access to effective treatment at home might obtain a residence permit "for humanitarian reasons." Depression was not a very good case, however, because state medical experts often refused to consider it as a valid reason and, in fact, often suggested that, back in the country of origin, the patient would benefit from returning to a traditional environment and forms of treatment. They nevertheless prepared a file but did not have time to send it to the immigration office for evaluation. A series of blood exams revealed that Marie was HIV+. With AIDS, the case was now legally "easy," and she did obtain a residence permit on the basis of "humanitarian reasons." What she had not been able to get as a right had finally been given to her by compassion.

Of the refugees, stateless people, and minorities whose number dramatically increased in the aftermath of World War I, Hannah Arendt (1951) writes: "Those whom persecution had called undesirable became the undesirables of Europe." In 1981, 20,000 foreigners sought asylum in France; out of these, 80 percent were recognized as refugees. In 1999, 30,000 applied for the same status under the Geneva Convention; however in that year, 80 percent were rejected (OFPRA 1996, 2004). Within less than two decades, the attitude of public authorities had completely reversed, from relative tolerance to general mistrust. This evolution became particularly clear at the end of the 1980s, a time when the political changes in Eastern Europe and the regional conflicts in the former Yugoslavia generated massive migrations toward Western Europe, tripling the number of asylum seekers between 1988 and 1990 (Berger 2000). Meanwhile, the National Front, an extreme-right xenophobic party, developed an aggressive rhetoric denouncing an "invasion" of France by immigrants from the South and grew in electoral significance from less than one percent of the vote in the early 1980s to 14.4 percent in the 1988 presidential election (Hargreaves 1999). Within this new political context, the number of foreigners benefiting from political asylum decreased sixfold in France during the 1990s, gradually stabilizing at around 2,000 refugees per year, not counting children who automatically became refugees on reaching the age of 18 (Legoux 1999). This decrease corresponds to two distinct trends sharing a common logic: the number of claims submitted was reduced by two-thirds and the proportion of accepted claims was halved.

Considering the international situation during this period, it would be hard to argue that this dramatic drop in the number of refugees had resulted from a reduction of conflict in the world. Rather, it is the consequence of two phenomena:

first, at all possible entrances to French territory, border officials were turning away an increasing number of potential asylum seekers before they could file their cases (Julien-Laferrière 2002); second, the civil servants who evaluated the claims were determined to lower the percentage of acceptances (Teitgen-Colly 1999). As a consequence of deep changes occurring in popular attitudes toward asylum, explicit orders had been given by the Ministries of the Interior and Foreign Affairs to their respective administrations, and police officers in the airports and bureaucrats of OFPRA have come to view asylum seekers with systematic suspicion: all candidates for refugee status are now considered, until there is evidence to the contrary, to be undocumented immigrants seeking to take advantage of the generosity of the European nations. Use of the expression "false refugees" to refer to "economic immigrants" who claim political asylum has become central to bureaucratic common sense (Valluy 2004). The Geneva Convention is thereby implemented in a more and more restricted way by governments who declare that it should be rewritten.

In contrast, during the same period, another category of immigrants were increasingly being granted residence permits: those with health problems, or more precisely, with severe pathologies for which they had no access to proper treatment in their home countries. This new criterion is officially designated as "humanitarian reasons" (Lochak 2001). It was invented in the early 1990s in response to pressure from medical NGOs like Médecins Sans Frontières and Médecins Du Monde but also from human rights associations who found themselves confronted by patients who suffered from life-threatening illnesses, such as AIDS or cancer, and who were at risk of being driven out of France for being undocumented. At first, the decisions concerning these cases were rare and arbitrary: they depended on the degree of social mobilization around each case and on the good will of the préfet. Progressively, however, the practice became more common and more publicized until the right-wing Minister of the Interior Jean-Louis Debré included a ban on expelling foreigners with severe health problems, whatever their legal status in the 1996 Immigration law. This fact is remarkable because it was the one concession made with "respect for individual rights" within a piece of legislation largely characterized by its "firmness against illegal immigration." Still, it was not a measure that granted full residence right, and beneficiaries were not allowed to enter the labor market. A few months later, with the installation of a new parliamentary majority, the 1998 Immigration law introduced by the socialist Minister of the Interior Jean-Pierre Chevènement was approved: for the first time, the existence of health problems could confer the right to a residence permit, social protection, and authorization to work. Under a humanitarian principle, the suffering body was now recognized as the main legal resource for undocumented immigrants (Fassin 2001b). The yearly number of foreigners awarded residence permits because of an illness increased sevenfold during the 1990s. By 2000, it had become equivalent to the number of political refugees recognized every year.

The chronological association between the marked drop in political asylum and the increasing recognition of humanitarian reasons is not a coincidence. The two phenomena are linked. Thus, as a high-level administrator of the Ministry of the Interior explained to me in an account of the 80,000 legalizations of undocumented foreigners they had processed in 1997–98, those categorized under humanitarian reasons had been treated "as a priority" while political asylum had been treated "as a subsidiary concern." In fact, many lawyers, human rights activists, and even local state officers in immigration services understood this new policy very clearly. For them, as well as for the undocumented immigrants themselves, "Article 12bis-11" of the law became the best hope for asylum seekers in the administrative jungle of immigration legislation: More specifically, the law mentions the right to a residence permit for "the foreigner living in France whose health status necessitates medical care, the default of which would have consequences of exceptional gravity, considering that he/she cannot have access to the proper treatment in the country from which he/she comes." (Groupe d'Information et de Soutien des Immigrés 1999) For asylum seekers seeking advice, advocates would ask: "don't you have an illness you could invoke?" and then suggest a visit to the doctor.

An African immigrant recalls what he was told by a volunteer in one of the main solidarity NGOs he had consulted: "I showed her my prescriptions. She said I surely had a severe disease. She told me to go to a doctor, and with good evidence it will not be a problem. I will have my residence permit. I just have to show that I cannot get treatment in my country." Paradoxically full of hope at the idea of an illness, the undocumented immigrants would go to their physician or to the hospital, sometimes with a letter from the préfet requesting "diagnosis, treatment, and perspectives on prognosis" under cover of "medical confidentiality." Often, on hearing the doctor say that "their disease is not severe enough to justify the claim," they would express their disappointment or their anger. Sometimes, as in the case of the young Haitian woman, they would obtain not only medical approval but also free health care with the *couverture maladie universelle*, the social protection system for the poor. As one of the beneficiaries of this administrative decision once said to me: "It is the disease that is killing me that now keeps me alive" (Fassin 2001c). He was from Nigeria and he had spent ten years in France and Germany without a legal permit. He had recently discovered that he had a severe form of AIDS. After having lived for such a long time under the threat of being sent back to his country, he had finally received the residence permit under this new article of the law and was undergoing intensive antiretroviral therapy free of charge.

No situation could reveal more obviously the recent change in European politics of life than this shift from political asylum to humanitarian reasons. For the French government and parliament, the legitimacy of the suffering body has become greater than that of the threatened body, and the right to life is being displaced from the political sphere to that of compassion. It is more acceptable and less dangerous for the state to reject an asylum claim, declaring it unfounded, than to go against medical expertise recommending a legal permit for health reasons. On Tuesday, October 7, 2003, access to French territory was refused to a woman from Chechnya and her two young children who had asked for political asylum. Her husband and father-in-law had been abducted by men with uniforms in Grozny; the former was never seen again and the dead body of the latter was discovered a few days later. When she started to search for her husband, she received an anonymous letter threatening her and her children with death if she continued her inquiry. The French administrator of the Ministry of Foreign Affairs who met her at the Roissy airport, however, concluded that she could not show sufficient evidence of exposure to threat, and thus a few hours later, before a lawyer could intervene in her defense, she was sent back to Moscow with her children (Fédération Internationale des Droits de l'Homme 2003).

This is one of the many examples in which asylum seekers are denied entry even before they can file their cases. Meanwhile, state medical experts face an increasing task of ruling on the "humanitarian reasons" of claims, and immigration services arc ordered to systematically "follow medical advice," except in cases in which there is a "menace to public order." It is much less politically risky for the government to deny entry to refugees than to expel a patient with AIDS or cancer. In Agamben's (1997: 9) terms, the full life (bios) of the freedom fighter or the victim of repression has less social value than the bare life (zoë) of the immigrant suffering from a severe disease. Many foreigners understand in their "flesh," to use Maurice Merleau-Ponty's concept (1964), that their presence in France is not recognized for the political risks they have taken or the dangers they face but rather for the physical or psychic distress they can demonstrate. Their access to French society is deeply marked by this often humiliating experience of having to use their biology rather than their biography as a resource to win the right to exist.

In his study of the "double absence," Abdelmalek Sayad (1999) asserted that "the immigrant is but a body" and that its dysfunctions reveal "embodied contradictions." A few decades ago, this body was legitimate for economic reasons and disease would be suspect. I suggest that the situation is reversed now. The body being useless for work, disease has become a social resource. Up to the 1970s, immigrants were workers whose labor was necessary for the reconstruction of European countries profoundly damaged by World War II: in those days, their work permit served as a residence permit. Their bodies had to be healthy, and if that was not the case, then they would be suspected of feigning illness to gain the benefits of the social security system. Times have changed. With the modernization of industry, which has replaced most of the unskilled labor by machines, their bodies have become superfluous because of real or supposed competition in the workforce, with the exception of certain economic sectors such as the building or clothing industries, in which illegal workers are still a necessary source of cheap labor (Morice 1997). In this new economic context, it is now the suffering body that society is prepared to recognize. The undocumented immigrants have understood this shift well, and some do not hesitate to engage in hunger strikes when seeking to have their rights recognized (Siméant 1998). Instead of provoking suspicion, illnesses now seem to be the most successful basis of claims for many undocumented immigrants, a condition I call "biolegitimacy" (Fassin 2000) – the legitimization of rights in the name of the suffering body. In the context of a consolidated European Union, which has strengthened control at its frontiers, the political economy of contemporary Europe has reduced immigrants from poor countries to what Hannah Arendt called "workers without work, that is, deprived of the only activity left for them" (1983: 38). Its moral economy has evolved toward a compassionate attention to individual suffering in which the search for a common humanity resides in the recognition of bare life, that of the physical alterations of the body.

However, in this paradigm, political asylum and humanitarianism still remain two separate and parallel entities that appear to represent distinct moral values.

The mere fact that a rejected asylum seeker can be encouraged to present his or her case again under a humanitarian rationale underscores that there are two different administrative realities governed by separate institutions: the OFPRA, under the Ministry of Foreign Affairs, and immigration services, under the Ministry of the Interior. However, recent evolution in political discourse and practice suggests that another paradigm is emerging, in which the two norms are becoming irrevocably linked, with the category of asylum increasingly subsumed under the category of humanitarianism.

The Humanitarianization of Asylum

The *East Sea* ran aground off the French Riviera on February 17, 2001. It had 900 persons on board, most of them Kurds. It was only one of many ships carrying thousands of people every year as they flee countries in Eastern Europe, Africa, and Asia to better their conditions of existence. The first public reaction was quite hostile. The wreck raised suspicions of what many political commentators described as a "planned" accident that would force France to receive the ship's passengers. During the days that followed, the socialist government as well as its right-wing opponents converged in denouncing the shipwrecked foreigners as "illegal immigrants" and condemning the "criminal organizations" that had helped them on their way to Europe. This discourse had the effect of disqualifying any claim to political asylum on the part of the passengers: they were to be considered as *clandestins* (illegal immigrants) rather than possible refugees. Publicly represented as such, they were parked in a "detention center" without any freedom of movement. Nevertheless, as the television coverage started to show images of destitute families, crying children, pregnant women, and sick old people behind barbed wired fences, indignant reactions were provoked from human rights associations as well as from the media and the public. This gave birth to a different rhetoric. They became "victims" of political oppression as well as of common misfortune. Surely, the "homeland of human rights" would not let them suffer in what was now referred to as a "camp." In response to this unexpected wave of collective sympathy, Prime Minister Lionel Jospin declared that each situation would be examined on the basis of "humanitarian criteria." He did not mention claims for asylum but instead evoked the sense of compassion one needed to have under such circumstances. As *Le Monde* commented approvingly: "The heart has its reasons, indeed even its reflexes, to which reason must listen" (2001a). This approximation of Pascal's aphorism eluded what could be more bluntly cast as the mere substitution of a political right by a moral sentiment. In fact, the residents of the "detention center" were relocated to small units dispersed all over the country, and their files were evaluated by the OFPRA, which recognized 83 percent of the claimants as refugees – an exceptionally high proportion in a period when this institution delivered political asylum to only 12 percent of all candidates. National emotion had indeed benefited them. Moreover, the demographic cost was low, because only 160 of the shipwrecked Kurds ultimately stayed in France, the rest of them preferring to go to other European countries, mainly Germany, where they had more effective networks.

Following Hannah Arendt's analysis (1951) of "the decline of the nation-state and the end of human rights," one can assert that the Geneva Convention was a response of the international community to the neglect of the 32 million refugees and stateless people during the 1930s and 1940s. However, beyond this ideological goal were the pragmatic objectives of meeting the concrete needs of "displaced persons," whose number reached seven million immediately after 1945, and of solving a series of demographic and economic problems linked to the losses of war and the requirements for reconstruction. In the case of refugees and stateless persons, one should certainly not idealize the conditions of the founding of a new world order on the UN's Universal Declaration of Human Rights (Noiriel 1991). If the "never again" leitmotiv in the wake of the Holocaust was a strong incentive for the consolidation of a specific status of "political asylum," the universal solidarity that it expressed in official rhetoric did not exclude national interests that manifested themselves through background discussions about the distribution of refugees and the stateless among European nations, mainly on economic grounds. Whatever the motives of governments, the Geneva Convention had a strong symbolic effect reversing the stigma that had affected "displaced persons" in the aftermath of the war (Cohen 2000). The international status they received in 1951 gave them a transnational nobility through recognition of the rightness of their political cause or, at least, of the wrongness of the violence to which they had been submitted.

Although it took some time to enter into administrative practice, the legitimacy of political asylum grew after the Geneva Convention. The "undesirables" became heroes for some, victims for many. They served as symbols of resistance to oppression, as in Chile after the 1973 coup, or of the suffering of the oppressed, as with the Vietnamese boat people of 1978. The level of protection they received during this period was a sign of this social recognition (Brachet 2002). In France, social rights for refugees obtained between 1975 and 1984, including authorization to work and social aid for the unemployed, were extended to asylum seekers in 1985. This evolution is all the more remarkable given that the period is also characterized by an overall setback in policies toward immigrant aliens, particularly the interruption of labor immigration in 1974, followed by the restriction of provisions for family reunion in 1984 (Weil 1991). In fact, until the early 1980s, refugees were the most legitimate figures within the implicit – and sometimes explicit – hierarchy of foreigners, and they thereby benefited from relatively privileged conditions. At that time, asylum seekers had a reasonable probability of achieving this socially valued status. But, as Giovanna Zincone (1997) suggests: "We tend to be better at practicing the virtue of tolerance when it is least needed." Generosity was not so difficult in those years because few benefited from it, and the rate of official recognition was high because the number of claims was small. France needed a labor force, as did other European countries, and instead of entering the long administrative path of asylum, most politically oppressed people preferred to get a work contract that entitled them to stay. In the mid-1970s, when the positive image of political asylum was at its peak and when the social rights associated with it were being extended, the presence of refugees in France had reached its lowest level since World War II. Moreover, during this period asylum seekers were mainly from Eastern Europe and East Asia, groups that were assumed to be easier to assimilate. This happy picture was to change rapidly during the 1980s.

The year 1989 represents a turning point. The number of asylum seekers entering France that year was the highest recorded in decades: 62,000 new files, compared to roughly 20,000 in the early 1980s and a meager 2000 in 1974 (OFPRA 1996, 2004). This spectacular increase was mainly the result of the end of the Cold War and the opening of the borders of formerly communist countries. However, it was more profoundly a sign of structural changes occurring in international migration. At the global level, the rapid transformation of a "new world order" determined an exacerbation of nationalisms and transnational processes resulting, on the one hand, in a series of regional conflicts and, on the other hand, in the development of clandestine immigration networks. Both phenomena led to an acceleration in the movements of human beings (Kearney 1995). In the local logic, with increasingly restrictive immigration laws, asylum became one of the only remaining "avenues of access" to legal status, thus facilitating a lack of distinction between political and economic motives (Watters 2001). Confronted by an increase in claims, the most common political reaction was to denounce the "crisis in asylum." The socialist Prime Minister Michel Rocard made his famous statement, "France cannot welcome all the misery of the world." This rhetoric reinforced the confusion between economic immigrants and political refugees, thereby discrediting the latter. Asylum seekers became suspect. Soon the dramatization of this discourse legitimized the use of more severe criteria for recognition of legal status and an increasing restriction of social rights.

As Aristide Zolberg (2001) has suggested: "Indeed the prevailing sense of an 'international migration crisis' has profoundly inflected the consideration of policy alternatives. In particular, it has been invoked to justify draconian measures to protect national borders, even at the expense of obligations towards refugees." The story of the *East Sea* illustrates how asylum has become a concern of ordinary policing, interrupted only by specific political emergencies that arouse temporary public sympathy toward victims. The dramas of Bosnia and Kosovo are examples of these fitful displays of generosity when the political elite tries to follow or even anticipate public opinion (Rosenberg 1995). However, the victims of violence very soon become mere illegal immigrants again, and they are hunted down as the Bosnians and Kosovares have been on the shores of Italy. Episodes of compassion toward refugees thus appear as privileged moments of collective redemption eluding the common law of their repression.

However, to make this repression socially acceptable, one has to disqualify asylum seekers. Here, the performative power of words is particularly effective in attaining this objective (Fassin 1996). The claimants are commonly designated as clandestins, thus justifying official actions against them, such as sending them to detention centers or driving them back to their countries. Even the services in charge of the reception of asylum seekers seem to have internalized this negative representation. A social worker in one of my studies explained, for example, that although such claimants had the official provisional status of asylum seekers, she considered them to be *sans-papiers* (i.e., undocumented) because she knew that most of them would end up as such. Her anticipation of the eventual outcome, which was statistically correct in more than eight cases out of ten, led her to deprive them of universal social security benefits, for which she substituted less beneficial and clearly stigmatized charitable medical aid. In this process of disqualification of refugees, successive French governments developed three strategies.

The first is dissuasive and based on the principle of deterrence through restrictions on welfare benefits (Düvell and Jordan 2002). It consists in reducing the social rights of the asylum seekers through suppression of the housing subsidy in 1989, the suppression of the authorization to work in 1991, and limitation of financial aid to one year and to a monthly allotment of $250 (one third of the poverty level). With this new situation, asylum is supposed to be less attractive – especially in relation to neighboring countries such as Britain. The second strategy is repressive and corresponds to a "criminalization of immigrants" (Palidda 1999). It includes driving back asylum seekers seeking to enter the national territory, confining them in fenced detention centers, implementing the unique French system of *double peine* (a double sentence), specific to aliens. Those who refuse to embark on planes are first condemned to prison and are then deported when they get out of jail. More generally, these immigrants are included in the category of ordinary "delinquency" as it appears in police statistics. The third strategy is distinctive and intended to restructure the status of refugees on a "discretionary" basis (Delouvin 2000). The 1998 law passed by the socialist government thus distinguishes "conventional asylum" from two other forms: on the one hand, "constitutional asylum," a category corresponding to the supposedly nobler and rarely granted status of "freedom fighter," and on the other hand, "territorial asylum," a category for victims of nonstate persecutors. Initially invented for Algerians, this last category actually appeared to be a disguised and precarious form of temporary status, as it is reevaluated every year to facilitate a return to the country of origin when the political situation there is deemed to be more democratic and stable. To harmonize European policies, this specific status was later abandoned but replaced by an even lower one.

Within this new context, the confinement of asylum seekers in transit camps becomes possible, and the government can pretend to forget that they are seeking asylum and generously offer them humanitarian treatment. A display of sympathy thus replaces the recognition of a right. The biopolitics of asylum must be understood as the substitution of a social order founded on "obligation" for a social order grounded in "solidarity," to use Georg Simmel's words (1998). The recognition of the refugee status by European nations appears as an act of generosity on the part of a national community toward a "suffering stranger" (Butt 2002) rather than the fulfillment of a political debt toward "citizens of humanity" (Malkki 1994). Constructed as illegal immigrants and commonly qualified as clandestins, asylum seekers oscillate between being objects of repression and compassion. On the one side lie the waiting zones, where 18,936 foreigners were detained in 2000 and where a state of exception reigns that has been denounced both by human rights activists and by the appeals court of Paris (Rodier 2002). On the other side lie humanitarian organizations that offer assistance by preparing narratives corresponding to the expectations of state officials and by testifying as medical doctors to physical and psychic traumas (Veisse 2003). The hierarchy introduced among refugees in the new French legislation appears to be a clear contradiction of the Geneva Convention as well as a paradoxical evocation of its deep historical significance. At the top of this hierarchy stands the eternal hero who (exceptionally) obtains constitutional asylum for his or her fight against oppression and his or her defense of liberty; next comes the permanent victim who (less and less frequently) receives through conventional asylum official protection for the violence inflicted; lower still comes the transitory victim who (increasingly) occupies a provisional status that is as precarious as possible to avoid future integration; and at the bottom lies the great mass of asylum seekers who will be classed as illegal immigrants and chased by the police. The harmonization of European policies after the Convention of Dublin in 1990 tends to pull this hierarchy downward, while at the same time appearing to be more subtle than the classical dualism between the "deserving" and the "non deserving" (Sales 2002). For instance, in the European Union in 1999, only one refugee in five had been recognized under the heading of conventional asylum, whereas four in five received the recently invented "subsidiary protection," also called "status B," which replaced the French territorial asylum (Bouteillet-Paquet 2002). But on the whole, both statuses left out several hundreds of thousands of rejected aliens who had sought in vain protection from the Geneva Convention.

The Last Camp

Agamben (1997: 195) posits two models of social organization, the camp and the polis, and concludes that the former and not the latter corresponds to our late modernity: "The biopolitical paradigm of the West today is not the polis, but the camp." And by this word, he meant the concentration, and even the extermination, camp. Commenting on this polemical sentence in *Le Monde* (2004), he insists that this is "a philosophical thesis and not a historical narrative." The pessimistic vision that it expresses has the merit of attracting our attention to the places where, and the moments when, the state of exception becomes the rule. These are the sites that Carl Schmitt (1985: 5) defined as the foundation of sovereignty in his political theology: "Sovereign is he who decides on exception." Certainly, from an anthropological perspective, this tension between the camp and the polis cannot be discussed as a desocialized space or in an ahistorical time. To put it bluntly, Sangatte was neither Auschwitz nor Guantanamo – the two camps positioned by Agamben (2003) as the horizons of contemporary biopolitics. In Sangatte, no citizenship was recognized, but human rights were respected; foreigners could claim asylum in France; the circulation of people was free as long as they did not try to cross the Channel; whereas humanitarian organizations, lawyers, journalists, and even ethnologists were allowed to cross freely. So, the parallel with Auschwitz or Guantanamo is misleading. However, as long as we avoid the intellectual perils of mere analogy, thinking about Sangatte in terms of the broader form of the camp might help to comprehend the profound nature of our treatment of refugees and in a broader sense the moral economy of our societies.

In the present French context, to designate Sangatte as a camp is a highly polemical act, because the memory of transit camps such as Drancy (from which French people, mainly Jews, were sent to Auschwitz after 1942) has been recently revived by historiography, literature, and cinema. Significantly, Smaïn Laacher, the sociologist who was contracted by Sangatte's director to write the history of the place and its occupants through a study of asylum seekers, refers to it as "Sangatte Center" in his book (2002), but the title of a lecture he gave to the League of Human Rights at the Ecole des Hautes Études en Sciences Sociales in 2003 referred to it as the "Camp of Sangatte." In the war of words that surrounds the issue of immigration, this expression has generally been used by those who denounced the site as shameful for France. In May 2002, Nicolas Sarkozy made his first official visit as the newly designated Minister of the Interior to Sangatte, immediately announcing that he would close it, but this was not just for "humanitarian considerations" or because it was "a facilitator of illegal networks" – as he declared on June 4, 2003 – but also and primarily because it was a "symbol" (Carrère 2002) through which the memory of the past could too easily and effectively be evoked by critics.

In fact, the history of camps in France began a little before World War II (Peschanski 2002). The confinement of undesirable foreigners in specialized centers had been decided in the decree of November 12, 1938, "in the interest of public order and security," as xenophobia and anti-Semitism were at their climax in France. The first camps, initially designated as "concentration camps" (an expression that later turned out to be difficult to keep using), served to gather Spanish Republicans fleeing Franco's dictatorship after the fall of Barcelona on January 29, 1939, and collected some half a million people in the south of France, the majority of whom were repatriated more or less voluntarily within a few months. During the weeks that followed the declaration of war against Germany, on September 3, 1939, 83 "confinement camps for the enemies" were progressively added to the eight camps already devoted to Spanish refugees. The French policies at that time were much more repressive than those of other countries such as Great Britain. After the defeat in June 1940 and the instauration of the Vichy regime, the camps served first to detain communists and then, increasingly, Jews, but it was not until the spring of 1942 that they became the antechamber of the final solution under the designation of "transit camps." When the war ended, the same camps ironically served to confine Nazi collaborators until May 1946.

One should certainly not confuse Sangatte, conceived at first to give shelter to candidates for immigration into Britain, with the transit camp of Drancy, the camp for "undesirable aliens which opened at Rieucros," the camp for Spanish refugees of Saint-Cyprien, the camp at Chateaubriand where communist detainees were arbitrarily executed, and the camp at Montreuil-Bellay where 1,000 nomad Gypsies were held, or the Conciergerie where collaborationists were imprisoned after the liberation of Paris. Each one of them had its own reason for being, its specific logic of confinement, and its particular rules of control. However diverse the social realities of the camps may be in these different moments of the dark side of French history, the permanence of the camp structure is in itself revealing. Indeed, Erving Goffman (1961) discovered a common functioning of what he called "total institutions" behind the different motivations that gave birth to the psychiatric hospital, the prison, and the convent, and it may be possible to transcend the historical variety of the camps to unveil their shared signification.

The camps correspond to a specific response to problems of public order by instituting small territories of exception. What justifies these local states of exception is an emergency that makes the gathering up of people appear as a practical solution. But the suspension of the usual social norms is accepted only because it is implemented for "undesirable" subjects. A situation that should be considered intolerable is in fact tolerated because the public order is threatened by immigrants, enemies, communists, gypsies, Jews, and collaborators. Therefore, because Sangatte is open for asylum seekers to come and go (under control of the police) and is administered by a humanitarian organization (with the collaboration of many volunteers), it cannot therefore be simply equated to other camps in modern French history. Nonetheless, the memory it disturbs tells us a profound truth. This memory says less about the center than about its inmates – who might be better described as "vagabonds," in Zygmunt Bauman's (1998) terms. From a long-term perspective, it becomes obvious that the opening of Sangatte recasts the asylum seekers as the new "unwanted" – a role they have long occupied, as Michael Marrus recalls (1985). The present reinvention of the camp reveals the continuity of the preoccupation: the camp draws attention to those who are constructed as living outside the polis – literally, the "alienated." The contemporary figure of the alien is the asylum seeker. As such, it became the theme of *Last Caravanserai*, an eight-hour play created by the famous director Ariane Mnouchkine in the Cartoucherie de Vincennes near Paris and later presented as the main event of the Avignon Festival: "The Théâtre du Soleil carries the voices of the refugees," ran the headline of *Le Monde* on April 1, 2003, indicating that the text had been based on "testimonies from Sangatte and other places." The drama of the asylum seekers had given birth to a national cultural performance.

Viewed from Europe, the figure of the asylum seeker is today essentially constructed within the framework of what Liisa Malkki (1995) calls the "emergence of refugees as a third world problem." On the one hand, it corresponds to a demographic reality crudely illustrated by statistics: most of the world's refugees come from poor countries. On the other hand, it reveals a political truth that is often neglected: the majority of them remain in poor countries. With 154,000 new refugees in 2002 and a total of 4.2 million refugees, Europe is only taking a limited share of the global distribution of the estimated 17 million victims of forced displacement in the world under the UNHCR responsibility (2004). And with 102,000 recognized refugees and 47,000 asylum seekers living in France, the so-called "crisis of asylum" is quite minor compared to small African countries such as Guinea, where more than 400,000 refugees are packed in camps (Wihtol de Wenden 2002). The dramatization of the situation in Western countries thus results far more from representations than from social facts; but then, one knows that in this matter, as in others, representations are social facts (Rabinow 1986). Bearing these paradoxes in mind, one can understand the biopolitics of asylum, which falls under a larger biopolitics of otherness in a polarized world, as a two-sided phenomenon.

On the one side is the polis within a protected European space of aggregated nation states, the highest protection being among the 25 nations of the European Union. Its core was delimited in 1985 by the Schengen Convention as a zone that should be defended against aliens. The Tempere Conference in 1999 defined a new common policy linking the forms of immigration that it was supposed to discourage with asylum that could then be more effectively restricted. Those who are identified as belonging within this European space are called *communautaires* (community members) and those who are identified as outside of it are, *étrangers* (foreigners). The protected zone is thought to be threatened by two kinds of security problems. First, public security at the national level menaced by terrorist attacks and at a local level by ordinary criminality and delinquency These have become the major issues of French politics during the early 2000s, as the combined result of the international situation after September 11 and a national political campaign based on everyday insecurity. Second, social security is threatened, whether it is thought of as an outcome of the welfare state present inside the French territory or extended, under certain conditions, to the wider European space. The argument that an influx of too many immigrants or refugees would endanger the welfare system is often presented as a reasonable justification for the implementation of draconian policies. A third dimension of the menace has recently become perceptible. Although difficult to name, as it is masked by cultural or religious, sometimes ethnic, description, it can be characterized most bluntly as racial security: it has to do with the protection of a European, Christian, and white civilization against Third World, Muslim, or black populations, as the debates surrounding the entrance of Turkey to the European community and the contestation about Islamic veiling in public institutions in France have revealed. Within this context, which has evolved far from the humanist principles of the Geneva Convention, asylum seekers and aliens in general are seen as potential threats to these three dimensions of European security.

On the other side of the biopolitics of asylum lies the camp as a territory of exception. Although Sangatte represents the most famous and symbolic image of this figure, it is only one of its numerous manifestations, and it is certainly not the worst. In the 122 "waiting zones" existing along France's borders, where asylum seekers are retained until official agents decide whether they will be allowed to present their file, human rights activists regularly criticize the indignity of the accommodations and the violence exerted by the police, the lack of communication with the outside, and the impossibility of receiving the legal assistance of lawyers, as well as the absence of any external control or judicial appeal. Of the detention centers where the undocumented foreigners, many of whom are rejected asylum seekers, wait to be deported, many reports, including some from the conservative senate, have denounced the inhumane conditions and the suspension of normal rights. The unique "double sentence" is applied to aliens accused of delinquent or criminal acts, which in most cases are simply acts of resistance to expulsion. These individuals are condemned to be imprisoned and then driven out of the country on release, no matter how long they have lived in France, in some cases from the time they were children. In the first months of 2003, two immigrants died of suffocation as they struggled against police officers attempting to secure them for detention. The aftermath of this case demonstrates how far one can go to get rid of the undesirable with apparent impunity and little public outcry. These scenes delineate a map of territories within the European political geography where the exception comes to be tolerated.

Contrary to Agamben's prophetic view that the camp, and not the polis, is the biopolitical paradigm of the West, I would rather say that these are the two sides of contemporary democracies. Because these regimes defend the polis for the happy few, they invent the camp for the undesirable. In the former, life is recognized as the political existence of the citizen, whereas in the latter, it is reduced to the bare life of the vagabond. Between the polis – however idealized it may be – and the camp – however marginal it may seem – the tensions are thus extreme. However, it would be cynical or simplistic to think that the collective renunciation manifested by the camp is the price we pay for the comfort of the polis. Indeed, these tensions between the two figures of our world explain why, with respect to asylum seekers and unwanted others in general, repression and compassion are so profoundly linked. Not only is there no separation between the humanitarian and the political but, in contradiction with Agamben, I suggest that the latter increasingly integrates the former, which in return redefines it. The increasing confusion between the humanitarian and the political is a structural feature of contemporary biopolitics.

Expressing sympathy for the asylum seeker or the undesirable immigrant holds fewer benefits for that figure than it has for us, as we show how humane we finally are. The medical doctor legalizing the unwanted refugee whose presence suddenly becomes legitimate because of a life-threatening disease, as in the case of the young Haitian woman, and the chief of government who asks civil servants to examine claims for asylum with humanitarian feelings, as in the case of the Kurds of the *East Sea*, both participate in a redefinition of the moral economy of our times: a unique combination of policies of order and a politics of suffering, in which the protection of security for the few within the polis is maintained while a compassionate treatment for those within the camps is assured.

The young Afghan hero of Michael Winterbottom's 2003 film *In This World* leaves a refugee camp resembling a city in Pakistan, which is the country in the world with the highest number of refugees. He crosses countries in buses and trucks, endures misfortunes, and confronts dangers to reach Istanbul. Later, he loses his older companion who dies asphyxiated in a container while traveling by boat to Italy. Finally, he reaches Sangatte, the last waystation before Britain, where he will subsequently succeed in becoming a dishwasher in a restaurant and obtain subsidiary protection until he reaches his legal majority. For him, Sangatte exists only as an episode in his journey, the last station as he enters the polis where he will join the ranks of the third world underclass. To get there, the risk he took was (merely) his life. The sympathy he arouses among the film's spectators makes them believe that, beyond his misery, they share a common humanity. For this moment of fictional illusion in our moral world, the film surely deserves the Golden Bear, the Prize of Peace, and the Prize of the Ecumenical Jury, all of which it received in Berlin in 2003.

REFERENCES

Agamben, Giorgio
  1997 *Homo sacer. I. Le pouvoir souverain et la vie nue.* Paris: Seuil.
  2003 *Homo sacer. II. État d'exception.* Paris: Seuil.

Arendt, Hannah
   1951   *The Origins of Totalitarianism*. New York: Harcourt-Brace.
   1983[1958]   *Condition de l'homme moderne* (*The human condition*). Paris: Calmann-Lévy.
Bateson, Gregory
   1958[1936]   *Naven*. Stanford: Stanford University Press.
Bauman, Zygmunt
   1998   *Globalization. The Human Consequences*. Cambridge: Polity Press.
Berger, Nathalie
   2000   *La politique européenne d'asile et d'immigration. Enjeux et perspectives*. Brussels: Bruylant.
Bloch, Alice, and Liza Schuster
   2002   Asylum and Welfare: Contemporary Debates. *Critical Social Policy* 22(3): 393–414.
Bouteillet-Paquet, Daphné
   2002   Quelle protection subsidiaire dans l'Union européenne? *Hommes et migrations* 1238: 75–87.
Brachet, Olivier
   2002   La condition du réfugié dans la tourmente de la politique de l'asile. *Hommes et migrations* 1238: 45–58.
Butt, Leslie
   2002   The Suffering Stranger. Medical Anthropology and International Morality. *Medical Anthropology* 21(1): 1–24.
Carrère, Violaine
   2002   Sangatte, un toit pour des fantômes. *Hommes et migrations* 1238: 13–22.
Cohen, Daniel
   2000   Naissance d'une nation: Les personnes déplacées de l'après-guerre, 1945–1951. *Genèses. Sciences sociales et histoire* 38: 56–78.
Daily Mail
   2001   "Asylum: Yes, Britain is a soft touch!" *Daily Mail*, February 11.
Delouvin, Patrick
   2000   The Evolution of Asylum in France. *Journal of Refugee Studies* 13(1): 61–73.
Douglas, Mary
   1986   *How Institutions Think*. Syracuse, NY: Syracuse University Press.
Düvell, Franck, and Bill Jordan
   2002   Immigration, Asylum and Welfare: The European Context. *Critical Social Policy* 22(3): 498–517.
Fassin, Didier
   1996   Clandestins ou exclus? Quand les mots font les politiques. *Politix* 34: 77–86.
   2000   Entre politiques du vivant et politiques de la vie. Pour une anthropologie de la santé. *Anthropologie et sociétés* 24(1): 95–116.
   2001a   The Biopolitics of Otherness. Undocumented Immigrants and Racial Discrimination in the French Public Debate. *Anthropology Today* 17(1): 3–7.
   2001b   Quand le corps fait loi. La raison humanitaire dans les procédures de régularisation des étrangers. *Sciences sociales et santé* 19(4): 5–34.
   2001c   Une double peine. La condition sociale des immigrés malades du sida. *L'Homme. Revue française d'anthropologie* 160: 137–162.
   2003   Justice Principles and Judgment Practices in Allotting Emergency State Financial Aid. *Revue française de sociologie* (annual English selection) 44: 109–146.
   2004   *Des maux indicibles. Sociologie des lieux d'écoute*. Paris: La Découverte.

2005   L'ordre moral du monde. Essai d'anthropologie de l'intolérable. In *Les constructions de l'intolérable. Etudes d'anthropologie et d'histoire sur les frontières de l'espace moral*. Didier Fassin and Patrice Bourdelais, eds. Pp. 17–50. Paris: La Découverte.

Fédération Internationale des Droits de l'Homme
2003   Une première au pays des droits de l'homme. Une femme et deux enfants tchétchènes expulsés vers Moscou. Electronic document, www.fidh.org/2003/fr1310f.htm, accessed October 20.

Foucault, Michel
1978   *The History of Sexuality. An Introduction*, Volume 1. New York: Vintage.

Geremek, Bronislaw
1987[1978]   *La potence ou la pitié. L'Europe et les pauvres du Moyen Age*. Paris: Gallimard.

Goffman, Erving
1961   *Asylums. Essays on the Social Situation of Mental Patients and Other Inmates*. Garden City, NY: Anchor.

Graham, Mark
2003   Emotional Bureaucracies: Emotions, Civil Servants, and Immigrants in the Swedish Welfare State. *Ethos* 30(3): 199–226.

Groupe d'Information et de Soutien des Immigrés
1999   "Article 12bis-11," 11 May 1998 Law. In *Le guide de l'entrée et du séjour des étrangers en France*. Paris: La Découverte-Syros.
2001   "Immigration Law Practitioners Association and Information and Support Group for Immigrants," press release. Electronic document, www.gisti.org, accessed February 5, 2005.

Hargreaves, Alec
1999   *Immigration, "Race" and Ethnicity in Contemporary France*. 2nd edition. London: Routledge.

Herzfeld, Michael
1992   *The Social Production of Indifference. Exploring the Symbolic Roots of Western Bureaucracy*. Chicago: University of Chicago Press.

Heyman, Josiah McC.
1998   *Finding a Moral Heart for U.S. Immigration Policy. An Anthropological Perspective*, 7. Arlington, VA: American Ethnological Society.

In This World
2003   Michael Winterbottom, dir. 88 min. BBC Films-The Film Consortium-Revolution Films-Film Council. London.

Julien-Laferrière, François
2002   Le traitement des demandeurs d'asile en zone d'attente, entre théorie et réalité. *Hommes et migrations* 1238: 32–44.

Kearney, Michael
1995   The Local and the Global. The Anthropology of Globalization and Transnationalism. *Annual Review of Anthropology* 24: 547–565.

Laacher, Smaïn
2002   *Après Sangatte. Nouvelles immigrations, nouveaux enjeux*. Paris: La Dispute.

Legoux, Luc
1999   Les pépites d'or de l'OFPRA. *Plein Droit* 44: 7–10.

Le Monde
2001a   "Droit d'asile," *Le Monde*, February 22.
2001b   "Une enquête a été ouverte après une rixe entre des réfugiés du centre de Sangatte," *Le Monde*, July 25.

2002a "A Sangatte, une bagarre entre réfugiés fait sept blesses," *Le Monde*, May 19.

2002b "Immigration: Europe strengthens its frontiers," *Le Monde*, May 30.

2002c "La préfecture dément que des policiers aient arrosé d'essence un blockhaus servant d'abri aux migrants près de Sangatte," *Le Monde*, November 24.

2002d "Sangatte emergency center, a small town of 1300 inhabitants who dream of England," *Le Monde*, May 30.

2002e "Un réfugié tué lors d'une rixe au centre de Sangatte," *Le Monde*, April 17.

2003 "The Théâtre du Soleil carries the voices of the refugees," *Le Monde*, April 1.

2004 "Un paradigme biopolitique," *Le Monde*, January 6.

L'Humanité

2001 "The English Recapture Calais," *L'Humanité*, February 12.

Libération

2002 "Farewell to Sangatte," *Libération*, December 3.

Lochak, Danièle

2001 L'humanitaire, perversion de l'Etat de droit. *Sciences sociales et santé* 19(4): 35–42.

Malkki, Liisa

1994 Citizens of Humanity. Internationalism and the Imagined Community of Nations. *Diaspora* 3(1): 41–68.

1995 Refugees and Exile: From "Refugee Studies" to the National Order of Things. *Annual Review of Anthropology* 24: 495–523.

Marrus, Michael

1985 *The Unwanted: European Refugees in the Twentieth Century.* Oxford: Oxford University Press.

Merleau-Ponty, Maurice

1964 *Le visible et l'invisible.* Paris: Gallimard.

Morice, Alain

1997 Quand la lutte contre l'emploi illégal cache les progrès de la précarité légale. In *Les lois de l'inhospitalité. La société française à l'épreuve des sans-papiers.* Didier Fassin, Alain Morice, and Catherine Quiminal, eds. Pp. 177–196. Paris: La Découverte.

Noiriel, Gérard

1991 *La tyrannie du national. Le droit d'asile en Europe, 1793–1993.* Paris: Calmann-Calmann-Lévy.

Nord Littoral

1998 "Calais, reflet du chaos," *Nord Littoral*, August 6.

1999a "Deuxième phase de l'opération," *Nord Littoral*, August 18.

1999b "Le refuge du parc Saint-Pierre," *Nord Littoral*, July 14.

1999c "Les réfugiés s'installent," *Nord Littoral*, August 22.

1999d "Première nuit d'un vrai accueil," *Nord Littoral*, April 24.

1999e "Reconcile humanitarian aid," *Nord Littoral*, August 11.

Office français de protection des refugiés et des apatrides [French Office for the Protection of Refugees and Stateless People] (OFPRA)

1996 *Activité statistique 1995.* 11 pp. Fontenay-sous-Bois: OFPRA.

2004 *Rapport d'activité 2004.* 70 pp. Fontenay-sous-Bois: OFPRA.

Palidda, Salvatore

1999 La criminalisation des migrants. *Actes de la recherche en sciences sociales* 129: 39–49.

Peschanski, Denis

2002 *La France des camps. L'internement 1938–1946.* Paris: Gallimard.

Rabinow, Paul
    1986   Representations Are Social Facts. In *Writing Culture: The Poetics and Politics of Ethnography*. James Clifford and George Marcus, eds. Pp. 234–261. Berkeley: University of California Press.

Red Cross
    2002   Sangatte, l'épine dans le pied de l'Europe. Press release, June. Electronic document, www.croix-rouge.fr, accessed February 5, 2005.

Rodier, Claire
    2002   Zones d'attente de Roissy: À la frontière de l'Etat de droit. *Hommes et migrations* 1238: 23–31.

Rosenberg, Göran
    1995   Sweden and Its Immigrants. Policies versus Opinions. Special issue, "The Quest for World Order," *Daedalus* 124(3): 209–217.

Sales, Rosemary
    2002   The Deserving and the Undeserving? Refugees, Asylum Seekers and Welfare in Britain. *Critical Social Policy* 22(3): 456–478.

Sayad, Abdelmalek
    1999   *La double absence. Des illusions de l'émigré aux souffrances de l'immigré*. Paris: Seuil.

Schmitt, Carl
    1985   *Political Theology. Four Chapters on the Concept of Sovereignty*, Cambridge, MA: MIT Press.

Scott, James
    1976   *The Moral Economy of the Peasant. Rebellion and Subsistence in South East Asia*. New Haven, CT: Yale University Press.

Siméant, Johanna
    1998   L'efficacité des corps souffrants. Le recours aux grèves de la faim en France. *Sociétés contemporaines* 31: 59–85.

Simmel, Georg
    1998[1908]   *Les pauvres*. Paris: Presses universitaires de France.

Sun
    2001   "Kurds on Way: But Will Jack Send Them Back?" *Sun*, February 23.

Teitgen-Colly, Catherine
    1999   Développements récents du contentieux des réfugiés. *Plein Droit* 44: 11–16.

Thompson, E. P.
    1971   The Moral Economy of the English Crowd in the Eighteenth-Century. *Past and Present* 50(1): 76–136.

UNHCR
    2004   *2003 Global Refugee Trends. Overview of Refugee Populations, New Arrivals, Durable Solutions, Asylum Seekers and Other Persons of Concern to UNHCR*, 15 June 2004. 94 Pp. Geneva: UNHCR.

Valluy, Jérôme
    2004   La fiction juridique de l'asile. *Plein Droit* 63: 17–22.

Veisse, Arnaud
    2003   Les lésions dangereuses. *Plein Droit* 56: 32–35.

Wacquant, Loïc
    1999   *Les prisons de la misère*. Paris: Raisons d'agir.

Watters, Charles
    2001   Avenues of Access and the Moral Economy of Legitimacy. *Anthropology Today* 17(2): 22–23.

Weber, Max

　1976　*The Protestant Ethic and the Spirit of Capitalism.* London: George Allen and Unwin.

Weil, Patrick

　1991　*La France et ses étrangers. L'aventure d'une politique de l'immigration de 1938 à nos jours.* Paris: Gallimard.

Wihtol de Wenden, Catherine

　2002　La crise de l'asile. *Hommes et migrations* 1238: 6–12.

Zincone, Giovanna

　1997　The Powerful Consequences of Being Too Weak. The Impact of Immigration on democratic regimes. *Archives européennes de sociologie* 38: 104–138.

Zolberg, Aristide

　2001　Introduction. Beyond the Crisis. In *Global Migrants, Global Refugees: Problems and Solutions.* Aristide Zolberg and Peter Benda, eds. Pp. 1–16. New York: Berghahn.

Part III
Roving Commodities

This part of the reader tracks the global flow of commodities, concentrating on the way the consumption of goods often mediates the "encounter" between peoples and cultures from around the world. Part of the aim of these essays is to suggest that the consumption of foreign goods does not necessarily lead to the eradication of local cultural traditions. They highlight how Third World consumers faced with a Western cultural commodity will not simply or necessarily assimilate its values, ideologies, and lifestyle positions. Instead, these subjects will often bring their own cultural dispositions to bear on such cultural goods, interpreting, translating, and/or rejecting them according to local conditions of reception. For example, Caldwell's article shows how Russians blur the boundaries between the personal and the public, the local and the foreign, by simultaneously drawing aspects of McDonald's into the intimate spaces of their everyday lives and personalizing the public McDonald's experience. More generally, the aim of these articles is to call attention to the increasing commodification of the world, to how more and more spheres of human life have become subject to the logics of the market. Thus, Hernandez-Reguant's essay shows how, as Cuba moved to salvage its economy from the deep crisis caused by the loss of its socialist trading partners, much of the state infrastructure of cultural production and distribution was turned into a network of for-profit semiautonomous enterprises and artistic labor and cultural products generally transformed into commodities. And Lakoff's contribution deals with the commodification of genetic material, focusing on the trade in DNA between Argentina and France.

SUGGESTIONS FOR FURTHER READING

Bestor, Theodore C.
   2001   Supply-Side Sushi: Commodity, Market, and the Global City. *American Anthropologist* 103(1): 76–95.
Borooah, Romy
   2000   Transformations in Trade and the Constitution of Gender and Rank in Northeast India. *American Ethnologist* 27(2): 371–99.
Chalfin, Brenda
   2006   Global Customs Regimes and the Traffic in Sovereignty: Enlarging the Anthropology of the State. *Current Anthropology* 47(2): 243–76.
Gewertz, Deborah and Frederick Errington
   1996   On PepsiCo and Piety in a Papua New Guinea "Modernity." *American Ethnologist* 23(3): 476–93.
Goldstein-Gidoni, Ofra
   2005   The Production and Consumption of "Japanese Culture" in the Global Market. *Journal of Consumer Culture* 5(2): 155–79.
Grewal, Inderpal
   1999   Traveling Barbie: Indian Transnationality and New Consumer Subjects. *Positions* 7(3): 799–826.
Mankekar, Purnima
   2002   "Indian Shopping": Indian Grocery Stores and Transnational Configurations of Belonging. *Ethnos* 67(1): 75–98.
Mazzarella, William
   2003   "Very Bombay": Contending with the Global in an Indian Advertising Agency. *Cultural Anthropology* 18(1): 33–71.
Patico, Jennifer
   2005   To Be Happy in a Mercedes: Tropes of Value and Ambivalent Visions of Marketization. *American Ethnologist* 32(3): 479–96.
Schein, Louisa
   1999   Of Cargo and Satellites: Imagined Cosmopolitanism. *Postcolonial Studies* 2(3): 345–75.
Scheper-Hughes, Nancy
   2002   The Ends of the Body: Commodity Fetishism and the Global Traffic in Organs. *SAIS Review* 22(1): 61–80.
Shannon, Jonathan H.
   2003   Sultans of Spin: Syrian Sacred Music on the World Stage. *American Anthropologist* 105(2): 266–77.

10

Domesticating the French Fry: McDonald's and Consumerism in Moscow

Melissa L. Caldwell

During my yearly research trips to Moscow, I periodically visited my friend Veronika who lives in a small town several hours outside the city. Concerned that Moscow's metropolitan setting was sapping my energy and giving me an atypical view of Russian life, Veronika insisted that these visits and her home-cooked meals would both rejuvenate me and provide a more 'authentic' Russian experience. Shortly after I had arrived at Veronika's apartment in summer 2000, my hostess arranged a large bowl, electric mixer, fresh strawberries from her garden and vanilla ice cream on her kitchen table. She explained that an acquaintance had told her about the latest craze in Moscow: the 'milk cocktail' (*molochnyi kokteil*). More commonly known as 'milkshakes' to American consumers, these milk cocktails were introduced to Russia by McDonald's in the early 1990s. Given that I am an American and presumably experienced in such matters, Veronika asked me to do the honors. When I was done mixing, my friend called her 85-year-old father, a decorated Second World War veteran, into the kitchen to have a sample. The older man skeptically took his glass and left the room. Within minutes, he returned with an empty glass and asked for a refill.

Today, with more than 75 outlets throughout Russia, McDonald's is a prominent feature in the local landscape. In Moscow, where the majority of restaurants are located, the physical topography of city streets and pedestrian walkways is shaped by large red signs with recognizable golden arches and arrows directing pedestrians

From *Journal of Consumer Culture* 4(1): 5–26. Copyright © 2004, SAGE Publications.

and motorists to the nearest restaurant, and local residents use McDonald's restaurants as reference points when giving directions to friends from out of town. Political demonstrators use McDonald's restaurants as landmarks for staging and dispersal areas such as during an anti-government and anti-American demonstration in early October 1998, when marchers first assembled at the McDonald's store at Dobryninskaia metro station and were then joined by additional supporters when the procession went past the outlet at Tretiakovskaia station. Muscovite acquaintances who participated in the demonstration ate lunch beforehand at the McDonald's at Dobryninskaia metro station.[1] Whereas school groups formerly took cultural excursions to sites such as Lenin's tomb, museums and factories, today these same groups take educational tours through McDonald's restaurants and the McComplex production facilities.

Muscovites' experiences of McDonald's offer an instructive intervention into theories about the nature of globalization and the local/global tensions that social scientists have ascribed to transnational movements. Specifically, Muscovites' efforts to incorporate McDonald's into their daily lives complicate the arguments proposed by Giddens (1990, 2000), Ritzer (2004), Tomlinson (1999) and others that the homogenizing effects of global movements such as McDonaldization elide meaning from daily life. Instead, Muscovites have publicly affirmed and embraced McDonald's and its products as significant and meaningful elements in their social worlds. More importantly, however, Muscovites have incorporated McDonald's into the more intimate and sentimental spaces of their personal lives: family celebrations, cuisine and discourses about what it means to be Russian today. In so doing, Muscovites have drawn McDonald's into the very processes by which local cultural forms are generated, authenticated and made meaningful. It is by passing through this process of domestication that McDonald's has become localized.

In this article, I am concerned with the ways in which Russian consumers' experiences with McDonald's depart from local/global paradigms that juxtapose 'the global' with an authentic and unquestionably indigenous 'local'. As I will describe, Russian consumers are blurring the boundaries between the global and the local, the new and the original, through a set of domesticating tactics grounded in flexible ideologies of trust, comfort and intimacy. Through the application of these principles, Russian consumers render McDonald's restaurants and food as locally constituted (and, more importantly, as locally meaningful) phenomena and not simply as transnational entities with local features or as local entities enmeshed in transnational forces. Ultimately, my task in this analysis is to explore how the 'local' itself is reinvented through processes of domestication.

This motif of 'domestication' calls attention to Russian practices of consumption that link ideas about home and intimacy with ideas about the nation. In Russia, after an initial period in the early and mid-1990s when foreign goods were valued precisely for their *foreignness*, Russian consumers have refocussed their attentions on the merits of domestically produced goods. When making selections in the marketplace, Russian shoppers consider such qualities as the cultural heritage and ethnic background of producers and their products (see also Humphrey, 1999; Patico, 2001). The appeal of the inherent *localness* of goods has only been heightened in the wake of Russia's August 1998 financial crisis, when the mass departure of transnational firms from the country not only created opportunities for domestic companies to meet market demands, but also prompted customers to support local industries for both patriotic and economic reasons. A nationwide 'Buy Russia' campaign that explicitly invoked the rhetorics of nationalism and insiderness associated with the segmentary system of *Nash* ('ours') appealed to Russian consumers to give priority to domestically produced goods.[2]

Because the flexible discourse of Nash invokes claims of intimacy and familiarity, it incorporates both the imagined space of the nation, occasionally rendered as *otechestvennyi* (which means 'fatherland' and 'domestic industry', also 'patriotic'), and the physical space of the home, usually rendered as *domashnii* (which means 'of the home'), or even more simply as *bytovoi* ('of daily life').[3] An approach that employs this dual sense of 'home' is critical for understanding the larger significance of McDonald's induction into Russian social life. At the same time that McDonald's and Muscovites' home lives intersect in intriguing and powerful ways, so that consumers are both taking McDonald's home with them and bringing their home lives to McDonald's, Russians' encounters with McDonald's also reflect their interest in nationally constituted local cultures.

More important, however, while the process of Nash typically evokes a sense of nationalist qualities, Russian consumers also use it more simply to demarcate feelings of intimacy that are not exclusively national. Specifically, the emphasis on sentimental familiarity, trust and comfort that is embodied in the Nash ideology transcends absolute distinctions between local and foreign and instead creates more abstract categories of insider and outsider. As I describe later in this article, the flexible and inclusive nature of Nash emerges clearly when Russians apply it to indicate that their relationships with foreign persons and products are intimate, ordinary and meaningful (see Caldwell, 2004). In this sense, a consideration of domestication as a form of Nashification approximates the process by which goods and values acquire a state whereby they seem natural and ordinary, which Ohnuki-Tierney (1993: 6) describes as 'naturalization'.

To pursue this theme of domestication, I first consider how recent analyses of globalization and localization approach the issues of meaning and home before turning to the specific case of McDonald's and an examination of the processes by which the company and its products have been incorporated into Muscovites' daily lives. This discussion resonates with other accounts of how transnational food corporations have entered foreign markets by simultaneously responding to local practices and cultivating new local interests oriented to the company's goals (Dunn, 1999; Lozada, 2000; Watson, 1997; Yan, 2000). From this discussion, I address the processes by which Muscovite consumers have encouraged and shaped the company's efforts to 'go native' and what these efforts reveal about Russian social practice.

The material on which this article is based derives from a larger ethnographic project on changing consumption practices and food provisioning in Moscow that I conducted between 1995 and 2002.[4] For the particular case study described here, I draw on archival materials; company brochures and advertisements; and personal visits, both alone and with friends, to various McDonald's restaurants in Moscow, the company's production and distribution facilities in a suburb outside the city and other restaurants, cafes and food shops in Moscow. Unless otherwise noted, all ethnographic observations are mine. These data are supplemented by surveys, formal interviews and informal conversations that I conducted between autumn 1997 and autumn 1998 with middle-class Muscovites ranging in age from school-children to elderly pensioners. Approximately 50 university students in Moscow completed written surveys describing their eating habits, food preferences, experiences with foreign foods and views on foreign food restaurants such as McDonald's. I conducted personal interviews with five university students. Group interviews were conducted at three schools in the Moscow region: two sets of interviews with nine children aged five to seven; two sets of interviews with nine children aged eight to 11; and three sets of interviews with 17 children aged 12 to 16. Interview questions focussed on students' eating habits, food preferences and experiences with McDonald's. My conversations with older adults (mid-thirties to mid-sixties) took place more informally over meals and visits to people's homes.

Locality, Home and Meaning in Globalization Theories

Themes of origins, home and homeland have been important in examinations of the intersection of food practices and global systems (Bestor, 2000; Freidberg, 2001; Goldfrank, 1994; Mankekar, 2002; Wilk, 1999). National origins have attracted particular attention as foreign products have been alternately accepted and rejected by local consumers precisely because of the national traits and tastes that are associated with those products (Miller, 1998; Terrio, 2000: 248–56; Wilk, 2002). In her work on foodscapes, Ferrero argues that, 'in transnational contexts, ethnic food is also seen as a vehicle for understanding the practices of "home cooking," where food practices represent a symbolic and cultural connection with the home-land' (2002: 194).

Issues related to the notion of 'home' have also emerged as key themes in localization/globalization studies. The increasing interconnectedness of peoples and cultures throughout the world facilitates the global colonization of local com-munities so that the individuals who inhabit the realm created by these processes are increasingly caught between the local spaces where they live their everyday lives and the global arenas where they interact with other global citizens (Featherstone, 1995; Ritzer, 2004; Robertson, 1992; Tomlinson, 1999). Through these processes of displacement or deterritorialization, distinctive and meaningful local communities are replaced by 'non-places' that are noticeable precisely because they are 'forms lacking in distinctive substance' (Ritzer, 2004: 10). Featherstone describes these processes thus: 'Localism and a sense of place give way to the anonymity of "no place spaces", or simulated environments in which we are unable to feel an adequate sense of being at home' (1995: 102). Building on this theme, Giddens notes (1990: 140) that this tension is 'a complex relation...between familiarity and estrange-ment', a feature that Hannerz describes in his observation that cosmopolitans 'are never quite at home again in the way real locals can be' (1990: 248). By extending this notion of the non-place, we can see, in Sassen's idea (1991) of the 'global city', a similar loss of the familiarity and intimacy that come with a 'home town'. Thus, local spaces characterized by familiarity and intimacy, such as those embodied in the notion of home, are accessible only via the imagination as an object of nostalgia (Ritzer, 2004; Tomlinson, 1999) or as a new postmodern imagined community (Appadurai, 1990, 1996).

At the same time, global processes present opportunities for localities not only to assert and affirm themselves, but also to recast the global according to locally particular and meaningful ways (Friedman, 1990; Jing, 2000; Metcalf, 2002; Miller, 1995; Watson, 1997; Wilk, 1995, 2002; Yan, 2000). In some cases, social actors refashion imported elements to fit pre-existing community standards and practices, such as Watson describes for the assimilation of McDonald's in Hong Kong (1997). In other cases, these actors appropriate imported elements and give them meaning as signs of local distinctiveness, as Wilk describes for Belizean cuisine (1995, 2002). What is common to both perspectives is that these processes are a 'culture's way of making new and unusual things part of itself' (Mintz, 1985: 120–1). Thus, localization involves processes of familiarization, domestication and shared belonging (Featherstone, 1995; Giddens, 1990; Lozada, 2000; Wilk, 2002).

The dynamic interplay between localities and globalities is captured in the notion of 'creolization', in which different cultural meanings are fused to create new forms (Friedman, 1994; Hannerz, 1987, cited in Barber and Waterman, 1995). A variation is that proposed by Robertson's idea of 'glocalization' (1992: 172) whereby 'the universal and the particular' coexist. Barber and Waterman caution, however, that despite Friedman's, Hannerz's and Robertson's visions of diversity and newly created cultural forms, models such as creolization and globalization in fact reify distinctions between '"indigenous" (traditional, local) and "imported" (modern, global) elements' (1995: 241). This warning raises an important point about the distinction between content and process. Specifically, implicit in localization theories such as those described above is an acceptance that it is possible to identify and preserve the specific cultural practices and beliefs that constitute local cultures. For Watson's subjects, for instance, there is something identifiably and predictably Chinese that is affirmed in the ways in which they interact with McDonald's (see also Lozada, 2000). This insistence on authentic original content also emerges in Bourdieu's (1984) schemas of cultural distinction and Ritzer's (2004) distinction between entities that possess meaning and value and those that do not.

This emphasis on cultural content is insufficient for conveying the complexities of the local/global experience in Russia where the origins of specific goods and behaviors are often less important than the values that Russians attach to them. Even as local and foreign observers depict McDonald's as the ultimate symbol of cultural imperialism (Love, 1986; Luke, 1990), many Russian consumers who support local businesses and commodities have transferred that support to McDonald's.[5] As McDonald's has lost its strangeness and become familiar and comfortable, it has become, in very tangible ways, domesticated. Thus, an approach that focusses on the processes by which the local is invented and rendered familiar is more productive for understanding the case of McDonald's in Moscow. As Appadurai notes (1996: 185), the production of the local is a continuous process of creativity and adjustment (see also Pilcher, 2002). What this means is that although the social processes of localization may be culturally specific, the content of local culture is continually invented.

In the rest of this article, I explore the processes by which Muscovites and McDonald's have collaborated to achieve this domestication. This process of domestication is twofold and reflects the cooperative efforts of McDonald's and Russian consumers. The first section presents a more familiar narrative of how McDonald's interprets local interests and carefully responds to – or exploits – them (Ritzer, 1996). The second section, however, presents an alternative vision of the domestication of McDonald's in Russia. Specifically, by illustrating how Russian customers actively rework McDonald's to fit their own needs and values, this section emphasizes the agency and autonomy of Russian social actors as they engage with global processes.

From the Exotic to the Mundane: Cultivating Friendship, Intimacy and Trust

Within consumption studies of postsocialist societies, McDonald's has emerged as a prime symbol of the processes and stakes at work in negotiations among local, regional, national and global forces (Czeglédy, 2002; Harper, 1999; Shekshnia et al., 2002; Watson, 1997; Yan, 2000). For the specific case of Russia, the foreign/local tension is particularly significant in light of McDonald's role among Russian institutions and its place within Russian culinary traditions. Throughout Russia's history, food has been both a celebrated aspect of Russian cultural, social and political life and an evocative symbol of national tastes and practices (Glants and Toomre, 1997). This importance was heightened during the Soviet period when, as in other socialist states, control of the food services sector provided a key venue for articulating and implementing political philosophies and social control (Borrero, 1997; Goldstein, 1996; Osokina, 1999; Rothstein and Rothstein, 1997).

Soviet leaders linked their visions of an egalitarian communist society with the goals of producing and distributing sufficient food supplies for the population.[6] To accomplish these tasks, authorities put the entire sphere of food services under state control; the culinary arts were standardized through the professionalization of food workers and the regulation of cuisine. Food production shifted from home kitchens and private restaurants to communal kitchens, state-owned cafeterias and food shops, work-place canteens and cafeterias run by consumers' societies (Borrero, 1997; Rothstein and Rothstein, 1997; see also Fitzpatrick, 1999; Kotkin, 1995). It was within this modernist vision of industrialized food services that privately owned transnational food corporations such as McDonald's first emerged.

After 14 years of negotiations with Soviet authorities, George Cohon, president of McDonald's Canada and *not* McDonald's USA – a distinction that Soviet leaders requested because of political tensions between the Soviet Union and the USA – opened Russia's first outlet in 1990. To attract new customers, the company quickly immersed itself in Russian daily life by highlighting not its novelty and foreignness, but its very ordinariness. Specifically, the company crafted itself as a place where ordinary people work and visit. In a continuing effort to cultivate these images of familiarity, responsiveness and accessibility, McDonald's periodically conducts market surveys. In 2000, I sat at a nearby table as a young female employee stopped young adults and asked them a series of questions about how much they would be willing to pay for different food items. The employee questioned respondents about how frequently they visited McDonald's and what they typically purchased. Then, pointing to pictures on a card, she asked respondents how much they would pay for particular items and if a specific price would be too expensive or acceptable.

More revealing, however, are McDonald's explicit efforts to position itself vis-à-vis Russians' cherished principle of Nash as a marker of trust, intimacy and sociality. First, McDonald's acknowledged the value that Russian consumers have historically placed on social networks and concepts of collective responsibility (Caldwell, 2004; Ledeneva, 1998; Pesmen, 2000) by situating itself as a responsive member of the local community. In addition to such activities as sponsoring athletic events and donating profits to a children's oncology program, the company has collaborated with local officials to develop fire safety programs in the city and established a Russian branch of the Ronald McDonald Children's Charity Fund. On a more individual level, McDonald's directly facilitates connections among consumers. In summer 2000, displays in several restaurants invited children to join a collectors' group to exchange toys and meet new people. Children treat the statue of Ronald McDonald that is invariably to be found in each restaurant as a friend with whom they sit and visit.

McDonald's officials next responded to local ideas about health and nutrition as essential qualities of Nash products (see also Gabriel, 2003). Russian consumers articulate food preferences through evaluations of the purity and healthiness of particular foods. Many Russians initially found the anonymity and technological regulation of McDonald's austere and sterile kitchen facilities, as well as the mass manufacture of foodstuffs, unnatural and disquieting.[7] One college student explained his discomfort with McDonald's by equating it to a transnational candy corporation that he had visited; referring to the latter, he commented, 'It was too clean'. A middle-aged Muscovite friend complained that McDonald's impersonal industrial kitchen was unsanitary, and several high school and university students complained that the types of food served at McDonald's were not as healthy as foods prepared at home.[8]

In contrast, Russians determine the healthiness and authenticity of foods according to where they are produced and by whom. More specifically, consumers privilege fruits and vegetables that are grown on farms in the Russian countryside or in gardens at private summer cottages (*dachas*) and then collected or prepared by friends or relatives. As one college student commented, authentically Russian foods 'grow here' and are eaten by Russians. This insistence on territorial origins emerged in the comments of many other informants such as Masha, a middle-aged mother who asserted that Russians are healthy precisely because they eat produce taken directly from the ground. Another college student acknowledged the importance of Russia's organic economy when she commented that Russian products are those grown by peasants. When buying commercial products, Muscovites claim to prefer domestically produced meats and dairy products over American and other products that are known to be filled with additives and preservatives. As part of their daily shopping practices, Muscovites ask salespersons and market vendors to verify the local origins of food items. For their part, salespersons attract customers by volunteering the information that particular products are locally grown or manufactured.

In their responses to these local preferences, McDonald's executives have joined other Russian companies in promoting the local origins of their produce.[9] Using billboards, signs on the sides of freight trucks and tray liners, McDonald's advertises its contract with a Russian agricultural corporation whose name explicitly invokes the symbolic power of the Russian countryside and personal gardening, *Belaia dacha* ('white cottage'). McDonald's thus reassures customers not only that its produce is Russian-grown, but also that it meets 'the standards accepted by the Russian Federation' and that it uses 'only the highest quality meat without additives and fillers'.[10] In 1998, tray liners guaranteed that 'The high quality of the products of the firm "McDonald's" begins with the highest quality ingredients.... "McDonald's" – it is quality!' Finally, special advertising supplements, available in Moscow restaurants in summer 2000, assured customers that McDonald's provides 'The taste that you love, the quality that you trust'.

McDonald's efforts to cultivate a sense of trust among Moscow consumers emerged most visibly when the company explicitly appropriated the rhetoric of Nash.[11] Russian marketers frequently include the word 'Nash' on their brand labels and present Nash goods with images and themes that invoke shared Russian origins and qualities. As such, Nash belongs to a larger discourse about the value of domestic production, such as was seen in a billboard slogan during a recent advertising campaign to promote domestically produced goods that reminded Muscovites, 'When we buy domestic, we live better' (*Pokupaem otechestvennoe – zhivëm luchshe*). More significant, however, is that although Nash is more exclusive than labels such as 'domestic' or 'Russian' because it delineates subgroups within larger national or ethnic groups, it in fact supersedes concrete origins and identities because of its emphasis on trust and familiarity. As Elena, a 28-year-old artist, explained: '[Nash] does not depend on one's nation....It is a spiritual belief. [Nash people] are the people to whom I tell my problems. You can switch from foreign [*chuzhoi*] to native [*rodnoi*] in a minute.' Elena concluded that Nash conveyed a sense of trust and helpfulness.

By summer 2002, McDonald's had begun invoking the rhetoric of Nash in posters that reminded consumers that the company was 'Our McDonald's' (*Nash Makdonalds*). This move enabled McDonald's to position itself within the parameters of the imagined – and, more importantly, *trusted* – collectivity to which its Muscovite customers belonged. Moreover, McDonald's claimed status as a local entity by cultivating what Feather-stone sees as the essential features of local culture: 'this sense of belonging, the common sedimented experiences and cultural forms which are associated with a place' (1995: 92).

Although Giddens argues that notions of intimacy, familiarity and tradition are themselves products of modernity (1990, 2000), they are nonetheless the markers by which Russians articulate their connections with local culture. It is perhaps more instructive, however, to consider how Russians are autonomous social actors who themselves encourage, accept, shape and discipline this sense of familiarity and intimacy. Rosaldo persuasively describes this process with his ideas about cultural invisibility: 'As the "other" becomes more culturally visible, the "self" becomes correspondingly less so' (1993: 202). As the Russian McDonald's case illustrates, this process is one that Russian consumers are actively producing and fashioning. In the next section, I turn to a discussion of how Muscovites express their autonomy by creatively incorporating McDonald's into their most intimate and personal activities: their home lives.

Feeling at Home: McDonald's as Comfort Food

Initially, Muscovites' relationship with McDonald's was framed through themes of novelty and exoticness.[12] In 1995, my landlady Anya, a retired geologist, recalled that when McDonald's and the pizza restaurants first opened in Moscow, it was precisely their foreignness that prompted long lines of curious customers.[13] Her brother-in-law expressed a sentiment similar to that I heard from other Muscovites when he commented that he and his teenaged son had tried McDonald's once simply for the experience, but that in general his family did not like the taste of McDonald's food and so had not returned. Several years later, during a dinner conversation on an unrelated topic, a close friend turned to me, asked if I had ever tried McDonald's food and then confessed that he had tried it and could not understand why a person would eat such food more than to try it once. Yet, even as urbanites such as my friends express their dislike for the taste of McDonald's food, they agree that the company has a certain appeal for the uninitiated and uncultured. In a 1998 interview, a Moscow university student remarked, 'People from the provinces, the first place they would go, I think, is McDonald's'.

Despite these individuals' emphasis on the novelty and social distinctiveness of McDonald's, what is more revealing is a more profound shift in Muscovites' attitudes towards McDonald's. Specifically, for many Muscovites, McDonald's has become so ordinary that it is no longer culturally marked. This shift to invisibility emerged vividly in conversations with schoolchildren and college students about what constituted Russian foods. Intriguingly, in their responses, students often included transnational foods such as McDonald's and Coca-Cola. When asked why they had included these items as 'Russian', students typically replied that they simply took them for granted and did not contemplate their origins. One college student put it this way: 'I am used to them. They are tasty and easy to buy.' In contrast, he said, new or foreign foods were those that he was not used to thinking about and with which he did not have a 'mental association': 'They do not appear in my mind.'

Another example that illustrates this process of domestication is the extent to which Russian consumers have accepted, and even facilitated, the inclusion of McDonald's foods in Russian cuisine. As in many countries, cuisine has occupied an important place in Russian culture and social life (Glants and Toomre, 1997), and Muscovite acquaintances express great pride in being able to prepare authentic Russian dishes.[14] Despite a long culinary history, however, Muscovites' food practices are changing as imported foods become more available. As one young woman observed: 'In Moscow it is impossible to distinguish between Russian and foreign foods because they are so mixed.' A specific example of these changes is evident in the 'milkshake craze' that my friend Veronika described when we prepared milkshakes at her home. By the end of the 1990s, milkshakes were available in both fast food and high-end restaurants throughout Moscow as well as at temporary sidewalk food stalls. Even vendors in the lobbies of Moscow's finest theaters and opera houses had added fresh milkshakes to their more typical intermission offerings of elegant chocolates, open-faced sandwiches, topped with smoked fish and caviar, and champagne. Russian restaurant owners now provide French fries with their main courses, and vendors at walk-up sidewalk stands include, among the usual assortment of candy bars, chips and nuts, Russian-made knock-offs named *Big mak* and *gamburgr roial* (as Quarterpounders are called in Russia).

Nevertheless, these examples point only to the spread of foods inspired by McDonald's throughout the commercial sphere. What is more intriguing is the extent to which Muscovites have incorporated McDonald's into their 'home cooking' (*domashchnaia pishcha*), a domain that Muscovites consider uniquely Russian. One college student, who said that she was able to identify distinctively Russian foods, explained: 'I remember what my grandmother cooked and how my mother cooked.' In a similar comment, another student observed: 'People who cook at home cook "Russian" because they buy ingredients and then cook like they did earlier.' An academic researcher in his mid-30s stated: 'I prefer home cooking [*domashnuiu pishchu*] because home is more comfortable.'

What was particularly instructive about these individuals' insistence that foods prepared at home are authentically Russian was that their repertoires of Russian cuisine included imitations of McDonald's foods. Like several middle-aged mothers I interviewed, my landlady Anya periodically attempts to make hamburgers at home to please her children and grandchildren, who want to eat at McDonald's, but are unable, owing to cost or time constraints, to do so. In some cases, cooks have resorted to highly creative culinary reinventions such as the meal described by one of my students. When the student's sister studied in Moscow, her host family offered to make McDonald's hamburgers at home. The promised meal turned out to be fried cabbage between two pieces of bread.[15]

More revealing, however, were the responses I received from school-children whom I interviewed about Russian cuisine in 1998. During two sets of interviews, one at a school in Moscow and another in a town located two hours away and without a McDonald's, I asked nine children aged five to seven to draw pictures of their favorite Russian foods. In response, four out of nine children independently depicted Russian-style fried potatoes (*zharennye kartoshki*), a staple in most families' meals, in recognizable McDonald's French fry boxes. In a similarly illuminating incident at a birthday party I attended, the guest of honor, a friend's four-year-old daughter who loved French fries, could barely contain her excitement at the news that we would have fried potatoes for dinner. When she was presented with the homemade French fries, however, she took one look at them and shrieked in horror: 'But they're not McDonald's!'

Collectively, these transformations in local food habits reveal that Muscovites have effectively turned the tables on McDonald's and transformed it not simply into something that is familiar and ordinary, but into something that is authentically indigenous as well as desirable and personally meaningful. More significantly, as the comments and actions of the schoolchildren whom I interviewed illustrate, McDonald's has become the local standard against which Russians' own food practices are measured. In this respect, as McDonald's has been more fully domesticated, it has lost its distinctiveness as something alien and visible and has instead become part of everyday life.

The routinization and habituation of McDonald's into the most ordinary and intimate aspects of Muscovites' daily lives are most vivid within the context of negotiations over the parameters of both domestic and domesticated space. As illustrated in the previous section, Muscovites are taking aspects of McDonald's into their homes. Yet, more and more, they are also taking their home lives into McDonald's, a practice that Muscovite employees facilitate by rarely limiting the amount of time that customers spend in the restaurants. For individuals without accommodation, such as visitors to the city and homeless persons, McDonald's serves as a surrogate home. I have frequently observed visitors using the bathrooms to bathe themselves and to wash out their clothes and dishes. Street children also find the restaurants to be safe havens. The store managers of a central Moscow McDonald's allow these children to sit at the tables and eat food that has been left on diners' trays. On one occasion, I watched as the store manager engaged several homeless children in friendly conversation and offered to help them with their problems. Even Muscovites who have apartments and jobs nearby elect to go to McDonald's to sit and enjoy their homemade lunches (and sometimes even a bottle of beer or two) that they have brought with them into the restaurant.

Other Muscovites have transferred their social lives to McDonald's. Instead of gathering for meals at someone's home, as was a more usual practice during Soviet days when meals in private kitchens were more cost-effective and safe from the prying eyes of others, friends, relatives and colleagues now meet at McDonald's to socialize or conduct business. One friend reported that when she and several other friends tried to organize an outing to a museum, one of the women decided which museum they could visit according to the location of the McDonald's where she wanted them to have lunch. Children and teenagers who live outside Moscow spend their weekends traveling to the city simply to visit McDonald's. During interviews that I conducted with a group of schoolchildren who lived several hours away from Moscow (and the nearest McDonald's), the students excitedly described how frequently they traveled to the city with their friends simply to have dinner at McDonald's. Similarly, several college students confessed that before they had come to Moscow to study, they were unfamiliar with McDonald's. After spending a few months in the city, however, they had quickly begun congregating at McDonald's with their friends for late night meals and conversations.

Birthday parties, which Muscovites generally observe at home or at the family cottage, now represent the most obvious example of these efforts to refashion McDonald's as a domestic and socially significant space. Brightly colored posters and flyers invite children to celebrate their birthdays with a formal party organized and hosted by McDonald's staff.[16] Such events occur regularly throughout the city and, on weekends, the restaurants are often busy with multiple parties taking place simultaneously. During one such party that I witnessed in September 1998, two female McDonald's employees supervised a group of about 15 10-year-olds. As several parents chatted and snacked at a nearby table, the children played games, gave presents to the birthday guest, ate hamburgers and French fries and drank sodas. After the party, the two employees cleaned up the area and removed birthday decorations from the walls. Muscovites with more limited resources organize their own birthday parties at McDonald's. I sat near one such party and watched as a group of children chatted and played together at a table that their parents had decorated themselves. The parents first delivered their food orders from the counter and later divided a cake and other sweets that they had brought with them from home.

As these examples show, the emphasis that Muscovites place on the comforts and intimacy associated with home emerges in the ways that they interact with McDonald's. For these individuals, McDonald's occupies an important space within the rituals and ideals that give meaning to their daily lives. As a place invested with meaning, value, delight and, more importantly, heightened sociality, McDonald's is an intrinsically and authentically local space (cf. Giddens, 1990; Ritzer, 2004; Tomlinson, 1999).

The Domestic Other: Creating the New Local

In many ways, Muscovites' experiences with McDonald's appear to resonate with the premises underlying the McDonaldization thesis: that the routinizing nature of McDonald's facilitates its insinuation into the organization and regulation of daily life and that McDonald's' inherent rationality replaces indigenous, and hence more authentic, meaning with its own set of values and practices. At this point in time, however, it is impossible to predict whether complete McDonaldization will eventually be achieved in Russia. Yet preliminary comparison of McDonald's with other food transnationals in Moscow suggests that, as of now, McDonald's has not yet achieved the same degree of rationality in Muscovites' everyday lives.

Specifically, we can look to the spread of coffee shops and sushi bars (sometimes coexisting in the same café) across Moscow during the past three years. There is an obvious sameness particularly among Russian coffee shops, as managers educate their clientele as to proper (i.e. American-style) coffee etiquette and tastes. The manager of one coffee shop boasted that his goal was to turn his Russian patrons into American coffee connoisseurs. Muscovite consumers have visibly adapted themselves to these changes by substituting cappuccinos and espressos for their more usual afternoon teas or instant coffees and by learning to debate the subtleties of muffins, bagels and other American pastries. Most noticeable is the change in social relations that has accompanied these shifts: previously, afternoon tea was a social occasion when co-workers would stop working for a few moments to sit and socialize with each other. In Moscow's coffee shops, however, it is common to see individuals sitting alone and working on school or work projects while drinking a cup of coffee. In contrast, even as Muscovites treat coffee shops as impersonal and generic settings, they continue to approach McDonald's as a trusted social space where they gather with friends and relax. More importantly, Muscovites are actively manipulating McDonald's by refashioning the eating experience to reflect their own ideas of what constitutes private space and personally meaningful activities. Hence, at this stage, McDonald's has not yet reached the same degree of homogeneity as that pursued and promoted by its competitors.

I have grounded my analysis in an ethnographic perspective (Caldwell, 2004) that proposes that Muscovites are autonomous social agents – even when their choices are constrained by external forces. Thus, by focussing on Muscovite consumers as individuals who actively engage with the institutions and forces with which they coexist, I have drawn attention to the ways in which Muscovites produce and enact the domesticating process of Nash. Although Muscovites may in some ways be complicit partners with McDonald's in this process, it is ultimately these consumers who set the indigenous standards that McDonald's must exploit and satisfy. Finally, because my intent in this article was to highlight the ways in which Muscovites are finding and making meanings within new cultural systems, a focus on the domesticating process of Nash as a particular form of localization calls attention to the ways in which Muscovites do not simply appropriate and refashion foreign elements as familiar and special, as happens in processes of glocalization, but rather reorient their attitudes, feelings and affections in order to experience and know the foreign as something mundane and, hence, part of the local landscape. Despite the power of McDonald's to position itself as local, Muscovites are the final arbiters of this distinction.

In this article, I have suggested that the uniqueness of McDonald's experience in Russia is evident in the ways that consumers affirm its place in local culture not simply by embracing it as just another part of the ordinary routines of daily life, but more accurately by taking it for granted. For many Muscovites, McDonald's has become, in Rosaldo's terminology, 'invisible'. Furthermore, at the same time as Muscovite consumers have accepted McDonald's as a local and personally meaningful experience, they have privileged it over other, more visibly foreign and uncomfortable, experiences. This quality of domestication emerged clearly when two Muscovite friends, a young middle-class married couple, recounted their driving vacation across the USA. Vera commented that because she and her husband were comfortable with the service and food at the McDonald's near their home in Moscow, they stopped at a McDonald's restaurant along an American interstate, but were surprised to find dirty facilities. They were even more astonished, she added, to discover that the food in the American McDonald's was not as tasty as that in Russia. Ultimately, Vera and her husband decided not to visit another McDonald's while they were on vacation, but to wait until they returned to Russia. As Vera noted, the McDonald's restaurants in Moscow were familiar and trustworthy and thus distinct from their North American prototypes.

By extending values of trust and intimacy to McDonald's, not only are Russian consumers reworking local understandings of such fundamental concepts as the private and the public, the domestic and the foreign, the personal and the popular, but they are also setting the standards that McDonald's must meet in order to flourish. McDonald's is more than a localized or a glocalized entity in Russia. By undergoing a specifically Russian process of localization – Nashification – it has become a locally meaningful, and hence domesticated, entity.

NOTES

1 A photograph that appeared in newspapers throughout the USA in 1999 captured the image of an elderly Russian veteran, dressed in a suit adorned with medals, eating at McDonald's following a political parade (Lovetsky, 1999).

2 For a more detailed discussion of these trends, see Caldwell (2002).

3 I thank an anonymous reviewer for adding *bytovoi*.

4 See Caldwell (2002, 2004).

5 Tim Luke describes the McDonaldization of the Soviet Union as the 'McGulag Archipelago' (Luke, 1990).

6 Food production offers a valuable insight into gender roles and expectations during the Soviet and post-Soviet period, particularly since industrial food production was intended to liberate women from the duties of the domestic realm. Because an extended analysis of this topic is beyond the scope of this article, I would refer interested readers to Goldstein (1996) and the essays in Glants and Toomre (1997).

7 This contrasts sharply with what Yunxiang Yan describes regarding Beijing consumers who see McDonald's as a paragon of nutrition and technoscientific development (Yan, 1997).

8 Cf. Ohnuki-Tierney (1997) for a related perspective on Japan.

9 I discuss this in more detail in Caldwell (2002).

10 These quotations were taken from McDonald's tray liners.

11 See also Humphrey (1995) for a discussion of the ideology of Nash in Soviet and post-Soviet practice.

12 See Campbell (1992) for a discussion of the role that novelty plays in consumer choice.

13 A writer for *Fortune* magazine ironically compared attendance at Moscow's McDonald's to that of another major Moscow attraction, Lenin's tomb. While the 1990 attendance rate at Lenin's tomb decreased to 3.2 million visitors (9000 daily average), the attendance rate at the new McDonald's just blocks up the street soared to almost 10 million (27,000 daily average). A young Muscovite professional explained her preference for standing in a two-hour line at McDonald's instead of at Lenin's tomb in this way: 'At least you can get something to eat here. Who wants to stand in line to see some dead guy?' (Hofheinz, 1990: 11).

14 Moscow's Museum of Public Dining offers a fascinating look at the important role that cuisine has played in Russian culture throughout the last several centuries. Former chefs guide visitors through impressive collections of cooking implements, menus, cookbooks and plastic food displays. As further proof of the value placed on cuisine, several walls in the museum are devoted to pictures honoring chefs and other individuals known for their contributions to Russia's culinary traditions.

15 One reviewer pointed out that the Russian *kotleta* might be analogous to this cabbage hamburger. I agree that this is likely, but it is nonetheless significant that the hostess in this story chose to call her dish a 'McDonald's hamburger'. I thank Mary Kay Taylor for this story.

16 Compare with Yan's descriptions of birthday parties in Beijing (2000: 216–17).

REFERENCES

Appadurai, Arjun (1990) 'Disjuncture and Difference in the Global Cultural Economy', *Theory, Culture & Society* 7: 295–310.

Appadurai, Arjun (1996) *Modernity at Large: Cultural Dimensions of Globalization.* Minneapolis: University of Minnesota Press.

Barber, Karin and Waterman, Christopher (1995) 'Traversing the Global and the Local: Fújì Music and Praise Poetry in the Production of Contemporary Yorùbá Popular Culture', in Daniel Miller (ed.) *Worlds Apart: Modernity through the Prism of the Local,* pp. 240–62. London: Routledge.

Bestor, Theodore C. (2000) 'How Sushi Went Global', *Foreign Policy* (Dec.): 54–63.

Borrero, Mauricio (1997) 'Communal Dining and State Cafeterias in Moscow and Petrograd, 1917–1921', in Musya Glants and Joyce Toomre (eds) *Food in Russian History and Culture,* pp. 162–76. Bloomington: Indiana University Press.

Bourdieu, Pierre (1984) *Distinction: A Social Critique of the Judgement of Taste* (trans. Richard Nice). Cambridge, MA: Harvard University Press.

Caldwell, Melissa L. (2002) 'The Taste of Nationalism: Food Politics in Post-socialist Moscow', *Ethnos* 67(3): 295–319.

Caldwell, Melissa L. (2004) *Not by Bread Alone: Social Support in the New Russia.* Berkeley: University of California Press.

Campbell, Colin (1992) 'The Desire for the New: Its Nature and Social Location as Presented in Theories of Fashion and Modern Consumerism', in Roger Silverstone and Eric Hirsch (eds) *Consuming Technologies: Media and Information in Domestic Spaces,* pp. 48–64. London: Routledge.

Czeglédy, André P. (2002) 'Manufacturing the New Consumerism: Fast-Food Restaurants in Postsocialist Hungary', in Ruth Mandel and Caroline Humphrey (eds) *Markets and Moralities: Ethnographies of Postsocialism,* pp. 143–66. Oxford: Berg.

Dunn, Elizabeth (1999) 'Slick Salesmen and Simple People: Negotiated Capitalism in a Privatized Polish Firm', in Michael Burawoy and Katherine Verdery (eds) *Uncertain Transition: Ethnographies of Change in the Postsocialist World,* pp. 125–50. Lanham, MD: Rowman & Littlefield.

Featherstone, Mike (1995) *Undoing Culture: Globalization, Postmodernism and Identity.* London: Sage.

Ferrero, Sylvia (2002) '*Comida Sin Par,* Consumption of Mexican Food in Los Angeles: "Foodscapes" in a Transnational Consumer Society', in Warren Belasco and Philip Scranton (eds) *Food Nations: Selling Taste in Consumer Societies,* pp. 194–219. New York: Routledge.

Fitzpatrick, Sheila (1999) *Everyday Stalinism: Ordinary Life in Extraordinary Times – Soviet Russia in the 1930s.* New York: Oxford University Press.

Freidberg, Susanne (2001) 'On the Trail of the Global Green Bean: Methodological Considerations in Multi-site Ethnography', *Global Networks* 1(4): 353–68.

Friedman, Jonathan (1990) 'Being in the World: Globalization and Localization', *Theory, Culture & Society* 7: 311–28.

Friedman, Jonathan (1994) *Cultural Identity and Global Process.* London: Sage.

Gabriel, Cynthia (2003) 'Healthy Russian Food Is Not-for-profit', paper presented at the annual Soyuz Symposium, University of Massachusetts, February.

Giddens, Anthony (1990) *The Consequences of Modernity.* Cambridge: Polity Press.

Giddens, Anthony (2000) *Runaway World: How Globalization Is Reshaping Our Lives.* New York: Routledge.

Glants, Musya and Toomre, Joyce (eds) (1997) *Food in Russian History and Culture.* Bloomington: Indiana University Press.

Goldfrank, Walter L. (1994) 'Fresh Demand: The Consumption of Chilean Produce in the United States', in Gary Gereffi and Miguel Korzeniewicz (eds) *Commodity Chains and Global Capitalism,* pp. 267–79. New York: Praeger.

Goldstein, Darra (1996) 'Domestic Porkbarrelling in Nineteenth-century Russia, or Who Holds the Keys to the Larder?', in Helen Goscilo and Beth Holmgren (eds) *Russia, Women, Culture*, pp. 125–51. Bloomington: Indiana University Press.

Hannerz, Ulf (1987) 'The World in Creolisation', *Africa* 57(4): 546–59.

Hannerz, Ulf (1990) 'Cosmopolitans and Locals in World Culture', *Theory, Culture & Society* 7: 237–51.

Harper, Krista (1999) 'Citizens or Consumers? Environmentalism and the Public Sphere in Postsocialist Hungary', *Radical History Review* 74: 96–111.

Hofheinz, Paul (1990) 'McDonald's Beats Lenin 3 to 1', *Fortune* 122(15): 11.

Humphrey, Caroline (1995) 'Creating a Culture of Disillusionment: Consumption in Moscow, a Chronicle of Changing Times', in Daniel Miller (ed.) *Worlds Apart: Modernity through the Prism of the Local*, pp. 43–68. London: Routledge.

Humphrey, Caroline (1999) 'Traders, "Disorder," and Citizenship Regimes in Provincial Russia', in Michael Burawoy and Katherine Verdery (eds) *Uncertain Transition: Ethnographies of Change in the Postsocialist World*, pp. 19–52. Lanham, MD: Rowman & Littlefield.

Jing, Jun (ed.) (2000) *Feeding China's Little Emperors: Food, Children, and Social Change*. Stanford, CA: Stanford University Press.

Kotkin, Stephen (1995) *Magnetic Mountain: Stalinism as a Civilization*. Berkeley: University of California Press.

Ledeneva, Alena V. (1998) *Russia's Economy of Favours*: Blat, *Networking and Informal Exchange*. Cambridge: Cambridge University Press.

Love, John F. (1986) *McDonald's: Behind the Arches*. New York: Bantam Books.

Lovetsky, Dmitry (1999) Photograph, *Christian Science Monitor* (10 May): 6.

Lozada, Eriberto P., Jr (2000) 'Globalized Childhood? Kentucky Fried Chicken in Beijing', in Jun Jing (ed.) *Feeding China's Little Emperors: Food, Children, and Social Change*, pp. 114–34. Stanford, CA: Stanford University Press.

Luke, Tim (1990) 'Postcommunism in the USSR: The McGulag Archipelago', *Telos* (84): 33–42.

Mankekar, Purnima (2002) '"India Shopping": Indian Grocery Stores and Transnational Configurations of Belonging', *Ethnos* 67(1): 75–98.

Metcalf, Peter (2002) 'Hulk Hogan in the Rainforest', in Timothy J. Craig and Richard King (eds) *Global Goes Local: Popular Culture in Asia*, pp. 15–24. Vancouver: University of British Columbia Press.

Miller, Daniel (ed.) (1995) 'Introduction: Anthropology, Modernity and Consumption', in *Worlds Apart: Modernity through the Prism of the Local*, pp. 1–22. London: Routledge.

Miller, Daniel (ed.) (1998) 'Coca-Cola: A Black Sweet Drink from Trinidad', in *Material Cultures: Why Some Things Matter*, pp. 169–87. Chicago, IL: University of Chicago Press.

Mintz, Sidney W. (1985) *Sweetness and Power: The Place of Sugar in Modern History*. New York: Penguin.

Ohnuki-Tierney, Emiko (1993) *Rice as Self: Japanese Identities through Time*. Princeton, NJ: Princeton University Press.

Ohnuki-Tierney, Emiko (1997) 'McDonald's in Japan: Changing Manners and Etiquette', in James L. Watson (ed.) *Golden Arches East: McDonald's in East Asia*, pp. 161–82. Stanford, CA: Stanford University Press.

Osokina, Elena (1999) *Our Daily Bread: Socialist Distribution and the Art of Survival in Stalin's Russia, 1927–1941*. Armonk, NY: M.E. Sharpe.

Patico, Jennifer (2001) 'Globalization in the Postsocialist Marketplace: Consumer Readings of Difference and Development in Urban Russia', *Kroeber Anthropological Society Papers* 86: 127–42.

Pesmen, Dale (2000) *Russia and Soul: An Exploration*. Ithaca, NY: Cornell University Press.

Pilcher, Jeffrey M. (2002) 'Industrial *Tortillas* and Folkloric Pepsi: The Nutritional Consequences of Hybrid Cuisines in Mexico', in Warren Belasco and Philip Scranton (eds) *Food Nations: Selling Taste in Consumer Societies*, pp. 222–39. New York: Routledge.

Ritzer, George (1996) *The McDonaldization of Society: An Investigation into the Changing Character of Contemporary Social Life*. Thousand Oaks, CA: Pine Forge Press.

Ritzer, George (2004) *The Globalization of Nothing*. Thousand Oaks, CA: Pine Forge Press.

Robertson, Roland (1992) *Globalization: Social Theory and Global Culture*. London: Sage.

Rosaldo, Renato (1993) *Culture and Truth: The Remaking of Social Analysis*. Boston, MA: Beacon Press.

Rothstein, Halina and Rothstein, Robert A. (1997) 'The Beginnings of Soviet Culinary Arts', in Musya Glants and Joyce Toomre (eds) *Food in Russian History and Culture*, pp. 177–94. Bloomington: Indiana University Press.

Sassen, Saskia (1991) *The Global City: New York, London, Tokyo*. Princeton, NJ: Princeton University Press.

Shekshnia, Stanislav V., Puffer, Sheila M. and McCarthy, Daniel J. (2002) 'To Russia with Big Macs: Labour Relations in the Russian Fast-food Industry', in Tony Royle and Brian Towers (eds) *Labour Relations in the Global Fast-food Industry*, pp. 117–35. London: Routledge.

Terrio, Susan J. (2000) *Crafting the Culture and History of French Chocolate*. Berkeley: University of California Press.

Tomlinson, John (1999) *Globalization and Culture*. Chicago, IL: University of Chicago Press.

Watson, James L. (ed.) (1997) *Golden Arches East: McDonald's in East Asia*. Stanford, CA: Stanford University Press.

Wilk, Richard (1995) 'Learning to Be Local in Belize: Global Systems of Common Difference', in Daniel Miller (ed.) *Worlds Apart: Modernity through the Prism of the Local*, pp. 110–33. London: Routledge.

Wilk, Richard (1999) '"Real Belizean Food": Building Local Identity in the Transnational Caribbean', *American Anthropologist* 101(2): 244–55.

Wilk, Richard (2002) 'Food and Nationalism: The Origins of "Belizean Food"', in Warren Belasco and Philip Scranton (eds) *Food Nations: Selling Taste in Consumer Societies*, pp. 67–89. New York: Routledge.

Yan, Yunxiang (1997) 'McDonald's in Beijing: The Localization of Americana', in James L. Watson (ed.) *Golden Arches East: McDonald's in East Asia*, pp. 39–76. Stanford, CA: Stanford University Press.

Yan, Yunxiang (2000) 'Of Hamburgers and Social Space: Consuming McDonald's in Beijing', in Deborah S. Davis (ed.) *The Consumer Revolution in Urban China*, pp. 201–25. Berkeley: University of California Press.

11

Copyrighting Che: Art and Authorship under Cuban Late Socialism

Ariana Hernandez-Reguant

Visitors to Havana are dwarfed by Ernesto Che Guevara's monumental face presiding over Revolution Square. A principal icon of the Cuban revolution and anti-colonial movements worldwide, Che Guevara has been the object of state worship since his death in 1967. So when Tomás Esson, a young graduate of Havana's prestigious Art Institute, scandalized the public in 1988 with an exhibit featuring an image of Che associated with sexual and scatological imagery, the Ministry of Culture quickly closed down the show.[1] In the words of one onlooker, the offending artwork depicted Che looking at "figures doing 'things'! Fornicating! People with horns! And one was sticking his horn up someone else's ass! And in the middle of that there were little Cuban flags! And *pioneros* climbing a cannon that was in fact a phallus!" (Garcia 1999).[2] Visitors were puzzled to see at a state gallery what appeared to be blasphemy. And to no one's surprise, the exhibit lasted only one day. Allegedly, it was the minister of culture himself, Armando Hart, who asked the artist to close it down. This incident marked the boundaries of Cuba's version of perestroika, a period of ideological opening and generational renewal in the Communist Party that brought about a thriving youth culture and unprecedented political humor. Barely two years later, perestroika, like the entire Soviet bloc, was a thing of the past, and Tomás Esson had moved to Miami. Some of his controversial paintings, however, remained in Cuba, since the government declared them to be "cultural patrimony of the Cuban nation" and therefore not permitted to leave the national territory (Plagens and Katel 1992).

From *Public Culture* 16(1): 1–29. Copyright © 2004, Duke University Press.

As Cuba moved to salvage its economy from the deep crisis caused by the loss of its socialist trading partners, much of the state infrastructure of cultural production and distribution was turned into a network of for-profit semiautonomous enterprises. The Cuban culture industries became a sort of "border zone" (Sassen 2000), "zone of contact" (Lomnitz 2001), or "zone of graduated citizenship" (Ong 1999) structured by the interests of a new array of stakeholders, both state and corporate. Within these zones, new social relations developed around the clash of socialist ethics and capitalist practices, along with new forms to imagine, mediate, and contest ideas of identification and community. On the whole, the inscription of cultural production, patterns of leisure, and approaches to labor and community within transnational circuits of mass culture and entertainment fostered alternative discourses and forms of social practice. This dynamic cultural formation defines a moment that, following Alexei Yurchak (1997), I refer to as "late socialism." And while the Communist Party still sought to reassert its command over artistic imaginaries and public discourses at home through ideological persuasion, capitalist mechanisms of control over cultural products extended the reach of patrimonial rights well beyond national jurisdiction. That is, to consider a cultural product, such as any depiction of Ernesto Che Guevara, as collective patrimony could be an arbitrary decision resting on state-appointed guardians of national ideology. But now, in addition, the control over such images was exerted through a seemingly neutral, internationally binding juridical resolution made on the basis of authorship. An international lawsuit pursued by a Cuban photographer in 1999, over the use and commerce of a picture of Che Guevara that he took in 1960 for a government newspaper, will exemplify the shift in notions of individualism, labor, and property occurring in Cuba throughout the 1990s.

Formerly valued according to socialist notions of aesthetic quality, cultural relevance, and ideological significance in the postperestroika period – known as the Special Period in Times of Peace – both creative labor and the cultural product became valued in relation to agents and processes outside the socialist state. This resulted in the separation of two distinct labor regimes, that is, in the differentiation between cultural and manual labor that was very much rejected under socialism but stands at the core of neoliberal capitalism. Economic and legal reforms throughout the 1990s turned cultural institutions into copyright industries structured by the dynamics of global markets of leisure and entertainment. Artists prospered, allowing the socialist state to renew, however precariously, its own legitimacy and public prestige, thereby revitalizing its articulation of national culture and identity with the revolutionary project. As a result, a group of musicians, artists, performers, and entertainers emerged as a highly visible elite with transnational connections – their jet-setting lives contrasting with the bleakness of everyday food deprivation, electricity blackouts, and water shortages. This *farándula* immediately became a symbol of a nascent capitalism that was not identified with a socialist ethic of work but with a system of valorization in which wealth accumulation appeared in the public consciousness to be disproportionate to the input of labor.

This article details the valorization of both artistic labor and the art product under a late socialist regime marked by the rise of hybrid modalities of value production and subjectivities that were as much the results of a burgeoning ideology of possessive individualism and new forms of transnational identification as the outcomes of a revolutionary ethos of work, community, and equality. It locates the Cuban government's social and economic privileging of independent creative work amid the transformations and turmoil wrought by the country's engagement with global markets structured by neoliberal regimes of value. And it examines the tensions and negotiations that ensued as cultural producers – exclusively – vied to convert their own labor into financial capital by entering directly and individually into contractual agreements with transnational stakeholders that now mediated and regulated Cuban fields of cultural production. The analysis identifies a decisive shift in signifying practices of authorship – now caught between socialist conceptions of collective redistribution and capitalist practices of individual profit and corporate speculation – whereby the cultural product of artistic labor assumed both a commodity form and a quasi-global copyright form.

Following a decade of cultural change in the 1990s, these developments emerged in the limelight of global media with the international legal dispute over the ownership of a revolutionary icon: Ernesto Che Guevara – or, rather, the photographic image that had become associated with him, in Cuba and abroad. Although the international press focused on the image itself, the issues at stake, when placed in the Cuban context, revealed enormous rearrangements of social relations and subjectivities around notions of labor, property, community, and culture. The copyrighting of Che, its ownership in Cuba and in the global circuits beyond, will serve as a starting point to illustrate the complexities of art and authorship, property and patrimony, and community and commodity for Cuban late socialism.

The Copyrighting of Che

On 15 September 2000, news agencies around the world reported that a Cuban photographer had finally won his copyright claim on a famous shot of Che Guevara that he had taken forty years earlier. The *Times* of London wryly recast this development as if it were the late Argentine revolutionary's own long and hard-fought victory. The newspaper declared: "After 40 Years, Che Beats Forces of Capitalism" (Bird 2000). CNN.com likewise dramatized the event, but with a slightly less ironic, and more-to-the-point, headline: "Social Justice, Sí. Vodka Advertisements, No." The claimant – Alberto Diaz Gutierrez, better known in Cuba as "Korda" – had sued a British advertising agency in the United Kingdom's High Court to stop the use of his 1960 Che photo in a marketing campaign for Smirnoff vodka. The ads depicted Che's face adorned with a pattern of hammers and chili-pepper sickles, not to foster communist consciousness in a creative redeployment of commodity fetishism, but simply to promote a new spicy line of Smirnoff vodka by invoking both strict Russian authenticity and fiery Latin masculinity.

There was never any official ruling on whether the depiction constituted a violation of copyright. But once the case was "sensibly and amicably" (Bird 2000) settled out of court, the offensive ad was removed, and the full rights of authorship over the Che picture were bestowed on Korda, along with $75,000 in damages. Korda had clearly triumphed, but so had all of Cuba, for he donated this substantial sum of hard currency to the cash-starved coffers of the country's welfare system. However, at the end of the affair, it was still unclear whether the now copyrighted Che – and his legacy to Cuban late socialism – had really beaten the forces of capitalism or rather surreptitiously joined them.

News stories focused on the image of Ernesto Che Guevara and the control of its meaning. It was amusing, no doubt, to see the former *guerrillero* posthumously caught in this tiff between a vodka brand and communism. But even more significant than the figure of Che Guevara was the fact that a relatively obscure Cuban citizen had demanded control of his artistic product, in a foreign court, claiming that he was its sole author and *therefore* its rightful owner. This was unprecedented in Cuban revolutionary history. Hence, the case of *Korda v. Lintas & Rex* was no ordinary international dispute over intellectual property. Korda was a citizen of socialist Cuba, where such individual rights were limited. Yet the Cuban government backed Korda's international claim to private ownership, even though, since Korda took the picture while working for a state-run newspaper, his actual property rights would be questionable under both Cuban and international law. Furthermore, Korda never objected to the Cuban government's profiting from the photo in the past, for example, in its dealings with Swatch regarding a Che watch. Since the Che photo had been used commercially countless times before, without protest from Korda or from the Cuban government, the advertising agency he sued argued that the picture was obviously in the public domain. It all seemed so abrupt: suddenly, at the turn of the millennium, Korda sought to assert his individual property right over a symbol of revolutionary socialism, an icon revered in the Cuban political imaginary as well as in the now shrinking horizons of international communism. Why did Korda claim ownership now and not during the previous thirty-plus years that the photo had been drawing profits for entrepreneurs around the world? Maybe he was truly outraged at the association of the Argentine revolutionary with "booze," as CNN reported. However, this was not the first time that the image was used to sell alcohol – a beer company had used it once before. So what impelled Korda to take action?

Korda himself inadvertently answered sometime earlier, when I was inquiring about the professional paths of graphic artists, writers, and photographers who, like him, began their careers in advertising in the 1950s, then joined the Revolution's propaganda apparatus, and were currently working again in the emerging advertising sector. Invariably, the subject of Korda's most famous picture, displayed prominently on his living room wall, came up. It was taken in 1960, when Korda worked as a photojournalist for the government newspaper *Revolución*, but because the print was slightly blurry it was never published. Several years later, the famed Italian communist editor Giangiacomo Feltrinelli got it from Korda while visiting Cuba to work with Fidel Castro on his memoirs. After Guevara's death in 1967, Feltrinelli obtained exclusive worldwide rights over Guevara's "Bolivian Diary" and put Korda's Che picture on the cover of what quickly became a bestseller. He also used the photo to print posters that became ubiquitous in the Paris uprising of May 1968 and that rendered Korda's Che into an icon for revolutionary movements around the world. According to Korda, Feltrinelli "sold one million posters, at five dollars each." Asked if he personally had profited, Korda responded: "Never. He did not even put my name on it. And I never disputed that, because in Cuba, the possibility of getting money from foreign countries did not exist" (Diaz 1999). Feltrinelli in turn absolutely denied having profited from the sale of either the Che book or the posters and claimed that he donated all revenues to both the Cuban government and various other revolutionary causes (Feltrinelli 2001). But Korda made a key observation: Up until the mid-1990s, Cuban authors did not have a say in these matters. They lacked the resources to fight international piracy, and most importantly, they lacked the legal protection of the Cuban state, which did not recognize – beyond wages – authors' economic rights over their creations; not domestically, much less inter-nationally. Consequently, no reciprocal agreements existed at the time between Cuba and capitalist countries regarding intellectual property. Cuban authors for the most part did not collect revenues for the use of their works in foreign countries, nor did foreign authors collect revenues in Cuba.

In hindsight, then, Korda's statement to the *Times* that the *Smirnoff* case "was fought to defend the principle that all creators have a moral and property right to their own work" (Bird 2000) was not an obvious one in the context of revolutionary Cuba. And with it, he provided clues to the deep transformation occurring in Cuban society throughout the 1990s. In itself, the fact that an artist would assert individual economic rights over the labor product signaled a radical shift in approaches to work, property, and community. But behind Korda's enunciation, and its expression of cultural change in Cuba, there was also the echo of a new privileged status accorded by the socialist state to individual cultural producers. In the context of Cuba's growing participation in global markets throughout the 1990s, this privilege paralleled the new value of cultural producers' work in transnational circuits. It also stemmed from the revolutionary government's desire to nurture a professional group that brought international prestige and legitimacy to one of the few remaining socialist states. And, over all this, there loomed the apparent contradiction of the Cuban state drawing on neoliberal notions of legality and property to protect, worldwide, revolutionary iconography – a development that expressed Cuba's new position in a globalizing world of transnational commerce as well as the Cuban state's strategy of using neoliberal opportunities to uphold socialism at home.

Korda's claims in international court thus revealed a change more profound than the policy and legal reforms that made it possible. The globalization of the Cuban economy, and particularly of its culture industries, fostered the emergence of an elite of cultural producers. That is, cultural producers were set apart from other workers in that they were able to assert a stake in the value of their labor product in their negotiations with foreign interest parties. But while the generation of the Revolution – Korda's generation – inscribed itself within revolutionary morality, a new generation of artists, entertainers, musicians, and media personalities had to learn to walk a thin line between politics and performance. Theirs were no longer the familiar faces associated with balding official intellectuals, protest singers, and media personalities dear to the regime. They were younger, blacker, and louder, and their home was not so much the *casas de cultura* and institutional forums as nightclubs and neighborhood plazas. They were musicians, performers, and media hosts with aspirations of travel, popularity, and financial gain. Their dashing flamboyance captured the popular imagination, and they quickly became symbols of a nascent capitalism that valued leisure as much as socialism valued labor.

In the following sections, I discuss the crucial preeminence of creative labor over manual work and its reshaping of Cuban socialist trajectories, with particular attention to the two elements that made this possible at the end of the century. The first was a partial liberalization of labor – specifically, the legalization of self-employment for certain professions, along with the possibility afforded to artists to perform freelance work and to negotiate their contracts directly with corporate intermediaries. The second element was the transformation of intellectual property into a profit-generating instrument, which, though originally intended for trademarks and patents, enabled a new type of relationship between individual workers and the state – a form of citizenship that was not expressed exclusively through labor, civic duty, and ideological acquiescence but also contractually through financial contributions in the form of taxes.

The Labor and Property of Cultural Producers

The rise of a *farándula* of cultural producers in the 1990s, during a time of harsh economic crisis, did not follow a logic of economic utility. The new valorization of creative labor was disproportionately greater than the modest revenue that artists generated for the Cuban economy. Why did the revolutionary regime permit internationally successful artists, writers, and entertainers to climb to the top of the economic scale while restricting other professionals capable of generating even higher earnings? One reason was Cuba's entry into a global economy structured by the neoliberal principles of the World Trade Organization (WTO). To encourage foreign investment per WTO stipulations, Cuba revised its intellectual property laws, recognizing patent, trademark, and copyright holders as proprietors with a right to compensation for the commercial use of their property. Individual copyright holders in Cuba were therefore afforded the possibility of profiting anew – additionally so, as new laws permitting some forms of self-employment allowed them to become independent entrepreneurs and as the infrastructure of cultural production was one of the first sectors to be inserted in transnational networks of distribution and consumption.

Indeed, the culture industries – which, under neoliberal capitalism, were refashioned as copyright industries – moved to the forefront of globalization processes, constituting what Saskia Sassen (2000) has called a "border zone": an economic sector privileged by the national state in terms of its advantageous participation in global economic networks and as a pull to the national economy. To benefit from global capital investments, the state mediates between transnational corporate interests and its citizen-workers, whose labor is valued not in terms of national standards but in terms of the needs of mobile transnational capital. Furthermore, as Aihwa Ong (1999) demonstrates in her study of transnational Chinese elites, workers in these privileged sectors develop new approaches to labor and self, often cultivating a differential relationship with the national state that is negotiable – a "graduated citizenship," as Ong terms it. These "zones," however, are not merely witnesses to a transformation in social relations. Claudio Lomnitz (2001), furthering Mary Pratt's (1992) idea of the "contact zone," has pointed out their creative potential. These zones, which develop at the interface of a national state with a particular historical logic and neoliberal transnational capitalism, often offer conditions for national discourses of identity and community to be challenged. It is precisely out of the disjunctured contact of hegemonic discourses and everyday practices that new forms of political imagination and cultural community may emerge. This is particularly relevant in the case of the culture industries, as their business is precisely the production and mediation of representations. Moreover, it is within the culture industries that labor ethics and practices are directly involved in the mediation of discourses and forms of entertainment that are projected onto public arenas and that are central to the development of consumer subjectivities on a transnational scale (Jameson 1998; Hardt and Negri 2000).

The culture industries, in sum, are enormous economic machines – and, in many instances, significant export sectors – that rely on creative labor as well as on the mediation of various state and corporate stakeholders. Far from being instruments of hegemony, as not only Max Horkheimer and Theodor Adorno but also the Cuban government would have it, the culture industries constitute institutional fields of power and possibility wherein competing interests struggle to influence public representations through negotiation and compromise in unequal and contingent ways (Bourdieu 1993; García Canclini 1989; Handler and Gable 1997). As such, in Cuba they constitute not only the institutional supports for the mediation and dissemination of mass cultural forms but also the sites of labor at which contradictory ethics and practices have converged in a sort of bureaucratic transculturation that has subverted, or at least hybridized, established socialist hierarchies of knowledge and power.

Artists, as creative workers, were therefore fundamental to the transformation of Cuban cultural production into an export sector. But this was not all. As a nationalist regime, the Revolution viewed artists as the soul of the nation, and the new generation was, in addition, an exponent of the revolutionary educational system. Hence they were nurtured as instrumental to the reproduction of revolutionary nationalist ideology. In contrast, middlemen and other workers in the emerging culture industries were policed in ways that constrained their ability to profit from the labor and rewards now exclusively adjudicated to artists. Artists were thus set apart from all other workers: they were now allowed to work independently, to negotiate the value of their labor with foreign parties, and to own and profit from the product of their work. Art was no longer regarded as a communal effort but rather legitimized as an individual and independent enterprise whose product was the sole property of its author. Nevertheless, the Cuban state inscribed this recognition of ownership in a quasi-global copyright form that attempted to reconcile socialist ethics with capitalist practices of authorship. This innovative appropriation of neoliberalism for the ends of socialism can be better understood in light of certain key developments in the conceptual history of intellectual property – the constitutive form crucial to the commodification of cultural labor under capitalism.

At the basis of international intellectual property jurisprudence are the philosophical pillars of Western modernity: seventeenth-century political philosophies of possessive individualism; Enlightenment notions of social progress and citizenship rights; nineteenth-century ideologies of civilization, culture, and national destiny;

and post–Cold War neoliberal precepts on free trade. After all, international property law – including patents, trademarks, and copyrights – developed alongside imperial capitalism as a state mechanism to control the transnational circulation of ideas and the transfer of technology. In 1886, a time of rapid decolonization, European colonial powers signed the Berne Convention for the Protection of Literary and Artistic Works to put forth and protect their – and their citizens' – rights of ownership over scientific advances and artistic works and to prevent their free use beyond their borders. Over the next century, many other countries followed suit in order to participate in international commerce.

The intellectual property laws and copyright regime that emerged from the Berne Convention reproduced a notion of the individual citizen as both a laboring subject and proprietor of his or her body, invested with rights and duties vis-à-vis the national state. Most importantly, the laws selectively extended property rights over the labor product to only certain kinds of workers. The laws championed the superiority of mental labor over manual labor, with the former construed as the expression of a sophisticated and educated mind and the latter as a mere application of bodily force and abilities – and it did so by adjudicating higher moral and economic rewards to creative workers. Hence, while the manual laborer was forced to sell his or her labor and remain alienated from both the means of production and the labor product, creative workers were accorded lifelong property rights over their ideas and the ability to profit whenever the materialization of those ideas was sold as a commodity or used as a service anywhere in the world. While not every country rushed to sign the Berne Convention, the United Nations and the World Trade Organization both eventually endorsed it and actively promoted the adoption of intellectual property regimes as a requirement for participation in international trade. For obvious reasons, socialist countries – revolutionary Cuba included – did not support the adoption of such legislation, since these tenets were regarded as fundamental to capitalist expansion and therefore contrary to socialist morality.

Under socialism, property rights were restricted. Socialist citizens could own property – within strict limits – but could not legally trade it for profit or extract rents. Furthermore, the socialist project of ending workers' alienation entailed a reassessment of both individual needs and the social value of labor. The Marxian notion of labor value rejected the essential distinction between mental and manual labor and any other distinction that would result in social inequalities. For Marx, what mattered was whether labor was productive or not productive, that is, whether it was inserted into social relations of production, generated surplus value, and thus contributed to the reproduction of capital and the creation of wealth. As formulated in his notion of abstract labor, all productive work, whether manual or mental, was equivalent, even indistinguishable when performed jointly – for example, an engineer working in team with a mason. This idea was at the core of socialist redistributive policies emphasizing social equality.

However, in an addition to volume 1 of *Capital*, entitled "Results of the Immediate Process of Production," Marx implicitly attributed a special quality to mental labor, allowing for the possibility of difference. This special quality derived from the immateriality of its product-idea: that of perdurability. Mental labor could be performed outside relations of production and therefore be unproductive, but this condition could change if the laborer – as proprietor of his or her labor, past and present – decided to sell the labor product, thereby transforming unproductive into productive labor even retroactively. Marx (1977: 1045) gave the example of a singer: "A singer who sings like a bird is an unproductive worker. If she sells her song for money, she is to that extent a wage laborer or merchant. But if the same singer is engaged by an entrepreneur who makes her sing for money, then she becomes a productive worker since she *produces* capital directly." Likewise, a poet is unproductive because the poet writes for the same reason that the "silkworm produces silk, as the activation of his own nature" (Marx 1977: 1045). If at some point the poet sells a poem, the poet then becomes a merchant. But if the poet writes books at the behest of a publisher, the poet becomes a literary proletarian, "nearly a productive worker" (Marx 1977: 1045). Thus an artist could be either a wage laborer, like any other worker, or a merchant (a "self-merchant") with the ability to turn the product of that labor into a commodity. This was precisely the point made by the intellectual property laws of the time to justify the rights derived from authorship, as opposed to the alienation attached to manual labor. This point would acquire enormous relevance one century later, when this signifying practice of authorship would index not only the ownership of commodity production but also the generation of a form of capital that rested in the copyright form itself. At the time, however, creative work – which Marx categorized as part of the service sector and as different from the directly capital-creating productive sector – seemed marginal to the accumulation of capital and the workings of the capitalist system. Work of this sort, wrote Marx (1977: 1045), "has scarcely reached the stage of being subsumed even formally under capital, and belongs essentially to a transitional stage."

Indeed, the economic importance of this work may have been minimal in Marx's time, and he could not have foreseen the economic significance of the culture industries in late capitalism, which capitalize on intellectual property in present-day neoliberalism. But with the advent of electronic and digital technologies of reproduction, the global reach of the mass media, and the transnational circulation of mass culture, the culture industries – which rely on creative labor and a general respect for intellectual property rights – have become export industries fundamental to the expansion of capitalism and related hegemonic projects. By the mid–twentieth century, the distinction between mental and manual labor contained in intellectual property law had acquired new significance. Authors' prospects for dissemination dramatically increased, while at the same time the tremendous scale of the field of circulation required authors not only to associate with other authors but often to release their rights to corporations that commercialized their works in exchange for royalties. The structures of surveillance needed to monitor usage rights worldwide gave them no choice but to rely on intermediary companies with the required resources to draw profits. These corporations turned copyrights into capital. That is, they derived profits from managing authors' intellectual property rights by charging fees to third parties who wished to use such property in any way. Specifically, other culture workers, such as musicians, may wish to perform or record compositions under the control of corporations, and likewise, mass media outlets may lease the right to broadcast them. In this process, independent creative workers became neither exclusively merchants nor wage workers, as Marx had envisioned, but both and more. Whether they worked under contract, for a corporation (e.g., a record label), or operated independently as merchants, as long as they retained ownership over the labor product (e.g., a composition), they would also become rentiers when their works were later reproduced. That is, they would collect royalties every time their intangible work (e.g., an idea, composition, or design) was harnessed and sold as the basis for a material commodity (e.g., a CD or poster).

Hence, forms of labor that may have seemed economically marginal and barely productive at the time of Marx have become central to what Fidel Castro has termed "casino capitalism" in order to capture the spectacular simulation of wealth generation through consumption and speculation rather than through labor (Comaroff and Comaroff 2000: 297). The centrality of the service economy under late capitalism has been noted by theorists of globalization (Castells 1996; Sassen 1998). Michael Hardt and Antonio Negri (2000), in particular, have stressed its reliance on a type of labor that was marginal to industrial capitalism and that they have termed "immaterial," because it produces no tangible commodities, strictly speaking, and in which labor and its product are indistinguishable. Although Hardt and Negri (2000) include creative work in this category, artistic labor may result in tangible or potentially tangible commodities (e.g., a painting or design) and, most importantly, in capital. That is, the product of creative work, such as a song, may generate revenues – surplus value – through the input of new labor by third parties. In the case of music, this value is created through its reinterpretation, in "sampling," "versions," and "remixes"; through its circulation in broadcasting and advertising; and in some cases, through its mere consumptive use, via a jukebox or Internet downloads. This is all crucial for understanding the intersections of Cuban late socialist structures and capitalist practices, for under neoliberal capitalism, capital is created not only through productive labor, but also through the circulation, use, and consumption of products as well as through speculation – in this case, with mass-cultural products that are also copyrights.

In this model, the intermediation of transnational corporations capable of operating across national borders is indispensable to the creation of wealth. Thus, authors' revenue does not depend so much on their labor as on the efficiency of their representatives in global markets of culture and entertainment. In fact, Jacques Attali (1985), in his study of music as a commodity, points out that authors are mere peons in the transnational economy of music. He argues that intellectual property law is nothing but a legal fiction, since it is eventually alienable by the state, typically some years after the author's death. But in the neo-liberal global economy, the state may still, indeed, be the ultimate copyright owner (at least, as it relates to patents and copyrights but not to trademarks). However, for the period provided by law – typically fifty to seventy-five years after an author's death – copyrights are frequently controlled by corporations, which are termed "legal persons" in Cuban intellectual property law. But unlike individual persons, corporations draw revenues not from the process of cultural production per se, but from the distribution and promotion of cultural materials. Thus in a corporate regime, individual intellectual property is still a fiction; not because the author's economic rights are not perpetual, as Attali (1985) has argued, but because authors must release them to corporations in order to collect profits. In short, even though authors benefit from this system, they control only marginally the use – and the fees to be paid for such use – of their work. Under these circumstances, individual intellectual property becomes not just a juridical issue of individual rights but also, and perhaps primarily, a transactional matter of contracts among corporate, state, and other parties.

In revolutionary Cuba, the rise of a class of individuals vested with the right to negotiate contracts with foreign corporations – a class whose labor was not valued according to the same standards as other workers – posed a challenge to the socialist government. This challenge was resolved through the presentation of cultural production as the product of socialist education and policies and through the implementation of mechanisms to ensure the ideological loyalty of artists. In a context of rapid change, where socialist state intervention confronted incoming capitalist practices, artists' labor became the most productive of all: it operated as capital itself. This revalorization of artistic labor according to the standards of a speculative type of global capitalism positioned artists at the top of the earning scale. But in all fairness, they had little competition, since the Cuban government limited all other forms of private accumulation. Artists were unique, as far as the Cuban government was concerned – and the reasons were not strictly economic. In the new economy, artists brought financial gain to themselves, but they also provided a far more precious capital for a Cuban government besieged in the post–Cold War era. Artists enjoyed high media visibility and international reputations, unparalleled by other professionals, that brought prestige to a socialist regime that derived its legitimacy, both at home and abroad, from its identification with national culture and identity. In addition, because the culture of socialism chastised the role of independent middlemen as nonproductive and parasitical, and because other creative labor (e.g., that of scientists) was under strict control as strategic to the country's economic and technological progress, artists emerged as the professionals to most benefit from these reforms – and therefore those with the most to lose.

Artistic Labor and Intellectual Property in Revolutionary Cuba

Korda's professional trajectory illustrates the consideration afforded to artistic labor and to the art product under socialism. Before the Revolution, he was a freelance fashion and advertising photographer who considered himself an innovator in the use of natural light and skinny female models. In 1959, shortly after the revolutionary victory, he won a prestigious award for his photos in a Pepsi-Cola campaign, but his "social zeal," as he put it, drove him to follow Fidel Castro and Che Guevara and to eventually become their personal photographer. By then, in a 1961 speech, Castro had proclaimed the social role of art under the Revolution, rejecting its commercialization and announcing that the state would replace private parties – regarded as corrupt intermediaries – in the distribution and dissemination of artwork. In return, cultural producers would have a responsibility as "organic artists" to raise social consciousness and support the regime. Furthermore, said Guevara ([1965] 1977), the rights of the revolutionary government to survive in a hostile environment shall prevail over those of the individual. Hence, artists should not subvert revolutionary discourse, which would be guarded by the government through the control of the ideological state apparatus, including the infrastructure of cultural production, education, and the mass media. By the end of the 1960s, all cultural production was under state control. All private operations were seized, such as recording studios, publishing houses, and art galleries, including Korda's own photography studio, where he still did some freelance work in addition to working for the *Revolución* newspaper. As he later recalled in an interview, being an acquaintance of revolutionary leaders did not help him resist the 1968 "Revolutionary Offensive" that resulted in the closing of all nightclubs and the relocation of musicians and performers to state agricultural farms as entertainers for farm workers (Diaz 1999).

With the nationalization of small businesses, the Offensive culminated the proletarianization of artists. As state cultural institutions took over private enterprises, artists became salaried employees at these new institutions, but only those deemed "professional" upon "technical evaluation" or by virtue of an art degree could work legally in the sector. In addition, income was determined by evaluation, according to set standards of quality, virtuosity, and craftsmanship, but it was no longer related to popularity and demand. From then on, gigs were assigned by a state-run management agency that considered orchestras and performing troupes as labor units, rarely authorizing any personnel changes. The employment relation between artist and agency was characterized as one of belonging (*pertenecer*); thus a musician would say "I belong" to such and such institution, suggesting the impossibility of independent work. This situation provoked Nueva Trova singer Silvio Rodríguez to state that "an artist is no more important than a worker, a bricklayer, a soldier or a clerk." His colleague Pablo Milanés added, "I am a worker who labors with songs, doing in my own way what I know best, like any other Cuban worker" (both quoted in Rohter 1987). Like all work, artistic work became wage labor. No profits derived from ownership over the labor product were recognized. Musicians, therefore, received no royalties from record sales, and authors were not paid copyrights.

The issue of copyrights was a thorny one because it revealed the most fundamental differences between socialism and capitalism regarding labor, private property and its accumulation, individual rights, and social equality. Socialist countries recognized moral rights to authorship but not economic rights beyond wages. At the time of the Revolution, Cuba had an intellectual property law that was passed under Spanish colonial rule in 1879, but the nationalization of the cultural apparatus, along with the U.S. embargo against the island, rendered it ineffective. The embargo, in place since 1960, precluded any payment to a Cuban resident of revenues generated in the United States or by U.S. companies and subsidiaries – a regulation also followed by U.S. allies, such as Mexico, and non-U.S. companies with interests in the United States. Furthermore, because Cuba stopped paying copyright fees to foreign authors, Cuban copyrights in those countries were, in return, not enforced. But in the 1970s, Cuban ensembles began to tour and record abroad and introduced a need for stronger copyright protection. In 1974, Cuba joined the United Nations World Intellectual Property Organization (WIPO), and, three years later, the Cuban National Assembly passed new legislation: Law 14 of the Protection of Intellectual Property Rights, which was modeled on Soviet law and which subordinated individual rights to those of the collective while also placing the state in charge of copyright administration. According to Article 6 of the law, "the need to disseminate culture broadly" will prevail over the individual rights of authors, which are protected "in harmony with the interests, goals and principles of our Socialist Revolution." The author's economic rights were limited to employment wages, and the state reserved the right to use artistic works freely without the author's permission or financial restitution.[3] Because Law 14 did not comply with international standards, no reciprocal agreements were established with nonsocialist countries. In addition, since the Cuban government did not have a favorable view of individual profit from intellectual property, no enforcement mechanism was ever put in place, thus rendering the law an expression more of the state's rights than of authors' protections. Although some of these policies were later modified, as far as authors were concerned the situation began to change only in 1988, when the Berman Amendment to the U.S. embargo lifted restrictions on the U.S. distribution of Cuban cultural materials. This reestablished copyright payments to Cuban authors for the use of their works in the United States – the country that has been, since the early twentieth century, the primary consumer of Cuban music.

It was in the 1990s, however, that the most dramatic changes occurred in the art professions as a result of economic reforms. As Cuba strengthened its intellectual property legislation to comply with the World Trade Organization and to offer guarantees against the piracy of trademarks and patents to encourage international trade, Cuban copyright holders ended up with the same economic rights as corporate trademark and patent owners that operated in the country. In 1997, Cuba signed the Berne Convention and agreed to update its intellectual property law to international standards, which allowed it to sign reciprocal agreements with foreign countries, thus enabling authors to collect hard-currency royalties.[4] In addition, the legalization of some forms of private enterprise, the circulation of the U.S. dollar, the employment of Cuban citizens in hard-currency sectors, and the mass arrival of foreign tourists all together fostered the emergence of a domestic consumer market for popular culture. This, along with the possibilities to market Cuban cultural production through transnational commercial networks, framed the transformation of the socialist organization of cultural production. The introduction of marketing principles and a human resource model of management in state enterprises accompanied the reconceptualization of culture industries as "copyright industries," now concerned with turning symbolic value into financial revenue through commercial expansion.

The relation between the industry and artists changed, as artists were able to become self-employed and either sell their products or contract their labor as freelancers. Unlike most workers' income, artists' earnings were no longer proportionally tied to labor intensity and labor time. Visual artists could now sell their works at market prices through an expanded network of state and private galleries. In the music profession, earnings – such as from record sales and concert bookings – once again became tied to popular success and, most importantly, could be negotiated and bargained between corporate parties and the artists themselves.[5] A new field, advertising, further expanded possibilities for both artists and cultural intermediaries of all sorts. As part of the process to revitalize state companies, their departments of propaganda were in many cases converted into advertising agencies for the new foreign and state companies competing for the emergent domestic market. In order to achieve profitability, these departments often laid off permanent employees and replaced them with writers, musicians, and graphic artists whom they hired on a per-project basis.[6] These freelancers, along with the entertainers and media personalities who lent their images to the promotion of a vast array of products, learned to leverage their popularity to associate their images with commercial products and services in exchange for bargained remuneration.

As a result of increased earnings and an international audience, the lives of many artists changed radically. Korda, for instance, who had retired from his photography job in 1992 and looked forward to living quietly off his modest retirement wages, became a jet-setter. Not only did he work again as an advertising photographer for a Brazilian-Cuban tobacco company, but he was able to claim international royalties for his Che Guevara picture:

> Since I am the author of that famous photo that is internationally considered the most reproduced in the history of photography, plus I took many other photos of Fidel Castro and the Revolution, I spend the entire year exhibiting them and traveling around the world. Last year, for instance, I was in Turkey in January, in March and April I went to the French Alps, then to Paris. . . . Where else? I don't even remember. I also went to São Paulo, then I came back. Then Los Angeles, Seattle, from there I went to Japan, and I visited Tokyo, Osaka, Kyoto, and Hiroshima. All because of that picture. And since two years ago, I have a team of lawyers in France and a team of lawyers in Asia that have the job to go after all those people who commercialize the image of Che. I could soon be a millionaire! (Diaz 1999)

And he was not the only one. Because of Cuba's new reciprocal agreements with foreign countries, artists were able to receive royalties generated elsewhere. Particularly after the Spanish SGAE (Sociedad General de Autores y Editores) set up shop in Havana in 1997 – immediately enrolling the top eight hundred Cuban artists – numerous rags-to-riches stories began circulating about those who joined the association. For instance, Isolina Carrillo, author of the famous bolero "Dos Gardenias" (included in the *Buena Vista Social Club* album), was said to have gone from near starvation to being driven in her own chauffeured car and treating her friends and acquaintances to lavish meals, all thanks to the hard-currency royalties she was now able to cash. Another bolero composer, Cesar Portillo de la Luz, followed a similar trajectory after his music was recorded by such famous stars as Luis Miguel and Christina Aguilera. In a country where the median monthly salary in 1999 was 223 pesos (or $10), top composers reported annual dollar incomes in the six-figure range.

Yet these composers were not permitted to form their own collections society – an association of authors such as the Spanish Sociedad General de Autores y Editores (SGAE) or the French Société des Auteurs Compositeurs Éditeurs de Musique (SACEM). The issue was hotly debated in the Cuban National Assembly, ultimately stalling calls for a brand new intellectual property law. The Cuban government was well aware of the dangers posed by the development of civil society and particularly of independent organizations based on profit, which had proven to be divisive in the USSR and Eastern Europe. The legalization of a citizens' association for the purpose of advancing business interests was considered unacceptable, because its financial power could eventually challenge the government's unity. As a compromise, in order to limit discontent and potential emigration, authors were allowed to join foreign collection societies to manage their works. In so doing, they had the opportunity to become equally wealthy, but what was most important to the Cuban government was that they not be united in a national association. The state still mediated their interests within Cuban borders. Beyond those borders, they were free to act and collect, as in the Korda case. And while some indeed joined foreign collections societies, others, particularly musicians and writers, coped with Cuba's weak intellectual property protection – particularly in international arenas – by releasing their economic rights to the corporations (e.g., publishers and labels, both state-owned and foreign) with which they signed contracts in exchange for royalties. These corporations became welcomed stakeholders in the up-and-coming Cuban arts commerce and were regarded by the Cuban government as reliable partners that posed no threat to its rule. Furthermore, their role was acknowledged in Cuban law by means of intellectual property amendments, including one that construed corporations to be "legal persons" whose rights to intellectual property, unlike those of individuals, could never be appropriated by the state as long as the corporation existed.[7]

Artists thus needed to hire corporations to manage their works and obtain profits from their worldwide usage. In so doing, artists became more than entrepreneurs. They became rentiers, because as copyright holders, they could sell their works while retaining rights to their representation, which translated into rights to its reproduction. A painter, for example, would collect a fee every time his or her painting was reproduced as a postcard or a poster. Thus the encounter between socialist structures and neoliberal forms of value in the cultural arena brought about not only the commodification of both artistic labor and cultural products, but also, most importantly, *the transformation of artistic products into capital* at unprecedented levels – especially since the transnational corporations that mediated these processes (commercializing, promoting, distributing, and administering the rights to cultural products) now could ensure copyright enforcement through expanded networks of information and exchange.

In a country proclaimed by the first article of its constitution to be made up of workers, the privileging of artistic labor – in which the socialist state remained complicit by gatekeeping access to the professions – and the capitalization of intellectual property gave rise to the possibility of a differential relationship between individuals and the state. This relationship was expressed through tax contributions and was therefore linked to the accrued value of labor and the labor product in global capitalist markets. A selective renegotiation of the social contract came hand in hand with this reconfiguration of society, for a new socio-economic stratification became most evident within fields of cultural production.

A Different Kind of People?

As more artists rose to the top of the earning scale, other cultural workers within the bureaucracy grew resentful. Whereas before art was viewed as the product of collective effort, now it was individual accomplishment that potentially brought fame and wealth to its author alone. And while artists could maintain ownership over their work – and thus generate earnings according to its market value – other workers in the cultural infrastructure still depended on the socialist earning scale. Art was no longer a social product, though the *Granma* newspaper, the official organ of the Communist Party, insisted otherwise even as late as 1996, if only to appease cultural wage workers during their annual conference: "[Culture] can be compared to an iceberg – only warmer. On the visible face, the smaller face, there are those in 'leading roles' (artists, journalists, writers). At the base, which is huge, are the roots, the pillars that sustain the visible part of the iceberg (technicians, workers, promoters). Both are part of 'the people,' which is synonymous with culture" (Partido Comunista de Cuba 1996).

From the perspective of workers at "the base," however, those in leading roles were living lavishly. Soon, mass media producers and managers, as well as others involved in the distribution and dissemination of cultural images and sounds, demanded a revalorization of their labor as that which facilitated the popularity and enrichment of artists and entertainers. Likewise, other professionals, such as radio playwrights and film production staff, resented receiving only wages, particularly when the resulting cultural products were successfully commercialized. Disgruntled, they demanded justice. The Communist Party responded by implementing a tax scale, allegedly to remedy economic stratification, while also waging a war against the illicit enrichment of these intermediaries "at the base." Not surprisingly, neither policy – taxation nor repression – solved social inequality, and those in intermediary positions began to take matters into their own hands. Employees in the new culture industries and at oversight agencies sought to benefit from their structural location, bargaining with new corporate stakeholders – such as advertisers and record labels – in exchange for their mediating access to the bureaucratic hierarchy of knowledge/power.

Mass media producers, who derived power from their influence over the viewing and listening publics and were positioned both within the bureaucracy and at the front lines of the incoming corporate capitalism, became the targets of anti-corruption campaigns. They fell under the scrutiny of the Communist Party in its combat against underground profit schemes. Radio and television shows, and their popular anchors, were pulled off the air periodically under accusations of payola practices. Only artists were morally entitled and legally empowered to seek profits from their work, because only those "who make and produce, have to also commercialize."[8] Cultural intermediaries were considered unproductive in the Marxist sense that they performed services but their labor did not result in tangible commodities. Consequently, their claims to the product of someone else's labor were dismissed, and they were chastised instead as parasites, "speculators, thieves, and violators of tax laws" (Partido Comunista de Cuba 1996). This repression of economic activity outside the state revealed a deeply rooted cultural bias against middlemen; moreover, the Cuban government had learned from the Eastern European experience that the main threat to state power was the emergence of an independent middle class. The repression was selective, however. Petty schemes among some state employees, like media workers, were tolerated at times to further state control. The selective and unpredictable enforcement of new anticorruption laws served to keep these workers on their toes while also instilling in them a sense of fragile privilege that would prompt them to maintain, rather than subvert, the late socialist status quo.

A new tax regime sought to level social stratification. Taxes and salary differentials, as expressions of individual contracts with the state, had been eliminated in the years following the revolutionary victory. The social contract was then established between the state and the masses on the basis of revolutionary allegiance, community service, and productive wage labor. In 1994, however, the Cuban government reintroduced taxes as a means to achieve "social justice by protecting the social segments with the lowest income, while stimulating both labor and production."[9] Taxable income excluded wages and included: (1) *profits from business activities*, including those generated by "intellectual, artistic, craftsmanship, and physical activities," particularly by the "creation, reproduction, interpretation, and application of knowledge and abilities"; and (2) *profits from capital*, which included rents and royalties. The new system of taxation acknowledged the role of the market in the parallel rise of social inequality and the differential value of labor – that is, the fact that some types of work had become more lucrative than others. But it also evidenced the government's bias against the emergent entrepreneurial middle class: taxes were not directly proportional to income but were levied most heavily on those in the middle-income brackets, severely limiting their ability to save and reinvest. Unlike petty entrepreneurs, artists brought prestige and legitimacy to a regime that prided itself on promoting national culture and the fine arts. They were nurtured as the children of the Revolution: they were born, raised, and schooled under socialism and often came from social segments, such as Afro-Cubans, that had benefited most from the redistribution policies of the Revolution.[10] Their preferential treatment extended not only to the amount of their financial contributions but to the actual bureaucratic practices surrounding taxation, as exemplified in one advertising designer's experience at the tax office:

> Since 1996, I have been an intellectual-artist self-employed worker in the field of advertising. I am registered at ONAT, the Tax Office. There I am just another self-employed worker. The only difference is that we independent creative workers get a differential treatment at ONAT. We don't get treated like, say, a shoe-repair person. …At every ONAT office, there is an employee dedicated only to independent creative workers. That is, even if the office is full, we don't have to wait, because we have our own specialist. The reason is because our work is artistic; it is intellectual. We are *a different kind of people!* (Gutiérrez 2001)

The price for all this was lip service to government ideology and policies, an inconspicuous display of wealth, and financial contributions to the state welfare system. In addition, high-profile artists and entertainers would often perform token acts of revolutionary allegiance by publicly donating significant amounts of money to the state coffers. For instance, Buena Vista Social Club's senior musician Compay Segundo auctioned his hat to a group of foreign tobacco executives at a meeting presided over by Fidel Castro, according to a press release issued 6 March 2001 by the Habanos tobacco company. Segundo donated the proceeds, $17,500, to the state's public health system – a move mimicked by Korda, who donated his financial settlement to Cuba's pediatric care system. In a more elaborate scheme, Nueva

Trova singers Silvio Rodríguez and Pablo Milanés established business partnerships with the Ministry of Culture in order to invest their hard-currency earnings. Among his other ventures, Rodríguez financed several commercial recording studios, while Milanés established a private foundation for the arts – a project that was abruptly closed down by the Ministry of Culture when its popularity and effectiveness threatened to compete with official channels.[11]

At the same time, artists permitted the Cuban government the free use of their works. For instance, popular songs were used at times without permission or compensation to advertise products by state companies or even in anti-U.S. propaganda campaigns, as in the case of the famous hit by Manolin (the "Salsa Doctor"), "Somos lo Máximo" (We are the max), which became a slogan of the Union of Communist Youth, much to Manolin's dismay. And indeed, Korda claimed intellectual property rights only *outside* Cuba, following the Cuban government's strategy of abiding by, and benefiting from, neoliberal market rules in international and transnational contexts while maintaining a mostly socialist administration at home. Although authors complained in private, they seldom spoke up. Their acquiescence corresponded to their sense of privilege and their wish to maintain residence on the island in a historical context in which dissent typically translated into exile. For many artists, like those associated with the Buena Vista Social Club project, international success was linked precisely to residency on, and association with, the island.[12] For others, such as young *timba* musicians, their music was locally specific, and most of their audience was on the island. Periodically, however, their flashy performances provoked a scandal in the Communist Party, for example, when La Charanga Habanera made a grand appearance at a rally of international Communist youth by descending in a helicopter borrowed from the Cuban air force, or when Paulito F. G. performed before thousands on a stage completely covered with commercial logos. In these instances, their options were to either abide by the sanctions imposed on them, usually entailing temporary broadcasting bans, or to go into exile. Most of them chose to stay and comply.

But not all artists were happy about the situation. For one thing, only a small fraction of them were accorded such an elite status: the professionalization system remained in place, excluding such groups as rappers and rockers. Moreover, those artists still trying to make inroads into international markets found the bottleneck system too stringent and often expressed the sort of resentment voiced by one salsa bandleader: "I am very annoyed that we are obliged to pay taxes. I give around 315 concerts a year, and from those about sixty I do for free. That's my way to contribute to society. In *NG La Banda* we are sixteen people, including the sound technician, and they need to be paid. I also need to buy equipment and instruments, which I pay in hard currency. . . . I don't know what they think we damn musicians make!" (José Luís Cortés, quoted in Manrique 1998). This musician, like others, believed that taxes were an added burden on those who were already fulfilling their revolutionary responsibilities in other ways and who did not feel they owed anything to a state that no longer provided them with an infrastructure of production (e.g., musical instruments).

Taxes failed to remedy social differences, but they did mark the end of an older conception of society as an undifferentiated mass by introducing a contractual relationship between the individual citizen and the state. This renegotiation of the social contract was still based on a labor relation, but it now acknowledged a qualitative differentiation between kinds of labor according to their economic value under capitalism without neglecting their moral value under socialism. And as the socialist state ceased to be a universal employer, it became, in practice, a sort of landlord. Those Cuban workers still employed by the state continued to contribute to the collectivity with their surplus labor. That is, they performed both remunerated labor and voluntary work in exchange for both wages and access to the welfare state programs. But those no longer employed by the state were now required to contribute with a monetary fee that was meant to express the price of the labor that the state was no longer alienating – a labor that could now be sold in open markets for higher remuneration than the one formerly provided by the state as employer. Taxpayers, however, often perceived this fee or tax not as a just contribution to society but as a penalty – particularly as it was proportionally higher for those sectors perceived to be closer to subverting Cuban revolutionary ethics and values, despite their potential in terms of actual revenues.

Culture Industries as Contact Zones

Still a part of the ideological state apparatus, the culture industries were turned into semiautonomous enterprises capable of competing in global markets. In the process, they constituted a sort of "contact zone," where transnational corporate capitalism came into contact with precisely the socialist state structures charged with the mission of transmitting and sustaining official ideology to the national public. As a result, the culture industries were required to mediate between a wide array of stakeholders, including corporate, state, and Communist Party agendas, and the desires of domestic audiences now empowered as consumers. As labor sites, they saw the emergence of new social relations as well as forms of identification in relation to labor, consumption, and community – with the particularity that the emerging hybrid subjectivities were formed around the negotiation of socialist morality and capitalist approaches to capital accumulation, at the level of both representation and practice.

Clearly, it was within the culture industries that the ideological hegemony of the revolutionary government was at risk. In response, the Cuban government sought to preserve the socialist hierarchy of power and knowledge by selectively granting privileges to certain cultural producers while policing any attempts to profit on the part of individual intermediaries. That is, it fostered the formation of selective elites loyal to the revolutionary project while containing the development of a middle class that could eventually challenge its rule. Likewise, while limiting private entrepreneurship at home, socialist institutions established ties with transnational corporations, thereby legitimizing them as players in the Cuban economy.

In this process, cultural producers, as copyright holders protected by intellectual property laws designed to promote free trade, became empowered to profit from their labor product for as long as they lived. Art ceased to be considered the product of a collective effort and became instead the property of an individual author who could prevent others from using it – a property that could be traded, sold, and invested in international markets at the will of its proprietor. Furthermore, this was a form of property whose value went beyond that of an exchangeable commodity. The product of artistic labor could now be turned into capital, generating profits merely through its use by other parties. In sum, in the encounter of socialist structures with neoliberal forms of value in the cultural arena, the creative product may become capital, while the author acts as a capitalist who collects rents and increases his or her estate without having to engage in any further work. That is, in contrast to other workers, creators gained the ability to become rentiers, as their earnings were not tied to labor time or other moral standards but to the successful speculation of their labor products by corporate parties.

Under late socialism, labor continued to define social worth, but it also acquired a new role in the making of subjectivities and social relations. In contrast to the social equality promoted by the socialist revolution and predicated in the egalitarian approach to work contained in the Marxist idea of abstract labor, a distinction emerged between what came to be viewed as essentially different kinds of labor, whereby mental labor, and particularly artistic labor, acquired preeminence over manual labor. As a result, first and foremost within the cultural zone of contact, social stratification developed following the accrued value of creative labor and its appropriated product in global markets. This proved crucial to articulations of citizenship: not only because the symbolic representations generated through this field – like Korda's photo of Che – form and inform the mediated contours of everyday life among national publics but because the dynamic negotiations surrounding the production and circulation of public representations harbored innovative practices – such as the copyrighting of Che – where we may locate the limit points, as well as the horizons, of state projects and laboring subjects.

Coda

The younger generations are the fundamental clay to build our legacy:
It is in the youth that we place our hopes, and therefore we'll pass
the flag on to them.
Ernesto Che Guevara, "El socialismo y el hombre en Cuba"

We're all marching along
in the full plaza
the flag floats ahead
it's carried by a girl,
her tits hanging out.
The fags and the druggies,
the hungry, the crazies
have marched already

. . . .

People look at our indecent faces
[and] show us their teeth.
Porno Para Ricardo, "La Internacional"

If in 1988 the socialist state appropriated some of Tomás Esson's controversial paintings without his consent, by declaring them to be the "cultural patrimony of the Cuban nation," fifteen years later that same state was less concerned with property than with profit. Nothing evidenced more the new attitude toward global markets than a 2003 Internet auction of contemporary Cuban art sponsored by the Ministry of Culture. Playing in the casino of capitalist speculation, the revolutionary state profited from its intermediary role in foreign market transactions as well as its monopoly over Internet access on the island. At the same time and in a less-visible way, the socialist state sanctioned the copyright form as the primary recipient of artistic value – as capital itself. This move contributed to create an illusion of ideological opening. But business imperatives did not override ideological concerns.

In 2003, punk rocker Gorki, leader of the band Porno Para Ricardo, copyrighted his own version of famed Communist symbols – specifically, a punk rendering of "The International" and the band's sickle-and-hammer logo – thereby inscribing them as his own private property in Cuba and beyond. More specifically, he wanted to protect his copyrights before signing a deal with an independent Mexican label. The new lyrics of "The International" re-created a Communist rally led by a topless girl carrying the Cuban flag, where homosexuals, drug addicts, and the destitute marched together, reaping only government scorn. The album cover, in turn, mocked official ideology by depicting a decrepit, half-open can of "meaty mass." Through this reference to Andy Warhol's *Campbell's Soup*, Porno's cover could be viewed as an instance of "socialist hyperrealism" were it not for its logo: a hammer-arrow-penis piercing a sickle-vagina. Both the song and the graphics exposed the fiction of the "masses" as a construction of socialistrationed consumption. To wit, a Cuban punk who dared to show up at a state office insisting that he was the author of such subversive depictions would have been unthinkable a few years earlier. But now, it seemed, ideological considerations could be disengaged from market practices. The ideological project of the Revolution was no longer linked to international socialism – even the new 1992 constitution had erased all references to it. Indeed, the state showed no interest in obstructing his record deal, much less in appropriating his works as "cultural patrimony" of the Cuban nation. But while control over public representations in transnational markets was exerted by appealing to a type of private ownership that was legitimized by the national state, within Cuba, the socialist state continued to maintain an iron hold over the domestic dissemination of cultural materials. Porno's music was often banned from public broadcasting, and soon after the copyrighting, the band's leader was given a serious warning: change the band's name and lyrics or face the consequences. He chose to face the consequences. Shortly after, in April 2003, as the Cuban government felt increasingly besieged by U.S. support to a growing dissident movement, it unleashed a severe crackdown that resulted in the imprisonment of not only self-proclaimed dissidents but many others, including Gorki.

During the so-called Special Period, following the collapse of the Soviet bloc, the socialist bureaucracy acquired an intermediary role among the increasingly globalized regimes of value and domestic subjects now participating in networks of mass culture as both producers and consumers. The resultant opening of new spaces for artistic expression threatened to weaken revolutionary hegemony at home. At the turn of the millennium and in a context of increasing international pressure for regime change, the Cuban government followed a carrot-and-stick approach to the control of discourse and, particularly, to underground avenues for both artistic expression and entertainment explored by young people. From the government standpoint, the ultimate control of discourse seemed more fundamental to regime preservation than economic well-being.

Che Guevara did not completely fall prey to the forces of capitalism, after all. Now more than ever, he stood as a symbol of an aging revolution. While his image became a commodity, his doctrine of governmentality was not forgotten. Indeed, his millenarian call to subordinate economic policy to ideological hegemony in order to create revolutionary subjects ([1965] 1977: 636) still seemed to guide cultural policy against all odds: "Sooner or later a new generation of revolutionaries will sing to the New Man as the authentic voice of the people. But this is a process that will take time."

NOTES

1   The exhibit was titled *A Tarro Partido* 2 and was shown at Galería 12 y 23 in Havana.
2   *Pioneros* refers to the Communist Children Organization. Its slogan is "Pioneers like Che."
3   Ley No. 14, Ley del Derecho de Autor, *Gaceta Oficial de la Republica de Cuba*, 30 December 1977, 757–62.
4   Resolución 61/1993 of the Ministry of Culture, *Gaceta Oficial*, 4 November 1993; and Resolución 42/1997 of the Ministry of Culture, *Gaceta Oficial*, 2 July 1997.
5   Decreto-ley 141, *Gaceta Oficial*, 8 September 1993; Decreto-ley 144, *Gaceta Oficial*, 19 November 1993; and Decreto-ley 145, *Gaceta Oficial*, 17 November 1993.
6   By 1999, about two-thirds of creative work in advertising was done by freelancers, according to the Cuban Association of Publicists and Propagandists.
7   Decreto-ley 156/1994, *Gaceta Oficial*, 14 October 1994, 230.
8   Resolución Conjunta 1/96 of the Cuban Ministry of Labor and Social Security and the Ministry of Finances.
9   Ley 73 del Sistema Tributario, *Gaceta Oficial*, 1 October 1994.
10 Upon seizing power in 1959, the new revolutionary government quickly moved to eliminate all forms of racial discrimination, integrating neighborhoods, schools, and public spaces and providing avenues for educational and professional advancement for all citizens regardless of race. Social prejudices, however, have been harder to eradicate (Fuente and Glasco 1997).
11 The Pablo Milanés Foundation operated from 1992 to 1995.
12 In addition, taxes in Cuba were lower than in other countries, while its monitoring system was inefficient, and contracts with foreign parties routinely underreported income.

REFERENCES

Attali, Jacques. 1985. *Noise: The political economy of music.* Minneapolis: University of Minnesota Press.
Bird, Steve. 2000. After 40 years, Che beats forces of capitalism. *Times* (London), 15 September.

Bourdieu, Pierre. 1993. *The field of cultural production*. Cambridge: Harvard University Press.

Castells, Manuel. 1996. *The rise of the network society*. Malden, Mass.: Black-well.

Castro, Fidel. 1961. Palabras a los intelectuales. *Bohemia* 53, no. 31.

Comaroff, Jean, and John L. Comaroff. 2000. Millennial capitalism: First thoughts on a second coming. *Public Culture* 12: 291–343.

Diaz, Alberto "Korda." 1999. Interview by author. Havana, 15 January.

Feltrinelli, Carlo. 2001. *Feltrinelli*. New York: Harcourt.

Fuente, Alejandro de la, and Laurence Glasco. 1997. Are blacks "getting out of control"? Racial attitudes, revolution and political transition in Cuba. In *Toward a new Cuba? Legacies of a revolution*, edited by Miguel Angel Centeno and Mauricio A. Font. Boulder, Colo.: Lynne Rienner.

Garcia, Heriberto. 1999. Interview by author. Havana, 3 June.

García Canclini, Néstor. 1989. *Culturas híbridas: Estrategias para entrar y salir de la modernidad*. Mexico City: Grijalbo.

Guevara, Ernesto Che. [1965] 1977. El socialismo y el hombre en Cuba. In *Escritos y discursos*, vol. 8. Havana: Editorial de Ciencias Sociales.

Gutiérrez, Aldo. 2001. Interview by author. Havana, 6 March.

Handler, Richard, and Eric Gable. 1997. *The new history in an old museum: Creating the past at Colonial Williamsburg*. Durham, N.C.: Duke University Press.

Hardt, Michael, and Antonio Negri. 2000. *Empire*. Cambridge: Harvard University Press.

Jameson, Fredric. 1998. Notes on globalization as a philosophical issue. In *The cultures of globalization*, edited by Fredric Jameson and Masao Miyoshi. Durham, N.C.: Duke University Press.

Lomnitz, Claudio. 2001. *Deep Mexico, silent Mexico: An anthropology of nationalism*. Minneapolis: University of Minnesota Press.

Manrique, Diego A. 1998. El músico José Luís Cortés refleja en su disco "Veneno" la gozadera de la música cubana. *El Pais*, 17 March, 39.

Marx, Karl. 1977. *Capital*, vol. 1, translated by Ben Fowkes. New York: Vintage.

Ong, Aihwa. 1999. *Flexible citizenship: The cultural logics of transnationality*. Durham, N.C.: Duke University Press.

Partido Comunista de Cuba. 1996. Political bureau report of March 23, 1996. *Granma International*, 10 April, 4.

Plagens, Peter, and Peter Katel. 1992. The next wave from Havana. *Newsweek*, 30 November, 76.

Pratt, Mary Louise. 1992. *Imperial eyes: Travel writing and transculturation*. London: Routledge.

Rohter, Larry. 1987. Troubadors of the Cuban Revolution. *New York Times*, 9 August, 2.

Sassen, Saskia. 2000. Spatialities and temporalities of the global: Elements for a theorization. *Public Culture* 12: 215–32.

——, ed. 1998. *Globalization and its discontents*. New York: New Press.

Yurchak, Alexei. 1997. The cynical reason of late socialism: Power, pretense, and the *anekdot*. *Public Culture* 9: 161–88.

12

Diagnostic Liquidity: Mental Illness and the Global Trade in DNA

Andrew Lakoff

Information is, at the end of the day, the coin of the genomics realm.[1]

Discussions of globalization processes typically describe an increasingly rapid flow of information, capital, and human bodies across national borders in the wake of technological innovation and political-economic transformation. As a number of analysts have noted, such increasing global circulation operates in relation to regulatory techniques and governmental strategies – at local, national, and transnational levels – that both encourage and constrain these flows.[2] Examples of such techniques include intellectual property regimes, immigration policies, and environmental standards. The negotiation of institutionalized regimes of coordination or harmonization – the linking of places through the creation of commensurable standards – is often necessary to make such circulation possible. By the same token, technical and regulatory regimes can also block the movement of goods or persons, as in the case of barriers to the sale of genetically-modified foods or ethical codes concerning the sale of human organs.[3] Recent studies of the creation and enactment of standards regimes provide helpful tools for the analysis of the micro-practices involved in creating zones of potential circulation.[4] This article combines an ethnographic description of the process of transnational standards-coordination with an analysis of the macro-political contexts in which such commensuration practices unfold. It

From *Theory and Society* 34: 63–92. Copyright © 2005, Springer.

follows a particular set of transnational flows, involving human DNA, biomedical knowledge, and capital, whose direction is intimately related to the relative presence of regulatory and technical regimes within different national spaces.

Specifically, I follow an attempt by a French biotechnology company to find and patent genes linked to psychiatric illness among a group of Argentine mental patients. This genomics research was significant in its institutional form, as well as in its potential implications for the reconfiguration of knowledge about mental illness. As an alliance between genomics and psychiatry across continents, and between public and private institutions, it represented a new type of assemblage oriented toward the understanding and regulation of human behavior. The central problem it raised – both practical and epistemological – concerned the *potential universality* of genomic knowledge about mental disorder. The success of the company's gene-hunting effort hinged on the global validity of a set of diagnostic standards that, it was hoped, would make possible the commensuration of divergent illness experience into a common classificatory scheme. Such commensuration, in turn, would enable psychiatric illness to be represented as genomic information, and would thus make the illness experience of Argentine patients convertible with that of patients in other parts of the world. How such experience was rendered liquid – that is, able to circulate and potentially to attain value as information – is the focus of this article. I show that in the case of mental illness, the effort to generate a space in which information flows seamlessly between biomedicine and the market is challenged by the difficulty of knowing just what a psychiatric disorder *is*. The extraction of valuable knowledge from patients' DNA relies on the development of diagnostic standards whose validity and extendibility remains in question.

Diagnostic Liquidity

In June 1997, the French genomics firm Genset announced a collaboration with the psychopathology department of a public hospital in Buenos Aires to collect and map the DNA of patients suffering from bipolar disorder. The genes or markers linked to susceptibility to bipolar disorder, if found, were to be patented by Genset as part of its strategy to enter into partnerships with major pharmaceutical companies for the development of new diagnostic and therapeutic technologies.

The process of gathering large amounts of data about the prevalence of illness in populations has historically been linked to public health initiatives: in order to gauge and improve the health of the population, national and transnational governmental agencies have, in collaboration with medical and scientific professionals, sought to accumulate epidemiological knowledge. What is distinctive about recent genomics research in places like China, Iceland, Russia, and Argentina is that it is often conducted by private database firms in collaboration with local clinics.[5] The case I describe here – in which the actual collection of DNA was carried out by local clinicians working in public hospitals, under contract to a genomics database firm – is not atypical of such arrangements. This pattern of collaboration is conditioned upon recent economic and techno-scientific developments: on the one hand, the emergence of health as a significant global marketplace, and on the other hand, the rapid development of DNA sequencing technology and bioinformatics in the wake of the Human Genome Project. For this reason, highly capitalized biotech firms have come to be interested in the possibility of attaining valuable genetic information through research on specific local populations. In the emergent space of exchange between industry and the life sciences, the role of government remains salient: the health marketplace as a target of technoscientific innovation is structured by the legal forms that ensure that biological information can attain value – i.e., intellectual property regimes.

It should be emphasized that this strand of genomics research targets health consumers in the advanced industrialized countries. The most valuable information in the health marketplace pertains to specific kinds of populations: North Americans and Europeans at risk of chronic illness, whose insurance will pay for the extended use of patented medications. In this context, the type of DNA collection and analysis I describe here seeks to demarcate specific illness populations that are simultaneously potential market segments. As this case illustrates, in other parts of the world patients serve as potential sources of knowledge rather than target markets, and they are often easier to access due to relaxed regulatory controls.

The Genset bipolar study was one of a number of transnational projects in the late 1990s involving newly minted genomics database firms based in the United States or Western Europe and health clinics in other parts of the world that were contracted to provide supplies of DNA from sample populations.[6] The sense was that there were hidden riches buried in the genomes of these clinically diagnosed patient populations.[7] As the Human Genome Project progressed, what legal theorist James Boyle called "an intellectual land grab" began as genomics database start-ups competed to find and patent genes or genetic markers linked to common, complex disorders.[8] While the value of such genes was still a matter of speculation, these genomics companies were confident that patented sequence information would prove a marketable resource in the burgeoning health marketplace. In Argentina, Genset sought to secure a supply of blood samples from an ethnically diverse patient population whose genetic background was similar to that of European and North American target markets, but without certain of the regulatory and legal complications that characterized such work in the North.

At stake in the process of gathering, analyzing, and developing proprietary knowledge from patients' DNA samples was the relation between truth and value in the global biomedical economy. At the scientific level, the translation from genetic material to significant information depended upon the validity of the diagnostic criteria used in gathering sample populations – criteria that in the case of psychiatric disorders had emerged in local and contingent circumstances. The economic value of such information, meanwhile, hinged on an intellectual property regime that granted monopoly rights to genomic innovation and on a market that structured demand for such information. Transnational epidemiology, in turn, made it possible to locate that market and gauge its size.

A key question emerged in Genset's research that focused attention on the classificatory devices to be used in gathering the sample population: to what extent could these criteria be claimed to measure the same thing across different spaces? How to know, for instance, whether a case of bipolar disorder in the United States was the same "thing" as a case of bipolar disorder in Argentina? Recent work in the social studies of science and medicine has investigated the processes through which the apparently universal validity of biomedical knowledge is materially and discursively forged via the standardization of practice across multiple domains.[9] This work indicates that the spread of standardized protocols does not necessarily produce equivalent practices in diverse sites.[10] In the case of the Genset study, what must be examined is the complex process of commensuration that was necessary for subjects with diverse histories to both recognize themselves as having bipolar disorder and to be so classified by doctors. At the same time, the difficulties faced in conducting the study illustrate local epistemic and political challenges to such commensuration.

To analyze the process of forging consistent illness populations so that Argentine patients' DNA could enter into circulation, I borrow the term "liquidity" from the field of finance. Bruce Carruthers and Arthur Stinchcombe analyze liquidity in futures markets as an example of the production of standardized value – the creation of generalized knowledge about value out of idiosyncratic personal knowledge.[11] They argue that producing equivalence out of specific entities involves both social regulation and political negotiation. Standardization is a social and cognitive achievement: buyers, market makers, and sellers have to share the conviction that "equivalent" commodities are really the same. Turning an illiquid asset into a more liquid one is a process of reduction and standardization of complexity.

To be transferable – liquid – an asset must lose its specificity and locality. Classificatory technologies work to simplify, stratify, and standardize such assets. Thus – to use Carruthers and Stinchcombe's example – a distinctive house becomes a liquid asset only when there are agreed-upon conventions for evaluating it in comparison with other houses. Similarly, William Cronon has shown how wheat was made into a liquid commodity in nineteenth-century Chicago through the invention of a set of technical standards for classifying the characteristics of specific bushels of wheat in terms of more general quality grades that made it unnecessary for buyers to inspect each bushel purchased.[12] Individualized evaluations of quality were thus shifted into collectively sanctioned criteria, enabling bushels of wheat to be abstracted and circulated as currency. In order successfully to implement such a system, the existence and legitimacy of a governing body that regulates the practice of measurement are crucial.

It is possible to consider the circulation of bipolar patients' DNA in terms of this process of abstraction through technical classification: the patients' illnesses assumed potential informational significance – and therefore, value – only insofar as their specific life trajectories could be brought into the same space of measurement. That is, their illnesses had to be made "liquid." From the vantage of genomics research, one should not need to know about the specific life trajectory of the person from whom DNA has been extracted in order to evaluate the significance of the information it bears. Diagnosis is the convention that produces such equivalence: in the case of bipolar disorder, what might seem like an implausible association then becomes natural: a young woman who has attempted suicide in Buenos Aires is brought into potential relationship with a middle-aged man in Chicago who goes bankrupt through risky business ventures. They are both members of a group of previously distinctive individuals now sharing a diagnosis.[13] The emergent group is alternately an epidemiological population, a market segment, and a community of self-identity.

Thus, while "liquidity" is typically understood in terms of finance, here techniques of classification enable biomedical knowledge to be assimilated to the domain of market exchange, shaping a hybrid commercial-epistemic milieu. In biomedicine, forging such a space of liquidity requires consistent classificatory practice among doctors – a problem that remains fraught in psychiatry, especially in Argentina. In what follows I describe how doctors in Buenos Aires performed classificatory work with psychiatric patients in order to render their illnesses liquid – that is, abstract and therefore exchangeable. This process involved the temporary extension of both a technical and an ethical standards regime. The setting of the DNA collection in Argentina revealed not only the reliance of techno-scientific objects, such as bipolar genes, on such regimes, but also the limits to their extension.

Circulatory Networks

The bipolar study crystallized through a contingent set of associations and opportunities. In 1997 Daniel Mendelson, an unemployed Argentine molecular biologist, was making a living by supplying genetic material from human organ tissue to Genset, a French biotech company that was building a cDNA library – a compilation of expressed human genes for use in detecting significant genetic information. Mendelson's work was a bit grisly. He would call up contacts who worked in forensic pathology laboratories in Buenos Aires hospitals, and ask them to send over healthy tissue from newly dead cadavers. Genset wanted various organs for its collection: kidneys, hearts, even brains. Once the tissue was sent over to him, Mendelson would process it in a lab he had rented at the Campomar Institute, a well-known biological research center near the Parque Centenario in Buenos Aires. He had been trained there before going off to do post-doctoral work at the Pasteur Institute in Paris with his wife, Marta Blumenfeld, also a molecular biologist. Now she was vice president of genomics at Genset, and he was struggling to establish a beachhead back home in Buenos Aires.

Mendelson had a new idea: they could expand their business of providing genetic material by obtaining DNA samples from patients with mental disorders. Genset was looking for populations of patients who had been diagnosed with schizophrenia and bipolar disorder for its gene discovery program in complex diseases. An old friend of Mendelson and Blumenfeld's from school now worked as a psychiatrist at a general hospital in Buenos Aires where patients could be recruited. After some back and forth negotiation, the details were worked out: Genset would give a hundred thousand dollars to Hospital Romero for structural improvements, and in exchange, doctors there would provide blood samples from two hundred patients diagnosed with bipolar disorder, types I and II.[14]

Genset was in a hurry to get hold of such material. As a genomics database company, its strategy depended upon finding and patenting genes linked to susceptibility to common, complex diseases. With its emerging patent portfolio and proprietary genomic search technologies in hand, Genset sought partnerships with large pharmaceutical firms to develop new diagnostic and therapeutic applications. It had recently formed strategic alliances with Abbott Pharmaceuticals, a leader in the diagnostics market as well as the maker of the leading medication for bipolar disorder, and with Janssen pharmaceuticals, producers of the antipsychotic Risperdal. Pharmaceutical industry strategists expected the next series of significant discoveries of drugs for mental disorder to emerge from the Human Genome Project; closer on the horizon was the prospect of diagnostic tests linked either to disease-susceptibility or medication-response. In order to have commercial rights to such products, Genset had to beat a number of competitors, in both the academic realm and the private sphere, to the relevant genomic loci. The alliance with Abbott was an early signal that major players in the pharmaceutical industry saw genomics as an important strategic arena. Given the possibility of royalties on a range of products, it seemed in the late 1990s – a moment of intense speculation in the life sciences, both conceptual and financial – that genomic information had potentially exponential value. As one biotech analyst wrote of the collaboration, "the Genset-Abbott deal is clearly geared toward creating a resource that the pair can sell again and again."[15]

The value of such resources relied first of all on the prospect that something scientifically significant would be found – which was by no means a foregone conclusion. Despite decades of academic research and a string of false alarms, no genomic loci had yet been confirmed to be linked to any of the major psychiatric disorders. According to Mendelson, it had only recently become possible to hunt seriously for such genes. First, developments in molecular biology and information technology now allowed genome-wide searches for disorders with complex genetic and environmental interactions. Genset's proprietary SNP (single nucleotide polymorphism) map provided dense markers to guide its researchers through the immense human genome, giving it an edge over academic and private-sphere competitors.[16] And secondly, it was now possible to forge coherent populations of clinically diagnosed patients: standardized criteria for diagnosing bipolar disorder had been spelled out in 1980 with the publication of the third edition of the diagnostic manual of the American Psychiatric Association (DSM-III) and had evolved in subsequent editions.[17]

Mendelson explained the process of looking for single nucleotide polymorphisms – natural variations in the genome – associated with bipolar disorder: if Genset could find a corresponding variation in multiple patients, it was likely that a susceptibility locus would be near, or statistically associated with, that variation. It was not a new or original scientific idea, he admitted, but it was one that was, practically speaking, incredibly daunting. Five years before it would have been technically unimaginable.

Once Mendelson and Blumenfeld made arrangements with Genset on the one hand, and with the hospital on the other, there was some delay in getting the DNA collection going. First, the Buenos Aires city government blocked the project on the grounds that it violated the law against trafficking in blood. After the concerned parties convinced the city's legal office that DNA was distinct from blood, and therefore saleable, another problem emerged: according to city regulations, a public hospital could not be paid by a private company for its services. This regulation was eventually circumvented, with the help of contacts in the municipal government, by changing the wording of the contract from payment to voluntary donation. By the time such regulatory hurdles had been taken care of, 6 months had passed.

Then when the study finally began, doctors at the hospital faced an unexpected problem: they could not find enough bipolar patients. It turned out that bipolar disorder was rarely diagnosed in Argentina. The North American diagnostic system in which it was recognized had not permeated the Argentine mental health world, nor had "bipolar identity" spread to raise awareness of the condition among potential patients.[18] Without such techniques of classification in place, the extraction and exchange of DNA could not begin. Doctors in the men's ward at Romero remained in need of donors even after recruiting at a nascent self-help group for patients with bipolar disorder, and were forced to make announcements in the newspapers asking for volunteers. In July 1998 a number of articles appeared in the city's major dailies describing the symptoms of bipolar disorder and promoting Romero's study.[19] These articles were in part geared to inform the public about what bipolar disorder was, given the absence of general knowledge of the condition. The publicity campaign turned out to be quite successful in drawing volunteers to the hospital, and by late September, psychiatrists in the men's ward were almost two-thirds of the way through their assignment to compile 200 samples. I was able to observe some of the collection process.

Collection (I)

Hospital Romero is located in a working-class neighborhood in the southern part of Buenos Aires. The hospital does not seem a likely place to be linked to cutting edge genomic research. Built in the 1930s, much of Romero is visibly crumbling, testimony to the current conditions of public health infrastructure in Argentina. The Psychopathology service is in especially poor shape – Genset's promised donation would go a long way, it turns out. On a Tuesday morning in September, a diverse group lingers around wooden benches in the entryway, all waiting to be attended: patients and family members, pharmaceutical company representatives, known as *valijas* or "briefcases" because of the satchels full of samples and promotional literature they carry around, and various cats who have wandered in from the hospital grounds. Through a swinging door at left, I enter the men's wing, passing a dozen old cubicles, where a few patients lie on sagging cots, on the way to the examination rooms. Some of the other patients are playing cards, or listening to the radio. The floors are of once-white, broken tile; the smell of ammonia is in the air.

A woman in her fifties, led by her daughter, is shown into a small room, bare except for a few chairs. They have traveled to Romero from a town about an hour away, having seen an article in *La Nacion* on the study of bipolar disorder being conducted there. After a preliminary phone interview, they were invited for an examination at the hospital. The mother and daughter do not seem particularly interested in the details of the gene study. They have come not so much to give blood as to ask for help: a diagnosis, a drug, a competent doctor. Gustavo Rechtman, a staff psychiatrist in his thirties, interviews them for about 5 minutes. He is formal and to the point, asking first whether the woman has had any depressions. Yes, she answers, looking to her daughter for reassurance. Very serious ones, adds the daughter – with suicidal thoughts. And are these sometimes followed by euphorias? She nods. Has she used any medications? She has taken anti-depressants in the past, and lithium – though, Rechtman notes, perhaps at too small a dosage. Her weight indicates that there might be a thyroid condition. Rechtman gives his diagnosis: bipolar disorder, type II – with hypomania. He mentions FUBIPA, the support group for bipolar patients and their families that helped publicize the study, but discourages the woman from seeking further treatment at Romero: it is very busy here, he says, and besides, this is a men's ward.[20] Instead, he will write a note to the doctor at her health clinic telling him of the diagnosis.

Rechtman then explains the scientific research to them: a French laboratory is doing a genetic study in order eventually to create a treatment, to see if the genes of patients are different from normal genes. It will have no direct benefit for her. Is she willing to participate? A glance at her daughter. Sure. A form is filled out: age, gender, marital status, occupation, ethnicity, financial status, familial antecedents, medication history. Then she is brought to a larger room, where test-tubes sit on the table, some already filled with blood. A male nurse, after considerable difficulty, finds a vein. A notebook is annotated, a code number put on the test tube. While the blood is drawn, the woman is handed a consent form, which she glances at briefly before signing. The blood will then travel the same route as the organ tissue before it – DNA will be extracted at Campomar and sent by special courier on to the Genset research campus at Evry, outside of Paris.

The transferability of genetic material depended not only on Genset's technical capacities to derive information from the patient's blood but also on the extension of an ethical-legal regime that sanctioned the technique: norms and regulations surrounding the circulation of genetic material between public institutions and private companies, and across national boundaries. The consent form legally detached the DNA from the patient. Drawn up by psychiatrists at Romero, it did not mention the possibility that the extracted genetic material might be patented. In a context where biomedical research was relatively rare and doctors retained significant authority, the consent form was not a well-recognized device, and therefore was something of a hollow ritual designed to meet the demands of the North Atlantic ethical sphere – it would be a part of the protocol that the firm would include along with any scientific achievements in a patent application or publication. What the patient received at the hospital was not a payment, but a diagnosis and a referral.

In general, the circumstances of the study did not especially concern observers I spoke with in Buenos Aires. Only a foreign company, some commented – and certainly not the Argentine state – could possibly do such advanced scientific work here, many told me. As for the role of the private sphere, given Argentina's recent history of state violence and political corruption there was little sense that the state was more trustworthy than private companies. And compared to some scandalous experiments that had recently been publicized, this one seemed fairly innocuous, involving only the taking of blood, and might lead to scientific advance.[21] Meanwhile, there was little worry over the political implications of finding genes linked to mental illness, no discussion of the return of eugenics – although, especially from members of the city's large corps of psychoanalysts, there was considerable skepticism as to whether anything significant would be found. Nor was the question of whether genes should be patentable much broached, except insofar as transnational bioethics discourse was beginning to be imported via global humanitarian networks.[22] Both anxieties and promises around the Human Genome Project, so prevalent in the North, had not yet arrived in Argentina.[23]

For some Argentine scientists, publicity around the study provided an opportunity to encourage more local attention to such issues. Mariano Levin, a molecular biologist who had worked in France with Genset's scientific director, Daniel Cohen, suggested that Argentina was an appealing place for the study precisely because of its lack of regulations on genetic research and patenting, not to mention that it was a good bargain for Genset. Cohen is a "marchand de tapis," he remarked, a rug merchant. For what was pocket change in the field of genomics, Genset would receive samples of diagnosed patients from a population whose ethnic origins were similar to those of target drug and diagnostic markets in Europe and North America. As Blumenfeld said, the city's "outbred population," predominantly of Italian, Spanish and Jewish descent, was one reason, along with its large supply of well-trained psy-professionals, that Genset chose to work in Buenos Aires.

Of several articles that appeared in the Argentine media concerning the gene study, only one, in the short-lived progressive weekly *Siglo XX*, was critical. This piece was accompanied by pictures of multiple Barbie and Ken dolls, and a table, translated from *Mother Jones*, showing multinational pharmaceutical companies' claims to patented genes. The article began with a joking reference to an Argentine penchant for melancholia:

> In Canada they study the gene for obesity. In Chile and in Tristan da Cunha, that of asthma. In Iceland, that of alcoholism. In Gabon, that of HIV. In the international partitioning of the body by the Human Genome Initiative...the French private company Genset chose Argentina to investigate the genetic roots of manic depression, as if this illness were an innate characteristic of the national being.[24]

The Genset study was used, in the article, as an opening for a discussion of the potential abuses of transnational genomics research. "It's a huge business straddling the frontier between medicine and biopiracy," said a geneticist who wished to remain anonymous. Why did Genset bother to go to Argentina to look for the genes? Mariano Levin was quoted in the article: "In this country there are no laws on genetic research and patenting, which diminishes the risks and costs if something goes badly, and increases the benefits if the research is successful." Levin's argument was not that such research should not be conducted in the country, but rather that Argentina needed to adopt and implement new forms of regulation – and ideally, to develop its own biotechnology research sector – in order to avoid being exploited by multinational firms seeking inexpensive genetic resources.

Alejandro Noailles, the director of Romero's Psychopathology ward, suspected that the peripheral status of Argentine clinicians made the country an especially good place for Genset to do the study. This is a private company, he emphasized in our first meeting, with a purely cost-benefit logic, and it is relatively inexpensive for them to do the study in Argentina. But even more, they won't have to share patent rights with those who do the work of collecting the samples: if the company were to do the study in Europe or the United States, he surmised, they might have to split the proceeds with the clinicians.

The key legal device making illness susceptibility genes potentially valuable was the agreement that well-characterized genes could be registered as intellectual property, which had been supported, though not without controversy, by European and United States patent offices since a landmark 1980 Supreme Court decision allowing living organisms to be patented.[25] Patents guarantee an exclusive license to commercialize discoveries for a limited period of time – normally 20 years. The question of what kind of information was sufficient to grant patent rights was a matter of some contention. In 1998, the Director of Biotechnology Examination at the U.S. patent and trademark office gave a provisional answer: "For DNA to be patentable, it must be novel and non-obvious in light of structurally related DNA or RNA information taught in nonpatent literature or suggested by prior patents."[26] After an initial stage of broad acceptance of patent claims on new genetic information, the tendency by the late 1990s was toward a more narrow vision of patentability – an insistence that the function and potential uses of the information be well demonstrated. Patent or no, the eventual value of such information was uncertain, as genomics-based products remained far on the horizon.[27]

Genset's research strategy of opportunistically seeking genetically heterogeneous patient populations was distinct from that of some other genomics companies, such as deCODE, which sought to leverage the ethnic homogeneity, detailed genealogical records and comprehensive clinical data available on the Icelandic population for its potential informational value.[28] Genset's research also provoked a far more muted response from the public than deCODE's work in Iceland: while deCode's project led to a national referendum and a spirited transnational debate on its ethical implications, research like Genset's remained mostly within the background noise of the 1990s biotech boom. An exception was a 2000 article in the *Guardian*, which noted that gene patenting was far from an exclusively North American phenomenon:

> European firms have become some of the most enthusiastic stakers of claims on human DNA. Patent applications on no fewer than 36083 genes and DNA sequences – 28.5% of the total claimed so far – have been filed by a single French firm, Genset. Andre Pernet, Genset's chief executive officer, said: "It's going to be a race. The whole genome will have been patented two years from now, if it hasn't been done already.[29]

Genset had fashioned itself as a company specializing in disorders of the central nervous system – specifically bipolar disorder and schizophrenia. As its founder Pascal Brandys said, "I believe that the brain is the next frontier, not just in genomics but in biotechnology as a whole."[30] Given the increasing size of the central nervous system (CNS) market, genes linked to mental illness that might provide new targets for drug innovation or lead to diagnostic technologies were potentially quite lucrative. Worldwide drug sales for CNS disorders were $30 billion in 1999, and CNS was the fastest growing product sector in the United States pharmaceutical market; by 2000 CNS disorders had overtaken gastroenterological illness as the second largest market segment, after cardiovascular conditions.[31] A venture capitalist noted the increasing interest in the CNS market, invoking the land rush image: "Every doctor knows that the brain is the final frontier of medicine, but VCs are just now starting to sniff opportunity. There'll be a lot of opportunities to play this sector because there are just so many problems that fall under the heading CNS."[32] Such opportunities ranged from Alzheimer's disease to attention deficit disorder, anxiety and schizophrenia. One question that was crucial to the eventual success of such ventures was whether illness populations as they had been classified according to the diagnostic standards of the American Psychiatric Association could be delineated at the genetic level.

Diagnostic Infrastructure

Noailles had recently returned from a visit to Genset's high-tech laboratory near Paris, stocked with millions of dollars worth of gene sequencing machines and high-speed computers. There a committee of European psychiatrists had gone over the research protocol for the study with Romero's staff to ensure consistent diagnostic practice. It was hoped that such standardized diagnostic protocols would mediate between the subjective interpretation of the clinician and the impersonal evidence of the gene.[33] Genset's protocol presumed that for the purposes of gathering consistent populations, psychiatric disorders were not inherently different from other common illnesses with complex inheritance patterns, like osteoporosis or diabetes. If this were the case, the process of making illness liquid should have been relatively straightforward, at least at the level of diagnosis. However, as Genset's experience in Argentina proved, the ecology of expertise and the dynamics of patient identity in psychiatric disorders are considerably distinct.

Genset's collection process was based on a more general assumption, in cosmopolitan psychiatry, of the existence of an undifferentiated global epidemiological space. The World Health Organization estimated that 2.5% of the world's population between the ages of 15 and 44 suffered from bipolar disorder.[34] If this was the case, where were the Argentine bipolar patients? Why was it so difficult for Romero's doctors to come up with 200 samples? Like the WHO, Genset's research protocol presumed that bipolar disorder was a coherent and stable entity with universal properties. But as a number of analysts of the production of scientific knowledge have argued, the existence of a given technoscientific object – here, bipolar disorder – is contingent upon its network of production and stabilization.[35] An individual experience of suffering becomes a case of a generalized psychiatric disorder only in an institutional setting in which the disorder can be recognized, through the use of specific concepts and techniques that format the complexities of individual experience into a generalized convention.

Beginning with the publication of the third edition of the Diagnostic and Statistical Model of the American Psychiatric Association [DSM-III] in 1980, a diagnostic infrastructure came to underpin diverse phenomena in U.S. psychiatry, ranging from drug development and regulation, to third party reimbursement, clinical research, and patient self-identity. The goal of these classificatory standards was reliability: if the same person went to two different treatment centers, he or she should receive the same diagnosis and treatment in each place. Such standards made it possible to forge comparable populations for research and to measure the relative efficacy of specific intervention techniques. The Research Diagnostic Criteria (RDC), forerunner to DSM-III, emerged in U.S. psychiatry in the 1970s for just this reason – the need to have a standard gauge so that researchers could meaningfully measure response to given medications across populations. The RDC was addressed to the problem of the low reliability of diagnostic procedures, which hampered large scale, comparative research in psychiatry. As its creators wrote, "a major purpose of the RDC is to enable investigators to select relatively homogeneous groups of subjects who meet specified diagnostic criteria."[36]

The connection between the RDC and the DSM-III is significant in that it shows how government regulations on market entry for pharmaceuticals – the FDA's clinical trial requirements – eventually played a key role in transforming psychiatric epistemology, structuring the need for diagnostic standards that led to the DSM revolution. Once enacted, these conventions then proved useful across a number of arenas of administration and practice – for insurance administration, transnational epidemiology, patient self-identification, and the re-biologization of psychiatry as a clinical research enterprise.[37] Diagnostic standardization in psychiatry thus made mental illness transferable between the domains of industry, government, and biomedicine.

However, physicians trained to see patients in terms of an individual life course are often resistant to the imposition of systems of standardized diagnosis.[38] Such classification presumes a distinctive model of illness, which Charles Rosenberg has described as the "specificity model" characteristic of modern biomedicine.[39] According to this model, which came to prominence in the mid-nineteenth century, illnesses are understood as stable entities that exist outside of their embodiment in particular individuals, and which can be explained in terms of specific causal mechanisms located within the sufferer's body. Disease specificity is a tool of administrative management: it makes it possible to mandate professional practice through the institution of protocols; to engage in large-scale epidemiological studies; to rationalize health practice more generally.[40] At the intersection of individual suffering and bureaucratic administration, the technology of standardized nosology "helps to make experience machine readable," as Rosenberg writes.[41]

While DSM met the demand for consistent diagnostic practice across diverse sites, the question remained whether the forging of such populations was based on valid – rather than simply reliable – criteria of inclusion.[42] Standardized psychiatric measures are founded on contingent agreements on rating scales among experts rather than on patho-physiological measures. This is where psychiatric genomics research such as Genset's faced a conundrum. On the one hand, this research required that codified diagnostic standards be in place. At the same time, it sought to remake these standards eventually by producing a new technology of measurement, the gene-based diagnostic tool.

The problem of how to recognize definitively a given illness phenotype remained critical to psychiatric genomics research, leading to professional reflection on the process of mutual adjustment between the surface and substrate of mental disorder. In a 2002 review of "psychiatry in the postgenomic era," two leading experts focused specifically on this challenge – as a conceptual as well as a practical problem:

There will be critical conceptual difficulties and none are more important than readdressing the phenotypes of mental disorders. The ability of genomic tools to find the appropriate disease-related gene(s) is limited by the "quality" or homogeneity of the phenotypic sample ... There will be a somewhat circular process of understanding phenotype as we gain a better understanding of genotype; this, in turn, will affect our understanding of phenotype. All of this circularity may seem unsettling and unsatisfying to philosophical purists and it is difficult to see any way out of a process of constant adjustment. However, in the meantime, it is critical that we collect broad and thoughtful phenotypic information and not be handcuffed by diagnostic criterion sets that have reliability as their strong suit but were never meant to represent valid diagnostic entities.[43]

Thus experts were at once using the agreed-upon definitions of illness phenotypes such as bipolar disorder and assuming that they were provisional and would necessarily be superseded by advances in genomics. Indeed, the psychiatrists who were gathering blood samples at Romero were skeptical that the diagnostic protocol given to them by Genset would be sufficient to find a gene: in our discussions they remarked that several different forms of the illness were being included in the study. A journalistic account of the study characterized this anxiety:

For the Argentine psychiatrists, this classification could be insufficient. As a matter of fact, they admit, other classificatory schemes point to the existence of up to six types of presentation of the illness, which for a long time was considered a psychosis and now is characterized as an affective disorder.[44]

Genotype and Phenotype

How did the modern form of "bipolar disorder" come into being in the first place? It is an especially intriguing category of illness because it seems to exist on both sides of certain key boundaries of mental disorder – the boundary between affective and thought disorder, or in psychoanalytic epistemology, between neurosis and psychosis. Moreover, its increasing visibility over the past two decades relates to the rise of pharmaceutical treatment in psychiatry.

From the early twentieth century until the introduction of psychopharmaceuticals in the 1950s and 1960s, the "functional psychoses" such as manic depression and schizophrenia were seen as chronic conditions requiring life-long institutionalization. With the introduction of psychotropic medication and then regulatory demands for randomized clinical trials, a drug market in anti-psychotics and mood stabilizers was created and populations for clinical research were delineated.[45] Following confirmation of the effectiveness of lithium in the 1960s, bipolar disorder became a rare success story within psychiatry, able to be managed if not cured.[46] Despite this relatively privileged place in the field, the boundaries of the disorder as well as its origins and its defining symptoms remained at issue up through the 1990s.

According to the American Psychiatric Association's 1994 DSM-IV – which guided Genset's protocol – bipolar disorder was characterized by fluctuations in mood, from states of manic excitement to periods of abject depression. The presence of affective disorders within the patient's family was also a diagnostic clue. There were at least two types of bipolar disorder: type I was "classic" manic depression, characterized by severe shifts in mood between florid mania and depression; type II included cases where severe depression is punctuated not by full-blown mania, but by mild euphoria, "hypomania."[47] The condition had to be diagnosed longitudinally, since in its synchronic state it could be difficult to differentiate the manic phase of bipolar disorder from the delusional symptoms of schizophrenia, or at the other extreme, from the melancholia of major depression.

But it was uncertain whether bipolar disorder was truly distinguishable from schizophrenia and/or depression, as the ambiguous status of "schizoaffective disorder" suggested. Genetic and neurological studies continued to confound researchers trying to establish consistent means of differentiation. Estimates of its prevalence in the population ranged from 0.5% to 5%, depending on the criteria of inclusion used.[48] Some psychiatrists argued that there was a "psychotic continuum" from bipolar disorder to schizophrenia, from predominately affective traits to thought disorder.[49] Meanwhile, expert advocates of the diagnosis claimed that many actual bipolar patients had been incorrectly diagnosed with unipolar depression and given anti-depressants, which could set off a manic episode.[50] Such proposals would radically expand the bipolar population. Geneticists struggled to define the disorder's boundaries in order to gather consistent populations for research:

> There is growing agreement that in addition to BPI [bipolar illness], MDI [manic depressive illness] encompasses several mood disorders related phenomenologically and genetically to BPI. These include bipolar disorder type II…some cases of major depressive disorder without manic symptoms…and some cases of schizoaffective disorder (in which symptoms of psychosis persist in the apparent absence of the mood disorder). The MDI phenotype may include other, milder manic-depressive spectrum disorders such as minor depression, hypomania without major depression, dysthymia, and cyclothymia, but this is less certain.[51]

Would finding susceptibility genes once and for all pin down the *thingness* of the disorder? In academic studies of the genetics of bipolar disorder, the late 1990s were a time of frustration. While twin and family studies had indicated heritable susceptibility since the 1930s, hopes that the advent of techniques for gene identification in molecular biology would quickly make it possible to find the biological mechanisms involved were disappointed. After a period of excitement in the 1980s as various reports of loci for linked genes appeared, a decade later the glow had receded after repeated failures to replicate such studies.[52] Experts gave dour assessments of the state of the field: "In no field has the difficulty [of finding genes linked to complex disease] been more frustrating than in the field of psychiatric genetics. Manic depression (bipolar illness) provides a typical case in point," wrote two Stanford geneticists in 1996.[53] By 2001, newly reported findings of a susceptibility locus on chromosome 10 were greeted warily by researchers.[54]

There were a number of possible suspects for the mixed results: "the failure to identify BP-I loci definitively, by standard loci approaches, probably reflects uncertainty regarding mode of inheritance, high phenocopy rates, difficulty in demarcation of distinct phenotypes, and presumed genetic heterogeneity," wrote a team at UCSF.[55] In other words, these researchers thought that conceptual difficulties around defining the phenotype for diagnostic purposes posed an insuperable technical challenge. The Stanford researchers, in contrast, argued that no dominant gene had been found because of the biological complexity of the inheritance mechanism.[56] Surveying the state of the field, some geneticists posed a worrisome question about the diagnostic entity they were looking at: "The question remains: do our modern definitions of clinical syndromes (at present considered as phenotypes) accurately reflect underlying genetic substrates (genotypes)?"[57] In other words, for the purposes of genetic studies, was there really such a thing as bipolar disorder?

The phenotype question created a paradox for these studies: on the one hand, genetic research promised to resolve such problems by making clear the underlying biological processes: "Currently the major problem is the unknown biological validity of current psychiatric classifications and it is worth bearing in mind that advances in molecular genetics are likely to be instrumental in providing the first robust validation of our diagnostic schemata."[58] In order for such validation to occur, researchers had to know what they were working with. Yet they lacked objective tools to do so: "In the absence of a clear understanding of the biology of psychiatric illnesses the most appropriate boundaries between bipolar disorder and other mood and psychotic disorders remain unclear."[59] Genetic studies might even turn out to undermine the notion of a clear distinction between these disorders:

> One of the exciting developments has been the emergence of overlapping linkage regions for schizophrenia and affective disorder, derived from studies on independently ascertained pedigrees. These results raise the possibility of the existence of shared genes for schizophrenia and affective disorder, and the possibility that these genes contribute to the molecular basis of functional psychoses.[60]

The unfulfilled promise of genetics led psychiatry back to an old curse, the problem of how to stabilize its objects – that is, how to ensure that its illnesses were "real" things, whose contours could be recognized and agreed-upon by diverse experts. Despite the discipline's adoption of neuroscientific models, and ongoing genetic and neuroimaging research into mental disorders, the question of the relation of psychiatry to biomedicine remained: to what extent could psychiatric conditions be considered equivalent to "somatic" illnesses? The effort to achieve such equivalence was one rationale for the re-biologization of U.S. psychiatry beginning in the 1980s.[61] Difficulties in confirming genetic linkage challenged the legitimacy of psychiatric knowledge, and the very existence of its objects. A leading researcher expressed frustration at the place of psychiatry in genetics research:

> [Psychiatric geneticists] continue to face an obstacle that does not hinder their colleagues who investigate non-psychiatric diseases; psychiatric phenotypes, as currently defined, are based entirely on clinical history and often on subjective reports rather than directly observed behaviors.... In no other branch of medicine have investigators (and practitioners) been called on to demonstrate time and again that the diseases they study really are diseases.[62]

Epistemic Milieu

This problem was especially palpable in Buenos Aires, as doctors struggled to locate patients who had been diagnosed with bipolar disorder. The dearth of bipolar subjects in Argentina was due not to a cultural difference in the expression of pathology or to the country's genetic heritage but to a different set of conceptions and practices, within its professional milieu, of the salient forms of disorder and the tasks of expertise.[63] The nosological revolution in North American psychiatry – the shift to DSM-III and its successors beginning in 1980 – had not extended to the Southern Cone. In Argentina, DSM faced professional resistance on both epistemological and political grounds. The pervasive presence of psycho-dynamic models among psy-professionals led to an emphasis on the unique clinical encounter between doctor and patient, and a suspicion of diagnostic categories that purported to generalize across cases. Meanwhile, there was political opposition to the incursion of such standards on the grounds that they were being imposed in the interest of managed care and pharmaceutical industry interests. Many Argentine psychiatrists associated the use of DSM with neoliberalism, the privatization of state industries and the dismantling of the welfare state.[64]

A number of absences also made resistance to standardization more feasible: in contrast to the North American situation, the Argentine psychiatric profession was not structured by a demand to forge populations for epidemiological or neuroscientific research. Disciplinary prestige did not come from producing scientific articles in transnational journals, and professional training did not include an emphasis on standardized diagnostic classifications. Further, insurance reimbursement systems did not require the use of "evidence-based" protocols in diagnostic and intervention decisions. Thus while the Argentine population had been made available for genomic research in ethico-legal terms by Genset's contract with Hospital Romero and the consent form, it had not been rendered equivalent in epistemological terms.

Across the hallway from where the genetic study was being conducted, the women's ward of Romero's psychopathology service achieved the surprising feat of practicing Lacanian analysis within a public hospital that served a predominantly poor and socially marginal population.[65] A number of times women who had received a bipolar diagnosis and then given blood samples for the Genset study in the men's ward were later hospitalized across the way during psychotic episodes. Such patients' claims to be bipolar were mostly disregarded by the physician-analysts there, who saw such self-diagnosis as a form of resistance to subjective exploration in psychoanalytic terms, and considered "bipolar disorder" to be a condition that owed much of its existence to the promotional efforts of the pharmaceutical industry.[66] As they saw it, their task was to penetrate beneath these generalizing categories to understand the distinctive life history and process of subject-formation of the patient.

Meanwhile there remained the question of how the patients themselves understood their condition. Given the prevalence of psychoanalysis in Argentina, and the absence of the kind of patient self-help movements that have transformed the North American milieu, it was not necessarily a receptive site for the inculcation of "bipolar identity." The problem for Genset was at one level a technical one: how to find a pool of patients that would prove amenable to genomic research. But insofar as psychiatric diagnosis also names a subjective mode the question involved self-identity as well. Bipolar self-identity – which emerged in the United States as part of a burgeoning self-help apparatus – was not widespread in Argentina. To what extent did subjects who entered Romero come to see their own life trajectories in terms of an illness characterized by extreme mood swings that had a biological underpinning? An unusual case during the sample collection illustrated some of the complex interactions between patient self-understanding and professional diagnosis that characterizes psychiatric conditions.

Collection (II)

On one Thursday morning in the men's ward, more potential DNA donors have come for their appointments. In one examination, a young woman does most of the talking, rapidly and in disjointed bursts. She is a psychoanalyst, she explains, and so she does not believe in genetic explanations. But a patient of hers, a friend – who had read about the study in the paper – told her that she had certain characteristics that seemed like they could be "bipolar," so she decided to come, just in case, out of curiosity. She does not want to give her name: professionally, she says, it would be bad for her reputation if it were known that she had come to find out about her genetic makeup. It soon becomes apparent that the woman thinks that there is already a genetic test available for bipolar disorder, and she has come to Romero to take it. She is not sure whether she really wants to know, or even if it would be possible to know such a thing through a blood test. When Rechtman finally makes it clear that in fact there is not yet a genetic test, but the hospital is collecting samples in the hopes of finding such genes, she begins to protest the very premise of the study.

"How can you possibly know a person's diagnosis if you haven't been treating them?" she demands. She cuts off Rechtman's response, explaining that in psychoanalysis, you have to establish a transferential relationship with the patient in order to see the psychic structure. The whole operation seems rather suspicious to her. She eyes the anthropologist: what is he writing down? Rechtman tries to calm her, explaining the rationale for diagnosis: "there are certain signs of the disorder – for instance, what was it that your friend noticed?" The woman lists a few symptoms: insomnia, cocaine use, depressions, an eating disorder. "My analyst says that I'm an obsessive," she explains.

"But the psychoanalytic clinic has its limits," she muses. "Perhaps if there were something physical?" They debate further, back and forth, and the discussion becomes acrimonious. Finally, Rechtman tries to close off the examination: "I wouldn't include you in the study, because it's not clear what you have." "But what else could it be?" she asks, now almost wanting to be convinced. "Maybe it's what your analyst says, obsessive neurosis," he suggests skeptically. "But I suspect that it is bipolar disorder." She muses for a moment, then poses another question: "What does Prozac have to do with all this?" Rechtman throws up his hands. At last, they reach a labored conclusion, agreeing to disagree. Her DNA will not be among the samples sent by courier to Paris. She has rescued her professional pride, and declined to shift her identity. Educated, middle class, and *porteña*, she retains her model of mental distress.

Despite her protestations, the woman's presence at the hospital indicated a certain urge to shift her conception of herself, to try new explanations and interventions. Because the experience of psychiatric disorder interacts with the characteristics of the disorder, its diagnosis is a moving target.[67] Psychiatry, in part because it depends on patients' subjective reports of their symptoms, has had a difficult time shifting the disorders under its purview into stable things in the world. The search for genes related to mental illness is, among other things, an attempt to turn mental disorders into more durable entities. Yet it seems that the discovery of loci of genetic susceptibility would not necessarily make such illnesses less complex. As the interaction above illustrates, knowledge of susceptibility is likely to add a layer of complexity to patient self-understanding, and provide a set of new possibilities of intervention rather than to reduce mental illness to purely organic determination.[68]

Local Conditions

Historian Ken Alder writes, "understanding the process by which artifacts come to transcend the local conditions in which they are conceived and produced should be one of the central tasks facing any satisfactory approach to technology."[69] DSM emerged from a specific conjuncture within North American psychiatry in the 1970s, and spread to other sites – both administrative and scientific – because of its ability to make behavioral pathology transferable across domains. DSM was not just an isolated set of technical innovations within psychiatry: its eventual widespread use in professional milieus (and resulting controversies from such use) had to do with its ability to serve a diverse set of needs: for drug development given regulatory guidelines; for insurance protocols based on "evidence-based medicine"; for the re-professionalization of psychiatry as a biomedical science.

As I have argued, technical protocols such as diagnostic standards structure the production of a space of liquidity: they mediate between the domains of science, industry, and health administration. Such technologies are part of an infrastructure, both material and conceptual, that enables goods, knowledge, and capital to flow across administrative and epistemic boundaries. They link social needs such as health to profit-seeking ventures and to scientific communities. The use of such technologies in material practices such as professional standardization and DNA collection underlies the abstraction of a global biomedical information economy.

But this case also points to the limits of such transcendence of the local. The setting in Argentina indicates that the extension of a diagnostic infrastructure does not occur uniformly across space but rather through networks, and must be supported or imposed by institutional and regulatory demands. The shift in North American and Western European psychiatry from "clinical" to "administrative" norms had not taken hold there by the late 1990s, despite efforts to privatize parts of health management along North American lines. The advance of DSM was an element in a health apparatus oriented toward bureaucratic management that had not suffused the Argentine milieu. Nor was there a significant patient-activist movement shaping collective action around the recognition and legitimacy of specific disorders. And a professional culture whose epistemological forms were incommensurable with DSM was entrenched. For these reasons, individual clinicians retained considerable autonomy in terms of diagnostic and therapeutic practices.

The difficulty of finding bipolar patients in Buenos Aires pointed to the halting extension not only of diagnostic standards, but also of modes of self-identification around illness labels such as bipolar disorder. In order to be a viable diagnostic entity, the disorder needed an epistemic niche in which it could take root and thrive. Bipolarity came into being temporarily in the men's ward of Hospital Romero, but only through the imperative to find a sufficient sample of patients for the Genset study. In turn, it disappeared when patients traveled to the women's ward. Patients' illnesses were rendered liquid without permanently transforming patient-identity, since a diagnostic infrastructure for managing health in terms of specific sub-populations was not in place. Thus, while information may be "the coin of the genomics realm," the extraction and circulation of such information is not a simple matter. In the case of mental illness, the value of genomic information depends upon the stabilization of the very thing it claims to represent – the disorder itself.

NOTES

1　Antonio Regalado, "Inventing the pharmacogenomics business," *American Journal of Health System Pharmacy* 56/1 (1999): 49.

2　Saskia Sassen, "Spatialities and Temporalities of the Global: Elements for a Theorization," *Public Culture* 12/1 (2000); Neil Brenner, "Globalization as Reterritorialisation: The Rescaling of Urban Governance in the European Union," *Urban Studies* 36/3 (1999). For the description of an emergent anthropology of global techno-scientific and administrative forms, see Stephen Collier and Aihwa Ong, "Global Assemblages, Anthropological Problems," in *Global Assemblages: Technology, Politics, and Ethics as Anthropological Problems* (Oxford: Blackwell, 2005).

3　For the case of the organ trade, see Lawrence Cohen, "Operability, Bioavailability, and Exception," in Collier and Ong, *Global Assemblages*. For the analysis of Europe as a "technological zone" see Andrew Barry, *Political Machines: Governing a Technological Society* (London: Athlone Press, 2001).

4　Geoffrey Bowker and Leigh Star, *Sorting Things Out: Classification and its Consequences* (Cambridge: MIT Press, 1999); Wendy Espeland and Mitchell Stevens, "Commensuration as a social process," *Annual Review of Sociology* 24 (1998); Ken Alder, "Making Things the Same," in *Social Studies of Science* 28/4 (1998).

5　The invention and dissemination of diagnostic standards that enable epidemiologists to constitute such collectivities can be seen as part of the more general task of fostering the health and welfare of the population, what Michel Foucault called biopolitics. Foucault, "The Birth of Biopolitics," in *Ethics, Subjectivity and Truth: Essential Works of Foucault, 1954–1984*, vol. 1, ed. Paul Rabinow (New York: The New Press, 1997).

6　A project conducted in rural China by Millennium Pharmaceuticals in collaboration with Harvard University and seeking genes linked to asthma provoked a scandal after an investigative report appeared in the Washington Post. Johan Pmfret and Deborah Nelson, "In Rural China, a Genetic Mother Lode," *Washington Post* Dec. 20, 2000, p. A1.

7   "Mining" was a common metaphor for the search for potential riches hidden in the human genome. As a 1996 article about a Genset research collaboration in China put it, quoting Genset's president: "China's population is a gold mine of genetic information. The country's rural populations have remained relatively static this century, so each region has a unique blend of genes and diseases. This makes it much easier to trace hereditary diseases back to defective genes, which are unusually abundant where the disease is prevalent. 'You can treat regional local populations almost like single families,' says Brandys." Andy Coghlan, "Chinese deal sparks eugenics protests," *The New Scientist*, November 16, 1996.

8   Boyle, *Shamans, Software and Spleens: Law and the Construction of the Information Society* (Cambridge: Harvard University Press, 1997), 9. The kind of mapping Genset was engaged in – which sought to find markers of genetic variation (SNPs) – did not presume a causal relation between a given DNA sequence and the presence or absence of disease; rather, it hypothesized that certain markers of variation could be correlated to greater *susceptibility* to that disease.

9   Examples include studies of organ donation, evidence-based protocols, and government-funded biomedical research. See Linda Hogle, "Standardization across Non-standards Domains: The Case of Organ Procurement," *Science, Technology and Human Values* 20/4 (1995); Stefan Timmermans and Marc Berg, "Standardization in Action: Achieving Local Universality through Medical Protocols, *Social Studies of Science* 27 (1997); Steven Epstein, "'One Size Does Not Fit All': Standardization, Resistance, and the Inclusion-and-Difference Paradigm in U.S. Biomedical Research," in preparation.

10 See, for example, Annemarie Mol and John Law, "Regions, Networks and Fluids: Anaemia and Social Topology," *Social Studies of Science* 24 (1994): 641–671.

11 Bruce Carruthers and Arthur Stinchcombe, "The Social Structure of Liquidity: Flexibility, Markets, and States," in *Theory and Society* 28/3 (1999): 356.

12 William Cronon, *Nature's Metropolis: Chicago and the Great West* (New York: Norton, 1991). Michel Callon describes the process whereby objects are "disentangled" from their immediate surroundings and made calculable as one of "enframing." Callon, editor, *The Laws of the Markets* (Oxford: Blackwell, 1998).

13 Genset would eventually check the validity of its findings of a "psychosis gene" among Quebecois and Russian populations against the sequence information extracted from its Argentine bipolar samples. Marta Blumenberg, et al., "Genes, Proteins and Biallelic Markers Related to Central Nervous System Disease," June 27, 2002. U.S. Patent and Trade Office, United States Patent Application 20020081584.

14 A note on the names used in this article: I have used pseudonyms both for the hospital and for the doctors where the research was carried out, to protect the privacy of my informants there. Because the Genset research is public knowledge, I have identified the firm and its employees by name.

15 Regalado, "Inventing," 45.

16 This strategic edge proved temporary: I interviewed Mendelson before the 1999 announcement of the "SNP Consortium," a collaboration designed to undercut the strategic position of database firms like Genset. See Note 27.

17 Its precursor, manic-depression, was first named by Emil Kraepelin around 1900. See Emil Kraepelin, "Stages of Maniacal-Depressive Insanity," in *Lectures on Clinical Psychiatry*, ed. Thomas Johnstone (London: Bailliere, Tindall and Cox, 1904).

18 Kay Redfield Jamison, *An Unquiet Mind* (New York: Random House, 1997).

19 As an article in *La Nacion* put it: "Currently, the hospital needs more sporadic patients to complete the sample that is awaited in France." Gabriela Navarra, "De la euforia a la depresion," *La Nacion*, July 22, 1998, Section 6, page 4.

20 Unlike patient groups in the U.S., FUBIPA and similar groups are relatively marginal phenomena in Argentina, and are typically run by local experts in the disorder rather than by patients and family members.

21 One highly publicized example was the Wistar Institute's 1986 field trial of a recombinant rabies vaccine in cattle outside of Buenos Aires, in which no Argentine authorities were informed of the experiment. See Bernard Dixon, "Genetic Engineers Call for Regulation," in *The Scientist* 2(8), May 2, 1988.

22 It appeared, for instance, via the UNESCO Bioethics initiative, represented in Argentina by legal scholar Salvador Bergel, who opposed the licensing of genetic material. Salvador Bergel, "Patentamiento de genes y secuencias de genes," in *Revista de Derecho y Genoma Humano* 8 (1998): 31–59.

23 To the extent that imagery of a dystopian genetic future entered the popular imagination, it was via the film *Gattaca*, rather than through newspaper editorials by vigilant watchmen. This can be contrasted with the deCODE case in Iceland. See Gisli Palsson and Paul Rabinow, "Iceland: The Case of a National Human Genome Project," *Anthropology Today* 15/5 (1999). On the other hand, Argentina was one of the first countries to ban cloning in the aftermath of Dolly, a result of the power of the Argentine Catholic Church to define the boundaries of human reproduction.

24 Walter Goobar, "De quien es esa naricita?" *Siglo XXI* 27 August 1998, 66.

25 Paul Rabinow, *Making PCR: A Story of Biotechnology* (Chicago: The University of Chicago Press, 1995); Sheila Jasanoff, *Science at the Bar: Law, Science, and Technology in America* (Cambridge: Harvard University Press, 1995).

26 John J. Doll, "The Patenting of DNA," in *Science* 280 (1998): 690. See also James Boyle, *Shamans*.

27 Indeed, a group of major pharmaceutical companies, in partnership with the Wellcome Trust, was able to circumvent the biotech effort to patent and license SNPs – by forming a consortium in 1999 to make such markers publicly available, significantly hindering the business strategy of companies like Genset. By 2000, Genset was forced to redefine itself as a drug development company, given the unproven profitability of genomic database firms.

28 See Palsson and Rabinow, "Iceland." Another difference was that the Argentine subjects of Genset's study were not prospective consumers of the technologies under development, whereas the deCODE project guaranteed Icelanders access to Hoffman-LaRoche products developed from the research.

29 James Meek, "Why you are first in the great gene race," *The Guardian*, Nov. 15, 2000.

30 *Genetic Engineering News*, July 2000.

31 Source: IMS Health. See www.imshealth.com.

32 Stephan Herrera, "The Biotech Boom: Revenge of the Neurons." *Red Herring*, Oct. 1, 2001.

33 The standardized diagnostic category was thus a potential "boundary object," in Geof Bowker and Leigh Star's sense: "those objects that both inhabit several communities of practice and satisfy the informational requirements of each of them. In working practice, they are objects that are able both to travel across borders and maintain some sort of constant identity." Bowker and Star, *Sorting Things Out*, 16.

34 World Health Organization, *World Health Report*, 2001. Typical estimates in the bipolar genetics literature were around 1%. But some experts thought it was as high as 5%. Much depended on the criteria of inclusion, and the means of distinguishing BPD from overlapping syndromes such as schizophrenia, unipolar depression, and attention deficit disorder.

35 For a description of how certain mental disorders come to thrive in specific political, cultural and professional niches, see Ian Hacking, *Mad Travelers: Reflections on the Reality of Transient Mental Illnesses* (Charlottesville: University Press of Virgina, 1998).

Bruno Latour discusses the ontological question of whether tuberculosis can be said to have existed in ancient Egypt, in "On the Partial Existence of Existing and Non-Existing Objects," in Lorraine Daston, editor, *Biographies of Scientific Objects* (Chicago: University of Chicago Press, 2000).

36 Spitzer and Endicott, "Research Diagnostic Criteria," in *Archives of General Psychiatry* 35 (June 1978).

37 In this sense DSM can be considered a potential "biomedical platform," as Peter Keating and Alberto Cambrosio describe, operating to connect clinical conventions with biological conventions, individuals with populations. See Keating and Cambrosio, "Biomedical Platforms," in *Configurations* 8 (2000): 337–387.

38 For the distinction between the clinical and the administrative as different modes of justification in medical work, see Nicolas Dodier, "Clinical Practice and Procedures in Occupational Medicine," in Marc Berg and Annemarie Mol, *Differences in Medicine: Unraveling Practices, Techniques, and Bodies* (Durham, N.C.: Duke University Press, 1998).

39 Rosenberg, "The Tyranny of Diagnosis: Specific Entities and Individual Experience," in *Milbank Quarterly* 80 (2002): 237–260.

40 For the relation between the standardization of illness categories and current efforts to administer health via "evidence-based medicine," see Stefan Timmermans and Marc Berg, *The Gold Standard: The Challenge of Evidence-Based Medicine and Standardization in Health Care* (Philadelphia: Temple University Press, 2003).

41 Rosenberg, "Tyranny," 23.

42 For a lucid analysis of questions of reliability and validity in psychiatric diagnosis, see Allan Young, *The Harmony of Illusions: Inventing Post-Traumatic Stress Disorder* (Princeton: Princeton University Press, 1996).

43 Kathy L. Kopnisky and Steven Hyman, "Psychiatry in the Postgenomic Era," in *TEN* 4/1 (2002): 27–31.

44 Navarra, "De la euforia a la depresion."

45 For the story of the emergence of the "specificity" model in psychopharmacology in relation to regulatory demands, see David Healy, *The Creation of Psychopharmacology* (Cambridge: Harvard University Press, 2002); for the history of FDA regulations and the demand for proof of efficacy and safety in clinical trials, see Harry M. Marks, *The Progress of Experiment: Science and Therapeutic Reform in the United States, 1900–1990* (Cambridge: Cambridge University Press, 1997).

46 Although discovered in 1949, lithium was not widely adopted until its effectiveness was confirmed in the early 1970s – in part because it was not a proprietary compound and so there was little marketing incentive for conducting the requisite clinical trials, but also because of lack of interest in biological treatment of manic depression among psychodynamic psychiatrists, then predominant in U.S. psychiatry.

47 American Psychiatric Association, *Diagnostic and Statistical Manual of Mental Disorders: DSM-IV* (Washington, DC: American Psychiatric Association, 1994).

48 A key difference is in whether both bipolar type I and type II are included. In the Romero study, both types were included. See R. C. Kessler et al., "The epidemiology of DSM-III-R bipolar I disorder in a general population survey." *Psychological Medicine* 27/5 (1997); J. Angst, "The emerging epidemiology of hypomania and bipolar II disorder," *Journal of Affective Disorders* 50/2–3 (1998): 143–151.

49 For example, psychiatrist Timothy Crow wrote, "The psychoses constitute a genetic continuum rather than two unrelated diatheses." T. J. Crow, "The Continuum of Psychosis and its Implication for the Structure of the Gene," *British Journal of Psychiatry* 149 (1986): 419–429.

50   Hagop S. Akiskal, "The Prevalent Clinical Spectrum of Bipolar Disorders: Beyond DSM-IV. *Journal of Clinical Psychopharmacology* 16/2 (1996), Suppl. 1, 4S–14S.

51   Dean F. MacKinnon, Kay Redfield Jamison, and J. Raymond DePaulo, "Genetics of Manic Depressive Illness," *Annual Reviews in Neurosciences* 20 (1997): 356.

52   Marion Leboyer et al., "Psychiatric genetics: Search for phenotypes," *Trends in neurosciences* 21/3 (1998): 102–105; Neil Risch and David Botstein, "A manic depressive history," *Nature Genetics* 12 (1996).

53   Risch and Botstein, "A manic depressive history," 351.

54   Jane Bradbury, "Teasing out the genetics of bipolar disorder," *The Lancet* 357 (May 19, 2001): 1596.

55   Michael A. Escamilla et al., "Assessing the Feasibility of Linkage Disequilibrium Methods for Mapping Complex Traits: An Initial Screen for Bipolar Disorder Loci on Chromosome 18," *American Journal of Human Genetics* 64 (1999): 1670–1678. In another paper, the same group placed blame on the uncertainty of the relation between phenotype and genotype, on the seemingly multiple ways the "underlying disease" expressed itself: "Genetic studies of psychiatric disorders in humans have been inconclusive owing to the difficulty in defining phenotypes and underlying disease heterogeneity." L. Alison McInnes, et al., "Mapping genes for psychiatric disorders and behavioral traits," *Current Opinion in Genetics and Development* 8 (1999): 287–292.

56   "We believe the explanation lies elsewhere [than genetic heterogeneity], namely that the genetic mechanism underlying the disease in these families is more complicated than postulated, leading to a reduction in [statistical] power." Risch and Botstein, "A Manic-Depressive History."

57   Leboyer et al., "Psychiatric genetics."

58   Dieter B. Wildenauer et al., "Do schizophrenia and affective disorder share susceptibility genes?" *Schizophrenia Research* 39 (1999): 107–111.

59   Ibid.

60   Ibid.

61   Andrew Lakoff, "Adaptive Will: The Evolution of Attention Deficit Disorder," *Journal of the History of the Behavioral Sciences* 36/2 (Spring 2000); Tanya Luhrmann, *Of Two Minds: The Growing Disorder in American Psychiatry* (New York: Knopf, 2000).

62   J. Gelernter, "Editorial: Genetics of Bipolar Affective Disorder: Time for Another Reinvention?" *American Journal of Human Genetics* 56 (1995): 1762, 1766.

63   Lawrence Cohen describes a similar problem in India: An apparent lack of Alzheimer's patients. In response to his queries, the argument initially made to him was that there was "no aging in India," that Alzheimer's was a disorder of modernity, of the bad family. Lawrence Cohen, *No Aging in India: Alzheimer's, The Bad Family, and Other Modern Things* (Berkeley: University of California Press, 1998).

64   Andrew Lakoff, *Pharmaceutical Reason: Technology and the Human at the Modern Periphery* (Cambridge: Cambridge University Press, 2005).

65   For the historical context of psychoanalysis in Argentina, see Mariano Plotkin, *Freud in the Pampas: The Emergence and Development of a Psychoanalytic Culture in Argentina* (Stanford: Stanford University Press, 2000); and Hugo Vezzetti, *Aventuras de Freud en el País de los Argentinos: De Jose Ingenieros a Enrique Pichon-Riviere* (Buenos Aires: Paidos, 1996).

66   I describe these dynamics in more detail in Andrew Lakoff, "The Lacan Ward: Pharmacology and Subjectivity in Buenos Aires," *Social Analysis* 47/2 (2003).

67   Ian Hacking suggests that psychiatric identity is an example of the type of classification he calls "interactive kinds." As opposed to "indifferent kinds" like trees, these are

classifications that interact with the thing being classified. Ian Hacking, *The Social Construction of What?* (Cambridge: Harvard University Press, 1999).

68   Paul Rabinow provides some guideposts for thinking about the way in which genetic identity might interact with new forms of political rationality. He identifies groups whose affiliation is based on a common disorder or genetic risk, and who influence health policy and scientific research, as emerging signs of such biosociality. "Such groups," he writes, "will have medical specialists, laboratories, narratives, and a heavy panoply of pastoral keepers to help them experience, share, intervene, and 'understand' their fate." Rabinow, *Essays on the Anthropology of Reason* (Princeton: Princeton University Press, 1996), 102.

69   Alder, "Making things the same," 501.

Part IV

Traveling Media

This part deals with the meanderings of the mass media, highlighting the increasingly important role they play in the quotidian realities of people all over the world. Like the last section on commodity flows, this one is also concerned with showing that people in the periphery are not passive in their encounters with foreign cultural products. For example, the chapter by Boellstorff focuses on how Indonesian men and women came to think of themselves as *lesbi* or *gay* through encounters with mainstream print and electronic mass media. This does not mean though that *gay* and *lesbi* subjectivities "originate" in the "West." Rather, they are distinctively Indonesian phenomena, formed through discourses of nation and sexual desire as well as a sense of linkage to distant but familiar Others. This section also aims to show that when it comes to global cultural influence, the West is not the only player in town. There are also quite a number of Third World countries – India, Mexico, and Taiwan, to name only a few – that exert a powerful cultural influence around the world, particularly on other countries of the periphery. Thus, Larkin's essay highlights how Indian films provide Nigerian men and women with meaningful cultural alternatives to the mass media productions of the West – alternatives that permit them to fashion modern forms of existing in the world without being weighed down by the ideological baggage of Western cultural imperialism. Finally, this part highlights the growing significance of digital technologies in a globalizing world. For example, Juris's essay focuses on how anti-corporate globalization activists have employed such technologies – Web pages, open editing software, e-mail lists, and so forth – to create networks, organize mass actions, engage in media activism, and practice an emerging political ideal of open communication and globally networked democracy.

SUGGESTIONS FOR FURTHER READING

Abu-Lughod, Lila
  1997   The Interpretation of Culture(s) after Television. *Representations* 59: 109–33.
Allison, Anne
  2000   A Challenge to Hollywood? Japanese Character Goods Hit the US. *Japanese Studies*
         20(1): 67–88.
Ginsburg, Faye
  1997   "From Little Things, Big Things Grow": Indigenous Media and Cultural Activism.
         In *Between Resistance and Revolution: Cultural Politics and Social Protest.* Richard
         G. Fox and Orin Starn, eds. Pp. 118–44. Berkeley: University of California Press.
Larkin, Brian
  2004   Degraded Images, Distorted Sounds: Nigerian Video and the Infrastructure of
         Piracy. *Public Culture* 16(2): 289–314.
Mankekar, Purnima
  2004   Dangerous Desires: Television and Erotics in Late Twentieth-Century India. *The
         Journal of Asian Studies* 63(2): 403–31.
Meyer, Birgit
  2003   Visions of Blood, Sex and Money: Fantasy Spaces in Popular Ghanaian Cinema.
         Visual Anthropology 16(1): 15–41.
Miller, Daniel
  1992   The Young and the Restless in Trinidad: A Case of the Local and the Global in Mass
         Consumption. In *Consuming Technologies.* Roger Silverstone and Eric Hirsch, eds.
         Pp. 163–82. London: Routledge.
Niezen, Ronald
  2005   Digital Identity: The Construction of Virtual Selfhood in the Indigenous Peoples'
         Movement. *Comparative Studies in Society and History* 47(3): 532–51.
Schein, Louisa
  2004   Homeland Beauty: Transnational Longing and Hmong American Video. *The Jour-
         nal of Asian Studies* 63(2): 433–63.
Whitaker, Mark P.
  2004   Tamilnet.com: Some Reflections on Popular Anthropology, Nationalism, and the
         Internet. *Anthropological Quarterly* 77(3): 469–98.
Wilk, Richard R.
  1993   "It's Destroying a Whole Generation": Television and Moral Discourse in Belize.
         Visual Anthropology 5(3–4): 220–44.
Yang, Mayfair Mei-hui
  2004   Goddess across the Taiwan Strait: Matrifocal Ritual Space, Nation-State, and
         Satellite Television Footprints. *Public Culture* 16(2): 209–38.

13

Dubbing Culture: Indonesian *Gay* and *Lesbi* Subjectivities and Ethnography in an Already Globalized World

Tom Boellstorff

As the 20th century begins to recede into historical memory, "globalization" presents itself as a completed project: We appear to live in a world that is already globalized (Appadurai 1996; Gibson-Graham 1996; Hannerz 1989; Miller 1995). Even with this state of affairs, however, globalization is more than background noise. Although a certain academic fatigue has set in concerning globalization, these processes are shifting and intensifying and so demand our continuing attention. Ethnography has an important role to play in such a refocused analysis, for it can show how even the most apparently "remote" communities are caught up in globalizing processes in ways that impact subjectivities as well as social circumstances (e.g., Tsing 1993).

Such are the foundational concerns of this article. In it, I bring an analysis of how Indonesians come to think of themselves as *lesbi* or *gay* through encounters with mass media together with a late 1990s controversy over the dubbing of foreign television shows and films into the Indonesian language, in order to develop a framework for rethinking ethnography in an already globalized world. (To keep *gay* and *lesbi* distinct from the English terms *lesbian* and *gay*, I italicize them.[1]) I call this framework "*dubbing culture*," where *to dub* means, as the Oxford English

From *American Ethnologist* 30(2): 225–242. Copyright © 2003, American Anthropological Association.

Dictionary phrases it, "to provide an alternative sound track to (a film or television broadcast), especially a translation from a foreign language" (*Oxford English Dictionary*, second edition, volume 4).

With regard to *lesbi* and *gay* Indonesians, my goal is to develop a theory that can account for a contingent, fractured, intermittent, yet powerfully influential relationship between globalization and subjectivities. Two additional requirements for such a theory are as follows. First, it must not mistake contingency for the absence of power; it must account for relations of domination. Second, such a theory must not render domination as determination; it must account for how *gay* and *lesbi* Indonesians transform this contingent relationship in unexpected ways.

More broadly, the framework of "dubbing culture" provides one way to conceptualize the relationship between persons and the cultural logics through which they come to occupy subject positions under contemporary globalizing processes. In particular, it does so without relying on biogenetic (and, arguably, heteronormative) metaphors like hybridity, creolization, and diaspora, which imply prior unities and originary points of dispersion. *Gay* and *lesbi* subjectivities do not originate in the "West" (they are not perceived as diasporic), nor are they a hybrid of "West" and "East"; they are distinctively Indonesian phenomena, formed through discourses of nation and sexual desire as well as a sense of linkage to distant but familiar Others.

Gibson-Graham (1996), in a feminist critique of globalization narratives, notes their similarity to rape narratives: Both present a masculinized entity (the rapist, global capitalism) as always already in a position of dominance and a feminized entity (the rape victim, the local) in a position of weakness. This is more than a metaphorical parallel: As narratives about relationality and transfer, stories of sexuality are stories of globalization and vice versa. Gibson-Graham hopes that "a queer perspective can help to unsettle the consonances and coherences of the narrative of global commodification" (1996: 144). In this spirit, I explore how "dubbing culture" might provide a way to understand globalization as susceptible to transformation. In queering globalization in this manner, I do not lose sight of the immense suffering and injustice it causes. Instead, I highlight that this suffering and injustice is caused not by a singular "globalization," but by a complex network of interlocking economic, political, and social forces that are not always in agreement or absolute dominance. In terms of the dubbing metaphor, we might say that the voice of globalization is powerful but that that voice does not "move" across the globe. Rather, it is dialogically reconstituted; it is in a constant state of "dubbing."

The framework of "dubbing culture" is crucially concerned with agency: It questions both deterministic theories that assume the hailing of persons through ideology and voluntaristic theories that assume persons voice and "negotiate" their subjectivities vis-à-vis structures of power. As a result, it aims to provide a more processual and conjunctural understanding of subjectivity: It gives us a new way to think through the metaphorical construal of hegemonic cultural logics as discourses. To "dub" a discourse is neither to parrot it verbatim nor to compose an entirely new script. It is to hold together cultural logics without resolving them into a unitary whole.

In this article, I first develop the concept of dubbing culture through a close ethnographic analysis of *gay* and *lesbi* Indonesians. Indonesia, the fourth most populous nation on earth and home to more Muslims than any other country, is a useful site from which to investigate emergent modalities of globalization. As a result, this article addresses itself to scholars with interests in contemporary Southeast Asia. Second, this article speaks to literature on the internationalization of gay and lesbian subjectivities, suggesting that this literature sometimes overemphasizes politics and activism, assuming that such globalization primarily takes place through channels like sex tourism, the consumption of "Western" lesbian and gay media, and the travel of non-"Westerners" to the "West." Third, I see this analysis as a contribution to mass-media theory. In much the same way that print capitalism presents a general precondition for national imagined communities, but in a manner open to reinterpretation (Anderson 1983), so contemporary mass media present a general precondition for dubbing culture, but not in a deterministic sense. I thus examine ways in which mass-mediated messages that might appear totalizing (because of their association with powerful political–economic actors) are, in fact, susceptible to contingent transformation. Just as the dubbed television show in which "Sharon Stone speaks Indonesian" does not originate in the United States, so the *gay* and *lesbi* subject positions I examine are Indonesian, not, strictly speaking, imported.[2] Yet just as the range of possibilities for a dubbed soundtrack is shaped by images originating elsewhere, so the persons who occupy subject positions that are dubbed in some fashion cannot choose their subjectivities just as they please. I move, then, from a literal, technical meaning of "dubbing" to a more speculative, analogical usage as a way to explore the relationship between social actors and the modes of subjectivation (Foucault 1985) by which such persons come to occupy subject positions.

Beyond these three audiences, however, the ultimate goal of this article is to speak at a broad level to the state of culture theory. Might it be that dubbing culture occurs in the context of globalizing processes not directly related to mass media, sexuality, or Southeast Asia? Indeed, at the end of this article I ask if the "dubbing of culture" Indonesians perform when they constitutively occupy the *gay* or *lesbi* subject position is all that different from the ethnographic project in an already globalized world. This article, then, has a reflexive (indeed, postreflexive) dimension. It asks if the ways in which much contemporary ethnography holds together, in tension, multiple cultural logics (like "the local" and "modernity") – in such a way that they are coconstitutive, not just juxtaposed – might not be productively interpreted in terms of dubbing culture.

Coming to *Lesbi* or *Gay* Subjectivity

It is late morning in the city of Makassar (the regional capital of South Sulawesi province on the island of Sulawesi), and I am recording an interview with Hasan, a 32-year-old *gay* man I have known for many years. We are speaking about Hasan's youth, and he recalls his first sexual relationship as a young teenager, which took place with an older friend at school. At that point Hasan had never heard the word *gay*.

Hasan: I didn't yet know. I was confused. Why, why were there people like that? What I mean is why were there men who wanted to kiss men? This got me thinking when I was at home. I thought: Why did my friend do that to me? What was going on? Was it just a sign, a sign of, what do you call it, just of friendship, I thought like that. I was still blind as to the existence of the *gay* world.

Tom Boellstorff: And to learn the term *gay* or about the *gay* world, how did that happen?

H: I knew later, when I was watching television. I saw on the "world news," there it showed a gay demonstration. And according to the information there ... the people who were demonstrating, um, wanted the government to accept the marriage of men with men. And that made me confused. Why was it like that? That's when I was in high school [about two years after his first sexual experience with a man].

TB: And when you saw that, about that gay demonstration, what was your reaction, your feelings?

H: I felt that an event like that could only happen outside; [that] in Indonesia there wasn't anything like that. I thought that maybe because we had a different state [*negara*], a culture [*kebudayaan*] that wasn't the same as [their] culture, so, maybe outside maybe it could be, and in Indonesia maybe it couldn't be, but, at that time I didn't think that there were people like that in Indonesia.

Hasan here recounts a moment of recognition, one that later leads him to look for other *gay* men and eventually call himself *gay*. Through an encounter with mass media, he comes to knowledge of what he takes to be the concept "*gay*" and retrospectively interprets his same-sex relationships before acquiring this knowledge in terms of "blindness." Readers familiar with debates in queer studies over the internationalization of lesbian and gay subjectivities (e.g., Adam et al. 1999; Altman 2001) might seize on the fact that Hasan saw a gay demonstration as evidence of activism driving this "globalization," but, in fact, this is the most unusual aspect of Hasan's narrative. Three other elements prove more typical in the Indonesian context: Sexuality is tied to mass-mediated language; an outside way of being becomes intimate; and the border dividing *gay* culture from other cultures is national, not ethnic or local.

Since 1992, I have spent about two years conducting ethnographic research on Indonesian nonnormative sexualities and genders, primarily in Surabaya (East Java), Bali, and Makassar (South Sulawesi). This research focuses on men and women who term themselves *gay* or *lesbi*, on *warias* (better known by the derogatory term *banci*) – what I roughly term male transvestites – and on persons calling themselves *tomboi* or *hunter*, who see themselves in some cases as masculine *lesbi* women and in other cases as men trapped in women's bodies.[3]

Throughout my fieldwork, I have taken great pains to investigate how it is that Indonesians come to *lesbi* or *gay* subjectivity. The reason for this is that unlike so-called traditional homosexual and transgendered subject positions or the waria subject position, *gay* and *lesbi* are not concepts with significant historical depth; they appear to have first arisen in Indonesia in the 1970s.[4] They are experienced as new, not something one learns from one's community, kin group, or religion.

Sometimes, as in Hasan's case, same-sex activity has taken place before thinking of oneself as *gay* or *lesbi*; in other instances such activity only begins after thinking of oneself as *gay* or *lesbi*.

Once *gay* men and *lesbi* women have come to *gay* or *lesbi* subjectivity and begin having homosexual relationships founded in that subjectivity, they usually begin to participate in what they call the "*lesbi* world" or "*gay* world" (*dunia lesbi, dunia gay*). These worlds are perceived to be nationwide, flourish primarily but not solely in urban areas, and are linked through travel, correspondence, and the informal publishing of small magazines. Later I describe some contours of these worlds, as well as the worlds of warias and "traditional" homosexualities and transgenderisms. For the purposes of this article, however, I focus on an early stage in the *lesbi* or *gay* life course, the process by which persons come to term themselves *gay* or *lesbi* in the first place.

This process appears, on first consideration, an ethnographic mystery. Most Indonesians, unless they are quite upper class or have traveled to the "West," are unaware of the terms *lesbi* and *gay* or think the terms (and *homo*) are English names for warias. Even *gay* men and *lesbi* women who went to elementary school in the late 1980s or early 1990s recall the use on the schoolyard of terms primarily for warias, such as *banci*, but rarely *gay* or *lesbi*. No local culture, ethnic tradition (*adat*), or religion sanctions *gay* or *lesbi* or even names them with any systematicity. How, then, do these subject positions take hold in the hearts of so many contemporary Indonesians?

A few Indonesians say that they first learned of the possibility of becoming *gay* or *lesbi* from friends (usually not *gay* or *lesbi* themselves). A few *gay* men say that they first knew that they could be *gay* after wandering into a public area frequented by *gay* men, and a few *gay* men and *lesbi* women say that they became aware of the subject positions after being seduced. It appears, however, that only a small fraction of Indonesians learn of the *gay* or *lesbi* subject positions through all of these routes to erotic knowledge combined.

Another possible avenue is through small magazines that *gay* men and *lesbi* women have been informally publishing since the early 1980s. These magazines might play a conduit role, importing and transmitting "Western" concepts of sexuality. No informants, however, have ever cited these magazines as the means by which they came to think of themselves as *lesbi* or *gay*. The primary reason for this is that Indonesians seem to access these magazines only after first occupying the *lesbi* or *gay* subject position (Boellstorff 2004).[5] It is also clear that *gay* and *lesbi* subject positions existed for several years prior to the appearance of the first *gay* publication in 1982. Despite impacting the subjectivities of those who read them, these magazines do not play a formative role. Although this may not remain the case in the future, particularly as greater press freedoms and increasing Internet access make the magazines more accessible, neither these magazines nor the other modes mentioned above explain how Indonesians have come to occupy the subject positions *lesbi* and *gay* to the present day.

For *gay* men and *lesbi* women, the element of Hasan's narrative with the greatest resonance is his description of a kind of "Aha!" moment when, during an encounter with *mainstream* print or electronic mass media, they come to think of themselves as *lesbi* or *gay*. Nearly 90 percent of my *gay* and *lesbi* informants cite mainstream mass media as the means by which they first knew they could understand themselves through the concepts "*lesbi*" or "*gay*." This is true whether the individuals in question are from Java, Bali, Sulawesi, or other islands; whether they are Muslim, Christian, Hindu, or Buddhist; whether they are wealthy, middle class, or impoverished; whether they live in cities or rural areas; and whether they were born in the 1950s, 1960s, 1970s, or 1980s. Rarely is a cultural variable distributed so widely across such a diverse population. (In cases where peers tell *lesbi* or *gay* Indonesians of these terms, those peers apparently learn of the terms through mainstream mass media.)

The critical role of mainstream mass media in the lives of *lesbi* and *gay* Indonesians is all the more notable when we compare the life narratives of *lesbi* women and *gay* men with those of warias. I have *never* heard warias cite mass media as the means by which they first saw themselves as waria; as I discuss later, they learn of the waria subject position from their social environs – schoolkids on the playground, a cousin, or neighbor – but not from mass media. Hasan's narrative rehearses a common story of discovery that most *gay* and *lesbi* Indonesians see as pivotal in their lives, a moment they recall without hesitation, as in the case of the following Javanese Christian man in Surabaya:

> In elementary school the only word was *banci [waria]*. For instance, a boy who walked or acted like a girl would get teased with the word *banci*. So I didn't know about the word *gay* until junior high. I heard it from books, magazines, television. And I wanted to know! I looked for information; if I saw that a magazine had an article about homos I'd be sure to read it. I knew then that a homo was a man who liked men. But I didn't know that homo meant *gay* at that time. So I tried to find out from books and things like that. I learned all of that stuff from the mass media. . . . So having someone come and tell me "It's like this," that never happened. I learned it all through magazines and newspapers. . . . And when I read those things, I knew that I was *gay*.

For this man "homo" is an impersonalized descriptive category, whereas "*gay*" is a framework for understanding the self's past motivations, immediate desires, and visions of an unfolding future. Abdul, a Muslim man who grew up in a small town in Sulawesi, tells his story in the following interview excerpt:

> TB: When you were in your teenage years, did you already know the term *gay*?
>
> Abdul: In my environment at that time, most people didn't yet know. But because I read a lot, read a lot of news, I already knew. I already knew that I was *gay*. Through reading I knew about the *gay* world . . .
>
> TB: What kinds of magazines?
>
> A: Gossip magazines, you know, they always talk about such-and-such a star and the rumors that the person is *gay*. So that broadened my concepts *[wawasan]*, made me realize, "Oh, there are others like me."

Because *lesbi* and *gay* representations mingle in these mass media, most *lesbi* women, like the following Balinese woman, also trace their subjectivities to encounters with mass media: "I didn't use the word *lesbi* because I didn't even know the term [when I was young]. I didn't hear about the word *lesbi* until about 1990, when I read it in a magazine. And right away, when I read about *lesbi* and what that meant, I thought to myself, 'That's me!'"

Consider the following narrative from Susie, a Muslim who terms herself a masculine *lesbi* woman *(hunter yang lesbi)*. Susie has been talking about sexual relations with other women in her early teenage years, and I ask her if she knew the terms *hunter* and *lesbi* at that point:

Susie: I didn't know *hunter* yet, but I already knew *lesbian, lesbi,* I knew. I'd already – I'd already read it, don't you know?

TB: Read it where?

S: In magazines, through hanging out with friends who mentioned it, through means like that.

Susie then talked about short articles in newspapers that would occasionally mention how women could have sex with women, concluding, "Through that I could know that I was *lesbi*" *(lewat itu saya bisa tahu bahwa saya itu lesbi)*. Indeed, the intertwining of *lesbi* and *gay* in mass media is so common that in at least one case a man who now calls himself *gay* termed himself *lesbi* for several years as a result of reading women's magazines, switching to *gay* only after reading a magazine "about historic English royalty...Richard someone."

The role of mass media is striking because to this day there is little coverage of openly *gay* Indonesian men or *lesbi* Indonesian women: What Indonesians usually encounter through mass media is gossip about Indonesian celebrities, but particularly gossip about "Western" celebrities and gay and lesbian "Westerners," real and portrayed.[6] And what they see is not a one-hour special on "Homosexuality in the West"; rarely is it even the kind of demonstration described by Hasan. *Gay* and *lesbi* Indonesians typically speak of brief, intermittent coverage: a single 15-second item on Rock Hudson's AIDS diagnosis one night in the 1980s, an editorial about Al Pacino's role in the movie *Cruising*, a gossip column about Elton John or Melissa Etheridge, or a short review of *The Wedding Banquet* or *My Best Friend's Wedding* (two films that had homosexual characters).[7] Although some *lesbi* women and *gay* men actually see such films, either because the films make it onto Indonesian screens or, increasingly, are available on video or DVD, these Indonesians also stress the role of print media, particularly newspapers and women's magazines like *Kartini* and *Femina*. References to Indonesians engaging in homosexual acts or terming themselves *lesbi* or *gay* in some fashion occasionally appear in these media, but in most cases the references to homosexuality are negative – psychologists presenting homosexuality as a pathology, or disapproving gossip columns. Sporadic coverage of same-sex scandals and arrests dates back to the early 20th century. The earliest extensive study of contemporary Indonesian homosexuality to my knowledge, sociologist Amen Budiman's 1979 book *Lelaki Perindu Lelaki* (Men Who Yearn for Men), notes that

in this decade [the 1970s] homosexuality has increasingly become an interesting issue for many segments of Indonesian society. Newspapers, both those published in the capital and in other areas, often present articles and news about homosexuality. In fact, *Berita*

Buana Minggu in Jakarta has a special column, "Consultation with a Psychiatrist," which often answers the complaints of those who are homosexual and want to change their sexual orientation. It's the same way with pop magazines, which with increasing diligence produce articles about homosexuality, sometimes even filled with personal stories from homosexual people, complete with their photographs. [1979: 89–90]

Budiman later adds, "It is very interesting to note that homosexuals who originate in the lower classes often try to change their behavior by seeking advice from psychiatric or health columnists in our newspapers and magazines" (1979:116). In the 1970s, however, and among my present-day informants (a few of whom became *gay* or *lesbi* in the 1970s or earlier), many *lesbi* and *gay* Indonesians are not changing behavior but coming to occupy what they see as legitimate and even healthy sexualities through these same mass media. From their beginnings to the present, these media have "exposed" not a fully articulated discourse of homosexuality, but a series of incomplete and contradictory references, in translation, sometimes openly denigrating and hostile. It is not a transmission of self-understanding so much as a fractured set of cultural logics reconfigured within Indonesia. Yet from "translations" of this intermittent reportage come subjectivities by which myriad Indonesians live out their lives.

Gay and *lesbi* subject positions thus lead us to a specific sociological problem. Indonesians learn of the possibility of thinking of oneself as *gay* or *lesbi* through the intermittent reception of messages from mass media. These messages do not intend to convey the possibility of a kind of selfhood. They are often denigrating and dismissive, but above all they are *fragmentary*. In the 1980s an Indonesian might encounter such reportage a few times a year at most, if an avid reader; in the 1990s it became more frequent but still was quite minimal given the universe of topics appearing in the mass media. The question, then, is how modes of subjectivation become established when the social field in which they arise establishes them neither as discourses nor reverse discourses. Indonesian mass media certainly do not intend to set forth the possibility of *gay* and *lesbi* subject positions, nor do the imported programs they frequently rebroadcast; in fact, they rarely take a *negative* stance on *gay* and *lesbi* subject positions. Yet it is these mass media that, in a very real sense, make *gay* and *lesbi* subjectivities possible, just as the national imagined communities that are so socially efficacious worldwide could not have existed before Gutenberg struck type to page.

Subjectivities and Subject Positions

Readers may have noticed three somewhat atypical dimensions to my analysis thus far. First, the term *identity* has not appeared in this article, and I speak instead of subjectivities and subject positions. Second, I treat Indonesia as a single ethnographic unit rather than segregating data from Java, Sulawesi, Bali, and elsewhere. Third, I do not segregate data by gender but bring together *gay* men and *lesbi* women as well as transgendered subjectivities like waria/banci. All of these methodological and theoretical moves relate to the concept of "dubbing culture." Addressing each in turn will foreclose some possible misunderstandings of this analysis and provide an opportunity to situate the narratives of Hasan, Susie, and the other informants in a wider ethnographic context.

In this article 1 eschew the identity–behavior binarism in favor of a language of *subject positions* (extant social categories of selfhood) and *subjectivities* (the various senses of self – erotics, assumptions about one's life course, etc. – that obtain when occupying a subject position, whether partially or completely, temporarily or permanently). As many scholars of sexuality have noted (e.g., Elliston 1995), "identity" versus "behavior" is a false dichotomy: Identity is not only simply a cognitive map but also a set of embodied practices, and behavior is always culturally mediated through self-narrative. As a result, focusing on subject positions and sub-jectivities turns attention to the total social fact of *gay* and *lesbi* selfhood. This is a basically Foucauldian framework that draws from the epistemological break between volumes 1 and 2 of *The History of Sexuality* (1978, 1985), wherein Foucault shifted from an emphasis on "the formation of sciences" of sexuality and the "systems of power" inciting sexuality to "the practices by which individuals were led to focus their attention on themselves, to decipher, recognize, and acknowledge themselves as subjects of desire, bringing into play between themselves a certain relationship that allows them to discover, in desire, the truth of their being" (1985: 4–5). This approach is attuned to the role of discourse in making subject positions intelligible historical and cultural possibilities, "an analysis of the 'games of truth,' the games of truth and error through which being is historically constituted as experience" (Foucault 1985: 6–7), a framework that situates agency in specific discursive contexts.

I think of "subject position" as a rough translation of *jiwa*, which means "soul" in Indonesian but often has a collective meaning; *lesbi* women will sometimes say "*lesbi* have the same jiwa;" warias will say they "have the same jiwa"; or *lesbi* women and *gay* men will sometimes say they share a jiwa. I think of "subjectivity" as a rough translation of *pribadi* or *jatidiri*, both of which mean approximately "self-conception"; a *gay* man once distinguished pribadi from jiwa by saying that "every person possesses their own pribadi." *Identitas* has a much more experience-distant, bureaucratic ring for most Indonesians: One *gay* man defined *identitas* as "biodata: name, address, and so on" *(biodata: nama, alamat, dan sebagainya).*[8]

The Indonesian Subject

This framework provides a useful place from which to consider the implications of treating Indonesia as an ethnographic unit for the case of the *lesbi* and *gay* subject positions. Subject positions are not always lexicalized, but like any aspect of culture they always have a history. They come into being at a certain period of time, which shapes them, and they also change through time as long as they persist. Subject positions also always contain within them "spatial scales" (or "spatial fixes"; see Brenner 1998; Harvey 2000). To be a "Yale student" has a different cultural logic of scale than to be a "New Yorker" or "Japanese." Additionally, the various subject positions through which we live at any point in time may not have isomorphic spatial scales: For instance, one's sense of self as a youth could be global, as a man local, and as a laborer national, all at the same time. Or, to be a youth could be both local and global at the same time, intersecting. As a result, three crucial issues in the ethnographic investigation of subject positions are (1) their historicity (that is, the way they are shaped by their embedded notions of their own history and what counts as history); (2) their spatial scales; and (3) how they intersect with other subject positions and the histories and spatial scales of those other subject positions.

In this regard, it may surprise readers unfamiliar with Indonesianist anthropology that the national imagined community has rarely represented a subject for ethnographic inquiry. Instead, anthropological research in the archipelago has been guided by what I term "ethnolocality" (see Boellstorff 2002). This mode of representation originated in the colonial encounter as a means of impeding the possibility of translocal spatial scales other than colonialism (in particular, nationalism and Islamic movements). As reified in the work of the Leiden school, "custom" (adat) was understood to belong not to the Indies as a whole but to groups framed in terms of the equation of ethnonym with toponym, an equation whose persistence has been noted by many scholars (e.g., Keane 1999:180). In this understanding (which can be emic as well as etic), culture is assumed to be the property of "the Balinese," "the Makassarese," "the Javanese," and so on. Under this formulation Indonesia is a field of anthropological study, but not the "field" in which one does "fieldwork" (Josselin de Jong 1977). Although a large body of anthropological scholarship has productively denaturalized ethnolocality, at the level of epistemology it remains influential. Indonesianist scholarship now typically acknowledges that in the decades since Indonesian independence a national culture has taken root – aided by the state-supported spread of the Indonesian language and commodity capitalism – but that national culture is often treated as a force impacting local culture rather than the possible location of a subject position in its own right. This issue is of particular importance in the post-Soeharto era, when movements for regional autonomy and adat "revitalization" threaten to renaturalize ethnolocalized conceptions of self and society.

But if ethnolocality can be problematized, if a subject of Java can be regarded as a subject of "Java" (Pemberton 1994), then can we dissolve the implicit scare quotes that prevent us treating a subject of "Indonesia" as a *subject of Indonesia*? Can there be such as thing as Indonesian adat? Can there be an ethnography of Indonesians? Are "the village" (Breman 1982), ethnolocality, and world religions like Islam and Christianity the only spatial scales shaping subject positions in contemporary Indonesia? Or could there be subject positions with spatial scales that are foundationally national, even if persons inhabiting such subject positions might consider themselves in terms of ethnolocality with respect to other aspects of their lives? Could one think of oneself, for instance, as "Madurese" with relation to conceptions of exchange, but "Indonesian" with relation to sexuality?

This ethnographic emphasis on locality is shaped by anthropology's emphasis on difference. In this tradition, difference is expected: unproblematic, obvious, and authentic. It asks nothing more than to be recorded, typologized, interpreted, and rhetorically deployed. Sameness, however, awakens disturbing contradictions. On the one hand, sameness is uninteresting: If you study the Other and they are the same, what is there to say? Are they a proper Other at all? At the same time, there is discomfort: Sameness cries out for explanation and modeling. It must have a reason: Is it diffusion or convergent evolution? There is a sense that contamination has occurred and authenticity has been compromised. In an already globalized world, however, anthropologies of similitude and translocality can illuminate new transformations of ostensibly "Western" discourses.

It goes without saying that there will be differences between different islands and ethnic groups, just as there is always difference between households or neighborhoods. At issue is the critical analytical moment when the ethnographer determines the boundaries of "the field" (Gupta and Ferguson 1997), deciding at what point the threshold from similitude to difference has been crossed. This is a culturally located act, and in the context of this act, this heuristic compromise, it seems methodologically sound to take into account our informants' senses of inhabiting subject positions with translocal spatial scales. James Siegel, in his classic *Solo in the New Order*, names this compromise when he says, "I want to stress how various Java is. Whatever claims I make about it should be understood to refer to [the city of] Solo alone, relieving me of the tiresome duty to qualify my statements in every instance" (1986:11). Although Siegel is certainly correct in pointing out the diversity of Java, the problem of spatial scale is not only one of overreaching but also of underreaching. It appears unlikely that Indonesians in Solo, even if ethnically Javanese – living in a city where one main cruising area for *gay* men is known as "Manhattan" – "refer to Solo alone" in their own cultural worlds. What Siegel points out here is the ethnographer's tiresome duty of looking not only for solid data but also for a methodological and theoretical construction of the field site pitched as closely as possible to the cultural geographies of those whose lives the ethnographer seeks to interpret. Questions of the ethnography of translocality link to *gay* and *lesbi* subject positions on an epistemological level: In both cases a crucial element of the research is theorizing the threshold between similarity and difference. This will prove to be the central problematic of "dubbing culture."

To date, most studies that consider the possibility of national subject positions in Indonesia focus on mass media or literature (e.g., Heider 1991). Although I foreground mass media in this article as well, mass media may simply represent the visible leading edge of a "superculture" that, as Hildred Geertz (1963: 35) noted some time ago, includes the impoverished as well as the middle class and extends beyond urban centers in many cases. Sexuality and gender have been central elements of this national culture since its inception, and much contemporary work on women in Indonesia examines the influence of the nation-state and, thus, at gendered subjectivities with a national spatial scale.[9] Looking at nonnormative genders and sexualities can contribute to this body of work and will provide important clues to the operations of "dubbing culture."

Gender and Sexual Relationality

National transvestites

The most enduring "Western" stereotype regarding homosexuality and transgenderism in Indonesia (and Southeast Asia more generally) is that these regions are "tolerant." Although it is true that there have been – and in some cases, still are – socially recognized roles for male-to-female transgenders as well as widespread acceptance of secretive homosexual behavior, transgenderism and homosexuality are hardly valorized in contemporary Indonesian society. Although homosexuality and transgenderism usually escape official comment, if directly asked, most religious and state authorities swiftly condemn transgenderism and homosexuality as sinful and incompatible with "Indonesian tradition."

Considerations of nonnormative sexuality and gender in Indonesia sometimes focus on what I term "ethnolocalized homosexual or transvestite professional" (ETP) subject positions, such as *bissu* transvestite priests in South Sulawesi or the homosexual relationships between male actors and their male understudies in East Java known as *warokgemblak* (Andaya 2000; M. Kennedy 1993; Wilson 1999). Although ETPs persist in some parts of contemporary Indonesia, I know of no cases where *gay* men and *lesbi* women see their subjectivities as an outgrowth of them (most appear to be unaware of their existence). This is not surprising, since ETPs are found only among some ethnic groups in Indonesia, are in most cases only for men and for only part of the life span, and are linked to adat ritual or performance. In fact, it is a misnomer to speak of ETPs as *sexualities*, as that term is understood in the "West," since they are above all professions, not categories of selfhood organized around sexual desire.[10]

Warias are far more familiar to Indonesians – *lesbi, gay,* or otherwise. Warias are better known to the Indonesian public by the rather derogatory terms *banci* or *béncong,* but themselves tend to prefer *waria,* an amalgam of *wanita* (female) and *pria* (male) coined in 1978. A succinct but inevitably incomplete definition of *waria* is "male transvestites." I use *transvestite* rather than *transgender* because most warias see themselves not as becoming female, but as men who (1) have the souls of women from birth, (2) dress as women much of the time, and (3) have sex with "normal" *(normal)* men. In contemporary Indonesia warias are truly "national": Warias can be from any ethnicity, religion, or part of the archipelago, including Papua and Aceh. Unlike the *gay* and *lesbi* subject positions, the national distribution of the waria subject position is really a colonial distribution; the subject position has significantly greater time depth than the *lesbi* and *gay* subject positions, dating to at least the mid–19th century and possibly earlier. Warias are much more visible than *gay* or *lesbi* Indonesians: Many dress as women 24 hours a day, but even those who do not are readily identifiable because of their feminine appearance (coded through tweezed eyebrows, long hair, and movements and speech deemed effeminate). In any Indonesian city and even in rural areas, you can encounter poorer warias on the street or in a park looking for sex work clients. Above all, you will find warias working at salons, and you would certainly hope to have a waria do the makeup and hairstyling for your daughter on her wedding day. It is this transformative power of warias to change the public appearances of others (in line with their ability to change their own public appearance) that is their *ilmu,* their great skill, in Indonesian society, and warias cite this as the reason they should be valued. Warias are part of the recognized social mosaic.

One consequence of this recognition is that, as noted earlier, warias do not come to that particular subjectivity through mass media as *lesbi* women and *gay* men typically do. This does not mean, however, that warias are absent from mass media and other public fora. You can see them in television comedy shows and Bayer Aspirin commercials or performing at amusement parks and Independence Day celebrations. In all of these contexts, warias are construed as artful, skilled in beauty, *and* as silly, worthy targets of disdain. In other words, although warias are acknowledged elements of contemporary Indonesian society, it would be a mistake to take seriously the orientalist claim that there is tolerance in anything but the barest sense of the term. The "Western" liberal assumption that to be public and visible implies acceptance (a notion that the concept of "coming out" reapplies to sexual subjectivity) does not hold here. Although the parents of warias usually release such children from the imperative to marry (particularly if the waria works in a salon and contributes economically to the household), some are thrown out of the family. Warias have been held underwater by angry fathers until they have almost drowned, have been tormented, stabbed, and killed by street youths, and have died of AIDS on an island far from home, rejected by their own families. At the same time, many warias enjoy steady incomes and relative social acceptance, and in some respects their condition is better than that of transgenders, lesbians, or gay men in much of the "West."

All in all, then, it seems difficult to hold up Indonesia as a transgendered nirvana. Nonetheless, warias see themselves as a significant element of Indonesian national culture. Like *lesbi* women and *gay* men, they typically assume that others sharing their subject position can be found across Indonesia, but an important difference is that they have only a weak sense that people like them exist in other parts of the world. Indeed, they often ask me, "Are there warias in America?"

Gay and lesbi Indonesians

I have never been asked such a question by a *lesbi* or *gay* Indonesian; just as the modern Indonesian nation-state is assumed to be one unique element in a global network of nation-states, so there is a strong sense that the *gay* and *lesbi* subject positions are Indonesian phenomena linked to the global existence of persons with homosexual subjectivities (even if this is, in my experience, rarely phrased in terms of a movement). For these Indonesians, the prerevelatory period of sexual subjectivity is usually experienced locally; the local is the social space of the not-yet *(belum)lesbi* or not-yet *gay*. What they describe when they encounter the concepts *lesbi* or *gay* through mass media is a moment of recognition, a moment that involves a shift in sexualized spatial scale; it is not only that same-sex desire can be constituted as a subjectivity, but also that its spatial scale is translocal. The deictic *"That's me!"* places the self in a dialogic relationship with a *distant but familiar other.*

On one level this spatial scale is national. One reason for this is that the mass media through which Indonesians come to *gay* or *lesbi* subjectivity employ the national language, Indonesian (not ethnolocalized languages like Javanese or Buginese) and emphasize themes of national unity and patriotism. A second reason is that, unlike ETPs, the concepts *lesbi* and *gay* are seen as self-evidently incompatible with ethnolocality: No one learns what *lesbi* or *gay* means through "Makassarese culture" or "Javanese culture." *Gay* and *lesbi* persons thereby think of themselves as *Indonesians* with regard to their sexualities – to the point that they sometimes use nationalist metaphors of the archipelago concept *(wawasan nusantara)* to conceptualize their community (Boellstorff 2005). On a second level (unlike waria) *lesbi* and *gay* Indonesians see their subjectivities as linked to a transnational imagined community: They regard themselves as one "island" in a global archipelago of gay and lesbian persons, a constellation including places like Australia and Europe as well as Malaysia and Thailand. They do not regard themselves as a "rerun" of the "West"; they view themselves as different, but this difference is not seen to create a chasm of incommensurability.

Based on my own fieldwork and that of other scholars, as well as the networks built by *lesbi* women and *gay* men, it seems clear that *gay* men and *lesbi* women can be found throughout Indonesia. Of course, this does not mean that they are found *everywhere* in Indonesia, but that they can be found both in major cities and in smaller towns and rural areas. Although some *lesbi* and *gay* Indonesians are wealthy and well educated, most are not, giving lie to the stereotype that gay men and lesbians outside the "West" are the product of wealth, decadence, or estrangement from tradition.[11] Indeed, if one common "Western" misconception about Indonesia (and Southeast Asia more generally) is that transgenders are always valued members of society, another misconception is that gay men and lesbian women are products of the executive, jet-setting classes. Here the cultural effects of globalization are thought to correlate with class in a linear fashion: The richer you are, the more you are affected by globalization, and thus the less authentic you are. The proletarian becomes the new indigene. As any Nike factory worker in Indonesia could tell you, however, class is poorly correlated with the degree to which someone is impacted by globalizing forces. And, indeed, most *gay* men and *lesbi* women in Indonesia are primarily lower class (90 percent of my *gay* informants make less than $60 a month), do not speak English, and have never traveled outside Indonesia. From the testimony of my informants, it appears that most have never met a "Westerner" before myself – gay, lesbian, or otherwise – particularly if they have never spent time in Bali or Jakarta. Like warias, many *gay* men work in salons, but because they are poorly visible to Indonesian society, they can also be found in other professions, from the highest levels of government to street sweepers. *Lesbi* women can also be found in a wide range of professions, but many are quite poor, particularly if they have a masculine appearance that renders them unfit for careers deemed women's work.

As noted earlier, most Indonesians still confuse the terms *gay* and *waria*, supposing that the former is an English rendition of the latter. *Gay* men and warias do not share this confusion, but they do see each other as sharing something: an attraction to men. Few *gay* men, however, speak of themselves as having a woman's soul. Not all are effeminate; though many *gay* men *déndong*, or "do drag" for entertainment purposes, in the rare cases where *gay* men begin to dress like women all of the time, they consider themselves to have become warias (and are so regarded by other *gay* men).[12]

Like *gay* men, *lesbi* women can be found throughout Indonesia. In fact, there appears to have been greater mass-media coverage of *lesbi* women than *gay* men when these subject positions first entered public awareness in the early 1980s, but this is probably an artifact of the greater scrutiny placed on women's sexuality in Indonesia more generally. As in the case of *gay* men, *lesbi* women can come from any class position – since they usually come to *lesbi* subjectivity through mainstream mass media, as *gay* men do, it is not necessary that they be members of feminist organizations, have a high level of education, or live in the capital of Jakarta.

There are many other similarities between *lesbi* women and *gay* men. Both usually describe their desires in terms of a "desire for the same" (*suka sama suka*). Another important similarity is that the *lesbi* and *gay* subject positions both have a national spatial scale. To this day *gay* slang (spoken by some *lesbi* women as well) is based only on Indonesian, the national language, not an ethnic language like Javanese or Balinese. I have never been able to discover consistent geographical variation for *lesbi* or *gay* subjectivities: no place where there exists an ethnic or island-specific network (though there is a national network), no place where expectations about heterosexual marriage differ from other parts of the country, no place where coming to *lesbi* or *gay* subjectivity takes place primarily through kinship networks, international tourism (even in Bali), or some modality other than mainstream mass media. Note that this is not a proscriptive argument. There is no reason that an ethnic-specific *lesbi* or *gay* subject position ("Sudanese *lesbi*" or "Batak *gay*," for instance) might not emerge in the future: The point is that from the 1980s until the present this has not been the case, nor have *lesbi* and *gay* Indonesians perceived this as a problem.[13] That the *lesbi* and *gay* subject positions have this national spatial scale (and are shaped by state discourse) does not mean these Indonesians have a greater investment in the nation-state than other Indonesians; it does not imply patriotism any more than the shaping of "Western" homosexual subject positions by sexological and psychoanalytic discourse (Foucault 1978) means that these "Westerners" are enthusiasts of psychoanalysis. Similarities between *lesbi* and *gay* Indonesians can be understood not only because of widely distributed conceptions of gender complementarity that de-emphasize gendered difference (Errington 1990), but also because *lesbi* and *gay* appear to have taken form in Indonesia more or less together, as gendered analogues, each implying the other and suggesting the (sometimes fulfilled) possibility of socializing between *lesbi* women and *gay* men.

A relational analysis, however, reveals differences between the *lesbi* and *gay* subject positions. Perhaps the most consequential of these is the relationship between what we could call masculine and feminine *lesbi* women. As noted above, *gay* men sometimes act in an effeminate manner. The distinction between masculine and effeminate *gay* men, however, is not an organizing sexual principle; some *gay* men will say they prefer "manly" men (*laki-laki yang kebapakan*), which can mean non-*gay* men, but this is seen to be a matter of personal taste and does not denote a category of person. In contrast, a distinction between masculine and feminine *lesbi* women is ubiquitous in Indonesia, and it is typically assumed that sexual relationships will be between masculine and feminine *lesbi*, not between two masculine or two feminine *lesbi*.

This state of affairs might seem to be an import from the "West," where a long tradition of butch–femme distinctions often plays an important role in lesbian communities (Halberstam 1998; Kennedy and Davis 1993), without a clear parallel in gay sexual norms. Indeed, some observers of *lesbi* Indonesians have characterized masculine and feminine *lesbi* women in terms of butch and femme (Wieringa 1999). Although not an intended interpretation, this could be seen to imply that the *lesbi* subject position, complete with an internal butch–femme distinction, is globalizing from the "West" except insofar as individual *lesbi* women "resist."[14] The key point, however, is that when *gay* took form in (not "globalized to") Indonesia, it did so in the context of the well-known waria subject position. The *gay* subject position thus came to structure "desire for the same" within the category of masculinity. Although *gay* men and warias are often friends, it is considered highly abnormal for them to have sex with each other, since *gay* men are understood to desire "the same" (i.e., other *gay* or normal men) and waria "real men" (*laki-laki normal/tulen/asli*).

Crucially, however, no female analogue to warias existed at the time that *lesbi* took shape in Indonesia: Masculine women and female-to-male transgenders certainly existed, but they were not publicly known as a category of person, as warias were. As a result, the subject position *lesbi* includes not only women attracted to women (of masculine or feminine gendering) but also persons born with women's bodies who feel themselves to have the soul of a man and strive to be considered social men. These persons, who usually call themselves "*tomboi*" (also *hunter* in Sulawesi and parts of Java, *cowok* [male] in parts of Sumatra, or *sentul* in parts of Java), tend to dress as men 24 hours a day and engage in stereotypically male activities (Blackwood 1998). Indeed, unless they speak, some are often mistaken for men on the street.

The consequences of this are manifold. First, like *lesbi* and *gay* (but unlike waria/banci), tomboi is understand to be a "foreign" concept that has been Indonesianized. *Tomboi* does not appear in a 1976 Indonesian dictionary (*lesbian* does, but *gay* is absent [Poerwadarminta 1976:592]); by 1991, however, it appears with the definition "an active girl, full of adventuring like a boy." That *tomboi* was Indonesianized by this point is indicated by the fact that the term could already occur with the circumflex *ke-an* to form the abstract noun *ketomboian*, "tomboi matters" (Salim and Salim 1991:1630). These common Indonesian uses of *tomboi*, however, do not mark a minoritized sexual subject position but indicate what is understood to be a temporary and benign characteristic of young girls.[15] The use of the term *tomboi* to label an adult sexual subject position builds from this understanding in a manner that has no parallel for the terms *waria, gay,* or *lesbi*. An important topic for future research will be to investigate how the tomboi subject position is "dubbed," both with relation to the "West" and to Indonesian popular culture, in a way that the *lesbi, gay,* and waria, subject positions are not.

The most important consequence of this dual "dubbing" is that there is active debate among tomboi as to whether they are a subcategory of *lesbi* – masculine *lesbi* (as Susie put it, a "hunter who is a lesbi" [*hunter yang lesbi*]) – or a separate transgendered subject position analogous to waria. For instance, the tomboi protagonist in the novel *Menguak Duniaku*, in the first of a series of pivotal encounters with mass media, reads about the first waria sex change operation (on Vivian Iskandar in 1973) and thinks to herself: "I wanted to tell my mother, my father, that I was the same as Vivian" (Prawirakusumah and Ramadhan 1988: 51).[16] This ambivalence regarding the *lesbi*-tomboi boundary does not appear to be localized to any one ethnic group or island: For instance, I have heard tomboi and *lesbi* women in both Bali and Sulawesi state, "Not all tomboi are *lesbi*, and not all *lesbi* are tomboi." The sense that tomboi and *lesbi* might be separate subject positions is complicated by the fact that, whereas *gay* men and warias rarely have sexual relationships, tomboi and *lesbi* are ideal sexual partners (although some tomboi also have relationships with "real women" who, they often assume, will eventually leave them for men). The "desire for the same" that characterizes *gay* subjectivity is thus more fractured for *lesbi* women. This analysis shows how considering tomboi in relation to warias, *lesbi*, and *gay* provides a better understanding of the gendering of the tomboi subject position and its spatial scale than could be reached otherwise.[17]

The "Problem" of Dubbing

> Eros and language mesh at every point. Intercourse and discourse, copula and copulation, are subclasses of the dominant fact of communication....Sex is a profoundly semantic act...human sexuality and speech [together] generate...the process... whereby we have hammered out the notion of self and otherness.
>
> George Steiner, *After Babel: Aspects of Language and Translation*

With this broader discussion of *lesbi* and *gay* life in mind, let us now return to the crucial role of mass media in Indonesians' coming to *lesbi* and *gay* subjectivity. The relationship between mass media and being Indonesian has a long history in the archipelago. From the late 19th century to the middle of the 20th century, print media played a central role in the formation of nationalism among the diverse and far-flung peoples of the Netherlands East Indies. Print media were also important in the establishment of Indonesian (a dialect of Malay formerly used as a lingua franca of trade) as the language of this new imagined community, a language that could permit communication among a populace speaking over 600 languages.[18]

In contrast to some other postcolonial states like India, imports now represent a substantial amount of cinematic and televised fare in Indonesia.[19] Although there is a long tradition of filmmaking in Indonesia dating back to the early 20th century and at some points garnering nationwide audiences, in the late 1990s the Indonesian film industry generally produced only 15–20 films per year, mostly low-budget erotic films that went directly to second- or third-run theaters (Ryanto 1998:42).[20] By the late 1990s, each of Indonesia's five private television stations was importing approximately seven thousand shows per year, many which originated in the United States (Republika 1996), and beginning in the 1990s dubbing became an increasingly popular way of presenting these broadcasts to Indonesian audiences (Lindsay 2003).[21]

It was in the context of this rise in imported television that, in a joint news conference on April 4, 1996, one year after one of Indonesia's private television stations went national for the first time, Minister of Information Harmoko and Minister of Education and Culture Wardiman Djojonegoro announced that "foreign films on television should no longer be broadcast in their original language version with Indonesian summaries or subtitles but were to be dubbed into Indonesian" (Lindsay in press). This regulation on dubbing (*dubbing, sulih suara* [to substitute sound]) was to take effect by August 16, in accordance with a soon-to-be-passed broadcasting law, which included the first set of broadcasting regulations to be issued in 18 years. This bill, which had been debated in parliament for several months at that point, was to become one of the most contentious legal documents of the New Order's twilight years (the "New Order" refers to the 30-year rule of Soeharto, Indonesia's second president, which ended in 1998). The requirement that all programs be dubbed into Indonesian was greeted with little fanfare: As the public relations manager of station TPI noted, many of the programs imported each year by private television stations were already dubbed in response to viewer demand. Acquiescing to the state's long-standing goal of building nationalism through language planning, the public relations manager of station RCTI added that the requirement was "a good policy that will help build Indonesian skills in society" (Republika 1996).

Within a month of the announcement, however, Aisyah Aminy, a spokesperson from the House of Representatives, suggested "this problem of dubbing is going to be discussed in more depth" (*Suara Pembuaran Daily* 1996). Revealing dissent within the state apparatus, Aminy expressed concern that "at present, foreign films on television are not dubbed selectively and show many things that do not fit well with the culture of our people" (*Suara Pembuaran Daily* 1996). The influential armed forces faction also weighed in against the measure, but the House forged ahead, incorporating the dubbing requirement in its draft broadcast law of December 6, 1996.

What made the broadcasting bill such a topic of discussion was the way in which it was debated and revised, extraordinary even for the typically arcane machinations of the New Order bureaucracy. A first draft of the bill was completed by a legislative committee early in 1996 and sent to parliament for approval. As usual in the New Order, the bill had been essentially crafted by the president and even bore his initials (McBeth 1997: 24). In December 1996, the parliament duly rubber-stamped the bill, returning it to Soeharto for his signature. After seven months, however, on July 11, 1997, Soeharto dropped a bombshell: In an official letter he refused to sign the draft broadcast law and returned it to parliament for revision, claiming that "several articles will be too difficult to implement from a technical standpoint" (Kompas 1997; Soeharto 1997). This unconstitutional act was *the first time in national history* a president refused to sign a draft law already passed by the House, a refusal made all the more perplexing by his approval of the original bill (Kompas 1997). House debate on the president's proposed revisions began on September 18, 1997, and was marked by unusual (for the Soeharto era) interruptions from parliament members and heated argument over executive-legislative relations.

In the wake of the president's refusal, government sources gave conflicting accounts of the issues at stake. One issue, however, stood out above the others for its cultural, rather than directly economic, emphasis: the edict on dubbing. What was notable was the total reversal that occurred during parliamentary revisions: When the dust cleared in December 1997, Article 25 of the draft law, concerning dubbing, "had been completely reversed. All non-English language foreign films henceforth had to be dubbed into English, and all foreign films shown with Indonesian subtitles" (Lindsay in press). Why this sea change? As one apologist later explained:

> Dubbing can create gaps in family communication. It can ruin the self-image of family members as a result of adopting foreign values that are "Indonesianized" [*diin- done- siakan*]...This can cause feelings of becoming "another person" to arise in family

members, who are in actuality not foreigners . . . whenever Indonesians view television, films, or other broadcasts where the original language has been changed into our national language, *those Indonesians will think that the performances in those media constitute a part of themselves. As if the culture behind those performances is also the culture of our people.* [Ali 1997: 341–342, my translation, emphasis added]

In the end, the final version of the bill indeed forbids dubbing most foreign programs into the Indonesian language. What is of interest for our purposes here, however, is the debate itself. Why, at this prescient moment in 1997 – as if foreshadowing the collapse of the New Order regime the following year – did translation become a focal point of political and cultural anxiety? What made the ability of Sharon Stone or Tom Cruise to "speak Indonesian" no longer a welcome opportunity to foster linguistic competency but, rather, a sinister force threatening the good citizen's ability to differentiate self from Other? Why, even with widespread discontent in many parts of the archipelago, was the state's fear suddenly recentered, not on religious, regional, or ethnic affiliation overwhelming national loyalty but on trans-national affiliation superseding nationalism and rendering it secondary? And what might be the hidden linkages between this dubbing controversy and the crucial role mass media play in *gay* and *lesbi* subjectivities?

Dubbing Culture

An error, a misreading initiates the modern history of our subject. Romance languages derive their terms for "translation" from *traducere* because Leonardo Bruni misinter-preted a sentence in the *Noctes* of Aulus Gellius in which the Latin actually signifies "to introduce, to lead into." The point is trivial but symbolic. Often, in the records of translation, a fortunate misreading is the source of new life.

George Steiner, *After Babel: Aspects of Language in Translation*

We now have two problems centering on mass media. First problem: How do Indonesians come to see themselves as *gay* or *lesbi* through the fragmentary recep-tion of mass-mediated messages? Second problem: Why would the question of dubbing foreign television shows into the Indonesian language provoke one of the greatest constitutional crises in Indonesia's history? Both of these problems raise issues of translation and authenticity in an already globalized world. I suggest that we might address the first problem through the second. In effect, we can "dub" these two sets of social facts together and in doing so discover striking convergences and unexpected resonances.[22]

It was long after becoming aware of the link between mass media and *gay* and *lesbi* subjectivities that I learned of the dubbing controversy. I had been struggling with the question of *lesbi* and *gay* subjectivities for some time without a clear conclusion, particularly concerning questions of agency. Were *gay* and *lesbi* Indo-nesians simply mimicking the "West"; were they severed from their traditions once they occupied the subject positions *lesbi* or *gay*? After all, as I discuss elsewhere (Boellstorff 1999), *gay* and *lesbi* Indonesians tend to view themselves in terms of a consumerist life narrative where selfhood is an ongoing project developed through treating one's life as a kind of career. Alternatively, were these Indonesians queering global capitalism, subverting its heteronormativity and building a movement dedicated to human rights? Were they deploying the terms *lesbi* and *gay* tactically, as a veneer over a deeper indigenousness?

A notion of "dubbing culture" allowed me to move beyond this impasse of "puppets of globalization" versus "veneer over tradition." Through individual encounters with mass media – like reading one's mother's magazines or an advice column in the local newspaper, or viewing television coverage of a gay pride march in Australia – Indonesians construct subjectivities and communities. *Construct* is the wrong word; it connotes a self who plans and consciously shapes something.[23] Better to say that these Indonesians "come to" *lesbi* and *gay* subjectivity through these entanglements with mass media; their constructive agency, and the *lesbi* and *gay* subject positions themselves, are constructed through the encounter. This is not a solely individual process; although the originary encounters with magazines or newspapers are typically solitary, as soon as the person begins to interact with other *lesbi*- or *gay*-identified Indonesians, he or she reworks these mass-mediated understandings of sexuality. Romance, for instance, is a crucial element of *lesbi* and *gay* subjectivities but rarely appears in media treatments of homosexuality.

A set of fragmented cultural elements from mass media are transformed in unexpected ways in the Indonesian context, transforming that context itself in the process. In other words, *lesbi* and *gay* Indonesians "dub" ostensibly "Western" sexual subjectivities. Like a dub, the fusion remains a juxtaposition; the seams show. "Speech" and "gesture" never perfectly match; being *lesbi* or *gay* and being Indonesian never perfectly match. For *lesbi* and *gay* Indonesians, as in "dubbing culture" more generally, this tension is irresolvable; there is no "real" version underneath, where everything fits. You can close your eyes and hear perfect speech or mute the sound and see perfect gesture, but no original unites the two in the dubbed production. This may not present the self with an unlivable contradiction, however, since in dubbing one is not invested in the originary but, rather, the awkward fusion. Disjuncture is at the heart of the dub; there is no prior state of pure synchrony and no simple conversion to another way of being. Where translation is haunted by its inevitable failure, dubbing rejoices in the good-enough and the forever incomplete. Dubbing is not definitive but heuristic, interpretative – like many understandings of the ethnographic project.

It is this dimension of dubbing that transcends the apparent dilemma of "puppets of globalization" versus "veneer over tradition." The idea of "dubbing culture" indicates that the root of the problem is the notion of authenticity itself, the colonialist paradigm that valorizes the "civilized" colonizer over the "traditional" colonized. In line with the observation that postcolonial nationalisms usually invert, rather than disavow, colonial categories of thought (inter alia, Gupta 1998: 169), the Indonesian state simply flips the colonial binary, placing tradition over modernity as the ultimate justification for the nation. To the obvious problem of justifying a recently formed nation in terms of tradition, the Indonesian state (like all national states) has worked ever since to inculcate a sense of national culture *(kebudayaan nasional)*. This is built on the pillar of the Indonesian language and propagated via mass media. Through mass media, citizens are to come to recognize themselves as authentic Indonesians, carriers of an oxymoronic "national tradition" that will guide the body politic through the travails of modernity. By speaking in one voice – in Indonesian – a hierarchy of tradition over modernity can be sustained and reconciled with statehood.

"Dubbing" threatens this hierarchy: It is lateral, rhizomatic (Deleuze and Guattari 1987), "a multiplicity that cannot be understood in terms of the traditional problems...of origins and genesis, or of deep structures" (Bogue 1989: 125). The authoritative voice is at odds with the visual presentation. "Dubbing culture" sets two elements side by side, blurred yet distinct. It is a performative act that, in linking persons to subject positions, creates subjectivities (Butler 1990); but this "dubbing" link is *profoundly not one of suture*, a term originating in film studies regarding "the procedures by means of which cinematic texts confer subjectivity upon their viewers" (Silverman 1983: 195). In "dubbing culture," subjectivity is constituted not through suture but collage. Yet this productively partial incorporation of the self into discourse is not a failed performance: In its iteration, its holding together of two ostensibly incompatible cultural logics without conflating them, a space for subjectivity appears.

The original television show or movie may preexist its Indonesian dub temporally, but to the interpreting audience neither voice nor image is prior. They happen together; neither dominates. Agamben, citing Benjamin's concern with the relationship between quotation and the new "transmissibility of culture" made possible by mass media, notes that quotation "alienat[es] by force a fragment of the past... mak[ing] it lose its authentic power" (1999: 104). But "dubbing culture" (in a literal sense as well as the metaphorical sense I develop here) is more than just quotation; it adds a step, first alienating something but then reworking it in a new context. The power of the "dub" comes not by erasing authenticity but by inaugurating new authenticities not dependent on tradition or translation. It disrupts the apparent seamlessness of the predubbed "original," showing that it too is a dub, that its "traditions" are the product of social contexts with their own assumptions and inequalities.

The Indonesian authorities were keenly aware of these disruptive implications during the dubbing controversy. For decades, Indonesian had been the vehicle allowing Indonesians to speak with one voice. But now the possibility that Sharon Stone could "speak Indonesian" meant that this vehicle was spinning beyond state control – into the control of globalizing forces but also into an interzone between languages and cultures, a zone with no controlling authority: "The Indonesian dubbing was so successful in making the language familiar that viewers lost any idea that it was strange for foreigners to speak Indonesian.... The language was too familiar, too much like real speech, too colloquial, and therefore the speech was too dangerous" (Lindsay in press).

The sudden shift during the dubbing controversy – from an insistence that *all* foreign television programs be dubbed into the Indonesian language to an insistence that *none* of them could be so dubbed – reveals a tectonic shift in the position of mass media in Indonesian society. For the first time, fear of this juxtaposition, of

"Westerners" "speaking" the national tongue, tipped the scales against a historically privileged concern with propagating Indonesian as national unifier. Now the ability of dubbing (and the Indonesian language itself) to explode the national imagined community – to show that one can be Indonesian *and* translate ideas from outside – presented a danger greater than the potential benefit of drawing more sharply the nation's archipelagic edges.

"Dubbing culture," then, is about a new kind of cultural formation in an already globalized world, one for which the idiom of translation is no longer sufficient. It questions *the relationship between translation and belonging*, asserting that the binarisms of import–export and authentic–inauthentic are insufficient to explain how globalizing mass media play a role in *lesbi* and *gay* subject positions but do not determine them outright. For queer studies, the lesson here relates to understandings of lesbian or gay non-"Westerners" in terms of "rupture or continuity" (Altman 2001) or "indigenous or Western import" (Jackson 1997: 186). Although tactically useful, such binarisms do not capture the possibility of subject positions with more nuanced and conjunctural relationships to the "West," ones that may stand outside usual definitions of identity politics.

In a metaphorical sense we might say that *lesbi* and *gay* Indonesians dub "Western" sexual subject positions: They overwrite the deterministic "voice of the West," yet they cannot compose any script they please; their bricolage remains shaped by a discourse originating in the "West" and filtered through a nationalistic lens. This process of dubbing allows *lesbi* and *gay* individuals to see themselves as part of a global community but also as authentically Indonesian. Unlike waria, they never ask, "Are there people like me outside Indonesia?" because it is already obvious – "built into" the dubbed subjectivities – that there are such people. These Indonesians imagine themselves as one national element in a global patchwork of lesbian and gay national subjectivities, not through tradition, because *lesbi* and *gay* have a national spatial scale.

More broadly, "dubbing culture" as a metaphor speaks to the nonteleological, transformative dimensions of globalizing processes. It is useful for questioning the ability of globalizing mass media to project uniform ideologies. Although it is true that contemporary mass media have enormous power, it is crucial to emphasize that this power is not absolute; it can lead to unexpected results – like *lesbi* and *gay* subject positions themselves. The metaphorical use of "dubbing culture" provides a useful fleshing-out of theories linking ideological apparatuses with Althusser's thesis that "ideology interpellates individuals as subjects" (1971: 160–162). By this, Althusser meant that ideology forms the subject positions by which individuals come to represent their conditions of existence to themselves and to others. Althusser terms this function of ideology interpellation or hailing and illustrates it in terms of a person on the street responding to the hail "Hey, you there!" When the person turns around to respond to the hail, "he becomes a *subject*. Why? Because he has recognized that the hail was 'really' addressed to him" (Althusser 1971: 163). Many social theorists, particularly those interested in mass media, have found this a useful analytical starting point. The question most commonly posed to this framework by these theorists concerns the issue of structure versus agency:

Although there would be no turning around without first having been hailed, neither would there be a turning around without some readiness to turn. But...how and why does the subject turn, anticipating the conferral of identity through the self-ascription of guilt? What kind of relation already binds these two such that the subject knows to turn, knows that something is to be gained from such a turn? [Butler 1997: 107]

Part and parcel of this dilemma of agency is the question: How are we to explain the circumstance when people "recognize" something the ideology does not intend? Indonesian mass media never meant to create the conditions of possibility for national *gay* and *lesbi* subject positions. One way to address this problem might be through the dubbing culture concept, where what is recognized in the hail *is itself a product* of transformation. This does not entail compliance with state ideology. Yet neither does it imply a freewheeling, presocial, liberal self-assembling of an identity from elements presented by mass media, independent of social context.

Gay and *lesbi* Indonesians often playfully employ the notion of authenticity *(asli)* – I have often heard gay men describe themselves as *asli gay*. In doing so, they implicitly challenge the state's monopoly on designating what will count as tradition in Indonesia. Authenticity is crucial for mass-media studies as well. For Benjamin, the very concept of authenticity is put under erasure by mass media. Because mass media depend on mechanical reproduction (no mass media circulate as a series of handcrafted originals) and for Benjamin "the presence of the original is the pre-requisite to the concept of authenticity," it follows that "the whole sphere of authenticity is outside technical...reproducibility" (1995: 220). Benjamin sees the most significant aspect of this reproducibility to be that of movement: "Above all, [technical reproduction] enables the original to meet the beholder halfway...the cathedral leaves its locale to be received in the studio of a lover of art; the choral production, performed in an auditorium or in the open air, resounds in the drawing room" (1955: 220–221).

Gay and *lesbi* subjectivities are not moved from one place to another, as Benjamin saw mechanical reproduction, but are the dubbing of cultural logics in new ways. "Dubbing culture" is thus articulation in both senses of the term, an interaction of elements that remain distinct – like the image of speech and the dubbed voice – and also the "speaking" of a (dubbed) subjectivity.[24] This lets us "queery" globalization without posing either an oppositionally authentic "native" or globalization as simple movement.

"Dubbing culture" also speaks to conceptions of translation in the age of mech-anical production. As Benjamin notes with reference to magazines, "For the first time, captions have become obligatory. And it is clear that they have an altogether different character than the title of a painting" (1955: 226). This is because captions are a guide to interpretation, juxtaposed to the work of art yet at a slight remove. They serve as "signposts" that "demand a specific kind of approach; free-floating contemplation is not appropriate to them" (Benjamin 1955: 226). They are a mediation internal to mass media, a translation within.

Dubbing, far more than a subtitle, is a caption fused to the thing being described. It comes from the mouth of imagic characters, yet is never quite in synch. The moving lips never match the speech; the moment of fusion is always deferred, as dubbed voice, translation-never-quite-complete, bridges two sets of representa-tions.[25] *Gay* and *lesbi* Indonesians dub culture as they live a subjectivity linked to people and places far away. They are completely Indonesian, but to be "completely Indonesian" requires thinking of one's position in a transnational world. In speaking of translation, Benjamin wrote that "unlike a work of literature, translation does not find itself in the center of the language forest but on the outside facing the wooded ridge; it calls into it without entering, aiming at that single spot where the echo is able to give, in its own language, the reverberation of the work in the alien one" (1955: 76). *Gay* and *lesbi* Indonesians have made of that echo subject positions that bespeak subjectivity and community even under conditions of oppression. They live in the echo, in the mass-mediated margin of incomplete translation, and find there authenticity, meaning, sex, friendship, and love.

Coda

As I noted as the beginning of this article, the concept of dubbing culture has a reflexive dimension for ethnography in an already globalized world. Indeed, to the extent we can consider translation a structuralist enterprise framing movement between languages and cultures in terms of grammar and meaning, many contem-porary ethnographers engage in "dubbing culture" when they employ poststructur-alist frameworks that question received understandings of the relationship among signifiers, and between signifiers and signifieds.

Additionally, "dubbing culture" need not be construed only in synchronic terms. There has been a striking retreat from the anthropology of postmodernity in recent years, perhaps induced by the lamentable vulgarization of "postmodern" from a specific theory of political economy, representation, and culture to an epithet hurled at methodologies or writing strategies one finds difficult to apprehend. Yet what is the emerging anthropology of alternative modernities – of modernity with-out metanarrative (Lyotard 1984) – if not an anthropology of postmodernity? And what is "dubbing culture" if not the antiteleological mode of historicity that produces postmodern bricolage, pastiche, the more-than-juxtaposition and less-than-unification of pasts, presents, and futures?

Contemporary ethnography, then, can be said to be engaging in dubbing culture when it brings together parts and wholes, data and theory. *Lesbi* and *gay* Indonesians engage in dubbing culture as they come to sexual subjectivity; they show not that "authentic Indonesian tradition" is a lie but that this authenticity is processual, constructed through active engagement with an unequal world. And if tradition and belonging are not given but constructed, they can be contested and transformed. The playing field is certainly not even – *lesbi* and *gay* Indonesians are not about to become fully accepted members of Indonesian society – but it is a playing field nonetheless, and there is space for change. Similarly, even in an already globalized world, non- "Western" cultures are not doomed to the status of reruns, even when confronted by "Western" hegemony.

NOTES

1 Although the term *lesbian* is sometimes used in Indonesian, *lesbi* is much more common and I use it here. The predominance of *lesbi* over *lesbian* is probably because of two factors: Prototypical words in Indonesian have two syllables, and in Indonesian *-an* is a suffix. In this article I also place the term *West* in quotes to indicate that I view it not in geographic terms but as "a particular historical conjugation of place, power, and knowledge" (Gupta 1998: 36). All italicized informant terms are Indonesian; in this article I follow standard Indonesian orthography except that the front unrounded vowel /é/ (spelled "e" in Indonesian, along with the schwa) is here written as "é" for clarity. All informant names are pseudonyms. All translations are my own.

2 The television reference comes from the title of Oetomo 1997, "When Sharon Stone Speaks Indonesian."

3 For further discussion of these issues, see my books, *The Gay Archipelago: Sexuality and Nation in Indonesia* (Princeton: Princeton University Press, 2005) and *A Coincidence of Desires: Anthropology, Queer Studies, Indonesia* (Durham: Duke University Press, 2007).

4 The appearance of the *lesbi* and *gay* subject positions in Indonesia in the 1970s is corroborated by a range of archival and oral historical data. In the 1988 novel *Menguak duniaku: kisah sejati kelainan seksual* (Revealing My World: A True Story of Sexual Deviance), the protagonist (a woman who feels like a man but does not appear to know of terms like *tomboi*) discovers a magazine article that dates the public existence of the terms *lesbi* and *gay* to "1976, more or less" (Prawirakusumah and Ramadhan 1988: 481).

5 One reason for this may be that even the most popular of these magazines (*GAYa Nusantara*, published from Surabaya) has a monthly circulation of about four hundred in a nation of over 200 million.

6 In recent years, the linguist and anthropologist Dédé Oetomo has gained some prominence in mainstream mass media, along with a handful of other *gay* men. *Lesbi* women appear much more rarely in mass media of their own accord: A 1997 edition of the television show *Buah Bibir* discussing lesbianism in Indonesia featured Oetomo as a speaker and a handful of *lesbi* discussants appearing with their faces blackened out.

7 Imported programs come from around the world – with many favorites from India, Latin America, and Japan. To my knowledge, however, concepts of *lesbi* and *gay* subjectivity seem to be formed exclusively with reference to programs originally in English and originating above all from the United States, as these examples indicate. My thanks to Margaret J. Wiener for reminding me to clarify this point.

8 This is because of the linkage between identitas and state surveillance, not just the fact that it is a loanword. Loanwords can become experience-near concepts in Indonesia, as borne out not only by *lesbi* and *gay* but also by *Muslim, Kristen*, and even *Indonesia* (coined by a European in the 19th century).

9 This literature is too vast to list here; see, for instance, Brenner 1998 and many articles in Blackburn 2001; Ong and Peletz 1995; Sears 1996; and Sen and Stivens 1998.

10 Thanks to Kathyrn Robinson for helping me develop this point.

11 See Murray 1999.

12 *Déndong* is a gay language transformation of standard Indonesian *dandan*, "put on makeup."

13   There are two primary reasons why I do not believe ethnic-specific *gay* or *lesbi* subject positions will emerge in the near future in Indonesia. First, the cultural dimensions of current moves toward regional autonomy have been predominantly expressed through conceptions of adat revitalization; that is, in terms of a return to tradition that may in some cases be seen to include ETPs, but certainly not *lesbi* or *gay* subject positions. Second, as noted earlier, subject positions are shaped by the historical circumstances during which they first took form, and since the *lesbi* and *gay* subject positions were formed during the New Order era, it seems likely they will retain national spatial scales and cultural logics for some time to come.

14   This might also be taken to imply a globalization earlier than the 1970s, since the butch–femme distinction dates to at least the early 20th century in the United States and elsewhere (Kennedy and Davis 1993).

15   For instance, in a television commercial shown nationally in 2000, a mother comments on her favorite brand of laundry detergent as her young daughter is shown walking home from school, wearing a school uniform and also a Muslim *jilbab* (a "veil" that covers the head and hair but not the face). As the little girl runs home, getting dirt and chocolate ice cream on her jilbab, the mother opines, "My girl is a real *tomboi*."

16   Not only have both tombois and warias during my fieldwork described themselves in terms of gendered analogues, but *gay* men also have occasionally noted this relationship as well, as when the members of the "Indonesian Gay Society" claimed in their zine *New Jaka-Jaka* that tombois and warias were "*biras* in regard to gender struggle"; *biras* is a kinship term referring to the relationship between two women marrying brothers or two men marrying sisters (IGS 1999: 15).

17   For example, what might be the implications of the apparent fact that tombois "in West Sumatra" think their subjectivities through the Indonesian language (Blackwood 1998), or that terms like *tomboi* are used elsewhere in Southeast Asia, whereas male to female trans-gender or transvestite terms do not transform "Western" terms (*waria* in Indonesia, but also *kathoey* in Thailand, *bantut* in the Philippines, and so on)? See Boellstorff 2007, ch. 7.

18   See, inter alia, Anderson 1983, Errington 1998, Maier 1993, Siegel 1997.

19   See Mankekar 1999.

20   The number of films and television shows produced has varied according to many factors, particularly the general state of the Indonesian economy and political conflict. See Heider 1991 and Sen 1994 for detailed historical and contemporary accounts of Indonesian cinema (both works were published before the rise of private television in Indonesia). Heider (1991: 19) notes that the number of films produced yearly in Indonesia has ranged from zero (in 1946 and 1947, for instance) to over one hundred in 1977 and 1989. There have been encouraging signs of a renaissance in Indonesian cinema since 1998.

21   The five private stations are RCTI, SCTV, TPI, Anteve, and Indosiar. Estimates of the proportion of shows originating outside of Indonesia range from two-thirds (Wahyuni 2000: 116) from the United States to 50 percent from the United States and Europe combined (Groves 1996: 42).

22   This seems possible despite the fact that *lesbi* and *gay* Indonesians themselves tended not to take much notice of the dubbing controversy. I have never heard a *gay* or *lesbi* (or waria) Indonesian bring up the topic. When I have explicitly asked them about the controversy, *gay* and *lesbi* Indonesians both respond that they prefer subtitles to dubbing for the following reasons: (1) you can learn the original language, "even if it is just 'buenos días' in Spanish," and (2) the dubbing "never follows the actor's lips exactly."

23 As does *negotiate*; these subjectivities are not negotiated in the sense that Maira (1999) speaks of an "identity dub" among South Asian Americans in the New York club scene. In that case the institutional context is not mass media but clubbing, and the individuals involved appear to be vastly more wealthy, English speaking, and mobile than *gay* and *lesbi* Indonesians.

24 Here I use *articulation* in its English sense. The term originally entered social theory through Marx, but *Gliederung* has only the first of the two meanings noted above. The root word, *Gleid*, means "limb" or "joint" but can also mean "penis" *(männliches Glied)*. Surely there is great potential in a psychoanalytic treatment that links the moment of speech to erection.

25 Lydia Liu notes that in studying how "a word, category, or discourse 'travels' from one language to another," we must "account for the vehicle of translation" and address "the condition of translation" itself (1995: 20–21, 26), a concern with a long history in anthropology as well (Asad 1986).

REFERENCES

Adam, Barry D., Jan Willem Duyvendak, and Andre Krouwel
   1999 *The Global Emergence of Gay and Lesbian Politics: National Imprints of a World-wide Movement*. Philadelphia: Temple University Press.

Agamben, Giorgio
   1999 *The Man without Content*. Stanford: Stanford University Press.

Ali, Novel
   1997 Sulih suara dorong keretakan komunikasi keluarga. In *Bercinta dengan televisi: ilusi, impresi, dan imaji sebuah kotak ajaib*. Deddy Mulyana and Idi Subandy Ibrahim, eds. Pp. 338–346. Bandung, Java: PT Remaja Rosdakarya.

Althusser, Louis
   1971 Ideology and Ideological State Apparatuses (Notes towards an Investigation). In *Lenin and Philosophy and Other Articles*. Louis Althusser, ed. Ben Brewster, trans. Pp. 121–173. New York: Monthly Review Press.

Altman, Dennis
   2001 Rupture or Continuity? The Internationalisation of Gay Identities. In *Postcolonial, Queer: Theoretical Intersections*. John C. Hawley, ed. Pp. 19–42. Albany: State University of New York Press.

Andaya, Leonard
   2000 The Bissu: Study of a Third Gender in Indonesia. In *Other Pasts: Women, Gender, and History in Early Modern Southeast Asia*. Leonard Andaya, ed. Pp. 27–46. Honolulu: University of Hawai'i Press.

Anderson, Benedict
   1983 *Imagined Communities: Reflections on the Origins and Spread of Nationalism*. London: Verso.

Appadurai, Arjun
   1996 Global Ethnoscapes: Notes and Queries for a Transnational Anthropology. In *Modernity at Large: Cultural Dimensions of Globalization*, by Arjun Appadurai. Pp. 48–65. Minneapolis: University of Minnesota Press.

Asad, Talal
   1986 The Concept of Cultural Translation in British Social Anthropology. In *Writing Culture: The Poetics and Politics of Ethnography*. James Clifford and George E. Marcus, eds. Pp. 141–164. Berkeley: University of California Press.

Benjamin, Walter

 1955 *Illuminations: Articles and Reflections*. New York: Schocken Books.

Blackburn, Susan, ed.

 2001 *Love, Sex, and Power: Women in Southeast Asia*. Clayton, Australia: Monash Asia Institute.

Blackwood, Evelyn

 1998 *Tombois* in West Sumatra: Constructing Masculinity and Erotic Desire. *Cultural Anthropology* 13(4): 491–521.

Boellstorff, Tom

 1999 The Perfect Path: Gay Men, Marriage, Indonesia. *GLQ: A Journal of Gay and Lesbian Studies* 5(4): 475–510.

 2002 Ethnolocality. *Asia Pacific Journal of Anthropology* 3(1): 24–48.

 2004 Zines and Zones of Desire: Mass Mediated Love, National Romance, and Sexual Citizenship in Gay Indonesia. *Journal of Asian Studies* 63(2): 367–402.

 2005 *The Gay Archipelago: Sexuality and Nation in Indonesia*. Princeton: Princeton University Press.

 2007 *A Coincidence of Desire: Anthropology, Queer Studies*, Indonesia. Durham: Duke University Press.

Bogue, Ronald

 1989 *Deleuze and Guattari*. London: Routledge.

Breman, Jan

 1982 The Village on Java and the Early Colonial State. *Journal of Peasant Studies* 9(4): 189–240.

Brenner, Neil

 1998 Between Fixity and Motion: Accumulation, Territorial Organization, and the Historical Geography of Spatial Scales. In *Environment and Planning D: Society and Space* 16(4): 459–481.

Brenner, Suzanne April

 1998 *The Domestication of Desire: Women, Wealth, and Modernity in Java*. Princeton: Princeton University Press.

Budiman, Amen

 1979 *Lelaki perindu lelaki: Sebuah tinjauan sejarah dan psikologi tentang homoseks dan masyarakat homoseks di Indonesia*. Semarang: Tanjung Sari.

Butler, Judith

 1990 *Gender Trouble*. New York: Routledge.

 1997 *The Psychic Life of Power: Theories in Subjection*. Stanford: Stanford University Press.

Deleuze, Gilles, and Félix Guattari

 1987 *A Thousand Plateaus: Capitalism and Schizophrenia*. Brian Massumi, trans. Minneapolis: University of Minnesota Press.

Elliston, Deborah A.

 1995 Erotic Anthropology: "Ritualized Homosexuality" in Melanesia and Beyond. *American Ethnologist* 22(4): 848–867.

Errington, Joseph

 1998 *Shifting Languages: Interaction and Identity in Javanese Indonesia*. Cambridge: Cambridge University Press.

Errington, Shelly

 1990 Recasting Sex, Gender, and Power: A Theoretical and Regional Overview. In *Power and Difference: Gender in Island Southeast Asia*. Shelly Errington and Jane Monnig Atkinson, eds. Pp. 1–58. Stanford: Stanford University Press.

Foucault, Michel
   1978   *The History of Sexuality*, vol. 1: *An Introduction*. Robert Hurley, trans. New York: Vintage Books.
   1985   *The History of Sexuality*, vol. 2: *The Use of Pleasure*. Robert Hurley, trans. New York: Vintage Books.
Geertz, Hildred
   1963   Indonesian Cultures and Communities. In *Indonesia*. Ruth McVey, ed. Pp. 24–96. New Haven, CT: HRAF Press.
Gibson-Graham, J. K.
   1996   *The End of Capitalism (as We Knew It): A Feminist Critique of Political Economy*. Cambridge, MA: Blackwell.
Groves, Don
   1996   Exhibition Still Modest in Indonesia. *Variety* 363(11): 42–44.
Gupta, Akhil
   1998   *Postcolonial Developments: Agriculture in the Making of Modern India*. Durham, NC: Duke University Press.
Gupta, Akhil, and James Ferguson
   1997   Discipline and Practice: "The Field" as Site, Method, and Location in Anthropology. In *Anthropological Locations: Boundaries and Grounds of a Field Science*. Akhil Gupta and James Ferguson, eds. Pp. 1–46. Berkeley: University of California Press.
Halberstam, Judith
   1998   *Female Masculinity*. Durham, NC: Duke University Press.
Hannerz, Ulf
   1989   Notes on the Global Ecumene. *Public Culture* 1(2): 66–75.
Harvey, David
   2000   *Spaces of Hope*. Berkeley: University of California Press.
Heider, Karl G.
   1991   *Indonesian Cinema: National Culture on Screen*. Honolulu: University of Hawai'i Press.
Indonesian Gay Society
   1999   Gay, gay gay. *New Jaka–Jaka* 6: 15–16.
Jackson, Peter A.
   1997   *Kathoey*><Gay><Man: The Historical Emergence of Gay Male Identity in Thailand. In *Sites of Desire, Economies of Pleasure: Sexualities in Asia and the Pacific*. Lenore Manderson and Margaret Jolly, eds. Pp. 166–190. Chicago: University of Chicago Press.
Josselin de Jong, Jan Petrus Benjamin de
   1977[1935]   The Malay Archipelago as a Field of Ethnological Study. In *Structural Anthropology in the Netherlands: A Reader*. Patrick Edward de Josselin de Jong, ed. Pp. 164–182. The Hague: Martinus Nijhoff.
Keane, Webb
   1999   The Materiality and Locality of Everyday Lives. *Indonesia* 68: 178–186.
Kennedy, Elizabeth Lapovsky, and Madeline D. Davis
   1993   *Boots of Leather, Slippers of Gold: The History of a Lesbian Community*. New York: Routledge.
Kennedy, Matthew
   1993   Clothing, Gender, and Ritual Transvestism: The *Bissu* of South Sulawesi. *Journal of Men's Studies* 2(1): 1–13.
Kompas
   1997   Presiden resmi minta DPR bicarakan lagi RUU penyiaran, July 25, 1997. Electronic document, http://www.kompas.com/9707/25/hiburan/mint.htm, accessed April 9, 1998.

Lindsay, Jennifer

In press Speaking the Truth: Speech on Television in Indonesia. In *Media Discourse and Performance in Indonesia and Malaysia*. Ben Arps, ed. Athens: Ohio University Press.

Liu, Lydia H.

1995 *Translingual Practice: Literature, National Culture, and Translated Modernity-China, 1900–1937*. Stanford: Stanford University Press.

Lyotard, Jean-François

1984 *The Postmodern Condition: A Report on Knowledge*. Geoff Bennington and Brian Massumi, trans. Foreword by Fredric Jameson. Minneapolis: University of Minnesota Press.

Maier, Hendrik Menko Jan

1993 From Heteroglossia to Polyglossia: The Creation of Malay and Dutch in the Indies. *Indonesia* 56: 37–65.

Maira, Sunaina

1999 Identity Dub: The Paradoxes of an Indian American Youth Subculture (New York Mix). *Cultural Anthropology* 14(1): 29–60.

Mankekar, Purnima

1999 *Screening Culture, Viewing Politics: An Ethnography of Television, Womanhood, and Nation in Postcolonial India*. Durham, NC: Duke University Press.

McBeth, John

1997 Technical Problems: Suharto Bends Constitution by Returning Broadcast Bill. *Far Eastern Economic Review* 160(36): 24.

Miller, Daniel

1995 Introduction: Anthropology, Modernity and Consumption. In *Worlds Apart: Modernity through the Prism of the Local*. Daniel Miller, ed. Pp. 1–22. London: Routledge.

Murray, Alison

1999 Let Them Take Ecstasy: Class and Jakarta Lesbians. In *Female Desires: Same-Sex Relations and Transgender Practices across Cultures*. Evelyn Blackwood and Saskia E. Wieringa, eds. Pp. 139–156. New York: Columbia University Press.

Oetomo, Dédé

1997 Ketika Sharon Stone berbahasa Indonesia. In *Bercinta dengan televisi: Ilusi, impresi, dan imaji sebuah kotak ajaib*. Deddy Mulyana and Idi Subandy Ibrahim, eds. Pp. 333–337. Bandung: PT Remaja Rosdakarya.

Ong, Aihwa, and Michael G. Peletz, eds.

1995 *Bewitching Women, Pious Men: Gender and Body Politics in Southeast Asia*. Berkeley: University of California Press.

Pemberton, John

1994 *On the Subject of "Java."* Ithaca: Cornell University Press.

Poerwadarminta, W. J. S.

1976 *Kamus umum Bahasa Indonesia*. Jakarta: Balai Pustaka.

Prawirakusumah, R. Prie, and Ramadhan K. H.

1988 *Menguak duniaku: kisah sejati kelainan seksual*. Jakarta: Pustaka Utama Grafiti.

Republika

1996 Stasiun TV menyambut, May 2, 1996. Electronic document, http://www.hamline.edu/apakabar/basisdata/1996/05/02/0041.html, accessed April 10, 1998.

Ryanto, Tony

1998 Indonesia Biz Resilient. *Variety* 373(3): 42.

Salim, Peter, and Yenny Salim

1991 *Kamus bahasa Indonesia kontemporer*. Jakarta: Modern English Press.

Sears, Laurie, ed.
  1996   *Fantasizing the Feminine in Indonesia.* Durham, NC: Duke University Press.

Sen, Krishna
  1994   *Indonesian Cinema: Framing the New Order.* London: Zed Press.

Sen, Krishna, and Maila Stivens, eds.
  1998   *Gender and Power in Affluent Asia.* London: Routledge.

Siegel, James
  1986   *Solo in the New Order: Language and Hierarchy in an Indonesian City.* Princeton: Princeton University Press.
  1997   *Fetish, Recognition, Revolution.* Princeton: Princeton University Press.

Silverman, Kaja
  1983   *The Subject of Semiotics.* New York: Oxford University Press.

Soeharto
  1997   *Indonesian Presidential Directive* R.09/jo/VII/1997. Jakarta, Indonesia.

Suara Pembuaran Daily
  1996   Kalangan DPR: Alih suara di TV sebaiknya tunggu UU penyiaran, May 3, 1996. Electronic document, http://www.hamline.edu/apakabar/basisdata/1996/05/03/0046.html, accessed April 10, 1998.

Tsing, Anna Lowenhaupt
  1993   *In the Realm of the Diamond Queen: Marginality in an Out-of-the-Way Place.* Princeton: Princeton University Press.

Wahyuni, Hermin Indah
  2000   *Televisi dan intervensi negara: Konteks politik kebijakan publik industri penyiaran televisi.* Yogyakarta: Penerbit Media Pressindo.

Wieringa, Saskia E.
  1999   Desiring Bodies or Defiant Cultures: Butch-Femme Lesbians in Jakarta and Lima. In *Female Desires: Same-Sex Relations and Transgender Practices across Cultures.* Evelyn Blackwood and Saskia E. Wieringa, eds. Pp. 206–229. New York: Columbia University Press.

Wilson, Ian Douglas
  1999   Reog Ponorogo: Spirituality, Sexuality, and Power in a Javanese Performance Tradition. Intersections: Gender, History, and Culture in the Asian Context 2. Electronic document, http://wwwsshe.murdoch.edu.au/intersections/issue2/Warok.html, accessed August 15, 2001.

14

Itineraries of Indian Cinema: African Videos, Bollywood, and Global Media

Brian Larkin

The tape recorder, the device that conveys love between the two main characters in the Nigerian (Hausa) video film *In Da So Da K'auna* (The Soul of My Heart, Ado Ahmad, 1994), is a mediating device, filtering, on several levels, the physical and symbolic boundaries among characters, societies, and technologies. Sumayya sits in her bedroom as a boy brings in a tape from her lover, Mohammed. The camera zooms in to a medium close-up as she turns on the tape recorder and hears her lover announce he will sing to her "Lambun Soyayya," (The Garden of Love). She sits still, for a full three minutes, as the camera moves to an extreme close-up on an immovable face. There is no reaction, no expression, and the viewer is forced to contemplate the unspectacular practice of listening. In this sensual, physical scene, a visceral declaration and acceptance of love occurs and in the intimacy of a bedroom lovers share the same space but only by virtue of the mediating capacity of the tape recorder. The tape recorder allows the presence of love, but preserves the segregation of the sexes as Mohammed, the lover, is only present by prosthesis. And in doing so the tape recorder also mediates between Indian films and Nigerian Hausa videos, enabling the declaration of love through song, so central to Indian films and their popularity in Nigeria, while preserving the sexual segregation necessary to Hausa Islamic values.

From *Multiculturalism, Postcoloniality, and Transnational Media*, ed. Ella Shohat and Robert Stam, pp. 170–92. New Brunswick. NJ: Rutgers University Press. Copyright © 2003, Brian Larkin.

The adoption of song-and-dance sequences in Hausa videos is one of the Bollywood-influenced intertextual elements that distinguish them from the Yoruba- and English-language videos, also made in Nigeria. For over forty years, Indian films,[1] their stars and fashions, music and stories, have been a dominant part of everyday culture of northern Nigeria. The rise of Hausa videomakers who borrow plots and styles from Bombay cinema are part of a proliferation of cultural forms that have resignified the global flow of Hindi cinema within Hausa culture. Here I will use the rise of a new genre of Hausa love films as an example of how transnational flows of Indian films can spawn a range of cultural phenomena as they are reworked in local settings. I use this example to rethink the idea of global media and the ways in which global cultural politics of identity are contested.

While Indian film is a hugely successful global media form that has been strikingly successful in competing with, and sometimes dislodging, Hollywood in the global arena, the specific and diverse reasons why Indian film travels have rarely been analyzed. For some, Indian film represents tradition, a space outside of, and alter to, the cultural spread of Western modernity; for others, the cultural address of Indian film is future-oriented, modern, and cosmopolitan. To understand the varying reasons why Indian film provides amenable spaces for global cultural imagining means taking seriously a decentered media theory, one whose premises start from the specificity of why media travel and the social context of their operation.

The popularity of Indian films with Arabic, Indonesian, Senegalese, or Nigerian youth reveals the mobilization of desire and fantasy that animates global cultural flows. These moments of borrowing are the choices individuals and cultures (in the case of extended, elaborated genres of music or film) make out of the range of mass-mediated cultural goods available to them in order to make those cultural goods do symbolic work locally. Stressing this range of cultural goods is important because discussions of global media are often structured around the dichotomy of the dominance or resistance to foreign (Western) media. This dominance is clear, but in many societies Hollywood *and* Indian films are popular; Egyptian *and* Indian *and* Hollywood *and* Hong Kong films are popular (in the case of the Middle East, for instance). If we take into account that most societies live in a diversified media environment, then we must shift our critical questions. What pleasures do Indian films offer that Hollywood films do not? What cultural work do Hollywood films accomplish that is different from Hong Kong films? The presence of one media flow – such as mainstream American films – does not mean the obliteration of others, as people take diverse meanings and different pleasures from various types of media available to them.

By examining the migration of Indian film outside of India, I will begin to analyze the diverse and often long-standing reasons Indian film travels. Following a more general discussion I will analyze the import of Indian film styles into Nigerian Hausa video. I argue that Indian film offers a "third space" for Hausa audiences that mediates between the reified poles of Hausa Islamic tradition and Western modernity (a false dichotomy to be sure, but one that remains deeply meaningful to people's political consciousness). Indian film offers Hausa viewers a way of being modern that does not necessarily mean being Western. This multifacetedness is key to their success and to their popularity. For Nigerian Hausa, Indian film offers a space that is alter to the West against which a cultural politics (but not necessarily a political one) can be waged. The story does not stop there, however, because Indian film also offers Hausa a cultural foil against other Nigerian groups, to wit, Igbo and Yoruba. The popularity of Indian film with Hausa audiences is so great that, in the north of Nigeria at least where Hausa are based, they are used by both Hausa and their others as means of defining identity and locating the temporal and political nature of that identity. When Hausa video-makers incorporate elements of Indian films into their videos they are thus engaging a complicated series of cultural hierarchies external and internal to the nation, setting our understanding of the operation of transnational media within a more complicated terrain.

The Global Flow of Indian Films

The popularity of Indian film in Nigeria reflects the extraordinary global reach of Bollywood – a cinema that has successfully marginalized Hollywood in certain world markets. Understanding this phenomenon is a means of revising the ways in which we understand what we conceive of as global media. In certain areas of the world Indian films have succeeded in establishing a cultural and aesthetic style outside the dominant genres of American media. In many cases audiences engage with Indian films as a means of establishing distance from the ideologically loaded presence of American film. This last statement needs careful contextualization so that the popularity of Indian films is not reduced to a simplistic notion of "resistance" to America, (although in many cases this is a self-conscious part of the process). Rather, this popularity is complexly grounded in history and cultural difference. Hausa videomakers, for instance, borrow from Indian films as a means of addressing an urban Hausa audience that is emphatically not Western and, just as important, not southern Nigerian, suggesting that some of the popularity of Indian film lies here in specific political and cultural relations well outside the knowledge of Indian filmmakers. If we examine this process we can see the diversity of audiences Indian films attract globally and suggest reasons for how it is that Indian films create narrative forms and modes of address and narrative that draw viewers in large numbers.

Indian film and the cultural production of diaspora

Perhaps most famously, Indian films have followed in the wake of Indian migration across the globe. In countries from England to the United States, Tanzania, Trinidad, Fiji, and elsewhere, these films play a complicated role in producing diasporic belonging, cultural knowledge, and even language training (for Fijian Indians, see Ray, 2000; for England, see Dhondy, 1985; Gillespie, 1995; Tyrell, 1998; Sardar, 1998). For many Indians, who are often internally divided by region, caste, and class, the archive of images, memories, and narratives produced by Hindi cinema creates a common cultural nostalgia in the diaspora, a cultural lingua franca that has the possibility to transcend difference. This role of Hindi film in mediating the connection between the diaspora and the homeland revolves around the tropes of loss, nostalgia, and pastness, where for diasporic Indians, India represents a way of life once present but now gone and film the means to reconnect with it. For second-generation diasporic Indians, Indian films play a role as ethnographic and cultural texts "teaching" migrant youth cultural knowledge about India. One British Asian woman commented that being taken as a child to see Indian films taught her "just about everything I know about religion, about India and my family traditions" (Tyrell, 1998, p. 20). Manas Ray argues that for Fijian Indians, separated from India by the historical rupture of indenture under British colonialism, this process of cultural ethnography is even more stark in that for Fijian Indians, the India represented in Indian films is a wholly imagined way of life (2000). The concept of India being mobilized here is one about transport, about using the images and narratives of film as a conduit back to the idealized world of India itself.

But while the link between Bollywood and Indian diasporic identity is growing stronger, Manas Ray warns against assuming that the reasons for this intensification are stable (2000). In his study of Fijian Indian migrants to Australia he argues that the consumption of Indian films in the diaspora varies greatly according to class, caste, and national origin. Whereas for some Bollywood might be a means of reconnecting with a homeland, Ray argues that for Fijian Indians (or Tanzanian or Trinidadian Indians) India remains an imagined entity and Indian films function as introduction to a whole way of life about which they know little and have experienced even less (2000). This points to what he terms the historical subjectivity of particular diasporic groups like Fijian Indians, for whom the mass culture of Hindi film provides a cultural repertoire of Indianness.

In recent years the style and nature of the way in which Hindi films have mediated the relation between the diaspora and the homeland have changed considerably. The introduction of liberalization in India, the rise of the diaspora abroad, the increase of middle-class incomes in India, and their ability to consume the same sorts of technological and cultural goods available to their diasporic cousins have heightened the shared cultural context between urban India and Indians overseas. This process has been mediated through satellite television, through the renewed interest in film-going among diasporic audiences, and through the emergence of a vibrant diasporic South Asian youth culture in the United States and especially in England. Indian films have in their turn recognized this cultural convergence in the production of a new genre of films centered on the diasporic experience and an increased awareness of the economic strength of the Indian market abroad. These changes exhibit a relation between the diaspora and India that is not based on issues of nostalgia and pastness, where India and Indian films represent the repository of enduring cultural values threatened by the modernity of Western diaspora. As Manas Ray argues, the dichotomies of past and present, inside and outside, are beginning to lose their analytical purchase. Rather, the relation is now one of cultural convergence and contemporaneity in which Indians in New York, London, Sydney, and metropolitan centers such as Mumbai and Delhi are engaged in the production of a transnational diasporic culture.

The renewed success of Indian films in the diaspora is signified by the return of diasporic audiences to cinematic exhibition and the rise of Bombay films specifically oriented toward a diasporic audience. *Dilwale Duhaniya Le Jahenge* (Braveheart

Will Win the Bride, dir. Aditya Chopra) was one of the first films to include a character from the diaspora at the center of the film; its huge success prompted the producer Yash Chopra to establish his own distribution company in the United States and United Kingdom. This opening up of the overseas market entailed a reorganization of the infrastructural distribution of Indian film. In an interview with *Business World India*, Chopra said that previously blockbuster Indian films had to appeal to a range of class, caste, and regional tastes (October 23, 2001). Now, the opening up of the diaspora market meant that Chopra could perfect a genre of light romantic comedy that addressed a cosmopolitan urban audience without worrying about how the film would play in the Indian hinterland. These films presume a mobile viewing subject equally at home in Mumbai, London, or New York. Chopra's first film after the opening of this distribution company was the massive hit *Dil to Pagal Hai* (1997, dir. Yash Chopra), a film that Rachel Dwyer argues set a new cool, urban visual style for Hindi films (1999).

Indian films have always been hugely popular on video. But because video is limited to the domestic sphere, the popularity of Indian films in the diaspora has rarely impinged on the mass cineplex public. That, however, is beginning to change. As cineplex managers, particularly in Britain, realize that Indian films can outperform Hollywood at the box office, there has been a movement of Indian films out of the dilapidated "flea pits" of old and into the best facilities available. These are often new multiplexes showing a mix of American and Indian releases. Major new releases of Indian films in Britain now premier at the Odeon, Leicester Square, the most prestigious cinema in Britain and formerly the site only of American and British film premiers. In 2000, the hosts of the Film Fare Indian film awards used the Millennium Dome in Greenwich, London (Britain's homage to fin de siecle, spectacle) as the site for the first ever Indian film awards ceremony held outside of India, an event broadcast on mainstream British TV. This demonstrates how Indian film has migrated from the realm of the family, the domestic, and the marginal in British society to a much more public arena, carrying with it a palpable sense of cultural self-assertion and self-confidence.[2]

Bollywood without Indians

While diasporic Indian engagement with Bollywood is a significant and intensifying phenomenon, perhaps more striking is the long-standing popularity of Indian films with non-Indian audiences in Asia, the Middle East, Africa, and Europe. It is this reach across the boundaries of nation, language, culture, and religion that makes Hindi films true global media. By the 1950s, Indian films were beginning to be exported all across the socialist world and into much of the Third World as a whole. In Russia, Bulgaria, Poland, and elsewhere, as relations with the West settled into the structured estrangement of the Cold War, Indian films found favor with socialist states.

It is this same fantastic, extra-real engagement with Indian films that we see mobilized in the continuing popularity of Bollywood in Africa and the Middle East, where the films' popularity was established outside of any meaningful connection with India itself (with the notable exception of the substantial Indian populations in parts of East and South Africa). Work on Indian film in African studies has stressed the ways in which Indian films offer a space for imaginative play for African audiences in which melodrama, love, and even action constitute spaces of alterity free from both Western media and local generational and gender hierarchies. Fugelsang (1994) and Behrend (1998) both argue that in Lamu, Kenya, love relations depicted in Indian film offer youths a subversive alternative to the control of relationships by elder kin. This was an important element in my own study of Hausa love literature in northern Nigeria and the intertextual borrowing from Indian films (1997). I argued that the imaginative investment of Hausa viewers with Indian films comes about because of the possibilities of narrative as a means of allowing readers to explore imaginatively social tensions in multiple connotations. The mass culture of Indian films, Hausa love literature, or Hausa videos develop this process of ambiguity by presenting various resolutions to similar predicaments in thousands of narratives extending over many years. Indian films become an attractive site for this investment. The massive popularity of Indian films in northern Nigeria stems, in part, from their ability to offer Hausa viewers a "third space," a way of engaging with forms of tradition different from their own while at the same time conceiving of a modernity that comes without the political and ideological significance of that of the West.

The work of the Kenyan photographer Omar Said Bakor presented and explored by Behrend (see Behrend, 1998; Wendl and Behrend, 1999) is a spectacular example of this identification. Bakor, a Swahili of Yemeni descent living in Lamu Island off of Kenya, worked as a street photographer before opening his own studio in 1962. He developed a style of portrait photography involving the superimposition of Indian film actresses over portraits of local Lamu men. In one photograph the film star Sridevi is superimposed next to a young Lamu man who is reaching over to embrace her. Another portrait shows Sridevi reclining against what looks like the hills of Kashmir (notable as the setting for legions of love songs). Superimposed over her heart is the portrait of another Lamu man.

These portraits play with themes of presence and absence, desire and imagination, in which Bakor sutures the fantasy space of Indian film into the indexical reality of portrait photography. Behrend argues that in the strict Islamic society of Lamu, images of Swahili women were seen as illicit and so the genre of lovers having their pictures taken together never developed. In this absence, she suggests, fantasy images of female Indian stars acted as substitutes. If this is the case, this intensifies the play between transgression and conformity, where the technological medium of photography allows imaginative transgression through disembodied representation. Photographs sutured together represent a mixing of images, not bodies, preserving the Islamic separation of the sexes. This preservation occurs, however, only if one follows the letter of Islamic law. In Lamu, Islam is syncretically mixed with older forms of magical practice. Photographs are often used for magical purposes by people who wish to secure the love and affection of the person photographed (Behrend 1998; Fugelsang 1994). This magical use often depends on the indexical and iconic qualities of the photographic image that insist on *connection* between the representation and the represented. Under Islamic law montage works because it keeps the sexes separate physically while uniting them visually. Local practices of love magic threaten to transgress those boundaries where magic worked upon the image will have consequences on the person to whom the image is tied. Behrend makes the fascinating point that the portrait of a man's head superimposed over a reclining Sridevi also has another ghostly image. Superimposed over Sridevi, but underneath the image of the man is the spectral, hard-to-see image of a second, African woman. Behrend argues this suggests love magic and the mixing of a real with an ideal partner. Who can say? But the use of the photographic space to bring into one field love and transgression, the (mass) mediated and the spirit world, the local and the global, makes it a rich site of imagination and transgression.

In Nigeria, Indian films offer ways of being modern and traditional that create a template for exploring the tensions of postcoloniality. In the Indian diaspora, Bollywood can be both a conduit into an essentialized, traditional past and the site for the production of a hip, hybrid present. Indian films betray a love/hate relation with both the West and a mythic India and in doing so open up interstices in which heterogeneity and ambivalence flourish, allowing the films to be both Westernized and traditional; corruptor of local values and a defender of them. Vasudevan (2000) analyzes the ways Indian films create a politics of cultural difference by reinventing themselves to establish dialogue with and assert difference from universal models of narration and subjectivity. He analyzes these workings internally to India, but the same process operates on a global stage. Indian films travel because they become a foil against which postcolonial identity can be fashioned, critiqued, and debated. They allow an alterity to Hollywood domination but offer their own aggressive commercialism in its stead that is at the same time traditional and modern. The reasons for the global popularity of Indian films – crucial to the ability to map and understand the phenomenon of global popular media – lie in this interwoven process where Western media, Indian media, and local cultural production interact, at times coalescing and at other moments diverging.

Before I turn to the relation between Indian film and Nigerian Hausa videos, I first wish to make a brief detour in order to contextualize the rise of Nigerian videos in the past ten years and what this means for our understanding of that discursive construct "African cinema."

Nigerian Video Films and the End of African Cinema?

By *cinema* in this heading I refer not just to a body of films but to the critical cultural project that is inherent to the idea of African cinema (see Cham and Bakari, 1996; Diawara, 1992; Pines and Willemen, 1989; Ukadike, 1994). This is clear in the overt political and aesthetic project of "third cinema" (Pines and Willemen, 1989) but more important has informed state media policy and practice in many post-colonial nations. The concept of "national cinemas" derives from a legacy where the nation-state is posited as the definer and defender of cultural values (cf. Meyer, 1999). The Nigerian state sponsored "Nigerian" cinema to preserve "Nigerian" values, and so on. The video industry, by contrast, emerged outside of state partici-pation, frequently in opposition to it and driven largely by commercial rather than political motives.

In what is truly a remarkable cultural renaissance in Africa, in the past eight years or so a mass media genre – Nigerian video film – has come to dominate local media production and to become regionally hegemonic in exporting media to other nations in West and East Africa. Over 3,500 of these video films have been released in the general market. These "films," shot and released on video but known locally as films, can be broadly broken down into three main categories according to language (and culture): Yoruba, English, and Hausa (for an introduction, see Haynes, 2000). The appearance of these films is remarkable in that the industry developed outside of state or foreign support, in a time of intense economic deprivation and based wholly on a mass viewing audience.

These films nearly all exhibit the qualities that Vasudevan (2000) associates with the cinema of "transitional" societies negotiating the rapid effect of modernity: the cinematic address is to a world governed by kinship relations; the plot is driven by family conflict; melodrama predominates, relying on excess, Manicheanism, and privileging the moral over the psychological. In "Nigerian" videos, the term used to refer to English-language videos (as opposed to Hausa or Yoruba videos), this melodrama is intensified by the use of horror and the supernatural. Here magic mixes with the world economy, and capitalist accumulation is only possible through occult means. Husbands sacrifice their wives to become rich, mothers bewitch their children, and the devil, through his intermediaries, is ever present in Nigerian life. In dramatizing the work of witches and the prevalence of human sacrifice, video films move from the world of melodrama into the suspense and gore associated with horror. Nigerian films, in particular, are known for their special effects, as humans transform into animals, witches fly through the night, and money is magically produced (for similar issues in Ghanaian film, see Meyer, 2003). It is the mixing of melodrama with horror and magic and the linkage of financial with sexual and spiritual corruption that makes the melodrama of Nigerian and Ghanaian video film distinctively African. In contemporary postcolonial West Africa, where the everyday suffering of the vast majority stands in stark contrast to the fantastic accumulation of the small elite, the tropes of sorcery, witchcraft, and supernatural evil have provided a powerful way to express the inequalities of wealth.

African cultural heritage here is rarely represented as the valued cultural patrimony we are familiar with from the debates around African cinema. Rather it is frequently represented as evil, a place where the forces of darkness operate unchecked, a representation that is the outgrowth of the emergence of what Meyer has termed (in another context) a Pentecostalist public culture (Meyer, 2003; Marshall-Fratani, 1998; Ukah, 2000) in which styles of Pentecostalist discourse have proliferated in a variety of popular cultural forms. Nigerian videos address a cosmopolitan public in which the modern and the Pentecostalist, consumption and Christianity, are intertwined. The realist verities of modernist development and cultural authenticity are rejected, as is any attempt toward a progressive political project. These videos represent the working out of a specific form of Nigerian melodrama in a society that is both modern and sacred. Peter Brooks's argument that melodrama rises when the traditional hierarchies of a sacred society are dissolved captures the sense of spiritual insecurity and permanent transition that marks Nigerian melodrama, but God, the devil, and the supernatural are the everyday forms through which modernity emerges (on melodrama as a postcolonial project, see Abu-Lughod, 2002).

The rise of these videos highlights several ironies inherent in the concept of African cinema. African cinema, for instance, has tended to refer to the films Africans *produce* rather than those they *watch*. Films that travel under the sign of African cinema are still much more readily available in festivals in London, Paris, and New York, than they are in Abidjan, Lagos, or Mombasa. The calls by African filmmakers for a "popular" film practice glossed over the fact that this cinema referred first and foremost to an auteur artistic practice that rarely had to rely upon the marketplace or a mass audience for its funding and survival. This now stands in stark contrast to the rise of local video film industries in countries such as Ghana and Nigeria that, while accused of being much more "Westernized," are successful in an African marketplace. Video filmmakers have been much less concerned with ideas of cultural authenticity and cultural value. Most clearly, Nigerian videos have indeed fashioned aesthetic forms and modes of cultural address based on the experiences of the societies they address rather than those of the West – a prime concern of third cinema – but this fashioning has emerged not so much in opposition to Hollywood and Western cultural values, but *through* and *out* of the history of that engagement.

So far I have used the term *Nigerian videos* or *Nigerian film* without unpacking the regional hegemony that is built into this concept. As Jonathan Haynes (2000) has pointed out, the scholarly and film festival circuits that have deployed the concept of "African cinema" have found it extremely difficult to deal with the issue of ethnicity and of subnational difference. This is in part the legacy of the struggle against colonialism and, later, against a cultural imperialism that downplayed ethnic allegiance in favor of identification with the nation-state. In part, it also has to do with the history of cinema studies, which has tended to concentrate on the dynamics of national rather than ethnic cinemas. Nigerian videos, however, are divided into Yoruba-, English-, and Hausa-language films. The term *Nigerian films* in fact often refers to *English*-language films primarily made by Igbo and minority group producers who address their productions to a pan-Nigerian, English-speaking urban subject.[3] This means the claim to "Nigerianness" has been constructed through exclusions, as a specific form of urban culture and experience serves as the sole basis of a a pan-Nigerian address. This is an urbanism marked by fast-growing capitalism, consumption, Pentecostalist Christianity, the occult, temptation, and corruption, the central themes around which the abstraction of "national" cinema and national subject is constructed.

If these videos address a cosmopolitan "modern," urban subject, then Muslim Hausa are the internal other against which that modernity is imagined. Hausa cosmopolitanism, focused as it is on dynamics in the Muslim world more than in the West, is readily stigmatized as "backward," "traditional," and "ignorant," in southern Nigerian stereotypes. For Hausa viewers and Hausa filmmakers, the melodramatic form of southern Nigerian videos – their focus on sexual and magical excess, their unrelenting materialism, the frequent stereotyping of Pentecostalist pastors as culture heroes – makes these videos an ambivalent space for cultural imagining. As one Hausa video storeowner said to me, while he sold southern videos, he wouldn't allow his family to watch them. This is not to say that southern Nigerian videos are not popular in the north, where they do sell well, but the form, content, and even distribution of Hausa videos have developed along strikingly different lines. And it is here that Indian films have proved to be a powerful intertexual presence.

Hausa Video Films

While magic, materialism, and corruption are all present to a certain extent in Hausa video films, perhaps the primary narrative difference is the focus on love and romance and the spectacular development of this through song-and-dance routines (*waka da rawa* in Hausa) – a generic convention rarely seen in English-language videos. The focus on love comes about for a number of reasons. Most obviously, the first Hausa videos evolved from a literary genre of local Hausa-language love stories, *soyayya* books (see Furniss, 1996; Larkin, 1997). These became hugely popular among youth just at the time that the first Nigerian videos were being produced in the south of Nigeria. The first Hausa videos tended to be adaptations of these "best-selling" books and maintained their preoccupation with love. This tendency was intensified, however, by several producers who sought to make films that were explicitly *not* like southern Nigerian videos and were closer to Hausa culture. In this search for alterity producers fell back on familiar cultural forms that were separate from southern Nigeria: *soyayya* books and Indian films.

Indian Films and Hausa Viewers

First imported by Lebanese cinema owners in the 1950s, by the early 1960s Indian films were, perhaps, the dominant film form in the north.[4] Since that time Indian films have remained an integral part of the Nigerian media landscape and form the everyday media environment through which people move. Stickers of Indian stars emblazon trucks, cars, and bikes of the north. Popular stars are given Hausa nicknames, such as *Sarkin Rawa* (King of Dancing) for Govinda, or *Dan daba mai lasin* (licensed hooligan – in the same way that James Bond is licensed to kill). Indian jewelry and clothing have influenced Hausa fashions and Indian film songs and stories have penetrated everyday Hausa popular culture (see Larkin, 1997).

In northern Nigeria there is a familiar refrain that Indian culture is "just like" Hausa culture. While indeed, there are many similarities between Hausa and "Indian culture" (at least how it is represented in Indian films) there are many differences, most obviously the fact that Indians are predominantly Hindu and Hausa are Muslim. The popularity of Indian films rests, in part, on this dialectic between difference and sameness – that Indian culture is both like and quite unlike Hausa culture. It is the gap between difference and sameness, the ability to move between the two, that allows Indian films to function as a space for imaginative play in Hausa society. The intra–Third World circulation of Indian film offers Hausa viewers a way of imaginatively engaging with forms of tradition different from their own at the same time as conceiving of a modernity that comes without the political and ideological significance of that of the West. Moreover, when Hausa youth rework Indian films within their own culture by adopting Indian fashions, by copying the music styles for religious purposes, or by using the filmic world of Indian sexual relations to probe the limitations within their own cultural world, they can do this without engaging with the heavy ideological load of "becoming Western."

The sense of similarity and difference is produced by the iconography and mode of address of the films themselves as well as by the ways in which Bollywood deploys a reified "culture" that acts as a foil against which Westernization in its myriad forms can be defined. Bollywood films place family and kinship at the center of narrative tension. Traditional dress is remarkably similar to that of Hausa: men dress in long kaftans similar to the Hausa *dogon riga* over which they wear long waistcoats much like the Hausa *palmaran*. Women dress in long sarees and scarves that veil their heads in accordance with Hausa moral ideas about feminine decorum. Indian films, particularly older films, express strict division between the sexes and between generations. Hausa audiences are not familiar with the main tropes of Indian religion, but they realize that the visual portrayal of Hindu religion and Indian tradition provides a cultural field that is frequently opposed to the spread of "Westernization" or modernity. It is this reified sense of tradition that Hausa refer to when they say that they "have culture" in a way that American films seem to lack. Britain and America are the structuring absences here and form the Other(s) against which Hausa can define their relation to Indian culture as similar. Hausa recognize the similarity in traditional dress; more, they realize the relational value of how one wears traditional dress. When characters code-switch from English to Hindi, when they elect to wear Western instead of Indian clothes, when they refuse to obey parents and follow their own desires, Indian films create a narrative in which action is based on moral choice. Ashis Nandy recognizes a communal mode of address in this moral choice in Indian film, arguing that commercial Indian cinema tends to "reaffirm the values that are being increasingly marginalized in public life by the language of the modernizing middle classes, values such as community ties, consensual non-contractual human relations, primacy of maternity over conjugality, priority of the mythic over the historical" (1995, p. 202). In short, the battle is against the values associated with Westernization.

It is the discourse around love, especially the tensions between arranged and love marriages, that has most influenced Hausa viewers. Indian films provide Hausa youth with an alternative style of sexual interaction, a different pattern of speech and bodily affect between the sexes. As these patterns of behavior have migrated to Hausa videos, the effect has been exhilarating. This migration is, of course, a matter of translation and accommodation and not merely copying. Like Indian films themselves, the act of borrowing plots, dance style, or visual effects entails detailed processes of rejection and addition, a stripping of superfluous detail and insertion of culturally relevant matter. Jeremy Tunstall's (1977) argument that Indian films were a dream factory locally assembling dreams manufactured 10,000 miles away (in America) has recently been decisively countered by the work of Tejaswini Ganti, who traces the transformations of narrative and form that go into the "copying" of an American film by an Indian one (Ganti, 2002). In the next section, I turn to this work of translation in the Hausa context, tracing the global flow of Indian film to Nigeria through the adoption of themes of love and song and dance sequences in Hausa video, concentrating on a transitional video, *In da So Da K'auna* (The Soul of My Heart, 1994) by the author/producer/director Ado Ahmad.

The introduction of new media forms always brings with it moments of ambivalence as the potential possibilities of the medium have to be reconciled within existing social and cultural norms. *In da* is a fascinating example of this ambivalence, especially when compared to the subsequent evolution of Hausa films. When *In da* was released in 1994, it was one of about four or five Hausa videos (there are less then ten Hausa feature films). In contrast, in 1999 alone, 125 Hausa videos were released in the market. *In da* inaugurates a new cultural form in a society where previously none existed, and introduces visual and narrative themes that have strong overlaps with Indian films. But because it is an innovation it foregrounds an uncertainty about how these themes should be handled and what the reception of this new form will be. *In da* treads delicately over themes that later videos represent unproblematically and is interesting because it is a transitional video that reveals the cultural *work* that goes into the process of cultural translation.

In da So Da K'auna

In da is set among the world of the urban elite in Kano, Nigeria. It follows the relationship between a rich girl, Sumayya (Ruk'ayya Mohammed), and a poor man, Mohammed. The theme of love and the sexual precociousness of the heroine signify the intertextual presence of Indian film. Sumayya initiates contact and pursues Mohammad, against his admonitions that their difference in status can never be overcome. In reality, as director Ahmad told me in an interview,[5] Hausa women are expected to be sexually modest, and such an open pursuit would be socially unacceptable. His dilemma as a director was how to invoke the desire and romance of Hindi cinema, while at the same time preserving a Hausa moral universe. The film treads delicately through the rituals of courtship in ways that seem unimaginable when compared to contemporary videos.

In one of the central scenes of the film, Mohammed declares his love for Sumayya. Until this point he had resisted her advances, wary of the gulf between them in terms of wealth and status. The scene consists of a series of parallel edits between the two. It opens with the lovers separated in space and time. Mohammed is in his dormitory at school; Sumayya is in her bedroom writing a letter to Mohammed. Music plays in the background as Sumayya writes. As the film cuts to Mohammed reading her letter, the same music continues to play, linking the lovers across the rupture of space and time. As the scene continues, Mohammed writes back. Their experience of each other is mediated by writing. The scene heightens when, as Sumayya receives her letter from Mohammed, his face is superimposed over the letter. As his voice-over reads the contents, the camera zooms in on Sumayya and his face appears again, superimposed over an extreme close-up of Sumayya.

Ahmad here preserves sexual segregation in the diagetic space of the film. While Mohammed's body is absent from Sumayya's room, his physical presence is made manifest through his voice and his superimposed face, permitting the lovers to share the same cinematic frame. This is a careful game that allows Ahmad to allude to the intimacy and sexual interaction familiar to Hausa viewers from Indian films while keeping its sexual excess safely separate. Ahmad repeats this narrative device frequently in the film, separating lovers in space and establishing that separation through a series of parallel edits and the a mediating device – a letter, a tape, or even dreams – to create a space for the lovers to unite through sound and montage.

The bedroom is a key space here. Sumayya first spies Mohammed as she passes him sitting outside with a group of friends. This is a male activity forbidden to Hausa women, especially wealthy ones, who are expected to remain inside the domestic space. Sumayya is narratively identified with her bedroom: this is where she writes her letter to Mohammed telling him she loves him; it is where she plays his tapes and where she returns to and listens to them after (later in the film) he tells her they should separate. Spatially and visually, then, Sumayya stays where a proper Hausa woman should be, restricted to the interior space of the house where men rarely are allowed to visit. It is only the fantasy of the film that allows her to move out of that space.

Visually these scenes are marked by restriction and immobility. In the song sequence I described in the introduction and in the scene where Sumayya first reads Mohammed's letter Sumayya is confined by both her bedroom and by the extreme close-up on her unmoving face. This restricted consummation of love is in stark contrast to the kinetic freedom of the dancing in Indian films. Here, the Hausa film stays within the bounds of cultural realism, adopting moral and bodily codes of Hausa expression, yet it always threatens to transgress that boundary with its constant mimetic reference to a fantasy world outside of local Hausa norms. This transgression was noted frequently by a group of young Hausa friends I watched the films with. The muted, minimalist nature of the love scenes seemed, to me, to bear little relation to the excess of Indian films, but for them the song scene was hilarious and immediately seemed culturally false. "Indian song!" one friend shouted as the scene began, "How can someone sing songs to a woman?" he asked in amused disgust.[6] Hausa viewers know that a sequence such as this, or scenes in which couples openly declare their love for each other or even spending unchaperoned time together, go against the conventions of Hausa sexual interaction. For them, such scenes are obviously derived from the style of courtship in Indian films.

In da, in its emphasis on love and relationships, and on the spectacular use of song-and-dance sequences, represents an early attempt at what is rapidly becoming an elaborate genre in Hausa cultural life. In contemporary films, song-and-dance sequences are common and few betray the cultural and religious delicacy of this transitional film. To take one example, the film *Daskin da Ridi* (dir. Aminu Mohd. Sabo) includes a love song sequence between Indo (Hauwa Ali Dodo) and her lover Yarima (Nasir Ismail). The song sequence opens with a medium shot of the couple splashing each other at a lakeside. It then cuts to them holding hands and running toward the camera and then, cutting again, to the two of them, still holding hands, running up a small hill. Still in medium shot, they begin to dance and sing to each other. As the sequence progresses, Indo dances away from Yarima. He follows, chasing her playfully, and they splash each other again. Here the use of Indian film style is blatant and unashamed: the lovers change clothes frequently during the song sequence; Indo sings in a high-pitched voice more reminiscent of the famous Indian playback singer Lata Mangeshkar than of a Hausa singer,[7] and the teasing, playful chasing is associated strongly with Hindi film.[8] The difference from Ahmad's delicate balancing act seems immense. When Ahmad adapted *In Da* from his book he changed one of the scenes so that Sumayya *dropped* a ring into Mohammed's hand rather than putting it on his finger as she did in the book. Unsure if Hausa audiences would tolerate physical contact of any kind, he developed a style that allowed sharing of filmic space while preserving strict physical separation.[9] In contrast, instead of being separated in space and time, nearly the entire *Daskin* sequence is filmed as a two-shot with both lovers constantly present in the frame.

In da and *Daskin* are revelatory of the deep intertextual influence that Indian films have had on the evolution of Hausa video film form. As I suggested elsewhere (Larkin, 1997), this influence has emerged because Indian films are useful repositories for Hausa audiences to engage with deeply felt tensions over the nature of individual freedom and familial responsibility, providing a safe imaginative space outside of the politicized contexts of western and southern Nigerian media. Indian films work for Hausa because they rest on a dialectic of presence and absence culturally similar to Hausa society but at the same time reassuringly distant. These films have allowed Hausa filmmakers to develop a genre of video films that are strikingly different from those of their southern Nigerian compatriots. This is not to say that the success of Hausa videos does not generate its own controversy. The engagement of Hausa with Indian films involves a sort of mimicry that carries with it the ambivalence of border crossing. As Hausa videos have boomed so has criticism of their cultural borrowing, leading in 2001 to a state ban on mixed-gender song sequences.[10] Interestingly the intense criticism has not focused on Indian films (which are unaffected by any censorship) but on the Hausa written and visual forms that are accused of translating their themes into Hausa social life.

Conclusion

Contemporary Indian film theorists have insisted on the "Indianness" of Hindi film. Chakravarty (1993) has elaborated on structuralist film theory to argue that Hindi film has developed a "communal" mode of address that interpellates an individual spectator as part of a wider national or religious community rather than as an isolated viewer. Vasudevan (1993, 2000) and others have examined the concept of the "darsanic" mode of vision enacted in Indian film. They argue that the formal construction of filmic meaning depends upon mobilizing extra-filmic cultural and ritual modes of knowledge in the (Indian) audience – at least in certain genres. These arguments emerge from the long-standing struggle against cultural imperialism and a desire to establish the cultural logics of a film form not totally subsumed by the Hollywood narrative and form. Studies of non-Western film therefore derived from the need to explicate the alterity and particularity of national cinemas partly, as Willemen has argued, to resist the "projective, universalizing, appropriation" that situates the Western experience of media as the model for the rest of the world (Willemen, 1991, p. 56; see also Shohat and Stam, 1994).

Similarly, in this essay, I have sought to decenter the Western experience of media, not by insisting on the alterity of Nigerian video but on its thoroughgoing intertextuality. At the same time, I have tried to place the historical and geographic spread of Hindi films at the center of an analysis of global media, rather than on the margins of a theory centered around Hollywood and the West (for a similar argument, see Ginsburg et al., 2002). Timothy Mitchell has recently argued that modernization continues to be commonly understood as a process begun and finished in Europe, that to be modern is to take part in a history defined by the West and against which "all other histories must establish their significance" (2000, p. 6). The privileging of Western media as the only "global" media has had a similar effect, downplaying the social significance of other long-standing global flows. By highlighting the global flow of Indian films, I do not mean to downplay the cultural and financial hegemony of Western media, especially since Indian films travel, in part, precisely because they counter Western media. I do want to suggest, however, that we must shift our focus to analyze the cultural flows of goods that do not necessarily have the West at their center.

The reasons Indian films travel and have traveled are diverse, evolving, and culturally specific. While southern Nigerians cite the popularity of Indian films among Hausa audiences as evidence of the northerners' "backwardness,"[11] for young British Asians sampling dance beats with Hindi film tunes, Indian films can be the source of a hip hybrid modernity (Sharma et al., 1997). Analyzing Indian films as global media entails revising the ways in which media scholars have tended to conceptualize national and transnational media. It necessitates revising our concept of African cinema to understand Indian films as part of *African* media. Similarly, the excellent work on the cultural particularity of Indian cinema, specifying the *Indianness* of Indian cinema, only goes partway in helping us to understand the phenomenal popularity of Hindi films in cultures, religions, and nations whose grasp of Indian and Hindu realities is weak. Central to this project should be the acceptance of diverse media environments in which audiences engage with heterogeneous cultural forms. Hausa youth, who listen to fundamentalist Islamic preaching, admire Steven Seagal, are captivated by the love tribulations of Salman Khan, and are voraciously consuming emerging Nigerian videos are part of a post-colonial media environment in which the Western domination is only a partial and contingent facet of global media flow.

NOTES

1   In recognition of local Hausa usage, I will use *Indian film* interchangeably with the more specific term *Hindi film* in this essay.
2   When the film *Taal* (dir, Subhash Ghai) was released in the United States in 1999, it entered the *Variety* list of the top grossing American films at number 20. The New York/New Jersey-based *Asian Variety Show* that caters to the South Asian population announced the news with the title: "Bollywood invades Hollywood." A few months later,

when *Hum Saath Saath Hain* (dir. Sooraj Barjatya) was one of the top grossing English films, the London *Times* reported, "Bollywood knocking Hollywood for six" (November 20, 1999).

3   It may be that the term *Nigerian* video came about from the popularity of English-language videos *outside* Nigeria in countries such as Ghana and Kenya.

4   To give an example, in May 1962, 33 Indian films were screened in Kano, the main city of northern Nigeria. This compared to 21 American films and 3 English ones. In June the numbers were 32 Indian, 23 American, and 1 English. In July there were 30 Indian films, 19 American, and 3 English (figures taken from the *Daily Comet, Kano*). Until the rise of Hausa Indian films videos were shown 5 nights a week on Kano screens compared to 1 night for American and 1 night for Hong Kong films.

5   Interview with Ado Ahmad, July 1996.

6   This is ironic give that only a few years later Hausa video films became famous precisely because of men singing love songs.

7   The credits for the video include listings of "Play Back Singers" (Fati Abubakar is the female singer) and "Music Director."

8   The radical novelty of this mode of romance was brought home to me during a discussion with an older Hausa (male) friend. He said that, as a youth in the 1970s, he went to see many Indian films at a time when they were mainly restricted to the cinema and thus to men. He said this caused problems when he got married, as in Indian films women openly declare their love for their partners and are passionate in their relations. In the 1970s, he continued, Hausa men were expecting, or wanting, this behavior from their wives but when he got married his wife, acting with the modesty that a "proper" Hausa wife should have, was initially reluctant to talk with him, or even spend much time with him alone, creating disappointment and friction in the relationship. He saw the problem lying in the fact he wanted the relationships he was used to in Indian films, but that this sort of relationship could not be realized within traditional Hausa gender relations.

9   Ibid.

10   For three months all filmmaking was prohibited., After intensive lobbying by the film industry, filmmaking was resumed but placed under the control of a new censorship board.

11   This was a common observation made to me by southerners living in northern Nigeria. They emphasized their participation in Western culture and especially what Gilroy calls a "black atlantic" world, listening to rappers like Tupac Shakur and Puff Daddy and watching Hollywood films. For them, Indian films were a marker of temporality, an index of marginalization from a history that is centered around the West. Abadzi makes the similar point when she argues that the popularity of Indian films waned in Greece at the moment during the 1960s when Greeks wished to emphasize their Westernness and their distance from the Eastern heritage.

REFERENCES

Abadzi, Helen. "Hindi Films of the 50s in Greece: The Latest Chapter of a Long Dialogue." http://www.sangeetmahal.com/journal_hindi_films_greece.asp.

Abadzi, Helen, and Emmanuel Tasoulas. *Indoprepon Apokalypsi* (Hindi-style Songs Revealed). Athens: Atrapos, 1998.

Abu-Lughod, Lila. "Egyptian Melodrama, Technology of the Modern Subject?" In *Media Worlds: Anthropology on New Terrain*, ed. Faye Ginsburg, Lila Abu-Lughod, and Brian Larkin. Berkeley: University of California Press, 2002.

Armbrust, Walter. "When the Lights Go Down in Cairo: Cinema as Secular Ritual." *Visual Anthropology* 10, no. 2–4 (1995).

Behrend, Heike "Love à La Hollywood and Bombay in Kenyan Studio Photography." *Paideuma* 44 (1998): 139–153.

Chakravarty, Sumita. *National Ideology in Indian Popular Cinema 1947–1987*. Austin: University of Texas Press, 1993.

Cham, Mbye. "Introduction." In *African Experiences of Cinema*, ed. Imruh Bakari and Mbaye Cham, pp. 1–14. London: BFI, 1996.

Cham, Mbye, and Imruh Bakari. *African Experiences of Cinema*. London: BFI, 1996.

Dhondy, Farukh. "Keeping Faith: Indian Film and its World." *Daedalus* 114, no. 4 (1985): 125–40.

Diawara, Manthia. *African Cinema: Politics and Culture*. Bloomington: Indiana University Press, 1992.

Dwyer, Rachel. *All You Want is Money, All You Need is Love*. London: Cassell, 1999.

Eck, Diana L. *Darsan: Seeing the Divine Image in India*. New York: Columbia University Press, 1998.

Fugelsang, Minou. *Veils and Videos: Female Youth Culture on the Kenyan Coast*. Stockholm: Studies in Social Anthropology, 1994.

Furniss, Graham. *Poetry, Prose and Popular Culture in Hausa*. Edinburgh: Edinburgh University Press, 1996.

Ganti, Tejaswini. "The (H)Indianization of Hollywood by the Bombay Film Industry." In *Media Worlds: Anthropology on New Terrain*, ed. Faye Ginsburg, Lila Abu-Lughod, and Brian Larkin. Berkeley: University of California Press, 2002.

Gillespie, Maria. "Sacred Serats, Devotional Viewing, and Domestic Worship: A Case Study of Two TV Versions of *The Mahabarata* in a Hindu Family in West Lond." In *Soap Operas Around the World*, ed. Robert C. Allen. London: Routledge, 1995.

Ginsburg, Faye, Lila Abu-Lughod, and Brian Larkin, eds. *Media Worlds: Anthropology on New Terrain*. Berkeley: University of California Press, 2002.

Haynes, Jonathan. *Nigerian Video Films*. Athens: Ohio University Press, 2000.

Larkin, Brian. "Indian Films and Nigerian Lovers: Love Stories, Electronic Media and the Creation of Parallel Modernities." *Africa* 67, no. 3 (1997): 406–440.

Marshall-Fratani, Ruth. "Mediating the Global and the Local in Nigerian Pentecostalism." *Journal of Religion in Africa* 28, no. 3 (1998): 278–315.

Meyer, Birgit. "Popular Ghanaian Cinema and 'African Heritage.'" *Africa Today* 46, no. 2 (1999): 93–114.

——. "Ghanaian Popular Cinema and the Magic in and of Film." In *Magic and Modernity: Interfaces of Revelation and Concealment*, ed. B. Meyer and P. Pels. Stanford: Stanford University Press, 2003.

Mitchell, Timothy. "The Stage of Modernity." In *Questions of Modernity*, ed. Timothy Mitchell. Minneapolis: University of Minnesota Press, 2000.

Nandy, Ashis. *The Savage Freud: And Other Essays on Possible and Retrievable Selves*. Princeton: Princeton University Press, 1995.

Pendakur, Manjunath, and Radha Subramanyam. "Indian Cinema Beyond National Borders." In *New Patterns in Global Television: Peripheral Vision*, ed. John Sinclair, Elizabeth Jacka, and Stuart Cunningham, pp. 67–82. Oxford: Oxford University Press, 1996.

Pines, Jim, and Paul Willemen, eds. *Questions of Third Cinema*. London: British Film Institute, 1989.

Ray, Manas. "Bollywood Down Under: Fiji Indian Cultural History and Popular Assertion." In *Floating Lives: The Media and Asian Diasporas*, ed. Stuart Cunningham and John Sinclair. Queensland: University of Queensland Press, 2000.

Sardar, Ziauddin. "Dilip Kumar Made Me Do It." In *The Secret Politics of Our Desires: Innocence, Culpability and Indian Popular Cinema*, ed. Ashis Nandy. London: Zed Books, 1998

Sharma, S. A. Sharma, and J. Hutnyk. *Disorienting Rhythms: The Politics of the New Asian Dance Music*. London: Zed Books, 1997.

Sheme, Ibrahim. "Zagon Kasar da Finfanan Indiya Ke Yi Wa Al'Adunmu" (The Danger of Indian Films to Our Culture.) *Gaskiya Ta Fi Kwabo* May 15, 1995, p. 5.

Shohat, Ella, and Robert Stam. *Unthinking Eurocentrism: Multiculturalism and the Media*. London: Routledge, 1994.

Tunstall, Jeremy. *The Media Are American: Anglo-American Media in the World*. London: Constable, 1977.

Tyrell, Heather. "Bollywood in Britain." *Sight and Sound* (1998): 20–22.

Ukadike, Nwachukwu Frank. *Black African Cinema*. Berkeley: University of California Press, 1994.

Ukah, Asonzeh F-K. "Advertising God: Nigerian (Christian) Video Films and the Power of Consumer Culture." Paper delivered to the Consultation on Religion and Media in Africa, held at Ghana Institute of Management and Public Administration (GIMPA), Greenhill, Accra, Ghana, May 20–27, 2000.

Vasudevan, Ravi. "Shifting Codes, Dissolving Identities: The Hindi Social Film of the 1950s as Popular Culture." *Journal of Arts and Ideas* 23/24 (January 1993).

——. "The Political Culture of Address in a Transitional Cinema." In *Reinventing Film Studies*, ed. Christine Gledhill and Linda Williams, pp. 130–162. Oxford: Oxford University Press, 2000.

Wendl, Tobias, and Heike Behrend. *Snap Me One! Studiofotografen in Afrika*. Munich: Prestel Books, 1999.

Willemen, Paul. "Negotiating the Transition to Capitalism: The Case of *Andaz*." *East-West Film Journal* 5 no. 1 (1991): 56–66.

15

The New Digital Media and Activist Networking within Anti-Corporate Globalization Movements

Jeffrey S. Juris

Following a second day of street battles and police riots on July 21, 2001, at the anti-G8 protests in Genoa, I walked over to the media center at around 8 p.m. together with my Catalan friends to catch up on the latest news. The *Caribinieri* (Italian police) had just attacked a peaceful march of nearly three hundred thousand demonstrators who had come together to challenge corporate globalization and denounce the murder of a young Italian activist killed the previous day. The center was teaming with protesters when we arrived, writing e-mails, conducting interviews, and posting audio and video clips. Pau, from the Catalan Movement for Global Resistance (MRG),[1] was still connected to the Internet via laptop sending out real-time updates, as he had been the entire week. He told us the buses would be leaving for Barcelona shortly, but I had planned to stay in Genoa for a few more days to take part in antirepression actions together with the Pink & Silver Bloc. Indeed, we had spent much of our time during the past two days running from baton charges and tear gas. Fortunately, protesters shot reams of digital footage documenting police abuses, which were compiled, edited, and uploaded at the Independent Media Center (IMC) on the floor above.

After the meeting, I went back to the computer lab to inform my Catalan friends that I had decided to stay. All of a sudden, we heard a terrible commotion in the streets, followed by loud banging on the media center gate out front. Several activists

From *The Annals of the American Academy* 597(January): 189–208. Copyright © 2005, *AAPSS*.

charged into the main room screaming, "Police, police!" Concerned about my pictures and field notes, I immediately grabbed my backpack and dragged it up to the fourth floor, where people were frantically running back and forth. As I wandered the hallway, two American direct action veterans threw me a sleeping bag and led me up to an empty room, where we hid under a table. As we waited in the dark, helicopters flew overhead, while the police began smashing computers and accessories at the IMC below. An Italian officer eventually entered the room and brought us to a second-floor corridor where police held us with roughly thirty others for nearly half an hour. Although dozens of activists were viciously beaten at the Diaz School across the way, the police left the media center as soon as they had destroyed large quantities of hardware and documentation. I was still somewhat rattled, so I ultimately decided to head back to Barcelona, joining a group of Catalans who had called for a taxi to bring them to a meeting point on the outskirts of town.

This anecdote suggests that government and police officials view Indymedia as a major threat. Indeed, there have been other similar incidents, though perhaps none so extreme. During the anti–Free Trade Area of the Americas (FTAA) protest in Quebec City in April 2001, for example, FBI agents appeared at the Seattle IMC demanding names and e-mail addresses of everyone who had visited the site during the previous two days. The following year, Spanish authorities monitored and tried to shut down several activist Web sites, including Indymedia, prior to the mobilization against the European Union (EU) in Barcelona. Finally, during November 2002, the police broke into IMCs throughout Italy after the European Social Forum in Florence. Riot cops have also repeatedly attacked media activists during protests, often leading to wider crackdowns. For example, at the beginning of a mobile street theater action during the anti-EU mobilization in Barcelona in March 2002, the police charged a group of video activists and then unsuccessfully tried to surround the larger crowd. The French police used a similar strategy with greater success to break up an immigrant rights action during a European No Border camp the following July.

The question thus arises as to why the forces of law and order specifically target media activists before, during, and after mass mobilizations? More generally, why do they consider independent media so threatening? On one hand, over the past few years Indymedia and other digital networks have helped mobilize hundreds of thousands of anti-corporate globalization[2] protesters around the world, while creating radical social movement publics for the circulation of alternative news and information. Clamping down on grassroots forms of media production, communication, and coordination thus has a practical effect. On the other hand, media activism and digital networking more generally are among the most important features of contemporary anti-corporate globalization movements, generating what Waterman (1998) has referred to as a "communications internationalism." Police are not only interested in collecting information and destroying evidence. Such attacks are also meant to intimidate, sending real-time shock waves through global activist networks, while targeting their most important symbolic expressions.

By significantly enhancing the speed, flexibility, and global reach of information flows, allowing for communication at a distance in real time, digital networks provide the technological infrastructure for the emergence of contemporary network-based social movement forms (cf. Arquilla and Ronfeldt 2001; Bennett 2003a, 2003b; Castells 1997; Cleaver 1995, 1999; Escobar 2004; Lins Ribeiro 1998). Regarding social networks more generally, Barry Wellman (2001) has argued that "computer-supported social networks" (CSSN) are profoundly transforming the nature of communities, sociality, and interpersonal relations. Although the prolifer-ation of increasingly individualized, loosely bounded, and fragmentary community networks predates cyberspace, computer-mediated communications have reinforced such trends, allowing communities to sustain interactions across vast distances.

The Internet is also being incorporated into more routine aspects of daily social life, as virtual and physical activities become increasingly integrated (Miller and Slater 2000; Wellman 2001; Wellman and Haythornthwaite 2002). Despite the shrinking yet still formidable digital divide, the Internet facilitates global connectedness, even as it strengthens local ties within neighborhoods and house-holds, leading to increasing "Glocalization" (Wellman 2001, 236; cf. Robertson 1995). Similar trends can also be detected at the level of political activity, where Internet use – including e-mail lists, interactive Web pages, and chat rooms – has facilitated new patterns of social engagement. Anti-corporate globalization movements thus belong to a particular class of CSSN: *computer-supported social movements*. Using the Internet as techno-logical architecture, such movements operate at local, regional, and global levels, while activists move back and forth between online and offline political activity.

The horizontal networking logic facilitated by new digital technologies not only provides an effective method of social movement organizing, it also represents a broader model for creating alternative forms of social, political, and economic organization. For example, many activists specifically view the open source devel-opment process – where geographically dispersed computer programmers freely improve, adapt, and distribute new versions of software code through global com-munication networks – as potentially applicable within wider social spheres.[3] As Steven Weber (2004) suggests, open source could potentially revolutionize produc-tion within other information-based sectors, such as primary care medicine or genomics. Although Weber maintains a strict definition of open source as involving only those processes that entail a new conception of property as the right to distribute, not the right to exclude, many activists view open source as a broader metaphor (cf. Lovink 2003, 195), which might one day inspire postcapitalist forms of political and social organization at local, regional, and global scales.

This article examines the innovative ways that anti-corporate globalization activ-ists have used new digital technologies to coordinate actions, build networks, practice media activism, and physically manifest their emerging political ideals. Since the protests against the World Trade Organization (WTO) in Seattle, and through subsequent mobilizations against multilateral institutions and forums in Prague, Quebec, Genoa, Barcelona, Porto Alegre, and other cities, activists have used e-mail lists, Web pages, and open editing software to organize actions, share information, collectively produce documents, and coordinate at a distance, reflect-ing a general growth in digital collaboration. Indymedia has provided an online forum for autonomously posting audio, video, and text files, while activists have also created temporary media hubs to generate alternative information, experiment with new technologies, and exchange ideas and resources. Influenced by anarchism and the logic of peer-to-peer networking, more radical anti-corporate globalization activists have thus not only incorporated new digital technologies as concrete networking tools, they have also used them to express alternative political imaginaries based on an emerging network ideal.

I have elsewhere explored the emergence of what I call the "cultural logic of networking" among anti-corporate globalization activists, or the broad guiding principles, shaped by the logic of informational capitalism, which are internalized by activists and generate concrete networking practices (Juris 2004).[4] This cultural logic specifically entails a series of deeply embedded and embodied social and cultural dispositions that orient actors toward (1) building horizontal ties and connections among diverse, autonomous elements; (2) the free and open circulation of information; (3) collaboration through decentralized coordination and directly democratic decision making; and (4) self-directed networking. It thus not only reflects the values associated with open source development, incorporated within GNU/Linux or the World Wide Web, it also forms part of a broader "Hacker Ethic" identified by Himanen (2001).[5]

This article is based on fourteen months of ethnographic research among Barcelona-based anti-corporate globalization activists, within Catalonia and the broader circuits through which they travel.[6] Specifically, I conducted participant observation during mass actions and gatherings in cities such as Barcelona, Genoa, Brussels, Leiden, Strasbourg, and Porto Alegre, and within sustained networking processes as a member of MRG's international working group. My research strategy thus involved situating myself within a specific node and following the transnational connections outward through virtual and physical formations, including Peoples Global Action (PGA) and the World Social Forum (WSF) process.[7] I had also carried out prior ethnographic research in Prague, Seattle, and among U.S.-based activist networks. My fieldwork was thus multisited but also rooted within specific network locales, constituting an example of what Burawoy (2000) calls a "grounded globalization," while affording me a strategic position from which to observe local, regional, and global networking practices. Finally, I also conducted qualitative interviews, media, and textual analysis as a complement to participant observation.

This article begins with an introduction to anti-corporate globalization movements and then continues with an exploration of how contemporary activists are appropriating new digital technologies as concrete networking tools. Next, I turn to the relationship between the Internet, decentralized network forms, and the cultural logic and politics of activist networking, with a specific emphasis on Spain and Catalonia. I then examine the new media activism, including independent media, culture jamming, and electronic civil disobedience. Finally, I conclude with some reflections about how new digital technologies and horizontal networking practices are generating new models of horizontal production and globally networked democracy.

The Rise of Anti-Corporate Globalization Movements

Nearly fifty thousand people took to the streets to protest corporate globalization at the WTO meetings in Seattle on November 30, 1999. A diverse coalition of environmental, labor, and economic justice activists succeeded in shutting down the meetings and preventing another round of trade liberalization talks. Media images of giant puppets, tear gas, and street clashes between protesters and the police were broadcast worldwide, bringing the WTO and a novel form of collective action into view. Seattle became a symbol and battle cry for a new generation of activists, as anti-globalization networks were energized around the globe.

On one hand, the "Battle of Seattle," packaged as a prime-time image event (Deluca 1999), cascaded through global mediascapes (Appadurai 1996), capturing the imagination of long-time activists and would-be postmodern revolutionaries alike. On the other hand, activists followed the events in Seattle and beyond through Internet-based distribution lists, Web sites, and the newly created IMC. New networks quickly emerged, such as the Continental Direct Action Network (DAN) in North America,[8] or MRG in Catalonia, while already existing global networks such as PGA, ATTAC, or Via Campesina also played crucial roles during these early formative stages. Although more diffuse, decentralized all-channel formations (Arquilla and Ronfeldt 2001), such as DAN or MRG, proved difficult to sustain over time, they provided concrete mechanisms for generating physical and virtual communication and coordination in real time among diverse movements, groups, and collectives.

Anti-corporate globalization movements have largely grown and expanded through the organization of mass mobilizations, including highly confrontational direct actions and countersummit forums against multilateral institutions. The anti-WTO protests were a huge success, and everywhere activists wanted to create the "next Seattle." Mass mobilizations offer concrete goals around which to organize, while they also provide physical spaces where activists meet, virtual networks are embodied, meanings and representations are produced and contested, and political values are ritually enacted. Public events can broadly be seen as "culturally constituted foci for information-processing" (Handelman 1990, 16), while direct actions, in particular, generate intense emotional energy (Collins 2001), stimulating ongoing networking within public and submerged spheres. Activists organized a second mass protest against the World Bank and International Monetary Fund (IMF) in Washington, D.C., on April 16, 2000, and went truly global during the subsequent mobilization against the World Bank/IMF in Prague on September 26, 2000. Protesters came from countries around Europe, such as Spain, Italy, Germany, and Britain, and other parts of the world, including the United States, Latin America, and South Asia. Solidarity actions were held in cities throughout Europe, North and South America, and parts of Asia and Africa.

The first WSF, organized in Porto Alegre, Brazil, in late January 2001, represented an important turning point, as activists began to more clearly emphasize specific alternatives. The success of the first WSF was magnified during the next two editions, which drew seventy thousand and one hundred thousand people, respectively. More than a conference, the WSF constitutes a dynamic process involving the convergence of multiple networks, movements, and organizations. Whereas PGA remains more radical, horizontal, and broadly libertarian,[9] the WSF is a wider political space, including both newer decentralized network-based movements and more hierarchical forces of the traditional Left. Meanwhile, mass actions continued to intensify and expand during spring and summer 2001, including the anti-FTAA protests in Quebec City and increasingly militant actions against the EU in Gothenburg, the World Bank in Barcelona, and the G8 in Genoa.

U.S.-based anti-corporate globalization movements, which were severely shaken by the September 11 attacks, reemerged when activists shifted their attention from the war in Iraq back toward corporate globalization, leading to mass mobilizations against the WTO in Cancun and the FTAA summit in Miami during fall 2003. In the rest of the world, mobilizations continued to grow after 9/11, including a half-million-person march against the EU in Barcelona in March 2002. Anti–globalization and anti–war in Iraq movements soon converged, leading to an antiwar protest of more than a million people during the European Social Forum in Florence in November. Meanwhile, the third edition of the WSF in Porto Alegre drew nearly one hundred thousand participants during January 2003. The following June, hundreds of thousands of anti-corporate globalization and antiwar activists descended on the border of France and Switzerland to protest the G8 summit in Evian, while the most recent World and European Social Forums were successfully organized in Paris in November 2003 and Mumbai, India, in January 2004.

Three broad features thus characterize anti-corporate globalization movements. First, although movement networks are locally rooted, they are *global* in scope. Coordinating and communicating through transnational networks, activists have engaged in institutional politics, such as global campaigns to defeat the Multilateral Agreement on Investments or abolish the foreign debt, and extrainstitutional strategies, including coordinated global days of action, international forums, and cross-border information sharing. Perhaps most important, activists *think* of themselves as belonging to global movements, discursively linking local activities to diverse struggles elsewhere. Second, anti-corporate globalization movements are *informational*. The various protest tactics employed by activists, despite emerging in different cultural contexts, all produce highly visible, theatrical images for mass mediated consumption. Finally, anti-corporate globalization movements are organized around a multiplicity of virtual and physical network forms.[10]

Computer-Supported Social Movements

Inspired by the pioneering use of the Internet by the Zapatistas (Castells 1997; Cleaver 1995, 1999; Olesen 2004; Ronfeldt et al. 1998) and early free trade campaigns (Ayres 1999; Smith and Smythe 2001), anti-corporate globalization activists have employed digital networks to organize direct actions, share information and resources, and coordinate activities. Activists have made particularly effective use of e-mail and electronic listservs, which facilitate open participation and horizontal communication. On one hand, given their speed, low cost, and geographic reach, e-mail lists have facilitated the organization of globally coordinated protests, such as the global days of action inspired by PGA. For example, the second PGA global day of action on June 18, 1999, involved demonstrations in more than forty countries around the world against the anti-G8 Summit in Cologne, while hundreds of thousands mobilized globally during the WTO Summit in Seattle the following November. On the other hand, the worldwide circulation of discourses, strategies, and tactics signals the emergence of a global web of alternative trans-national counterpublics (Olesen 2004; cf. Fraser 1992).

Although anti-corporate globalization activists primarily use e-mail lists to facili-tate planning and coordination, they also create temporary Web pages during mobilizations to provide information, resources, and contact lists; post documents and calls to action (cf. Van Aelst and Walgrave 2002); and sometimes house realtime discussion forums and Internet relay chat rooms. Indeed, interactive Web sites offering multiple tools for coordination are becoming increasingly popular. These include open publishing projects like Indymedia or sites that incorporate collabora-tive production software, such as the Infospace in Barcelona (see below). Moreover, particular movement networks and processes – such as PGA, the WSF, or ATTAC – have their own, more narrowly focused Web pages, where activists post reflections, analyses, updates, calls to action, and links along with more logistical information.

Internet use has complemented and facilitated face-to-face coordination and interaction, rather than replacing them. During my fieldwork in Barcelona, activists used listservs – both within broad convergence spaces (Routledge 2004), such as the campaigns against the World Bank and EU and within specific networks like MRG or the Citizens Network to Abolish the External Debt (XCADE) – to stay informed about activities and events and to perform concrete logistical tasks. However, complex planning, political discussions, and relationship building often took place within physical settings. My own time thus largely involved attending meetings nearly every evening, followed by long hours of online work late into the night. At the same time, the phone remained an important tool of communication. For example, after sending various e-mails back and forth between MRG International and activists from a Dutch collective during planning for a European PGA meeting, we had to pick up the phone on several occasions to work out disagreements, which were impossible to solve without interactive communication.

Despite these cautionary remarks, the Internet has proven absolutely crucial, allowing key "activist-hackers" (cf. Nelson 1996) to carry out relay and exchange operations, receiving, interpreting, and distributing information out to diverse network hubs and nodes.[11] For example, when an MRG-based activist developed a system for instantly sending messages out to hundreds of listservs around the world, he turned to me and exclaimed, "Now I can reach thousands of activists at the touch of a button every time we want to communicate something important!" Activist interviews further illustrated how the Internet has facilitated long- distance coordination and horizontal collaboration, as Joseba, from Indymedia-Barcelona, recalled:

> I learned how a group of people, some in the U.S., others in London, and others, who knows where, coordinated through a global listserv. Suddenly someone would send an e-mail saying, "I think this story is important, what do you think?" In less than a week, ten people had answered, one or two saying it wasn't clear; but most feeling it was important, so we distributed the tasks: "I'll reduce it to so many characters," "I'll translate it into German," and "I'll do Italian." The next day we started working, and the messages began arriving: "Spanish translation done," "Italian done," "French

done." Then someone sent a photo, "What do you think about this picture?" The comments went around, and then someone sent another picture, and suddenly we had created an article![12]

Digital Technologies and the Cultural Politics of Activist Networking

The Internet does not simply provide the technological infrastructure for computer-supported social movements; its reticulate network structure reinforces their organizational logic (Arquilla and Ronfeldt 2001; Bennett 2003a; Castells 1997; Cleaver 1995, 1999; Escobar 2004; Juris 2004). Decentralized, flexible local/global networks constitute the dominant organizational forms within anti-corporate globalization movements. The absence of organizational centers within distributed networks makes them extremely adaptive, allowing activists to simply route around nodes that are no longer useful. Moreover, the introduction of new digital technologies significantly enhances the most radically decentralized all-channel network formations, facilitating transnational coordination and communication among contemporary movements.

For example, MRG-Catalonia, which grew up around the World Bank/IMF protests in Prague, was conceived as "a network of people and collectives against economic globalization and unitary thinking...a tool for providing local struggles with global content and extension."[13] Activists wanted to create a flexible mechanism for communication and coordination among diverse local struggles, including environmentalists, squatters, Zapatista supporters, solidarity and antidebt activists, and EU opponents. Rather than top-down command, activists preferred loose, flexible coordination among autonomous groups within a minimal structure involving periodic assemblies, logistical commissions surrounding concrete tasks, and several project areas, including a social movement observatory and resource exchange. In contrast to traditional leftist organizations, open participation was favored over representation: "MRG is a movement 'without members;' membership...leads to static, non-dynamic structures and to a clear and distinct, rather than a more diffuse sense of belonging."[14]

MRG activists also took part in broader regional and global networks, including PGA, which itself represents a diffuse all-channel network involving communication and coordination among diverse local movements around the world. Like MRG, PGA has no formal members but rather seeks to provide an instrument for coordination to help "the greatest number of persons and organizations to act against corporate domination through civil disobedience and people-oriented constructive actions."[15] Any person or collective can participate as long as they agree with the network hallmarks, which include a clear rejection of capitalism and all systems of domination, a confrontational attitude, a call to direct action and civil disobedience, and an organizational philosophy "based on decentralization and autonomy."[16]

Within movements such as MRG or PGA, networking logics have given rise to what many grassroots activists in Barcelona call a "new way of doing politics." While the command-oriented logic of leftist parties and unions is based on recruiting new members, developing unified strategies, political representation through vertical structures, and the pursuit of political hegemony, network-based politics involve the creation of broad umbrella spaces, where diverse organizations, collectives, and networks converge around common hallmarks while preserving their autonomy and specificity. Rather than recruitment, the objective becomes horizontal expansion and enhanced "connectivity" through articulating diverse movements within flexible, decentralized information structures allowing for maximal coordination and communication.

For example, when the Barcelona campaign against the World Bank was formed in early 2001, MRG-based activists brought their horizontal networking praxis to bear within this broader political space. Leftist parties and larger NGOs initially wanted their institutions to figure prominently within the campaign, which more grassroots activists interpreted as a strategy for gaining members or increasing electoral support. Formal organizations also favored structures based on representative voting, where influence would be determined by membership size rather than actual contribution. On the other hand, activists from MRG, XCADE, and other grassroots groups felt the best way to encourage broader and more active participation was to create open, assembly-based structures where everyone would have an equal say through consensus decision making, while establishing a rotating group of spokespersons to issue public declarations. This open networking model ultimately won out, but it did not lead to an absence of conflict. Rather, collective decisions would be restricted as much as possible to technical coordination as opposed to abstract political debates, allowing diverse actors to organize within a common platform.

Networking logics are thus unevenly distributed, as more established organizations tend to incorporate new digital technologies into existing communication routines, while smaller, resource-poor organizations often use technologies more innovatively, taking advantage of their low cost to forge horizontal linkages (Bennett 2003a). What many observers view as a single anti-corporate globalization movement is actually a congeries of competing, yet sometimes overlapping, social movement networks that differ according to issue addressed, political subjectivity, ideological framework, political culture, and organizational logic. Struggles within and among different networks, which I call the "cultural politics of networking," largely shape the way specific networks are produced, how they develop, and how they relate to one another within broader social movement fields.

For example, following the mobilization against the World Bank in Barcelona, the more institutional sectors created their own representative structure called the Barcelona Social Forum. Meanwhile, many traditional Marxists wanted the broader campaign to become a permanent statewide platform. Activists associated with MRG and XCADE opposed this idea, arguing against what they considered a return to more traditional organizational forms. They felt it was important to maintain open spaces for communication and coordination but that such spaces should facilitate the continual reconfiguration of fluid ties. The assembly finally agreed to bring the World Bank campaign to a close in September 2001, giving rise to a new coordinating space later that fall to plan for the upcoming mobilization against the EU. Moreover, militant squatters, who had created an anticapitalist platform against the World Bank, would take part within the wider campaign this time around, as parties and unions had forged a space of their own.

Radical anticapitalists thus face a continual dilemma about whether to operate within more strictly defined political formations, at the risk of being marginalized, or participate within broader spaces involving more reformist and traditional actors. Complex patterns of shifting alliances also operate at the transnational scale. For example, activists associated with PGA and other radical grassroots networks often create "autonomous spaces" during the world and regional social forums, conceived as "separate, yet connected" to official events. However, specific networks will move between the larger forums, autonomous spaces, or not participating at all, depending on the political context. Digitally powered social movement networks are thus "rhizomatic" (Cleaver 1999; cf. Deleuze and Guatarri 1987) – constantly emerging, fusing together, and hiving off – yet it is important to consider how such contradictory processes are actually generated in practice through concrete networking politics, which are always entangled within complex relationships of power rendered visible through long-term ethnographic research.

W. Lance Bennett (2003a, 154) has argued that contemporary Internet-driven campaigns are not only flexible and diverse, they are also "ideologically thin," allowing "different political perspectives to co-exist without the conflicts that such differences might create in more centralized coalitions." Although Bennett is right to highlight diversity within such campaigns, he may overstate their internal cohesion and ideological thinness. At the very least, these features will vary according to political culture and context. For example, his case studies involve U.S.-based corporate campaigns against Microsoft and Nike. My own research among broader anti-corporate globalization spaces revealed somewhat different dynamics. For example, activists generated a great deal of ideological discourse within the Barcelona campaigns against the World Bank and EU, or the world and regional social forums more generally, but decision making tended to involve practical matters, while political debates were often coded as conflicts over organizational form. Indeed, activists increasingly express their utopian imaginaries directly through concrete political, organizational, and technological practice, as Geert Lovink (2002, 34) suggests: "Ideas that matter are hardwired into software and network architectures."

The New Digital Media Activism

Contemporary independent media activists have made particularly effective use of new technologies through alternative and tactical forms of digital media production (cf. Meikle 2002). Alternative media constitute independent sources of news and information beyond the corporate logic of the mainstream press. John Downing (2003, v) defined what he called "radical media" as diverse small-scale outlets that "express an alternative vision to hegemonic policies, priorities, and perspectives." Such alternative or radical media also tend to be independently operated and self-managed through horizontal participation rather than top-down command. Not only do they incorporate a broader networking logic, they are also increasingly Internet based.

Alternative media.   Indymedia is perhaps the most emblematic of the new alternative digital media projects (Downing 2003; Halleck 2002; Kidd 2003; Meikle 2002). Using open publishing software developed by Australian programmer Mathew Arnison, the first IMC was established during the anti-WTO mobilization in Seattle. Indymedia journalists reported directly from the streets, while activists uploaded their own text, audio, video, and image files. Indymedia sites would soon be up and running in Philadelphia, Portland, Vancouver, Boston, and Washington, D.C., while the network quickly expanded on a global scale to places like Prague, Barcelona, Amsterdam, Sao Paolo, and Buenos Aires. There are now more than 120 local sites around the world, while the global network receives up to 2 million page views per day.[17]

During mass actions and gatherings, Indymedia centers become dynamic communication hubs, particularly among more radical sectors. During the December 2001 mobilization against the EU in Brussels, for example, the official convergence center was situated in a large open-air tent, which principally housed NGO information tables, generating an institutional feel. The IMC, on the other hand, was organized in an old squatted theater in the center of town. The main computer lab buzzed with activity as media activists and protesters uploaded images and audio files, swapped reports and information online, and edited video files. Meanwhile, the entire floor below was transformed into a project called Radio Bruxxel, which featured 24-hour programming about the EU, immigration, economic exclusion, war, and self-management.

Such temporary spaces of digital production provide a crucial terrain where activists carry out several concrete tasks. First, they send e-mails to each other and to their friends and families, facilitating action coordination, while rapidly circulating information about events on the ground. Second, activists generate formal updates, which are instantly posted and distributed through global distribution lists. Third, protesters can also immediately upload and disseminate video and image files. Fourth, IMCs also provide workshops for carrying out more complex operations, including live video and audio streaming as well as documentary film editing. While in the past activists had to rely on experts and the mass media to circulate their messages, largely due to high transaction costs and time constraints, they can now use new digital technologies to take on much of this work themselves, assuming greater control over the media production process, while enhancing the speed of information flow. Finally, such temporary media labs have also facilitated the exchange of information, ideas, and resources, as well as experimentation with new digital technologies through which media activists inscribe their emerging political ideals within new forms of networked space, a practice I call "informational utopics."[18]

During mass actions, hundreds of media activists thus take to the streets to record video footage, snap digital photos, and conduct interviews. At the mobilization against the EU in Barcelona during March 2002, for example, Meri, from MRG, exclaimed, "Everyone is filming everyone else!" Indeed, contemporary social movements are uniquely self-reflexive (Giddens 1991), as activists circulate their own texts and images through global networks in real time. Moreover, activists have also used digital technologies to help plan and organize mass direct actions themselves.

Beyond e-mail lists, protesters have also made innovative use of cell phone technology to coordinate tactical positions, report on police activities, and provide real-time updates. However, the use of cell phones should not be exaggerated. For example, even though organizers created an intricate communications structure in Prague, the system broke down when the Czech police blocked cellular transmissions. Activists have certainly used mobile phones, but not with the "military-like" tactical precision often suggested in more popular accounts.

Beyond specific mobilizations, Indymedia also incorporates a broader networking logic, as open publishing software allows activists to independently create, post, and distribute their own news stories regarding concrete actions, ongoing campaigns, and thematic issues. Open publishing reverses the implicit hierarchy dividing author and consumer, empowering grassroots users to freely participate in the production process, as programmer Evan Henshaw-Plath pointed out: "It's all about using technology to disintermediate the authority and power structure of the editor."[19] The refusal of editorial control allows users to draw their own conclusions about the veracity and relevance of particular posts. Moreover, the open publishing process facilitates active participation through the provision of concrete networking tools and nonhierarchical infrastructures, as Henshaw-Plath explained: "I see my task as building technological systems where people can exert power through egalitarian systems that will reproduce horizontal cooperative social relations and institutions."[20] Open editing thus represents an important example of informational utopics, as broader values related to horizontal collaboration, open access, and direct democracy are physically inscribed into Indymedia's network architecture.

Tactical media.   Rather than creating alternative counterpublics, tactical media aim to creatively intervene along dominant media terrains (Lovink 2002, 254–75; Meikle 2002, 113–72). This can involve either the juxtaposition of incommensurate elements to generate subversive meanings, as in "guerrilla communication" (Grupo Autónomo A.f.r.i.k.a. et al. 2000), or the playful parodying of corporate advertisements and logos to produce critical messages, which activists call "culture jamming" (cf. Klein 2000, 279–310; Lasn 2000). First theorized and put into practice during the "Next 5 Minutes" festivals in the Netherlands (Meikle 2002, 119), tactical media emphasize the use of new technologies, mobility, and flexibility. Geert Lovink (2002, 265), activist and Internet critic, put it in the following terms: "It is above all mobility that most characterizes the tactical practitioner. . . . To cross borders, connecting and re-wiring a variety of disciplines and always taking full advantage of the free spaces in the media."

Tactical media interventions do not necessarily take place in cyberspace, but new digital technologies are almost always crucial. For example, the Canadian-based Adbusters, founded by Kalle Lasn, provides multimedia culture jamming resources online, allowing local participants to download materials and participate in global campaigns, including Buy Nothing Day. Anti-corporate globalization activists have built clone sites like the "World Trade Organization/GATT Home Page" during the anti-WTO protests in Seattle. After the WTO secretary general publicly denounced the clone site, the story was picked up by CNN (Meikle 2002, 118), involving what Bennett (2003a, 161) called "micro-to-mass media crossover."

Within Catalan anti-corporate globalization movements, the "Agencies," a Barcelona-based political art and media collective, has developed numerous tactical media projects using digital technologies to produce and distribute physical and virtual materials, including posters, flyers, stickers, and videos. Its latest project, called "YOMANGO," combines guerrilla communication, culture jamming, civil disobedience, and sabotage. "Mango" is a Spanish-owned multinational clothing chain, while the slang "Yo Mango" also means "I steal." The campaign provides materials and information encouraging people to steal clothing and other items from transnational corporations. YOMANGO also involves public events including collective shoplifts and banquets featuring stolen food. Reflecting an open networking logic, the project aims to create "tools and dynamics that flow and proliferate, in order to be re-appropriated and circulate,"[21] Moreover, the project ironically promotes, "the free circulation of goods!"[22]

"Hacktivism" or "electronic civil disobedience" constitutes a final dimension of tactical media (Meikle 2002, 140–72; Wray 1998). Just as power moves through nomadic electronic circuits, Critical Art Ensemble (CAE; 1996) argued that activists should also operate along virtual terrains, using digital trespass and blockade tactics. Whereas CAE insisted that electronic civil disobedience should remain underground, Electronic Disturbance Theater (EDT) and its principal theorist Stefan Wray have promoted a more public approach to digital protest (Meikle 2002, 141). During the "virtual sit-in," for example, activists gather at a preannounced Web site and are automatically transferred en masse via FloodNet software to a target site, overwhelming its server. EDT has staged successful sit-ins against the Mexican government in support of the Zapatistas, while the "Electrohippies" flooded the WTO Web site during the protests in Seattle. Other digital tactics include the "e-mail bomb" and the "hijack," where surfers are automatically redirected from one Web site to another. Virtual actions rarely succeed in completely shutting down their targets, but they often generate significant media attention (Meikle 2002, 154–55).

Beyond specific tactical objectives, alternative and tactical media both involve ongoing experimentation with new technologies, forming part of an emerging digital activist networking culture. Moreover, grassroots media activists increasingly express their broader political values by projecting them onto both physical and virtual terrains through horizontal forms of digital collaboration. Contemporary activist gatherings, including No Border camps, PGA conferences, or the world and regional social forums, thus also provide concrete spaces for the practice of informational utopics. For example, the July 2002 Strasbourg No Border camp was specifically designed to challenge the nearby Schengen Information System (SIS), which tracks movement across EU space, but the camp was also conceived as a broader experiment in collective living and grassroots self-management. Activists transformed an empty swath of parkland along the Rhine River into a bustling two-thousand-person tent city, involving mobile kitchens; makeshift showers and latrines; video zones; dance spaces; and domes for logistical, first-aid, legal, security, and action planning. Organizers also devised a directly democratic decision-making structure based on autonomous neighborhoods that coordinated through larger assemblies. The scheme often broke down in practice, yet it represented an attempt to manifest a horizontal networking logic in the design and management of social space.

The alternative media center, ironically called "Silicon Valley," was among the most vibrant zones in the camp, housing an IMC, an Internet café running open source software, a radio tent, Web-based news and radio, and a double-decker tactical media bus from Vienna called the Publix Theater Caravan, which itself featured video screening, Internet access and streaming, and a bar and lounge. Pau and I first visited the media space on the second day of the camp and immediately ran into Karl, a friend from Indymedia-Berlin, who was typing something on his laptop outside the Internet café. He explained the entire zone was equipped with WiFi (wireless) connection and that he was sending e-mail. He then took us over to the radio tent, which was equipped with a fifty-watt transmitter and produced 24-hour simultaneous Web and broadcasts.

There were also numerous workshops within a project called d.sec (database systems to enforce control), which explored links between freedom of movement and communication, as well as physical and virtual struggles against growing mechanisms of control. Specific themes included open source, guerrilla communication, technology and the body, and media activism. More generally, d.sec was conceived as a space for experimentation with open networking, self-organization, and horizontal collaboration, as the project flyer explained:

> d.sec is... an open structure where activists, anti-racists, migrants, hackers, techs, artists and many more put their knowledge and practices into self-organized inter-action: a space to discuss and network, skill share, and produce collaborative knowledge. A laboratory to try out ways to hack the streets and reclaim cyberspace with crowds in pink and silver; experiment with virtual identities, Linux, and open source... explore the embodiment of technology, learn about the meanings of physical and virtual border crossing.

d.sec was a platform for generating new ideas and practices that physically embodied an emerging network ideal. Moreover, together with the broader media zone, which featured always-ready Internet connection, live audio and video streaming, and interactive peer-to-peer file sharing, activists had created an innovative, networked terrain fusing the "space of flows" and the "space of places" (cf. Castells 1996). If revolutions are characterized by their production of new spatial forms (Lefebvre 1991), then informational utopics also constitute a concrete mechanism for imagining and experimenting with alternative digital age geographies.

Conclusion: Digitally Networking Democracy?

Anti-corporate globalization movements have not only generated widespread visibility surrounding issues related to global economic justice and democracy, they have also pioneered in the use of new digital technologies. On one hand, grass-roots activists have developed highly advanced forms of computer-mediated alternative and tactical media, including Indymedia, culture jamming, hacktivism, and electronic civil disobedience. These practices have facilitated the emergence of globally coordinated transnational counterpublics while providing creative mechanisms for flexibly intervening within dominant communication circuits. On the other hand, activists have appropriated the Internet into their everyday routines, largely through e-mail lists and Web sites, favoring the rise of highly flexible and decentralized network forms. At the same time, the network has also emerged as a broader cultural ideal, as digital technologies generate new political values and vocabularies (cf. Wilson and Peterson 2002, 453), which are often directly inscribed into organizational and technological network architectures, suggesting a powerful dialectic among technology, norm, and form, mediated by human practice. Finally, activists are building a new digital media culture through the practice of informational utopics, involving experimentation with new technologies and the projection of utopian ideals regarding open participation and horizontal collaboration onto emerging forms of networked space.

Although the use of new digital technologies has helped mobilize hundreds of thousands of people around the world in opposition to corporate globalization, it remains to be seen whether new horizontal networking practices can be incorporated into more everyday forms of social, economic, and political life. This was precisely the motivation behind the development of a new media project by anti-corporate globalization activists in Barcelona called the "Infospace," which combines virtual tools, including an Internet server and social movement directory, with physical tools, including publishing and editing services; activist research and documentation; a solidarity economy project; and a physical storefront housing reception, meeting, and digital workspace. The physical and virtual are thus completely intertwined. For example, activists use Internet-based collaborative software (twiki) to collectively produce documents regarding real-world initiatives, while virtual projects are coordinated through both online and offline interaction.[23] Regarding the project's long-term goal, Pau had this to say: "We are building autonomous counterpower... by networking movements... and creating our own alternatives without waiting for the government... and helping others to achieve them as well."

Activists in Barcelona and elsewhere are thus increasingly turning to technological paradigms as a way to promote social transformation. Many specifically view open source as a harbinger of new self-organized forms of horizontal collaboration coordinated at multiple scales. For example, theorists associated with the German-based Oekonux project have debated how open software principles might potentially "migrate" into other contexts, perhaps leading to postcapitalist forms of economic production (cf. Lovink 2003, 194–223).[24] At the political level, electronic democracy advocates are interested in how "the technical possibilities of cyberspace make innovative forms of large-scale direct democracy practical," not via Internet alone, but rather through "collective and continuous elaboration of problems and their cooperative, concrete resolution by those affected" (Lévy 2001, 176). Anti-corporate globalization activists have similarly developed the European Social Consulta as a way to build political alternatives and exchange resources among local assemblies coordinated regionally through digital networks.[25]

Although such long-term networking projects, and the practice of informational utopics more generally, may not produce immediate results, they should be seen in another light. Indeed, as Alberto Melucci (1989, 75) once argued, new social movements are cultural innovators that challenge dominant cultural codes while also developing new "models of behavior and social relationships that enter into everyday life." Beyond the production of alternative values, discourses, and identities, however, contemporary anti-corporate globalization movements are perhaps best understood as social laboratories, generating new cultural practices and political imaginaries for a digital age.

NOTES

1   The Catalan Movement for Global Resistance (MRG) was ultimately "self-dissolved" in January 2003 as a response to declining participation and a broader political statement against the reproduction of rigid structures. Pseudonyms have been used throughout to hide activist identities.

2   I use "anti-corporate globalization" here to emphasize that most activists do not oppose globalization per se but rather those forms of economic globalization viewed as benefiting transnational corporations. "Global justice" is increasingly preferred by English-speaking activists but is not common elsewhere.

3   Open software is based on the "copyleft" principle, requiring that original source code be released and distributed with new program versions (cf. Himanen 2001; Raymond 1999; Lovink 2003, 194–223).

4   I adapt this term from Jameson (1991), who refers to postmodernism as the cultural logic of late capitalism; and Ong (1999), who explores a specific type of late capitalist cultural logic-transnationality.

5   Citing the hackers' jargon file, Himanen (2001, vii–viii) defined hackers as "people who 'program enthusiastically' and who believe that 'information-sharing is a powerful positive good.'"

6   Barcelona-based fieldwork was carried out from June 2001 to August 2002 for my doctoral dissertation titled "The Cultural Logic of Networking: Transational Activism and the Movement for Global Resistance in Barcelona," supported by the Wenner-Gren Foundation for Anthropological Research and the Social Science Research Council (with Andrew W. Mellon funding).

7   MRG was a co-convener of Peoples Global Action (PGA) Europe, while MRG-based activists also took part in the social forums.

8   The Continental Direct Action Network (DAN) process came to a standstill during the year after Seattle.

9   This brand of left-wing "libertarianism" should be distinguished from the variety prevalent in the United States. The former involves a radical critique of both the market and the state, while the latter is oriented toward limiting the role of the state in order to unleash the dynamic potential of the free market.

10   These include hierarchical circle patterns, intermediate wheel formations, and the most decentralized all-channel configurations (Kapferer 1973, 87), which refer to those where every node is connected to every other (Arquilla and Ronfeldt 2001). Networks can be defined more generally as sets of "interconnected nodes" (Castells 1996, 469).

11   Diane Nelson (1996) employed the term "Maya-Hacker" to characterize Mayan activists engaged in cultural activism and transnational networking.

12   Unless otherwise stated, quotations are from personal interviews.

13   Cited from "La Organización del MRC" in *EIMA* (February-March 2001), a Catalan activist journal.

14　Cited from a document sent to the global@ldist.ct.upc.es listserv on October 18, 2000.

15　See PGA Network Organizational Principles (www.nadir.org/nadir/initiativ/agp/cocha/principles.htm).

16　See PGA Hallmarks (www.nadir.org/nadir/initiativ/agp/gender/desire/nutshell.htm).

17　See Indymedia FAQ page, retrieved from http://process.indymedia.org/faq.php3 on March 14,2004.

18　With regard to radical activism more generally, Hetherington (1998, 123) refers to the spatial practice of "utopics," whereby "a utopian outlook on society and the moral order that it wishes to project, are translated into practice through the attachment of ideas about the good society onto particular places."

19　Interview with Evan Henshaw-Plath: http://lists.indymedia.org/mailman/public/mediapolitics/2001-November/000041.html, retrieved on March 18, 2004.

20　Ibid.

21　Cited from http://www.sindominio.net/lasagencias/yomango/ES/textos/10sugerencias.html, retrieved on March 15, 2004.

22　Cited from www.sindominio.net/lasagencias/yomango/ES/acciones/presentacion_1.html, retrieved on March 15, 2004.

23　"Tiki Wiki" is an open source content management system based on Wiki technology, which allows users to collaboratively create and edit content using any Web browser (http://tikiwiki.org).

24　See http://www.oekonux.org/. Also, see King (2004) for a critical perspective regarding the idea of openness as an organizing principle for social movements and other aspects of society.

25　This more ambitious version of the European Social Consulta has not yet generated widespread support around Europe, but Spanish and Catalan activists decided to move forward with a statewide referendum during the 2004 European parliamentary elections. See www.consultaeuropea.org.

REFERENCES

Appadurai, Arjun. 1996. *Modernity at large*. Minneapolis: University of Minnesota Press.

Arquilla, John, and David Ronfeldt. 2001. *Networks and netwars*. Santa Monica, CA: Rand.

Ayres, Jeffrey M. 1999. From the streets to the Internet. *Annals of the American Academy of Political and Social Science* 566: 132–43.

Bennett, W. Lance. 2003a. Communicating global activism. *Information, Communication & Society* 6 (2): 143–68.

——. 2003b. New media power. In *Contesting media power*, ed. Nick Couldry and James Curran. Lanham, MD: Rowman & Littlefield.

Burawoy, Michael. 2000. Grounding globalization. In *Global Ethnography*, ed. Michael Burawoy, Joseph A. Blum, Sheba George, Zsuzsa Gille, Teresa Gowan, Lynne Haney, Maren Klawiter, Steve H. Lopez, Sean Riain, and Millie Thayer. Berkeley: University of California Press.

Castells, Manuel. 1996. *The rise of the network society*. Oxford, UK: Blackwell.

——. 1997. *The power of identity*. Oxford, UK: Blackwell.

Cleaver, Harry. 1995. The Zapatistas and the electronic fabric of struggle. http://www.eco.utexas.edu/faculty/Cleaver/zaps.html (accessed March 18, 2004).

——. 1999. Computer-linked social movements and the threat to global capitalism, http://www.eco.utexas.edu/faculty/Cleaver/polnet.html (accessed April 1, 2004).

Collins, Randall. 2001. Social movements and the focus of emotional attention. In *Passionate politics*, ed. Francesca Polletta, James M. Jasper, and Jeff Goodwin. Chicago: University of Chicago Press.

Critical Art Ensemble. 1996. *Electronic civil disobedience*. Brooklyn, NY: Autonomedia.

Deleuze, Gilles, and Félix Guatarri. 1987. *A thousand plateaus*. Minneapolis: University of Minnesota Press.

Deluca, Kevin Michael. 1999. *Image politics*. New York: Guilford.

Downing, John D. H. 2003. The Independent Media Center movement. In *Contesting media power*, ed. Nick Couldry and James Curran. Lanham, MD: Rowman & Littlefield.

Escobar, Arturo. 2004. Actors, networks, and new knowledge producers. In *Para Além das Guerras da Ciência*, ed. Boaventura de Sousa Santos. Porto, Portugal: Afrontamento.

Fraser, Nancy. 1992. Rethinking the public sphere. In *Habermas and the public sphere*, ed. Craig Calhoun. Cambridge, MA: MIT Press.

Giddens, Anthony. 1991. *The consequences of modernity*. Palo Alto, CA: Stanford University Press.

Grupo Autónomo A.f.r.i.k.a. et al. 2000. *Manual de Guerrilla de la Comunicación*. Barcelona, Spain: Virus.

Halleck, DeeDee. 2002. *Hand-held visions*. New York: Fordham University Press.

Handelman, Don. 1990. *Models and mirrors*. Cambridge: Cambridge University Press.

Hetherington, Kevin. 1998. *Expressions of identity: Space, performance, politics*. London: Sage.

Himanen, Pekka. 2001. *The hacker ethic*. New York: Random House.

Jameson, Fredric. 1991. *Postmodernism*. Durham. NC: Duke University Press.

Juris, Jeffrey S. 2004. Networked social movements. In *The network society*, ed. Manuel Castells. London: Edward Elgar.

Kapferer, Bruce. 1973. Social network and conjugal role. In *Network Analysis*, ed. Jeremy Boissevain and J. Clyde Mitchell. The Hague, the Netherlands: Mouton.

Kidd, Dorothy. 2003. Indymedia.org. In *Cyberactivism*, ed. Martha McCaughey and Michael D. Ayers. New York: Routledge.

King, Jamie. 2004. The packet gang. *Metamute* 27. http://www.metamute.com (accessed March 18, 2004).

Klein, Naomi. 2000. *No logo*. New York: Picador.

Lasn, Kalle. 2000. *Culture jam*. New York: Quill.

Lefebvre, Henri. 1991. *The production of space*. Oxford: Oxford University Press.

Lévy, Pierre. 2001. *Cyberculture*. Minneapolis: University of Minnesota Press.

Lins Ribeiro, Gustavo. 1998. Cybercultural politics. In *Cultures of politics, politics of cultures*, ed. Sonia E. Alvarez, Evelina Dagnino, and Arturo Escobar. Boulder, CO: Westview.

Lovink, Geert. 2002. *Dark fiber*. Cambridge, MA: MIT Press.

———. 2003. *My first recession*. Rotterdam, The Netherlands: V2_/NAi Publishers.

Meikle, Graham. 2002. *Future active: Media activism and the Internet*. New York: Routledge.

Melucci, Alberto. 1989. *Nomads of the present*. Philadelphia: Temple University Press.

Miller, Daniel, and Don Slater. 2000. *The Internet: An ethnographic approach*. Oxford, UK: Berg.

Nelson, Diane M. 1996. Maya hackers and the cyberspatialized nation-state. *Cultural Anthropology* 11 (3): 287–308.

Olesen, Thomas. 2004. *Long distance Zapatismo*. London: Zed Books.

Ong, Aihwa. 1999. *Flexible citizenship*. Durham, NC: Duke University Press.

Raymond, Eric. 1999. *The cathedral and the bazaar*. Cambridge, MA: O'Reilly.

Robertson, Roland. 1995. Glocalization. In *Global modernities*, ed. Mike Featherstone, Scott M. Lash, and Roland Robertson. London: Sage.

Ronfeldt, David, John Arquilla, Graham E. Fuller, and Melissa Fuller. 1998. *The Zapatista "social netwar" in Mexico*. Santa Monica, CA: Rand.

Routledge, Paul. 2004. Convergence of commons. *The Commoner*, Autumn/Winter. www.thecommmoner.org (accessed March 18, 2004).

Smith, Peter Jay, and Elizabeth Smythe. 2001. Globalisation, citizenship and technology. In *Culture and politics in the information age*, ed. Frank Webster. London: Routledge.

Van Aelst, Peter, and Stefaan Walgrave. 2002. New media, new movements? The role of the Internet in shaping the "anti-globalisation" movement. *Information, Communication & Society* 5 (4): 465–93.

Waterman, Peter. 1998. *Globalization, social movements, and the new internationalisms*. London: Mansell.

Weber, Steven. 2004. The success of open source. Cambridge, MA: Harvard University Press.

Wellman, Barry. 2001. Physical place and cyberplace. *International Journal of Urban and Regional Research* 25 (2): 227–52.

Wellman, Barry, and Caroline Haythornthwaite, eds. 2002. *The Internet in everyday life*. Malden, MA: Blackwell.

Wilson, Samuel M., and Leighton C. Peterson. 2002. The anthropology of online communities. *Annual Review of Anthropology* 31: 449–67.

Wray, Stefan. 1998. On electronic civil disobedience. http://cristine.org/borders/Wray_Essay.html (accessed March 18, 2004).

Part V

Nomadic Ideologies

This final part of our reader explores the circulation of Western ideologies, focusing on how these narratives both constrict the lives of and create new subject positions for the peoples of the periphery. Using the female inheritance movement in Hong Kong as a case study, Merry and Stern argue that the localization of global human rights ideas depends on a complicated set of activist groups with different ideological orientations along with intermediaries who translate rights narratives from the arena of international law and legal institutions to specific situations of suffering and violation. Sylvain's piece focuses on how the San (Bushman) of southern Africa – who are currently engaged in global activism and local struggles for rights as indigenous people – are being encouraged to promote a stereotypical image of themselves as isolated, pristine primitives. Such primordial expressions of identity reflect how the globalization of an essentialist idea of culture functions as an instrument of exploitation that masks the lived reality and marginalized existence of the San. And Misra's essay focuses on how the concept and practice of "confidentiality" circulated to India through a transnational expert infrastructure set up to deal with AIDS. It suggests that this notion constituted a key discursive site reflecting changing and contested definitions of health, configurations of citizenship, and arrangements of governance in Indian society.

SUGGESTIONS FOR FURTHER READING

Bielefeldt, Heiner
    2000 "Western" versus "Islamic" Human Rights Conceptions? A Critique of Cultural Essentialism in the Discussion on Human Rights. *Political Theory* 28(1): 90–121.
Chin, Elizabeth
    2003 Children Out of Bounds in Globalising Times. *Postcolonial Studies* 6(3): 309–25.

Comaroff, John L. and Jean Comaroff
   1997   Postcolonial Politics and Discourses of Democracy in Southern Africa: An Anthro-
      pological Reflection on African Political Modernities. *Journal of Anthropological
      Research* 53(2): 123–46.
Geismar, Haidy
   2005   Copyright in Context: Carvings, Carvers, and Commodities in Vanuatu. *American
      Ethnologist* 32(3): 437–59.
Holston, James
   2001   Urban Citizenship and Globalization. In *Global City-Regions: Trends, Theory,
      Policy*. Allen J. Scott, ed. Pp. 325–48. New York: Oxford University Press.
Jacka, Jerry K.
   2005   Emplacement and Millennial Expectations in an Era of Development and Global-
      ization: Heaven and the Appeal of Christianity for the Ipili. *American Anthropologist*
      107(4): 643–53.
Jolly, Margaret
   2005   Beyond the Horizon? Nationalisms, Feminisms, and the Globalization of the
      Pacific. *Ethnohistory* 52(1): 137–66.
Liechty, Mark
   1996   Paying for Modernity: Women and the Discourse of Freedom in Kathmandu.
      Studies in Nepali History and Society 1(1): 201–30.
Merry, Sally Engle
   2006   Transnational Human Rights and Local Activism: Mapping the Middle. *American
      Anthropologist* 108(1): 38–51.
Sharma, Aradhana
   2006   Crossbreeding Institutions, Breeding Struggle: Women's Empowerment, Neoliberal
      Governmentality, and State (Re)Formulation in India. *Cultural Anthropology* 21(1):
      60–95.
Speed, Shannon
   2002   Global Discourses on the Local Terrain: Human Rights and Indigenous Identity in
      Chiapas. *Cultural Dynamics* 14(2): 205–28.
Weeratunge, Nireka
   2000   Nature, Harmony, and the Kaiyugaya: Global/Local Discourses on the Human-
      Environment Relationships. *Current Anthropology* 41(2): 249–68.

16

The Female Inheritance Movement in Hong Kong: Theorizing the Local/Global Interface

Sally Engle Merry and Rachel E. Stern

In the spring of 1994, everyone in Hong Kong was talking about female inheritance. Women in the New Territories were subject to Chinese customary law and, under British colonialism, still unable to inherit land. That year, a group of rural indigenous women joined forces with Hong Kong women's groups to demand legal change. In the plaza in front of the Legislative Council building, amid shining office buildings, the indigenous women, dressed in the oversized hats of farm women, sang folk laments with new lyrics about injustice and inequality. Demonstrators from women's groups made speeches about gender equality and, at times, tore paper chains from their necks to symbolize liberation from Chinese customary law (Chan 1995: 4). Across the plaza, a conservative group representing rural elite interests, the Heung Yee Kuk, gathered in large numbers to protest female inheritance on the grounds that it would undermine tradition. One banner held the plaintive message "Why are you killing our culture?" (p. 30).

The starting point for this research was the odd juxtaposition of rural women wearing farm hats and the transnational rhetoric of rights and gender equality that they employed to lobby for legal change. The majority of these women had never been in the central business district before. How did they become part of a

From *Current Anthropology* 46(3): 387–409. Copyright © 2005, The Wenner-Gren Foundation for Anthropological Research.

movement that framed their grievances as a violation of their human rights when they needed directions even to find downtown? How did they recognize the potential of legislative change to solve their particular problems? In other words, how were human rights made local? To what extent were they indigenized, that is, translated into local terms that made sense to rural village women?

On a small scale, the 1993–94 female inheritance movement is a case study of globalization. There is a widespread assumption that the global circulation of ideas is increasing cultural homogeneity, but, as Appadurai (1996: 7) suggests, global ideas circulated through the mass media also spark resistance, selectivity, and agency, creating vernacular forms of globalization.[1] Scholars emphasize the global circulation of ideas and images but rarely examine how transnational ideas and discourses become localized. The female inheritance movement offers an opportunity to examine a vernacular form of globalization and to think about how global ideas are reinterpreted in terms of local categories of meaning.

This process of localization is a high-stakes question in the universalism-versus-relativism debate. Although the idea of human rights creates universal standards (Donnelly 2003), proponents of Asian values, most famously Lee Kuan Yew of Singapore, argue that it is based on Western individualism and does not readily apply to more collectivist Asian societies (see Bauer and Bell 1999: 3–23). Although support for Asian values has diminished, it is common for members of non-European societies to argue that the idea of human rights is an alien, Western concept which does not fit into their cultural framework. By focusing on how human rights are interpreted in local cultural terms and gain legitimacy within local communities, localization offers one way to bridge the divide between universalism and relativism. Anthropological research on human rights, for example, focuses on processes of appropriating rights and critiques the notion of an opposition between universalism and relativism (Wilson 1996, Cowan, Dembour, and Wilson 2001). Abdullahi An-Na'im also argues that "human rights are much more credible... if they are perceived to be legitimate within the various cultural traditions of the world" (1992a: 3, see also An-Na'im 1992b, 2002). He advocates a cross-cultural approach in which rights are "conceived and articulated within the widest possible range of cultural traditions" as a way of increasing their credibility, legitimacy, and efficacy (1992a: 2).

From another angle, there is a growing body of research on transnational social movements that blends social movement theory with transnational network analysis. This work asks how transnational movements and actors promote normative and political change at the global level (Keck and Sikkink 1998, Khagram, Ricker, and Sikkink 2002, Risse, Ropp, and Sikkink 1999). There is much discussion of norm creation because the political impact of transnational nongovernmental organizations (NGOs) often depends on the use of information, persuasion, and moral pressure (Khagram, Ricker, and Sikkink 2002: II). Framing, defined as "action-oriented sets of beliefs and meanings that inspire and legitimate the activities and campaigns of a social movement organization," is also an important ingredient in movement success as well as a way to push the creation of new norms (Snow and Benford 2000: 614; see also Tarrow 1998). Work on framing, transnational networks, and norm creation generally explores interaction between domestic

NGOs, transnational NGOs, movements, and states. Case studies often look at how coalitions both take advantage of existing international norms and institutions and create new ones. For example, Alison Brysk (2000) shows that Latin American indigenous people turned to international institutions only after efforts to frame their grievances in terms of rights had failed at home.

This scholarship on transnational movements, however, pays little attention to how local actors come to see their everyday grievances as violations of human rights or negotiate between their existing cultural frame-works and rights concepts. For those sympathetic to An-Na'im's argument, there is little detailed exploration of what a dialogic approach to human rights means in practice. How do places like Hong Kong manage to employ rights language in a way that taps the power of universalism while responding to local conditions? Using an anthropological perspective, we examine the female inheritance movement in its historical, social, economic, and political context as an example of meaning-making at the grass roots in a rights-based movement. We develop a framework for thinking about process – charting how and why human rights ideas moved from their global sites of creation to local social movements. Two ideas are important here: *layers* and *translators*.

We see the female inheritance movement as a coalition of distinct layers. We call the different camps "layers" rather than "groups" as a way of conceptualizing their relationship to rights language and their relative distance from transnational ideas. Following the pioneering work of Stuart Scheingold (1974) and other socio-legal scholars (e.g., McCann 1994, Engel and Munger 2002), we see rights as a resource, albeit a limited one. The layers of the female inheritance movement formed a rough hierarchy in terms of the degree to which they tapped into this resource. For example, one layer emphasized the rights dimension of female inheritance while another framed the issue in terms of patriarchy and feudal thinking. The indigenous women themselves, whose stories formed the narrative core of the movement, generally saw themselves as the victims of unfeeling and rapacious make relatives, although they also came to see themselves as subject to gender discrimination. The movement was an amalgamation of the ways in which these different layers perceived the issue, incorporating both particularistic understandings of grievances and the more generalized framework of human rights.

Despite significant ideological differences, these layers were able to communicate through the services of people whom we term "translators." Translators were able to switch between different ways of framing the problem, facilitating collaboration between people in various layers who did not necessarily say the same thing or think about the issue in the same way. Translators, for example, helped the indigenous women recast their stories as violations of a right to protection from gender discrimination, something guaranteed by the Hong Kong government. These few intermediaries provided critical bridges between a human rights discourse connected to modernity and universalism and more particular and individualized ways of thinking about injuries.

This discussion of layers and translators shows that the human rights framework can play an important role even when rights talk only trickles down to protagonists through the mediation of translators. For a focus on human rights to be an effective political strategy, the idea of rights need not be adopted by participants at all levels of the movement and need not be culturally legitimate throughout the society. However, timing is critical. The Chinese crackdown at Tiananmen Square in 1989 and the anticipated handover to China in 1997 worried Hong Kong leaders and citizens concerned about protection for individual rights (Petersen 1996; Chan 1995: 27). At this historical juncture, human rights were an important source of what Kevin O'Brien terms "rightful resistance" (1996). By citing the gulf between international norms and the situation in Hong Kong, the women and their allies gained both legitimacy and public support.

Our research on the movement relies on ethnographic studies done at the time of the movement and subsequent field research in 2002–3, including interviews with many of the protagonists. These interviews took place nearly ten years after the movement. While they provided insight into how people saw the issue, we have relied heavily on secondary sources to reconstruct a timeline of events. Eliza Chan's (1995) master's thesis in anthropology at the Chinese University of Hong Kong was particularly valuable because Chan spent significant time with the indigenous women during the movement and placed emphasis on how they perceived events at the time. It was Chan's insightful analysis of the difference between the way indigenous women saw the movement and the way it was understood by others that started us on a further exploration of the female inheritance movement as a way of understanding the process of localizing human rights.

The Female Inheritance Movement

The central actors in the female inheritance movement are people labeled "indigenous," a term used in Hong Kong to describe the descendants of the population living in the New Territories at the time of the British colonial takeover in 1899. In anthropology, the term "indigenous" is usually used to refer to relatively homogeneous groups that were the initial inhabitants of a territory and have now been incorporated into larger national states. They often occupy a subordinate status within the state. In contrast, the New Territories is an ethnically diverse region that has experienced continuous immigration and settlement of various ethnic groups, largely Cantonese, Hakka, and Punti, over a long period of time (see Watson 1985). Groups typically claim indigenous identity on the basis of prior residence, custom, and community and use these claims as the basis for entitlements to land and resources. Thus, indigeneity is a political claim as well as a cultural status. In the Hong Kong context, "indigenous" was a label first imposed by the British and locally adopted to differentiate those with pre-1899 roots from more recent urban arrivals.

The catalyst for the movement was an indigenous woman, Lai-sheung Cheng, who became a key leader by tracking down other aggrieved women in the New Territories and contacting Hong Kong women's groups to push their claims. When Ms. Cheng's father died without a will (a common occurrence in the New Territories),[2] her two brothers inherited his house in Yuen Long. In May 1991 the brothers decided to sell the house to a developer. Ms. Cheng was still living on the second floor of the house, and she refused to leave unless she was given a share of the proceeds from the sale, citing a Qing-Dynasty custom allowing unmarried women to reside indefinitely in the family's home after a father's death (*South China Morning Post*, August 23, 1993, and Cheng interview, 2003). For the next two years she was harassed by the buyer of the house to force her to leave. The buyer routinely broke into the house, once smearing excrement and urine around the interior and on another occasion releasing mice (*Sunday Telegraph*, October 24, 1993, and Cheng interview, 2003). The harassment was so intense that Ms. Cheng said she had to call the police nearly every night.

Fed up, Ms. Cheng decided to make her story public. Her first step was to write a letter to Chris Patten, then governor of Hong Kong, saying, "I was persecuted because of the law" (Cheng interview, 2003). Not content with alerting Governor Patten, she wrote a letter to the Chinese newspaper *Oriental Daily* explaining her situation. The *Oriental Daily* did not publish the letter, but someone at the paper put Ms. Cheng in touch with Linda Wong, a social worker at the Hong Kong Federation of Women's Centres who was known to the staff because her organization was lobbying hard for a women's commission (Wong interview, 2003). Ms. Cheng told Linda Wong that she knew several other indigenous women in a similar situation, including Ying Tang, a patient at Ms. Cheng's Chinese-medicine clinic. She also said that several women had contacted her after they saw her name and story in a Chinese newspaper, the *Wah Kui Daily*. Ms. Wong asked Ms. Cheng to contact these women and bring them to a meeting, which she did in late 1993 (Wong interview, 2003). After this first meeting, the women began to publicize their stories. They met informally with various government officials, including members of the Hong Kong Legislative Council Anna Wu and Christine Loh, to explore their legal options. Their first formal step was a meeting at the Complaints Division of the Office of Members of the Legislative Council (Wong interview, 2003).

Framing the Issue

As the indigenous women were organizing, prohibition of female inheritance in the New Territories was gaining prominence as a political issue. On the most basic level, the conflict over female inheritance stemmed from Hong Kong's dual legal system regarding land. While Hong Kong Island and Kowloon, the two other regions of Hong Kong, are governed by laws and a legal system imported from Britain, the New Territories fall under the 1910 New Territories Ordinance, which recognizes Chinese customary law. Although the original legislation makes it sound as if courts had the option of using Chinese customary law to resolve land cases ("the courts have the power to enforce Chinese custom or customary right"), the *Tang v Tang* decision (1970) established that application of Chinese custom to New Territories land cases was mandatory (Selby 1991:48; see also Loh 1997). As a result, there were two laws governing inheritance in Hong Kong in 1994: one in urban Hong Kong and another in the rural New Territories.

Discrimination against New Territories women had been on the radar screen of women's groups for a long time. When the Association for the Advancement of Feminism (AAF) was founded in 1984, abolishing discriminatory laws in the New

Territories was mentioned in its position paper (Tong 1999: 64). In addition, five women's groups asked the government to set up a working group to look into New Territories discrimination in July 1990 (Howarth et al. 1991: 17). The issue of female inheritance took on increased importance after a 1991 shadow report by the Hong Kong Council of Women prepared in conjunction with Hong Kong's report to the Human Rights Committee in Geneva on compliance with the International Covenant on Civil and Political Rights (ICCPR).

NGO reports on UN treaties tend to vanish into the ether of documents surrounding UN work. However, this particular submission came at a high point of interest in human rights in Hong Kong. Hong Kong's Bill of Rights had been passed in July 1991,[3] and in the wake of the events in Tiananmen Square Hong Kong was newly concerned with civil liberties and discrimination (Petersen 1996; see also Petersen and Samuels 2002: 47–48). Although the Heung Yee Kuk, a political organization representing rural villages, had lobbied to exempt "traditional rights" of male villagers from the Bill of Rights, it had failed to win an exemption (Petersen 1996: 353–55).[4] As a result, the Hong Kong Council of Women's report was able to claim that this was a form of gender discrimination that contravened the newly passed Bill of Rights (Howarth et al. 1991: 16).

The shadow report was important because it framed the female inheritance issue in human rights terms. The four authors, all Western women with strong academic backgrounds, argued that male-only inheritance violated both the Convention on the Elimination of Discrimination Against Women (CEDAW) and the ICCPR (Howarth et al. 1991: 12).[5] They further explained that Hong Kong's legislation governing succession – the Intestates' Estate Ordinance and the Probate and Administration Ordinance – did not apply to New Territories women (p. 14). The report included a well-reasoned argument as to why male-only inheritance was not protected by either the Joint Declaration or the Basic Law, the two documents outlining the terms of the handover (pp. 16–17). These legal arguments provided the critical intellectual framework for activists and legislators to push for equal inheritance. They also helped clear up confusion about the complicated dual legal system. The government could no longer claim, as the attorney general did in 1986, that they were "not aware of any provisions of [Hong Kong] law which discriminate against women" (quoted in Lui 1997: chap. 3, 5). The report called male-only inheritance a "feudal" result of a patriarchal Confucian social order and noted that it persisted in Hong Kong long after its abolition in China, Taiwan, and Singapore because the New Territories Ordinance had "led to a rigidification of customary law" (pp. 13, 15, 17).

The most important contribution of the report, however, was its discovery that the jurisdiction of the New Territories Ordinance was based on territory, not on indigenous identity, and therefore its prohibition of female inheritance applied to all residents of the New Territories. In 1994, 42% of the population of Hong Kong lived in the New Territories (Tong 1999: 53). Most of the people lived in public housing estates or private flats that were not exempted from the New Territories Ordinance. As a result, women were ineligible to inherit property throughout most of the New Territories (Petersen 1996: 341; Jones interview, 2003).[6] Amazingly, practically no one had realized this. The news of this discovery broke in the Chinese newspaper *Ming Pao* on September 6, 1993, and immediately created a crisis for the government (Wong 2000: 299; see also Fischler 2000: 215).[7] The 340,000 owners of apartments and houses in urban parts of the New Territories suddenly discovered that Chinese customary law applied to them (Home Affairs Branch 1993). Clearly, the New Territories Ordinance would have to be amended to allow female urban residents to inherit property when the owner died intestate, following the laws in place in urban Hong Kong.

On November 19, 1993, the government introduced the New Territories Land (Exemption) Bill. The bill exempted urban land, land generally inhabited by Hong Kong residents who had moved into the New Territories, from the New Territories Ordinance. This change was not contested by the rural political leaders or the government. It was only when a legislator proposed extending the right to inherit family land to rural indigenous women that a wave of protest erupted. Giving rural women the right to inherit family land was a dramatic departure from a practice dating back at least a hundred years. The first step in making this momentous change came with the creation of the Anti-Discrimination Female Indigenous Residents Committee.

The Anti-Discrimination Female Indigenous Residents Committee

On October 3, 1993, the indigenous women lodged their complaint with the Complaints Division of the Legislative Council. Less than a week later, the Legislative Council passed a nonbinding motion calling for female inheritance in the New Territories (*South China Morning Post*, October 14, 1993). Despite two hours of fierce debate, the motion passed easily, with 36 in favor and only 4 opposed. The Anti-Discrimination Female Indigenous Residents Committee was founded about the time of this debate (Wong 2000: 299; Chan 1995: 47). In addition to the indigenous women, it included Linda Wong, a representative of the AAF, a Radio Television Hong Kong reporter, an anthropology graduate student, and a labor organizer.[8] With the help of these outsiders, the indigenous women began to tell their stories to a wider audience. Most important, they learned to tell these stories in a way that was politically effective.

In the beginning, the women saw their situations as personal wrongs perpetrated by particular relatives and stressed that they had been denied affection by their natal and marital relatives (Chan 1995: 72). According to Linda Wong, the women were not thinking about changing the law until the first demonstration outside the Legislative Council. Rather, they were hoping that Legislative Council members would address their individual cases (interview, 2003).[9] Chan (1995) argues that most of the women saw their claims in terms of kinship obligations, not equal rights. Most of the women did not criticize the patrilineal kinship system itself but blamed particular relatives who had reneged on their kinship obligations to provide them financial and emotional support in lieu of their fathers' land. One woman interviewed by Chan was most angry that her relatives had failed to keep in touch with her, forgetting that she was her father's "root and sprout" and "flesh and blood." If she had inherited, she said, she would have allowed her relatives to live in her father's house as long as they maintained close ties with her (pp. 88–89).

When the women did make inheritance claims, they justified them on the basis of their filial ties to their father and sought to assert their membership in the lineage (Chan 1995: 39). In telling their stories, several of the women emphasized the role they had played in their fathers' funerals to underscore their close ties to their fathers (pp. 82–85). Because they had been filial, affectionate daughters, they argued, they were entitled to inherit.[10] By using kinship ties to justify inheritance, they reinforced the patrilineal family system even as they asserted their rights (p. 97). Tellingly, only one of the women in the Anti-Discrimination Female Indigenous Residents Committee had a brother. The rest of the women were all "last-of-line" daughters (*juefangnu*) and, as a result, their fathers' land had been inherited by distant male relatives.[11] In Chan's interviews, most of the women said they would have been willing to give up their inheritance rights if they had had brothers (Chan 1995: 72). Regardless, many villagers criticized them for behaving unreasonably in demanding a share of their natal family's property (p. 39). As the women began lobbying for a change in the law, they came under pressure for being "ungrateful" and for being "collaborators" with the Westernized "outsiders" (p. 126).

Through the Anti-Discrimination Female Indigenous Residents Committee, the indigenous women learned how to translate their kinship grievances into the language of rights and equality. This translation was critical because, in order to be politically persuasive, the women needed to phrase their needs in a language acceptable to those hearing their claims (Chan 1995: 56). The Legislative Council and the media were interested not in family disputes over property but in stories that spoke to wider themes of gender equality and human rights. The women had to "learn" to put on an "elitist and rational pose," to present themselves as victims with a "detached" attitude, in language devoid of personal grievances and emotions (p. 100).

Although the Hong Kong Federation of Women's Centres claimed that the "women took all the initiatives by themselves while the Centre just concentrated on providing resources support," the process was more complicated (Hong Kong Federation of Women's Centres 1994: 20; see also Lui 1997: chap. 4, 20). Chan describes how outsiders on the Residents Committee played an important role in framing the indigenous women's stories and, more generally, facilitating the transition to a more generalized, rights-based perspective (1995: 119). The social workers drilled the women, teaching them not to use slang and how to present themselves to the public (p. 120). They learned to ask for a broad change to an unfair law rather than mediation and a more equal division of property. On several occasions the outsiders in the group groomed the women in dealing with the media, particularly in how to respond to reporters. The emphasis, beyond avoiding slang and speaking with sufficient detachment, was on keeping the women's stories short and quotable. They wanted the women to reiterate a standard claim rather than telling their personal stories so that the movement did not appear to be motivated only by personal interest (p. 117). The women practiced responding to questions such as "There are some women in the New Territories who say that they do not need the rights of inheritance. Why do you still insist on it?" and "What experience of yours in the New Territories aroused you to speak out so boldly?" pp. 117–19; see also Chan interview, 2003, and Cheng interview, 2003). In one session, the social worker imitated the tone of the reporters in asking this question and taped the response given by one of the women. She then played the tape for the group to illustrate the power of placing an individual story in a wider context. For one woman, the principle of gender equality and human rights enabled her to claim inheritance even though her natal kin claimed that she was only an adopted, not a biological daughter (pp. 119–20). Under the human rights framework, she had rights regardless of her adopted status.

In addition, the Residents Committee helped the women branch out into different modes of expression, creating dramas and songs to illustrate the injustice of male-only inheritance. A labor organizer in the group became the "stage director" for the drama. As one interviewee put it, "She put together elements to strike those cameras," such as suggesting that the women dress in traditional clothes (Chan interview, 2003; see also Cheng interview, 2003). As part of this dramatization, the women needed to present a united front regardless of differences in age, ethnicity, and education. They had to negotiate a common identity as indigenous women, an identity forged through a series of small decisions within the group. When the women rewrote a traditional song to include new lyrics about injustice, for example, they had to find a song that everyone knew. In the end, they chose a Hakka mountain song (*shan ge*) even though the majority of the indigenous women were not Hakka (Cheng interview, 2003).

In creating the dramas, the organizers were responding to the stereotypes that they knew the media wanted to see. The media had long seen the New Territories as a bastion of outdated tradition. In a documentary on New Territories life entitled *An Indigenous Village: A Case for Concern*, aired on Radio Television Hong Kong June 20 1986, the narrator closed with the thought that "traditional modes of thinking vastly out of step with the modern world are still deep-rooted in the hearts of indigenous villagers in the New Territories." During the female inheritance movement, the Kuk was portrayed as traditional, rural, and male while the female inheritance coalition was urban, modern, and female (Chan 1995: 50). For the most part, the indigenous women were seen as victims of "tradition" and lineage hegemony (p. 100). One TV series broadcast during the movement depicted the lineage system as a "living fossil" of Chinese tradition (p. 107). Other reporters posed the women in front of ancestral halls staring into the distance, using the elegant Chinese calligraphy as a foil for the women's apparent helplessness (p. 103). The press encouraged the women to wear the loose-fitting black suits and large-brimmed hats traditionally associated with rural women, a departure from their normal attire (p. 53).

Indigenous women who failed to generalize their particular grievances into stories of rights violations were silenced (Chan 1995: 131–32). In the middle of one Legislative Council debate, for example, an indigenous woman, the oldest participant in the movement, suddenly interrupted the chairperson and started shouting in Hakka about how badly her relatives had treated her. The chairperson cut the woman off, saying, "Your story is not related to our discussion." A representative of the Kuk then told her that her story was just a family dispute and should be filed with the Kuk (pp. 131–32). Portraying the women's stories as individual disputes without broader significance was an important way of discrediting the indigenous women (p. 5). During the debate over the passage of the land exemption bill, one legislator dismissed the indigenous women by saying, "As regards the case of Ms. Cheng Lai-Sheung... her family members have already clarified publicly that it was only a matter of dispute on fighting for legacy" (Hong Kong Hansard 1994: 4553).

In contrast, the women's stories were very effective when filtered through the lens developed in the Anti-Discrimination Female Indigenous Residents Committee and presented as examples of gender inequality. Social movement scholars have noted the degree to which individual testimonials can help legitimate a cause and, by extension, rally support behind it (Keck and Sikkink 1998: 19–20). In the female inheritance movement, the women's stories played a critical role in giving a human face to the problem and discrediting the Kuk's claim that it was the sole voice of indigenous villagers. During the October 1993 motion debate, several of the legislative councillors mentioned having met the indigenous women and having been moved by the women's stories. These women's stories also refuted Kuk claims that no one complained about male-only inheritance (Hong Kong Hansard 1993: 249, 253, 256).

It would be easy to believe that the indigenous women lost control of their stories and were exploited for political change, as has occurred elsewhere (Keck and Sikkink 1998: 20). The reality, however, is more nuanced. While the outsiders on the Residents Committee helped the women present themselves to the outsiders world, the women themselves played an active role in shaping the strategy. The idea of writing new lyrics for indigenous songs, for example, came from the women (Chan 1995: 108; see also Cheng interview, 2003). The idea was a public relations coup: the image of indigenous women singing traditional songs became an incon of the movement. The women also had a voice in the wider women's movement through the chairperson of the Residents Committee, Ms. Cheng, who attended meetings of a coalition of women's groups. Perhaps most important, the women spoke for themselves. While the outside members of the Residents Committee coached the women, they also felt strongly that the women should have their own voice (Chan 1995: 117; see also Wong interview, 2003).

As the indigenous women learned to tell their stories differently, they moved from framing their problems as kinship violations to presenting them as a product of discrimination and gender inequality. This shift in consciousness seems to have been an additive process. Although the women developed a new perception of the problem as gender discrimination, they retained their old sense of individual wrongs perpetrated by male relatives. Consciousness is slippery and unquantifiable, and it is difficult to know how completely the indigenous women assimilated the gender-equality framework. One woman told her story using terms such as "gender discrimination" and "injustice," for example, terms that she had not known before joining the Residents Committee (Chan 1995: 146). The Hakka mountain song that the women developed also refers to injustice. The first two lines of the song show an awareness that the indigenous women stand together as an oppressed group with common concerns: "Female indigenous women are the most unfortunate people / This world is unfair to them" (p. 98). The second two lines go farther, asking the Legislative Council to address the problem and, by implication, change the law: "The Hong Kong society is unjust / I hope that the Legislative Councillors will uphold justice" (p. 98).

Yet the Hakka song does not mention rights, and there is little evidence that the indigenous women developed a sustained critique of their problems based on human rights. Despite one women's statement that "now and after [the handover in] 1997, I will continue to bravely stand up and fight for the rights of indigenous women," the indigenous women dropped out of the women's movement after the land exemption ordinance was passed (Hong Kong Women Christian Council 1995: 126; see also interviews). No doubt they were tired of fighting, but this may also be a sign that their concerns were rooted in their particular problems with uncooperative male relatives rather than a larger struggle for gender equality. The women's frustration with demonstrations that did not focus exclusively on them is another sign that the rights perspective never entirely replaced the kinship-violation frame. Moreover, Chan reports that some of the women were upset when their stories were subsumed by the larger themes of gender equality or antidiscrimination (1995: 116, 146).

Passage of the Bill

After the initial debate and the formation of the Anti-Discrimination Female Indigenous Residents Committee, events began unfolding rapidly. Inside the Legislative Council, Christine Loh took up the female inheritance cause for the rural indigenous women. Loh, educated in both Hong Kong and England, says that the issue appealed to her because she thought it was "very odd" that indigenous women had "less rights" than everyone else in Hong Kong (interview, 2003). On January 31, 1994, she submitted an amendment to extend the land exemption ordinance to include rural land. If passed, it would have allowed female indigenous women to inherit family property, although not the ancestral trust lands held by lineages.

For a few months after Loh submitted her amendment, things were quiet. The Heung Yee Kuk, relying on old-style colonial politics, ignored the issue because it assumed that the amendment would never receive government support. But on March 10 the government announced that it would not oppose Loh's amendment. This was a turning point, particularly because it had initially seemed that extending female inheritance to indigenous women would be an uphill battle. While the outcome seems inevitable in retrospect, the colonial government had long courted the support of the Kuk to ensure that rural development was not met with serious resistance, and many thought the government would continue to back it on the inheritance issue. In fact, it is not clear why the colonial government had a change of heart. Some Kuk members felt that the government had sold them out because it no longer required Kuk support to develop the New Territories (*South China Morning Post*, March 27, 1993). The Kuk's pro-Beijing stance and opposition to Governor Patten's political reforms may also have played a role (*South China Morning Post*, March 27, 1993).

In response to the change in the government's position, the Kuk organized a rally on March 22 attended by over 1,200 supporters (*South China Morning Post*, March 23, 1993). At 3:50 p.m., 20 incensed indigenous villagers broke through security barriers during a protest outside the Legislative Council building. They attacked people demonstrating for equal inheritance rights, ripped up banners, threw water bottles, and shouted curses (*South China Morning Post*, March 23, 1994; see also Tse interview, 2003). Lee Wing-tat, a legislative councillor caught in the fray, fell to the ground after a punch to the back. After March 22, both sides realized the strength of the opposition and the scale of the fight ahead of them. At that point, 12 women's groups formed the Coalition for Equal Inheritance Rights to fight for rural women's inheritance rights in the New Territories (Tong 1999: 55–56).[12] Three days later, the Kuk formed the Headquarters for the Protection for the Village and Defense of the Clan (p. 58). For the next three months, these two groups worked hard to gain support, holding frequent demonstrations and facing off dozens of times.

In both the March 22 rally and subsequent demonstrations, the Kuk positioned itself as the defender of tradition and culture.[13] Traditionally, women left their home village and became part of their husbands' lineages. Allowing female inheritance, the Kuk argued, would lead to a disintegration of clan identity because land would eventually be owned by nonlineage members (Chan 1998: 45). To buttress its claim, it appealed to the authority of the ancestors. Male-only inheritance is "in accordance with the wishes of [the] ancestors" and, as a result, "any outsider tampering with these customs shall not be tolerated" (Heung Yee Kuk Proclamation, quoted in Chan 1998: 45). In order for this claim to be seen as legitimate, the male-dominated Kuk realized that it would need the support of indigenous women. It found women who agreed with Angela Li York-lan: "[We] do not think we are discriminated against. We love our traditions. We have the right not to accept any change" (*South China Morning Post*, April 4, 1994). At one demonstration, the Kuk vice chairman, Daniel Lam, said, "We have shown the community that villagers are able to demonstrate endurance, calm and reason in the fight against the destruction of our customs" (*Hong Kong Standard*, April 12, 1994).

As defenders of tradition, the Kuk placed emphasis on being Chinese. One song often sung at demonstrations was "The Brave Chinese," renamed "The Brave New Territories People" (Chan 1998: 47). Being Chinese meant renewing attention to the anticolonial strands of indigenous history. In April 1994, 1,000 villagers gathered to commemorate an 1899 uprising against the British at Tai Po (p. 45; see also *South China Morning Post*, April 18, 1994). Ironically, it was the first time the uprising had ever been publicly commemorated (p. 46). Kuk demonstrations lend themselves to dramatic media coverage. The inheritance issue remained in the public eye from October 1993 (the motion debate) through June 1994 (the passage of the bill) because Kuk members did things such as beheading a doll representing Governor Pattern (*South China Morning Post*, April 18, 1994). On another occasion, angry villagers threatened to rape Loh if she dared set foot in the New Territories (*South China Morning Post*, March 26, 1994). When it came to media attention, Loh said, "One couldn't have better opponents than the Heung Yee Kuk" (interview, 2003).

Although there were times when the outcome of Loh's amendment was unclear, the issue was pretty much settled by May 1994. The public overwhelmingly supported female inheritance rights, by a margin of 77% in favor to 9% opposed (*South China Morning Post*, May 9, 1994).[14] There was little sympathy for the Heung Yee

Kuk both because people generally believed in gender equality and because they were resentful of what they saw as the special privileges granted to indigenous villagers. Recognizing the extent of public support for extending female inheritance rights from urban women in the New Territories to indigenous women, the government incorporated Loh's amendment into its own bill, along with suggestions from several other legislative councillors (Tsang and Wang 1994: 13). On May 24, 1994, the Bills Committee of the Legislative Council accepted the government's amended bill and voted down Heung Yee Kuk Chairman Lau Wong-fat's suggestion of a referendum in the New Territories to settle the issue (Tsang and Wan 1994: 12). By the time of the actual vote on June 22, the result was a foregone conclusion. The New Territories Land (Exemption) Ordinance passed easily, with 36 votes in favor, 2 against, and 3 abstentions (Hong Kong Hansard 1994: 4656).

Creating Custom: The History Behind the Debate

The female inheritance movement is full of deep ironies about the meanings of tradition and modernity. Most basically, it was a struggle over land rights and political power in which powerful male leaders claimed to be defending culture, tradition, and the lineage while poor indigenous women and their elite urban allies claimed to speak for gender equality and universal human rights. Yet this dichotomy between tradition and modernity was a constructed truth, created both by the protagonists and by the historical legacy of colonialism.

Colonial roots

Hong Kong's dual legal system was the result of the unusual circumstances under which the British gained control of the New Territories. In contrast to Hong Kong Island and Kowloon, which were ceded to Britain in perpetuity, the terms of the 1899 Convention of Peking specified that the New Territories would be leased to Britain for 99 years. This was the lease that expired on July 1, 1997, when Hong Kong (including Hong Kong Island and Kowloon) was handed back to China. The limited scope of Britain's right to rule was one reason to preserve local custom as much as possible (Petersen 1996: 339; Jones 1995: 167–70). After gaining control of the New Territories, the British issued a number of proclamations assuring New Territories villagers that the New Territories would be "governed … according to the laws, customs and usages of the Chinese by the elders of villages, subject to the control of the British magistrate" (quoted in Chan 1999: 234). The 1899 Blake Proclamation, often cited as the grounds for deference to Chinese custom, further reassured villagers that "your usages and good customs will not in any way be interfered with" (Lockhart 1900: appendix no. 9). Before World War II, villagers were governed by local elders according to Chinese custom and law with a British district officer to resolve disputes.

    This strategy was dictated by economics and a desire to avoid conflict. Remembering the expensive and bloody 1857 Sepoy Rebellion in India, British colonial administrators decided that adherence to Chinese customary law in the

New Territories was the best way to ensure local support for colonialism at minimal cost (Chiu and Hung 2000: 226; see also Jones 1995: 168). Because the British never believed that the New Territories would be particularly profitable (Chun 2000: 48), they saw the New Territories villagers in terms of culture and kinship, not as potential laborers. In contrast to Hong Kong Island, which saw rapid change, the New Territories villages were treated as bearers of tradition, isolated and expected not to change. For many colonial administrators, preserving village life became a romantic goal (Jones 1995: 180). Until urbanization and industrialization hit the New Territories in the 1970s and 1980s, the area was seen as "a virtual laboratory for the study of rural Chinese society" (Watson 1983: 486).

The New Territories were dominated by powerful patrilineages, corporate groups that traced membership through male descent. While multilineage villages did exist, most males in a community could trace their family back to a common ancestor. The members of the patrilineage had common land, held celebrations to worship common ancestors, and cooperated for political purposes (Watson 1983: 486). In contrast to the situation in the rest of Hong Kong, it was permissible in the New Territories to make gifts of land to ancestral trusts in perpetuity. In 1948 about one-third of the land was held in such ancestral trusts, with sale permitted only by all beneficiaries (Strickland Report 1953: 62). The female inheritance dispute focused not on lands held in ancestral trusts but on family lands.

Despite a common belief that patrilineages were unified corporate groups, there was considerable inequality in the villages and within lineages. Watson's (1985) careful ethnographic study from the 1970s reveals that small-holder tenants were heavily dependent on their wealthy agnates.[15] These two classes were quite distinct, with different forms of marriage, levels of education, kinds of houses, and social lives for wives and daughters. Although it was important for the lineage to present itself as a unified corporation to the outside world and to its members, it existed in a highly stratified society. Moreover, during the last quarter of the twentieth century, inheritance patterns slowly started changing. Local lawyers sometimes found ways around the ban on women's inheritance of family land, particularly if the village head was supportive. In the absence of a male heir, widows or daughters occasionally inherited land or acquired the cash after the properties were sold (Chan 1997: 169). Sometimes a woman could keep land if she did not remarry. Her position was, in essence, "trustee for life" (Selby 1991: 73).

Defining custom

Since Chinese custom was not codified, it was typically interpreted by British magistrates serving in the New Territories and the courts (see, e.g., Coates 1956, Wesley-Smith 1994). For colonial administrators, preserving local customs meant identifying them, a problematic process. Despite references to homogeneous "Chinese customs," there was variation in customs among lineages, villages, and districts (Wesley-Smith 1994: 218; Strickland Report 1953: 13). No doubt overwhelmed by this diversity, the British began an effort to record Chinese customs in 1899. The result was a particularly idealized version of Chinese custom because their informants were mostly village elders and scholars, men – they were all men – with an interest in preserving the status quo (Chan 1999: 236). District officers developed a "bible" of points of custom, which they passed on to others. Coupled with testimony from expert witnesses alive in 1899, these notes were used by British district officers to resolve land disputes according to traditional Chinese law until they were lost in the 1941–44 Japanese occupation (Wesley-Smith 1994: 206).

This was an ironic situation. Despite their confessed ignorance, British district officers functioned as upholders of Chinese tradition.[16] Perhaps as a result of uncertainty, district officers tended to be conservative, with the result that adherence to Chinese law and custom was reinforced and solidified (Wesley-Smith 1994: 206, 222–23). The additional irony is that other Chinese societies, such as Taiwan and Mainland China, reformed Chinese law and custom to allow equal inheritance. By refusing to allow this kind of change, the British froze New Territories life in a mythic, imagined past. This model of colonial administration worked in the prewar era because the New Territories were still largely rural. In 1931 the population of the New Territories was 98,000. Most residents were still farmers, and district officers could hear most disputes (Watson 1983: 484). Most important, the New Territories were isolated enough from urban Hong Kong to maintain a different legal system and set of rights. This isolation ended in the postwar era.

Postwar changes: the end of village life

The end of World War II brought a wave of migrants from China. Residents who had fled Hong Kong during the Japanese occupation returned, accompanied by refugees from the Chinese civil war. Between 1945 and 1950 the population of Hong Kong jumped from 600,000 to between 2 and 2.5 million, an increase of roughly 400% (Bray 2001: 16; see also Chun 2000: 111). This jump in population created an intense need for new public housing. After a 1953 fire in the Shek Kip Mei squatter community, the Hong Kong government decided to build public housing on a massive scale. Urban Hong Kong was already overcrowded, so the new public housing estates had to be built in the New Territories. The government built seven New Towns in the New Territories, each of which included industry, public housing, community services, and infrastructure (Scott 1982: 660).

This development was tremendously disruptive to rural life. In the most direct measure of disruption, about 50 villages were physically moved to make room for the New Towns and another 25 villages were moved in order to create reservoirs to meet the water needs of the expanding urban population (Hayes 2001: 72). Not surprisingly, the old district officer system could not keep up with population growth and the new burdens of New Towns administration. Starting in 1961, land dispute cases were resolved by the courts; the district officers were no longer "father mother officials" (*fu mu guan*) but pure administrators.

Most important, development changed the economy of the New Territories by creating new sources of wealth. Land for the New Towns was largely purchased from New Territories villagers, either with cash or through a land swap (Nissim 1998: 102). Between 1984 and 1997, the period just before reunification with China, there was a rapid increase in wealth based in part on the skyrocketing value of real estate (Smart and Lee 2003: 167; see also Chan 2001: 272). In 1993 one legislative councilor said, "When I was small, people were still talking about 'country people' with 'feet covered with cow dung' and 'illiterate.' But today we see that the members of the Heung Yee Kuk are all tycoons in smart suits and traveling in Rolls Royces" (Hong Kong Hansard 1993: 240). The development value of land was part of a larger move away from an agricultural economy. Cheap rice imports from Thailand flooded Hong Kong in the 1950s. Rice farming, the traditional occupation in the New Territories, was suddenly unprofitable (Watson 1983: 483). Some farmers switched to vegetables, but many others decided to emigrate. Suddenly, villages were transformed from physical communities based on a shared physical space to transnational communities based on shared traditions and birthplace (Chan 2001: 280).[17] As the rural wealthy became absentee landlords, a group of new entrepreneurs, distinct from the old elite of wealthy landlord-merchants, emerged. The new entrepreneurs were supported and nurtured by colonial officials because they were more willing to cooperate with Hong Kong officials in their development plans than the old elite (Watson 1985: 147–48). In addition, they tended to be less concerned with lineage unity (p. 148).

It was against this backdrop of urbanization, industrialization, and dislocation that the rural women stepped forward to protest their inability to inherit land.

Layers and Translators: Theorizing the Movement

The story of how indigenous women came to demand a change in inheritance shows how international human rights can be used to address local grievances. Yet this is not a simple story of elite outsiders introducing or imposing rights language. Rather, rights language, mediated through translators, was adopted, modified, supplemented, and ignored by the various participants. Here, we introduce four layers as a way of thinking about the degree to which actors were tied to international rights language. These four layers – expatriates, the Legislative Council, women's groups, and indigenous women – differed significantly from each other in ideology, level of education, extent of international travel, degree of international rights consciousness, and language.

Expatriates

Expatriates played a critical role in bringing the female inheritance issue to prominence and framing it in rights terms. Although it is difficult to remember in hindsight, there was no reason male-only inheritance had to be addressed through legislative change. In 1993, five indigenous women had applied for legal aid to sue for equal inheritance. They were denied legal aid, but their efforts show that the inheritance issue could have been settled on a case-by-case basis by the courts instead of by legislative change (*South China Morning Post*, October 23, 1993). Inheritance was resolved through legislation because, in the course of preparing its ICCPR report, the Hong Kong Council of Women discovered that female inheritance was illegal throughout the New Territories, not just in the villages (Jones interview, 2003).

After securing the necessity of changes to the New Territories Ordinance, expatriates lobbied for female inheritance as a question of international law. The Hong Kong Council of Women's report clearly stated that male-only inheritance "should have been declared *unlawful* long ago, as [it is] contrary to Article 26 of the ICCPR" and is "in conflict with the principle of equality between sexes contained in the internationally accepted Declaration of Elimination of Discrimination Against Women" (Howarth et al. 1991: 16, 12). These expatriates were primarily academics and lawyers, several of whom dealt with international law professionally. They were mostly from the United States, Britain, or Australia and spoke English fluently, if not as a first language. On a local-global continuum they were undeniably global, and they saw denying women inheritance rights as a violation of women's right to protection from gender discrimination.

The Legislative Council

The Legislative Council, Hong Kong's national elite, saw female inheritance primarily as a choice between tradition and modernity. In the final debate over the land exemption ordinance, opponents of the bill claimed that it would "attack the age-old fine tradition of the clan system" and "disturb the peace in the countryside" (Hong Kong Hansard 1994: 4579).[18] Others sympathetic to the Kuk complained about the pace of change.[19] In the words of one legislator, "This is an attempt to change the social customs of the indigenous population. Such thinking will gradually be overtaken by newer concepts. In view of this, should we take the hasty move of enforcing the changes through the legislative process?" (p. 4544). Not even Kuk supporters, however, dared question the tenet of gender equality (Lee 2000: 248). Chairman Lau Wong-fat maintained that the indigenous women "are not actually treated unequally. In fact, they are equal in other respects. Many of them may even often bully their husbands" (Hong Kong Hansard 1994: 4559).

On the other side of the debate, supporters of the bill argued that Hong Kong could not be an international city as long as it had laws that discriminated against women. As one legislator put it, "Hong Kong is a prosperous and progressive metropolis. The fact that the indigenous women of the New Territories are still openly discriminated against is a disgrace for the people of Hong Kong" (Hong Kong Hansard 1994: 4565). Others made an explicit connection between the Kuk's rowdy behavior and support for the land exemption ordinance: "When the 20th century is coming to a close, that someone should so shamelessly and overtly threaten to rape is indeed a shame on this modern international city of Hong Kong. Today members of this Council must use their vote to remove such a stigma on Hong Kong" (p. 4542).

Christine Loh, originally attracted to the issue because she saw it in rights terms, continued to talk about equality and human rights: "The idea of human rights is that we have to protect every individual's basic right. Not to mention that there are 200 indigenous women complaining, even if there were only two of them, we as legislators still have the responsibility of ensuring their equal right before the law" (quoted in Lee 2000: 250). Some legislators also referred to international rights, echoing the rhetoric used by the expatriate layer. Legislative Councillor Anna Wu, herself a lawyer, was one of the first to pick up the connection between female inheritance and international law. In a December 1993 letter to members of the Bills Committee, she wrote: "The 1976 extension of the ICCPR to Hong Kong and the 1991 enactment of the Bill of Rights Ordinance should have cast serious doubt on the continuing validity of the system established by the NTO (New Territories Ordinance)" (1994: 1).

For legislators, there were two appealing aspects of international law. First, international law could be used to shame the government into action. In question-and-answer sessions with government representatives, Legislative Council members occasionally inquired about international covenants as a way of holding the government responsible to the ideals expressed in UN documents (Hong Kong Hansard 1993: 156–57, 159–60). The other appealing aspect of international law was its perceived connection to modernity. In the debate over the passage of the land exemption ordinance, Legislative Councillor Fung called it "both out of date and inappropriate to deprive women of their land rights," particularly because the Bill of Rights, the ICCPR, and CEDAW all stated that all citizens should be equal before the law (Hong Kong Hansard 1994: 4547).

Most supporters of the bill were not much concerned about the abolition of custom, perhaps because neither they nor their constituencies would be affected by the change in law. "Outdated customs are a burden," declared one legislator (Hong Kong Hansard 1993: 139; see also 1994: 4542). However, Anna Wu was concerned that the ordinance would inadvertently abolish a positive tradition: women's rights under Chinese customary law to maintenance from the estate (see also Loh 1997: 6). Although these customary rights were never enforced by the courts, male relatives were traditionally responsible for the ongoing maintenance of widows and unmarried daughters. Ms. Cheng's original complaint, for example, was that her brothers had violated Chinese custom by refusing to allow her to stay in her father's house. In a March 1993 letter to the members of the Bills Committee, Wu expressed her concern that the bill would be "placing in jeopardy the welfare" of women "dependent on the residual customary obligations of the landowner" (1993: 2). While not widely shared, her apprehension showed sensitivity to the strengths of the old system. It suggests that her vision of the problem bridged the perspectives of the expatriate, national, and local groups.

Women's groups

In 1989, 20 women's groups formed a coalition to lobby for a women's commission and the extension of CEDAW to Hong Kong (Wong 2000: 60–61). Until the Coalition for Equal Inheritance Rights was founded in March 1994, the women's groups shared information and coordinated action on female inheritance through regular meetings of this coalition. In contrast to the Legislative Council or the expatriates, the coalition functioned entirely in Cantonese. Like the wider women's movement, it consisted primarily of middle-class, educated women, including students and social workers (see Tong n.d.: 648).

The women's groups conceptualized the female inheritance issue mainly in terms of gender equality. T-shirts and banners from the movement often carried the logo "♀ = ♂." In keeping with this theme, one women's group issued a statement that "based on the principle of equality, land inheritance right is the right of every indigenous inhabitant. If women inhabitants are not entitled to it because of their gender, it is blatant discrimination, something we cannot accept" (quoted in Lee 2000: 250). The women's groups treated gender equality as a self-evident tenet and, for the most part, saw no need to justify it in terms of law. When they did talk about the law, women's groups borrowed their arguments and even their language from the ICCPR report. One AAF publication directly quoted the report, saying that male-only inheritance rights "should have been declared *unlawful* long ago" (Association for the Advancement of Feminism 1993: 14). Like the legislative councillors, the women's groups made an explicit connection between gender equality and modernity. Male-only inheritance was "archaic and out of step with society's development." The Hong Women Christian Council went so far as to say, "Gender equality is a shared goal of the modern world" (quoted in Wong 2000: 192). Along with the legislative councillors, the women's groups focused on changing the law, not on providing solutions for individual women.

However, there were some important differences in perspective between the women's groups and the legislative councillors. The women's groups saw male-only inheritance as a product of patriarchy, a strand of thought that never emerged in the Legislative Council.[20] One group accused the Heung Yee Kuk of "patriarchal hegemony" (Wong 2000: 192). Another suggested that the majority of indigenous women were not aware of their oppression because of "patriarchal socialization.... A harmony that conceals injustice is not one to be applauded" (quoted in Lee 2000: 250–51). This critique of patriarchy was closely mixed with antifeudalism, a term associated with postre-volutionary thought in China. The term "feudalism" functioned as a kind of shorthand to connote backward customs in need of change. During the rally outside the Legislative Council in connection with the October motion debate, demonstrators shouted "Down with feudal traditions!" (*Hong Kong Standard*, October 14, 1993). Antifeudalism was the theme of the May 4, 1994, demonstration outside the Legislative Council in honor of China's May 4th movement (Cheung 1994: 7). By "feudal traditions" the women's groups generally meant gender inequality, usually stemming from patriarchy. Male-only succession was said to reinforce "the feudalistic idea that women are inferior to men" (Association for the Advancement of Feminism 1993: 7). One women's group wrote that "depending on fathers, husbands and children is exactly what the 'three subordinations' teaches in feudal society" and is in opposition "to the principle of independence for women" (quoted in Lee 2000: 250).

In striving toward modernity and renouncing "backward" customs, women's groups and legislative councillors were drawing on themes familiar from twentieth-century Chinese history. Both May 4th reformers and Cultural Revolution zealots fought against custom and feudalism in the name of progress. Nevertheless, many of the concepts used by the women's groups – gender equality, human rights, and patriarchy – were appropriated from Western thought. Gender inequality based on the critique of patriarchy is a standard feminist message, as familiar to the U.S. National Organization of Women as to Hong Kong's AAF. The women's groups' techniques of activism – demonstrations, T-shirts, and banners – are also familiar from Western feminism, as is the ♀ = ♂ logo. While the broader themes were appropriated from abroad, local symbols were used to express international ideas. Singing their modified Hakka songs, the women wore traditional hats colloquially known as "Hakka hats" – an ironic choice of symbols given that Hakkas are a denigrated group in the New Territories. Even the slogans about feudalism were a way to put gender equality in a regional historical context.

The overarching appropriation of Western feminist concepts and activist techniques is interesting because many of Hong Kong's women's groups were founded specifically to indigenize Western feminism. AAF, for example, was founded "to bring together people who speak our language and share a similar background" and "work within our own culture" (AAF founder quoted in Choi 1995: 95).[21] Still, even if ideas and tactics were borrowed from abroad, the women's groups were indigenized in the sense that the leaders were Hong Kong women and discussions were conducted primarily in Cantonese. In discussing the role of the Hong Kong Women Christian Council, one of the founding members emphasized the importance of local leadership: "[We are] a local Christian women's group, not the expatriates. If they join us, then they may play a supporter's role ... but we have a local basis" (quoted in Choi 1995: 97).

Indigenous women

The indigenous women's were the only lower-class voices in the female inheritance movement. While 200 indigenous women signed petitions supporting the movement, only 6 had high-profile roles (Chan 1995: 17). Of these 5 were relatively poor, 4 had very limited education, 3 were Hakka, and 1 spoke only Hakka (pp. 42–46).[22] One spoke fluent English and had been educated at a local university, traveled widely, and worked as a reporter (pp. 46, 95); while the other women hoped to recover their parents' property and assert their identities as lineage members, this woman participated in the movement to support gender equality and human rights (pp. 40, 42, 46). Comparing these six women with the Kuk elite, it is clear that there was a class-struggle aspect to the movement. One of the indigenous women remarked, "Before, when all the villagers were poor, we helped each other out. Now we are enemies" (pp. 30–32). However, the movement focused on gender, not class. One of the few references to class came from Ms. Cheng: "Before we had nothing while the male villagers had everything. There was a wide gap between rich and poor, and women were inferior at that time" (interview, Asia Television News, February 27, 2001). In her mind, class and gender were intertwined. Women were inferior not just because they were women but because they were poor.

The indigenous women slowly shifted from seeing their stories as individual kinship violations to broader examples of discrimination. The theme of rights and gender equality was prominent in documents collectively written by the Residents Committee. In an article published in the Hong Kong Federation of Women's Centres annual report, the committee called the denial of female inheritance "a century-long discriminatory barrier to the indigenous women's basic rights" (Hong Kong Federation of Women's Centres 1994: 88). A submission to the Legislative Council talked about the "inherent right" to succession and mentioned "the protection to women that has been laid down in the United Nations Universal Declaration of Human Rights" (Anti-Discrimination Female Indigenous Residents Committee 1994). Because the majority of the indigenous women were illiterate, it is probable that such articles and statements were guided, if not written, by Linda Wong or the other outsiders on the Residents Committee.

On an individual level, Ms. Cheng was both the person most comfortable talking about female inheritance in terms of equality and rights and the person most comfortable talking to the press. In one interview she said, "What I am fighting for is sexual equality" (*Sunday Telegraph*, October 24, 1993). At another point she said that if the government refused to change the law it "would be violating the Bill of Rights" (*Hong Kong Standard*, October 14, 1993). In contrast, another indigenous woman's critique of the New Territories Ordinance was limited to the fact that "the legislation does not take care of situations where families do not have any sons, which is my case" (*South China Morning Post*, February 25, 1993). Because she spoke rights language, Ms. Cheng could bring the women's concerns to a wider public.

Translators

There were relatively few points of contact between the four layers. After their initial work framing the issue, the expatriates attended rallies but rarely went to coalition meetings. The fact that coalition meetings were held in Cantonese was an important barrier. The women's groups informed Christine Loh about upcoming demonstrations, but there was little dialogue with Loh or her office. And the indigenous women had little contact with any of the other layers except to attend formal Legislative Council hearings and rallies. Nevertheless, these four layers formed a coalition that made the female inheritance movement possible. Each layer was aware that it had to work with the others for the movement to succeed. For example, when the head of the Kuk, Lau Wong-fat, claimed that respect for the traditions of indigenous people helped promote harmony in society, a supporter of the movement in the Legislative Council retorted that they had received complaints from female indigenous residents that they were "oppressed by the sexist traditions" (*South China Morning Post*, October 14, 1993). The legislator was able to call on indigenous women's voices to refute the Kuk's call for respecting tradition.

A few translators connected the layers. Translators can move between layers because they conceptualize the issue in more than one way and can translate one set of principles and terms into another. They created a movement in which rights language and indigenous women's stories could come together to create political change. Although the women did acquire some consciousness of rights through participation in the Residents Committee, rights language was mainly promoted by others. Through translators, the indigenous women joined their stories to a larger movement concerned with human rights and discrimination.

Our research uncovered at least three people who acted as translators: Lai-sheung Cheng, Linda Wong, and Anna Wu. Ms. Cheng, in essence, created the Residents Committee by finding other women with similar stories who were ready to step forward. Through her participation in coalition meetings and her contacts with the media, she brought the women's concerns to a wider audience. She was able to generalize individual kinship grievances and lobby for a change in the law. By having a voice in the coalition's strategy, she was also able to shape how the women's stories were used in the movement.

Although she did not have a formal leadership title, Linda Wong was a critical link between the indigenous women and the broader world. The women were able to tell their stories in the Legislative Council because Linda Wong created the opportunity and showed them how to do it. With the help of other outsiders, she helped frame the women's stories in terms of equality and rights so that they were politically viable. In contrast to the indigenous women, who rarely traveled outside of the New Territories, Wong had experience in activism and had a good idea what the media and the public would find appealing. The carefully orchestrated dramas and songs had, in the words of one participant, a "symbolic meeting" that "became an icon for the whole movement" (Chan interview, 2003). Wong also literally translated the Cantonese and Hakka used by the indigenous women into English. Using English ensured that the women's stories reached a wider audience and were taken seriously by elites. In a sense, both Linda Wong and Laisheung Cheng translated "up"; they took stories anchored in a local kinship idiom and talked about them in global rights language.

In the Legislative Council, Anna Wu was a translator of quite a different kind. With help from other legislative councillors, Wu brought international law, a concern mainly expressed by the expatriate layer, into the Legislative Council debate. However, it is clear from her attempt to codify indigenous women's customary rights that she also understood and appreciated the kinship system.[23] By bringing the kinship system into a dialogue about rights, she helped to localize the debate. This localization could have gone farther if other legislative councillors had been sensitive to the kinship dimension. The issue died quietly because the discussion was dominated by the tradition-versus-rights debate.

Local as a matter of degree?

Taking about the female inheritance movement in terms of layers is implicitly a discussion about what it means to be local and global. As an international import, rights talk is, by definition, global. More global layers tended to see female inheritance as an international human rights issue, more local layers as a kinship violation. However, the terms "global" and "local" are not particularly useful. They are often a stand-in for social class. To say that the indigenous women are local while the expatriates are global is to say that the expatriates are educated, mobile, and rich while the indigenous women are illiterate, fixed, and poor. In an international city like Hong Kong, it is not even clear that there is any "local." Global influences are so pervasive that "local" is a matter of degree.

"Local" is a particularly slippery word because no one in the female inheritance movement is a truly local actor. The indigenous women seem local, for example, but one of the core members of the Residents Committee lived in Holland; she had found out about the inheritance debate during a visit home (Wong and Chan interview, 2003). The Heung Yee Kuk is actually a transnational group because so many villagers have emigrated but retain their New Territories identity. They help pay for celebrations, and many come back to reconnect with their villages during yearly rituals (Chan 2001: 276). They feel strongly about preserving the past, and, as a result, indigenous tradition is largely financed, protected, and promulgated by people who no longer live in Hong Kong. Overseas villagers were encouraged to participate in demonstrations against the female inheritance movement, and the Headquarters for the Protection for the Village and Defense of the Clan even established a U.K. branch (Tong 1999: 58).

As a transnational actor, the Kuk was attuned to the persuasiveness of human rights language. In the late 1960s it had closely watched Britain's behavior in Gibraltar and learned that indigenous people were entitled to certain rights (Chan 1998: 41). In a 1994 proclamation, the Kuk appealed to international norms to protect local tradition: "The indigenous inhabitants of any country in the world all have their legitimate traditions and customs well protected by law.... Therefore the existing provisions in the legislation to safeguard the traditional customs of New Territories indigenous inhabitants are ... a primary obligation of the Hong Kong government" (quoted in Chan 1998: 42). It was a stretch, but during the October 1993 motion debate one legislative councillor argued that female inheritance would violate the human rights of ancestors. "There should not be a double standard in human rights," he said. "As we have to respect the human rights of our contemporaries, we have also to respect the human rights of our ancient ancestors" (Hong Kong Hansard 1993: 268).

"Global" and "local" become particularly meaningless in the context of international politics. Against the backdrop of the 1997 handover and the larger question of Sino-British relations, every issue in Hong Kong had a global dimension. The Kuk lobbied hard for China's support as a way of putting pressure on individual legislators to vote down the land exemption ordinance.[24] Although China's top leaders did not comment on the inheritance question, China was initially supportive of the Kuk. Both the Xinhua news agency, China's de facto embassy in Hong Kong, and the Hong Kong and Macau Affairs office released statements in March 1994 warning the Hong Kong government that the amended ordinance violated the Basic Law (Lui 1997: chap. 4, 13; Wong 2000: 187). Following up on this, Kuk representatives met China's ambassador in England on April 5 (Tsang and Wan 1994: 10) and found the ambassador supportive. China's support noticeably waned, however, as the vote on the ordinance drew closer. The internal workings of the Chinese Communist Party (CCP) are opaque, but it must have decided that international bad press about lack of support for gender equality was not worth the support of the Kuk.[25]

Moreover, the "local" problem of female inheritance was created by the world's ultimate global system – colonialism. The root of the problem was, of course, the preservation of Chinese customary land law under the British, but this was not the root cause of the Kuk's opposition to the land exemption ordinance. Customs were slowly changing in the New Territories, and it was becoming more and more common for women to inherit money, if not land (Chan 1997: 169). The Kuk was not horrified by the idea of female inheritance per se; it wanted to protect the profits guaranteed under another colonial policy, the 1972 small-house policy. The small-house policy allowed any male villager who could trace his lineage back to 1898 to obtain a 700-square-foot piece of land, free of land premium, to build a house for himself within the borders of the village (Chan 2003: 72).[26] All New Territories men, even those overseas, are eligible for this once-in-lifetime land grant. The original aim of the policy was to replace temporary housing and allow for natural growth in the New Territories, but a glut of small houses has led to rapid development (Hopkinson and Lei 2003: 2). Although the small-house policy was originally considered a privilege that would be abolished if abused, it has come to be seen as a right (Hopkinson and Lei 2003: 4, 31), and because of rising land values it is a very valuable one. Although the Kuk cites clan continuity as the primary justification for the policy, houses are often sold or rented to outsiders for a profit (Chan 1999: 238–40). During the female inheritance movement it was an open secret that the Kuk was concerned that female inheritance would lead to the repeal of other indigenous rights, particularly the small-house policy (see Chan 2003). The village elder Bruce Kan even said publicly, "The next thing the government would do is cancel our rights on applying for land" (*South China Morning Post*, March 27, 1993).

But the zeitgeist was simply against the Kuk. The years 1989–97 were the high tide of human rights consciousness in Hong Kong (Petersen interview, 2003). The 1991 passage of the Bill of Rights, based on the ICCPR, encouraged everyone, including women, to think in terms of human rights (Petersen and Samuels 2002: 24). Greater awareness of human rights coincided with Patten's democratic reforms, particularly the 1992 reform package and the 1991 introduction of direct elections to the Legislative Council. Democratization led to increased attention to local problems.[27] As Christine Loh said, "It was the golden age of democracy in Hong Kong, and I was honored to be the salad tosser" (Loh interview, 2003).

Conclusion

The female inheritance movement illustrates the localization of global ideas. Gender equality, feminism, and human rights are ideas borrowed from another cultural context, spread through the UN system of treaties and major world conferences which draw government and nongovernmental activists together from all parts of the globe. This language was clearly critical to this movement at all levels, although to varying degrees. Much has been written about the importance of technology, particularly the Internet, as a force behind the globalization of ideas, but the female inheritance movement underscores the importance of people. Much of the rights discourse was introduced by expatriates. It was subsequently picked up by Hong Kong residents who had either spent time abroad, like Christine Loh and Anna Wu, or been exposed to this kind of language by others. As people flow across borders in search of jobs or education, they carry ideas with them. Cultural translators reinterpret these ideas in ways that make sense in more particular and local terms.

Success is important to the spread of traveling theories such as that of human rights. During the campaign, the indigenous women expected that the new law would allow them to inherit their fathers' property, although some also filed lawsuits (Chan 1995: 48). However, the land exemption ordinance was not retroactive, so the original claimants whose fathers had already died did not benefit. They had to file lawsuits under Chinese customary law and could only sue for compensation for male relatives' failure to fulfill their kinship obligations (pp. 18, 50, 134). Lack of success probably contributed to these women's disappearance from rights-based movements. Yet some of the indigenous women in the movement continued to talk about their misfortunes in terms of gender discrimination, injustice, and the land exemption ordinance. They still articulated their grievances in rights terms, even if they did not regain their property or become recognized as daughters in the lineage system (p. 146). In contrast, the passage of the law gave the women's groups, some legislators, and the expatriates a dramatic victory. And it is these groups rather than the indigenous women who sustained a long-term commitment to a rights framework.

The female inheritance movement shows that the power of rights discourse lies in its flexibility and contingency. As the recent literature on rights suggests, the broad umbrella of rights language can allow people with very different conceptions of the issue to work together (see Milner 1986, McCann 1994, Gilliom 2001, Goldberg-Hiller 2002, Goldberg-Hiller and Milner 2003). Through a system of layers and translators, women at the grass roots used rights language in a far more contingent and limited way than elites. Moreover, the rights frame was layered over the kinship frame, producing a kind of double consciousness. The female inheritance movement shows that rights mobilization does not require a deep and abiding commitment. Rather, it can be adopted in a more transitory and tentative way contingent on success. Although framing rights in local terms may increase their legitimacy and effectiveness, this analysis shows that not all participants in a movement need to be deeply committed to this framework.

The female inheritance movement also shows that rights language is appropriated because it is politically useful, not because it is imposed. In 1994 Hong Kong, rights had political currency precisely because they were associated with the international world and modernity. Both citizens and the government were concerned about losing Hong Kong's liberal traditions after the 1997 handover. Allegiance to gender equality and human rights was a sign, both to the people in Hong Kong and to the outside world, that things in Hong Kong were not going to change – that Hong Kong deserved a place in the "civilized" community of nations.

NOTES

1   Some studies show that global ideas build on local referents to establish their meaning and value, as in transnational fashions and music (see, e.g., Feld 2001).

2   Wills are considered bad luck in traditional Chinese culture because of their association with death. For this reason, wills detailing the division of property are rare. However, men occasionally leave "voice from the grave" wills that exhort family members to behave well or give a widow permission to remarry (Selby 1991: 72–73; see also Wong 2000: 173).

3   There were calls for a Bill of Rights prior to 1989, but the proposal was not endorsed by the government until after Tiananmen (Petersen 1996: 350). In a tricky bit of legislation drafting, Hong Kong's Bill of Rights was modeled on the ICCPR to make it harder to

repeal after the handover. China had already agreed in the Joint Declaration (the document outlining the terms of the handover) that the ICCPR would remain in force.

4   The Heung Yee Kuk, founded in 1926, has acted as a leader in protecting the interests of indigenous villagers, particularly with reference to land, and is the highest tier of the representative organization of the villagers (Chan 2003: 67, 87). Kuk members consist of the chair and vice chair of each of 27 rural committees made up of representatives elected by their villages (Asian Television Network, February 27, 2001). These conservative clan leaders have in the past opposed development, but since the late 1950s they have stopped doing so and sought to increase compensation for land from the government (Chan 2003: 71).

5   The Hong Kong Council of Women was formed in 1947. Because of an explosion in the number of local women's groups during the 1980s, membership in the early 1990s was limited to a small number of expatriate women.

6   The Hong Kong Council of Women also discovered that women had once been permitted to administer New Territories property after the death of a husband, father, or son, but 1971 changes to the laws governing inheritance had eliminated this possibility (Carol Jones, personal communication, October 14, 2003).

7   By the time the news broke, the Hong Kong Council of Women had already informed the government of the problem. In June 1993 the government started automatically exempting all new grants of lands (with the exception of land grants to indigenous villagers) from the New Territories Ordinance (*South China Morning Post*, March 11, 1994).

8   The exact number of members of the Residents Committee is unclear. Chan (1995: 39) cites six active members, although one is a news reporter without a grievance. Wong and Chan (interview, 2003) list seven core members. Most likely, there was some flux over time.

9   This is a matter of dispute. In a 2003 interview Ms. Cheng claimed that the women knew that the law had to be changed from the start.

10 In some cases, affection and kinship were valid criteria for female inheritance. Chan (1997: 155–59) discusses a case from the 1970s in which a village council ruled that a daughter could become trustee of her father's land because she was the person closest to her father.

11 All Chinese terms are in Mandarin. For a more extended discussion of what it means to be a "last-of-line" daughter, see Chan (1995: 40, 60–63).

12 The Coalition included the following groups: Anti-Discrimination Female Residents Committee, Hong Kong Federation of Women's Centres, Association for the Advancement of Feminism, Hong Kong Women Christian Council, Women's Rights Concern Group of the Chan Hing Social Service Centre, Hong Kong Women Workers Association, AWARE, Hong Kong Council of Women, Business and Professional Women, the Hong Kong Federation of Women, and two other community groups (Tong 1999: 64–65; see also Wong 2000: 62).

13 This appeal to tradition is an old argument. Defenders of the practice of keeping concubines argued that it was "an institution ... sanctioned by immemorial Chinese law and customs; it has been preserved by the Colony's Charter; it has received the highest judicial recognition" (quoted in Lee 2000: 232).

14 This was a survey of all of Hong Kong.

15 In a New Territories region that Watson studied, a small merchant and landowning elite headed lineages made up of tenant farmers (1985: 54). The landlord-merchants controlled crucial resources such as land, ancestral estates, markets, pawnshops, boats for cargo, and factories. They employed fellow lineage members as well as outsiders in their many enterprises (p. 81). James Hayes notes that "Watson mainly worked with the oldest, biggest lineages and class divisions were less marked in the majority of New Territories lineages, many of which were quite small" (personal communication, October 2003).

16 On the bench there was a minority view that custom should be allowed to change with the times. In a 1956 decision (*Wong Ying-kuen v Wong Yi-shi and Ors*) J. Briggs held that "the correct law to apply is the Qing law and custom as it existed in 1842 with such modifications in custom and in the interpretation in the law as have taken place in Hong Kong since that period" (quoted in Selby 1991: 50).

17 In a study of two villages, Watson (1985: 150) found that one-third of the households had one or more members living abroad.

18 This debate took place in both English and Cantonese, the two official languages of Hong Kong.

19 The Hong Kong Federation of Women, a conservative women's group founded in 1993, also favored a more gradual approach: "We aim at progress without upsetting stability" (Hong Kong Federation of Women 1994). Peggy Lam, a founding member of the federation as well as a legislative councillor, argued that haste to pass the amended land exemption ordinance had caused anxiety and conflict that could have been avoided (Hong Kong Hansard 1994: 4548–49).

20 Some later criticized the female inheritance movement because it failed to offer a fundamental challenge to patriarchy (Lui 1997: chap. 4, 22).

21 Fanny Cheung, the founder of the Hong Kong Federation of Women's Centres, says that it takes a "community approach" that differs from Western feminism; in addition to mobilizing community resources, it seeks to avoid confrontation and militancy (Lee 2000: 253).

22 According to interviews with Wong and Chan in 2003, of the seven indigenous women who formed the core of the Residents Committee, four were illiterate. None were educated beyond secondary school.

23 In an early meeting with the indigenous women, Wu suggested that the women might be able to sue male relatives for failing to live up to their responsibilities. Compared with other legislative councillors, Wu left the indigenous women with a sense that her view of the issue was closest to theirs (Wong interview, 2003).

24 The tactic of appealing to China continued even after the ordinance was passed. In 1997, the Kuk lobbied the Preparatory Committee, the body reviewing Hong Kong's laws in preparation for the handover, to repeal female inheritance in the rural New Territories. When the Preparatory Committee let the land exemption ordinance stand, the Kuk appealed to the National People's Congress. Ultimately, this tactic also failed.

25 At the time, China was under substantial international pressure because of its human rights record. In contrast, China had a relatively good record on gender equality, and this must have been something that the CCP wanted to preserve (Petersen interview, 2003).

26 In 1995 the UN Committee on Economic and Social Rights complained that the small-house policy discriminated against women (Hopkinson and Lei 2003: 23). Although the policy has been under review since 1996, extending it to include women is not seen as an option because there is simply not enough land.

27 A great deal of attention has been given to the connection between democratization and increased support for women's rights (see Fischler 2000; Lui 1997; Tong 1999, n.d.).

REFERENCES

An-na'im, Abdullahi. 1992*a*. "Introduction," in *Human rights in cross-cultural perspective: A quest for consensus.* Edited by Abdullahi Ahmed An-Na'im. Philadelphia: University of Pennsylvania Press.

——. 1992*b*. "Toward a cross-cultural approach to defining international standards of human rights: The meaning of cruel, inhuman, or degrading treatment or punishment," in *Human rights in cross-cultural perspective: A quest for consensus*. Edited by Ahmed An-Na'im. Philadelphia: University of Pennsylvania Press.

——. Editor. 2002. *Cultural transformation and human rights in Africa*. London: Zed Books.

Anti-Discrimination Female Indigenous Residents Committee. 1994. Submission on the green paper on opportunities for women and men. MS.

Appadurai, Arjun. 1996. *Modernity at large: Cultural dimensions of globalization*. Minneapolis: University of Minnesota Press.

Association for the Advancement of Feminism. 1993. New Territories women denied right to inherit. *Women's News Digest* 29: 13–14.

Bauer, Joanne R., and Daniel A. Bell. Editors. 1999. *The East Asian challenge for human rights*. London and New York: Cambridge University Press.

Bray, Denis. 2001. "Recollections of a cadet officer Class II," in *Hong Kong, British Crown Colony, revisited*. Edited by Elizabeth Sinn. Hong Kong: Centre of Asian Studies, University of Hong Kong.

Brysk, Alison. 2000. *From tribal village to global village: Indian rights and international relations in Latin America*. Stanford: Stanford University Press.

Chan, Eliza Chong-Lai. 1995. Negotiating daughterhood: A case study of the female inheritance movement in the New Territories, Hong Kong, M.A. thesis, Chinese University, Hong Kong.

Chan, Selina Ching. 1997. "Negotiating tradition: Customary succession in the New Territories of Hong Kong," in *Hong Kong: The anthropology of a metropolis*. Edited by Grant Evans and Maria Tani. Honolulu: University of Hawai'i Press.

——. 1998. Politicizing tradition: The identity of indigenous inhabitants of Hong Kong. *Ethnology* 37: 39–54.

——. 1999. Colonial policy in a borrowed place and time: Invented tradition in the New Territories of Hong Kong. *European Planning Studies* 7: 231–42.

——. 2001. Selling the ancestor's land: A Hong Kong lineage adapts. *Modern China* 27: 262–84.

——. 2003. Memory making, identity building: The dynamics of economics and politics in the New Territories of Hong Kong. *China Information* 17: 66–91.

Cheung, Choi Wan. 1994. New Territories indigenous women reclaimed inheritance rights. *Women's News Digest* 32–33: 6–7.

Chiu, Stephen, W. K., and Ho-Fung Hung. 2000. "Rural stability under colonialism: A new look at an old issue," in *Social development and political change in Hong Kong*. Edited by Siu-kai Lau. Hong Kong: Chinese University Press.

Choi Po-King. 1995. Identities and diversities: Hong Kong women's movement in 1980s and 1990s. *Hong Kong Cultural Studies Bulletin* 4: 95–103.

Chun, Allen. 2000. *Unstructuring Chinese society: The fictions of colonial practice and the changing realities of "land" in the New Territories of Hong Kong*. New York: Harwood Academic Publishers.

Coates, Austin. 1969. *Myself a Mandarin*. New York: John Day. New York: Harwood Academic Publishers.

Cowan, Jane, Marie-Benedict Dembour, and Richard Wilson. Editors. 2001. *Culture and rights*. Cambridge: Cambridge University Press.

Donnelly, Jack. 2003. *Universal human rights in theory and practice*. Ithaca: Cornell University Press.

Engel, David M., and Frank W. Munger. 2002. *Rights of inclusion: Law and identity in the life stories of Americans with disabilities*. Chicago: University of Chicago Press.

Feld, Stephen. 2001. "A sweet lullaby for world music," in *Globalization*. Edited by Arjun Appadurai. Durham: Duke University Press.

Fischler, Lisa Collynn. 2000. Women at the margin: Challenging boundaries of the political in Hong Kong. Ph.D. diss., University of Wisconsin at Madison, Madison, Wis.

Gilliom, John. 2001. *Overseers of the poor: Surveillance, resistance, and the limits of privacy.* Chicago: University of Chicago Press.

Goldberg-Hiller, Jonathan. 2002. *The limits to union: Same-sex marriage and the politics of civil rights.* Ann Arbor: University of Michigan Press.

Goldberg-Hiller, Jonathan, and Neal Milner. 2003. Rights as excess. Understanding the politics of special rights. *Law and Social Inquiry* 28(3).

Hayes, James W. 2001. "Colonial administration in British Hong Kong and Chinese customary law," in *Hong Kong, British Crown Colony, revisited*. Edited by Elizabeth Sinn. Hong Kong: Centre of Asian Studies, University of Hong Kong.

Home Affairs Branch. 1993. *Legislative Council brief: New Territories Land (Exemption) Bill.* CNTA/L/CON/26/21/Pt. II.

Hong Kong Federation of Women. 1994. Statement on conflict arising from New Territories women's right of succession. MS.

Hong Kong Federation of Women's Centres. 1994. *Annual report: 1993–1994.* Hong Kong.

Hong Kong Hansard. 1993. *Proceedings of the Legislative Council.* http://www.legco.gov.hk/yr93–94/englihs/lc_sitg/hansard/h931013.pdf.

——. 1994. *Proceedings of the Legislative Council.* http://www.legco.gov.hk/yr93–94/englihs/lc_sitg/hansard/h940622.pdf.

Hong Kong Women Christian Council. Editor. 1995. *Uncertain times: Hong Kong women facing 1997.* Hong Kong.

Hopkinson, Lisa, and Mandy Lao Man Lei. 2003. *Rethinking the small house policy.* Hong Kong: Civic Exchange.

Howarth, Carla, Carol Jones, Carole Petersen, and Harriet Samuels. 1991. *Report by the Hong Kong Council of Women on the Third Periodic Report by Hong Kong under Article 40 of the International Covenant on Civil and Political Rights.* Hong Kong: Hong Kong Council of Women.

Jones, Carol. 1995. "New Territories inheritance law: Colonization and the elites," in *Women in Hong Kong*. Edited by Benjamin K. P. Leung and Veronica Pearson. Hong Kong: Oxford University Press.

Keck, Margaret E., and Kathryn Sikkink. 1998. *Activists beyond borders: Advocacy networks in international politics.* Ithaca: Cornell University Press.

Khagram, Sanjeev, James V. Riker, and Kathryn Sikkink. Editors. 2002. *Restructuring world politics: Transnational social movements, networks, and norms.* Minneapolis: University of Minnesota Press.

Lee, Ching Kwan. 2000. "Public disclosures and collective identities: Emergence of women as a collective actor in the women's movement in Hong Kong," in *The dynamics of social movements in Hong Kong*. Edited by Stephen Wing Kai Chiu and Tai Lok Lui. Hong Kong: Hong Kong University Press.

Lockhart, J. H. Stewart. 1900. *Report on the New Territory at Hong Kong.* London: Darling & Son.

Loh, Christine. 1997. *Inheritance rights of indigenous women of the New Territories.* http://www.christineloh.bizland.com/cloh/vz_mainframe.htm.

Lui, Yuk-Lin. 1997. The emergence and development of the feminist movement in Hong Kong from the mid-1980s to the mid-1990s. M.A. thesis, Chinese University, Hong Kong.

McCann, Michael W. 1994. *Rights at work: Pay equity reform and the politics of legal mobilization.* Chicago: University of Chicago Press.

Milner, Neal. 1986. The dilemmas of legal mobilization: Ideologies and strategies of mental patient liberation. *Law and Policy* 8: 105–29.

Nissim, Roger. 1988. *Land administration and practice in Hong Kong.* Hong Kong: University of Hong Kong Press.

O'Brien, Kevin. 1996. Rightful resistance. *World Politics* 49(1): 31–55.

Petersen, Carole. 1996. Equality as a human right: The development of anti-discrimination law in Hong Kong. *Columbia Journal of Transnational Law* 34: 335–87.

Petersen, Carole, and Harriet Samuels. 2002. The International Convention on the Elimination of All Forms of Discrimination Against Women: A comparison of its implementation and the role of non-governmental organizations in the United Kingdom and Hong Kong. *Hastings International and Comparative Law Review* 26: 1–51.

Risse, Thomas, Stephen Ropp, and Kathryn Sikkink. Editors. 1999. *The power of human rights: International norms and domestic change.* Cambridge: Cambridge University Press.

Scheingold, Stuart. 1974. *The politics of rights.* New Haven: Yale University Press.

Scott, Ian. 1982. Administering the New Towns of Hong Kong. *Asian Survey* 22: 659–75.

Selby, Stephen. 1991. Everything you wanted to know about Chinese customary law (but were afraid to ask). *Hong Kong Law Journal* 21: 45–77.

Smart, Alan, and James Lee. 2003. Financialization and the role of real estate in Hong Kong's regime of accumulation. *Economic Geography* 79(1): 153–71.

Snow, David, and Robert Benford. 2000. Framing processes and social movements: An overview and assessment. *American Review of Sociology* 26: 611–39.

Strickland Report: Report of a Committee Appointed by the Governor in October, 1948. 1953. *Chinese law and custom in Hong Kong.* Hong Kong: Government Printer.

Tarrow, Sidney. 1998. 2d edition. *Power in movement: Social movements and contentious politics.* Cambridge: Cambridge University Press.

Tong, Irene. 1999. "Re-inheriting women in decolonizing Hong Kong," in *Democratization and women's movements.* Edited by Jill M. Bystydzienski and Joti Sekhon. Bloomington: Indiana University Press.

———. n.d. The women's movement in Hong Kong's transition. MS, Department of Politics and Public Administration, University of Hong Kong.

Tsang Gar Yin and Chi Kie Wan. 1994. Campaign for equal inheritance rights. *Women's News Digest* 32–33: 8–13.

Watson, James L. 1983. Rural society: Hong Kong's New Territories. *China Quarterly* 95: 480–90.

Watson, Rubie S. 1985. *Inequality among brothers: Class and kinship in South China.* Cambridge: Cambridge University Press.

Wesley-Smith, Peter. 1994. *The sources of Hong Kong law.* Hong Kong: Hong Kong University Press.

Wilson, Richard A. 1996. "Introduction: Human rights, culture, and context," in *Human rights, culture, and context: Anthropological perspectives.* Edited by Richard A. Wilson. London: Pluto Press.

Wong, Pik Wan. 2000. Negotiating gender: The women's movement for legal reform in colonial Hong Kong. Ph.D. diss., University of California, Los Angeles, Los Angeles, Calif.

Wu, Anna. 1993. Letter to the members of the Bills Committee considering the New Territories Land (Exemption) Bill. MS.

17

Disorderly Development: Globalization and the Idea of "Culture" in the Kalahari

Renée Sylvain

In postapartheid Namibia, the San (Bushmen) have been increasingly exposed to the effects of liberalizing trade markets, the global flows of capital and people associated with a booming tourism industry, and a massive proliferation of nongovernmental organization (NGO) activity.[1] Since Namibian independence from South African rule in 1990, the San have become engaged in rights-based activism as indigenous peoples. With the assistance of the Working Group of Indigenous Minorities in Southern Africa (WIMSA), San people throughout southern Africa now participate in international indigenous peoples' rights forums and are organizing as a vocal and sophisticated political community. The current integration of the San into the new global order introduces important opportunities for empowerment and "development" but is also fraught with contradictions and challenges inherent to local identity politics and global indigenous activism. One of the most puzzling features of postcolonial life for the San is that, at the very moment they are beginning to travel the world, speak at international conferences, and keep in regular e-mail communication with interested parties overseas, primordialized and essentialized representations of primitive "Bushmen" are being vigorously reasserted in mainstream media and NGO rhetoric. These representations are often difficult to distinguish from colonial stereotypes.

From *American Ethnologist* 32(3): 354–70. Copyright © 2005, American Anthropological Association.

In this article, I examine the environment for development that globalization is currently creating in the Kalahari and, more specifically, how globalization is influencing San struggles for rights, recognition, and resources. I first bring into focus one form of collusion between the processes of globalization and the indigenous peoples' movement that results in the promotion of a particular idea of culture – one that meshes uncomfortably with the idea of culture inherent in the anthropology of "separate development" in southern Africa. I then illustrate how this idea of culture is played out in the Omaheke Region of Namibia.

My case study examines three interconnected processes. I first describe how local systems of class exploitation are shaped by racial and ethnic stereotypes about "primitive" Bushmen, and I juxtapose these stereotypes with a description of the class-shaped cultural life of the Omaheke San. I then describe the promotion of primordial and essentialized expressions of Bushman identity by ethnic entrepreneurs who capitalize on the confusion, chaos, and corruption associated with post-independence administrative vacuums and a proliferation of uncoordinated NGO activity. Finally, I outline the convergence of so-called ethnodevelopment and the commodification of culture in the tourism industry.

Globalization and Culture

The central problematic in most analyses of globalization is the relationship between global forces and local-level responses. Specifically, scholars seek to address the apparent paradox between "the homogenizing tendencies which appear inherent to globalization" and the "continued or even intensified [cultural] heterogeneity" asserted on the local level (Meyer and Geschiere 1999: 1; see also Appadurai 2000 and Kalb and van der Land 2000). Many studies of the cultural aspects of globalization focus on how the content of global capitalist culture, global consumer culture, or global political culture influences the content of local cultures. As a result, reified notions of culture are often embedded in definitions of globalization, and global culture is assumed to be homogeneous. For example, Peter Kloos describes globalization as "the emergence of a world economy, a world polity, and perhaps a *world culture*" (2000: 281, emphasis added; see also Giddens 1991). Ulf Hannerz asks how local cultural processes "affect the way the periphery is drawn into *world culture*" (1997: 116, emphasis added; see also Wolff 1997).[2]

This focus on the interactions of global and local cultural content contributes to a picture that pits global homogenization against local resistance to it. With this view of globalization operating in the background, explanations of the ubiquity of ethnic assertions on the local level standardly resort to universalistic (and essentialist) assumptions about psychological needs. The uncertainty that globalization creates – the political, economic, and cultural shifts – results in ethnic movements that reflect "a search for fixed orientation points" (Meyer and Geschiere 1999: 2) or a search for "solid ground" (Hall 1997: 35–36); they are a means for people to "regain their bearings" (Wallerstein 1997: 104; see also Friedman 1994) or "fix the flow" (Meyer and Geschiere 1999: 7; see also Appadurai 2000; Featherstone 1990). Kloos, for example, explicitly resorts to speculative psychology when he claims that people's awareness of global forces beyond their control "results in feelings of insecurity and a quest for configurations people feel they can trust" (2000: 291).

These explanations, however, are unsatisfying for three reasons. First, such explanations are tautological: People fix ethnic boundaries because they feel the need to fix ethnic boundaries. Second, they tend to limit their characterization of local-level responses to parochial reactions against globalization – a mere circling of the wagons. Finally, this view also neglects the widespread phenomenon that Richard Falk describes as "globalization-from-below," which "consists in an array of transnational social forces [especially NGOs] . . . [dedicated to] the strengthening over time of the institutional forms and activities associated with global civil society" (1993: 39). One may be able to get around the apparent paradox between universalizing, homogenizing tendencies of globalization and the intensification of local, primordialized ethnic heterogeneity – and better understand why identity movements, particularly ethnic assertions, are such a common local response – if one asks what it is that is being globalized and homogenized. Stuart Hall addresses this question by claiming that globalization produces a "global mass culture" that entails a "homogenizing *form of representation*" (1997: 28, emphasis added). According to Hall, global mass culture recognizes and absorbs "differences within the larger, overarching framework of what is essentially an American conception of the world" (1997: 28). But one important component of a Western conception of the world is a Western idea of "culture." So I would put Hall's point differently and suggest that it is not, or not only, a U.S. or Western culture that is being globalized but also a Western idea of what culture is – specifically, the idea that cultures are bounded, ahistorical "facts of nature."[3] This is already implicit in Hall's claim that "forms of representation" are being homogenized; but, as researchers, we need to make explicit that among those forms of representation is a particular way of representing culture.

Rather than narrowly viewing identity politics as distress-driven attempts to impose order on an increasingly chaotic world, we should also consider the extent to which people on the ground are manipulating the idea of "culture" as a tool for securing political, economic, and development resources. The international indigenous peoples' movement is an important example of "globalization-from-below" (see also Appadurai 2000), and it is a good example of a global deployment of a particular Western idea of culture.[4]

Important examinations of cultural essentialism in indigenous identity politics focus on its strategic value, or potential dangers, in fields of unequal engagement (see, e.g., Conklin 2002; Dombrowski 2002; Hodgson 2002; Jacobs 1988; Ramos 1994; Turner 1991). Adam Kuper notes that the current conception of culture that dominates U.S. multiculturalism "often comes to serve as a politically correct euphemism for race" (1999: 240), and he expresses a common misgiving about contemporary culture talk when he claims that "in the rhetoric of the indigenous peoples movement the terms 'native' and 'indigenous' are often euphemisms for what used to be termed 'primitive' " (2003: 389). Although interrogating particularly powerful ideas is important, so, too, is examining the dynamics that make these ideas powerful. So, here, I focus instead on the ways that this idea of culture is advanced as an outcome of struggle in contexts of disorder and corruption. I suggest that the ubiquity of essentialized notions of indigenous culture is less a result of the power of activist discourse than of the ways in which "places of recognition" (see Hall 1995 and Li 2000) are shaped by ambiguities produced at the intersection of class inequalities, identity politics, and privatized development initiatives, particularly ethnotourism ventures.

Ethnotourism is a site at which identity politics joins with market demand, and this union has inspired concerns about the commodification of culture, the perpetuation of Western imperialist nostalgia, and the promotion of a neocolonial quest for the authentic exotic Other (see Bruner 1995; Bruner and Kirshenblatt-Gimblett 1994; Crick 1989; Greenwood 1989; MacCannell 1973, 1984; Nash 1989; Urry 1990; van den Berghe 1994). Ethnotourism's appeal as a development strategy is enhanced by its perceived value as a "pedagogical instrument" (see Lanfant 1995: 4): The industry increasingly accommodates tourists seeking a cultural encounter of the anthropological kind. Edward M. Bruner notes that "colonialism, ethnography, and tourism occur at different historical periods, but arise from the same social formation" (1989: 439). A naturalized and territorialized conception of culture is advanced most conspicuously at the confluence of ethno-tourism and international indigenous identity politics: Here the ubiquity of localizing and essentializing identity-based movements is not a paradoxical result of globalization at all but a very understandable outcome of the globalization of a particularly potent idea.

My picture at this point suggests that the proliferation of essentialist claims to identity is owed to a globalizing idea of culture that proves useful for generating income and securing recognition, particularly for indigenous peoples. The situation, however, is more complex. My case study shows how a globalized idea of culture, embodied in the identity expectations imposed by donor agencies and the tourism industry, converges with historical habits of racially based misrecognition operating within a context of local corruption and disorder. Ironically (but not paradoxically), this convergence both promotes essentialized and primordialized images of indigenous Bushmen and perpetuates their underclass status.

Indigenous Identities in Southern Africa

Indigenous peoples' activism arose largely in response to the disenfranchisement and dispossession that followed from development strategies dominated by megaprojects and imposed by states and multilateral agencies during a wave of developmentalism in the 1960s and 1970s (Bodley 1990; Brysk 2000; Maybury Lewis 1997; Ramos 1998; Wright 1988: 377). The roots of the indigenous peoples' movement are commonly located in the post-World War II elaboration of an international human-rights apparatus (see, e.g., Kymlicka 1999; Niezen 2003; Warren 1998). Ronald Niezen identifies four features of the postwar world that facilitated indigenous rights activism: First, the Holocaust in Europe sensitized the world to issues of racial discrimination and the need to protect minorities. Second, the process of decolonization established new international norms that could be used to promote self-determination for indigenous peoples. Third, assimilationist policies produced an educated elite equipped to organize and lobby for rights. Finally, a rapidly expanding global NGO community provided support structures through which indigenous elites could network and promote their cause on an international scale (Niezen 2003: 40–42). The first two trends encourage indigenous activists to couch their demands in the language of decolonization and self-determination (Muehlebach 2003; Warren 1998: 6–7). Establishing a basis for particular rights for indigenous peoples involves crafting a unique, locally grounded but globally recognizable indigenous identity, which would bear enough of a family resemblance to nationhood to be suitable for some form of self-determination.[5] Indigenous elites associated with the Center for World Indigenous Studies and the promotion of Fourth World Theory provide an important example of a global self-fashioning of essentialized indigenous identity.

Fourth World Theory emerged during the 1970s as a critique of the emphasis placed on Third World development and of the general failure within the development industry to acknowledge that decolonization did not apply to Fourth World peoples but, rather, made them subject to internal colonization under current state systems (Seton 1999: 12). The term *Fourth World* came into popular usage in 1974, following the publication of *The Fourth World: An Indian Reality*, authored by Chief George Manuel, a Shuswap Native from British Columbia, founding president of the World Council of Indigenous Peoples, and cofounder of the Center for World Indigenous Studies. The International Work Group for Indigenous Affairs (IWGIA) adopted Manuel's definition of the Fourth World, outlined by Roxanne Dunbar Ortiz in the following terms: "the name given to the indigenous peoples descended from a country's aboriginal population and, who today are completely or partly deprived of the right to their own territories and its riches. The peoples of the 4th world have only limited influence or none at all in the national states to which they belong" (1984: 82). The UN Working Group on Indigenous Populations, the most significant site for the articulation of a global indigenous identity (Muehlebach 2001; Niezen 2003), draws from the definition of *indigenous* provided by the International Labour Organization (ILO) Convention 169 (1989) and from the working definition provided by UN special rapporteur José Martínez Cobo:

> Indigenous communities, peoples and nations … form at present non-dominant sectors of society and are determined to preserve, develop and transmit to future generations their ancestral territories and their ethnic identity, as the basis for continued existence as peoples in accordance with their own cultural patterns, social institutions and legal systems. [1986: 1]

Both the ILO's and Cobo's definitions of indigenous peoples remain true to the original formulation of Fourth World peoples; the elaborations on the significance of territorial roots for indigenous identity are also in keeping with the emphasis placed on the link between territory and identity emphasized by Fourth World theorists. According to Fourth World theorists, Fourth World nations are "aboriginal peoples who have special, non-technical, non-modern exploitative relations to the land in which they live and are 'disenfranchised' by the States within which they live" (Seton 1999; see also Griggs 1992).

At the heart of indigeneity is an overt link between cultural, or "national," identity and a unique relationship with "the land" (see also Beckett 1996 and Muehlebach 2001). The idea of culture mobilized here is adapted from familiar nationalist rhetoric. As Niezen notes, indigenous identity developed within the institutional framework of successful nationalisms: "International legislative bodies of states have provided the conceptual origins and practical focus of indigenous identity" (2000: 121). Indigenous peoples come to represent the most natural of nations, however, through what Liisa Malkki calls "sedentarist metaphysics" (1992: 32), in which territorial – and familial – metaphors naturalize nations as discrete, territorially grounded and bounded entities (Malkki 1992: 32).[6] Alan Barnard evokes these naturalizing and territorializing metaphors in his description of (Khoi)San national identity: "Khoisan identity through 'blood' ... is only really meaningful as a sense of belonging conferred by the land" (1998: 54).[7]

Such territorial conceptions of national culture provide the basis for a "globalized aboriginality," which Maximilian Forte describes as "the embryonic creation of a worldwide indigenous macro-community seemingly with its own indigenous macro-culture" (1998). One need not doubt the utility of a concept of culture, or even that some groups see their identities as owing to a particular relationship to the land, to recognize that essentialist conceptions of national culture assume a discomfiting salience in postapartheid southern Africa, where conflated notions of "culture" and "race" have been politicized as natural, territorial national units more explicitly and consequentially than in most other areas of the world. The essentialized idea of culture mobilized by the global indigenous movement – particularly its "blood and soil" rhetoric and its perceived agenda of "ethnic separatism" – conjures up images of apartheid "homelands" (Muehlebach 2001: 439) and harks back to the Herderian Romanticism that so strongly influenced apartheid anthropology.[8]

One would be hard-pressed to find a more "natural" nation than the Bushmen, whose colonial designation explicitly signifies a land-linked, organic identity. The historical processes of Bushman iconography are too vast and complex to address here (but see Dubow 1995; Gordon and Douglas 2000; Guenther 1980; Suzman 2000; Wilmsen 1989). It is widely recognized, however, that the trope of the Bushmen as the ultimate African Ur-race figured prominently in the colonial formulation of a "civilized" white racial and national identity (see Gordon 1988: 43). Bushmen came to embody the original, primitive condition of humanity, generally, first as "brutal bandits" and later as "harmless people" or "noble savages" (see Guenther 1980). Mathias Guenther notes that "the motif of the noble Bushman... consists of such themes as ecological sensitivity and responsibility, the innocent, the beauty, the humanness, and the harmony" (1980: 123).

Today, the San's activism as indigenous people is most positively received in public forums when they present themselves, in stereotypical terms, as Bushmen whose identity is organically linked to the land. For example, the South African ≠Khomani San won 65,000 hectares of land in and around the Kalahari Gemsbok National Park in March 1999, and, as Steven Robbins notes, "Media representations of the San land claim comprised a series of stereotypical images of timeless and primordialist San 'tribes' reclaiming their ancestral land" (2001: 833–834). Robbins also points out, however, that "the colonial stereotype of the pure and pristine bushman hunter gatherer" has also been "embraced 'from below'" (2001: 839). For example, Dawid Kruiper, the traditional leader of the ≠Khomani San community, has publicly promoted the image of primordial, hunting-and-gathering San by claiming that he is "an animal of nature" (White 1995: 19).

Although arguments have been made for the use of such "strategic essentialism" (see Lattas 1993; Lee 2000), what is important here is that the San are not asserting ethnic or national identities in an effort to get their bearings so much as they are mobilizing an idea of culture made available by globalization to secure resources and social, economic, and cultural rights. Rather than circling the wagons, the San are responding to identity expectations placed on them by the local mainstream society, the state, NGOs, and the international donor community, all of whom expect to find a bounded cultural entity to which rights can be attached and a discrete target group for development (see also Robbins 2001). Nevertheless, although the idea of culture may be a useful tool in the hands of some, it can also serve to obscure other groups of San, whose living cultures and identities are, in the vernacular of globalization, of the "hybrid" variety.

Taming the "Wild" Bushmen

The Omaheke San, whose identity is owed to a confluence of race, class, and ethnic relations, is one such hybrid group. The San are the third largest ethnic group in the Omaheke Region (Central Statistics Office 1996: 19). The largest group is the Bantu-speaking Herero, who raise cattle in the former reserves–homelands, now known as the "communal farming areas." Nama-Damaras are the second largest group, and they, along with the San, constitute the largest proportion of farmworkers in the region. A small minority of Bantu-speaking Tswanas raise cattle in the communal areas in the south of the Omaheke. The German and Afrikaner descendants of white settlers constitute only eight percent of the population but own 65 percent of the land in the Omaheke, where they operate approximately 900 cattle ranches in what is known as the "commercial farming block" (Suzman 1995: 4).

The 6,500 San in the Omaheke belong to three main language groups: Ju/'hoansi are found in the central and northeastern parts of the region; Nharo-speakers are concentrated in the east, along the Botswana border; and !Xûn-speakers live primarily in the south. These groups of San are not self-contained; because they are highly mobile, a great deal of intermarriage has occurred, not only among Ju/'hoansi, Nharo, and !Xûn but also between these groups and Nama-Damaras. Ethnicity is often reckoned opportunistically, depending on employment opportunities and the proximity of kin who can provide support and assistance during periods of economic distress.

The class system in the Omaheke was shaped by deeply essentialist notions of bounded and territorially grounded cultural entities. Stereotypes of "feral" foragers – and the definition of the Bushmen as an ethnic group – did not, however, result from a straightforward imposition of colonial ideologies onto passively subaltern San (contra Gordon and Douglas 2000; Suzman 2000; and Wilmsen 1989). Rather, these stereotypes emerged out of struggles over land, labor, and political position as white settlers attempted to secure a livelihood in the Omaheke.

Large-scale white settlement began in the region in the 1920s, as poor whites moved in from South Africa and, especially, after a substantial number of Afrikaners from Angola were resettled in the Omaheke in 1928 and 1929 (van Rooyen and Reiner 1995: 40).[9] Most new arrivals were poor *bywoners* (tenants) and were highly dependent on the colonial administration for subsidies and infrastructural inputs. The settlers required two things to establish viable farming ventures: land and cheap labor. Both were supplied by the dispossession of local Africans. Hereros and Tswanas were relegated to overcrowded reserves (later, ethnic homelands), whereas the San and Namas were eventually completely encapsulated as white farms overtook their traditional territories.

The San did not simply acquiesce to land dispossession. They retaliated by stealing and mutilating the intruders' livestock. Many farmers saw this behavior as evidence of the innate wildness of the Bushmen: Being beyond the bounds of civilization, Bushmen were unable to distinguish between game and domesticated animals, and so were seen as hunting the farmers' cattle out of ignorance. Other farmers interpreted the mutilation of their livestock as evidence of the innate cruelty and depravity of "brutal Bushman bandits" (see also Suzman 2000: 32–33). Although white settlers were concerned to protect their livestock from "Bushman depredations," calls for tougher measures to deal with "the Bushman problem" were also demands to have recalcitrant natives pressed into service on the farms. Furthermore, efforts to pacify the Bushmen and acquire cheap labor were at the same time attempts by white settlers to assert greater political influence. For example, a 1923 letter to the newspaper *Swakopmund Zeitung* from farmers in Grootfontein (just north of the Omaheke) asked:

> Why is it not possible to enact a law empowering the Magistrate – or better still forcing him – to send idle natives or those who have offended against the laws requiring passes to some farm for a definite period where they would have the opportunity of getting used to hard work? Unfortunately nothing can be looked for in this respect so long as we have the infamous "One Man Government" and have no say ourselves. [National Archives of Namibia 1923]

White farmers and colonial administrators were not always like-minded when it came to defining the Bushman problem. In 1927, the native commissioner responded to complaints of stock theft in the following way: "As is well known, the Bushman by instinct is not a thief but changed circumstances are driving him to slaughter cattle when game and 'veldkos' [bush food] are not available" (National Archives of Namibia 1927). The existence of a few sympathetic explanations of San behavior reflects the divergent class interests and ethnic–national backgrounds that divided the white community. Whereas a few administrators – many of whom were British South Africans enjoying a more privileged social position – could afford to assume a benignly paternalistic stance toward the San, impoverished Afrikaners were struggling to secure a livelihood and gain a political voice.

Although land expropriation secured cheap labor by undermining traditional subsistence patterns, it failed to ensure a stable labor force, especially in the case of the San. Initially, San only selectively participated in the white economy, working on the farms during the dry season when veld food was scarce and returning to the veld to forage when the rains came. This dual subsistence strategy was a response to inadequate subsistence resources both on the farms, where workers were inadequately remunerated, and off the farms, where the diminishing and increasingly denuded veld was unable to sustain full-time foraging. Many in the white community, however, consistently interpreted the San's dual subsistence strategy as evidence of an innately feral nature. For example, in 1939, the magistrate of Grootfontein expressed an attitude that many white farmers hold today: "[The Bushman] is independable [sic] as, after the rains have fallen, he often cannot resist the call of the wilds and simply deserts from his master's service. For this reason farmers prefer more reliable native labour, although at a considerably higher wage" (National Archives of Namibia 1939).

By the 1930s, farmers were becoming increasingly aggressive in their attempts to bind San workers to the farms year-round. One method was to recruit San children for apprenticeships (often a euphemism for slavery in southern Africa [see Morton 1994]), which not only provided cheap and steady labor but also ensured the "good behavior" of nearby "wild" Bushmen. Such coercive tactics were rationalized by an elaborate system of stereotypes centered on the distinction between "wild" and "tame" Bushmen. Initially, coercive forms of labor recruitment were justified on the grounds that taming the Bushmen required exposing them to the civilizing effects of hard work. After white settlement had reached its peak in the 1950s and the San were completely encapsulated within the white political economy, more nostalgic sensibilities prevailed: Exposing the Bushmen to civilization threatened to bring about the disappearance of these "children of nature." The discordant vocabulary that developed during the process of class formation served to rationalize the widespread exploitation and marginalization of the San.

The Omaheke San Today

Today, the San in the Omaheke exist at the bottom of the local ethnic labor hierarchy as third- and fourth-generation farm laborers and domestic servants. On white farms, they are the first to be laid off when drought hits or when market conditions deteriorate; they face the greatest difficulties securing employment because white farmers generally prefer to hire non-San workers; and they are paid on average less than half the wages of non-San workers.[10] Remuneration for farmwork consists of a balance between monthly wages and weekly rations.[11] The wages and rations are usually inadequate to support an entire household, and so the San are compelled to purchase food from the farmer on credit, leaving many San families tied to the farms through a system of debt bondage.

About one-third of the Omaheke San work on Herero or Tswana cattle posts in the communal areas. San men tend livestock and San women cook and do laundry.

They receive some food or only homemade beer for their labor. San children, usually girls, are recruited by Hereros and "adopted" as servile household members.

After independence, jobs on white farms became scarce as farmers adapted to liberalizing markets, new labor legislation, and drought by retrenching large numbers of San workers. Life on Herero or Tswana cattle posts, however, is often one of extreme poverty and eventual alcoholism and, so, is unattractive to many San. Thus, many San are on the road in a perpetual search for employment, traveling from farm to farm where they have friends or family who can provide food and shelter while they ask local farmers for jobs. These job hunters often must squat illegally because farmers discourage visitors. Many prefer to stay with friends or kin in the squatters' villages along the edges of urban centers and in government resettlement camps, which were established to resettle indigent people shortly after independence. The majority of the more permanent resettlement camp residents are San, many of them too old or too sick to work on the farms. In the camps, the San have access to sporadic supplies of drought-relief food, water, housing, small plots of land for kitchen gardens, and grazing land for those who have livestock. The major source of personal income is old-age pensions. Those not old enough to collect pensions gather camelthorn seeds and truffles (tsotso) to sell to local farmers or sign on for piecework when farmers come into the camps to fill their pickup trucks with seasonal, casual laborers. A few San men tend livestock for absentee Herero, Tswana, or Nama-Damara stock owners in return for milk and a small wage. Very often, however, the wages offered are never paid or are only paid after intervals of several months, during which time the San must get by without money. San women are able to get extra food by tending the gardens and doing the laundry of non-San camp residents. Given the alternatives – camp life or the cattle posts – most San prefer more steady work on white farms, where historically entrenched stereotypes continue to sustain their underclass status.

Today, white farmers frequently report that San workers will disappear without giving notice, only to return months or years later asking for their old jobs. The explanation usually given by the farmers is that Bushmen are incorrigibly – perhaps even innately – nomadic. Whereas farmers explain the San's "unreliability" in terms of their innate ethnic character, the San themselves provide class-based explanations for their disappearances. One former San farmworker explained the situation to me this way:

> It's about money. If you are on a farm and they [the farmers] are not very good and don't give enough money, then you have to go to another farm. If that farmer is not very good, he gives enough money, but the rations are not very good, then you leave for a different farm. If there is enough food and money, but he is cruel, then you leave and go to another farm.

Other justifications for lower pay continue to be under-written by reference to "traditional" Bushman culture. Farmers claim that, just as San ancestors gorged themselves after a kill and then went hungry for long periods before the next successful hunt, the contemporary San spend all of their wages on payday, with no thought of saving for the days ahead. Many farmers are still unable to see the San in terms of their class position, and so they often miss an important part of how the San see themselves.

Many San I spoke to differentiated themselves from non-San – and especially white farmers – on the basis of moral behavior. San widely consider "stinginess" the most iniquitous vice (see Lee 1993) and often attribute it to white farmers and other non-San employers. By contrast, the San insist on high standards of generosity among themselves – and this expectation contributes to San self-definition as a community. The widely scattered farm San maintain community ties through elaborate networks of kinship and mutual support. Widespread visiting, child fostering, and generalized reciprocity sustain a dynamic moral community. San struggling with unemployment or cash shortages can count on kin and friends to supply food, money, and shelter as they are able, and few San, whether kin or not, are denied such assistance (which explains why the San are "unable to save money"). Generosity is a highly valued personality trait, not just because it is culturally prescribed but also because it enables the San to cope with the hardship of their underclass condition. Their coherence as a community – the dynamics of cooperative conflicts that characterize their own forms of sociality – is shaped by the ways in which they are compelled to engage with others as Bushmen in their efforts to cope with their material conditions.[12]

Despite the existence of the class-shaped and dynamic cultural life of the Omaheke San, the general conviction that Bushman culture and character are innate was expressed by a phrase repeated to me by a number of Omaheke farmers: "You can take the Bushman out of the bush, but you can't take the bush out of the Bushman!" (see also Suzman 2000). Farmers with more romantic and nostalgic sensibilities lament that there are no "real" Bushmen in the Omaheke anymore – because the Omaheke San no longer hunt and gather, they are no longer "wild" and "authentic" Bushmen, but only detribalized workers dressed in tattered Western clothing. Thus, the Omaheke San must negotiate a complex and contradictory terrain at the intersection of class and cultural identity politics: Whereas their definition as "Bushmen" consists of a number of stereotypes that justify their exploitation as an underclass, their status as an underclass also disqualifies them from counting as "real" Bushmen.

The formation of the idea of the "Bushmen" was as disorderly and discordant as the process that turned various groups of San into an ethnic underclass. This process was characterized by hegemonic struggles within the white community; by genuine, if ideologically driven, misinterpretations of San strategies of resistance and survival; and by opportunistic stereotyping that continues to justify their exploitation. Although the nature of uncertainty and disorder has changed in the Omaheke since independence, the modes of ethnic differentiation and class exploitation developed during the colonial encounter are sustained and intensified.

Disorder, Corruption, and Class Consciousness

The argument that assertions of primordial ethnic identities are defensive responses to forces of globalization suggests too tidy a picture. As the case of the Omaheke San demonstrates, identity is formed and negotiated in contexts of power asymmetries.

An analysis of the politics of identity politics will need to include a consideration of local power struggles – unfolding in contexts of chaos, corruption, and class exploitation – and the role they play in promoting primordial expressions of identity.

Africanists have recently turned their attention to two trends associated with globalization and the decline of the state: on the one hand, the suggestion of democratization, associated with the increasingly important role that NGOs are assuming as agents of civil society; on the other hand, the escalation of disorder and conflict.[13] Patrick Chabal and Jean-Pierre Daloz suggest that these trends derive from the "instrumentalization of political disorder," which is a "process by which political actors...seek to maximize their returns on the state of confusion, uncertainty and sometimes even chaos" (1999: xviii). As I show in the following discussion, the "instrumentalization of political disorder" contributes to both the promotion of an essentialized definition of Bushmen identity and the exploitation of the San as an underclass.

In the Omaheke, liberalizing trade markets, contracting economies, and the decline of state resources have shifted the responsibility for economic and social upliftment onto NGOs and private entrepreneurial ventures. Postcolonial Namibia, however, has also witnessed a general deterioration of human-rights standards and an alarming increase in corruption (see Bauer 2001). This situation, combined with an explosion of uncoordinated NGO activities, has created new opportunities for the exploitation of the Omaheke San and for the exploitation of their popular image as pristine Bushmen.

When I first arrived in the Omaheke Region in 1996, I met/In!gou, shortly after his cattle had been stolen by a group of local Hereros. As is common practice in the Omaheke, /In!gou was required to track the cattle thieves, locate his stolen cattle, and then report to the local police (who are also Herero). /In!gou located his cattle and went to the police with the names of the men who had stolen them. A few weeks later, /In!gou made the day-long journey to the police station to inquire about the status of his case. He was told his cattle had been recovered and that charges were pending; to get his cattle back, he need only sign the document the police put in front of him. /In!gou informed them that he could not read English, so the police explained that the document outlined the details of the case. He signed the document and returned to his home in a nearby resettlement camp. A few weeks later, he returned to the police station to inquire, again, about his stolen cattle. He was then told that he had already signed a document stating that his cattle had been returned and that he had dropped the charges.

While /In!gou was struggling to recover his cattle, the San people in the resettlement camp in which he lived were dealing with an even larger problem. The camp manager – who had gained her position through her connections with the ruling South West African Peoples Organization – was withholding the monthly supplies of government drought-relief food. She gave some rations to San people who agreed to work for her. For instance, Gase, an elderly man with one leg, cut the grass in the area surrounding the manager's house, crawling on his belly with a pair of sheep shears, in return for mielie meal, a tin of fish, and some cooking oil. The San who worked for the camp manager received only a small portion of the drought-relief food; the rest the manager fed to her pigs.

Overt corruption is not always necessary to create conditions in which the San are vulnerable to exploitation – general disorder and ambiguity are often sufficient. For example, since my first visit in 1996, the number of areas set aside for indigent people in the Omaheke has grown from two resettlement camps (Skoonheid and Drimiopsis) to an indeterminate number. By June 2001, nobody was clear about how many such areas existed or which areas inhabited by indigent people counted as resettlement camps, government farms, squatters' areas, or simply well-populated cattle posts on abandoned farms.

Most San refer to these ambiguous areas as "reserves," falling back on the colonial term for land designated for nonwhites; most non-San refer to them as "resettlement camps," even if their official status is not known. The distinction is important because resettlement camps fall under the jurisdiction of the Ministry of Land, Resettlement and Rehabilitation, which is accountable for management practices and utilization of resources in the camps. Within the political and administrative vacuum in these areas, non-San designate any settlement area a resettlement camp, assume positions of power, and control the distribution of resources.

When I first visited one of these informally proclaimed resettlement camps near the border of Botswana, I was advised by the San residents to present myself to a Damara man who was described as the "manager" and ask him for permission to visit. When I enquired about the official status of the camp, the "manager" replied, "Well, I guess I *could* call this a resettlement camp." I later learned, from other San informants, that several other Damaras also claimed to be the camp "manager." These various "managers" were not in competition with each other, but all claimed official power over the San in the camp. A number of Damara residents also formed a "water committee," took control of the borehole, and charged the San N\$10 per month for water. The San were not convinced that the water committee was legitimately empowered to impose these fees, but they were coerced into paying for water after Damaras placed guards at the communal borehole. Few San could afford to pay for the water, and so they were forced to sell their livestock and to seek work on nearby commercial farms or work for their Damara neighbors in return for food and a small wage.

Taking control of land and water, by assuming positions of power in unregulated areas off the farms, is one common method non-San use to keep the San in servitude. One enterprising group of Mbanderus (an ethnic group linguistically related to Hereros) found a more novel way to profit from the San's identity and labor by manipulating newly opened channels of development funding. In 1993, a group of Mbanderus in the northern Omaheke secured funding from the aid organization Terre des Hommes for what was ostensibly a San development project. They received development inputs, such as breeding cattle and infrastructural equipment, and relocated 50 San people onto a newly designated farm project. While the San labored on the new farm, the Mbanderus made all the decisions; they also limited San presence on the farm to three years (just long enough for the San to build the fences and drill the boreholes). In effect, the Mbanderu were simply building a new farm, financed by Terre des Hommes, and using unpaid San labor. The San's Bushmen image made them an attractive target for donor money, and their underclass status made them easily exploitable labor.

Experiences of corruption and exploitation convinced many San of the need for a San leader in the Omaheke. With the assistance of WIMSA, two chiefs-designate were elected by the San who live in communities off the farms, and both now regularly attend leadership training workshops initiated by WIMSA. Of course, a leader must have a community to lead, and so WIMSA's activities are contributing to the formation of a self-consciously cultural community – locally referred to as a "nasie," or a "nation" – among the widely scattered farm San. The formation of a self-conscious and increasingly politicized pan-San cultural community in the Omaheke, however, is not entirely a result of efforts to defend culture; it is also a result of the widely recognized need to address the twin problems of exploitation and corruption that keep the San in conditions of servitude and poverty.

Moving Targets

Corruption and confusion are not the only factors that contribute to development difficulties in the Omaheke. The majority of San in the region are farmworkers who do not live on land they own or to which they have de facto rights. Also, as I have shown, the San's extreme economic vulnerability means that many are compelled to move almost constantly in search of employment. Those San who are able to maintain steady employment on a farm are isolated and largely inaccessible. Thus, the Omaheke San do not constitute a sedentary, fixed, and territorially contained community. Nevertheless, much mainstream development theory and practice is dominated by Malkki's "sedentarist metaphysics," and the combination of conventional development wisdom and indigenist agendas of ethnodevelopment encourage the San to reinvent themselves as a culturally homogeneous, bounded and territorially grounded ethnic community. The incongruity, however, between popular conceptions of indigeneity and the daily realities the Omaheke San must deal with creates problems for putting development models into practice.

The need to address the problems faced by the San, as a group stigmatized and exploited on the basis of their identity, suggests an approach to development that emphasizes empowerment along ethnic and cultural lines. Any development or advocacy work that addresses San issues will therefore also inevitably contribute to the creation of an identifiable and manageable San constituency (see also Garland 1999 and Robbins 2001). As Robbins notes, the "strong interest of international donors in the 'cultural survival' of vanishing cultures and languages" (2001: 849) contributes to the pressure put on indigenous communities to be recognizably indigenous, according to the terms of global indigenist discourse. As a result, the Omaheke San are, ironically, encouraged to conform to the very picture of pristine Bushmen that continues to justify their exploitation as an underclass.

These pressures also cause some difficulties for local NGOs, which must struggle with the contradictions inherent in their role as advocates for the San: On the one hand, they are committed to promoting the San's human rights, which involves challenging the stereotypes that denigrate and dehumanize them; on the other hand, securing funding and promoting cultural survival means that they are compelled to strategically adopt the very stereotypes they challenge. These difficulties become even greater when mainstream development wisdom and global indigenist agendas confront the untidy realities of San life on the ground. For all that culture brokering is inevitable and even necessary, the primacy placed on culturalist conceptions of indigenous identities and issues has important consequences for the definition of target groups in the NGO community and also for what development entails. The Omaheke San, as an underclass of indigenous people, therefore present important challenges to both Third World development paradigms and to Fourth World models of ethnodevelopment.

In 1998, WIMSA facilitated the establishment of the Omaheke San Trust (OST), an NGO concerned exclusively with the San people in the Omaheke. The OST and WIMSA have been instrumental in the establishment of culturally appropriate educational programs, building "traditional" leadership structures, and supplying development inputs for a range of projects.[14] The aims and activities of the OST are commendable, but its strategies also reveal the implications of an almost exclusive emphasis on the cultural aspects of ethnodevelopment.

In its first report, the OST notes that "the San work as farm laborers for commercial farmers and wealthy communal farmers who often pay them the lowest wage" (Moore with Omaheke San Trust Board of Trustees 2000: 3). Yet the description of its target group reads as follows: "The majority of the population of the Omaheke lives on communal land or resettlement farms and it is in these areas that the San *communities* eke out a living" (Moore with Omaheke San Trust Board of Trustees 2000: 3, emphasis added). The OST recognizes 26 such communities: 25 are clusters of San people living in small pockets off the farms, many of them in conditions of servitude with non-San neighbors in "resettlement camps." The remaining community – more than two-thirds of San residing in the Omaheke – consists of farmworkers and domestic servants scattered widely throughout the commercial farms and cattle posts in the communal areas. Each community is entitled to elect two representatives to attend OST meetings, vote, and exercise membership rights on behalf of their community (Omaheke San Trust 1999: 4). The result is that a minority of San who live off the farms have 50 representatives, whereas the majority of farm-dwelling San have two.[15] Many of the San in the 25 communities off the farms only live there part-time, compounding this representational balance. Many leave to look for employment when food runs out and return when government drought relief appears. The OST's definition of "community" remains true to both Third World and Fourth World development models, insofar as both assume sedentarism and territorial boundedness. Labor relations are largely beyond the scope of the OST's mandate, and so the majority of the Omaheke San remain invisible to the one NGO in the region that explicitly targets San people.

Although there are practical constraints to addressing class issues in the Omaheke – namely, the difficulties associated with accessing San living on the private property of farmers – class exploitation is also a common feature of San life off the farms, and, so, one could fairly say that ideological reasons exist for marginalizing class in the OST's mandate. Whereas indigenous discourse has politicized culture to great strategic advantage, class has become depoliticized and, to be recognized as indigenous people, the San are compelled to present themselves as largely uncorrupted by historical and political–economic contexts. As I have already suggested, one important component of this essentializing move has been to insist on a special relationship to the land. Thus, one finds that struggles over land rights are often couched in terms of retaining or regaining a traditional (primordial) cultural identity.[16] But, in the Omaheke, San calls for land also reflect their self-consciousness as an underclass. ≠Oma described the problems of the Omaheke San this way:

> You must improve things or resettle. If you resettle then they [Damaras and Hereros] will steal your things. The government says we must develop things here, like a garden. But if you do it the other people will just destroy it. We should get a place of our own so that we know what we can do with it, so that the government can work directly with the San.

N≠isa, a middle-aged San woman living in one of the communities near the Botswana border, described the situation this way: "When we stay together with the Damara people we are not free. When will we get our freedom? That is the most difficult thing. Like now, we must pay for the water. Where will we get the money? Now, we are asking ourselves, 'Where will we have a place to stay?'" N≠isa is a respected traditional healer, and on the same day she said these things to me, she and other woman from her community dressed themselves heavily in bead-work and animal skins to perform what they described as a "traditional dance." But it is still class consciousness that shines through in her complaints. Whereas indigenist discourse emphasizes the relationship between indigenous peoples and the land, the Omaheke San emphasize the relationship between themselves, the land, and non-San peoples with whom they are in unequal relationships.

NGO networks in the Omaheke are quite new, and so NGO activity is still relatively chaotic and uncoordinated. Many of the directors of local NGOs do not know each other, and they have no idea how many or even which NGOs are working in the region. The San themselves are unfamiliar with NGOs and are not clear on the distinctions among development projects, government or church-funded food-for-work programs, drought-relief programs, and temporary employment opportunities. All of these efforts are broadly described by the San as "projects."[17] The San are, thus, vulnerable to exploitation as local Hereros, Tswanas, and Damaras approach unemployed San to initiate what they describe as incomegenerating "projects." One fairly typical such project used San women at a remote community to knit sweaters; Herero women dropped off large quantities of wool, returned after a couple of months to collect the sweaters, and sold them in town. The San women were never paid. Other so-called projects – which draw explicitly on the San's cultural image – enlist the San to perform their traditional dances at local political events and tourism venues.

Ethnic Entrepreneurs and Ethnotourism

The globalized idea of culture – specifically, the notion of a primordial indigenous culture – is also reinforced in a context of local disorder, in which identity-based entrepreneurial ventures, both formal and informal, take on development functions.

Koba described how a Damara woman approached her and five other San women and offered them money to perform in various venues:

> The first dance we did was in Gobabis. . . . Then we went to dance at Buitepos [on the border of Botswana] when the [trans-Kalahari] road was opened. . . . The work was not good for me. If you dance there, you are not wearing any clothes. We are wearing the !gu, like we were wearing in the old time. [But] we didn't get any money [and no food].

//Aese, who lives on a cattle post in a communal area 250 kilometers (about 155 miles) south of Koba's camp, told me about his community's experiences performing for tourists at the behest of Hereros:

> They were there, the people from other countries. . . . The Hereros came and picked up the San people to dance – they said it was a concert. My son was also a performer. But he didn't get money in his hands. All the money goes to the Hereros – the money that comes from other hands [i.e., from the tourists].

In a village settlement approximately 200 kilometers (124 miles) northeast of Koba's camp, Tchi!o, a middle-aged San woman, described how a group of Hereros offered the women in her village an opportunity to earn money by performing at a cultural festival:

> The Hereros came and took us from here. When we got [to the town], they took off our clothes in front of many people. And they put a !gae [a leather apron] on us and they took off our doeks [head scarves] and tied them between our breasts. And our breasts were out. Hereros made us like that so that we could go and dance for them. They said, "You must come and play. You will be paid, and you will also get some food. Come and eat. You are suffering a lot." . . . The women said, "Let's go and get food and money!" That's why all of us stood up and went – we were hungry. When we came back home, they gave us a small packet of tea and sugar and soup . . . [but] no money! They wasted us. They made us dance, and made us naked, and they left us with nothing.

In Tchi!o's story, the Hereros transformed their San recruits according to a familiar conception of what pristine primitives should be – naked dancers. The San who were recruited, most of whom were unemployed former farmworkers and domestic servants, clearly saw these ventures as income-earning opportunities, not as opportunities for cultural assertion.

Informal ethnic entrepreneurial activities represent an extreme form of cultural exploitation. The same dynamics, however, are often reproduced in formal-sector cultural marketing because the conditions for "acceptable" expressions of identity and the conditions sustaining class inequalities are often the same. The IMF now considers tourism a viable export strategy for debt-ridden countries, and tourism is being promoted by industry members and states as a means for achieving sustainable development (World Travel and Tourism Council 2001b).[18] Tourism is also one of the fastest growing industries in Namibia, with a projected growth rate of ten percent per year (United Nations 1999).[19] Tourism is also one of the least-regulated industries in the world, and the Namibian farming sector – in which most commercialized ethnotourism ventures are initiated – is itself characterized by a lack of regulation, especially with respect to the enforcement of labor laws.

Many white farmers, feeling the pinch of liberalized trade markets and decreased government subsidies, have begun to diversify into the tourism sector, using the Bushmen to draw tourists to their newly established guest farms. A visitor to the Omaheke Region can now find brochures marketing Bushmen as tourist attractions. For example, the brochure for San World invites tourists to "meet the last survivors of an ancient society...living in close harmony with nature" and to "come and explore the secrets of the Bushmen." San World is a guest lodge owned and run by a local white farmer and had been, prior to 2001, a cattle ranch where San worked as farm laborers.

A recent brochure for Bona Safaris, a tour company based in Gobabis, provides the following description of the Omaheke San for potential customers:

> Amid these desolate expanses [of the pristine Kalahari] the Bushman clans have wandered for thousands of years. ... This race of people is ancient – as shown in their ability to store fat reserves in their buttocks, to be used when food is scarce. Bushmen live on game and wild fruit. They are still mainly hunters and gatherers. ... They are unable to comprehend what happens beyond their world.

According to the itinerary, tourists will visit, not the pristine Kalahari, but a lion farm, a leopard farm, and an ostrich farm. This tour is careful to perpetuate a mythical image of the hunting and gathering Bushman, and this requires that the real San in the Omaheke – the farmworkers and domestic servants – remain invisible.

Unfortunately, the working conditions on many of the guest farms differ little from those on the cattle ranches. San I spoke to complained that they were not getting paid, their nations were inadequate, and the farmers kept the money that the tourists offered to the San role-players. Oba, an elderly man from /In!gou's resettlement camp, was recruited by the owners of the lion farm promoted by Bona Safaris. At the farm, they replaced his tattered clothing with a loincloth and put him to work showing tourists how to track animals and make arrows. He described his experience on the guest farm in the following way:

> I bought food [from the farmer] with the money I received from the government – my pension. I received nothing from [the farmer]. ... When [the tourists] came to see me, they were only interested in my weapons like my spear, the hunting equipment that I made; [we danced for them], but they gave me nothing ... they took pictures, but they gave us nothing. ... When I refused to give [the farmer] my pension money, he stopped giving us food.

Oba worked on the guest farm for less than a year before returning to the resettlement camp, where at least he could get drought-relief food each month. By this time, the camp manager had ceased feeding drought-relief food to her pigs, so conditions in the camp had improved enough for Oba to believe that life there would be better than on the lion farm.

Other ventures capitalize on the recent trend toward ecologically and politically responsible tourism. In August 1998, members of the !Xûn community – a group of unemployed farmworkers in the southern Omaheke Region – entered into a joint tourism venture with Intu Afrika Lodge (located outside of the Omaheke Region). With the assistance of WIMSA, a contract was drawn up to ensure appropriate housing and remuneration for the San and to secure a share in the returns from the venture (Working Group of Indigenous Minorities in South Africa 1998:40). The lodge promotes itself to tourists by claiming that

> the Intu Afrika corporation has developed a project that it believes will provide a blueprint for the successful implementation of development projects with the Bushmen and other indigenous minority peoples. ... The objective of the Intu Afrika Bushman project is to empower the community in order to regain their dignity and pride. This has been done by creating employment opportunities and giving the Bushmen scope to practice cultural activities that utilize traditional Bushman skills in order to generate income for the community. [Intu Afrika Game Lodge n.d.]

The only identity given scope for expression, however, is the one that is marketable; that is, the traditional foraging identity as it is defined largely by stereotypes feeding the demand for this kind of ethnotourism. The manager of Intu Afrika Lodge even contributed his own idea of authentic Bushmen behavior and required the men to rub the blood from a recent kill onto their legs while tourists watched.[20]

Problems plagued Intu Afrika almost as soon as it was opened. Before the lodge owner recruited the Omaheke !Xûn, he had tried to import Bushmen from the Schmidtsdrift army base in South Africa. These San had been relocated to Schmidtsdrift from the Caprivi strip in northern Namibia, where they had been recruited by the South African Defence Force to fight in covert operations units during Namibia's liberation struggle.[21] The lodge owner had inadvertently hired a motley crew of ex-combatants. Even worse, they were not the Bushmen of popular imagination but the tall, dark Kxoe "river Bushmen." The irate lodge owner eventually sent the Kxoe back to Schmidtsdrift because "they were not short and yellow" but were merely "ordinary folk" who "wore trousers, shirts and dresses" and "did not appreciate having to sport animal skins"; some drank too much and "refused to behave like 'genuine bushmen' " (Mail and Guardian 1995).

The lodge owner's concern to have "real" Bushmen working at his lodge was only in part a product of apartheid stereotypes: Market demand also imposes an authenticity imperative on such ventures. For example, shortly after the South African ≠Khomani San signed a historic land deal in 1999, the *Cape Times* uncovered the "Great Bushman Tourism Scam" (Robbins 2001:839). According to the *Cape Times* exposé, "fake bushmen" were being marketed at the world-famous Bushman village at Kagga Kamma – the lodge's bogus Bushmen were at worst actually "Coloured" people and at best not "one hundred percent pure Bushmen" (Robbins 2001: 839).[22]

This was not the first time Kagga Kamma had been accused of marketing inauthentic Bushmen. In October 1997, an article entitled "The Search for Authenticity," published in the *Nation*, complained that the Bushmen at Kagga Kamma were wearing "Mets baseball caps and Nikes" and so were obviously not the "real thing." The author eventually found "real" Bushmen in Namibia:

> My search for authentic Bushmen finally took me to the northern extremity of the Kalahari Desert. ... I had hoped to make some contact with "the wild Bushmen in all of us" – the free spirit that once resided in all men and that all men still hanker for; the way we were, *uncomplicated*, uncluttered, at peace. I'd been told that the Ju/'wasi Bushmen in this desolate outpost were as close as I would get, and this turned out to be true. ... Any doubts I had about their authenticity were obliterated the day I went hunting with the village elder, a wiry man in his late 60s named Old Kaece. ... They say a true Bushman twangs with the bush and watching Old Kaece sniffing and twitching and sensing everything around him ... *it was as if he was a part of the natural world himself.* [Boynton 1997: 19, emphasis added]

Complaints from those on the consumer side of the tourism industry (including journalists) consistently cite the failure of real San to conform to idealized images of "Bushman Noble Savages." The expectation of an organic link between the Bushmen and the land or nature – already imposed by donor behavior in the development industry – is now reinforced by market demand. Where Bushmen ethnotourism ventures – whether in the formal or informal sectors – are in the hands of non-San, the same disturbing pattern recurs. The very people who help to sustain the myth that the Omaheke San remain pristine foragers, in need of nothing but game and wild fruits, are the first to believe that myth when payday comes.

The San are themselves quite critical of others marketing their identity. One San man told me, "At the lodges – the places of the white people – they are just busy making money for themselves." A San woman I spoke to exclaimed, "Everybody likes to steal our traditions!" At the same time, the San recognize tourism as an opportunity to both make money and express cultural pride. The same woman who spoke out against tradition theft told me that she is hopeful that she and other San living at a small cattle post in the southern Omaheke will be successful in their own tourism scheme because "our culture is very good to us ... it is beautiful." When I asked Koba, the San woman who had been recruited by Damaras to perform traditional dances, if she was still interested in identity work, she said, "Yes, so that our traditions don't die out." Kxao Moses ≠ Oma and Axel Thoma argue that ethnotourism can revitalize traditional culture and that "the recent introduction of tourism-based undertakings among San communities has made the San aware that their culture is a valuable social and economic asset" (2002: 40).

Involvement with WIMSA and the OST has already produced a visible impact on the ways the San choose to present themselves to outsiders. During my fieldwork in 1996 to 1997 – before WIMSA and the OST were operating in the Omaheke – when the San I visited learned that I had a camera, they often asked to be photographed. To prepare themselves, San living on the farms put on the best clothes they could borrow and posed with their most prized possessions – usually with radios or, if one was available, with a bicycle. Those who had no such symbols of affluence often asked to be photographed standing in front of, or leaning against, my truck. But now, in the communities in which the OST is active and development work has begun, an opportunity to be photographed sends the San residents to dress up in beadwork and animal skins. However inextricably class and culture are interwoven in the lives of the Omaheke San, their images are easily separated for the camera. For all that, the displays of the San in beadwork and animal skins were genuine expressions of cultural pride.

Conclusion

I suggested at the outset that one part of the explanation for intensified ethnic and cultural assertions in the face of globalization relates to the globalization of an increasingly essentialized idea of what culture is, and, so, ethnic and cultural assertion is often an expression of globalization rather than a reaction against it. In the confusion that follows in the wake of globalization, the idea of culture becomes an instrument in the struggle for resources and, in the processes by which it is instrumentalized, culture is also essentialized. The international indigenous peoples' movement, as a form of "globalization from below," adds another layer of essentialism to the idea of culture by using it to provide a crucial part of the contrast between indigenous peoples and impoverished "ordinary folk." Predicating the survival or resurgence of an indigenous identity on a unique relationship to the land – itself an essentializing move – has proven a strategically useful tool in the struggle for resources. Furthermore, discrete and bounded communities make easy targets for donors and for ethnodevelopment projects. Finally, a booming global industry in ethnotourism, which requires that indigenous culture be a suitable subject for photography, contributes a glossy finish to how a pristine culture looks in the global marketplace.

The Omaheke San illustrate the consequences of these instrumentalizing and essentializing trends. When the idea of culture becomes instrumentalized in the struggle for resources, then, in situations of extreme marginalization and class inequality, it easily becomes another instrument for continued exploitation. And, as the idea of culture becomes essentialized, the San's own distinctive but class-shaped culture – the lived patterns of practices and beliefs that make up their moral identity – goes unnoticed.

NOTES

1   From 1884 to 1915, Namibia (then South West Africa) was a German colony. In 1920, South West Africa was mandated by the League of Nations to South Africa as a Trust Territory. After a lengthy liberation struggle (1966 to 1989), led by the South West Africa Peoples Organization (SWAPO), Namibia achieved independence on March 21, 1990.

2   More sophisticated analyses of the cultural effects of globalization examine the process of hybridization, which Jan Nederveen Pieterse defines as "the ways in which forms become separated from existing practices and recombine with new forms in new practices" (2000: 101–102; see also Appadurai 2000). As a "counterweight to introverted notions of culture" (Pieterse 2000: 105), these studies are valuable. Nevertheless, they are unable to explain why "introverted notions of culture" are such a common feature of identity movements. Interestingly, even studies of cultural hybridization attempt to examine the logic of global culture, as though global culture were a coherent, homogeneous

whole (or an introverted culture). For example, Roland Robertson claims that "the unitary view of the nationally-constituted society is *an aspect of global culture*" (1997: 87). Thus, Robertson sees ideas of "nationally constituted societies" as a feature of a homogeneous global culture rather than as ideas that have been globalized (i.e., as an aspect of global-ization) and so misses a rather obvious explanation for why ethnic–nationalist movements are such a common feature of localization. Such frameworks that pit global culture against local culture produce a paradox that encourages opaque descriptions of the relationship between global and local dynamics, such as that offered by Arjun Appadurai: "The central feature of *global culture* today is the politics of the mutual effort of sameness and difference to cannibalize one another and thereby proclaim their successful highjacking of the twin Enlightenment ideas of the triumphantly universal and the resiliently particu-lar" (2000: 330, emphasis added).

3 Some scholars have associated identity movements with the history of modern national-isms. But the standard focus on the logic of a global culture has prevented most from exploring how this influenced a globalized definition of cultural identity (see Appadurai 2000; Hall 1997: 26–27; King 1997; Pieterse 2000; Robertson 1997; but see Buell 1994 and Wallerstein 1990 for promising approaches to this issue).

4 I focus here on one particular idea of culture – that is, the popular notion of culture as a bounded and territorially grounded entity that corresponds to a nation – because explor-ing the various ideas of culture that have developed in popular and academic discourse is beyond the scope of this article. Adam Kuper (1999) discusses the evolution of various concepts of culture, from mid-20th-century European traditions to the U.S. postmodern turn, and criticizes contemporary identity politics as politically dangerous and atavistic (see also Kuper 2003). His argument entails a problematic dichotomy, however, between essentialist conceptions of culture and identity and constructionist approaches, and his characterizations of each rely on problematic presuppositions about what it would take to make a culture (or cultural identity) "real."

5 Will Kymlicka locates the substance of debates surrounding indigenous peoples' rights in the gap between article 1 of the UN Charter, which establishes the right of all "peoples" to self-determination, and article 27 of the International Covenant on Civil and Political Rights, which establishes the right of "members of minorities" to "enjoy their own culture... in community with other members of their group" (1999: 283). Nonetheless, as Kymlicka notes, "the right to 'self-determination' is too strong, for it has traditionally been interpreted to include the right to form one's own state," whereas article 27 is "too weak, for 'the right to enjoy one's own culture' has traditionally been understood to include only negative rights of non-interference, rather than positive rights to assistance, funding, autonomy or public recognition" (1999: 284). Because article 27 is too weak to address the concerns of indigenous minorities, "self-determination" has dominated the vocabulary of indigenous activists. Because this right is traditionally understood as the right to form an independent state, however, it is limited by the "salt water thesis," which restricts the right to self-determination to peoples colonized by overseas powers (Kymlicka 1999: 284). Given that most indigenous activists are not seeking secession, a weaker sense of self-determination needs to be articulated and accepted by the international community.

6 James Clifford also notes that "the idea of culture comes with it an expectation of roots, of a stable, territorial existence" (1988: 38).

7 The term *Khoi* is often used to refer to Nama-speaking peoples, who are linguistically and culturally similar to San.

8 The anthropological wisdom that shaped the apartheid system saw nations as "fundamen-tal human entities" (Gordon 1988: 541). The particular conception of culture that under-pinned the ideology of apartheid was developed by Afrikaans-speaking anthropologists

who, drawing from their training in Germany in the 1920s and 1930s, adapted the German ethnological notion of "volkgeist" to the South African context. Werner Willi Max Eiselen – widely recognized as the intellectual architect of apartheid – was among these German-trained anthropologists, was one of the founding members of South African *volkekunde* anthropology, and was, according to Robert Gordon, "obsessed with the organic analogy" (1988: 540). Eiselen insisted that culture, not race, determined behavior (Gordon 1988: 540; see also Kuper 1999: xii). But for Eiselen, culture was itself conceived in terms of biological metaphors – that is, as an organism. Another member of the volkekunde school, J. P. Bruwer, served on the Odendaal Commission, the body responsible for the establishment of ethnic "homelands" in South West Africa (Namibia) in the 1960s (Gordon 1988).

9   The Angola Boers were the recipients of the largest and most expensive resettlement and financial-aid scheme in the territory's history. They were the descendants of the Dorsland Trekkers who had passed through the Omaheke en route to Angola 50 years earlier and who returned in the late 1920s to constitute the largest single influx of settlers into the region.

10   On the farms I surveyed in 1996, the average wage for San male workers was N$82.00 per month (equivalent to US$20.50). This compares to an average monthly cash wage of N$166.12 for non-San farmworkers, or N$300 a month if payment was made in wages only (Devereux et al. 1996: x, 23). The average wage for San domestic servants was N$45.00 per month (US$11.25). Wages for non-San domestic servants reported by the Namibian Domestic and Allied Workers Union averaged N$221.90 per month (Fuller and Hubbard 1996: 114–115).

11   Rations usually include mielie meal, coffee, sugar, tea, milk, and, sporadically, meat.

12   For details on the intersection of San class and culture, see Sylvain 2002. For a description of the intersections of race, class, and gender inequalities, see Sylvain 2001.

13   For recent work on disorder, corruption, and the "criminalization" of states in Africa, see Bayart et al. 1999 and Chabal and Daloz 1999.

14   WIMSA and the OST initiated a Devil's Claw harvesting project in two small communities off the farms and are assisting the !Xûn San in the southern Omaheke with establishing a tourist camp site.

15   The chief-designate of the northern Omaheke San suggested a remedy for this imbalance by pointing out that farm San could be counted as belonging to the community located closest to the farm on which they work.

16   This is also illustrated by the case of the ≠ Khomani San in South Africa (see Robbins 2001).

17   This was the situation as of June 2001. WIMSA and the OST have been working tirelessly to raise awareness of their activities and to forge fruitful networks with other local development and advocacy organizations.

18   According to the World Travel and Tourism Council (2001a), tourism, which represents 11 percent of the global Gross Domestic Product (GDP) and 8.2 percent of world employment, is one of the world's biggest industries and one of the world's largest employers.

19   According to the World Travel and Tourism Council (2001b), tourism contributed 7.8 percent to Namibia's GDP in 2001. The director of tourism at the Ministry of Environment and Tourism estimates that "tourism will be the largest contributor to the national GDP in six or seven years" (United Nations 1999).

20   For a detailed description of the touristic experience at Intu Afrika, see Guenther 2002.

21   In the mid-1970s, the South African army began recruiting Ju/'hoan and Kxoe as trackers and reconnaissance troops in covert operations units against SWAPO's armed wing, the Peoples' Liberation Army of Namibia (PLAN; see Gordon and Douglas 2000; Lee 1988).

22 In his study of the Kagga Kamma settlement in the Western Cape, Hylton White
    (1995: 42) describes many of the same stereotypical justifications for low wages that
    I found in the Omaheke: "Bushmen" are too primitive to handle money, and besides,
    "real" Bushmen have no need for it anyway.

REFERENCES

Appadurai, Arjun
    2000[1990] Disjuncture and Difference in the Global Cultural Economy. In *The Globali-*
    zation Reader. Frank Lechner and John Boli, eds. Pp. 322–330. Malden, MA: Blackwell.
Barnard, Alan
    1998 Problems in the Construction of Khoisan Ethnicities. *Proceedings of the Khoisan*
    Identities and Cultural Heritage Conference – Cape Town 12–16 July 1997. Andrew
    Bank, ed. Pp. 51–68. Cape Town: Institute for Historical Research, University of Western
    Cape, and Infosource.
Bauer, Gretchen
    2001 Namibia in the First Decade of Independence: How Democratic? *Journal of Southern*
    African Studies 27(1): 33–55.
Bayart, Jean-François, Stephen Ellis, and Béatrice Hibou
    1999 *The Criminalization of the State in Africa.* Stephen Ellis, trans. Oxford: Inter-
    national African Institute and James Currey.
Beckett, Jeremy
    1996 Contested Images: Perspectives on the Indigenous Terrain in the Late 20th Century.
    Identities: Global Studies in Culture and Power 3(1–2): 1–3.
Bodley, John H.
    1990 *Victims of Progress.* 3rd edition. Mountain View, CA: Mayfield.
Boynton, Graham
    1997 The Search for Authenticity: On Destroying the Village in Order to Save It. *The*
    Nation 265(10): 18–19.
Bruner, Edward M.
    1989 Of Cannibals, Tourists, and Ethnographers. *Cultural Anthropology* 4(4): 438–445.
    1995 The Ethnographer/Tourist in Indonesia. In *International Tourism: Identity*
    and Change. Marie-Françoise Lanfant, John B. Allock, and Edward M. Bruner, eds.
    Pp. 224–241. Studies in International Sociology, 47. London: Sage.
Bruner, Edward M., and Barbara Kirshenblatt-Gimblett
    1994 Maasai on the Lawn: Tourist Realism in East Africa. *Cultural Anthropology* 9(4):
    435–470.
Brysk, Allison
    2000 *From Tribal Village to Global Village: Indian Rights and International Relations in*
    Latin America. Stanford, CA: Stanford University Press.
Buell, Frederick
    1994 *National Culture and the New Global System.* Baltimore: Johns Hopkins University
    Press.
Central Statistics Office
    1996 *Living Conditions in Namibia: Basic Description with Highlights. 1993/1994*
    Namibia Household Income and Expenditure Survey, Main Report. Windhoek,
    Namibia: Central Statistics Office and National Planning Commission.

Chabal, Patrick, and Jean-Pascal Daloz
  1999 *Africa Works: Disorder as Political Instrument*. Oxford: International Africa Institute and James Currey.
Clifford, James
  1988 *The Predicament of Culture: Twentieth-Century Ethnography, Literature, and Art*. Cambridge, MA: Harvard University Press.
Cobo, José Martínez
  1986 *The Study of the Problem of Discrimination against Indigenous Populations*. Document E/CN.4/Sub.2/1986/7/Add.4. Geneva: Office of the United Nations High Commissioner for Human Rights.
Conklin, Beth A.
  2002 Shamans versus Pirates in the Amazonian Treasure Chest. *American Anthropologist* 104(4): 1050–1061.
Crick Malcolm
  1989 Representations of International Tourism in the Social Sciences: Sun, Sex, Sights, Savings, and Servility. *Annual Review of Anthropology* 18: 307–344.
Devereux, S., V. Katjiuanjo, and G. van Rooy
  1996 *The Living and Working Conditions of Farmworkers in Namibia*. Windhoek: Legal Assistance Centre, Farmworkers Project and Social Sciences Division, Multi-Disciplinary Research Centre, University of Namibia.
Dombrowski, Kirk
  2002 The Praxis of Indigenism and Alaska Native Timber Politics. *American Anthropologist* 104(4): 1062–1073.
Dubow, Saul
  1995 *Illicit Union: Scientific Racism in Modern South Africa*. Cambridge: Cambridge University Press.
Falk, Richard
  1993 The Making of Global Citizenship. In *Global Visions: Beyond the New World Order*. Jeremy Brecher and John Brown Childs, eds. Pp. 39–49. Boston: South End Press.
Featherstone, Mike, ed.
  1990 *Global Culture: Nationalism, Globalization and Modernity*. London: Sage.
Forte, Maximilian C.
  1998 Renewed Indigeneity in the Local-Global Continuum and the Political Economy of Tradition: The Case of Trinidad's Caribs and the Caribbean Organization of Indigenous People. Electronic document, http://www.centrelink.org/renewed. html, accessed November 11, 2001.
Friedman, Jonathan
  1994 *Cultural Identity and Global Processes*. London: Sage.
Fuller, B., and D. Hubbard
  1996 *The Living and Working Conditions of Domestic Workers in Namibia*. Windhoek, Namibia: Legal Assistance Centre.
Garland, Elizabeth
  1999 Developing the Bushmen: Building Civil(ized) Society in the Kalahari and Beyond. In *Civil Society and the Political Imagination in Africa: Critical Perspectives*. John L. Comaroff and Jean Comaroff, eds. Pp. 72–103. Chicago: University of Chicago Press.
Giddens, Anthony
  1991 *Sociology*. Cambridge: Polity Press.
Gordon, Robert
  1988 Apartheid's Anthropologists: On the Genealogy of Afrikaner Anthropology. *American Ethnologist* 15(3): 535–553.

Gordon, Robert, and Stuart Sholto Douglas
  2000   *The Bushmen Myth: The Making of a Namibian Underclass.* 2nd edition. Boulder,
         CO: Westview Press.
Greenwood, Davydd J.
  1989   Culture by the Pound: An Anthropological Perspective on Tourism as Cultural
         Commoditization. In *Hosts and Guests: The Anthropology of Tourism.* 2nd edition.
         Valene L. Smith, ed. Pp. 171–185. Philadelphia: University of Pennsylvania Press.
Griggs, Richard
  1992   Background on the Term "Fourth World." Fourth World Documentation Project
         reprint, 28 May 1992. Electronic document, ftp://ftp.halcyon.com/FWDP/fourthw.txt,
         accessed November 2002.
Guenther, Mathias
  1980   From "Brutal Savages" to "Harmless People." *Paideuma* 26: 123–140.
  2002   Ethno-Tourism and the Bushmen. In *Self- and Other-Images of Hunter-Gatherers.*
         Henry Stewart, Alan Barnard, and Keiichi Omura, eds. Pp. 47–64. Senri Ethnological
         Studies, 60. Osaka, Japan: National Museum of Ethnology.
Hall, Stuart
  1995   Negotiating Caribbean Identities. *New Left Review* 209 (January–February): 3–14.
  1997   The Local and the Global: Globalization and Ethnicity. In *Culture, Globalization
         and the World-System: Contemporary Conditions for the Representation of Identity.*
         Anthony D. King, ed. Pp. 19–39. Minneapolis: University of Minnesota Press.
Hannerz, Ulf
  1997   Scenarios for Peripheral Cultures. In *Culture, Globalization and the World-System:
         Contemporary Conditions for the Representation of Identity.* Anthony D. King, ed.
         Pp. 107–128. Minneapolis: University of Minnesota Press.
Hodgson, Dorothy
  2002   Precarious Alliances: The Cultural Politics and Structural Predicaments of the
         Indigenous Rights Movement in Tanzania. *American Anthropologist* 104(4): 1086–1097.
International Labour Organisation
  1989   Convention (No. 169) concerning Indigenous and Tribal Peoples in Independent
         Countries. Electronic document, http://www.unhchr.ch/html/menu3/b/62.htm, accessed
         June 2003.
Intu Afrika Game Lodge
  N.d. Intu Afrika Game Lodge. Electronic document, http://www.namibweb.com/intuafri-
         ca.html, accessed June 2003.
Jacobs, Jane
  1988   The Construction of Identity. In *Past and Present: The Construction of Aboriginality.*
         Jeremy Beckett, ed. Pp. 31–44. Canberra: Aboriginal Studies Press.
Kalb, Don, and Marco van der Land
  2000   Beyond the Mosaic: Questioning Cultural Identity in a Globalizing Age. In *The
         Ends of Globalization: Bringing Society Back In.* Don Kalb, Marco van der Land,
         Richard Staring, Bart van Steenbergen, and Nico Wilterdink, eds. Pp. 273–280. Lanham,
         MD: Rowman and Littlefield.
King, Anthony D.
  1997   Introduction: Spaces of Culture, Spaces of Knowledge. In *Culture, Globalization
         and the World-System: Contemporary Conditions for the Representation of Identity.*
         Anthony D. King, ed. Pp. 1–18. Minneapolis: University of Minnesota Press.
Kloos, Peter
  2000   The Dialectics of Globalization and Localization. In *The Ends of Globalization:
         Bringing Society Back In.* Don Kalb, Marco van der Land, Richard Staring, Bart van

Steenbergen, and Nico Wilterdink, eds. Pp. 281–297. Lanham, MD: Rowman and Littlefield.

Kuper, Adam
1999 *Culture: The Anthropologists' Account.* Cambridge, MA: Harvard University Press.
2003 The Return of the Native. *Current Anthropology* 44(3): 389–395.

Kymlicka, Will
1999 Theorizing Indigenous Rights. *University of Toronto Law Journal* 49(2): 281–293.

Lanfant, Marie-Françoise
1995 Introduction. In *International Tourism: Identity and Change.* Marie-Françoise Lanfant, John B. Allock, and Edward M. Bruner, eds. Pp. 1–23. Studies in International Sociology, 47. London: Sage.

Lattas, Andrew
1993 Essentialism, Memory and Resistance: Aboriginality and the Politics of Authenticity. *Oceania* 63(3): 240–268.

Lee, Richard B.
1988 The Gods Must Be Crazy but the State Has a Plan: Government Policies toward the San in Namibia. In *Namibia: 1884–1984: Readings on Namibian History and Society.* Brian Wood, ed. Pp. 181–190. London: Namibia Support Committee and United Nations Institute for Namibia.
1993[1969] Eating Christmas in the Kalahari. In *The Dobe Ju/'hoansi.* Pp. 183–188. Fort Worth, TX: Harcourt Brace.
2000 Indigenism and Its Discontents: Anthropology and the Small Peoples at the Millennium. Keynote address, American Ethnological Society Annual Meetings, Tampa, Florida, March 25.

Li, Tania Murray
2000 Articulating Indigenous Identity in Indonesia: Resource Politics and the Tribal Slot. *Comparative Studies in Society and History* 42(1): 149–179.

MacCannell, Dean
1973 Staged Authenticity: Arrangement of Social Spaces in Tourist Settings. *American Journal of Sociology* 79(3): 589–603.
1984 Reconstructed Ethnicity Tourism and Cultural Identity in Third World Communities. *Annals of Tourism Research* 11(3): 375–391.

Mail and Guardian
1995 Whose Land Is This? Mail and Guardian Online, February 17. Electronic document, http://www.sn.apc.org/wmail/issues/950217/wm950217-56.html, accessed October 5, 2001.

Malkki, Liisa
1992 National Geographic: The Rooting of Peoples and the Territorialization of National Identity among Scholars and Refugees. *Cultural Anthropology* 7(1): 24–44.

Manuel, George
1974 *The Fourth World: An Indian Reality.* Toronto: Collier-Macmillan Canada.

Maybury-Lewis, David
1997 *Indigenous Peoples, Ethnic Groups, and the State.* Needham Heights, MA: Allyn and Bacon.

Meyer, Birgit, and Peter Geschiere
1999 Globalization and Identity: Dialectics of Flow and Closure: Introduction. In *Globalization and Identity: The Dialectics of Flow and Closure.* Birgit Meyer and Peter Geschiere, eds. Pp. 1–15. Oxford: Institute of Social Sciences and Blackwell.

Moore, Anna, with the Omaheke San Trust Board of Trustees
2000 *Omaheke San Trust Annual Report, March 1999 to February* 2000. Windhoek, Namibia: Working Group for Indigenous Minorities in Southern Africa.

Morton, Fred
    1994   Slavery and South African Historiography. In *Slavery in South Africa: Captive Labor on the Dutch Frontier*. Elizabeth Eldredge and Fred Morton, eds. Pp. 1–9. Boulder, CO: Westview Press; Pietermaritzburg: University of Natal Press.
Muehlebach, Andrea
    2001   "Making Place" at the United Nations: Indigenous Cultural Politics at the U.N. Working Group on Indigenous Populations. *Cultural Anthropology* 16(3): 415–448.
    2003   What Self in Self-Determination? Notes from the Frontiers of Transnational Indigenous Activism. *Identities: Global Studies in Culture and Power* 10(2): 241–268.
Nash, Dennison
    1989   Tourism as a Form of Imperialism. In *Hosts and Guests: The Anthropology of Tourism*. 2nd edition. Valene L. Smith, ed. Pp. 171–185. Philadelphia: University of Pennsylvania Press.
National Archives of Namibia
    1923   Draft of letter to administration, November 10, 1923. SWAA A521/3: Farm Labour, Desertions, 1928–1941. National Archives of Namibia, Windhoek.
    1927   Minute from the Native Commissioner to the Magistrate of Gobabis, November 3, 1927. SWAA A50/67: Native Affairs, Bushmen, 1926–1947. National Archives of Namibia, Windhoek.
    1939   Memorandum, Magistrate of Grootfontein, February, 1939. SWAA A198/26: Ethnological Inquiry into Control of Bushmen, 1934–1947. National Archives of Namibia, Windhoek.
Niezen, Ronald
    2000   Recognizing Indigenism: Canadian Unity and the International Movement of Indigenous Peoples. *Comparative Studies in Society and History* 42(1): 119–148.
    2003   *The Origins of Indigenism: Human Rights and the Politics of Identity*. Berkeley: University of California Press.
≠ Oma, Kxao Moses, and Axel Thoma
    2002   Will Tourism Destroy San Cultures? *Cultural Survival Quarterly* 26(1): 39–41.
Omaheke San Trust
    1999   *Constitution of the Omaheke San Trust. Drawn up by the Board, 9/7/99*. Windhoek, Namibia: Working Group for Indigenous Minorities in Southern Africa.
Ortiz, Roxanne Dunbar
    1984   The Fourth World and Indigenism: Politics of Isolation and Alternatives. *Journal of Ethnic Studies* 21(1): 79–105.
Pieterse, Jan Nederveen
    2000[1995]   Globalization as Hybridization. In *The Globalization Reader*. Frank Lechner and John Boli, eds. Pp. 99–105. Malden, MA: Blackwell.
Ramos, Alcida Rita
    1994   The Hyperreal Indian. *Critique of Anthropology* 12(2): 153–171.
    1998   *Indigenism: Ethnic Politics in Brazil*. Madison: University of Wisconsin Press.
Robbins, Steven
    2001   "Bushmen" and Double Vision: The ≠Khomani San Land Claim and the Cultural Politics of "Community" and "Development" in the Kalahari. *Journal of Southern African Studies* 27(4): 833–853.
Robertson, Roland
    1997   Social Theory, Cultural Relativity and the Problem of Globality. In *Culture, Globalization and the World-System: Contemporary Conditions for the Representation of Identity*. Anthony D. King, ed. Pp. 69–92. Minneapolis: University of Minnesota Press.

Seton, Kathy
  1999   Fourth World Nations in the Era of Globalization: An Introduction to Contemporary Theorizing Posed by Indigenous Nations. Fourth World Journal 1–2. Electronic document, http://www.cwis.org/fwj/41/fworld.html, accessed November 11, 2001.
Suzman, James
  1995   *Poverty, Land and Power in the Omaheke Region.* Windhoek, Namibia: Oxfam.
  2000   *Things from the Bush: A Contemporary History of the Omaheke Bushmen.* Basel, Switzerland: P. Schlettwein.
Sylvain, Renée
  2001   Bushmen, Boers and Baasskap: Patriarchy and Paternalism on Afrikaner Farms in the Omaheke Region, Namibia. *Journal of Southern African Studies* 27(4): 717–737.
  2002   "Land, Water, and Truth": San Identity and Global Indigenism. *American Anthropologist* 104(4): 1074–1084.
Turner, Terence
  1991   Representing, Resisting, Rethinking: Historical Transformations of Kayapo Culture and Anthropological Consciousness. In *Colonial Situations: Essays on the Contextualization of Ethnographic Knowledge.* George Stocking, ed. Pp. 285–313. Madison: University of Wisconsin Press.
United Nations
  1999   Africa Recovery Online: Country Report. Electronic document, http://www.un.org/ecosocdev/geninfo/afrec/vol12no4/namibxs.htm, accessed November 2, 2001.
Urry, John
  1990   *The Tourist Gaze: Leisure and Travel in Contemporary Societies.* London: Sage.
van den Berghe, Pierre L.
  1994   *The Quest for the Other: Ethnic Tourism in San Cristobal, Mexico.* Seattle: University of Washington Press.
van Rooyen, P. H., and P. Reiner
  1995   *Gobabis: 1845–1895–1995.* Gobabis, Namibia: Municipality of Gobabis.
Wallerstein, Immanuel
  1990   Culture as the Ideological Background of the Modern World System. In *Global Culture: Nationalism, Globalization and Modernity.* Mike Featherstone, ed. Pp. 31–55. London: Sage.
  1997   The National and the Universal: Can There Be Such a Thing as World Culture? In *Culture, Globalization and the World-System: Contemporary Conditions for the Representation of Identity.* Anthony D. King, ed. Pp. 91–106. Minneapolis: University of Minnesota Press.
Warren, Kay B.
  1998   *Indigenous Movements and their Critics: Pan-Mayan Activism in Guatemala.* Princeton: Princeton University Press.
White, Hylton
  1995   *In the Tradition of the Forefathers: Bushman Traditionality at Kagga Kamma.* Cape Town: University of Cape Town Press.
Wilmsen, Edwin
  1989   *Land Filled with Flies: A Political Economy of the Kalahari.* Chicago: University of Chicago Press.
Wolff, Janet
  1997   The Global and the Specific: Reconciling Conflicting Theories of Culture. In *Culture, Globalization and the World-System: Contemporary Conditions for the Representation of Identity.* Anthony D. King, ed. Pp. 161–174. Minneapolis: University of Minnesota Press.

Working Group of Indigenous Minorities in Southern Africa

    1998 *Working Group of Indigenous Minorities in Southern Africa, Report on Activities, April 1998 to March 1999*. Windhoek, Namibia: Working Group of Indigenous Minorities in South Africa.

World Travel and Tourism Council

    2001a Decrease in Tourism Demand Signals the Loss of Millions of Jobs Worldwide. Electronic document, http://www.wttc.org/resourceCentre/mediaCentre/releases/01010924/Demand Decreases.asp, accessed November 15.

    2001b World Travel and Tourism Council Forecast Places Tourism among Leading Economic and Employment Generators. Electronic document, http://www.wttc.org/resourceCentre/mediaCentre/releases/1010508Forecast2001.asp?, accessed November 15.

Wright, Robin

    1988 Anthropological Presuppositions of Indigenous Advocacy. *Annual Review of Anthropology* 17: 365–390.

18

Politico-moral Transactions in Indian AIDS Service: Confidentiality, Rights, and New Modalities of Governance

Kavita Misra

Kya aap HIV/AIDS se prabhavit hain? Jaaniye apney adhikaar" ("Are you infected with HIV/AIDS? Know your rights")

– Laywer's Collective Pamphlet[1]

Events, Ethnographic and Critical

Two months into my fieldwork at Garv, the urban North Indian non-governmental AIDS service organization where my ethnography is located, one of the staff was fired in quite a dramatic fashion. A meeting of all the staff was convened and Shraddha Menon, the founder and executive director, put the gentleman in question (I will call him NS) through a kind of public interrogation. What had he done? The simple answer would be that he had indulged in gossip. Word had leaked to Shraddha that NS had bad-mouthed Garv, its activities and its leadership to members of another organization. The precise nature of this gossip was lost to me, but it had involved criticism of Garv's employment practices and salaries. It was also clear

From *Anthropological Quarterly* 79(1): 33–74. Copyright © 2006, Anthropological Quarterly.

that this was not the first time that such a thing had happened. Shradhha, who was sensitive, emotional and impulsive, saw this incident not only as a sign of disloyalty both to the organization and to her personally, but also, interestingly, as a breach of the principles of confidentiality that Garv espoused and swore by as being among the central pillars of its organizational philosophy.

The meeting was called with no advance notice and nobody seemed to know its purpose. When everyone was finally gathered together, Shraddha threw out a question: "What does confidentiality mean to you?" ("Aap sub ke liye, gopniyeta kya maaine rakhti hai?") The question was posed in Hindi, repeated in English, and throughout the rest of the conversation the words "gopniyeta" (Hindi for confidentiality or secrecy) and confidentiality were used interchangeably. Various persons responded: it meant that information about the organization and what went on within it, as well as any information pertaining to clients would never be discussed with persons other than those who were approved with the client's consent. One of the staff of the male sexual health program noted that since most persons who came to support group meetings had not made their sexual practices, preferences or orientation known to their families and friends, secrecy was crucial. Often, he revealed, he would not acknowledge or speak with persons who might have come to support groups or who he might have seen during outreach work if he saw them in another context. Some of the staff became vocal about loyalty. Finally, Shraddha concluded that if a person could not keep information about the organization confidential then it was likely the same could happen with sensitive information about clients. Following this, one of the program managers revealed that NS had betrayed the confidence of the organization by talking about affairs that were internal to it. NS was silent and shame-faced during this time and protested his innocence, claiming that while he had had conversations about Garv with persons from another organization, his intention had not been to malign the organization or to give away information. His protests did not appear to impress anyone and his services were terminated.

As my fieldwork unfolded, I saw how the idea and practice of "confidentiality," in all its nebulous and contested manifestations, and embedded within it, the juridico-moral lexicon of "rights," underlay many crucial negotiations in work related to AIDS. The uses of this language by AIDS experts came to signify all that was deemed culturally absent but desirable and ideal for AIDS prevention and management in the Indian context (indeed, in all non-Euro-American contexts), and all that constituted socio-political impediments to health. Thus, discussions on the individual and on privacy, medical ethics, information, consent, stigma and discrimination, institutional neglect, poor resources, lack of education, and governmental apathy could all be invoked in the use of the notion of "confidentiality" and central to it, that of "rights." This article focuses on such politico-moral transactions occasioned by the AIDS crisis and occurring in the space of AIDS service, and how they reflect changing arrangements of governance, configurations of citizenship and redefinitions of health.

The extent to which health in modern societies and polities is perceived as a static condition rather than as experience is exemplified in the articulation of the WHO, which defines health as "a state of physical, mental and social well-being." In her critical examination of the way we have come to think of health today, Veena Das (1990) argues that this perception is linked to the idea of disease as located in body populations rather than only in individual bodies and therefore, that the management of disease and the maintenance of the health of the *populus* are seen as the responsibility of the state. The state is implicated in the health of individual bodies and body populations through its functions of governance, policing, and as *parens patriae* (Das 1990, Foucault 1972). However, in the way that modern "governmentality" (Foucault 1991) is deployed, the state seems to fragment, to disappear or to be rendered spectral. A marked effect of governmentality is this process of depoliticization or the shift towards the invisible presence of the state, through the diffusion of its disciplinary capacities into institutions that provide technical intervention which, because of their scientific nature are objective and apolitical (Adams 1998). In this Foucauldian governmental rationality then, the conduct of individuals and societies is structured by the systematic organization of knowledge and activities built into authoritative agencies like medicine, psychology, education and law (Hunt and Wickham 1994). Thus, human life circulates within a biopolitics constituted through technologies and constellations of knowledge and power that measure, evaluate, discipline, subject and control persons and populations (Biehl 1999, Foucault 1965, 1972, 1973, 1978, Petryna 2002, Rabinow 1989, 1996). "Bio-power," according to Foucault's well-known formulation, brings the realm of life into the realm of calculations (1978).

Calculations characterize modern "risk society" (Beck 1992, Luhmann 1993) where decision-making is based on informed choices about future losses and benefits and where information and expert knowledge are tied to structures of decision making and risk taking. In such a political contract, the legitimacy of governments is contingent on the use of scientific knowledge in the evaluation and management of risk. An event such as an epidemic presents a crisis in legitimacy by pointing to the failure of the state to perform its duties as an informed decision maker and the preserver of the health of its subjects. The way that statistics and epidemiological information are deployed by the state, by non-governmental agencies and by international bodies, appears both paradoxical and instrumental. Numbers are made visible, carefully fashioned into discursive objects that serve to create "viable" crises. On the one hand these numbers seem to betray the ineptitude of the state in the preservation of the health of its people, this seen as delegitimizing and an indicator of poor government and of a society that falls short of the desired characteristics of modernity. On the other hand, statistics, figures and surveillance data show how the state possesses the knowledge of its weaknesses and uses techniques and information in order to respond to crises, thereby relegitimizing itself as well as opening up the market for international resources. This cyclical story of problem, obstacle, struggle and triumph is told in many an annual report of government programs. These strategies are not restricted to institutions of the state. Both government and the non-governmental must continually renew and reaffirm themselves through the construction and management of crises, which are made visible through an intricate process of focusing the gaze of authorities, that is, the constellation of expert knowledge, on specific objects borne of a transnational political and moral economy. AIDS is one such transnationally circulating object.

AIDS constitutes a "critical event" (Das 1995) in the life of modern India.[2] Its critical nature lies undoubtedly in the enormity of suffering it causes, but also in how it draws attention to the role and the legitimacy of the state in its management of health and risk, involves new actors and relationships in such management, raises questions about cultural and moral codes and ideas of tradition, including ideals of marriage and family and notions of sexuality, brings disen-franchised and marginal groups into the fold of public health and development, produces new communities and political actors, forges links between local and global communities, and compels discussion on the meanings of citizenship and belonging.[3] While it is not possible here to elaborate on the entire spectrum of these processes, in what follows, I instantiate some of them and signal to others by documenting some of the micro-dynamics, or the minute, everyday transactions through which organized responses to the epidemic arose. As I have pointed out, through the ethnographic moment that opens this article, confidentiality and the underlying articulation of rights are crucial discursive sites where some of the transformative potential in AIDS work comes to be distilled. The newness and volatility of AIDS, the unstable nature of knowledge-practices around it and the history of its representation imply that the domain of AIDS service itself tends to involve a complex configuration of the political and the moral.[4] Its politics lie in how it must constitute itself as a legitimate actor within the social world, and stake a claim within the social imagination and projects of health and welfare. Its moral nature rests in the fact that its claims are based on experiences of suffering, marginality and questions of ethics and human values. As I see it, in this context, the political and the moral live an entangled existence, and I refer to this duality as the politico-moral. In the politico-moral, transactions around power and governance, the limits of state and civil society, and claims to nodes of authoritative speech are enmeshed with struggles to deal with pain and grief, the reevaluation of networks of kinship, affect, and faith, and the interrogation and redefinition of tradition, culture, citizenship and social belonging. My observations are based on fieldwork conducted between 2000 and 2001, in an urban North Indian non-governmental organization (NGO) called Garv that worked on HIV/AIDS care, prevention and advocacy, and sexual health. One of the focal points of my ethnographic work is Garv's role as part of the AIDS NGO Network, a set of seven organizations that dealt with different aspects of HIV/AIDS and related issues such as sexuality, sexual health, and drug use.[5]

AIDS Experts in the Non-governmental: Interrogations and Simulations of the State

The nineties witnessed a proliferation of responses to AIDS in the country – what I refer to as "AIDS service."[6] This novel biosociality (Rabinow 1996) encompassed agencies of the government (at the national level in the form of the National AIDS Control Organization or NACO, and at the state level in the form of State AIDS Cells) as well as a multitude of non-governmental organizations or NGOs working on AIDS and related issues like sexual and reproductive health and drug rehabilitation.[7] India, according to statistics compiled by national and international surveillance mechanisms, was evolving into the new epicenter of the pandemic.[8] Responding to this epidemiological crisis, and buttressed by technical and financial assistance from a combination of the Indian government and international donor agencies,[9] the non-governmental world has become instrumental in the way that knowledge and expertise about the disease, but also about sexuality, culture and society are produced and disseminated in the country.[10] This knowledge, often unroutinized and experimental, is produced through dialogue, confrontation and negotiation among different social actors who make up AIDS service, and who are situated across the realms of the governmental, non-governmental and private. These include scientists, biomedical practitioners and paramedical workers, policy makers, legal experts, non-governmental and other voluntary and welfare organizations, and identity based communities that have materialized as a product of AIDS related mobilization. The AIDS crisis in India has thus produced a community of expertise, a set of transnationally mobile individuals and groups, many of whom are situated in the realm of the non-governmental. This space of expert knowledge acts as a self-critical source of cultural commentary as well as transformative trends. It is a conduit for globally established scientific and ideological material to be delivered to local spaces, and the medium through which such material came to be contested, critiqued and reformulated before finding its way back into global sites. As Lawrence Cohen notes in his recent work on AIDS and the rise of same sex politics in India, AIDS acts as a "vehicle" for the circulation of global developmental capital to previously peripheral sites, marking a domain of "AIDS cosmopolitanism" (2005:300). AIDS and the institutions that surround it thus have a crucial global and globalizing potential (Altman 1999).

Garv's history and activities manifested the cosmopolitanism of AIDS service and the transnational character of modern networks of advocacy and activism (Keck and Sikkink 1998). The organization, as has been noted of NGOs, issue based associations and networks, voluntary or non-profit groups, or the "third sector" (Hemment 2004), represented a burgeoning transnational civil society or public sphere (Clark, Friedman and Hochstetler 1998, Fisher 1997, Florini 2000, Guidry, Kennedy and Zald 2000, Khagram, Riker and Sikkink 2002).[11] It was initiated in 1994 by Shraddha Menon, a young woman who had returned to India from the United States in order to work on what she saw as an emerging crisis. She had substantial social work experience in the US where she had conducted HIV/AIDS and sexual health education and peer education training with minority communities. Her work as a journalist in India and her acquaintance with AIDS and gay rights activism in the US and with the language of international human rights had equipped her with essential intellectual and social tools for advocacy. Shraddha's international contacts and mobility were also evidenced in the number of conferences she attended, her professional contacts that spanned the globe and the presence of international volunteers and researchers (like me, for instance) at Garv.

The impetus for Shraddha Menon to found an NGO in India had come from strong personal motivation to "make a difference." In the course of her travel between India and the United States, Shraddha had attended meetings on HIV/ AIDS and had witnessed "misinformation" being disseminated at public forums. Describing the denial that was common in both official and popular discourses, she states that she was "shocked at how closed we were, and not accepting of the various behaviors that do exist in our culture and I felt like I had nothing to lose by being an open person and by taking the bull by its horns." She began to make forays into funding to set up an NGO focusing on training and counseling, as she had noted an acute "lack of trained people in HIV and AIDS issues." During this effort she began to converse with Triloke Akhtar, the founder and director of Garv (London), an organization that worked with minorities in the UK on problems of sexuality and sexual health and HIV/AIDS. Akhtar was interested in starting a project on sexual health and HIV in India. He and Shraddha negotiated an arrangement whereby Shraddha would set up an independent organization to work on sexual health and HIV/AIDS with endorsement and advice from Akhtar's organization.

Garv (India) was able to procure funding with ease. This was due, in part, to the backing of Garv (London), a reputable organization with the credible leadership of Akhtar, and in part to Shraddha's own background and experience in non-profit work in the US. It was also due, quite significantly, to the fact that donors were keen to pump resources into HIV prevention and control at a time when NGOs working in the area were still few. Shraddha's meeting with her American funders had been "remarkably informal." These funders took a "leap of faith" convinced by Shraddha's ideas and plans for how her proposed organization would address HIV awareness and prevention. After a few years of continued aid and work, Shraddha now had more confidence in her organization and was therefore able to negotiate with funding agencies to get grants on "her own terms." Her experience with funders was varied. There were those who had "fixed agendas" that they wanted to push, and "preconceived notions" of what NGOs in India were or ought to be. Shraddha felt this was blatantly disrespectful. Other funders, in contrast, seemed to show faith in the capabilities of local NGOs and provided the finances for projects without dictating terms, and with only the expectation of positive outcomes. This enabled a space for local organizational development of programs and goals. Mistrust of NGOs by donor agencies arises from a certain "history" that involves corruption in the form of misappropriation of funds, fraudulent claims to services and results, concocted data, and nepotism. However, most persons involved in NGO work will point to the variety amongst non-governmental agencies and hence the folly of generalizations, as well as to the fact that corruption was widespread and not simply restricted to this sector.[12]

Garv grew gradually as more funding became available from foreign donors. Its activities were organized into discrete programs, each with its own source of international aid. At the time that I began fieldwork at Garv, there were multiple projects functioning out of the organization, dealing with "male sexual health," in particular "men who have sex with men," "women's sexual health," counseling, testing and care services for persons living with HIV/AIDS, and a training program, in addition to several telephone help lines dealing with sexual health, same sex issues, and HIV/AIDS. Garv had recently concluded a project on "peer education" revolving around sexual health and HIV awareness and education activities among young people, especially college and some high school students. Further, it served as the physical base and location for meetings and activities of two groups, one for lesbian and bisexual women, known as Mitali ("female friend"), and the other, for gay men, called Aashiana ("dwelling"). The internal organizational structure of Garv revolved around the pivotal, authoritative figure of Shraddha. Such charismatic leadership, borne of the ideals, ideology and personal convictions of one or a set of persons is seen as typical of NGOs (Streeten 1997, Willetts 1982). I saw this manner of leadership not only at Garv but also in the other NGOs that I encountered. The life trajectory of the organization is tied to that of the leader as the repository of knowledge, of ideas, ideology and expertise, much of which, as I have pointed out, is the product of a transnational, cosmopolitan situation. It is incumbent on this individual to be the face and mouthpiece of the organizational agenda and activities, and to keep it alive through material resources. These resources, while increasingly plentiful for work on AIDS, are also sought by a host of similar organizations. The competing claims for legitimacy of different NGOs and those who represent them have at their center not just ideological motivations but economic ones, the combination of which, gives them the distinction and the profile they have and that, in turn, is tied to the idiosyncrasies of the individuals at their helm. Thus, Shraddha was the primary decision maker in the organization, formulating and controlling the agenda, with advice and input from consultants and colleagues. The hierarchical nature of the distribution of power and decision-making was subject to influence on the basis not just of expertise or even simply of position in the organization's hierarchy, but at times on the basis of personality and affective relations. Finally, and centrally, global trends and norms of the cultural politics of HIV/AIDS, sexuality, human rights and bioethics suffused these decisions.

The structured appearance of the organization belied its internal malleability. The boundaries of the programs were fluid, intersecting with one another's functioning and altering with changes in circumstances, funding, or demand for services. For instance, if the need or opportunity arose, an individual working in the male sexual health program could gradually be trained as a counselor and move to do counseling or care work, or then training staff could be asked to temporarily take on the work of manning the telephone help lines. This structure of non-structure was common to many NGOs. It reflected a deliberate self-presentation of the non-governmental as antithetical to the rigidity of government bureaucracies and as embodying a counterposition to the formal manner in which state agencies functioned. This informality was also manifested in interpersonal relations within the organization, which were friendly and some bordering on a kind of familial intimacy. Kinship terms (like "didi" or older sister) were often used among staff to mark respect. Meals at the organization were a ritual of familiarity and a careful and self-conscious negation of class, caste, religious and national divisions, as well as of distinctions between those who might have HIV and those who did not. Everyone sat on the floor, pooled their food, and ate out of one another's plates, a significant act, given the taboos around food, purity and pollution, and various rules of commensality in India. Finally, the quasi-kinship like relations and behavior gave the organization an aura of transparency in the way that its affairs were run, again in direct contrast to the mechanics of state structures and their opacity.

The fluidity of the programs was evidence of conceptual and practical linkages. Shraddha's agenda was to formulate strategies to deal with awareness, prevention and care through "empowerment." Empowerment, a key term in the literature on NGOs (Fisher 1997), is a central discursive strategy of the "participatory" approach to development, influenced by grassroots movements and especially women's mobilizing. From the model of top-down filtering of welfare, the goal became to enable growth and progress through the creation of awareness and desire for transformation from below, from the level of the community, and through structural mechanisms that would allow communities that had thus far been powerless, to assert themselves as politically relevant actors (Fisher 1997, Stein 1997, Zellerer and Vyortkin 2004).[13] The equation of knowledge and power was key to this process – knowledge of one's rights and responsibilities, knowledge of one's history, of one's body, of the polity and the economy, and the power to exercise this knowledge. These ideas were at the heart of democratic governance, but the domain of the political itself had now shifted to encompass a wider scope. The reason that Shraddha chose to work with certain groups was because they were disempowered and because they "impacted the way that the epidemic was spreading." However, while she did work with "targeted groups" designated by public health authorities, her scope was not restricted to them.[14] She resisted this practice as it tended to ghettoize the epidemic and to perpetuate the notion that AIDS was circumscribed within these groups. She did not, for instance, consider HIV/AIDS an infection that was particular to men who had sex with men, even though this group was one of the focal points of Garv's work. Her attention to men who have sex with men centered around the fact that they were "a marginalized community" and that, moreover, their behavior had "an impact on the life of women," also marginalized.

Shraddha Menon's vision had been to build a web of organizations that would exceed the bounds of the local urban settings and reach the most remote recesses of the country. Her attempt was to aid in the creation of this far-reaching network through the methodology of "training" groups and individuals through intensive workshops and seminars. This was the key to promoting awareness of AIDS and to the building of a discursive space to address sexuality, sexual health, rights and empowerment. Through the gradual process of "training," Garv could go on "to build larger coalitions," a chain of knowledge and power, that would provide a support structure for advocacy. Training activities also did the work of pulling together groups of people that otherwise would not have the chance to work together. All this would serve to bring different organizations with varying programs under one "large umbrella" to cooperate when it came to advocating changes in law and policy around HIV/AIDS care and treatment, and sexual and reproductive health.[15]

NGO staff and volunteers, while many of them from upper class or elite backgrounds, tend to work closely with the communities that they delineate and thus have a less mediated relationship with them than does the government. Garv relied for its information and planning on a combination of official statistics and publications, and "anecdotal data" generated from their own observations and experiences from within the groups they worked with. Shraddha had come into contact, "by word of mouth," with many individuals who had become infected recently. The more she became known as somebody who worked on HIV, the more people began to inform her of cases. As she describes the situation:

I knew the reality at some level. And even though I had no formal study to go by, I knew anecdotally what was happening and if it was happening to one person I knew there had to be a lot more. And of course the behavior I was seeing, the complete promiscuity…maybe promiscuity is the wrong word, but the amount of sexual activity that exists in this culture is phenomenal. And it was something that I was totally unaware of because we never talk about it. It is so hidden, and if you are not looking for it you don't become aware of it because it is also part of the class where you are brought up, you are protected and then it hits you in the face. And when I started seeing it I felt I absolutely had to do something. I had to acknowledge that these behaviors existed and it actually got me to start questioning our culture which, I think, was the hardest part because it meant questioning myself, questioning who I am as an individual, what triggers my responses, why do I treat certain people in certain ways.

Shraddha was thus confronted with an Indian reality distinct from that she was accustomed to. The heterogeneity of the Indian social world and the complex divisions and overlaps of caste, class, education, region and religion result in parallel realities that, while they coexist, can also be utterly segregated. Her narrative also tells of the collective dissimulations that societies participate in and the stories they tell about themselves in the production of locality (Appadurai 1996). Shraddha's observations, like those of many others who grappled with issues of behavior, attitudes and practices because of the very nature of their work, were instrumental in generating larger introspective questions about the meanings of cultural values and traditions. These questions ultimately become the metanarrative for the work of organizations such as Garv, whose tasks might begin with the pragmatic functions like the delivery of certain services like health and education, but culminate in self-examination and interrogative moments that disrupt the idea of an unchanging or homogenous cultural self.

Representative and indicative of the way in which modern NGOs are connected and perpetuated through networks (Keck and Sikkink 1998, Riles 2001), Garv operated in a globally and nationally situated web of governmental and extra governmental agencies. It was part of a local coalition of seven NGOs based in Nagar, who, in 1996, had formed the AIDS-NGO Network, in order to have a consolidated front for advocacy and the provision of services. The participants in "the Network," as it was referred to – Asra ("support"), Roshni ("light"), the Group to Fight AIDS (GFA), Bal Vikas ("progress of the child"), Women's Support Organization (WSO), and the Organization for AIDS Education and Prevention (OAEP) – had diverse histories of involvement in social justice and welfare. Some had existed for decades as welfare groups working with the poor and destitute, and, because of the demands of the times and the circumstances and the needs of the people whom they catered to, had incorporated HIV/AIDS into their existing mandate. Others established themselves in the wake of the HIV/AIDS crisis with the express agenda to work on this issue. The scope of their services ranged from drug rehabilitation work, to services and advocacy for women, commercial sex workers, and street children, to clinical work on sexually transmitted diseases and infectious diseases, to information and communications design and implementation. In coming together in form of the AIDS NGO Network, the vision and main purpose of the various organizations had been to facilitate advocacy and to organize and conduct the activity of voluntary counseling and testing for HIV in one of the largest government hospitals in Nagar.[16] In order to organize themselves in this manner, they had to dialogue extensively with hospitals and with the government and look for funding that was disbursed primarily through NACO. Thus, in establishing the Network, they underwent a process of remarkably intimate interaction and dialogue with the government. They met with ministers of health and other bureaucrats, advocated extensively and conducted awareness and sensitization campaigns. The individual trajectories of the organizations intersected through their engagement in AIDS service. This intersection is evidence of how the formation of a community of AIDS experts arose from a disparate set of organizations with varying agendas and ideological histories, how they carved out a place within the new forms of social intercourse that were occasioned by the epidemic, and how discursive practices, particularly around "rights" were arranged within this novel sociality.

The consensus among the members of the Network that I conversed with was that the growing prominence of the non-governmental sector was evidence of the increasing withdrawal of the state from its functions as provider, and its failure at equitable governance. A shift occurred in the late eighties and early nineties in the wisdom and practice on the part of international development and donor agencies like the World Bank and the UN, from reliance purely on state structures and the bureaucracies that they entailed, to the inclusion of the voluntary sector in the execution of development models (Edwards and Hulme 1996, Fisher 1997). NGOs were also seen as the harbinger of social change and critique, disseminating alternative discourses of development, social welfare and equity (Escobar 1992) and evidence that the responsibility for projects of social uplift were no longer the sole responsibility of the state and markets (Fernando and Heston 1997). Whereas in its initial avatar, the Indian state had taken on the responsibility of fulfilling most of the welfare and development functions for its citizens, in its more recent form, the onset of the free market and liberalization has encouraged it to delegate these tasks (Kamat 2001). Under pressure from the global economic and political order, the national government has come to cooperate increasingly with the non-governmental sector to achieve goals of development. This complicates the role of NGOs as critics of the state.

While all the members of the Network defined themselves and their *modus operandi* as distinct from the state, some were moderate and others radical in the way that they articulated these differences. This variety had to do with the particular history of each organization, its leadership, the kinds of groups and communities that they worked with and the distinct "political fields" (Ray 1998, 1999) that they had encountered and occupied in their respective trajectories.[17] There was no uniformity of opinion within the Network on exactly what "non-governmental" really entailed. The definition of "non-governmental" for some NGOs meant not only being able to question and monitor the government, but being inherently an antithesis of everything that government represented and embodied. This critique of the state as well as of market processes is where NGOs tend to derive meaning and legitimacy. Moreover, given the lack of clarity about the precise scope and parameters of what constitutes an NGO, being what the state and the market is not becomes the way the non-governmental comes to be defined (Fernando and Heston

1997, Leve and Karim 2001).[18] Shraddha for instance, was contemptuous of the government and articulated Garv's position as directly opposed to the state. She "got into trouble" on many occasions not only with government officials but also with her colleagues in other NGOs because of her relentless censure of state projects. Persistent antagonism towards the government and the refusal to conform to its agenda created problems for organizations. In the case of Garv, these problems came in the form of arbitrary and frequent audits by state agencies, or simply a tacit denial of their role in AIDS service, refusal to acknowledge their work and undermining the value of their contribution.

Official renditions of the history of the AIDS epidemic in India are found in documents of the Ministry of Health and NACO (Annual Reports and Annual Country Scenarios). Competing reconstructions of the progression of the AIDS crisis that emerged from the non-governmental sector hinged on narratives of the short-comings of the state apparatus. Official documentation suggests quite clearly that the Government of India had surveillance mechanisms in place to investigate the spread and the patterns of transmission of HIV in the country, and had acknow-ledged by 1994, when Garv came into being, that AIDS was "a national crisis."[19] Shraddha however, maintained that when she was beginning work in India, the government was still saying that "they didn't have a problem" and that they continued to state this. According to her, there was "complete political denial" of the existence of HIV, even though a body like NACO had been set up in 1992 solely for the purpose of dealing with HIV/AIDS in India. Others in the Network men-tioned their experience with government agencies, and how, at the level of individual commitment and conviction, many NACO officials either did not "really believe" that AIDS was a problem, or if they did, then they did not consider it economically viable to spend the state's resources on it. There is a schism between what exists at an institutional and discursive level and what exists at the level of individual under-standing, an internal bad faith on the part of the state. This kind of institutional ambivalence that is common to governments (South Africa's denialism exemplifies this) also complicates the very notion of crisis and emergency and how it is consti-tuted. Several of my interlocutors who worked in the AIDS service industry testify that, for a long time after it came into existence, people within NACO did not really believe that "AIDS was a problem;" some actually did not care that it was, as it was believed to afflict only those who engaged in unhealthy and immoral practices. The story told by statistics produced through mechanisms of state surveillance and global epidemiological tools, as well as the sheer size of the loans and funding flowing into the country from international aid agencies and donors did not appear to match individual conviction on the part of functionaries of the state in the magnitude of the problem. The material and ideological resources that came into the country represented the "agenda" of donors. It was the belief within a certain segment of the NGO sector that the state set up institutions and structures to conform to this agenda and to satisfy the conditions and stipulations that accom-panied aid monies. They were convinced that unlike voluntary and non-governmental work that arose from personal convictions, government work was simply a "job" and that the lack of commitment reflected on the quality of work. This kind of framing of the position and the "mentality" of the state as an actor became a place where the non-governmental sector of AIDS service inserted itself and how it came to define its own position within the domain of the political.

While AIDS service experts in the NGOs that I describe experienced the state largely as corrupt, inept and unable to deliver services to the groups that they worked with, they also acknowledged its indispensability to the evolution and transformation of policies and legislation. Law and policy were embodiments of the state, and in so far as such organizations saw their role as protecting marginalized or disenfranchised persons from unjust or inefficient legislative formulations, they often pit themselves squarely against the government. Anti-discrimination policies to protect the rights of persons with HIV/AIDS were always the subject of discussion as was the infamous Section 377 of the Indian Penal Code, on the basis of which, homosexuality was considered illegal.[20] An institutionalized mode of registering protest and of conducting systematic social action that NGOs utilized thoroughly and effectively was that of public interest litigation or PIL. This is a form of legal action in which an individual or organization has the standing to file a case in higher courts on behalf of a particular social group or segment of population, or in the interest of society in general (Madsen 1997). Several PILs pertaining to issues around HIV/AIDS were filed against the state by NGOs. The first and most significant one was filed to appeal the AIDS Prevention Bill of 1989, which called for random, mandatory testing of blood of all designated risk groups, especially commercial sex workers. The bill never reached the status of an act and was finally repealed because of protest and the PIL filed on the part of AIDS Bhedbhav Virodhi Andolan or ABVA (Movement against AIDS related Discrimination), a group of activists led by doctors and lawyers. In response to a PIL filed by Common Cause, another NGO, the Supreme Court of India directed the Union of India and the State governments to take steps toward revamping the entire Blood Transfusion Services through measures such as the licensing of all blood banks and putting a stop to professional blood donation. The government followed the directive by setting up a National Blood Transfusion Council and State Blood Transfusion Councils, issuing licenses to blood banks and ensuring that no unlicensed blood banks be permitted to provide transfusion services, and banning all professional blood donating activities. Apart from taking immediate measures, a Draft National Blood Transfusion Policy was formulated for the purpose of providing the necessary guidelines and directions for better management of blood transfusion services and to improve the availability of safe and adequate blood and blood products.

Whatever the modes of its manifestation, the work of advocacy is a constitutive part of AIDS service NGOs. The relationship between state and the non-governmental is predicated on calling into question the logic of government with respect to its practices of governance. This work can be carried out in different forms ranging from a combination of the highly performative marches and demonstrations to privately circulated letters and memos to functionaries of the government, to statements in the media and legal recourse in the form of writ petitions and public interest litigation through which the state can be brought to court. While NGOs can be said to mediate between citizens and the state, this should not necessarily be taken as evidence of spontaneously erupting grassroots social action, or of an increased democratization that originates from these grassroots but rather as representative of selective elite and expert organizing, where these organizations are professionalized brokers with links both to centers of power as well as to the communities they represent (Hemment 2004, Madsen 1997, Routledge 1993). However, uncritical collaboration with the government could mean a dilution of the mission and the goals of NGOs because of the tendency of the government to subsume or co-opt the goals and ideals of the non-governmental sector. Shraddha knew that it was difficult to resist such co-optation and that hence NGOs had to be clear about the boundaries that separated them from the state. "I am not saying that NGOs should not work with the government," she argued, "but I think that you have to have a very clear understanding of the extent to which you can do this...I know if I start collaborating with the government, tomorrow they are going to start stomping all over me and saying you should be working in this area or that area. How does one stop that?" There was also very little clarity on what exactly it meant for NGOs to work with the government, to cooperate or to collaborate. "Does this collaboration mean financially, politically or intellectually, I don't know. Very often, it means towing the government's line, it means compromising your own philosophy," said Shraddha. This kind of ideological desire to be completely autonomous of the state, expressed by so many NGOs has been described as the "autonomy fetish" (Sanyal 1997).

The rigid separateness from state structures that many persons in the non-governmental world would like to maintain is illusory (Fernando and Heston 1997). In fact, the analytical divisions between state, civil society and the market, or state, civil society and the private sector that are utilized in development discourse have indistinct boundaries. The language used by the United Nations Development Program (UNDP) for instance, reveals a conceptual framework and imagination of how social and political life is structured, within which the global operationalization of development takes place. The neat categorization of distinct sectors involved in diverse social, economic and political activities can be seen in the following definitions: "The state creates a conducive legal and political environment. The private sector generates jobs and income. And civil society facilitates political and social interaction – mobilizing groups to participate in economic, social and political activities" (UNDP Report on Governance and Sustainable Development 1997: iv). However, as this ethnography documents and as has been argued by others concerned with the issue, NGOs occupy a place somewhere between state, market and civil society, and the sectors themselves overlap far more than schematic definitions suggest (Fernando and Heston 1997, Fisher 1997). The slippage between the government and non-governmental is evident in the manner that statistics and data on health and disease are collected and managed, the way that aid monies are dispensed, and in the institutional structures that are set up for the delivery of services. An imaginative, experiential and narrative scheme of the world divided into government and non-government, or those who govern and those who are subjected to governance, is embedded in episodes in the life of Garv and its networks. The uneasy space that the non-governmental occupies in relation to the state becomes a site where the possibilities and limits of particular forms of entitlements and expectations come to be expressed. In the section that follows, I document one such expression, that of "confidentiality" and the emerging lexicon of "rights" that it enfolds.

Negotiating Confidentiality: Politico-moral Predicaments and a Vocabulary of Rights

Central to evolving forms of governance, is the conceptualization of the individual who is both the subject of and a participant in governance – the citizen invested with rights and duties. New ways of theorizing citizenship have reconstituted the citizen in excess of the political, delineating intimate spaces within which belonging or exclusion are enacted. Citizenship now comes to encompass not only political but also moral, affective, sexual and biological domains (Biehl 2004, Carver and Mottier 1998, Das and Addlakha 2001, Petryna 2002, Plummer 1995, 2003, Rapp and Ginsberg 2001, Scheper Hughes 1994, Waites 1998). In the setting of my work, novel means for social recognition and inclusion take the shape of assertions of rights for particular sets of individuals, who are marginalized, disenfranchised, stigmatized and discriminated against, and the situation of such rights within a universalizing language of human rights. Such a vocabulary comes to frame, both explicitly and implicitly, the interrelated practices around confidentiality, privacy, consent, information and ethics in the management of AIDS and in the deployment of sexual health as a site where AIDS might be preempted. At stake within these discussions is the tension between public health as collective good on the one hand, and the autonomy and wellbeing of the individual on the other. Locally evolving frameworks around these ideas and what lies in the domain of legislation are informed by and negotiated in global forums. These discursive practices can be dissonant from local historical and cultural memory and knowledge. An unwieldy and hybrid corpus of expert knowledge results from such a circulation of ideas, its goals often at odds with the scope of their realization, their translation often awkward and sometimes impossible. The set of ethnographic observations that follow reveal how the debate on confidentiality becomes a site at which AIDS service experts in India tackle the complexity of an emergent discourse.

The emphasis on confidentiality and professional ethics around the maintenance of privacy and personal information is one of the most urgent and robust expressions of the language of rights that permeates AIDS service networks in India. The extent to which these principles were emphasized at Garv was manifested in the careful way that it arranged it's material and human resources. Counseling rooms were set apart from other areas of the organization as was the clinic where testing and consultations took place, so that the visibility of clients to others was at a minimum. Files and records pertaining to clients were stored in securely locked filing cabinets in a locked room and only counselors and the doctor had access to such documents. Notes and case studies that were written up for training purposes or for reports always used pseudonyms. Staff were trained on a regular basis on the significance of maintaining the private nature of interactions within the organization and on the importance of discretion in handling clients. Any volunteers, interns, and volunteer/ researchers (like me) in the organization had to sign a form committing to keeping information pertaining to the organization confidential. The centrality of preserving confidentiality on patients and clients was also obvious from the kinds of conflicts that the members of the organization got entrenched in. Many of these conflicts arose because of the discordant relationship between state policy, institutional and bureaucratic practices, and biomedical cultural particularities in the Indian context.

The overt philosophy of the state as embodied in official written and spoken language was to ensure that rights of individuals were not violated in the process of managing AIDS. Consider the statement in the NACO Report of 1999 with regard to the debate on mandatory testing for HIV:

> Testing for HIV is more than a mere biological test for it involves ethical, human and legal dimensions. The government feels that there is no public health rationale for mandatory testing. On the other hand such an approach could be counterproductive as it may scare a large number of suspected cases from getting detected and counseled to take appropriate measures to improve his quality of life and prevent spread of infection to other persons in the community. HIV testing carried out on a voluntary basis with appropriate pre-test and post-test counseling is considered to be a better strategy and is in line with the national policy on HIV testing and also the WHO guidelines ... Any health program that does not maintain the dignity of a patient or deprives him of his basic right to employment or access to medical care or social support is harmful on a long-term basis. The question that must be asked before a testing procedure is how this result will be used for the benefit of the individual or the community; whether there is a policy and means to support the group under testing following the test result; and whether the same principle of intervention applies even if people refuse testing.

While NACO had prescribed guidelines on informed consent, confidentiality and testing, it did not have structures in place to ensure that these guidelines were followed, and to monitor practices within government run institutional bodies. Neither did there exist any legal framework to address the breakdown and violation of these codes. Such discrepancies between the official line and the actual practices of the government represented by government health workers, doctors, bureaucrats and policy makers, were glaring to those who had to deal with its representatives on a daily basis. It was not coincidental that many of them described "the state" despairingly and cynically as "hypocritical" and "double-faced." Shraddha mocked it openly. In her words: "If you read any of NACO's documents it seems like the most progressive government in the world has written it ... look at the politically correct language! But where is it getting translated into anything? I don't see it. Unless I am blind!" Because NGOs like Garv saw it as central to their work to propagate the principle of confidentiality and to ensure that the rights of their clients were upheld, their relationship with government hospitals tended to be ambivalent. While they required the infrastructural possibilities afforded by the state to be able to do much of their work, they saw themselves as posed against these very state structures, which they experienced *not* as facilitators but rather as impediments for services for people with HIV/AIDS.

Confidentiality in the case of HIV/AIDS was seen as crucial to the survival and life chances of clients because of the intensity of stigmatization of infected persons. The secrecy that surrounded the disease, and its lack of visibility were symptomatic of the potential for discriminatory attitudes and practices. Organizations had good reason to stress confidentiality; there had been innumerable instances of ostracization of persons afflicted with HIV from neighborhoods, villages and work places, of their rejection from families and of the denial of medical services to them. Counseling staff in the Network reported that clients were often encouraged by doctors to take tests even though they did not want them, and without being provided a clear rationale for testing. They surmised that hospitals conducted testing as surveillance and triage. This identification of HIV positive persons through testing most commonly became a means to *withhold* medical care rather than to facilitate treatment and management of the illnesses related to AIDS. Doctors argued that the principle of confidentiality and patients' rights to privacy of information were simply impractical, unrealistic and even of questionable ethical value in a situation like the Indian one, where the health-care system was under tremendous pressure due to high patient volume and low funding, where the lack of adequate resources did not allow for adherence to "universal precautions,"[21] and consequently where the rights of the HIV-positive person may be directly counterposed to the rights of medical personnel who worked under those conditions, as well as to the interests of public health.[22]

These issues were debated regularly at Network meetings. Meetings took place at least once a month and more often if there were immediate problems that needed to be discussed. This "urgent" need to convene happened invariably and frequently. One such "emergency meeting" was suddenly scheduled three weeks into my field-work at Garv, opening a window onto the vexed nature of practices of confidentiality as well as of conflicting views within the AIDS service industry. Not permitted to attend this particular meeting, I pieced together a narrative from two separate accounts of Charu and Mita, both counselors at Garv. The last time Charu had been on her round of the Network's counseling center at the hospital, she had been asked by the Head of the Skin and Sexually Transmitted Diseases Department, to reveal the HIV status of one of the clients she had counseled. Charu had refused and had been reprimanded by the Head for this. This resulted in tension between her and the department, and with this doctor in particular. According to Charu, this doctor was antagonistic to all counselors. This was gradually corroborated by the other counselors. The Network had become implicated in the situation, as the activity of counseling was seen as representative of the collective entity of the Network rather than of the individual organizations. This meant that the group as a whole had to find a way to ease the tension, and this meeting was where this issue was going to be discussed and resolved.

For Charu, the problem was straightforward: "confidentiality" was to be adhered to at all costs and in doing this, she had come into conflict with a party who would have her compromise this principle. Following what she understood as the organizational ethics of Garv, she took confidentiality to imply that absolutely nobody aside from the clients themselves, could be apprised of their HIV status. Other counselors from other organizations, or even from Garv, could interpret these categories differently, but in this case, Charu's unwavering refusal to reconsider her stance and to reveal such information to the treating doctor at the hospital had not only caused the conflict between the hospital's medical staff and her, but had also brought to light a lacuna in the functioning of the Network. The problem revolved around the absence of clear guidelines to address the boundaries of ethics, confidentiality and consent with relation to revealing the HIV status of the client to the treating doctor, or to doctors directly concerned with the running of the department in question. In the absence of such guidelines and rules, it was left to the discretion of individual organizations and their counselors, to interpret the meaning of these concepts. Previously, the other NGOs in the Network had agreed to two things that the doctors at the hospital had demanded. One, that any person who came to be tested for HIV, even if it was entirely voluntarily, be sent for STD (sexually transmitted diseases) screening, and two, that the doctors at the hospital be told the HIV status of a patient. These demands were now contested by Garv.

There was speculation among Garv staff that the coordinator of the counseling center, Dr. Thomas, had taken a unilateral decision regarding disclosure of HIV status to hospital authorities. This stipulation regarding disclosure was confounding to most staff at Garv, who felt that the decision needed to be reviewed. Liam, a Canadian volunteer who had been at Garv for over a year, pointed out that this practice was clearly against the clauses of confidentiality that the patient as well as the NGO agreed to when they signed the consent form. The hospital needed to conduct their own testing if they wanted to know the HIV status of a patient. Further, NGOs could not be used as an extension of the services of the hospital; they were autonomous and independent, running a service out of the premises of the hospital, not acting as a proxy for it. Information about a client could be revealed only if the patient agreed explicitly to it and wanted the doctor to know his or her HIV status. The initiative or pressure could not come from the hospital authorities. Charu additionally voiced complaints of how lightly and callously the hospital treated confidential information in general and how they disregarded the patients. She described instances of how privacy was breached in hospital situations with laboratory personnel yelling out into the hallway for all to hear: "CD4 test for HIV!" There were times when the laboratory technicians might refuse to draw blood to conduct CD4 counts, complaining that their low status as government employees meant that they could be made to do just about anything, that their lives were not valued, and that they would be forced to take extra precautions while dealing with HIV positive persons. The precautions, Charu remarked, were those that they should be taking anyway, as per the guidelines of the WHO on universal precautions.

Mita, also a Garv counselor framed the problem in the form of larger, more abstract statements about her work and her calling. It was as though the incident with Charu and the doctor had prompted her to think about her own position in non-governmental AIDS service. She believed very firmly that even though they were an NGO, they had to work within the structure of the government to achieve their goals. Garv had as the center of its focus, "the client, especially the (HIV) positive client" and that she believed it was necessary to keep this focus in mind and to do what was in the best interests of the client. She was disturbed by the way that Shraddha, the spokesperson of the organization took an aggressively anti-government stand, saying that they were opposed to state policies, that they were not governmental agencies, hence could, in fact, be radically opposed to the government. The reality of the situation, according to Mita, was that they had to deal with the state and had to function alongside government officials. She herself often "hated" having to deal with the bureaucratic structure and personalities that accompanied it, but had made compromises with the best interests of her clients in mind. "How," she exclaimed, "can we work without the hospitals?! We need them, we should not antagonize them but try to find some sort of middle ground." She said that she "hated" activism, even though she realized that it had its place in certain situations. In this case, she felt it was not justified. She noted that the organization was alienating both the hospital authorities as well as NACO by taking such an aggressive stance. Moreover, because of the vociferous nature of the organization's executive director, as well as the fact that Garv was, for the moment the executor and the representative of the Network, other organizations had no choice but to go along with its decisions. She noted that the very concepts of confidentiality, informed consent and universal precautions, which were being debated and fought over, were concepts alien to the Indian reality. In her words: "The reality here is very different than what people imagine. The doctor thinks he has the right to know the status of his patient. Isn't this the case everywhere in the world? He should have this information if he is treating the patient. He also has to be responsible for the other staff in the hospital. It is not just the client who has human rights, what about the human rights of the medical and paramedical staff?" She was alluding to the fact that universal precautions were not the norm in Indian hospitals, that the combination of scarce resources, corruption, pilfering and black markets made necessary items like disposable needles, syringes and gloves harder to come by. This being the case, it was only when the staff was aware of a risk, would they use extra precautions to avoid infection. Mita was thus, in her rendition of this episode, narrating "an Indian reality," a reality that was at odds with the framing of rights in the context of biomedical privacy, information and consent. Her concerns echo larger philosophical and political debates on weighing collective versus individual good in the deployment of governance and in the construction of health as a site of governmentality.

While Charu saw this episode as a kind of victory for Garv, for the principles of confidentiality that it stood for, as well as for its struggle against the government, Mita perceived it as a problem in the way her organization functioned, and was frustrated by it. She perceived it as ultimately counter-productive and detrimental to the interests of those who they served – the "clients," the persons with HIV/AIDS and their families. The differences between the way Mita and Charu narrated and interpreted the situation were indicative of a deeper divide that existed between persons engaged in the business of doing non-governmental AIDS service – about the meaning of non-governmental, about their personal roles within the structure of organizations, about the relationship between state and non-governmental, and about what to do with the problems of "culture" and the translation of global concepts into the local idiom. As I attended subsequent Network meetings, the fissures within the coalition became apparent. One of the most crucial points of dissent within the Network was over how "confidentiality" was to be defined, how it had been dealt with so far and how it was to be addressed in the future. The situation at the hospital between the doctor and Charu had revealed and indeed deepened cleavages within the Network on the idea and practice of confidentiality. At one meeting, a question was posed as to whether the Network was willing to compromise the principle of confidentiality. It was taken for granted that this principle meant the same thing for all parties concerned. Some wanted to be able to negotiate this issue, among themselves as also with the doctors and with officials of the government and to discuss this with a view to arriving at some kind of consensus. However, Shraddha was adamant that confidentiality remain "non-negotiable." Others disagreed, saying that while confidentiality itself was vital, the scope and the definition of its boundaries needed to be reviewed. Margaret, one of the founders of the Group to Fight AIDS (GFA) argued that while everybody in the Network prized confidentiality, it was unrealistic to assume that a doctor could go without being told the HIV status of his or patient, and that revealing this information would have in any way constituted a breach of confidentiality. This information was in fact, indispensable to him. Shraddha retorted that the doctor could only be told with the express permission of the client, and that this needed to be made explicit to the client, before the test. Margaret conceded, but emphasized that the client be informed of the utmost importance for the attending doctor to be apprised of his or her HIV status. Jake, a founding member of the organization Roshni, pointed out that there were no guarantees of any commitment on the part of the doctors to maintain confidentiality as they were not "conscientized" with respect to their responsibilities to the rights of patients to privacy. In this regard, he saw confidentiality as "a gray area" in the Indian context. Apparently the notion of confidentiality did not form a practical part of the professional training and ethical expectations from doctors in India and this absence manifested itself in the looseness with which they handled patient information.

There were those who saw different sides to the situation and even though they were firm about the rights of persons with HIV or AIDS to treatment and care, they were sympathetic to the larger structural problems associated with the apathy of medical personnel in government-run hospitals. Ina, who worked at Asra, saw the problems faced by doctors in public hospitals as contributing to their callousness towards HIV positive persons. This is how she felt about the dilemma:

> You can't always blame the doctors . . . you should see the queues over there (at the hospitals). How can you expect someone in a government hospital to give so much time, to focus; it isn't possible. The whole system is like that. If you look after the doctors, look after their needs, you make sure that thirty patients is all he can see, you provide more facilities in terms of the size of the population . . . So how can you even blame the doctors for saying, these guys are going anyway, let us look after the ones that will live. There are ninety people coming in, who do I save my energy for? We saw from the doctors' point of view how frustrating it was . . .

Ina was also torn about how to deal with the ethics of maintaining confidentiality. She felt that every individual had an ethical obligation to judge each situation on its own merit rather than to follow an organizational principle blindly. She put this problem to me by asking me what I would do if I knew my best friend's lover was HIV positive and had not disclosed it to her. I didn't have a ready answer. She went to ask rhetorically:

Is our responsibility only to one individual who is HIV positive? HIV positive is not the beginning and the end of our society. Is it? If it were your sister, or your own brother, or your own husband, or your own kid, think of it then. Easy to talk when it is someone else's life, someone else's wife, some other person.

Once again, in Ina's statements, we get powerful reminders of the many unresolved moral dilemmas posed by novel and as yet unroutinized knowledge practices. Once more, her questions betray the tensions between the primacy of individual good versus the virtues of collective welfare that vexes the business of governance.

The situation that I describe reflected not only a conflict of interest between the medical perspective on the one hand and the view of the counselors and the NGOs on the other, but a larger, more profound chasm between the way the two construct the objects and the objectives of their fields. NGOs appear to pose themselves as bearers of services catering to the more "human" dimensions of social issues, to the interests of their clients as individuals and as people not just with a disease, but rather as suffering individuals and persons with rights. NGOs situate themselves carefully in the position of caretakers of such rights, and, in this way, carve out a domain for themselves and their services. At the outset it appeared that there were two clear positions, one for, and one against the medical establishment and the way that it approached its human subjects. It gradually became clear that opinions and sentiments were divided on this issue, with people vacillating, and a great deal of uncertainty and ambivalence. What might have looked like unequivocal positions at first glance were, on closer scrutiny, complicated and not very clear at all. So, while it had initially seemed that the only organization in the group that had aligned itself with the hospital by virtue of a now controversial and challenged decision, was Bal Vikas, in the person of Dr. Thomas, himself a medical doctor, what later emerged was that even individuals in Garv were not always convinced of its philosophy of confidentiality. Others in different NGOs of the Network also expressed similar doubts and tended to oscillate between being completely antithetical to the doctors, and being sympathetic to them.

The conflicts around confidentiality and the resulting contentious atmosphere in Network meetings brought questions of organizational ideology and ethics to the surface. It spurred people to talk about the origins and goals of the Network and of the structural problems that were plaguing it. Shraddha expressed concern that the Network's program was being co-opted by the doctors in the hospital and that it appeared to be operating on behalf of the medical community and not of the client. Dr. Thomas reported that the hospital authorities perceived the Network and the Counseling Center as appendages of the hospital's service, that there was a general misconception amongst the medical staff that the Network had been "hired by them" and that they were thus accountable to them. In addition to the disputes on the everyday practices around confidential information, the future of their very existence in the hospital setting was becoming uncertain. This was in part because their presence in the hospital was not really welcome, but also due to a rumor that had begun to circulate in the Network. People had heard that the local State Government had plans to begin running other such counseling centers, or what they called "voluntary testing centers" and to employ their own counselors for this purpose. In this case, the counseling center of the Network would become defunct. However, as Dr. Thomas and Jake revealed, government representatives had expressed the desire to continue the involvement of the Network and its trained and experienced counselors for this work, in this way trying to amalgamate the functions of the government and the non-government. Shraddha expressed a lack of confidence in the state's capabilities to run such a service. Others thought that while their internal disagreements and politics had to be examined and the principles and functioning reevaluated, the purpose of the Network was far from achieved and that it should continue. Yet others thought that it might continue with a different make-up even if some members were to withdraw from it. In the face of resistance from the hospital administration and other state agencies, it was deemed crucial to have "internal cooperation," and to "suspend judgment and criticism" of organizations within the Network. The strength of a coalition such as the Network, as one member put it, was the presentation of a united front for advocacy to fight for changes in the structure of service delivery and legislation. Better results in this fight were assured if they battled as a group rather than as a divided set of individual organizations. Moreover, the Network as well as the individual organizations in it had a responsibility to their clients to continue providing the service of counseling. There was consensus, however, that if the Network did continue to exist then they had to address their relationship with the government, in particular with NACO, as also with the government run hospitals where they worked, and develop clarity and "terms of engagement" to negotiate with these parties.

The counselors in the Network often complained that the work of counseling itself was considered by many government doctors as marginal and unnecessary in the handling of HIV. A continual tension existed between NACO along with the doctors, on the one hand, and AIDS service NGOs on the other about the expertise of counselors and the value of their work. There was an insecurity associated with being engaged in the activity of counseling, as yet a new and somewhat liminal category of expertise and practice, and not seen by bearers of other kinds of scientific and administrative knowledge as being entirely authoritative, established or legitimate. Exacerbated by the disagreement amongst the members of the Network, this insecurity was beginning to manifest itself in accusations of betrayal and complaints that in times of crisis, counseling staff were not shown support by the rest of the Network. Dr. Thomas also revealed that the Head of the STD Department through which the service was run, had expressed dissatisfaction with the way that the counselors related to the clinicians and had stated that if the counselors could not cooperate with the doctors then they should leave the hospital and close down the service. From the discussion it was evident that the medical community's general opinion of counselors was that they posed a barrier to testing, and that because of the stipulations of consent and confidentiality, HIV tests were more difficult to conduct. Also it seemed that doctors were expressing concern about provision of services to HIV positive persons for fear that this would lead to a higher occupancy in hospitals of HIV positive persons and consequently to a higher statistic.

Dr. Praful Niranjan, a UN official who I interviewed about the evolution of AIDS service organizations in India, stated to me that most government employed medical practitioners did not respect the practice of counseling and considered it "a menial job." He himself had encountered resistance to training in counseling techniques that he conducted for doctors. These doctors would argue that counseling was "a Western concept and practice" and that it would not work in India. Many doctors simply informed individuals that they were HIV positive and that they would likely die within ten years. Dr. Niranjan reported that that while doing some research on counseling for the WHO, he had noted that there was no "appropriate Indian language world for counseling." He told me that the concept of counseling was "not cultural" to India; what was "cultural" was "advice, which is paramarsh in Hindi... you have come to me and I gave you paramarsh...I tell you to do this... which is not counseling, which is not helping you to make a decision, to choose your own path." Dr. Niranjan's observations were echoed in the career trajectory and experiences of Dr. Thomas, the counseling coordinator of the Network. These reaffirmed the tenuous nature of counseling in relation to medical education in India. He had not encountered the concept or the practice during his medical studies and noted that counseling was still absent from mainstream medical curricula... "There is no training even now on concepts of confidentiality or informed consent. HIV is just one chapter in the Harrison's Book of Medicine that we have to study for Medicine and it only covers the medical aspects of HIV. And when I was doing undergraduate work, HIV was just two or three pages in Harrison's Book of Medicine. So there was not much information at the time that I was studying. It was an absolutely theoretical thing. For most of the doctors and most of the health care workers it was just a theoretical thing..." Before his work in Bal Vikas, he had never really been exposed to the "social side" of HIV/AIDS. His training in HIV/ AIDS through his specialization in Skin and STD had only dealt with its clinical aspects. This clinical knowledge had also been theoretical as very few cases were reported during the time that he was a student and he had gone through medical school without ever observing first hand a case of HIV or AIDS. Later, he had become interested in the intricacies of AIDS and began to research it, underwent training, and then linked up with the AIDS-NGO Network in 1996, to become part of "the community of AIDS service providers," one of the central tasks of which became to provide "the specialized service of counseling." It was only after his collaboration with other NGOs that he had realized the existence of counseling as a well-formed practice in other parts of the world. He declared Shraddha Menon's work as instrumental in the recognition of the legitimacy of counseling as an expert practice, as also the significance and centrality of confidentiality to work on HIV.

The uneasy and often antagonistic relationship between the form of authority embodied in the medical profession and that in the profession of counseling was, in the particular case of the Network, also the result of the spatial location of the counseling service. Its functioning out of the STD department of a government hospital meant that it was expected to cater to the needs of the hospital rather than create a niche of needs for itself and for its clients. It also meant that the persons the counseling service sought to produce in a different category, that is, as "clients" of the service, rather than as the patients in the hospital, became, in a sense, the objects of a dispute of ownership. The problem between the medical community and the counselors was complicated by another variable, that is, whether the medical personnel were government employees or then private or voluntary doctors. This meant that one 'face of the state', or a medium through which the effects of the state were felt was located in the doctors employed in public hospitals. When the NGOs and voluntary workers spoke of the "state" in reference to AIDS work, it meant the state as seen in the garb of government-employed medical personnel, in addition to the policy makers and bureaucrats such as those in NACO. This messed up the category of "medical community," dividing it along lines drawn between state and non-state, government and non-government, among others.

The ambiguity of confidentiality as a concept and practice, and the paradoxical rigidity with which certain individuals following organizational principles held on to it, had become the subject of another debate. In this case, the tension between "research" and "service" came to a head around the question of confidentiality and informed consent in research using HIV positive persons as informants. Roshni, the organization collaborating in a research project funded by an international think tank, had brought a proposal to the Network to solicit their help and support with procuring data. Dr. Thomas was directing the project and the research was aimed at designing interventions to improve the state the of hospital services for persons with HIV/AIDS. The question was of whether researchers should be permitted, under the aegis of the Network, to conduct research and collect data from HIV positive clients was discussed within organizations before coming to a decision. When the issue was presented to the group of counselors within Garv, Charu emerged as the most vociferous critic of research. In her opinion, there were no benefits to the clients from research of the sort that was being proposed. She saw only the benefit of medical or clinical research and frowned upon social science research. She also expressed the opinion that clients were ignorant of "their rights," that they knew little about what was in their best interests and that they relied heavily on the judgment of counselors for decision-making. Many clients referred to her as "doctor," that is to say, thought that she was a medical doctor, a figure that comes with a great deal of authority, and when asked to sign consent forms for tests, wanted to defer to her opinion, saying that if she thought testing was good for them, then they believed that it was in fact, good for them. Charu felt very strongly that it was the duty of counselors to "protect" the interests of clients and because the clients relied on them for direction, she felt she could not even give them information about the research project as it might be construed as a suggestion for participation.

Some in the Network felt that it was time that the epidemic became "more public," and that facilitating research would help alleviate the silence around it. Others felt that confidentiality, which was still an unstable practice, would be threatened by allowing researchers access to clients. The representative of the research team was asked to attend a Network meeting where she spoke about their protocol and how it was very strictly formulated to ensure that no information could be solicited without an elaborate and long consent procedure with the client. This, she explained, would be done through the counselors, who would first mediate between the research team and the clients, explaining to the latter the existence of the project, its purpose and then ascertaining whether they would participate in it; they would then administer a consent form. Also, she clarified, there would be no names, no addresses, nothing to reveal the identity of the client. It would be anonymous data collection. The argument continued, with some saying that this was breach of confidentiality because then, the researchers would know who the HIV positive persons were. How, asked the researcher, will it be a breach, if the only way that the researcher will know is if the client agrees to it and does so by signing the consent form. "Yes, but..." "No, but...," and it went on like this. There was skepticism of the ritual administering of the consent form. It was noted that most persons to whom consent forms were administered did not really comprehend it or its implications, in spite of efforts at explanation, and that the very concept of confidential information was lost on them. They looked to the counselor for advice; they looked to the counselor, in fact, to make the decision for them. Clearly, the right to choose to test or not test and the right to withhold information is assumed awkwardly by persons for whom the language of privacy and that of rights is as yet incompletely translated.

Further complicating the issue of research was the question of gains to informants or subjects. Results needed to be immediately visible to people working in the service delivery sector. The assumption of tangible benefits and changes underlay all activities. Because the benefits of research were not easily measured, it was often judged as voyeuristic and exploitative, thereby reinforcing an imaginary divide between those who "acted" and those who "observed." Implicit in this divide was the demarcation and maintenance of territorial lines within which "the client" was produced and for whose protection and wellbeing the NGO existed. Confidentiality was the right of this client, one of the interests that were to be protected by the NGO. The discourse of confidentiality had become petrified, the implications and ramifications of which were not always clear to those participated in it. This ideological rigidity with its lack of reflection was heightened by the fact that the concept itself was as yet alien and still nascent both to biomedical culture in India and to the underlying sociocultural fabric where it could not find a comfortable place and be buttressed by well defined ideals of the private, and the individual invested with rights in the same way as one finds in Euroamerican societies.[23]

The lived space of non-governmental AIDS service as I have shown, is not undifferentiated but rather involves a wide spectrum of ideology, agenda and practices. This was manifested in the private and public interactions amongst the members of the Network, and the way that its programmatic life was enacted. At the same time, the pressure to conform to a polarized, schematic division between government and non-government, and to present a homogenous and unified face to those on the outside of non-governmental worlds tended to obliterate the nuances, the differences and the points of contention amongst groups and organizations. These organizations thus moved between moments of consensus and those of conflict, between cooperation and contestation around crucial cultural, political and economic points and definitions; it was this mobility that characterized the coalition that I documented. The Network was a space where ideological transitions around rights particularly embodied in the practices of confidentiality, medical ethics, privacy and scientific triage, could be seen in the process of being formulated, experimented with and threshed. Thus, new possibilities for transformation in the political and moral landscape within which the health of individuals and the collective is constituted can be said to emanate from this AIDS related biosociality.

Conclusion: Sites of Cultural Politics and Transformation

As I talked to various AIDS service experts during my fieldwork about what had changed in the years that they had been involved in social service, they all noted the increasing acquisition by common people of the language of rights. The proliferation of mass media, for instance, had been influential in bringing images and new perceptions about how things were around the world. People now desired things they believed other people had – commodities, information, lifestyles, rights. They would no longer simply accept the kind of services they received from the state, they would now hold it accountable for its failures and its transgressions. Neither would those who were marginalized, disenfranchised or under-privileged, (in this case, sexual minorities, injection drug users, that is those at risk for HIV, and persons living with HIV/AIDS) continue life as always; they now had recourse to spaces to representation. Initiating, mediating and facilitating this dialogue between state, citizen and the social world was the community of AIDS experts, represented in no small part, by the non-governmental.

While the state continues to be the primary locus where accountability for the health of the population rests, the way in which practices of surveillance and of the administration of services are organized have been reorganized notably, with the government delegating large portions of this responsibility to the non-governmental realm. In the case of the HIV/AIDS epidemic, the pressure on the government to work with NGOs comes both from international donors as well as from the recognition on the part of local state agencies that the situation demands action the government is not equipped to take without multisectoral collaboration. However, non-governmental AIDS service is not a passive collaborator or arm of state programs; through politico-moral transactions around justice, equity, and the value of human life, it questions, resists and offers alternative models to the vision and methods of the state. Nor is it simply an alternative to government; rather, it relies on state structures in order to conduct its work and forms a site of governmentality and the enactment of biopolitics. At times when the state seems to have receded from the sphere of service and social justice, it might take its place and simulate it, at other times it might upbraid the state and remind it of its functions. If the non-governmental mobilizes for social and political change and thus challenges the state, but at the same time serves as the vehicle for governmental agendas of development, modernization and governance, if it subverts existing legal structures but puts into place new ones, if it facilitates the flow of transnational concepts like confidentiality, but seeks recognition of these by agencies of the government, then dichotomies of state and civil society, or government and non-government break down.[24] What we have instead is the reconfiguration of the sites at which politics takes place. AIDS service in fact represents the mutation of the political into the politico-moral, where questions and struggles of power and those of suffering, shared experience and the value of human life come together inextricably.

The discursive and performative activity that the AIDS crisis has effected makes up a distinct domain of cultural politics in India. That AIDS service and the new biosociality that it engenders, particularly in non-governmental spaces challenges the cultural and legal order at every step, and that the work of prevention and care entails a questioning of the very fundamentals of citizenship and political and social rights, the relationship between the individual, the family, community and the state, points to its profoundly transformative nature. If the social expression of resistance, the language in which social actors express discontent, and the spaces in which specific sanctions and action takes place are to be considered in the analysis of cultural politics (Escobar and Alvarez 1992), then it becomes evident that even the day to day activities of AIDS service in India can be construed as a battle to reconstitute the structures of governance within which health is deployed and managed.[25] Its very existence is political and moral as it implies an interrogation of existing norms, in the way that it deploys "arts of resistance" through cultural idioms of protest, whether they be "hidden transcripts" or public ones (Scott 1990). By evaluating existing laws and demanding the formulation of new legislation, through symbolic protest against discriminatory practices of the state, of society and of the medical community against certain groups, especially HIV positive persons, and the creation of spaces where cultural identities can be nurtured and communities can be formed, such collective formations make up a quasi movement that represents a variety of marginal groups bound together by virtue of their vulnerability to AIDS. They are enacting a cultural politics by opening up and defining notions of individual and collective health, the body, sexuality, tradition and culture itself. They are constituting social practices framed by "rights" – sexual rights, the right to information, the right to confidentiality and privacy, the right to choose to test or not to test for HIV, the right to marry, the right to access to medical services and medication, the right to employment and livelihood, the right not to be discriminated against.[26] The theoretical premise in descriptions of new social movements rests on the emergence of a novel, diffuse and plural social actor as one of the main features of organized bids for social change (Brysk 1994, Escobar and Alvarez 1992). AIDS service embodied in non-governmental spaces should be taken as one such emergent social actor.[27] In this sense, rather than conceptualize movements for social and political change as having clearly defined homogenous modes of being, one can imagine them as fluid entities – sometimes taking the shape of a series of sporadic, visible, dramatic events such as marches, public demonstrations, public interest litigation, media events and other times, a long chain of quiet, mundane activities like training, information dissemination, sensitization activities, and counseling that nonetheless do the work of infusing social and political life with the language of rights, and transforming governance and the meaning of citizenship, if not by violent defiance then by subtle persuasion.[28]

NOTES

1   The Lawyers Collective is a national level non-governmental organization formed by a set of legal specialists and practicing attorneys that concerns itself with legal advocacy, research and public interest litigation on behalf of a range of marginalized groups. It is the most influential non-profit legal organization in the country and has been responsible

for several landmark cases and public interest litigation. It conducts many of its activities in tandem with other NGOs. Some of the groups that the Lawyers Collective represents are men who have sex with men, sex workers and persons living with HIV/AIDS. Most of the funding to this organization comes from the European Union. The Lawyers Collective has been trying to promote a "rights-based" approach to the AIDS epidemic in India.

2   I use the concept of a critical event here, even though AIDS is an ongoing epidemic, precisely to challenge the notion of temporal closure. Any moment that has historical import and that results in "new modes of action" and the "redefinition of traditional categories" (Das 1995: 6) should be seen as a critical event, whatever the duration of its occurrence. In fact, the kinds of events that Veena Das reflects on – the Bhopal gas incident, the 1947 Partition of India for instance – have profound and continuing effects and by no means should be treated as anything but ongoing.

3   UNAIDS estimated the number of HIV positive persons in India at the end of 2003 to be 5,100,000, or an adult rate of 0.9%. Since the detection of the first case in 1986, HIV has been reported in all states and union territories, with a total of 68,809 cases reported to NACO by March 2004. The majority of cases are situated in Maharashtra, Tamil Nadu, Pondicherry and Manipur and while heterosexual transmission is seen to be the predominant mode, the epidemiological profile is said to differ among regions. For details see UNAIDS Epidemiological Fact Sheets by Country 2004.

4   It is not my contention that the newness of AIDS is inherently or solely responsible for its political import. The combination of its emergence and social production as a new and poorly understood infectious disease and the spaces/populations in which it was thought to originate, can be situated within a genealogy of racist and homophobic science and geopolitics. The singularity of the epidemic lies in the cumulative and persistent effects of its construction – from apocalyptic and religious imagery and metaphors, allusions to moral and social decay, conspiracy theories of biological warfare, racist and culturally discriminatory language, to the medical and epidemiological discourse on risk groups and behaviors, and the kinds of national and international institutions that were set up to deal with AIDS (Martin 1994, Sontag 1989, Treichler 1999). It has been refered to, in fact, as "the most political of all epidemics" (Altman 1986: 11). The global nature of its life as well as responses to it is undoubtedly a factor of the hyper-mobile, and mass mediated world that we inhabit. Moreover, the biological characteristics of HIV and AIDS cannot be separated from its social construction and its difference from other diseases – that is, its routes of transmission, the highly complex and mutable nature of the virus which has made vaccine development particularly challenging, and the complexity of its management and treatment. Arguments have been made for and against the construction of AIDS as a phenomenon completely different from epidemic diseases in the past (Farmer 1999, Grmek 1990, Scheper-Hughes 1994). While it is true that the responses to AIDS are reminiscent of historically significant diseases like the plague, cholera, leprosy and syphilis, it is quite clear that no other disease has generated this magnitude of social commentary, movements for social change, and the materialization of a newly organized language of rights and ethics. Stephen Epstein's detailed work on the AIDS movement in the US and its relationship to scientific language and practice shows, for instance, how this movement was unique and served as a model for others. Its particularity and impact lay in the fact that the social definition of AIDS lay at "the intersection of cultural discourses about sexuality, the body and identity" (Epstein 1996: 20).

5   I spent ten months in the year 2000 and two months in 2001 as a participant observer and volunteer at Garv (Hindi for pride). I was introduced to the organization and specifically to Shraddha Menon the founder and executive director by a former colleague who was on the board of directors of the organization. My presence at the organization was predicated

on my being available to assist the organization in any way that they thought appropriate. This usually took the form of helping in writing and editing reports, attending meetings and taking minutes. Prior to this, I had been involved, as a volunteer and as a future researcher, in various NGOs, since 1997. For purposes of confidentiality, the names of all the organizations and individuals described and quoted in the article have been altered. I have attempted to convey the spirit of the names of organizations in their altered form, and also the regional or religious affiliation of individuals, to preserve the particularity of the situation. I refer to the urban locale in which the work was done as Nagar, the Hindi word for "city" or "urban settlement." All these strategies have been employed in good faith; it is inevitable that to persons familiar with this terrain, the identity of some of the individuals and organizations might be apparent.

6   In using the term AIDS service, I am making a reference to Cindy Patton's (1990) analysis of the "AIDS-service industry" in the US. Her work on the politics of AIDS and its rise as a discursive social phenomenon looks closely at the processes by which the AIDS epidemic became the grounds for collective action. This "industry" is one site where discourses on AIDS are generated, and where the categories and social definitions related to the disease are crystallized. The AIDS-service industry for Patton encompasses broadly "the private-sector non-profit organizations devoted exclusively to AIDS work – because it implies a set of social relations based on shared norms and styles of organizational behavior institutionalized through patterned power relations, rather than a collusion of the powerful who maintain an 'establishment' by coercion or conscious exclusion, or to act purely as a conduit for government monies to communities" (Patton 1990: 13). I have expanded the scope of AIDS service to include both governmental and non-governmental responses, precisely because, as my work shows, the boundaries that delineate them are not as clear in practice as they seem in theory. While I acknowledge the differences between the privatized, insurance based health care system of the US that Patton describes, and the Indian healthcare system that combines public/government run and funded with a parallel highly heterogeneous private sector medical service, I believe that many of the practices and norms that formed the basis of the AIDS service industry in the US are also what bind communities of AIDS experts, not just in the Indian context, but also, I would wager, in the global one.
     What Patton does specifically for AIDS is preceded by work in the sociology of medicine such as Carroll Estes' (1979) on "the aging enterprise," which documents the professional and political arrangements around which medical care of the aged is organized – "the programs, organizations, bureaucracies, interest groups, trade associations, providers, industries and professionals that serve the elderly in one capacity or the other" (Estes 1979: 2).

7   Paul Rabinow's formulation of biosociality takes place in the context of the social aggregations that arise from the identification of genetic conditions and the naming of specific genes. He speaks of the likelihood of "the formation of new individual and group identities and practices arising out of these new truths" (1996: 101). Ethnographic explorations of various forms of biosociality can be found, for example, in Rayna Rapp's (1999) study of the associations that form around Down's Syndrome and Adriana Petryna's (2002) work on the social formations and practices that arise in Ukraine around claims for restitution and welfare on the basis of radiation induced damage due to the Chernobyl nuclear accident.

8   Statistics on HIV and AIDS cases are compiled, for instance, by the Ministry of Health, local State governments, the WHO and UNAIDS. UNAIDS estimated the number of HIV positive persons in India at the end of 2003 to be 5.1 million, second in the world only to South Africa, whose numbers are estimated at 5.3 million. Since the detection of the first

case in 1986 in a sex worker in Madras, HIV has been reported in all states and union territories, with a total of 68,809 cases reported to NACO by March 2004. The majority of cases are situated in Maharashtra, Tamil Nadu, Pondicherry and Manipur and while heterosexual transmission is seen to be the predominant mode, the epidemiological profile is said to differ among regions. For details see UNAIDS Epidemiological Fact Sheets by Country, 2004. Elsewhere, I have traced the progression of AIDS in India in more detail.

9   Ford, Macarthur, UNDP, WHO, World Bank, Oxfam, DFID, Norad, SIDA, among others. Also important as funding actors are private foundations like the Richard Gere Foundation, the Packard Foundations and more recently, the Clinton Foundation that works with NACO on care and treatment and specifically antiretroviral roll out, and the Bill and Miranda Gates Foundation. The Gates Foundation notably has committed two hundred million dollars to the Indian AIDS initiative called Avahan ("clarion call") (for details of the India AIDS initiative see www.gatesfoundation.org). It has been known to have introduced a distinctly corporate model into the world of AIDS service.

10 Until the eighties, the Indian state did not actively define or acknowledge in any formal or institutionalized way, the place of voluntary agencies and the non-governmental sector in processes of national development. The tendency had been to equate the work of the voluntary agencies with only local level charity work, rather than with a sustained participation in the growth of the nation, its economy and its goals of social welfare. Realizing the centrality of the globally envisioned idea of "participatory development" to the national project of modernization and progress, the Sixth Five Year Plan Document voiced the importance of NGOs as social actors who could access and mobilize people and who could achieve the increasing goals of developmental programs. They came to be constructed as "the eyes of the government" at the level of the village and the community. The Seventh Five Year Plan (1985–1990) emphasized an even more active role for voluntary agencies in working towards empowerment and self reliant communities (Jain 1997).

11 Much attention has been devoted, particularly by political scientists and international relations scholars, to the growing and robust nature of a transnational political arena and particularly, the involvement of non-state actors in it. The traditional concepts of civil society and public sphere have evolved into dynamic entities that, in the globalizing world, have taken on global implications and incarnations. Keck and Sikkink, for instance, describe the political influence of what they see as a new actor in the global political area, and what they term as the "transnational advocacy network." These, according to the authors, are bound and motivated by "shared principal ideas or values" (1998: 30) that are moral rather than instrumental. The edited works by Florini (2000), Guidry, Kennedy and Zald (2000) and Khagram, Riker and Sikkink (2002) all demonstrate through cases of social movement activity, and various forms of political mobilization from a multitude of cultural contexts, the ways in which state and non-state actors relate, the processes by which advocacy, protest and pressure groups may or may not become efficacious and underlying this, the flows of ideas, resources and power between local and global in the making of transnational spheres of political activity. Clark, Friedman and Hochstetler analyze the involvement of three NGOs in global conferences in order to examine empirically, the scope and limits of a global civil society. They conclude that the visibility and presence of NGOs in the world political scene is undeniable and that there is evidence of a growing community of global NGOs that thrive through their transnational interconnectedness and relationships. However, while they see global civil society as a sector that is in the making, they do not see it either as a *fait accompli*, or as transcending the relative autonomy of nation states. As they argue, the limits of a global civil society are set by the bounds of national sovereignty.

12   The processes by which funding agencies produce and deploy knowledge have been
     addressed in such anthropological studies of development as Judith Justice's (1986)'s
     analysis of the culture of bureaucracies in Nepal and James Ferguson's (1994) scrutiny of
     the systematic discursive production of objects of uplift in Lesotho. Various aspects and
     theoretical implications of the relationship between the state, donor organizations and
     NGOs, its implications for the interests of the groups that NGOs represent, and issues of
     dependency have been examined by Fowler (1992), Gordon (1997), Hulme and Edwards
     (1997), Lewis (1997), Stirrat and Henkel (1997). Justice's work also provides an insight-
     ful contextualization of local administrative practices and their resilience as a way to
     address questions of corruption.

13   There is a plethora of literature in development, anthropology, sociology and politics that
     uses the concept of empowerment. Much of it does not trace the genealogy of the term
     and its usage. Zellerer and Vyortkin point out the centrality of the concept in "feminist
     perspectives." Based on review of literature, they cite the definition of empowerment as a
     process in which "oppressed persons gain some control over their lives by taking part
     with others in development of activities and structures that allow people increased
     involvement in matters which affect them directly" (2004: 441). Stein's work reviews
     processes of empowerment of women and their importance in improving their health.
     For a critique of the use of "empowerment" in neoliberal agendas and structural adjust-
     ment policies by agencies like the World Bank, see Elyachar 2002.

14   A central component of the National AIDS Control Program run by NACO is "targeted
     interventions" (TIs) approach, according to which, a concentrated focus on particular
     vulnerable and marginal groups, in order to reduce the rate of HIV transmission among
     them. The target groups that NACO addresses are sex workers, intravenous drug users,
     men having sex with men, truckers, migrant labour and street children (http://www.na
     coonline.org/prg_sche_targetint.htm)

15   Instances of advocacy and attempts to transform laws and legal language are discussed in
     sections that follow.

16   Health care services in India are characterized by a "multiprovider" distribution between
     the government, private and non-governmental (Bhat 2000). This reflects the nation's
     mixed economy manifested in what has been called "state managed capitalism" (Kamat
     2001). The economy liberalized gradually in the late eighties through the early nineties
     and this has seen increasing privatization of many essential services.

17   Activism, voluntarism and social mobilization in India are highly variegated according to
     the region in which they are situated. A comparative study of organizational activity
     across regions would yield such specifics. My observations are limited to a specific set of
     AIDS service organizations in urban North India, and as such a discussion of the
     comparative politics of NGO activity in India is beyond the scope of this article. Raka
     Ray's (1998, 1999) comparative analysis of women's organizing in Calcutta (Kolkata)
     and Bombay (Mumbai) reveals the centrality of the workings of power and culture in the
     local political structures and environments within which protest movements live and to
     which they respond, in determining the ideological and programmatic agendas that they
     follow. She offers the concept of the "political field" to encapsulate this and to address
     the divergences and seeming paradoxes between women's mobilizing in the states of
     Maharashtra and West Bengal.

18   The reification of the non-governmental in the literature and the discourse of inter-
     national development agencies like the UN belies the internal inconsistencies of the
     category of NGO. The use of the term "non-governmental organization" or NGO was
     first documented in with the formation of the United Nations in 1949. The term was used
     to describe a wide spectrum of organizations, the likes of which go back to the nineteenth

century. For an overview of the scope and history of NGOs, see the introductions to special journal issues dedicated to the analysis of NGOs by Fernando and Heston (1997) and Leve and Karim (2001). Several ethnographic projects on non-governmental organizations have been undertaken in recent years. Michael Fisher's (1997) review and Leve and Karim's introduction to the symposium on NGOs, Power and Development point this out. The latter also notes that the anthropological practice around the study of NGOs has even given rise to the nomenclature "NGOgraphies" (2001: 55).

19 From Annual Reports of the Ministry of Health and from those of the National AIDS Control Organization, as well as newspaper reports.

20 Section 377 of the Indian Penal Code, instituted in 1861, under British Common Law, and first proposed by the Indian Law Commission in 1837 reads: "Unnatural offences – Whoever voluntarily has carnal intercourse against the order of nature with any man, woman, or animal shall be punished with imprisonment for life, or with imprisonment of either description for a term which may extend to ten years and shall also be liable to fine. Explanation – Penetration is sufficient to constitute the carnal intercourse necessary to the offence described in this section." The law does not state explicitly that it addresses homosexuality *per se*, but talks only of "carnal intercourse against the order of nature," which might be interpreted to imply any kind of sexual intercourse whose purpose is not reproductive.

21 According to WHO guidelines: "Universal precautions are simple infection control measures that reduce the risk of transmission of bloodborne pathogens through exposure to blood or body fluids among patients and health care workers. Under the "universal precaution" principle, blood and body fluids from all persons should be considered as infected with HIV, regardless of the known or supposed status of the person. Improving the safety of injections is an important component of universal precautions." (http://www.who.int/hiv/topics/precautions/universal/en/#what)

22 From informal unstructured interviews conducted with counselors and medical practitioners in the Network.

23 I am not suggesting here that there is no concept of an individual self in India, rather that it has evolved as a discursive object in the west differently, and that it is this discursive formation that has given rise to legal and ethical constructs like "confidentiality."

24 Such dichotomies are posited in literature on social movements, on non-governmental organizations, and, as I have already pointed out earlier, in the discursive practices of development agencies like the UNDP.

25 Vincanne Adams' work on the movement for democracy in Nepal and the role of medical professionals in this movement concludes that medicine is not about neutral universal scientific truths but is highly political and contingent and that very practice of healthcare is about politics (Adams 1998).

26 The legal crystallization of these particular instantiations of rights can be found in specific debates and public interest litigations. A compilation of these can be found in the Lawyers Collective Manual on HIV/AIDS, Volumes I and II, 2000 as well as www.lawyerscollective.org. Local efforts are intimately linked to the global political landscape which is increasingly morphing by virtue of rights based language and practices. International human rights movements act as moral guardians and voices for a global community. Progressive governments are said to be based on rights based constitutions, such as in the new Republic of South Africa.

27 The framework of "new social movements" was primarily concerned with understanding organized attempts at social change that were distinguishable from formations like the labor or agrarian movements which had a clearly demarcated class base, which used formal institutional political conduits to make their assertions, and whose demands were

primarily material. One of the characteristics that made for the newness of new social movements was the unique way that collective action of the kind embodied for instance in environmental/ecological movements, tribal movements, students movements, and the women's movement, however variegated it might be, brought to the fore a novel, plural social actor involved in redefining the boundaries of the political, and in the social expression of cultural identity, and whose concerns, though often articulated as affective, sought to change the nature of civil society. Social movements may be considered to have a transformative potential at two levels; on the one hand they embody the constitution of a different kind of "sociopolitical citizenship," linked to people's struggle for social acknowledgment and for public and political spaces of expression; on the other hand, the transformation or the taking over of the cultural domain by these new actors that emerge in social movements, the assertion of identity and the affirmation of difference.

28   In the scope of my work, the efficacy of AIDS service is documented in the effects that it produces in the social universe. That aspect of the "success" of AIDS service that is measured in terms of statistical outcomes, were beyond the scope of this particular study, in that I have not systematically collected and analyzed rates of HIV and AIDS in certain groups before and after the advent of AIDS service networks in the area.

REFERENCES

Adams, Vincanne. 1998. *Doctors for Democracy. Health Professionals in the Nepal Revolution*. Cambridge: Cambridge University Press.

Altman, Dennis. 1986. *AIDS in the Mind of America. The Social, Political and Psychological Impact of a New Epidemic*. Garden City, NY: Anchor.

——. 1999. Globalization, Political Economy and AIDS. *Theory and Society* 28(2): 559–584.

Appadurai, Arjun. 1996. *Modernity at Large. The Cultural Aspects of Globalization*. Minneapolis: University of Minnesota Press.

Beck, Ulrich. 1992. *Risk Society: Towards a New Modernity*. London: Sage Publications.

Biehl, João Guilherme. 1999. *Other Life: AIDS, Biopolitics, and Subjectivity in Brazil's Zones of Social Abandonment*. Ann Arbor: UMI Dissertation Services.

——. 2004. "The Activist State: Global Pharmaceuticals, AIDS, and Citizenship in Brazil." *Social Text* 22(3): 105–132.

Brysk, Alison. 1994. *The Politics of Human Rights in Argentina: Protest, Change and Democratization*. Stanford: Stanford University Press.

Carver, Terrell and Veronique Mottier, eds. 1998. *Politics of Sexuality. Identity, Gender, Citizenship*. London: Routledge.

Clark, Ann Marie, Elisabeth J. Friedman and Kathryn Hochstetler. 1998. "The Sovereign Limits of Global Civil Society: A Comparison of NGO Participation in UN World Conferences on the Environment, Human Rights, and Women." *World Politics* 51(1): 1–35

Cohen, Lawrence. 2005. "Kothi wars: AIDS Cosmopolitanism and the Morality of Classification." In Vincanne Adams and Stacy Leigh Pigg, eds. *Sex in Development: Science, Sexuality, and Morality in Global Perspective*. Durham: Duke University Press.

Das, Veena. 1990. "What do we mean by Health?" In J.C. Caldwell, ed. *What We Know About Health Transition, Volume 1*. Canberra: Australian National University.

Das, Veena and Renu Addlakha. 2001. "Disability and Domestic Citizenship: Voice, Gender and the Making of the Subject." *Public Culture* 13 (3): 511–531.

Edwards, Michael and David Hulme, eds. 1996. *Beyond the Magic Bullet: NGO Performance and Accountability in the Post Cold War World*. West Hartford, Conn.: Kumarian Press.

Elyachar, Julia. 2002. "Empowerment Money: The World Bank, Non-Governmental Organizations, and the Value of Culture in Egypt." *Public Culture* 14 (3): 493–513.

Epstein, Steven. 1996. *Impure Science. AIDS, Activism and the Politics of Knowledge*. Berkeley: University of California Press.

Escobar, Arturo. 1992. *Encountering Development: The Making and Unmaking of the Third World*. Princeton: Princeton University Press.

Escobar, Arturo and Sonia Alvarez, eds. 1992. *The Making of Social Movements in Latin America: Identity, Strategy and Democracy*. Boulder: Westview Press.

Estes, Carroll. 1979. *The Aging Enterprise. A Critical Examination of Social Policies and Services for the Aged*. San Francisco: Jossey Bass Publishers.

Farmer, Paul. 1999. *Infections and Inequalities. The Modern Plagues*. Berkeley: University of California Press.

Ferguson, James. 1994. *The Anti-Politics Machine: "Development," Depoliticization and Bureaucratic Power in Lesotho*. Minneapolis: University of Minnesota Press.

Fernando, Jude and Alan W. Heston. 1997. "Introduction: NGOs between States, Markets, and Civil Society." *Annals of the American Academy of Political and Social Science* 554 (The Role of NGOs: Charity and Empowerment, November): 8–20.

Fisher, William F. 1997. "Doing Good? The politics and antipolitics of NGO practices." *Annual Review of Anthropology* 26: 439–64.

Florini, Ann, ed. 2000. *The Third Force: The Rise of Transnational Civil Society*. Tokyo/Washington: Japan Center for International Exchange/Carnegie Endowment for International Peace.

Foucault, Michel. 1965. *Madness and Civilization. A History of Insanity in the Age of Reason*. New York: Random House.

——. 1972. "The Politics of Health in the Eighteenth Century." In Colin Gordon, ed. *Power/Knowledge*. Sussex: Harvester Press.

——. 1973 (1963). *The Birth of the Clinic: An Archaeology of Medical Perception*. London: Tavistock.

——. 1978. *The History of Sexuality. An Introduction*. London: Random House.

——. 1991. "Governmentality." In Graham Burchell, Colin Gordon, Peter Miller, eds. *The Foucault Effect. Studies in Governmentality with Two Essays by and an Interview with Michel Foucault*. Chicago: University of Chicago.

Fowler, Alan. 1992. "Distant Obligations: Speculations on NGO Funding and the Global Market." *Review of African Political Economy* 20(55): 9–29.

Gordon, Leonard A. 1997. "Wealth Equals Wisdom? The Rockefeller and Ford Foundations in India." *Annals of the American Academy of Political and Social Science* 554 (The Role of NGOs: Charity and Empowerment, November): 104–116.

Grmek, Mirko. 1990. *History of AIDS: Emergence and Origin of a Modern Pandemic*. Princeton: Princeton University Press.

Guidry, John A., Michael D. Kennedy and Mayer N Zald, eds. 2000. *Globalizations and social movements: Culture, Power, and the Transnational Public Sphere*. Ann Arbor: University of Michigan Press.

Hemment, Julie. 2004. "The Riddle of the Third Sector: Civil Society, International Aid, and NGOs in Russia." *Anthropological Quarterly* 77(2): 215–241.

Hulme, David and Michael Edwards, eds. 1997. *NGOs, states and donors: too close for comfort?* New York : St. Martin's Press.

Jain, RB. 1997. "NGOs in India: Their Role, Influence and Problems." In Noorjehan Bava, ed. *Non-Governmental Organizations in Development: Theory and Practice*. New Delhi: Kanishka.

Justice, Judith. 1986. *Policies, Plans and People: Culture and Health Development in Nepal.* Berkeley: University of California Press.

Kamat, Sangeeta. 2001. *Development Hegemony: NGOs and the State in India.* New Delhi: Oxford University Press.

Keck, Margaret and Kathryn Sikkink, eds. 1998. *Activists without Borders: Advocacy Networks in International Politics.* Ithaca: Cornell University Press.

Khagram, Sanjeev, James V. Riker, and Kathryn Sikkink, eds. 2002. *Restructuring world politics: Transnational Social Movements, Networks, and Norms.* Minneapolis : University of Minnesota Press.

Leve, Lauren and Lamia Karim. 2001. "Privatizing the State: Ethnography of Development, Transnational Capital, and NGOs." *PoLAR* 24 (1): 53–58.

Lewis, David J. 1997. "NGOs, Donors and the State in Bangladesh." *Annals of the American Academy of Political and Social Science* 554 (The Role of NGOs: Charity and Empowerment, November): 33–45.

Luhmann, Niklas. 1993. *Risk: A Sociological Theory.* New York: A. de Gruyter.

Madsen, Stig Toff. 1997. "Between people and the state: NGOs as troubleshooters and innovators." In Staffan Lindberg and Arni Sverrisson, eds. *Social Movements in Development: The Challenge of Globalization and Democratization.* New York: St. Martin's Press.

Martin, Emily. 1994. *Flexible Bodies. The Role of Immunity in American Culture from the Days of Polio to the Age of AIDS.* Boston: Beacon Press.

Patton, Cindy. 1990. *Inventing AIDS.* New York: Routledge.

Petryna, Adriana. 2002. *Life Exposed. Biological Citizens After Chernobyl.* Princeton: Princeton University Press.

Plummer, Ken. 1995. *Telling Sexual Stories: Power, Change, and Social Worlds.* London: Routledge.

——. 2003. *Intimate Citizenship: Private Decisions and Public Dialogues.* Seattle: University of Washington Press.

Rabinow, Paul. 1989. *French Modern. Norms and Forms of the Social Environment.* Chicago: University of Chicago Press.

——. 1996. "Artificiality and Enlightenment: From Sociobiology to Biosociality" In Paul Rabinow. *Essays on the Anthropology of Reason.* Princeton: Princeton University Press.

Rapp, Rayna. 1999. *Testing Women, Testing the Fetus: The Social Impact of Amniocentesis in America.* New York: Routledge.

Rapp, Rayna and Faye Ginsburg. 2001. "Enabling Disability: Rewriting Kinship, Reimagining Citizenship." *Public Culture* 13(3): 533–556.

Ray, Raka. 1998. "Women's Movements and Political Fields: A Comparison of Two Indian Cities." *Social Problems* 45(1): 21–36.

——. 1999. *Fields of Protest: Women's Movements in India.* Minneapolis: University of Minnesota Press.

Riles, Annelise. 2001. *The Network Inside Out.* Ann Arbor: University of Michigan Press.

Routledge, Paul. 1993. *Terrains of Resistance. Non-violent Social Movements and the Contestation of Place in India.* Westport: Praeger.

Sanyal, Bishwapriya. 1997. "NGOs' Self-Defeating Quest for Autonomy." *Annals of the American Academy of Political and Social Science* 554 (The Role of NGOs: Charity and Empowerment, November): 21–32.

Scheper-Hughes, Nancy. 1994. "AIDS and the Social Body." *Social Science and Medicine* 39 (7): 991–1003.

Scott, James. 1990. *Domination and the Arts of Resistance. Hidden Transcripts.* New Haven: Yale University Press.

Sontag, Susan. 1989. *Illness as Metaphor and AIDS and its Metaphors*. New York: Farrar, Strauss and Giroux.

Stein, Jane. 1997. *Empowerment and Women's Health: Theory, Methods, and Practice*. London: Zed.

Stirrat, RL and Heiko Henkel. 1997. "The Development Gift: The Problem of Reciprocity in the NGO World." *Annals of the American Academy of Political and Social Science* 554 (The Role of NGOs: Charity and Empowerment, November): 66–80.

Streeten, Paul. 1997. "Nongovernmental Organizations and Development." *Annals of the American Academy of Political and Social Science* 554 (The Role of NGOs: Charity and Empowerment, November): 193–210.

Treichler, Paula A. 1999. *How to Have Theory in an Epidemic. Cultural Chronicles of AIDS*. Durham: Duke University Press.

Waites, Matthew. 1998. "Sexual Citizens. Legislating the Age of Consent in Britain." In Terrell Carver and Veronique Mottier, eds. *Politics of Sexuality. Identity, Gender, Citizenship*. London: Routledge.

Willetts, Peter. 1982. "The impact of promotional pressure groups on global politics." In Peter Willetts, ed. *Pressure Groups in the Global System. The Transnational Relations of Issue Oriented Non-Governmental Organizations*. London: Frances Pintner.

Zellerer, Evelyn and Dmitriy Vyortkin. 2004. "Women's Grassroots Struggles for Empowerment in the Republic of Kazakhstan" *Social Politics: International Studies in Gender, State and Society* 11(3): 439–464.

Index

Note: "*n*" after a page reference indicates a note on that page.

CPSIA information can be obtained
at www.ICGtesting.com
Printed in the USA
BVHW070543060722
641390BV00022B/283